The Future of Excellence in Public Relations and Communication Management

Challenges for the Next Generation

LEA's COMMUNICATION SERIES
Jennings Bryant/Dolf Zillmann, General Editors

Selected titles in Public Relations (James Grunig, Advisory Editor) include:

Austin/Pinkleton • Strategic Public Relations Management: Planning and Managing Effective Communication Programs

Culbertson/Chen • International Public Relations: A Comparative Analysis

Dozier/Grunig/Grunig • Manager's Guide to Excellence in Public Relations and Communication Management

Fearn-Banks • Crisis Communications: A Casebook Approach, Second Edition

Grunig • Excellence in Public Relations and Communications Management

Grunig/Grunig/Dozier • Excellent Public Relations and Effective Organizations: A Study of Communication Management in Three Countries

Hearit • Crisis Management by Apology: Corporate Response to Allegations of Wrongdoing

Lamb/McKee • Applied Public Relations: Cases in Stakeholder Management

Ledingham/Bruning • Public Relations as Relationship Management: A Relational Approach to the Study and Practice of Public Relations

Lerbinger • The Crisis Manager: Facing Risk and Responsibility

Mickey • Deconstructing Public Relations: Public Relations Criticism

Millar/Heath • Responding to Crisis: A Rhetorical Approach to Crisis Communication

Spicer • Organizational Public Relations: A Political Perspective

For a complete list of titles in LEA's Communication Series, please contact Lawrence Erlbaum Associates, Publishers at www.erlbaum.com

The Future of Excellence in Public Relations and Communication Management

Challenges for the Next Generation

Edited by

Elizabeth L. Toth
University of Maryland

2007

LAWRENCE ERLBAUM ASSOCIATES, PUBLISHERS
Mahwah, New Jersey   London

Lawrence Erlbaum Associates, Inc., Publishers
10 Industrial Avenue
Mahwah, New Jersey 07430
www.erlbaum.com

Cover design by Tomai Maridou

Library of Congress Cataloging-in-Publication Data

The future of excellence in public relations and communication management : challenges for the next generation / edited by Elizabeth
   L. Toth.
          p.   cm. (LEA's Communication Series).
   Published on the occasion of the retirement of James E. Grunig
   and Larissa A. Grunig from university education and to present
   the advances made because of their IABC Excellence Study.

   Includes bibliographical references and index.
ISBN 0-8058-5595-5 (cloth : alk. paper)
ISBN 0-8058-5596-3 (pbk. : alk. paper)
1. Public relations.   2. Communication in management.   I. Grunig,
   James E.   II. Grunig, Larissa A.   III. Toth, Elizabeth L.   IV. Excellence in public relations and communication management / edited by James E. Grunig with David M. Dozier ... [et al.].   V. Series.
HD59.F827   2006
659.2—dc22   2005057746
                                                              CIP

Books published by Lawrence Erlbaum Associates are printed on acid-
free paper, and their bindings are chosen for strength and durability.

Printed in the United States of America
10 9 8 7 6 5 4 3 2 1

Contents

Preface

On the occasion of the retirement from university education of James E. Grunig, PhD, and Larissa A. Grunig, PhD, this book presents the advances that have been made in the study of public relations and communication management because of the groundbreaking publications of the IABC Excellence Study, a three-country examination of best practices of public relations. The book is also a challenge to future public relations scholars to consider other theoretical research problems that lead to solving the problems of public relations practice.

Most public relations scholars would agree that the IABC Excellence Study was the most comprehensive research project done in the field of public relations. The research team, directed by James E. Grunig, and with co-authors Larissa A. Grunig and David M. Dozier, sought to test theories from multiple disciplines—such as management, communication, public relations, sociology, psychology, and philosophy—that could explain how public relations contributed to organizational effectiveness (the excellence factor) and what indicators actually made up public relations excellence. The resulting study, in three nations, presented public relations professionals and academics with a set of standards to which they could benchmark their own practice of public relations.

Although there were many significant theoretical advances revealed by the Excellence Study results—such as the new model of symmetry as two-way practice, the demand-delivery cycle, integrated communication reconceptualized, and the necessity of the symmetrical model to internal communication—perhaps the most important outcome was the bridge constructed between theory and practice. The purpose of the Excellence Study was to find out what effective public relations looked liked, and to explain to practitioners how they could carry out effective public relations. It exemplified the best in scientific research by modeling how the gathering of information can have both theoretical and practical contributions.

The Excellence Study was no simple feat. Methodologically, there was no existing list of organizations that modeled excellent public relations for the researchers to examine. Eventually, organizations that participated in the study volunteered themselves as having "best practices" or were chosen and invited to participate as award winners and media list designees of "best organizations." Theoretically, the excellence team built a set of hypotheses, based on the literature available in 1992, that were aimed at examining what public relations people did, who they reported to, and how the management of communication led to value to the organization. The study did not focus directly on the contributions to society of excellent public relations, nor did it directly consider whether society was better off because organizations practiced excellent public relations (which critics would claim was a weakness in the study). However, the excellence team dealt with the implications of their work and its limitations, and the team challenged future researchers to test their findings with more recent theory and findings, particularly of how to apply the work on the global scale.

Theory building in public relations would have gained no significant foothold without the work of James E. Grunig, Larissa A. Grunig, David M. Dozier, and their research team colleagues. These scholars have provided us with the most valid evidence yet of how public relations management contributes to organizational effectiveness. At the same time, these scholars would be the first to challenge us to build, modify, enlarge, or deepen the understanding of public relations that their study offered. Research findings are meant to be benchmarks into the future. On the occasion of their retirement, Jim and Lauri Grunig have encouraged all of us to keep developing the many ideas and conclusions that their research provided. The contributors to this book have done just that—advanced our understanding of public relations excellence and challenged our community of researchers to continue to do so. On behalf of the contributors, we express our appreciation for the Excellence Study and the dedication of Jim and Lauri Grunig to our theory-building enterprise. Thanks, Jim and Lauri, for all you've done for our profession and discipline.

—*Elizabeth L. Toth*

ACKNOWLEDGMENTS

I would like to thank many colleagues and friends who made this project possible. My first thanks go to the contributing authors, whose chapters illustrated so superbly how the results of the Excellence Study have initiated new theories and applications. I would like to express my appreciation to Linda Bathgate, Editor at Lawrence Erlbaum Associates, Publishers, for her support, and to the Erlbaum staff for their help with production. I would also like to thank the Department of Communication at the University of Maryland for its support and resources. Finally, I would like to acknowledge Maria Russell for introducing me to the festschrift; and express my very profound gratitude to Jim and Lauri Grunig for their guidance and friendship.

Brief Biographies

JAMES E. GRUNIG

Dr. James E. Grunig, professor emeritus at the University of Maryland at College Park, is the foremost scholar of public relations theory. He has written six books and edited five books, one of which won the National Communication Association PRIDE Award, the most prestigious award given for public relations publications. Three books detail the excellence in public relations and communication management study, the most influential research study to date on best practices in public relations. Dr. Grunig has contributed 38 book chapters, written 4 monographs, and published 56 refereed journal articles. He has written extensive research reports and published widely in professional publications. He has presented over 75 juried papers at conferences, and spoken to global audiences. His Excellence Theory and the situational theory of publics are his legacy to the body of knowledge in public relations.

Teaching

Dr. Grunig has guided and mentored 73 master's students to the completion of their theses. He has advised 20 doctoral students to the completion of their dissertations. Many of these students are now established scholars and leaders in public relations education, such as Larissa A. Grunig, Kathleen Kelly, K. Sriramesh, and Yi-Hui Huang. Many of his students' theses and dissertations have received prestigious awards, given by the Institute for Public Relations and the International Communication Association.

Service and Honors

Dr. Grunig established and co-edited for 6 years the first scholarly journal in the field of public relations, *The Journal of Public Relations Research*. He has contributed his leadership on numerous editorial boards and academic and professional associations, and consulted with U.S. government agencies, corporations, and public relations firms. For his service, Dr. Grunig has received many of the highest honors bestowed by professional and academic associations: "One of Five Legends" of the Public Relations Society of America; PRSA's 1989 Outstanding Educator Award; the Jackson, Jackson & Wagner Award for Behavioral Science Research in Public Relations; and the first Institute for Public Relations Pathfinder Award. In 1996, the Maryland State Senate gave him a special commendation on the occasion of the University of Maryland Public Relations Sequence being voted the Number 1 graduate program in public relations in the United States by *U.S. News and World Report*. In 2000, *PR Week* named him as one of the 10 outstanding public relations educators in the United States.

LARISSA A. GRUNIG

Dr. Larissa A. Grunig, professor emerita at the University of Maryland at College Park, is one of the most published scholars in the field of public relations. Her work in the area of gender and public relations and in public relations ethics as an underlying dimension of the practice of public relations places her as one of the most influential scholars of the public relations field. She co-conducted the landmark Excellence Study in public relations and communication management research, and co-authored the three books about the Excellence Study. She has authored three books, edited three books, and contributed 29 chapters to refereed books. She has authored over 37 refereed journal articles and contributed to numerous professional publications. She has presented over 80 juried and invited academic conference papers. She has presented her work in numerous international settings, including China, Slovenia, Great Britain, Australia, Germany, Italy, Poland, South Africa, Taiwan, and Hong Kong. Among the many research awards she has received for public relations research are the two most prestigious: the 1994 Jackson, Jackson & Wagner Behavioral Science Prize of the Public Relations Society of America, and the 1989 Institute for Public Relations Pathfinder Award.

Teaching

Dr. Grunig has advised over 30 master's thesis projects, three of which won the Institute for Public Relations outstanding master's thesis competition. She has chaired six doctoral dissertations. These doctoral students are now outstanding public relations scholars and educators, including Linda Hon, University of Florida; Bey-Ling Sha, San Diego State University; and Shannon Bowen, University of Maryland at College Park. For Dr. Grunig's teaching, she received the 1996 Public Relations Society of America Outstanding Educator Award. In 1996, the State of Maryland Senate honored her for the University of Maryland at College Park's top ranking for graduate education in public relations in the United States by *U.S. News and World Report*.

Service and Honors

Dr. Grunig has provided her leadership to numerous academic and professional organizations, such as the International Communication Association's Public Relations Division and the Association for Education in Journalism and Mass Communication's Public Relations Division. She established and co-edited for 6 years the first scholarly journal in the field of public relations, *The Journal of Public Relations Research*. She served the University of Maryland at College Park as the President's Special Assistant for Women's Issues from 2000 to 2003. In 2000, *PR Week* named her as one of the 10 outstanding public relations educators in the United States.

James E. Grunig and Larissa A Grunig are honored by the contributing authors of this book for their extraordinary contributions to our understanding of excellence in public relations.

Introduction

Elizabeth L. Toth

The purpose of this book is to provide the public relations scholarly and professional communities with the advanced research and commentary to come from the IABC Excellence Study. Theory and research are always in process. The contributors to this book illustrate this by reporting on how they tested, questioned, and sought to fill gaps based on the IABC Excellence Study's findings and conclusions. The IABC Excellence Study has provided us with a set of theoretical benchmarks by which to help solve the practice problems of public relations. Contributors to this book illustrate how the study of what is excellence in public relations and communication management and how it contributes to organizational effectiveness continues to evolve and change through research and theory. The contributors to this book inform us of their advancing findings and challenge us to continue the work.

I have organized these contributions according to the original three spheres of public relations and communication management excellence found in the *Manager's Guide to Excellence in Public Relations and Communication Management* (Dozier, Grunig, & Grunig, 1995). The *Manager's Guide* describes the structure of excellence as consisting of a core of communication knowledge, a middle sphere of shared expectations about public relations and communication management, and an outer sphere made up of organizational culture. I end the book with some challenges to public relations educators.

The most significant indicators of excellence in public relations and communication management suggested that practitioners had to have the requisite knowledge to conduct excellent public relations. This knowledge has been readily available, and practitioners have sought it out and integrated it into their work. Linda Hon, in chapter 1, presents practitioners who are knowledgeable about excellence practices and describes how they have put excellence to use in their careers. Hon includes voices of former students of Jim and Lauri Grunig.

Parts II and III of this book consider the middle layer of public relations and communication management. This middle layer of significant factors focuses on communication and management. In Section II, Advances in Understanding Excellence and Communication, several contributors provide deeper perspectives and challenges around the concepts of symmetry and asymmetry. In chapter 2, Christopher H. Spicer addresses when collaborative advocacy or symmetrical communication is warranted between an organization and its stakeholders. In chapter 3, Robert L. Heath offers important conceptual depth to the place of advocacy in management and communication strategy. In chapter 4, Don W. Stacks and Marcia L. Watson seek to find quantitative ways to measure two-way symmetrical communication, arguing that most quantitative research only measures asymmetrical communication. In chapter 5, Kenneth D. Plowman advances our understanding of conflict resolution as a strategy of two-way symmetrical and asymmetrical communication by explicating the concept of mediation. In chapter 6, Yunna Rhee expands the excellence team's research by exploring the use of interpersonal communication strategies in one organization's symmetrical public relations program. In chapter 7, Priscilla Murphy considers how complexity-based thinking complements the symmetrical model of communication.

In Part III, the contributors advance the Excellence Study research on public relations as strategic management. In chapter 8, Benita Steyn explicates organizational strategy formation through her review of studies on shared expectations between public relations and senior managers, and explores further what is meant by the strategic management role. In chapter 9, Minjung Sung provides a case study of how strategic public relations management includes scenario building to strengthen public relations' contribution to organizational effectiveness. In chapter 10, Ursula Ströh discusses public relations and communication strategy through the lens of postmodernism. In chapter 11, Bruce K. Berger considers the concept of organization power as being more fluid than fixed in organizational decision making.

The middle sphere concerns how public relations and communication management contribute to "bottom-line" organizational effectiveness. In chapter 12, Yi-Hui Huang returns to the topic of symmetrical communication and its strategic management use. In chapter 13, Jennifer Scott describes how one public relations firm applied relationship measures to client practice.

In their final project conclusions, the excellence authors challenged others to consider ethics as a dimension of public relations practice. In chapter 14, Shannon A. Bowen responds with a conceptualization of ethical public relations decision making. The excellence authors commented on the relationship of the public relations functions to other functions in the organization. In chapter 15, Kirk Hallahan reviews the excellence authors' conclusions on integrated communication, proposing another view on how organizational communication functions should work together.

The third sphere of excellence considers the culture of organizations as a significant indicator of whether excellence can flourish. In part IV of this book, I've addressed this area by looking at culture as being made up of publics (including activist groups), diversity, and organizational responses to crises. In chapter 16, Linda Aldoory and Bey-Ling Sha extend this perspective with theoretical and practical challenges of the situational theory of publics. In chapter 17, Derina R. Holtzhausen developed our understanding of activist publics. In chapter 18, Bey-Ling Sha and Rochelle Larkin Ford redefine "requisite variety" to reflect internal and external multicultural audiences. In chapter 19, Linda Aldoory describes the gender perspective in the Excellence Study and challenges researchers to reconsider gender in public relations research. In chapter 20, Linda M. Hagan offers a case study examining how excellence in public relations and communication management aid in a crisis.

Finally, the Excellence Study researchers concluded with propositions for generic principles of public relations that would be found in all nations and societies. In part V of this book, the following chapters test these propositions. In chapter 21, Chun-Ju Flora Hung emphasizes relationship cultivation and a dialectical approach for relationship management from her program of research in China and Taiwan. In chapter 22, Yi-Ru Regina Chen provides a first look at effective government relations in mainland China using theories of excellence as her starting point. In chapter 23, K. Sriramesh argues for a more prominent role for the concept of culture in public relations research. In chapter 24, Ana Tkalac applies the situational theory of publics to case studies of publics in Croatia. In chapter 25, Robert Wakefield summarizes the fledgling research that has been conducted to establish a global theory of public relations excellence.

Part VI of this book returns to the responsibilities of educators and practitioners to develop, share, and integrate the requisite knowledge into public relations practice. This section challenges educators to study and teach their theories and practice to solve public relations practice problems. In chapter 26, Donald K. Wright and Judy VanSlyke Turk report that although the principles of excellence are available to the field, there still is a disconnect between educators and practitioners seeking public relations knowledge. They describe the barriers that continue to hinder professional acknowledgment for public relations education. In chapter 27, Maria P. Russell of the Syracuse University distance learning master's program in communication management presents one graduate educational model that provides professionals with the knowledge that they need.

REFERENCES

Dozier D. M., Grunig, L. A., & Grunig, J. E. (1995). *The manager's guide to public relations and communication management.* Mahwah, NJ: Lawrence Erlbaum Associates.

Contributors to This Volume

Linda Aldoory, PhD, is an associate professor in communication at the University of Maryland. She edits the *Journal of Public Relations Research* and directed the Center for Risk Communication Research. She has published numerous articles and book chapters on gender and public relations. Her current research interests include exploring the utility of the situational theory of publics for health communication and the impact of gender on public relations.

Bruce K. Berger, PhD, is professor and chairman of the advertising and public relations department at the University of Alabama. He also is director of the Plank Center for Public Relations Studies at the university. Previously, he was corporate vice president of PR for Whirlpool Corporation and president of the Whirlpool Foundation.

Shannon A. Bowen, PhD, is an assistant professor at the University of Maryland. She has authored numerous book chapters, won a grant from IABC to study communication ethics, advised the *Encyclopedia of Public Relations*, and published research in the *Journal of Public Relations Research*, *Journal of Pubic Affairs*, and the *Journal of Business Ethics*. Her research interests include moral philosophy, organizational communication, and issues management.

Yi-Ru Regina Chen, PhD, is an assistant professor at University of Macau. She has published book chapters and articles on Chinese public relations, government affairs, risk management, and conflict resolution of public policy. She was given top paper awards by the International Communication Association and the International Academy of Business Disciplines.

Rochelle Larkin Ford, PhD, APR, is an assistant professor and coordinator of the advertising/public relations sequence at Howard University. She writes the monthly column "Diversity Dimensions" for *Public Relations Tactics* newspaper and has published other work on diversity and pedagogy.

Linda M. Hagan, PhD, APR, is a visiting assistant professor in the department of advertising, public relations, and retailing in the College of Communication Arts and Sciences at Michigan State University. She teaches undergraduate courses in principles of public relations, public relations techniques, public relations campaigns, and advertising account planning, along with graduate courses in public relations strategic management and media relations.

Kirk Hallahan, PhD, is an associate professor in journalism and technical communication at Colorado State University. His research interests include strategic communication, publicity, online technologies, and applications of behavioral and organizational theories to public relations practice. He is a winner of the Jackson, Jackson & Wagner Behavioral Science Prize from the PRSA Foundation.

Robert L. Heath, PhD, is professor of communication at the University of Houston. He is the author or editor of 12 books and 80 articles and chapters. His specialty is the rhetorical approach to public relations, issues management, crisis communication, and risk communication. He is the recipient of the NCA PR Division Pride Award, the Institute for Public Relations Pathfinder Award, and the PRSA Foundation Jackson, Jackson & Wagner Behavioral Science Prize.

Derina R. Holtzhausen, PhD, is an associate professor at the School of Mass Communications, University of South Florida. She has published extensively on postmodernism, social change, and activism in public relations. She won the Institute for Public Relations Pathfinder Award. She is completing a book entitled *Public Relations Activism: A Postmodern Exploration of Public Relations Theory and Practice*.

Linda Hon, PhD, is a professor and graduate coordinator in the department of public relations at the University of Florida. She also holds the title of Al and Effie Flanagan Professor of Journalism and Communications. Hon was editor of the *Journal of Public Relations Research* from 2000 to 2005. In 2001, she received the Pathfinder Award given by the Institute for Public Relations for best recent program of research in public relations.

Yi-Hui Huang, PhD, is a professor in the department of advertising of the National Cheng-Chi University in Taiwan. Her research interests include public relations, crisis communication, conflict and negotiation, public relations, and cross-cultural communications/relationship. She has published numerous articles and book chapters on relationship measurement. She studied conflict resolution at Harvard University.

Chun-Ju Flora Hung, PhD, teaches at Hong Kong Baptist University. Her research interests are relationship management, strategic management, crisis communication, reputation management, conflict resolution, negotiation, and intercultural communication. She has won several awards and has published articles in journals and books. She is a senior research fellow for the International Public Relations Research Center founded by the China International Public Relations Association and Fudan University.

Priscilla Murphy, PhD, is a professor in the department of strategic and organizational communication at Temple University in Philadelphia. She has published numerous articles on public relations and activism, chaos theory, and public relations models. Her recent research has focused on the application of network analysis and complexity theory to media reputation, crisis communication, and communication of science issues by special-interest groups.

Kenneth D. Plowman, PhD, is an associate professor at Brigham Young University, specializing in strategic management and conflict resolution in public relations. He spent 15 years in the field, the majority of that on Capitol Hill. He is also a public affairs officer in the U.S. Army Reserve. He edits *Teaching Public Relations.*

Yunna Rhee, PhD, is an assistant professor in the division of communication, Hankuk University of Foreign Studies, Seoul, Korea. She is winner of the 2003 Ketchum Excellence in PR Research Award and 1999 Master's Thesis Award from the Institute for Public Relations. She has presented several top papers at national conferences.

Maria P. Russell directs Syracuse University's S.I. Newhouse School of Public Communication's interdisciplinary, limited/residency distance learning program for mid-career public relations professionals, leading to a master's degree in communications management. She was chair of the school's public relations department from 1990 to 1992 and from 1994 to 2002, and has more than 16 years of professional public relations experience.

Jennifer Scott, PhD, is managing director, Insights and Research, Ogilvy PR Worldwide. Her work informs organizational positioning, issue management, branding, and marketing campaigns. Dr. Scott received her doctorate from Oxford University, England.

Bey-Ling Sha, PhD, APR, is an assistant professor at San Diego State University. Previously, she taught at the University of Maryland, College Park, and the American University of Paris. She also served as public affairs officer with the U.S. Census Bureau and as communication consultant for numerous public and private organizations.

Christopher (Kit) H. Spicer, PhD, is the dean of the College of Fine Arts & Communication at Towson University, Maryland. He authored *Organizational Public Relations: A Political Approach*. His current research interests include academic leadership and trust in organizations.

Don W. Stacks, PhD, is professor and director of the University of Miami's School of Communication Advertising and Public Relations Program. He has written books on public relations research methods and communication theory and research. He received the Institute for Public Relations Pathfinder Award and the PRSA Foundation's Jackson, Jackson & Wagner Behavioral Science Prize.

Benita Steyn, APR, is a senior lecturer at the Cape Peninsula University of Technology, Cape Town, South Africa. She teaches in the Web-based master's program in public relations management and is the co-author of *Corporate Communication Strategy*. She is director of Digital Management AG, a Swiss company that developed a comprehensive software solution that guides strategy formulation and performance management in public relations.

K. Sriramesh, PhD, is associate professor in the School of Communication and Information at Nanyang Technological University, Singapore. He has received the Pathfinder Award from the Institute of Public Relations and the NCA PR Division PRIDE award for best book (2003). He has co-edited the *Global Public Relations Handbook: Theory, Research, and Practice* and edited *Public Relations in Asia: An Anthology*.

Ursula Ströh, PhD, lectures at the University of Technology, Sydney. She started her research career in South Africa, where she received the merit award for research from the Human Sciences Research Council in 1989. She has published research on chaos and complexity theories and public relations. The Public Relations Institute of Southern Africa chose her as Educator of the Year for 1999–2000. She has performed training and consulting work in strategic communication management and change.

MinJung Sung, PhD, teaches public relations at Chung-Ang University, Seoul, South Korea. She received her PhD from the University of Maryland, College Park. Prior to joining Chung-Ang University, she was an assistant professor at Baruch College, City University of New York. Her main research interests include strategic management of public relations, global public relations, issues management, and corporate communication.

Ana Tkalac, PhD, is an assistant professor of marketing communications and public relations at the Graduate School of Economics and Business, University of Zagreb, Croatia. Her major research interests are focused on attitude change in public relations. She has published in the area of public relations and marketing communications and participated in leading conferences.

Elizabeth L. Toth, PhD, is a professor in the department of communication at the University of Maryland. She has published widely on gender and public relations, co-authoring *Women and Public Relations: How Gender Influences Practice*. She has received the PRSA Outstanding Educator Award, the Institute for Public Relations Pathfinder Award, and the PRSA Foundation Jackson, Jackson & Wagner Behavioral Science Prize.

Judy VanSlyke Turk, PhD, is director and professor at the School of Mass Communications at Virginia Commonwealth University. She is a member of the Commission on Public Relations Education and in 1992 was named Educator of the Year by the PRSA. She is a co-editor of *Journalism Studies*, an international refereed journal. She was cowinner of the Institute for Public Relations Pathfinder Award.

Robert I. Wakefield, PhD, is an associate professor of communications at Brigham Young University, and an author and researcher emphasizing cross-cultural effects on reputation in multinational organizations. He also served as director of communications for BYU–Hawaii, and as director of global public affairs for Nu Skin International. He was chair of PRSA's International Section and a consultant to the PRSA Global Initiatives Committee.

Marcia L. Watson, MA, is a doctoral student in the University of Miami School of Communication.

Donald K. Wright, PhD, is professor of communication at the University of South Alabama, the immediate past president of the International Public Relations Association (IPRA), and a member of the Board of Trustees of both the Arthur W. Page Society and the Institute for Public Relations. He has been conducting research on communication ethics since the 1970s. He has worked full time in corporate, agency, and university public relations, and has been a corporate communications consultant for 3 decades.

I

Excellence: The Practitioner's Responsibility

Chapter 1

How Public Relations Knowledge Has Entered Public Relations Practice

Linda Hon
University of Florida

The purpose of this chapter is to showcase how academic theory in public relations has entered practice. The focus here is on the major components of Excellence Theory (Dozier, Grunig, & Grunig, 1995; Grunig et al., 1992; Grunig, Grunig, & Dozier, 2002) and their application to the profession (see also Botan & Taylor, 2004; Cornelissen, 2000; Hallahan, 1993; Murphy, 1989; Sallot, Lyon, Acosta-Alzuru, & Jones, 2003). This chapter also celebrates and honors the role that James and Larissa Grunig have played as educators and mentors to their many former students who are now working in the public relations industry.

RESEARCH PROCEDURE

To meet this chapter's goals, it seemed appropriate and necessary to capture the voices of these professionals and ask them to speak about their perceptions and experiences as they relate to Excellence Theory. Thus, the first step was to ask Lauri and Jim to provide me with the names and contact information for former students now in practice.[1]

The 41 practitioners for whom a mailing address was available received an initial letter from me, explaining the nature of the project and encouraging their participation. Two of these were returned as undeliv-

---

[1]The initial list contained 50 names, although the Grunigs acknowledged that some of their information may not have been current. In cases for which this had been indicated, I made attempts, most of which were successful, to find up-to-date e-mail addresses for the students by searching online.

erable. At this point, I also received several unprompted e-mail messages from former students indicating that they would be honored to participate, and each of these students wrote fondly of Jim and Lauri. One referred to them as "wonderful people and teachers." Another wrote that she would look forward to discussing Lauri's "profound impact" on her career and life. As she noted, "I actually would relish discussing it! Thank you so much for the opportunity to reminisce about a woman whom I admire and respect more than I can express. I will forever be in her debt."

Each professional for whom an e-mail address was available received an e-mail message from me, with the letter of invitation and the study's informed consent protocol attached.[2] In the text of the e-mail, recipients were directed to a link that accessed an online survey containing six open-ended questions.[3]

Ultimately, 48 potential participants were sent the e-mail with the letter, protocol, and link information. Four of these e-mails were returned as undeliverable. Three former students responded and said that they had looked at the survey and did not feel they could answer the questions: One was no longer working in public relations; one believed that the questions did not fit the nature of her job (small agency), although she did provide some written feedback in a separate e-mail about her job and experiences at University of Maryland; and one felt that his education predated the excellence research program. However, the latter practitioner also provided some written comments about Jim's teaching and theories and their positive impact on his professional life.

Fifteen former students completed the survey. Each of these 15 answered every question. Their answers generated approximately 30 pages of single-spaced comments that were printed and analyzed by the researcher.

The chapter does not aim to present the results of this survey as necessarily representative of any larger group of practitioners' perceptions and experiences. However, certainly the main themes uncovered resonate with many of the topics discussed in the trade and academic literature in public relations. I also do not attempt to answer formal research questions by making comparisons in relation to variables such as respondents' industry, job title, gender, and so on, other than where participants did so themselves or when identifying these descriptors is necessary to make points clear. I enthusiastically admit my mission here is single-minded—to uncover in the voices of professionals the demon-

---

[2]The protocol was approved by the Institutional Review Board at the University of Florida.

[3]I thank University of Florida doctoral student Eyun-Jung Ki for constructing and maintaining the site during the survey period.

strated and potential efficacy of Excellence Theory for understanding and practicing public relations (for other perspectives see, e.g., Berger, 2005; Cancel, Cameron, Sallot, & Mitrook, 1997; Heath, 2001; Holtzhausen, Petersen, & Tindall, 2003; L'Etang & Pieczka, 1996; Miller, 1989; Roper, 2005; Toth, 1992). In doing so, I also hope to reveal some of the current and future challenges that practitioners face when trying to make excellence happen for their organizations and clients. Obviously, I recognize that the professionals who chose to respond to this study's survey no doubt share my belief that Excellence Theory is the field's most well-researched and efficacious positive theory and normative model. And, clearly, their comments indicate that their admiration and affection for Jim and Lauri parallel my own. This chapter therefore is also unabashedly personal.

SURVEY QUESTIONS

The questionnaire first asked respondents to provide descriptive, background information about their career in public relations, including their present job title and responsibilities. They then were queried about how their formal education in public relations, specifically their experiences at University of Maryland, had or had not impacted their career.

Question three, which included multiple items, was the main focus of the survey. Here, participants were asked to explain whether and to what degree characteristics of excellence are or are not reflective of their work experience in public relations. The characteristics that were probed included the main components of excellence—*empowerment of the public relations function, roles, organization of the communication function*, and *models of public relations*.[4]

For each of these characteristics, criteria were provided on the survey to help respondents relate the theoretical principles to their work experience. Empowerment included the following descriptions: The senior public relations executive is involved with strategic management, communication programs are developed for strategic publics identified through the strategic management process, and the senior public relations executive is a member of the dominant coalition or has a direct reporting relationship to senior managers who are members of the dominant coalition. Excellence as it relates to practitioner roles was explained by stating that the public relations unit is headed by a manager rather than a technician, the senior public relations executive or others in the unit have the knowledge needed for the managerial role; and diversity is embodied in all roles.

---

[4]The organization of the questions on the survey followed the format and wording of the excellence criteria as specified in Grunig, Grunig, and Dozier (2002).

Organization of the communication function was specified by two criteria. The first was that the communication function is integrated or provides a mechanism for coordinating programs managed by different departments. Second, public relations is a management function separate from other functions.

Finally, the section on models of public relations stated that communication programs reflect a two-way symmetrical model. Also specified was that practitioners have mixed motives: They are loyal to both their organization and the publics of their organization.

A fourth question and a fifth question investigated the environmental and organizational context for excellence, respectively. Respondents were asked to discuss if and how activism, crises, or other sources of conflict have or have not moved the organizations where they have worked toward excellence. They then were queried about whether the organizations they have worked for have or have not embodied excellence internally. This internal dimension was explained by listing the following: participative rather than authoritarian culture, organic rather than bureaucratic structure, equal opportunity, and high job satisfaction.

A final section asked participants to include additional comments, if they desired. Eleven respondents offered more information here.

PROFILE OF PARTICIPANTS

These professionals are well qualified to address the questions about excellence. Each has significant professional experience in public relations and many hold or have held the top public relations post in their organizations, or have served at the highest level of major agencies. Most of them have moved through a variety of positions, each with increasing responsibility and, in most cases, stature.

Worth noting is that six of the participants, after serving successful stints in organizational positions, are now independent consultants. The other nine practitioners hold a variety of positions—director of marketing for a performing arts center, senior public relations counselor specializing in technology management for a *Fortune* 350 company, senior vice president of corporate affairs for a major airline, director of public relations (no industry given), president and CEO of a NGO with operations in 11 countries, lobbyist within a European ministry of defense, director of public affairs for the U.S. Air Force, a senior consultant to multinational companies in China, and a senior vice president at a top global public relations agency.

The industries or job sectors in which respondents are working or have worked are diverse. They include arts, airline, biotechnology, biomedicine and science, civil engineering, computers and technology, consumer products, educational services, environment, financial services, food, global entertainment, health care, health care insurance, higher education, hospital, international hotel, military, pharmaceutical, politics and government, public school system, and telecommunications.

These practitioners also have worked in all types of organizations—government, trade associations, nonprofits, corporations, and public relations agencies. The latter group includes many leading firms, such as Hill & Knowlton, Fleishman-Hillard, Ketchum, Ogilvy, Porter Novelli, and APCO Worldwide.

The vastness of the expertise among these professionals is impressive. When describing their current and former positions, the following tasks and responsibilities were mentioned: advertising, business planning (proposals), community relations, consumer affairs, corporate giving, corporate social responsibility, crisis management, donor relations, employee communications, environmental relations, global communications, government affairs and lobbying, grant writing, integrated communications, investor relations, issues management, market branding and positioning, marketing communications, media relations and training, member communications, photography services, public affairs, publications/production of collateral material, risk communication, sales, security and policy review, special events and trade shows, spokesperson, visitor hospitality, and Web site development/maintenance. One also teaches college English, communication, and business writing part time.

As could be expected, most of the respondents' earlier jobs focused on technical work, such as writing for the media and producing publications. In their current positions, the majority emphasize what one described as "strategic communications planning," whereas others mentioned a counseling role.

SURVEY RESULTS

Role of Education in Excellence Theory

All but one of the participants had received a degree at University of Maryland. Although the questionnaire did not ask for respondents to indicate whether they had an undergraduate or graduate degrees (or both), six of the professionals mentioned the importance of their graduate degree from University of Maryland. The one practitioner who did not have formal education in public relations said that he had entered the field via MBA courses and the "marketing gate," but he discovered that marketing's perception of public relations was too narrow. He mentioned reading Jim and Todd Hunt's textbook, *Managing Public Relations* (Grunig & Hunt, 1984), meeting the Grunigs, and then later becoming a visiting scholar at University of Maryland.

Several themes are apparent in respondents' descriptions about the impact that Lauri and Jim's teaching and research have had on their professional careers. The most striking theme is that participants believe that their education at University of Maryland provided them with a powerful mental conceptualization of public relations practice that has served them well. The terms they used to refer to this conceptualization include *philosophy, construct, perspective, grounding, mindframe, core belief, mindset, and schemata.*

For example, one said:

> The philosophy [of public relations] espoused by Jim and Lauri Grunig was one I agreed with whole-heartedly and one I felt good about adopting myself. While some practitioners might view the Grunigs' philosophy as "idealistic" or "not real-world enough," I totally disagree and I have put their philosophy into practice and seen it succeed.

Another spoke of receiving a "useful, practical, wise, and progressive construct (i.e., what is now known as Excellence Theory) for approaching the field of public relations and its practice in the real world." This practitioner went on to say that his education supplemented whatever good judgment and common sense he had, so that even early in his career he jumped right into advising CEOs and vice presidents on public relations strategy with credibility and confidence. He also said that the excellence construct allowed him to make sound arguments for having the public relations function involved at the highest levels of the organization.

Still another credited Excellence Theory for a successful career in public relations:

> Learning the Excellence Theory has provided me with a unique perspective (different) from the public relations colleagues at the organizations in which I have worked to see and understand the big picture and to think strategically about the practice of public relations. Throughout my career, I have strived to implement the components of Excellence Theory.... My colleagues told me that they learned what public relations really was and "should be" during my time at [name of former employer].

Within the broad theme of Excellence Theory as a mental conceptualization, these professionals also commented on several elements of excellence as being key to their education and professional socialization. Dimensions cited include public relations as a strategic function, two-way communication, and ethics, which also was linked to professional maturity and credibility (see also Bowen, 2004, 2005; Sallot, Cameron, & Weaver-Lariscy, 1998; Wylie, 1994).

Respondents noted that although their academic preparation had taught them important skills, such as writing for the media, learning about public relations as a management discipline was critical to their practice. They noted in particular that conducting research was key to practicing public relations as a strategic management function. Several mentioned the importance of conducting empirical research prior to launching a campaign or a program. Additionally, one cited the value of secondary research—"best practices, industry standards/norms, and new trends."

Public relations as two-way communication also was a predominant theme. Perhaps this perspective was captured best by a participant who said that his experience at University of Maryland was a "once-in-a-lifetime" treasure that taught him the importance of two-way communication. To make this point, this practitioner referred specifically to Jim's situational theory of publics (Grunig & Hunt, 1984): "Before starting a campaign, now I ask myself: 'How can we reduce the constraints [recognition] and how can we increase problem recognition and level of involvement?' I think of it [public relations] from the needs of the different publics."

Other practitioners echoed this theme of two-way communication, with one noting that the most effective public relations is that which "relies on two-way communication and takes into account the interests of stakeholders." Another said that "the communications theory I learned at University of Maryland has helped me plan programs that consider all of the publics of my clients."

These respondents also seem to believe in the ethical norms underlying Excellence Theory and the enhanced credibility and professionalism that these ethical standards bring to the practice of public relations. Making this point, one participant said that Excellence Theory is a "useful, ethical, practical, wise, and progressive approach to the role of public relations and its practice in the real world." This professional went on to say that Excellence Theory:

> helped prepare me especially for situations where ethics came into play [practitioners have mixed-motives situations] and helped give me the confidence to stand my ground and not compromise my integrity. [It] allowed me to sleep at night, knowing I conducted myself as a professional and adhered to a high code of ethics. I am not sure how I would have been better prepared.

Another practitioner referred to academic knowledge in public relations as a "professional framework":

> It gave me ... a set of standards that I then held every company I worked for up to and, more important, as a consultant, I advised my clients based on these standards. Clients often expect consultants to do this, but often, consultants bow to the clients' standards instead of offering higher ones.

Still other participants noted that learning and putting public relations theory into practice had helped their career progression. Mentioned here were respect and credibility from colleagues, more and better job opportunities, and a more rapid rise from technician to management rank (see Broom & Dozier, 1986; Broom & Smith, 1979).

Components of Excellence Theory

As could be expected, the answers to questions about empowerment, roles, organization of the communication function, and models of public relations were not mutually exclusive. Respondents tended to describe how these excellence components work together to make public relations the most effective.

Empowerment.   Practitioners' responses about the power of the public relations department ran the gamut. Several had worked or were working in organizations for which public relations was highly valued, whereas others had experienced instances of both empowerment and devaluation.

One respondent argued that the that value management places on public relations is related to performance that positively impacts the company: "As the public relations teams deliver continuously improved results, the more trust and access we have" (see Hon, 1997; Pieczka, 2000). This professional went on to note, however, that empowerment can be double-edged: "When executives' ears are open, their eyes are as well."

A couple of practitioners were unequivocal in describing their organization's support for public relations. A good example was provided by the respondent who is employed by the U.S. Air Force:

> The senior PAO [public affairs officer] either is an active member of the dominant coalition or reports directly to the senior commander who leads the dominant coalition. In most Air Force organizations, the PAO is a member of the senior commander's personal staff and has direct unfiltered access.

Another participant described how, when he was negotiating for his current job, he was successful at making sure that the company structured the public relations function according to the principles of Excellence Theory. He attributed this empowerment of public relations to the company's later success at managing the "difficult and unpopular" issues he has encountered since joining the company—Chapter 11 filings, labor negotiations/concessions, corporate downsizings, and "speculation about the company's future."

Taking the opposite stance, one professional described a somewhat bleak outlook for the empowerment of public relations in China:

> To my disappointment, most of the ... excellence characteristics are not reflective of my work experience in public relations.... Most companies in

China don't involve senior public relations executives with senior management. Public relations is mostly treated as a department responsible for communicating internally or externally. The dominant coalition for the most part doesn't include public relations people. There is no formal research or study to identify strategic publics, but mostly [the decisions about public relations] are based on experience and gut feelings.

This practitioner's experience is an interesting contrast to another who worked in China, and who argued that all of the elements of the Excellence Theory are at work there (see also Chen & Culbertson, 1996; Grunig, Grunig, Sriramesh, Huang, & Lyra, 1995; Rhee, 2002; Synnott & McKie, 1997). This 25-year industry veteran noted that public relations has become more empowered and strategic overall, and mentioned client work in China to make that point:

I think about my time in China in this regard [the value of public relations]. The public relations function was essential to most of my clients doing business in China. They assigned senior managers to direct the function and to manage us [the public relations agency]. They understood the need to identify and communicate with specific, targeted publics in China that could influence their success. And the knowledge, insights, and recommendations of my clients' public relations functions most certainly influences the "home office" and related departments.

Most professionals' experiences with empowerment were mixed, depending on the mindset of other managers at the organization about public relations, the function's position in the organizational structure, and type of industry. Several said that they were fortunate to work with enlightened managers who truly valued public relations or, as one noted, were easy to convince: "I made it clear to the CEO and shareholders that there is no way but to report to the CEO or myself being part of the dominant coalition.... This worked out very positively and was most effective." Two described how the empowerment of public relations was linked to its relationship with the marketing department. In one case, restructuring public relations to report to the marketing director was a positive step, because the marketing director listened to and valued the respondent's input. However, another participant described how important it was to "respect" public relations and marketing as "separate entities" and ensure that public relations is a "management function in its own right." Still others noted that because they worked in high-profile industries, such as biotechnology, they have always enjoyed an environment in which public relations is highly valued.

Roles. Not surprisingly, because the professionals surveyed here have the knowledge to enact the managerial role, they described their own positions and work this way. As mentioned before, some had held positions earlier in their careers in which they performed mostly technical work. One respondent in particular argued for a dual role as the ideal: "The role of the senior public relations executive requires a delicate balance of strategist, manager and technician.... [T]o instill confidence and build support, a good manager will roll up his/her sleeves and do the heavy lifting when necessary."

One response was especially indicative of the excellence principle having to do with knowledge needed for the managerial role:

> During my way through public relations positions, I met journalists as well as managers as heads of public relations departments.... Journalists in these functions often fail to develop, communicate, and share any strategic plan with their staff. This does not mean they did not have such a plan, but they are not likely to be able to give their staff direction. Thus, from my experience, technicians, especially journalists, are often less effective.

One pattern in several of the answers about roles is that some organizations recruit public relations technicians from other functions (e.g., customer service) or promote technicians to managerial ranks without adequate experience or training. When this happens, as these practitioners noted, the potential of the public relations function is diminished.

Statements about diversity among the survey participants were somewhat scant. Those who did address this issue tended to share perspectives that have been documented in academic literature (see Grunig, Toth, & Hon, 2002; Hon & Brunner, 2000; Kern-Foxworth, 1989; Pompper, 2004). For example, one said, "I find that most of the profession is female and the representation of minorities differs with each client." The practitioner who works in China commented that most professionals there are women, and men tend to have higher positions in organizations. However, the senior PAO for the Air Force noted that a number of Air Force PA offices are headed by women.

Organization of the Communication Function.   Clearly, these professionals' experiences and perceptions mesh with the excellence principle that the communication function should be integrated or coordinated. One respondent's comments about a former position seem especially descriptive of this notion:

> I was able to bring together communication directed to all of the organization's key publics under one roof. I was able to put together a team that I personally hired. Each of the people who worked for me (and by extension, their staff) were responsible for key audiences. During any corporate-wide initiative, we were able to sit down and establish a comprehensive communication strategy that took each audience into consideration and allowed us to present a consistent image and message to everyone.

Some of the statements about public relations as a management function separate from other functions had to do with public relations and marketing (both the positive and negative). One participant, however, eschewed thinking about public relations as being anything less than synonymous with top management:

> In our organization, public relations and strategic management have merged. They have become one. The internal and external communication (as well as publics and image considerations) are an integral part of the decision-making process. If you truly think about this excellence principle in full consequence to the end ... public relations is the thinking heart of an organization, of management.

Several of the practitioners saw lack of integration or coordination among communication departments as the function's "major weakness," as one said. Another felt frustrated by the lack of opportunity to coordinate communication programs and the "useless waste of energy" that results from turf confrontations.

Other professionals pointed out how important it is for public relations to build relationships with other departments beyond communication. Perhaps the best example was provided by a consultant:

> Many of my clients are product managers who are subject to the medical and legal regulatory folks of their overall companies. These MLR folks have a lot of control and make decisions that are not based on the product communication strategy but rather what is allowed under ... SEC, FDA, and other regulations.

Models of Public Relations. All of the respondents were advocates of the two-way symmetrical model of public relations, and most had been able to enact it or were working toward that goal. They also understood and acknowledged the importance of mixed motives for the public relations function.

One participant linked two-way symmetrical public relations to the overall management philosophy of his company. He described the organization's mind-set about communication as "systemic," noting that the company cares as much about input as output and that "information from outside is the blood that keeps the system alive."

The Air Force professional provided a strong endorsement for the two-way symmetrical model of public relations, and clearly articulated the corresponding principle of mixed motives:

> There are times when the PAO will represent and advocate the interests of the media/public regarding information ... affecting Air Force issues and operations. While ultimately, PAOs are loyal to the Air Force and DoD (Department of Defense) organizations, they are duty bound to provide

trusted counsel and advice to commanders regarding how to communicate news and information—good and bad—to the public, employees, and the media.

Several practitioners described how they had helped or were helping their organizations develop two-way symmetry. One noted that when she began working at a state college, the school practiced the one-way, asymmetrical, public information model (Grunig & Hunt, 1984). However, when she left 13 years later, although elements of public information were retained, she had set in place the two-way symmetrical model and had written this term into departmental policy documents. Another respondent acknowledged that his corporation needs to improve in the area of two-way symmetrical communication. However, he said that, with "blogs and new media, this model is getting easier."

A consultant described how her clients vary in terms of sophistication about public relations. She said that one was striving to have communication programs that reflected the two-way symmetrical model but was "not quite there" because so many of its public relations managers had been promoted within from other functions. In contrast, another of her clients has a more sophisticated understanding and organization of public relations and values "transparency, corporate social responsibility, and the importance of getting feedback."

One respondent thought that, overall, public relations agencies are more likely than corporate America to practice two-way symmetrical communication. She argued that practitioners in agencies have to listen to and serve the needs of their clients and employing agency. She went on to say that companies tend to be more removed from external publics and more loyal to internal publics, such as the board of directors, who can significantly impact companies' financial fate.

However, a participant from the corporate sector said that because loyalties are always mixed (organization and public), the two-way symmetrical model "meets the test for being most effective." He maintained that public relations professionals therefore should always strive to practice two-way communication and utilize research. And, as he added, "[Even in the] worst case, you can speculate on the interests, motivations, and reactions of key stakeholders and try to take that into account when making a decision, implementing a tactic, etc. That way, the two-way symmetrical model is only an arm's length away."

Again, the most dire response came from the respondent working in China, who maintained that two-way symmetrical public relations is rarely practiced there: "Most organizations just care about their own interests. Practitioners seldom have loyalty to their publics." Later in the survey, however, this professional did note the following:

> I want to stress that the Excellence Theory is really a great theory to guide
> public relations. However, the reality is often very disappointing in China.
> Public relations is a new industry here. Few organizations can really prac-
> tice excellent public relations. But I do believe things will get better soon as
> the industry matures.

Activism, Crises, and Conflict.   All of respondents acknowledged
the potential of excellent public relations for helping organizations respond to activism, crises, and conflict (see also Benoit, 1997; Coombs,
1998; Murphy, 1996; Murphy & Dee, 1996; Plowman, 1998; Susskind
& Field, 1996). They also were able to cite examples of how these forces
helped their organizations or clients better appreciate public relations.
One respondent made this point particularly well:

> I have often found that organizations rarely see the true value of public rela-
> tions until a crisis hits. That is usually when they are able to see all of the
> moving parts. If conflict stems from one "public," organizations will tend to
> react to that public/conflict in a silo, without taking the time to look at all
> audiences. Clearly, in my experience, when the communications function
> has a pulse on all publics, we have been better able (and sometimes the
> *only* ones able) to see the larger picture.

Another participant also argued that conflict situations can enhance
the reputation and stature of public relations: "The more high-profile
problems you solve with minimal pain, the more public relations will be
trusted and invited into the management suite." This practitioner went
on to say that solving the communication and relationship problems
that underlie conflict is a tangible and distinct contribution of effective
public relations that is also easier to quantify than are outcomes such as
sales. However, he noted that although crises are an opportunity for
public relations, if handled poorly, they also have the potential to move
the function "down the ladder."

One consultant mentioned that, among her clients, "crises have allowed public relations to be an important part of the response team,
from anticipation and planning through execution." She argued that
this happens because public relations "allows for strategies and tactics
that cannot be achieved via other communication routes such as advertising." She also noted that activism can help advance organizational
goals by providing opportunities for third-party alliances and engaging
negative publics to change opinions or actions on both sides.

The NGO president provided a compelling story of a recent crisis involving an employee with whom the group lost contact after war broke
out in the West African country where she was working. He attributed
the NGO's success at responding to the crisis to the "contingency plan"
in place, an approach he said he learned from another graduate student
at University of Maryland. He went on to say that, for his organization,

"'crisis' doesn't have negative connotations," but rather is a challenge and a chance for excellence:

> Now, we communicate more in advance (risk communication) and take all stakeholders into account (even the parents and family members of our employees). It's sometimes a daunting task, but necessary and rewarding. It's a strategic investment decision. We invest in people, in human capital, in relationships. The return on investment (ROI) is a bargain.

Other professionals cited examples of having helped their organizations through crises and the resulting positive effects for public relations. Some, however, did mention frustrations and constraints. For example, one said that during his organization's Chapter 11 period, he felt the company was definitely more open to strategic communication counsel and deferred to the public relations department's expertise. However, after the crisis was over, a new department head, whom he described as a "tactician," seemed to propel the organization into "backslide."

Another respondent's experiences echoed this dilemma:

> No question—activism, crises, and other sources of conflict have moved clients/companies I have worked for in the direction of excellence. Whether they acted on their newfound knowledge to make permanent changes is another question. I have been out of the corporate environment for close to 10 years now, but I would say that, up until I left, there was not a total buy-in to the two-way symmetrical model.

Still another practitioner mentioned that although she wanted to direct her organization toward a philosophy of issues management, the farthest she could get was the "crisis communication model"—that is, implementing her organization's first crisis communication plan, inserting the public relations director into the primary information loop (a first), and educating others to realize that public relations must be "in on issues from the beginning, not just brought in at the end to deal with the media."

One consultant speculated on the dynamics that may cause some organizations to turn away from the excellence principles during times of environmental turbulence:

> In corporate communication, when the CEO is in the spotlight for positive or negative reasons, the internal ranks seem to close and unify to defend him [sic] and sustain the corporate image. All other goals or differences have seemed to vanish in the face of that current crisis. Other types of conflict or crisis (such as when the technology sector slumped so badly in the early 2000s) have caused organizations, especially agencies, to close up, become paralyzed even in their internal communication—that is, have drastically changed otherwise open and two-way communication environ-

ments—with dire results (loss of good staff, plummeting stock, the lost of client confidence). Other forms of activism (e.g., a luxury retailer was beset by animal activists protesting its sale of fur coats) have resulted in a shutting off of communication with one or more publics, rather than creating more openness that could have better overall results for the organization.

Culture, Internal Communication, Structure, Equal Opportunity, and Job Satisfaction.   Overall, participants' experiences reflected how the internal characteristics of excellence are predictive of effective public relations. Again, many believed that they had helped move or were trying to move their organizations and clients toward internal excellence. Among the latter group, some recalled specific organizational variables that they thought were inhibitors of excellence.

A former consultant who now works in corporate public relations provided a cogent layperson description of Excellence Theory as it relates to internal organizational factors:

> The best examples I have seen are where organizations offer multiple feedback channels and then promote how that feedback has been acted on, and if not, why not. Good organizations are confident, open, and trust their coworkers. I have seen other organizations that try to manage by fear. Doing that, though, degrades coworker loyalty. Our company has a guiding principle that happy coworkers lead to happy customers.

Perhaps the most philosophical description of internal excellence came from the NGO head who took a somewhat postmodern stance (Holtzhausen, 2000; Toth, 2002) by rejecting the concept of structure. For him, the essence of his organization is not structure, but being a "learning company." He described his organization using the oxymoron "flat hierarchy," and said that it is "99 percent participative" with a "360-degree feedback system" and multidirectional information flows. He argued for this approach, stating that the 20th century brought the realization that "uncertainty crumbles in your hand," "control is an illusion," and "we cannot any longer have a fixed, certain view of anything." Thus, in his organization, communicators are "uncertainty managers" and employees are rewarded for "talking about failure" (i.e., without blame) and listening to others:

> It's funny but it works. You can't get more two-way communication (input, suggestions, discussions, and feedback) as when you commit to listen. Every decision maker has to go and sit with stakeholders for 5 hours a week—and just listen (I call it the shut-up approach). I feel as if we are not only a learning organization but a "listening organization." We celebrate it. We cultivate it. It can be fun—and it pays off.

Another strong endorsement for internal excellence came from, ironically, the practitioner working with multinational companies in China.

This professional attributed the organization's positive internal environment to managers who cultivate free expression among employees and then act on employee suggestions. Job turnover is high, however, due to heavy workload demands.

At the other end of the spectrum was a participant who seemed to question some of the internal excellence components, saying he thought they existed more in theory than the "real world." This professional explained that most of the organizations he had worked for were too small to have a "planned and managed internal communications culture." Additionally, he argued that when an organization becomes big enough to plan and manage internally, it tends to automatically develop a bureaucratic structure.

Most of the respondents described working in organizations or with clients somewhere in the middle range for most of these internal dimensions (i.e., strived to be excellent but were necessarily somewhat or altogether bureaucratic) or had moved back and forth in culture and structure due to changes in management personnel or environmental forces. As one said, many organizations could be characterized as authoritarian "disguised as participative ... with well-meaning intentions." To make her point, she cited widespread use of "task forces, brainstorming, SWOT teams, etc., that do allow for broader and more equal input." However, she argued that despite these improvements, "internally there is much work to be done." Another noted that her organization "just changed in that direction (toward excellence) out of pressure from the internal community, changes in the business world, and market pressures."

One professional indicted public relations agencies for failing as examples of internal excellence, arguing that "people stay mostly because they are holding onto their jobs rather than fulfillment." This practitioner thought that in corporate communication environments, internal excellence is more evident because "companies are run by people with management and business training who are committed to successful businesses, not just creative or interesting communication."

A participant from the corporate sector, however, talked about how difficult it is to enact two-way symmetrical communication internally when dealing with organized labor: "Labor-management disputes, work rules, and contracts all contribute to a difficult environment, and it limits your ability to be creative, open, and as effective as one would like."

Many of the respondents believed that employee job satisfaction was highly dependent on factors beyond internal communication. One cited "commitment to the company's core values" as key, whereas several others mentioned "passion" for the organization's mission. A good example of the latter was provided by a practitioner who works for a performing arts center:

> I tend to have a lot of job satisfaction because I love the strategy of marketing and public relations and I am in the position to develop and implement programs with the input from my department that feeds my professional drives, while still doing something that adds to the quality of life for the community in which I live.

Only three of the participants addressed the internal excellence dimension of equal opportunity explicitly (see Aldoory & Toth, 2002, 2004; Grunig, Toth, & Hon, 2001; Toth, 2001), and two were quite positive. One noted that all of the organizations she had worked for provided equal opportunity, and another said that three fourths of the managers at his organization are women. One practitioner, however, hinted at the reality that the workplace is not a perfect meritocracy. This professional, who identified herself as a young female, mentioned hiring "older, gray-haired male" consultants (and, in one case, "a gray-haired, very experienced, and well-respected female" consultant) to help "sell" her strategies and ensure that her advice "would be heard."

Final Thoughts: Challenges and Accolades

In the "additional comments" section on the survey, one respondent took the opportunity to address challenges for the field. Two others had made similar comments in their earlier answers, so it seems appropriate to group these together here.

These practitioners were concerned about the relationship of public relations to business. One wished for more "fly or die/make or brake" involvement in the public relations business as part of the university curriculum. Another felt that more business courses would help practitioners "better understand the language of businesspeople," or the "key internal stakeholders who can have at least as much impact on job performance as external stakeholders." This assertion seems implicit in the third professional's response about the challenges that public relations faces:

> Public relations must add the disciplines of business to its profession in order to truly achieve the qualities of excellence. A major change also must occur inside public relations agencies before the profession will change its reputation into one of a necessary business function, tied to business profits, growth, and overall success, rather than a supporting one.

The remainder of the participants provided personal thoughts about the Grunigs. These former students were effusive in describing the effect that Lauri and Jim have had on their personal and professional lives. One said it was "very sad for future students" that the Grunigs have retired. Another spoke of the "debt of gratitude" owed to Jim and

Lauri for "their intellectual curiosity, their research, and their tireless push to give public relations greater stature within organizations, more sophisticated responsibilities, and more importance in society overall."

Several former students addressed Excellence Theory specifically in their final comments. One response in particular seems to reflect everyone's feelings:

> I just think the world of the education I received at University of Maryland from Lauri and Jim, and feel very fortunate to have learned and grown under them. You hear so many people say that the education they received *for their field* gave them little practical knowledge/skills once they were in the work world. Not the case for me. To have received such a progressive, sophisticated, thorough, and inspiring education is such a gift of great fortune. And, I think my education was so good that it helped me continue to grow and learn in my profession for years after I left. Each year, there are countless occasions where I put into practice Excellence Theory with good results, and find that when aspects of excellence aren't followed, fairly predicable, less-than-desirable results follow.

CONCLUSION

This chapter has attempted to provide insights into how academic theory in public relations has entered practice. To do so, the perceptions and experiences of 15 practitioners as they relate to the excellence program of research have been analyzed and presented.

Overall, these respondents believe that Excellence Theory provides a conceptually rich framework for understanding public relations. Excellence is also powerful at the operational level. Participants provided real-life testimony about their successes with enacting Excellence Theory, while also discussing other variables that contribute to or hinder the effectiveness of the public relations function at their organizations or among their clients.

It is my hope that, taken together, these practitioners' voices bring Excellence Theory out of the pages of textbooks and into the day-to-day opportunities and challenges of public relations practice. I close by offering a sentiment shared by one professional that reflects my own feelings. Her comment also delivers a compelling charge to all of those committed to advancing public relations as an academic and professional discipline: "I believe that studying under and working with Drs. Jim and Lauri Grunig and learning the Excellence Theory have taught me to be a true public relations professional, and I hope to pass on the Excellence Theory and move the field of public relations forward."

REFERENCES

Aldoory, T., & Toth, E. L. (2002). Gender discrepancies in a gendered profession: A developing theory for public relations. *Journal of Public Relations Research, 14*(2), 103–126.

Aldoory, L., & Toth, E. (2004). Leadership and gender in public relations: Perceived effectiveness. *Journal of Public Relations Research, 16*(2), 157–183.

Benoit, W. L. (1997). Image repair discourse and crisis communication. *Public Relations Review, 23*(2), 177–186.

Berger, B. K. (2005). Power over, power with, and power to relations: Critical reflections on public relations, the dominant coalition, and activism. *Journal of Public Relations Research, 17*(1), 5–27.

Botan, C. H., & Taylor, M. (2004). Public relations: State of the field. *Journal of Communication, 54*(4), 645–661.

Bowen, S. (2004). Expansion of ethics as the tenth generic principle of public relations excellence: A Kantian theory and model for managing ethical issues. *Journal of Public Relations Research, 16*(1), 65–92.

Bowen, S. (2005). A practical model for ethical decision making in issues management and public relations. *Journal of Public Relations Research, 17*(3), 191–216.

Broom, G. M., & Dozier, D. M. (1986). Advancement for public relations role models. *Public Relations Review, 12*(1), 37–56.

Broom, G. M, & Smith, G. D. (1979). Testing the practitioner's impact on clients. *Public Relations Review, 5*(3), 47–59.

Cancel, A. E., Cameron, G. T., Sallot, L. M., & Mitrook, M. A. (1997). It depends: A contingency theory of accommodation in public relations. *Journal of Public Relations Research, 9*(1), 31–63.

Chen, N., & Culbertson, H. M. (1996). Guest relations: A demanding but constrained role for lady PR practitioners in mainland China. *Public Relations Review, 22*(3), 279–296.

Coombs, W. T. (1998). An analytic framework for crisis situations: Better responses from a better understanding of the situation. *Journal of Public Relations Research, 10*(3), 177–191.

Cornelissen, J. P. (2000). Toward an understanding of the use of academic theories in public relations practice. *Public Relations Review, 26*(3), 315–326.

Dozier, D., Grunig, L., & Grunig, J. (1995). *Manager's guide to excellence in public relations and communication management.* Mahwah, NJ: Lawrence Erlbaum Associates.

Grunig, J., Dozier, D., Ehling, W., Grunig, L., Repper, F., & White, J. (1992). *Excellence in public relations and communication management.* Hillsdale, NJ: Lawrence Erlbaum Associates.

Grunig, J., Grunig, L., Sriramesh, K., Huang, Y., & Lyra, A. (1995). Models of public relations in an international setting. *Journal of Public Relations Research, 7*(3), 163–186.

Grunig, J., & Hunt, T. (1984). *Managing public relations.* New York: Holt, Rinehart & Winston.

Grunig, L., Grunig, J., & Dozier, D. (2002). *Excellent public relations and effective organizations: A study of communication management in three countries.* Mahwah, NJ: Lawrence Erlbaum Associates.

Grunig, L., Toth, E., & Hon, L. (2001). *Women in public relations. How gender influences practice.* Mahwah, NJ: Lawrence Erlbaum Associates.

Hallahan, K. (1993). The paradigm struggle in public relations practice. *Public Relations Review, 19*(2), 197–205.

Heath, R.L. (2001). *Handbook of public relations.* Thousand Oaks, CA: Sage.

Holtzhausen, D. R. (2000). Postmodern values in public relations. *Journal of Public Relations Research, 12*(1), 93–114.

Holtzhausen, D., Petersen, B., & Tindall, N. (2003). Exploding the myth of the symmetrical/asymmetrical dichotomy: Public relations models in the new South Africa. *Journal of Public Relations Research, 15*(4), 305–341.

Hon, L. C. (1997). What have you done for me lately? Exploring effectiveness in public relations. *Journal of Public Relations Research, 9*(1), 1–30.

Hon, L., & Brunner, B. (2000). Diversity issues in public relations. *Journal of Public Relations Research, 12*(4), 309–340.

Kern-Foxworth, M. (1989). Status and roles of minority PR practitioners. *Public Relations Review, 15*(3), 39–47.

L'Etang, J., & Pieczka, M. (1996). *Critical perspectives in public relations.* London: International Thomson.

Miller, G. R. (1989). Persuasion and public relations: Two p's in a pod. In C. H. Botan & V. Hazelton, (Eds.), *Public relations theory* (pp. 45–66). Hillsdale, NJ: Lawrence Erlbaum Associates.

Murphy, P. (1989). Game theory as a paradigm for the public relations process. In C. Botan & V. Hazleton (Eds.), *Public relations theory* (pp. 173–192). Hillsdale, NJ: Lawrence Erlbaum Associates.

Murphy, P. (1996). Chaos theory as a model for managing issues and crisis. *Public Relations Review, 22*(2), 95–113.

Murphy, P., & Dee, J. (1996). Reconciling the preferences of environmental activists and corporate policymakers. *Journal of Public Relations Research, 8*(1), 1–33.

Pieczka, M. (2000). Objectives and evaluation in public relations work: What do they tell us about expertise and professionalism? *Journal of Public Relations Research, 12*(3), 211–233.

Plowman, K. (1998). Power in conflict for public relations. *Journal of Public Relations Research, 10*(4), 237–261.

Pompper, D. (2004). Linking ethnic diversity and two-way symmetry: Modeling female African American practitioners' roles. *Journal of Public Relations Research, 16*(3), 269–301.

Rhee, Y. (2002). Global public relations: A cross-cultural study of the Excellence Theory in South Korea. *Journal of Public Relations Research, 14*(3), 159–184.

Roper, J. (2005). Symmetrical communication: Excellent public relations or a strategy for hegemony? *Journal of Public Relations Research, 17*(1), 69–86.

Sallot, L. M., Cameron, G. T., & Weaver-Lariscy, R. A. (1998). Pluralistic ignorance and professional standards: Underestimating professionalism of our peers in public relations. *Public Relations Review, 24*(1), 1–19.

Sallot, L. M., Lyon, L. J., Acosta-Alzuru, C., & Jones, K. O. (2003). From aardvark to zebra: A new millennium analysis of theory development in public relations academic journals. *Journal of Public Relations Research, 15*(1), 27–90.

Susskind, L., & Field, P. (1996). *Dealing with an angry public.* New York: Free Press.

Synnott, G., & McKie, D. (1997). International issues in PR: Researching research and prioritizing priorities. *Journal of Public Relations Research, 9*(4), 259–282.

Toth, E. L. (1992). The case for pluralistic studies of public relations: Rhetorical, critical, and systems perspectives. In E. L. Toth & Robert L. Heath (Eds.), *Rhetorical and critical approaches to public relations* (pp. 3–15). Hillsdale, NJ: Lawrence Erlbaum Associates.

Toth, E. L. (2001). How feminist theory advanced the practice of public relations. In R. L. Heath (Ed.), *Public relations handbook* (pp. 237–246). Thousand Oaks, CA: Sage.

Toth, E. L. (2002). Postmodernism for modernist public relations: The cash value and application of critical research in public relations. *Public Relations Review, 28*(3), 243–250.

Wylie, F. W. (1994). Commentary: Public relations is not yet a profession. *Public Relations Review, 20*(1), 1–3.

II

Advances in Understanding Excellence and Communication

Collaborative Advocacy and the Creation of Trust: Toward an Understanding of Stakeholder Claims and Risks

Christopher H. Spicer
Towson University

In his introduction to the *Handbook of Public Relations*, Heath (2001) listed 20 words and phrases that he identified as constituting an "emerging vocabulary" representative of the "heart and soul of current intellectual ferment" in the discipline (p. 2). The terms included *relationships, shared control, trust, social capital, shared meaning, argumentativeness, openness, multiple publics* (stakeholders and stakeseekers), *legitimacy gap, power,* and *collaborative decision making,* among others. Heath continued his introductory essay by suggesting that "no term is more important to understanding relationships than is *community*" (p. 3, italics in original). It is the concept of community as stakeholder that this current chapter addresses.

As I read the words linked to the emerging vocabulary, I could not help but be struck by how many of them emanated one way or another from the work of Jim Grunig and his many colleagues, especially the historical and continuing impact of the two-way symmetrical model of public relations. I can think of few instances whereby a concept has had such a profound and lasting effect in a communication discipline as has the two-way symmetrical model (Grunig, 2001; Grunig & Hunt, 1984). The model has spawned scholarly work as well as best public relations practices. The discipline we know as public relations would be intellectually and pragmatically poorer without the articulation of the two-way symmetrical model of organizational public relations.

That said, I have also been impressed over the years in the ways in which the original model has been challenged, tweaked, morphed and revised to the current "mixed-motive" model incorporating both two-way asymmetrical as well as two-way symmetrical communication between an organization and its publics (Dozier, Grunig, & Grunig, 1995; Grunig, 2001). The efficacy and ethical nature of the symmetrical model has been confirmed to the point that it is generally accepted; the asymmetrical model can be used effectively and even ethically "depending on the rules used to ensure ethical practice" (Grunig, 2001, p. 29). We seem to have arrived at a theoretical and pragmatic understanding that both persuasion and dialogue may be necessary independently or compatibly given the situation, the goals of the organization, the goals of the stakeholders, and existing external constraints (e.g., legal mandates or cultural mores). This combination is what I labeled *collaborative advocacy* in an earlier work (Spicer, 1997).

What is less clear at this time are more fundamental questions about stakeholders, particularly those loosely identified as "the community." These questions emanate from Freeman's (1984) seminal book, *Strategic Management: A Stakeholder Approach*, in which he defined a stakeholder as "any group or individual who can affect or is affected by the achievement of the firm's objectives" (p. 25). From the very beginning, scholars and practitioners have struggled with the broadness of Freeman's definition. Is any group with the ability to influence the organization a stakeholder ("who can affect")? How wide a net needs to be cast to discover all of the entities possibly affected by an organization's decisions or actions ("is affected")? Which stakeholders warrant a manager's attention? Which stakeholders have a moral claim on the organization? Attempts to answer these and other, similar questions have driven stakeholder scholarship for the past 20 years.

Seeking a more collaborative stance between a firm and its stakeholders has been championed recently within the management and business ethics literatures, attesting to a maturing articulation of a stakeholder model of the firm (Friedman & Miles, 2002; Jonker & Foster, 2002; Rowley, 1997). These models range from ones in which a more or less traditional managerial structure attempts to manage stakeholders such that the goals of the firm can be better achieved, thereby enhancing shareholder wealth, to ones in which multiple critical stakeholders have an immediate say in actually establishing the goals of the organization. Simmons, for example, (2004) viewed "organizational systems as the negotiated outcome of salient stakeholder groups [thereby] facilitating a more democratic form of accountability ..." (p. 602). Starck and Kruckeberg (2001) suggested that "a different and broader accountability method is in order, one that takes into account as much as possible all entities among the environmental constituencies that are potentially affected by the corporation" (p. 55). In either case, but especially the latter, collaboration is essential in maintaining the viability of the stakeholder firm.

In the broadest sense, there are three approaches to thinking about stakeholders that are evident in the literature: instrumental, descriptive, and normative. The *instrumental approach* focuses on a managerial, quasi-shareholder model that is primarily concerned with enhancing the organization's ability to produce "organizational wealth" (Preston & Donaldson, 1999). Those working from a *descriptive approach* attempt to describe what a firm actually does in responding to stakeholder influences or claims, building theory from the ground up. Finally, the *normative approach* is grounded in writings on business ethics and corporate responsibility and examines organizational and stakeholder relationships from a moral perspective. In this chapter, I intend to follow the tradition established by several authors by drawing from both instrumental and normative approaches (Mitchell, Agle, & Wood, 1997; Phillips, 2003).

My purpose in this chapter is to examine recent stakeholder literature to assess what it might add to our knowledge of when collaborative or symmetrical communication is warranted between an organization and its stakeholders. I am interested in the reciprocal nature of stakeholder claims, risk, and trust. I place particular emphasis on the "community" stakeholder. The importance accorded to relationships with community notwithstanding (Heath, 2001; Kruckeberg & Stark, 1988; Stark & Kruckeberg, 2001), communities are often dependent on the organization, vulnerable to risk from an organization's behavior. In a nutshell, my argument is that an imbalance of power in favor of an organization increases the vulnerability of those stakeholders without power, which leads to increased risk that can only be alleviated through the creation of trust that comes about, in part, from collaborative advocacy. I begin by examining ways in which the concept of stakeholder has been defined.

DEFINING STAKEHOLDERS

Donaldson and Preston (1995) wrote, "It is essential to draw a clear distinction between influencers and stakeholders: ... some recognizable stakeholders (e.g., the job applicants) have no influence, and some influencers (e.g., the media) have no stakes" (p. 86). Coombs (1998) noted that "stakeholders are more precisely conceptualized as two distinct variants: primary and secondary" (p. 292). Drawing from Donaldson and Preston (1995), Coombs defined primary stakeholders as those who can harm or benefit the organization, and secondary stakeholders (or influencers) as "those who can affect or be affected by the actions of an organization" (p. 292), but not to the critical degree that primary stake-holders can.

Clarkson (1995) proposed that only those stakeholders who are risk bearers—have some form of financial or human capital and, therefore, something to lose or gain—should be considered stakeholders of the firm. Those with something to "lose or gain" hold a claim on the organization to having their interest acknowledged or served. Kaler (2004) aptly distinguished between claimant and influencer when he commented, "I am favoring what ... I label a 'claimant' definition of stakeholder status over the alternative of an 'influencer' definition: that is to say, a characterization in terms of an ability to aid or impede whatever strategic aims an organization happens to have" (p. 75). The claimant definition "tells us what the goals of an organization should be (namely, to serve stakeholder interests), an influencer definition does not.... It simply says that here is a grouping that can aid or impede whatever goals an organization has" (Kaler, 2004, p. 76).

Assumption 1: Stakeholders with claims incur risks, influencers do not.

Much of the recent stakeholder scholarship based on an instrumental approach is grounded in resource dependency theory (Frooman, 1999; Jawahar & McLaughlin, 2001; Mellahi & Wood, 2003). Resource dependency theory (RDT) emanates from open systems theory, placing the organization within a larger environment of suppliers, competitors, government agencies, customers, and the like. Working from a resource dependency approach led Kochan and Rubinstein (2000) to propose a definition of stakeholders based on:

> "(1) the extent to which potential stakeholders contribute valued resources to the firm (2) the extent to which they put those resources at risk ... and (3) the power they have in or over an organization." (p. 369)

This definition is typical of most working from a RDT framework in that it incorporates the necessity of a resource or claim, the potential of negative consequences or risk, and the ability to influence the focal organization or power.

Assumption 2: Stakeholders with a claim and the power to influence the satisfactory achievement of that claim will be more likely to receive managerial attention than will stakeholders without a claim and/or without power.

In stakeholder models based on resource dependency theory, the degree to which an organization is dependent on a stakeholder (and vice

versa) is determined by a combination of the nature of the resource provided and the ability of the stakeholder to influence the organization.
The matrix in Fig. 2.1 indicates under what conditions a firm or stakeholder is independent of one another and under what conditions they
are closely linked or interdependent. In Fig. 2.1, for example, power is
judged to be relatively equal in Quadrant 4, lopsided toward one party
or another in Quadrants 2 and 3, and nonexistent or not applicable in
Quadrant 1.

It is not clear, however, from a resource dependency model, that a
stakeholder located in Quadrant 3 of Fig. 2.1, might still have a claim on
the organization. Noting that Freeman's (1984) definition yielded two
types of stakeholders—those that can affect the organization and those
affected by the organization—Goodpaster (1991) labeled the former
strategic stakeholders and the latter *moral stakeholders*. Although this
parsimonious distinction is still debated, it serves to move us from an
entirely resource-dependent distinction and introduce Simmons' (2004)
concept of a "silent stakeholder" who may incur risk given the outcomes of organization decisions. Given their typology based on power,
legitimacy, and urgency, Mitchell et al. (1997) described dependent
stakeholders as having legitimate urgent claims but no power with
which to pursue them.

Stakeholder Power

		Low	High
Organization Power	Low	1.No dependence	2.Organization dependent on stakeholder
	High	3.Stakeholder dependent on organization	4.Interdependent

FIG. 2.1.   Dependency matrix.

Assumption 3: If a stakeholder is without the power to pursue a claim, the claim can only be addressed by a third party who has power or the benevolence of the organization.

In his summary of the literature on trust in social structures, such as organizations, Hosmer (1995) concluded that "trust is generally accompanied by an assumption of an acknowledged or accepted duty to protect the rights and interests of others" (p. 392). In the absence of third-party intervention to press the claims of silent or dependent stakeholders, managers may have a duty to protect the rights and interests of others, even if those others have no apparent claim stemming from resource dependency theory and/or no power to influence the firm.

RESPONSIBILITIES AND DUTIES

Kaler (2003) proposed a helpful way of thinking about the organization's obligation to silent stakeholders using the nature of responsibilities and duties. Briefly, Kaler (2003) suggested that there are general and role-specific responsibilities:

> The former hold for people in general and are such fundamental responsibilities as the duty not to kill, cheat, steal, and so on. The latter do not hold generally but are particular to people in specific sorts of positions or relationships; in short those fulfilling a particular social role. (p. 76)

The role of the public relations practitioner is just such a "particular social role," one that includes a basic role set of responsibilities, both to the organization as well as to others (Berger, 2005).

Kaler (2003) continued by delineating two types of duties, perfect and imperfect, such that "with the perfect there is a corresponding right to the performance of that duty whereas with the imperfect there is not" (p. 76). Kaler noted that the admonition not to kill is a general duty corresponding with the perfect responsibility to a universal right to life. He continued, "Likewise, corresponding to the role-specific duty of parents to care for their offspring is the role-specific right of those offspring to be cared for" (p. 76). Included in the imperfect duties are "duties of *benevolence to look after the interests of others*: duties of generosity, consideration, kindness, and so on" (p.76, italics added).

Assumption 4: In that the resolution of claims of dependent or silent stakeholders are bestowed through third-party intervention or the benevolence of the organization, managers will judge them to be imperfect duties and, as such, consider their fulfillment only morally desirable rather than obligatory.

THE PLACE OF COMMUNITY IN THE PANTHEON
OF STAKEHOLDERS

When asked to delineate the stakeholders of a firm, a fairly common list emerges that includes shareholders, employees, customers, suppliers, competitors, government agencies, and communities in which the firm is physically located. More enlightened lists include the natural environment, society in general, future generations, and the like. In a speech titled "Walking the High Wire: Balancing Stakeholder Interests," the then-chairman and CEO of Eastman Chemical Company, Earnie Deavenport, listed five: "employees (of which management is a subset), our customers, suppliers, various publics, and investors" (1996, p. 1). He spoke positively, noting a variety of mutually beneficial programs that supported relationships with employees, customers, suppliers, and investors. Of the communities in which his firm operated, Deavenport said:

> If a company has the reputation for poor labor practices, or is perceived as a poor environmental steward, or simply extracts value rather than giving something back, the general public will take recourse. They can boycott your products. They can generate adverse publicity to hurt you in the market place.

> They can bring down upon you the wrath of local, state, and even federal government. The public can do any number of things to make life miserable if they feel they have been shut out as a stakeholder. (p. 3)

Although this is an accurate description of what a community might do if its members felt shut out or neglected, Davenport did not allow as to how the relationship should be managed proactively or positively to enhance mutual benefit. What he did describe, and vividly so, was the extent of *third-party intervention* available to a community adversely affected by an organization's actions. He did not, however, include *organizational benevolence* as a prime consideration or strategy.

In a test of their contingency theory of accommodation, Cancel, Mitrook, and Cameron (1999) found that all of the 18 senior public relations practitioners they interviewed could provide positive examples of interactions between their corporations and communities. The most notable predisposing variable for accommodation via community relations was the dominant coalition's support for community relations activities. If the CEO in particular supported community relations activities, then they were accomplished; if the CEO did not support or perceive a value to community relations, they did not occur.

Although empirical evidence is scant, several studies of organizational stakeholder prioritizing and bottom-line effect lend support to my assumption that duties owed to communities are imperfect at best. For example, in a study of CEOs in 80 large U.S. firms, Agle, Mitchell, and Sonnenfeld (1999) discerned that CEOs paid more attention to those stakeholders "that are part of the traditional production function view of the firm—shareholders, employees, and customers" than they did to stakeholders "that are part of the expanded stakeholder view of the firm: governments and communities" (p. 520). Berman, Wicks, Kotha, and Jones (1999) correlated stakeholder relationships with the financial performance of the firm and discovered that only employees and stakeholders identified with product safety/quality positively affected financial performance. Stakeholder variables associated with "community, diversity, and the natural environment ... failed to exhibit statistically significant impacts on firm financial performance" (p. 501).

Although the importance of community is recognized and often nurtured in a wide variety of ways by organizations, especially through corporate philanthropy, it appears safe to conclude that other stakeholders are often thought to be more important to the continuing success of the firm. Mellahi and Wood (2003) maintained that "managers—especially CEOs ... pay more attention to stakeholders who control resources critical to the organization than to stakeholders who do not control such critical resources" (p. 186).

Assumption 5: As a stakeholder, the community is often perceived by managers of the firm to be dependent, subordinate to those stakeholders who have a claim and therefore risk associated with critical resources necessary for the firm to achieve its strategic goals.

STAKEHOLDER RISK

Sheppard and Sherman (1998) elaborated a number of dimensions concerning risk that vary given the nature of the organizational and stakeholder relationship based on relationship form and depth. Relationship form is described as being either dependent or interdependent, whereas relational depth as either shallow or deep. Once again, a two-by-two matrix can be created identifying four quadrants: shallow dependence or shallow interdependence and deep dependence or deep interdependence. I am most interested in the risks associated with relationships characterized by deep dependence, in that they are most like Simmons' (2004) silent stakeholders, without power but dependent on the organization. The risks associated with this relational form include acts of commission such as cheating, in that the dependent party is not aware of an action (e.g., holding back necessary information). They also include risks of omission, in that one's interests can be ignored. In this instance, Sheppard and Sherman (1998) wrote that "employees, shareholders, or other constituent groups regularly risk that the managers of a firm will not consider their interests in key decisions made privately" (p. 425).

The authors continued by identifying and characterizing qualities of trustworthiness that the four relational types should seek, given the particular risks associated with the form and depth of the relationship. Interestingly, in light of Kaler's (2003) work on perfect and imperfect duties, Sheppard and Sherman (1998) suggested that stakeholder relationships characterized by deep dependence should look for *integrity, concern,* and *benevolence. Concern* and *benevolence* fall into Kaler's description of imperfect duties, in that their performance is "merely morally desirable" opposed to "morally obligatory." An action or behavior that is only desirable as opposed to obligatory is one that may be ignored or treated lightly by an organization's management. It is in addressing the risk inherent in dependent situations like these that the development of trust between stakeholder and organization is critical. As Wicks, Berman, and Jones (1999) noted, "trust becomes both possible and important in contexts where parties have something at risk" (p. 104).

STAKEHOLDER TRUST

Although definitions of trust abound, there is a centrality to the idea that trust is born of risk, with risk often defined in terms of vulnerability and power. A commonly accepted definition is that "trust is a psychological state comprising the intention to accept vulnerability based upon positive expectations of the intentions or behavior of another" (Rousseau, Sitkin, Burt, & Camerer, 1998, p. 395). Commenting on the definition proposed by Rousseau et al., Fichman (2003) agreed that "both risk and interdependence are necessary conditions for trust to matter" (p. 135). Other definitions of trust have incorporated similar understandings of risk and vulnerability (Kramer, 1999; Morrow, Hansen, & Pearson, 2004; Wicks & Berman, 2004).

Moving closer to a description of the nature of trust between an organization and its stakeholders is the definition of general trust offered by Morrow et al. (2004): "to refer to one's overall belief that another individual, group or organization will not act to exploit one's vulnerabilities" (p. 50). Or, as Hosmer (1995) wrote, "[T]rust generally occurs under conditions of vulnerability to the interests of the individual and dependence upon the behavior of other people" (p. 390).

Generally, the literature has agreed that the greater the vulnerability, the greater the risk, and potentially the greater the obligation for trust. Wicks et al. (1999) noted that "where dependence (i.e., risk) exists, trust becomes a potential coping mechanism; as it increases so too does the potential need for trust" (p. 104). I would argue that stakeholders in Quadrant 3 are potentially vulnerable to decisions and behaviors made by the organization's managers, if not the outright misuse of the organization's power.

Assumption 6: Dependent stakeholders, such as communities, are in the vulnerable position of having to trust the organization in times when a strategic decision is made that might adversely affect their well-being.

PROPOSITIONS

A stakeholder without apparent claim from a resource dependency theoretical perspective and/or lacking power to directly influence the firm is often vulnerable to decisions made by the managers of the firm. This vulnerability is especially acute when the firm's decision results in a degree of risk—potential negative consequences—to the dependent stakeholder. The vulnerability created by the firm becomes in and of itself a claim on the part of the dependent stakeholder. Subsequently, the resolution of the vulnerability-based claim can be resolved by third-party intervention or the benevolence of the firm. Benevolence from the firm through the actions of its managers comes about through the creation of a long-term relationship characterized by trust between the firm and the dependent stakeholder. Ultimately, trust becomes a critical coping mechanism for stakeholders dependent on the benevolence of a firm.

Given that there can be stakeholders who are dependent, that these stakeholders may be put at risk by the firm and thereby vulnerable to the firm's actions, that the act of making someone vulnerable ascribes a claim to the vulnerable party, and, finally, that the vulnerable party seeks to trust the focal organization, I propose the following:

Proposition 1: Organizational managers have an imperfect duty to a dependent stakeholder when the actions of the organization do not put the stakeholder at risk given its vulnerability. In other words, managers are not morally obligated to include dependent stakeholders in two-way symmetrical collaborations to establish organizational goals or strategy, although they may choose to do so.

Proposition 2: Organizational managers have a perfect duty to a dependent stakeholder when the actions of the organization put that stakeholder at risk. The nature of a perfect duty is such that the managers are morally obligated to engage in two-way symmetrical collaboration with the dependent stakeholder in order to alleviate as best they can the risk entailed in the decision.

In the case of dependent stakeholders—those vulnerable to risk from a firm's actions and necessarily forced to trust the organization on their behalf—managers are obligated to engage in two-way symmetrical communication. The very vulnerability of the powerless stakeholder creates a claim sufficient and necessary to be "heard" by the organization's managers. Dependent stakeholders trust the focal firm to engage them in collaborative dialogue when the conditions of a perfect duty materialize within the decision-making process of the firm.

GENERATING TRUST THROUGH COLLABORATIVE ADVOCACY

It is timely at this juncture to note that "organizations cannot trust, only individuals within organizations are capable of trust (Morrow et al., 2004, p. 51). Not only is trust generated between individuals, it also is derived from cooperation. As Hosmer (1995) concluded, "[T]rust is generally associated with willing, not forced, cooperation and with the benefits resulting from that cooperation" (p. 390). In that the creation and nurturing of trust is a critical coping mechanism for pressing the claims of dependent stakeholders, collaborative symmetrical communication between the firm and the stakeholders is critical (Das & Teng, 1998). A body of research on the benefits of collaborative advocacy in establishing public policies regarding the management of natural resources is indicative of the trust-building power of symmetrical dialogue (Frame, Gunton, & Day, 2004; Gray, 2004; Paretti & Tech, 2003; Schusler, Decker, & Pfeffer, 2003; Weible, Sabatier, & Lubell, 2004).

Although the success of these efforts varied, several benefits regarding collaborative communication procedures are emerging:

1. Improved stakeholder relations, skills, and knowledge.
2. The development of evolving common purpose.
3. A greater likelihood of understanding other views.
4. A greater willingness to trust the process and the others.

For example, 83% of the participants in a collaborative venture devoted to the management of natural resources in the Lake Ontario Islands Wildlife Management Area in upstate New York "reported that through the search conference [a collaborative dialogue] they gained trust in others to a moderate or great extent" (Schusler et al., 2003, p. 317). Similarly, "better communication and enhanced levels of trust were identified as outcomes that were exceeding the expectations" of participants in a study of 30 collaborative initiatives partnered by the USDA Forest Service (Selin, Schuett, & Carr, 2000, p. 741).

The natural resource studies also indicated that a predisposition to value dialogue on the part of the stakeholders involved was important to the ultimate outcome of the collaboration (Weible et al., 2004). Additionally, effective leadership committed to the collaborative model was critical to its success (Selin et al., 2000).

CONCLUSION

The managers of a firm may eventually find themselves making decisions that put dependent or silent stakeholders at risk. The dependent stakeholders can employ trust in the managers of the firm as a coping mechanism to try to allay their vulnerability. By increasing the vulnerability of these stakeholders, the managers incur a claim owed to the stakeholders—a claim that, I argue, must be addressed by engaging in two-way symmetrical communication. The two-way symmetrical model of public relations suggests that the public relations practitioners in the firm may well find themselves leading the charge for collaborative engagement with the dependent stakeholders.

In a cogent article summarizing research on the role of the public relations practitioner in the dominant coalition, Berger (2005) cautioned that "doing the right thing" might not always be possible. In discussing several roles that a practitioner might take on, Berger (2005) noted that "those who seek to serve the interests of the organization and greater society are likely to find their roles to be complex and constrained" (p. 23). At the end of his article, Berger (2005) suggested that:

> acknowledging the power that organizations hold over public relations practices and possibilities, as well as the pressures for conformity and complicity in the exercise of this power, seems an important step on the way to opening up and realizing alternative public relations conceptions and possibilities. (p. 25)

I suggest that one way of achieving what Berger posited is to examine and more critically define the public relations practitioner's role responsibilities in relation to his or her duties to the organization and stakeholders (Kaler, 2003). I have attempted to briefly (and I am the first to admit this is but a sketch) show how the relationship between a vulnerable stakeholder leads to a claim on the organization that thereby puts the stakeholder and organization at risk. Risk can be ameliorated by trust—trust between the stakeholder and the organization that arises from two-way symmetrical communication.

REFERENCES

Agle, B. R., Mitchell, R. K., & Sonnenfeld, J. A. (1999). Who matters to CEOs? An investigation of stakeholder attributes and salience, corporate performance, and CEO values. *Academy of Management Journal, 42*(5), 507–525.

Berger, B. K. (2005). Power over, power with, and power to relations: Critical reflections on public relations, the dominant coalition, and activism. *Journal of Public Relations Research, 17*(1), 5–28.

Berman, S. L., Wicks, A. C., Kotha, S., & Jones, T. M. (1999). Does stakeholder orientation matter? The relationship between stakeholder management models and firm financial performance. *Academy of Management Journal, 42*(5), 488–506.

Cancel, A. E., Mitrook, M. A., & Cameron, G. T. (1999). Testing the contingency theory of accommodation in public relations. *Public Relations Review, 25*(2), 171–197.

Clarkson, M. B. E. (1995). A stakeholder framework for analyzing and evaluating corporate social performance. *Academy of Management Review, 20*, 92–117.

Coombs, W. T. (1998). The internet as potential equalizer: New leverage for confronting social irresponsibility. *Public Relations Review, 24*(3), 289–303.

Das, T. K., & Teng, B. S. (1998). Between trust and control: Developing confidence in partner cooperation in alliances. *Academy of Management Review, 23*(3), 491–512.

Deavenport, E. (1996). Walking the high wire: Balancing stakeholder interests. *Executive Speeches, 10*(4), 1–3.

Donaldson, T., & Preston, L. E. (1995). The stakeholder theory of the corporation: Concepts, evidence, and implications. *Academy of Management Review, 20*(1), 85–91.

Dozier, D. M., Grunig, L. A., & Grunig, J. E. (1995). *Manager's guide to excellence in public relations and communication management.* Mahwah, NJ: Lawrence Erlbaum Associates.

Fichman, M. (2003). Straining toward trust: Some constraints on studying trust in organizations. *Journal of Organizational Behavior, 24*(2), 133–157.

Frame, T. M., Gunton, T., & Day, J. C. (2004). The role of collaboration in environmental management: An evaluation of land and resource planning in British Columbia. *Journal of Environmental Planning & Management, 47*(1), 59–83.

Freeman, R. E. (1984). *Strategic management: A stakeholder approach.* Englewood Cliffs, NJ: Prentice-Hall.

Friedman, A., & Miles, S. (2002). Developing stakeholder theory. *Journal of Management Studies, 39*(1), 1–22.

Frooman, J. (1999). Stakeholder influence strategies. *Academy of Management Review, 24*(2), 191–205.

Goodpaster, K. (1991). Business ethics and stakeholder analysis. *Business Ethics Quarterly, 1*, 53–73.

Gray, B. (2004). Strong opposition: Frame-based resistance to collaboration. *Journal of Community & Applied Social Psychology, 14*, 166–176.

Grunig, J. E. (2001). Two-way symmetrical public relations: Past, present, and future. In R. Heath (Ed.), *Handbook of public relations* (pp. 11–30). Thousand Oaks, CA: Sage.

Grunig, J. E., & Hunt, T. (1984). *Managing public relations.* New York: Holt, Rinehart & Winston.

Heath, R. L. (2001). Shifting foundations: Public relations as relationship building. In R. Heath (Ed.), *Handbook of public relations* (pp. 1–9). Thousand Oaks, CA: Sage.

Hosmer, L. T. (1995). Trust: The connecting link between organizational theory and philosophical ethics. *Academy of Management Review, 20*(2), 379–403.

Jawahar, I. M., & McLaughlin, G. L. (2001). Toward a descriptive stakeholder theory: An organizational life cycle approach. *Academy of Management Review, 26*(3), 397–414.

Jonker, J., & Foster, D. (2002). Stakeholder excellence? Framing the evolution and complexity of a stakeholder perspective of the firm. *Corporate Social Responsibility and Environmental Management, 9*, 187–195.

Kaler, J. (2003). Differentiating stakeholder theories. *Journal of Business Ethics,*
  46, 71–83.
Kaler, J. (2004). Arriving at an acceptable formulation of stakeholder theory.
  Business Ethics: A European Review, 13(1), 73–79.
Kochan, T. A., & Rubinstein, S. A. (2000). Toward a stakeholder theory of the
  firm: The Saturn partnership. *Organizational Science, 11*(4), 367–386.
Kramer, R. M. (1999). Trust and distrust in organizations: Emerging perspectives, enduring questions. *Annual Review of Psychology, 50,* 569–598.
Kruckeberg, D., & Starck, K. (1988). *Public relations and community: A reconstructed theory.* New York: Prager.
Mellahi, K., & Wood, G. (2003). The role and potential of stakeholders in "hollow
  participation": Conventional stakeholder theory and institutionalist alternatives. *Business and Society Review, 108*(2), 183–202.
Mitchell, R. K., Agle, B. R, & Wood, D. J. (1997). Toward a theory of stakeholder
  identification and salience. Defining the principle of who and what really
  counts. *Academy of Management Review, 22*(4), 853–886.
Morrow, J. L., Jr., Hansen, M. H., & Pearson, A. W. (2004). The cognitive and affective antecedents of general trust within cooperative organizations. *Journal of Management Issues, 16*(1), 48–64.
Paretti, M. C., & Tech, V. (2003). Managing nature/empowering decision-makers: A case study of forest management plans. *Technical Communication Quarterly, 12*(4), 439–459.
Phillips, R. (2003). Stakeholder legitimacy. *Business Ethics Quarterly, 13*(1), 25–41.
Preston, L. E., & Donaldson, T. (1999). Stakeholder management and organizational wealth. *Academy of Management Review, 24*(4), 619–620.
Rousseau, D. M., Sitkin, S. B., Burt, R. S., & Camerer, C. (1998). Not so different
  after all: A cross-discipline view of trust. *Academy of Management Review,
  23*(3), 393–404.
Rowley, T. J. (1997). Moving beyond dyadic ties: A network theory of stakeholder influences. *Academy of Management Review, 22*(4), 887–910.
Schusler, T. J., Decker, D. J., & Pfeffer, M. J. (2003). Social learning for collaborative
  natural resource management. *Society and Natural Resources, 15,* 309–326.
Selin, S. W., Schuett, M. A., & Carr, D. (2000). Modeling stakeholder perceptions
  of collaborative initiative effectiveness. *Society and Natural Resources, 13,*
  735–745.
Sheppard, B. H., & Sherman, D. M. (1998). The grammars of trust: A model and
  general implications. *Academy of Management Review, 23*(3), 422–437.
Simmons, J. (2004). Managing in the post-managerialist era: Towards socially
  responsible corporate governance. *Management Decision, 42*(3/4), 601–611.
Spicer, C. (1997). *Organizational public relations: A political perspective.*
  Mahwah, NJ: Lawrence Erlbaum Associates.
Starck, K., & Kruckeberg, D. (2001). Public relations and community: A reconstructed theory revisited. In R. Heath (Ed.), *Handbook of public relations* (pp.
  51–59). Thousand Oaks, CA: Sage.
Weible, C., Sabatier, P. A., & Lubell, M. (2004). A comparison of a collaborative
  and top-down approach to the use of science in policy: Establishing marine
  protected areas in California. *The Policy Studies Journal, 32*(2), 187–207.
Wicks, A. C., & Berman, S. L. (2004). The effects of context on trust in firm–
  stakeholder relationships. *Business Ethics Quarterly, 14*(1), 141–160.
Wicks, A. C., Berman, S. L., & Jones, T. M. (1999). The structure of optimal
  trust: Moral and strategic implications. *Academy of Management Review,
  24*(1), 99–116.

Chapter 3

Management Through Advocacy: Reflection Rather Than Domination

Robert L. Heath
University of Houston

For more than a century, public relations practitioners—especially those in the United States—have discussed public relations as a professional practice. Robust dialogue, innovative thinking, and hurt feelings characterize this playing field of ideas. About mid-20th century, academics began to weigh in on the discussion, and the concept of dialogue slowly emerged as a defining theme for the study and practice of public relations. The past 3 decades witnessed a robust debate of the ethical standards and societal role of public relations. Now, some academics feature "the public" and "community" as defining paradigms, as well as "symmetry."

Several concepts have emerged as fertile ground for healthy debate. *Management, systems, process, relationship, strategy, counseling, symmetry, control, interest, trust, problem recognition, involvement, power, activism, marketing, meaning, community,* and *publics,* among other terms, salt academic and professional normative best practices discussions. Ideas—some coarse and others quite sophisticated—have found their way into an increasingly broad and deep literature.

The occasion of this current reflection on contributions to and the future of the field allows for retrospection as well as proposed new agendas. As a reviewer of *Excellence in Public Relations and Communication Management* (J. Grunig, 1992), now more than a decade old, I predicted that the book could set an agenda for subsequent research. Indeed, that has been the case, as is the mark of excellent academic work. Scholarly work is best when it is considered to be not definitive, but rather founda-

41

tional. If it is definitive, or is treated as such, it can stifle innovation and controversy. Robust debate is the stuff of academic, scholarly, and professional advance, not the sign of weakness. Strong ideas foster strong ideas. Unprovocative ideas waste away.

Out of this legacy, one line of analysis has been particularly dear to me: Knowledge of and support for ethical and savvy management as a centerpiece in public relations research and practice. Ancient Roman teaching of rhetoric brings me to champion this advice to a speaker: Be a good person who can therefore speak well (Quintilian, 1951). As organizations have replaced individuals as key figures in society, we must analyze what it means to be a good organization communicating well. Out of this logic arise ideas for how management advances its strategic planning and operations, as well as relationship development through advocacy.

What follows is a discussion of management and rhetoric, with special interest on advocacy, the challenge I was invited to address by the editor of this project. Central to my position on this theme is the need for organizations to be good citizens by adding value to the ideas in communities where they work; to do so requires that they engage as advocates and listeners with the propositions afloat in those communities. Advocacy centers on citizenship and the propositional nature of discourse. That good news can be offset in the minds of some as the bad news of partisanship. At issue is the ability to reconcile advocacy, partisanship, symmetry, and mutually beneficial relationships.

From the outset of this discussion, advocacy needs to be reconciled with symmetry. Accepting themes suggested by many others, Grunig (2001) acknowledged that advocacy is not inherently contradictory to symmetry. He reasoned, "If, after dialogue, one side finds that it cannot accommodate the other side, then the symmetrical approach suggests that advocacy of its interests or withdrawal from the dialogue is ethically reasonable" (p. 16). This logic suggests that if two parties cannot negotiate or collaborate in reconciling differences of fact, value, and policy, they can then engage a larger audience—other publics that have an interest in the discussion. In this view, and depending on one's definition of dialogue, the enlargement of the number of participants may broaden the dialogue. If the standard is that dialogue is not propositional discourse, then it may be called *debate*—statement and counterstatement on various sides of the contested proposition(s).

In the rhetorical tradition, advocacy is at odds with manipulation and propaganda, and acknowledges how discourse entails statements that suffer counterstatement. In its worst form, advocacy can be limited to bellicose monologue. Sethi (1976), who examined the innovation of advocacy discourse in the 1970s, cautioned against such discourse, calling it advocacy advertising. His case studies demonstrated that it is used often by the companies "most" deserving of criticism. Advocacy, in this sense, was used retroactively to defend against and deflect criticism rather than to respond in more proactive and positive ways to differing opinions in the public policy arena. In the worst case, if an advocate "listens," it is *only* to locate weakness as a means to refute others' statements rather than to learn from and appreciate them.

The sort of advocacy that would be comfortable with symmetry presumes that participants engage in dialogue in which they can learn by recognizing the merits of others' statements as well as understanding where and how challenges may refine ideas at play in the public sphere. This paradigm assumes that ideas grow in quality through dialogue as a win-win outcome. As such, advocacy is a virtuous management and communication strategy and philosophy. This theme guides the rest of this chapter.

DEFINITIONS AND PERSPECTIVES

Definitions count. Terms need definition. What is the best of the myriad definitions of public relations? Beauty is in the eyes of the beholder. One definition, useful to this discussion, reads as follows: *Public relations is the management function that entails planning, research, publicity, promotion, and collaborative decision making to help any organization's ability to listen to, appreciate, and respond appropriately to those persons and groups whose mutually beneficial relationships the organization needs to foster as it strives to achieve its mission and vision.*

Management planning and implementation is best, cautioned John Budd, Jr. (1995), if it is realized that communication does not define, and can diminish, the practice of public relations. Thinking of communication as the result of management, he reasoned, "[C]ommunication is the last act in the process of public relations—a process that should appropriately begin with policy and decision-making" (p. 178). In this context, Budd used communication as a strategic option—an outcome variable after management decision making and improvements are conceived and implemented. With a bit of adjustment, we can view communication as a precursor variable used to learn and plan, rather than merely to respond to opinions and preferences expressed by others.

The legendary John W. Hill (1958) suggested the need to understand management as the initial step toward appreciating the roles and challenges facing public relations. He cautioned:

> It is not the work of public relations—let it always be emphasized—to outsmart the American public in helping management build profits. It is the job of public relations to help management find ways of identifying its own interests with the public interest—ways so clear that the profit earned by

> the company may be viewed as contributing to the progress of everybody
> in the American economy. (p. 21)

He added, "Big companies, if they are properly managed, have a keen sense of public responsibility. They guide their policies in keeping with the public interest and make sure that each of their plants is a good neighbor in its respective community" (p. 39).

Hill's position squares with the advice offered by Quintilian and captures the richness of the rhetorical tradition. Seeing the need for management to learn from the variety of propositions advocated by various voices, Hill (1958) observed, "Good corporate public relations depends, first, upon sound policies truly in the public interest and second, upon clear and effective communication, explanation, and interpretation of policies and facts to the public" (p. 163). The interests of private sector organizations can never be indifferent to the public interest, but must achieve symmetry with that interest. This logic values a synergism between both interests based on process and cocreation of shared meaning. Both interests can be adjusted to one another by organizations moving closer to the public interest, via understanding and appreciating it as well as communicating about the ways in which the organization operates in the public interest. From this position, Hill (1963) reasoned:

> Business managements are concerned with the problems of conducting their corporate or industry affairs in ways that they may feel are contributive to public progress. They must arrive at effective policies that go far beyond their economic and operating functions into the complex realms of social, governmental, and political relationships. The large majority push forward into these policy areas as a matter of choice. But in terms of the long-range survival of corporate enterprise, there is little choice involved; it is a matter of essentiality. (p. 230)

All interests better understand one other through a process of advocacy whereby positions are set forth, appreciated, considered, weighed, and responded to through appropriate means. The best logic is not "What is in the interest of General Motors is in the public interest." The better logic is "What is in the interest of the public is in the interest of General Motors." Thus, management can understand and learn from positions advocated by its critics as well as supporters.

Thought of this kind helps refine the concept of symmetry. Social responsibility through symmetry is a management challenge—a logic supported by systems theory, rhetorical theory, and social exchange theory. Understanding public relations, Moss (2005a) argued, begins with insight into the nature of management. Moss noted Fayol's (1949) view that management involves forecasting and planning, as well as organizing, commanding, coordinating, and controlling. *Control* is one of

the problematic terms in this definition. It can imply that managements, especially those of large organizations, can and must control
opinions and all other factors relevant to their needs and self-interests.
Surely, as Moss (2005a) reasoned, control is vital, because "management can be seen as focusing on identifying and guiding those activities
that transform business inputs into outputs" (p. 499). However, control
must be symmetrical.

Management can be imagined as a juggernaut, but Moss called on the
history of management theory to suggest that it "is often a very fre-
netic, unstructured, and largely reactive activity in which managers are
forced to engage in a constant process of negotiation, bargaining, and
compromise to get things done" (p. 499). By this logic, Moss set the
stage for addressing management through advocacy. What drives management? It is driven by information and the judgment of what that information means—opinion, evaluation, understanding, agreement,
and motivation. Management, then, can be viewed as strategic and operational value-laden choices implemented through budgets designed to
achieve outcomes in an iterative fashion in an environment more characterized by disorder and difference than by order and consensus. Advocacy is a characteristic of this disorder, and potentially a source of its
remedy.

For many reasons, advocacy is problematic in the context of this
book's study of public relations. The term *advocacy* recurs in the rhetorical tradition, but is rarely singled out for special consideration. L.
Grunig (1992) listed it as one of several perplexing issues in public relations. L'Etang (2004) referred to ethics discussion during the 1980s in
Britain; at least one person, J. Harvey Smith, could distinguish between
"public relations as advocacy or persuasion and public relations as
straight communication" (p. 173). Such distinctions may not be universally clear or necessary unless advocacy is seen as a bête noire. Who
knows how many practitioners and academics cannot so easily distinguish persuasion/advocacy from something called "straight"
communication?

Jasinski's (2001) *Sourcebook on Rhetoric* obliquely mentioned advocacy in the discussion of epideictic rhetoric. Sloane's (2001) monumen-
tal *Encyclopedia of Rhetoric* did not feature the term as a separate entry.
Thus, it is not easy to dredge up telling definitions to set the tone for
elaborating on management through advocacy as a rationale for
excellent public relations.

One recent discussion of advocacy occurred in the *Encyclopedia of
Public Relations*. When discussing accommodation through contingency
theory, Reber (2005) commented, "Contingency theory defines pure accommodation as the polar opposite of pure advocacy in public relations.
Advocacy occurs when public relations practitioners attempt to meet

the needs or desires of their organization *or* a stakeholder group to the exclusion of the needs or desires of the other side" (p. 1). This view of advocacy may be spurred by the sense of advocacy advertising, one forerunner of what is today called *issues management*. Advocacy advertising is a vehicle for responding to corporate critics—stakeholder groups that challenge corporate management policy and action.

Advocacy plays out on Google in association with grassroots groups such as the Advocacy Institute. The Advocacy Institute's mission statement includes these laudable goals: "To enable social justice advocates to gain access and voice in the decision-making of relevant institutions," "to change power relationships," and "to bring a change in people's lives" (Advocacy Institute, n.d.). Is this view of advocacy uncomfortable or compatible with the kind Reber (2005) cautioned against as the polar opposite of accommodation? It seems that contingency theory would view advocacy, as described here, as a voice to which organizations would at least consider accommodating. The Advocacy Institute offers a positive view of advocacy as a benefit to society, rather than one steeped in recalcitrance.

Further digging opens another seam to be explored. Reber (2005) observed, "Accommodation has been compared to symmetrical public relations practice, whereas advocacy has been compared to asymmetrical practice. Symmetry and asymmetry are concepts articulated by James E. Grunig and colleagues in their seminal program of public relations theory building known as the Excellence Study" (p. 1). Thus, by this connection, we have essential theories locked into agreement over accommodation, but what about advocacy? Can contingency theory and Excellence Theory be advanced by a different and more positive view of what advocacy is and how it can contribute to managements and the communities in which they operate? At this point in one's scholarship, an author invited to write about management through advocacy might look at the Excellence Study for advice for defining advocacy. Neither J. Grunig's (1992) *Excellence in Public Relations and Communication Management* nor Grunig, Grunig, and Dozier's (2002) *Excellent Public Relations and Effective Organizations* featured advocacy in any way.

This plot thickens. For instance, Dozier and Lauzen (2000) called on public relations to increase the effectiveness of activist community interest groups by strengthening their criticism of large institutions (private and public) that might impose policies on communities that those residents find offensive. Does this sound like advocacy for stakeholders of large organizations? If so, what does that process entail? Can large organizations advocate in response? Perhaps that question would be best answered by Reber and others. Reber (2005) observed, "Contingency theorists argue that there are times when it would be inappropriate to accommodate a public. They have advised organizations against accommodation of 'the Hitlers of the world'" (p. 1; on this point Reber cited Yarbrough, Cameron, Sallot, & McWilliams, 1998).

At this moment, public relations and its allied disciplines seem to disagree on *advocacy*. One can, however, imagine that the term does focus on the nature of communication as being propositional and the work of good citizenship, including corporate citizenship. Is public relations "nonpropositional" communication? Are there instances in which propositional discourse—external as well as internal—is a valuable part of "communication management" or the "use of communication in management"—the "use of advocacy in management"?

Recognizing the inevitability and virtue of partisanship, Karen Miller (1995) engaged in an important colloquy over advocacy. She wrote that John W. "Hill believed practitioners should serve as advocates for their clients. But he did not situate advocacy 'versus some higher ethic'" (p. 5). To Hill, client selection was crucial. Do not represent a client who has no worthy (or an unworthy) case to make; this was his rule. Miller commented, "One might dislike some of the causes that Hill and Knowlton advocated, but Hill thought the public interest is best served when practitioners advocate causes they believe are right" (p. 5).

The PRSA Member Code of Ethics (2004) discussed advocacy in similar fashion, offering two bulleted guidelines on the role of advocacy in practice:

- We serve the public interest by acting as responsible advocates for those we represent.
- We provide a voice in the marketplace of ideas, facts and viewpoints to aid informed public debate. (p. B17)

These guidelines seem to be narrow to the extent they do not mention internal advocacy that can bring management teams to know the strength of cases they would challenge as well as those they would build and advocate. The rhetorical tradition realizes that advocacy is a two-way street. It is not advocacy in a vacuum, but rather in the marketplace of ideas, where the strength of all ideas must be considered

This point was made by Curtin and Boynton (2001) in their examination of a social responsibility approach to public relations ethics. The essence of their critique was that the power differential of large organizations can keep ideas from the public, rather than increasing the opportunity for the public to receive, reflect, and make decisions based on open exchange of ideas in what Curtin and Boynton called "the marketplace of ideas." Such analysis acknowledges that advocacy must indeed grow from an examination of the arguments and counterarguments being made. At least, this review cannot assume that open advocacy is inherently pure, but rather questions if it can be workable within the guidelines of symmetry and the public good. That seems to be the challenge. It requires that the advocates listen, regard, and learn from counterstatements as opposed to simply advocating their position as indifferent to or superior to those ideas of other advocates in the marketplace.

Quite germane to the concern over advocacy is the work of Edgett (2002). She blended persuasion and rhetoric, as she noted, to create an ethical standard for advocacy. In fact, her work relied on leading treatises on persuasion, and none on rhetoric. It is problematic to assume that rhetoric and persuasion are the same. In modern times, the former has been driven by social science researchers examining the factors of social influence, which relies heavily on examination of messages and cognitive processing leading to decision making. Rhetorical studies have traditionally examined the dynamics of social influence, but from a humanities perspective much more comfortable to advocacy than are social scientific views of persuasion, which can morph into propaganda. Whereas the ethics of propaganda centers on outcomes (the goodness of the cause), the rhetorical heritage features the ethics of process, the ethical quality of the process by which outcomes can be achieved—and, one could add, mutually beneficial outcomes. Edgett's analysis sought an ethical framework for the process of discourse, dialogue, and even debate.

Such analysis features the logic of communication (discourse/dialogue) as centering on what is true/false, just/unjust, moral/immoral, or expedient/inexpedient. Such decisions must be driven by some analytical and communicative process. Anchoring one end of that logic, Plato took the elitist position that a highly qualified philosopher king had the right and responsibility to make such decisions for others who were less qualified. Others—for instance, Aristotle—have reasoned that policy conclusions can and must be formed by advocacy: stating claims and examining or demonstrating the merits of such claims through assertion and counterassertion. Thus, advocacy is a means by which to determine factuality, morality, and wise policy—to make enlightened decisions.

As comfortable as this paradigm is for some, others might find it less so. To some people, advocacy signifies one-way asymmetrical (monologue) or two-way asymmetrical (strategic and manipulative dialogue to the advantage of one party and the potential disadvantage of another) communication. Others see it as recalcitrant bellicosity. Advocacy as a concept and strategy can imply propaganda, manipulation, win-lose conflicts, deep-pockets advocacy, and a sense of the loudest voice serving as winner take all. That notion of advocacy is anathema to excellent public relations and the approach to public relations advocated by Budd and Hill, as described earlier.

The rhetorical heritage grew out of and has led the study of strategies of social influence, such as the techniques of suasory discourse, or persuasion. From its origins in ancient Greece, rhetoric has recognized advocacy as process as well as a tool or tactic. Plato bitterly criticized rhetoric as allowing advocacy to be used against the character of Socrates, thereby leading to his death. In this sense, Plato shunned rhetoric and favored dialectic (as a tool of the philosopher king) to bring truth into public judgment.

This position and other incentives (essential to metaphysics, ethics, and politics) motivated Aristotle to offer an alternative view. Advocacy occurs in public. People can, by hearing the sides of an issue, learn and weigh facts, consider evaluations, judge character (credibility), and weigh the expediency of policy. The paradigm is debate arising from and initiating rhetorical problems: guilt or innocence (forensic rhetoric), expedience or inexpedience (deliberative rhetoric), or just or unjust reward (epideictic rhetoric with its companion, apologia).

Rhetoric, by this ancient paradigm, exists because people can and must make decisions in the face of uncertainty and differing opinions. Discourse may produce the best decisions as sides advocate opposing views. Rhetoric, predicated on advocacy, was the essence of democratic government in ancient Greece; this motivated Aristotle to support rhetoric while acknowledging the intellectual contributions of dialectic. Rhetoric, in his judgment, was the counterpart of dialectic (Aristotle, 1952c).

What then, for purposes of definition, is advocacy? It is the content and process of the discourse used by the good person when "speaking" well to some proposition in response to a rhetorical problem. It depends on contests of substance of fact, value, and policy advocated by individuals who demonstrate their character by adhering to high principles. It is characterized by form (structure), mode of delivery, and style. It presumes the process and content of statement and counterstatement. It can entail courtship among parties in varying degrees of merger and division to transcend differences and achieve identification. Symmetry, in this view, is more a matter of the relative excellence of ideas than power parity or disparity. At its best, it can produce superior judgments because only the best idea and argument survives in open, public, and robust debate. However Pollyanna this view might be, Lentz (1996) reasoned, "Truth should prevail in a market-like struggle where superior ideas vanquish their inferiors and achieve audience acceptance" (p. 1). It empowers people who examine claims made in answer to rhetorical problems (Bitzer, 1968). It can lead to win-lose outcomes if one side's ideas are vastly inferior to others, but prefers ultimate resolution through win-win outcomes and can occur among an organization's leadership as well as in public. A public relations practitioner can assist an organization by engaging in dialogue inside of an organization, by making people aware of the ideas at play in society. This brief gives management the opportunity to listen to and learn from others' ideas, not merely to craft rebuttal but to make valid assertions. Such internal dialogue can improve management planning and implementation.

Reflections on the good or evil of rhetoric are not new. One such colloquy occurred in the 1987 volume of *Critical Studies in Mass Communication*, and focused on rhetoric as a search for truth versus being a tool for acquiring and keeping power. Truth and power are interlinked in ways that have been considered for centuries. Posing the central question, Jasinski (1987) observed, "[P]ublic communication, considered at its most elemental level as discourse that attempts to guide collective conduct or represent group sentiment, constitutes an impure, unstable, and irreducible mixture of power and truth" (p. 424).

Rhetoric fosters truth as best as can be done; it serves to solve problems that confront the public. To support this claim, Bitzer (1987) featured principles of the rhetorical heritage. One principle was that *"public communication ... depends on its subjective matter and its function: its subject matter is constituted of problems, questions, information, proposals, and the like that are related to the public's business or affairs; the function of public communication is consideration and conduct of that business"* (p. 425, italics in original). As many others have, Bitzer drew on John Dewey's sense of public as forming around shared problems. A collective of publics becomes aware of a problem and has conflicting thoughts, ideas, and interests on these matters. People experience and respond to problems with personal concern and constraint—the classic rhetorical context.

A public can be an advocate as well as the target of others' appeals. Second, as Bitzer reasoned (1987), advocates contend with one another as representatives of the public in the public interest: *"[T]heir messages and judgments are shaped significantly by their perception (whether purposeful or not) that their values, interests, and premises accord with—and, as it were, derive authority from—the public"* (p. 425, italics in original). Each public advocate stands in for others who are silent but intellectually interested in the debate. A third principle of public communication, Bitzer contended, centers on norms of excellence. This practice reflects decisions in statement and principle that are *"as excellent as they can be in probable and contingent circumstances"* (p. 426, italics in original). The fourth characteristic of public communication realizes that *"communicator and audience are participants, both are centers of intelligence, both are obliged to weigh evidence and reason soundly, and both must be prepared to express information, objections, and arguments to the end that, in the contest of ideas, the probable truths and the most reliable decisions will emerge"*

(p. 426, italics in original). Interests and wills of the participants are explicit and implicit to the process, but never independent of it. In all, "The functions of discourse are to portray or argumentatively establish the truth and reveal and correct the false" (p. 427).

In partial response to Bitzer, Goodnight (1987) took a constitutive approach suggesting that meaning varies by public. Human communication is a strategic response to some problem. This paradigm centers on reconciling difference and is fraught with consequences for the participants in the dialogue. In this sense, he reasoned, "While public discourse makes open and common collective preference, it also provides an arena where interests conduct controversy and openly struggle for power" (p. 429). Communication occurs as and seeks to shape relationships. Goodnight argued, "Because the interrelationships among the spheres of discourse are contingent, persuasion is necessary to construct and legitimate the ongoing process of communication. Such rhetorical argument may even be deployed to redraw the boundaries of ordinary communication" (p. 429). Such discourse can be genuine or surrogate for some alternative line of reasoning or other sphere of discourse. It may be ingenuous or oblique. Communication of all kinds is controversial and born and sustained through interest. Goodnight maintained, "Controversy may be extended to the contents of judgment, the prudence of choices selected to constitute action, to the rights and obligations or interests, to questions of communal value, and to the viability and potential of discourse to recomport domains of communication" (p. 431). Dialogue arises from controversy; it allows the opportunity, incentive, and even imperative for advocacy and counter advocacy: "In sum, the public may be understood as that domain of discursive practices open to those whose opinions count in contesting a decision of consequence to a community" (Goodnight, 1987, p. 431). And thus, what is the prospect of a promising outcome? Goodnight focused on the pragmatism and idealism of the discourse: The public sphere "offers the only place to fashion the self-directed, critical communication requisite to collective action and forbearance" (p. 431). The burden of being an advocate is suffering counteradvocacy. The burden of placing ideas, values, facts, opinions, and policies into play requires the forbearance of response.

Is that the essence of management through advocacy? Strategic issues management requires a strategic balance of four organizational challenges: sound strategic management in a tug of war among multiple stakeholders/stakeseekers; high standards of corporate responsibility that demonstrate appropriate levels of character and foster mutually beneficial relationships as a citizen of society; issues monitoring, which keeps the organization vigilant to the vagaries of the environment in which it operates; and issue communication that can entail advocacy based on fact, value, policy, and identification. In this mix, organizations and other members of any community accommodate to better facts, evaluation, policy, and identification.

By this view, instead of accommodating "Hitlers," the responsible organization advocates against the claims they advocate. This process of statement and counterstatement, whether existing in public or a boardroom strategic planning session, exhibits the virtues of what advocacy can bring to the dance. Through advocacy, ideas can be tested or contested. The symmetrical weight of an idea is its ability to sustain itself under scrutiny. One can imagine, then, why the Advocacy Institute fosters itself as a public good, a means for community empowerment. Empowerment occurs through the worthy disputation of ideas—the rationale of advocacy as a citizenship responsibility in the rhetorical heritage.

Advocacy can achieve understanding, agreement, reinforcement, and motivation. The opposite is also true: Advocacy can bring about misunderstanding, failure to understand, disagreement, diminished belief, and demotivation. The process is dialogue; feedback occurs as advocates listen to one another, consider responses, weigh options, learn, appreciate others' ideas, and reconsider positions held. Feedback, in this sense, is a learning process, rather than one narrowly tuned to manipulation or refutation. It is characterized by reflection.

The public, community, and dialogue become intertwined. Community embraces publics as a symbolic and functional principle in the academic approach to theory and practice (Hallahan, 2004). The symbolic aspect of community includes the meaning around which publics develop and adhere. Thus, community is a more embracing concept than is "a public." At the functional level, dialogue constitutes efforts to achieve concurrence and consensus cocreated by members of the community; on this issue, rhetorical heritage suggests that dialogue, debate, and advocacy are key functions to that end. Recognizing the idealism, and perhaps even Pollyannalike view of community, Hallahan focused attention on the potentiality of polarization and division to fracture community. It can be, but it is also the source of healing. At the marketing level (and the market level; Gandy, 1992), products/services are pitted against one another, as are the organizations that offer them in the community. Community, by definition, is not seamless. It can be intimidating as well as liberating. Polarization can be a detriment to community. As Hallahan (2004) wisely observed, "Indeed, healthy conflict is possible only within the context of supportive community" (p. 263). Is this, then, the nexus of the role of excellent strategic public relations, as a feature of reflective communication management?

MANAGEMENT THROUGH ADVOCACY

The journey continues. Reflection is a key. Management entails making choices that depend on qualitatively different processes of communication and its content as argumentative claims. This process cannot escape the virtue and pitfalls of advocacy. Cutlip (1994) focused attention on this reality in his historical analysis of public relations:

> I held, and still hold, that only through the expertise of public relations can causes, industries, individuals, and institutions make their voice heard in the public forum where thousands of shrill, competing voices daily re-create the Tower of Babel. I did not and do not deny the harm done by the incompetent, the charlatan, and those who serve dubious causes. (p. ix)

Through the lens of history, Cutlip saw public relations as an "unseen power." This profession can achieve good and bad ends, but it is a social influence: "Public relations strategies and tactics are increasingly used as weapons of power in our no-holds-barred political, economic, and cause competition in the public opinion marketplace, and thus deserve more scholarly scrutiny than they have had" (Cutlip, 1994, p. xi).

A moment of reflection suggests that such findings deserve caution. First, a case can be made that formalized and strategic efforts to influence through what can be called public relations may be timeless. The antecedents of modern public relations stretch back to the dawn of human society (Heath, 2005). However, distant from the name used for the practice and profession today, the skills, tactics, counseling, and managerial elements of public relations are ageless. Monarchs, priests, tribal leaders, organizers of war, celebrants of victory, organizers of fairs where produce and other goods are hawked—these are either the practitioners or the employers of such practitioners.

These practitioners have debated issues and shaped—as well as damaged—images. They have "got the word out." They have created awareness, diverted attention, forged allegiances, and destroyed alliances. They have created identifications and engaged in courtships. They have engaged in government relations, investor relations, alumni relations, and employee (follower and supporter) relations. As much sound advice and caution as appears in the extensive writing of Edward Bernays and John Wiley Hill, the advice in Machievelli's *The Prince*, Adolph Hitler's *Mein Kampf,* and work of the Congregatio de Propaganda Fide cannot be ignored, even if it is found wanting and even loathsome. The pervasiveness of this profession was closely noted by Cutlip (1994): "Propagandist, press agent, public information officer, public relations or public affairs official, political campaign specialist, lobbyist—whatever their title, their aim is the same: to influence public behavior" (p. xi). The foundation of behavior is some simple or complex matter of opinions, beliefs, values, and policy preferences—as well as identifications. It can include images and reputations as well as product and service preferences, even brand equity.

Understanding the good, the bad, and the ugly side of management through advocacy requires acknowledging the scary and unethical as well as the pure and irreproachable forms, strategies, content, and uses of discourse, as well as the ends to which it is put. Central to this point is the recognition that even the efforts to engineer consent are restricted by the efficacy of countermeasures that limit such engineering. Limits to any management's efforts to dominate discourse, large or small, come from voices that challenge the claims made. Even silence is a form of discourse.

The ancient Greeks were keenly interested in the limits and benefits of discourse. Isocrates' (1929) opinions on rhetoric were coupled with his sense of how citizens prepare to serve their community. They need civic education that each generation hands on to each following one. Education shapes how they govern. They must understand the power of persuasion and its responsible role for collective decision making in the public interest. Communication is not an art in which a facile mind and a quick wit should rule; rather, the best rhetor is a thinker devoted to truth in service to society.

As did Aristotle, Isocrates (1929) observed that rhetoric was essential to any effective and ethical society. Such is the case:

> because there has been implanted in us the power to persuade each other and to make clear to each other whatever we desire; not only have we escaped the life of wild beasts, but we have come together and founded cities and made laws and invented arts; and, generally speaking there is no institution devised by man which the power of speech has not helped us to establish. For this it is which has laid down laws concerning things just and unjust, and things honourable and base; and if it were not for these ordinances we should not be able to live with one another. It is by this also that we confute the bad and extol the good. Through this we educate the ignorant and appraise the wise; for the power to speak well is taken as the surest index of a sound understanding, and discourse which is true and lawful and just is taken as the surest index of a sound understanding, and discourse which is true and lawful and just is the outward image of a good and faithful soul. (p. 327)

The key to discourse is not its nature alone, but also its citizenship role in the service of community.

This conceptual foundation supports the challenge to manage through advocacy as rationale for the study and practice of public relations. As many researchers (see, e.g., Deetz, Tracy, & Simpson, 2000; Heath, 1994; Van Ruler & Vercic, 2005) have affirmed, managers perform communication roles as well as other roles that depend heavily on communication. Management calls for coordinated choices. It requires an understanding of the communication process in addition to meaning or content, as ideas are contested in concert.

In their discussions of public relations management, scholars often feature process and ignore meaning. Understanding advocacy can help them enrich their understanding of management as well as communication management. This analysis affirms the logics used by Van Ruler and Vercic (2005) to justify their view of public relations as reflective management of communication.

Efforts to blend meaning and management are not new. Both are needed for strategic issues management (Heath, 1997). Strategic management is the central concern of organizational leaders. Those who manage organizations engage in forecasting and planning, as well as organizing, commanding, coordinating, and controlling. These strategies transpire in context, and under varying degrees of chaos, uncertainty, and risk. How this planning occurs depends on issue monitoring and market research, as well as changing and adaptive standards of corporate responsibility. As organizations engage in communication, they make statements that are expected to meet resistance by customers, publics, and audiences. This discourse may tout products and services; solve customer problems; create human resources through culture and climate; contest issues; and build, maintain, and repair relationships.

Many authors have stressed that this activity occurs in and for the betterment of community (Starck & Kruckeberg, 2001). Community consists of process and meaning. Exploring the virtues of using communitarianism as a metatheory for public relations, Leeper (2001) reasoned:

> The communitarian approach to ethics seems to be a virtue approach, which puts the emphasis on character development and on Aristotle's golden mean. The teaching of this approach would necessarily involve dialogue as to what it means to be virtuous. What it means to be ethical would not focus on rule following but on the situation and the interaction of the parties involved. (p. 170)

This dialogue cannot successfully occur independent of any community, which consists of power resources and meaning that is proposed and contested.

The claimed good of the community alone is not the telling point in making these decisions. As Brummet (1995) warned, the opinions of a community may actually stifle better thought rather than liberate it. People may resist change by arguing that some position, advocated perhaps by an interest group, is contrary to conventional wisdom of the community and therefore wrong. One can recall the rhetoric of abolition encountering such resistance. If a Hitler exists, he or she is likely to challenge, ridicule, and perhaps severely punish advocates of opposing ideas.

Enlightened choice is the centerpiece in this effort. Advocacy is the essence of decision making (Nichols, 1963). It examines which claims are best demonstrated to be true and therefore warrant acceptance, support, and implementation until otherwise successfully challenged. This is the process of science, social science, and humanities. This logic drives scholarship.

Management of any organization makes decisions and implements policy that reflects its choices. Such choices are not wisely made in a vacuum. Their latitude is bound by other choices, by opinions, and by issue positions. This tradition, as Campbell (1996) concluded, champions rhetoric as "the study of what is persuasive. The issues it examines are social truths, addressed to others, justified by reasons that reflect cultural values. It is a humanistic study that examines all the symbolic means by which influence occurs" (p. 8). Persuasion is a process of advocacy. Claims made narratively, expositionally, and statistically are foundational to this analytical process.

Management is strategic, by definition, because it must make enlightened choices and recommend decisions persuasively. None of this exists in a vacuum. Strategy, summarized Moss (2005b), takes permutations:

> Strategy as plan introduces the idea of intention, emphasizing the role of conscious leadership; strategy as pattern focuses on action, introducing the notion that strategies can emerge; the idea of strategy as a position introduces context, rooting strategy in the situation that the organization finds itself in, encouraging the consideration of competition and cooperation; and perspective emphasizes that strategy may be nothing more than a concept, and focuses attention on the question of how intentions diffuse through a group to become shared as norms and values and how patterns of behavior become deeply ingrained in the group. (pp. 824–825)

Centered in this way, strategy is part of a learning process.

Strategy, then, is dialogue, subject to cybernetics, and requires acts, encountering success and resistance, and learning ways to respond. The richness of advocacy is to achieve knowledge by learning from what others say and do. Such learning results from engagement. It demands appreciation for the ideas of other as well as the motives behind what is said and done.

Ideas compete through advocacy; the forging of sound ideas, Burke (1983) reasoned, evolves dialectically: "(a) one acts; (b) in acting, one encounters the resistance to one's purpose; (c) one learns by suffering the punishment dealt by such resistance" (pp. 22, 26). Burke also stipulated, "Beginning with the particulars of the world, and with whatever principle of meaning they are already felt to possess," dialectic "proceeds by stages until some level of generalization is reached that one did not originally envisage, whereupon the particulars of the world itself look different, as seen in terms of this 'higher vision'" (Burke, 1969a, p. 306). This vision is the essence of legitimacy.

Through dialogue, people can seek better ideas, justice, higher morals, wise policies, and sound identifications. Meaning that enriches all parts of the community—its various publics—matures through cocreation. In the worst case, people encounter propaganda, lies, deceit, and misframing, and sham. Those who recognize—even adore—the role of rhetoric in this process believe that only those propositions that are justifiable and ethical can sustain themselves against the scrutiny of counterrhetoric. On this point, Quintilian (1951)—scholar of rhetoric in ancient Rome—was firm: "My ideal orator, then, is the true philosopher, sound in morals and with full knowledge of speaking, always striving for the highest" (p. 20). He continued, "If a case is based on injustice, neither a good man [or woman] nor rhetoric has any place in it" (p. 106). People who adhere to Quintilian's timeless advice agree with Burke (1946), who asked: "How can a world with rhetoric stay decent, how can a world without it exist at all?"

Practitioners can't properly engage in management through advocacy if they are unwilling or unable to learn from the claims proposed by others. Society, according to Kenneth Burke (1969a), is a marketplace of competing ideas. This marketplace requires rhetoric that addresses "the Scramble, the Wrangle of the Marketplace, the flurries and flare-ups of the Human Barnyard, Give and Take, the wavering line of pressure and counter pressure, the Logomachy, the onus of ownership, the War of Nerves, the War" (p. 23). For society to function at its best, actions of people need to be coordinated based on shared, cocreated meaning.

Rhetoric has a larger purpose than to distort, win at any cost, and propagandize. The process is very much, as Bryant (1953) thought, a matter of adjusting ideas to people and people to ideas. It has, as its substance, good reasons (Wallace, 1963). All of this should serve the public interest and transpire in the public sphere.

As Leeper (2005b) observed, "The public sphere is the space where public opinion can be formed.... The public sphere mediates between the realms of the private and the state, and the guarantees of the basic rights of citizens in the liberal state depend on the demarcation between the two. For such mediation to be effective, discourse in the public sphere must be critical and rational" (p. 710). Interpreting public sphere, Bentele (2005) noted that "The public sphere in this perspective is defined as a 'forum for communication,' an open 'communication system' that, in principle, is open for all actors who want to inform themselves about something, who want to communicate, or want to observe the communication of others" (pp. 708–709). Sharing his views on public sphere, Leeper (2005b) concluded, "A space where issues can be rationally discussed, critical opinions formed, and that is inclusive in scope is, ultimately, in the best interest of any and all particularized private interests. At its best, public relations has a positive role to play in achieving that ideal" (p. 712). To fully appreciate management through advocacy, the "public space" must include the "decision-making space" of each organization. The public space and the private space of the organization can both be served by advocacy and counteradvocacy, by the careful examination of arguments, claims, and conclusions that serve as the rationale for plans, policies, and actions. How well these "spaces" blend is a measure of the extent to which meaning has been cocreated as shared social reality.

LET THE FORCE BE WITH YOU

As they pushed the boundaries of theory, Van Ruler and Vercic (2005) pulled together very useful themes that they extracted from enactment theory and J. Grunig's (1992) concept of public relations as communication management. They drew on Heath's (2001) views of public relations as rhetorical enactment. Rhetorical enactment as rationale for public relations postulates that all of what an organization does and says can be meaningful and therefore helpful or harmful to the relationships that the organization needs to accomplish its mission and vision through its strategic business plan, public policy plan, and communication plan. By this logic, meaning is vital to the relationship between organizations and those who hold and seek stakes valuable to the organization's interests. The likelihood of harmony increases as relevant parties cocreate meaning that gives them a compatible social reality.

By featuring the good organization communicating well, this rationale for public relations not only stresses the character of the organization as the basis for and result of its communication and business planning, but it also centers corporate responsibility in the practice of public relations. Enactment theory reasons that people cocreate and enact narratives that facilitate harmony or suffer harmful conflict. Through the management of this enactment, organizations seek harmony, work through conflict, and "accommodate" their stakeholders to the extent that good reasons (Wallace, 1963) justify that outcome. Herein rests the essence of symmetry, which is featured not only in the power dimensions of each relationship but also in the quality of the ideas on which it rests. As the parties consider the quality of the relationship, they examine the quality of the ideas—the meaning—that serves as its rationale. Participants' legitimacy plays a crucial role in this search for symmetry. A legitimacy gap of varying degrees can strain the relationship (Sethi, 1977; see also Heath, 1997).

Legitimacy results from the process and content of rhetorical dialogue whereby ideas are critiqued and opinions forged along the dimension of the certain, probable, possible, and plausible (Campbell, 1996). This kind of critique requires, as Campbell reasoned, a candid and insightful awareness as to the agreement between each organization's management's preferred position on many issues and the positions advocated by others in the dialogue. Productive dialogue finds the best ideas not merely those favored by management.

Dialogue is preferred to monologue, as Pearson (1989) advised: "The goal of public relations is to manage these communication systems such that they come as close as possible to the standards deduced from the idea of dialogue. This is the core ethical responsibility of public relations from which all other obligations follow" (p. 128). In this way, rhetoric, according to Pearson (1989), is "the use of symbols to achieve agreement, to persuade, or to induce cooperation" (p. 113). Rhetoric is needed because collective, socially relevant decisions are predicated on probabilities instead of certainties. It is a means for achieving wise choices in the face of ambiguity and alternatives not reducible to absolutes.

One sense of this dialogue is that information is shared. This view of public relations communication is narrow and naïve, for several reasons. Campbell (1996) compared scientists for whom "the most important concern is the discovery and testing of certain kinds of truths," whereas "rhetoricians (who study rhetoric and take a rhetorical perspective) would say, 'Truths cannot walk on their own legs. They must be carried by people to other people. They must be explained, defended, and spread through language, argument, and appeal'" (p. 3). From this foundation, Campbell reasoned, rhetoricians take the position "that unacknowledged and unaccepted truths are of no use at all" (p. 3). Thus, we can't reasonably suggest that public relations is based on communication best characterized as sharing or exchanging information as a means for achieving understanding. Beyond understanding, agreement is a goal to be achieved through cocreated views and perspectives.

One of the most affective advocates of dialogue, Buber (1965) featured the preposition *between*. Derived from the Greek word *dialogos*, dialogue blends *logos* (word) and *dia* (through or across). Taken this way, dialogue is:

> both a quality of relationship that arises, however briefly, between two or more people and a way of thinking about human affairs that highlights their dialogic qualities. Dialogue can identify the attitudes with which participants approach each other, the ways they talk and act, the consequences of their meeting, and the context within which they meet. (Cissna & Anderson, 1998, p. 64)

Dialogue, as viewed by Buber (1965), depends on whether the participants have "in mind the other or others in their present and particular being and turn to them with the intention of establishing a living mutual relation between" themselves and the others (p. 19).

Dialogue highlights the communal character of society. Ideas grow in one's mind as well as through social interaction, because any idea only survives in contest with other ideas. Advancing this analysis, Fairclough (1995) compared two approaches to discourse. One views discourse as "social action and interaction, people interacting together in real social situations" (p. 18). The other view, Fairclough suggested, is more vital; it treats "discourse as a social construction of reality, a form of knowledge," "the ideational function of language" (p. 18).

Thus, one can argue that public relations through rhetoric reflectively engages in advocacy. This advocacy can proclaim ideas and interpretations an organization believes to be the best. Such claims require proofs that increase probative force through reasoning, evidence, and the character of the contestants. This dialogue transpires in ways in which both parties can learn from one another and consider the strengths of each other's arguments as well as the weaknesses of their own. Thus, they can adjust themselves as well as others to ideas as they adjust ideas to themselves (Bryant, 1953). This dialogue centers on relevant rhetorical problems (Bitzer, 1968). Rhetorical problems occur because of doubt produced by the circumstances of life as well as exigencies posed by those engaged in the dialogue. Both sides—all sides—can learn and reflect on the process as well as the content and product cocreated in the process.

Pursuing this theme, Burke stressed the power that words, especially idioms, have to create identification (1969b). For Burke, "Identification is affirmed with earnestness precisely because there is division. Identification is compensatory to division" (1969b, p. 208). Identification— cocreated views of reality and identity—results from the human tendency to engage in merger and division.

Along a line of thought similar to these, Van Ruler and Vercic (2005) offered an advance to excellence and communication management theory. The goal, so this theory reasons, is for each or any organization to achieve legitimacy in the community where it operates and in the judgment of people whom it affects and who can affect it. Properly employed, the principles of reflective management will "enable the organization to emerge, develop and prosper" (p. 263). Each organization emerges and succeeds through meaning, the social construction of its public identity. In sum, *it is about maximizing, optimizing, or satisfying the process of meaning creation using informational, persuasive, relational, and discursive interventions to solve managerial problems by co-producing societal (public) legitimation* (p. 266).

What links reflective communication management and principles of management through advocacy? Here is the answer: "What distinguishes communication managers from other managers when they sit down at the table is that they contribute special concern for broader societal issues and approaches to problems" (Van Ruler & Vercic, 2005, p. 264). This connection suggests an awareness of the claims advocated by and for the legitimacy of the organization by others and by the organization. This dialogue can be viewed from two vantage points: as existing as wrangle in the marketplace of ideas and wrangle in the boardroom.

In the boardroom, the wrangle can be reconstructed by issue managers/public relations managers. Discussion centers on public policy issues as well as concerns about products and services, for nonprofit, governmental, and private sector organizations. Creating and sustaining the legitimacy of an organization requires being responsive to the claims advocated by others. These claims relate to all aspects of organizational legitimacy, constitute conflicting perspectives, and raise rhetorical problems to be addressed by what the organization does or says by its rhetorical enactment.

Such reflection seeks not what is narrowly good for the organization, nor does it innocently accommodate to the complaints, views, and concerns asserted by others. The end to which all discourse should be aimed, Aristotle (1952c) reasoned, is the good of society. Two ethical standards guide the choices of those who engage in rhetoric. One is the need to demonstrate through evidence the factual basis for any claims advocated. The second is to demonstrate through the values espoused that the person (or organization) has a high sense of what is good. What distinguishes character? Aristotle (1952c) answered, "good sense, good moral character, and goodwill" (p. 623). Standards of the "good" are basic to rhetoric that "exists to affect the giving of decisions" by listeners (readers or viewers) who then decide among the positions presented to them (p. 622). Such decisions serve the good of society:

> Every state is a community of some kind, and every community is established with a view to some good; for mankind always acts in order to obtain that which they think good. But, if all communities aim at some good, the state or political community, which is the highest of all, and which embraces all the rest, aims at good in the greater degree than any others, and at the highest good. (Aristotle, 1952c, p. 445)

Dialogue can manage mutual needs and interests to some shared advantage. Isocrates (1929) reasoned that society is the benefactor when persons are trained to be effective and ethical communicators. Today, corporate citizens must learn and apply the principles of strategic and ethical communication, not in the service of some participant's self-interest, but rather the collective interest. As Isocrates argued, "With this faculty we both contend against others on matters which are open to dispute and seek light for ourselves on things which are unknown; for the same arguments which we use in persuading others when we speak in public, we employ also when we deliberate in our own thoughts" (p. 327). Contention and advocacy, thus, are not inherently bad, but instead are a great good if applied to that larger end.

LOOKING FORWARD AT RESEARCH HORIZONS

Themes featured in this view of public relations fit into what Botan and Taylor (2004) categorized as the cocreational perspective. This conclusion is founded on themes central to theories of organizations–publics relationships: community theory, coorientation theory, accommodation theory, dialogue theory, symmetrical/Excellence Theory, and rhetorical enactment theory. As Botan and Taylor prophesied, the next generation of scholarship will seek to isolate and build on the best of these theories. Such advances are likely to realize that the competitive weight of views, ideas, or perspectives constitutes the true essence of symmetry; efforts to forge concurrence and consensus are the essence of excellence in the service of a fully functioning society.

One of several challenges for researchers' and practitioners' best practices will be to examine and refine what is meant by *reflexivity* and *reflective management*. Coupled with that will be a continuing investigation of the connections between the interests of those who are targeted and/or receive messages that advocate one position in favor of another.

Personal interest seems to be a potentially corrupting factor in the selection of the arguments and the framing of a case. Researchers need to understand and build advice for organizations to be reflective by taking into consideration the honest and candid interest of those targeted or likely to receive advocacy messages. How is society enriched by a symmetrical balance of interests that becomes expressed in the substance and framing of such messages?

Although one can acknowledge that at times one side is truly superior to the competing sides of a controversy, the essence of dialogue results when the society in which it occurs benefits as a whole because of the dialogue. Can researchers increase our understanding of how advocacy can enrich society and obtain superior conclusions that encompass the needs and benefits of the entire community?

If public relations is going to assist efforts to make society more fully functional, can it advise managements on how to learn from and appreciate the substance and conclusions, as well as value recommendations, that occur through advocacy and counteradvocacy? Advocacy seems likely to fail over the long run if it merely advances the cause and interest of part of society. This is especially the case if the communication is steeped in the assumptions and strategies typical of propaganda. Being reflective by listening and learning, public relations practitioners can discover the merit in others' advocacy. How is this discovery best brought into management decision making?

To these ends, this chapter offers a glimpse of the rhetorical heritage. Many thinkers have sought solutions to these questions. They will continue to offer research and introspection for future generations of academics and working professionals.

REFERENCES

Advocacy Institute. (n.d.). *Mission statement*. Retrieved January 18, 2005, from www.advocacy.org

Aristotle. (1952a). Nichomachean ethics. (W. D. Ross, Trans.). In R. M Hutchins (Ed.), *Great books* (Vol. 2, pp. 333–436). Chicago: Encyclopaedia Britannica.

Aristotle. (1952b). Politics. (B. Jowett, Trans.). In R. M Hutchins (Ed.), *Great books* (Vol. 2, pp. 445–548). Chicago: Encyclopaedia Britannica.

Aristotle. (1952c). Rhetoric. (W. R. Roberts, Trans.). In R. M Hutchins (Ed.), *Great books* (Vol. 2, pp. 593–675). Chicago: Encyclopaedia Britannica.

Bentele, G. (2005). Public sphere (Öffentlichkeit). In R. L. Heath (Ed.), *Encyclopedia of public relations* (pp. 707–710). Thousand Oaks, CA: Sage.

Bitzer, L. (1968). The rhetorical situation. *Philosophy and Rhetoric, 1*, 1–15.

Bitzer, L. (1987). Rhetorical public communication. *Critical Studies in Mass Communication, 4*, 425–428.

Botan, C. H., & Taylor, M. (2004). Public relations: State of the field. *Journal of Communication, 54*, 645–661.

Brummet, B. (1995). Scandalous rhetorics. In W. N. Elwood (Ed.), *Public relations inquiry as rhetorical criticism: Case studies of corporate discourse and social influence* (pp. 13–23). Westport, CT: Praeger.

Bryant, D. C. (1953). Rhetoric: Its function and its scope. *Quarterly Journal of Speech, 39*, 401–424.

Buber, M. (1965). *Between man and man*. (R. G. Smith, Trans.). New York: Macmillan.

Budd, J., Jr. (1995). Commentary: Communications doesn't define PR, it diminishes it. *Public Relations Review, 21*, 177–179.

Burke, K. (1946, October 22). *Letter to Malcolm Cowley*. Kenneth Burke file, Pennsylvania State University.

Burke, K. (1969a). *A grammar of motives*. Berkeley: University of California Press.

Burke, K. (1969b). *A rhetoric of motives*. Berkeley: University of California Press.

Burke, K. (1983). Counter-gridlock: An interview with Kenneth Burke. *All Area, 4*–35.

Campbell, K. K. (1996). *The rhetorical act* (2nd ed.). Belmont, CA: Wadsworth.

Cissna, K. N., & Anderson, R. (1998). Theorizing about dialogic moments: The Buber-Rogers position and postmodern themes. *Communication Theory, 1*, 63–104.

Curtin, P. A., & Boynton, L. A. (2001). Ethics in public relations: Theory and practice. In R. L. Heath (Ed.), *Handbook of public relations* (pp. 411–421). Thousand Oaks, CA: Sage.

Cutlip, S. M. (1994). *The unseen power: Public relations. A history*. Hillsdale, NJ: Lawrence Erlbaum Associates.

Deetz, S. A., Tracy, S. J., & Simpson, J. L. (2000). *Leading organizations through transition*. Thousand Oaks, CA: Sage.

Dozier, D. M., & Lauzen, M. M. (2000). Liberating the intellectual domain from the practice: Public relations, activism, and the role of the scholar. *Journal of Public Relations Research, 12*, 3–22.

Edgett, R. (2002). Toward an ethical framework for advocacy in public relations. *Journal of Public Relations Research, 14*, 1–26.

Fairclough, N. (1995). *Media discourse*. London: Edward Arnold.

Fayol, H. (1949). *General and industrial management* (C. Storrs, Trans.). London: Pitman.

Gandy, O. H., Jr. (1992). Public relations and public policy: The structuration of dominance in the information age. In E. L. Toth & R. L. Heath (Eds.), *Rhetorical and critical approaches to public relations* (pp. 131–164). Hillsdale, NJ: Lawrence Erlbaum Associates.

Goodnight, G. T. (1987). Public discourse. *Critical Studies in Mass Communication, 4*, 428–432.

Grunig, J. E. (Ed.). (1992). *Excellence in public relations and communication management*. Hillsdale, NJ: Lawrence Erlbaum Associates.

Grunig, J. E. (2001). Two-way symmetrical public relations: Past, present, and future. In R. L. Heath (Ed.), *Handbook of public relations* (pp. 11–30). Thousand Oaks, CA: Sage.

Grunig, L. A. (1992). Toward the philosophy of public relations. In E. L. Toth & R. L. Heath (Eds.), *Rhetorical and critical approaches to public relations* (pp. 65–91). Hillsdale, NJ: Lawrence Erlbaum Associates.

Grunig, L. A., Grunig, J. E., & Dozier, D. M. (2002). *Excellent public relations and effective organizations*. Mahwah, NJ: Lawrence Erlbaum Associates.

Hallahan, K. (2004). "Community" as a foundation for public relations theory and practice. In P. J. Kalbfleisch (Ed.), *Communication yearbook 28* (pp. 232–279). Mahwah, NJ: Lawrence Erlbaum Associates.

Heath, R. L. (1994). *Management of corporate communication: From interpersonal contacts to external affairs*. Hillsdale, NJ: Lawrence Erlbaum Associates.

Heath, R. L. (1997). *Strategic issues management*. Thousand Oaks, CA: Sage.

Heath, R. L. (2001). A rhetorical enactment rationale for public relations: The good organization communicating well. In R. L. Heath (Ed.), *Handbook of public relations* (pp. 31–59). Thousand Oaks, CA: Sage.

Heath, R. L. (2005). Antecedent of modern public relations. In R. L. Heath (Ed.), *Encyclopedia of public relations* (pp. 32–36). Thousand Oaks, CA: Sage.

Hill, J. W. (1958). *Corporate public relations: Arm of modern management*. New York: Harper & Brothers.

Hill, J. W. (1963). *The making of a public relations man*. New York: David McKay.

Isocrates. (1929). Antidosis. (G. Norlin. Trans.). *Isocrates* (Vol. 2, pp. 181–365). Cambridge, MA: Harvard University Press.

Jasinski, J. (1987). Perspectives on public communication. *Critical Studies in Mass Communication, 4*, 423–424.

Jasinski, J. (2001). *Source book on rhetoric: Key concepts in contemporary rhetorical studies*. Thousand Oaks, CA: Sage.

Leeper, R. V. (2001). In search of a metatheory for public relations: An argument for communitarianism. In R. L. Heath (Ed.), *Handbook of public relations* (pp. 93–104). Thousand Oaks, CA: Sage.

Leeper, R. V. (2005a). Communitarianism. In R. L. Heath (Ed.), *Encyclopedia of public relations* (pp. 168–171). Thousand Oaks, CA: Sage.

Leeper, R. V. (2005b). Public sphere discourse. In R. L. Heath (Ed.), *Encyclopedia of public relations* (pp. 710–712). Thousand Oaks, CA: Sage.

Lentz, C. S. (1996). The fairness in broadcasting doctrine and the Constitution: Forced one-stop shopping in the "marketplace of ideas." *University of Illinois Law Review, 271*, 1–39.

L'Etang, J. (2004). *Public relations in Britain: A history of professional practice in the 20th century.* Mahwah, NJ: Lawrence Erlbaum Associates.

Miller, K. S. (1995), Letter to the editor. *Public Relations Strategist, 1*(2), 5.

Moss, D. A. (2005a). Management theory. In R. L. Heath (Ed.), *Encyclopedia of public relations* (pp. 499–501). Thousand Oaks, CA: Sage.

Moss, D. A. (2005a). Strategies. In R. L. Heath (Ed.), *Encyclopedia of public relations* (pp. 823–826). Thousand Oaks, CA: Sage.

Nichols, M. H. (1963). *Rhetoric and criticism.* Baton Rouge: Louisiana State University Press.

Pearson, R. (1989). Business ethics as communication ethics: Public relations practice and the idea of dialogue. In C. H. Botan & V. Hazleton, Jr. (Eds.). *Public relations theory* (pp. 111–131). Hillsdale, NJ: Lawrence Erlbaum Associates.

PRSA Member Code of Ethics. (2004). *Public relations tactics: The blue book* (pp. B17–B19). New York: Public Relations Society of America.

Quintilian, M. F. (1951). *The institutio oratoria of Marcus Fabius Quintilianus* (C. E. Little, Trans.). Nashville, TN: George Peabody College for Teachers.

Reber, B. H. (2005). Accommodation: Contingency theory. In R. L Heath (Ed.), *Encyclopedia of public relations* (pp. 1–3). Thousand Oaks, CA: Sage.

Sethi, S. P. (1976). Dangers of advocacy advertising. *Public Relations Journal, 32*(11), 42, 46–47.

Sethi, S. P. (1977). *Advocacy advertising and large corporations: Social conflict, big business image, the news media, and public policy.* Lexington, MA: D. C. Heath.

Sloane, T. O. (Ed.). (2001). *Encyclopedia of rhetoric.* Oxford, England: Oxford University Press.

Starck, K., & Kruckeberg, D. (2001). Public relations and community: A reconstructed theory revisited. In R. L. Heath (Ed.), *Handbook of public relations* (pp. 51–59). Thousand Oaks, CA: Sage.

Van Ruler, B., & Vercic, D. (2005). Reflective communication management: Future ways for public relations research. In P. J. Kalbfleisch (Ed.), *Communication Yearbook 29* (pp. 239–273). Mahwah, NJ: Lawrence Erlbaum Associates.

Wallace, K. R. (1963). The substance of rhetoric: Good reasons. *Quarterly Journal of Speech, 49*, 239–249.

Yarbrough, C. R., Cameron, G. T., Sallot, L. M., & McWilliams, A. (1998). Tough calls to make: Contingency theory and the Centennial Olympic Games. *Journal of Communication Management, 3*(1), 39–56).

Chapter 4

Two-Way Communication Based on Quantitative Research and Measurement

Don W. Stacks
Marcia L. Watson
University of Miami

This chapter examines the quantitative research and measurement associated with Grunig's (1976; Grunig & Hunt, 1984) two-way symmetrical model of public relations. Based on a review of relevant published literature and a critique of previous research, two proposed methodological advances are suggested. The chapter argues that to adequately measure and test symmetrical communication, a move away from regression-based, variable-oriented methodology to a relational-based methodology from both metric and nonmetric data approaches to measurement and research is needed. That is, most two-way public relations models follow "asymmetrical" rather than "symmetrical" models.

What constitutes "symmetry"? The symmetrical/asymmetrical model comes from interpersonal and organizational communication theory. A *symmetrical model* represents a balanced flow of communication whereby all parties are communicating with each other as equals, seeking to maintain a relationship based on mutual understanding and needs. An example of a historical model would be the political model of "mutually assured destruction," or MAD, that described the relationship between the United States and the former Soviet Union from the late 1940s to mid-1980s. In this instance, the relationship was symmetrical because each had a credible and equal ability to destroy the other.

An *asymmetrical model*, on the other hand, suggests that the balance of the relationship is tipped toward one of the relational parties. This is

found in the traditional superior–subordinate organizational communication literature (see, Tompkins, 1984) or in a one-up/one-down relationship in which some form of power (e.g., French & Raven, 1968)
establishes inequality among participants. Examples of asymmetrical
relationships are found in a variety of corporations in which communication is top-down or occurs between a provider and a providee (e.g.,
automobile leasing company and the lessee). Both relationships are typically based on formal contracts specifying particular roles and power
relationships.

In both the asymmetrical and symmetrical models, two-way communication is essential for successful outcomes. In the public relations
literature, however, the vast majority of quantitative research falls into
the asymmetrical model.

How, then, can symmetrical public relations research be conducted?
As explained in this chapter, much of the symmetrical research conducted to date has been focused on qualitative methodologies—in-depth
interviews and case studies in which the researcher had the advantage of
knowing in advance the relational outcome of the subject of study.
Some quantitative, primarily survey-based research has begun to explore variables of symmetry, but that research employs analytical tools
that are more appropriate for asymmetrical models.

This chapter introduces the reader to two different approaches to
two-way symmetrical research. The first seeks to describe the actual
communication paths as a sociological approach to "who says what to
whom." The second goes beyond a simple description to an understanding of the impact of two-way symmetrical communication by exploring the communication relationships between agents or agencies of
interest. Thus, the first model quantitatively maps the flow of communication between organizations and publics—both internal and external—and the second adds to that map by examining the relational
variables of interest and testing them for effect. Hypothetical models of
both approaches are offered as models for future two-way symmetrical
research and measurement.

AN OPERATIONAL DEFINITION

For the purposes of this chapter, *public relations* is operationally defined
as the "management of credibility" (Stacks, 2002). What is being managed is the credibility of an organization, an issue, a product, and so
forth. *Credibility* is defined as the relationship among perceptions of
trust, reputation, and relationship. *Trust* is defined as a perception that
the evaluation of the organization or public(s) is dependable. *Relationship* is defined as the association between the organization and its pub-
lic(s) and lies somewhere between zero (0), asymmetric, and one (1),

symmetric. *Reputation* is defined as the historical relationship between the organization and its public(s). An additional variable that affects credibility is the organization's or public(s)'s reward power (cf., French & Raven, 1968). Assuming that the publics of interest are internal (employees) and external (stockholders), a public relations campaign may establish a set of expectations (ROE) that, in turn, will impact on organizational return on investment (ROI). Thus, from the problem's point of view, credibility is dependent on the trust between the organization and its publics, which is highly correlated with both reputation and relationship (see Fig. 4.1).

For instance, an organization could be viewed by a public as credible—its reputation is bad on a particular issue and that the public believes future issues will be handled similarly. This relationship would be asymmetrical and the expectation negative. The question, of course, is where does feedback fit in? Who can the organization work with to establish a more symmetrical relationship? Return of expectations by this public will be negative.

A problem with Fig. 4.1 is that it reflects a one-way process—from credibility to ROI—and does not include feedback. If it did include feedback, it would look like Fig. 4.2 (feedback is designated as ROE with reversed arrow). However, does the negative sign indicate negative feedback or no feedback? What if the correlation between credibility, trust, reputation, relationship, and feedback was zero (0)? Perhaps a "self-loop" regarding some clique or rumor campaign is accounting for the negative expectation. In a study examining the impact of "leader–member exchange" and feedback seeking, Campbell (2002) found such a relationship in a path analytic model. Given that there was no measurement of the actual communication networks in the study (the study

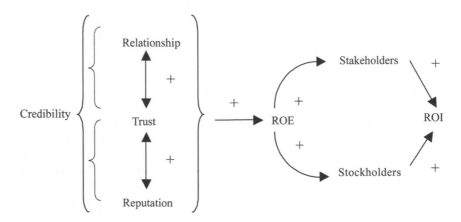

FIG. 4.1. Traditional relationship between credibility and ROI.

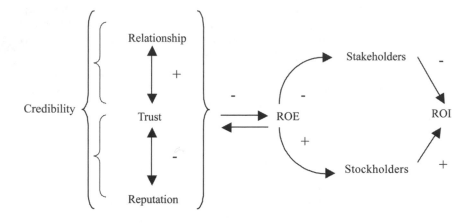

FIG. 4.2.   Revised relationship between credibility and ROI.

employed a role-playing scenario with no indications of what communication networks were in play), a network analysis could not have
been completed.

HISTORICAL OVERVIEW

As Fig. 4.3 demonstrates, in 1976, Grunig published his first study developing categories to describe public relations practitioner behavior
by building on past research (see Cutlip & Center, 1952; Goldman,
1948). In this study, he quantitatively analyzed 16 public relations activities into Thayer's (1968) concepts of *synchronic* (at one time) and
diachronic (at two times) communication. Building on the limited success of this study, Grunig (1984) changed the terms to *asymmetrical*
and *symmetrical*.

Grunig and Hunt (1984) were the first to define the four models of
public relations as: press agentry, public information, two-way asymmetrical, and two-way symmetrical. Since then, these models have received a considerable amount of attention. In this study, Grunig and
Hunt identified the press agentry and the public information models as
one-way approaches to public relations because they were the dissemination of information. Grunig and Hunt described (a) the two-way
asymmetrical model as being propaganda or persuasion based, with
practitioners both giving and seeking information from publics, and (b)
the two-way symmetrical model as truthful interpretations of the
public and the organization to each other.

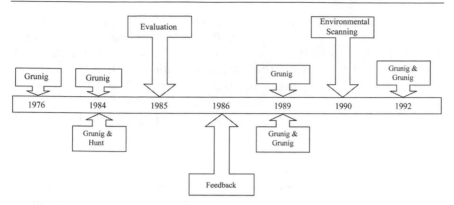

FIG. 4.3. Two-way communication timeline.

Grunig (1984) further developed these models by identifying the variables of direction and purpose. *Direction* referred to one-way communication as a monologue (or the dissemination of information) and two-way communication as a dialogue (or the exchange of information). For purpose, he described asymmetrical communication as imbalanced because, with this, the organization stays the same but it tries to change the public; whereas symmetrical was defined as balanced, because the relationship between the organization and the public is adjusted. Grunig and Grunig (1989) further conceptualized press agentry as a one-way asymmetrical model and public information as a one-way symmetrical model. Then, Grunig (1989) changed his mind and reexplained public information as a selective dissemination of information and therefore an asymmetrical model. Grunig and Grunig (1992) argued that the two-way symmetrical model is a characteristic of "excellence in public relations and communication management" (p. 320).

Major Theoretical Advances

Two-way communication is concerned with the organization's environment, evaluation, and feedback; however, the models differ in their goals. Symmetrical models seek cooperation, whereas asymmetrical models seek "environmental domination" (Grunig & Grunig, 1992, p. 346).

Environmental Scanning. According to Dozier (1990), open-systems theory suggests that the structure and function of public relations should be based on an organization's environment. He defined environmental scanning as the "detection of environmental turbulence or change likely to affect the homeostasis of the system … 'What is going on out there'" (p. 5). Essentially, it is a form of communication from publics to organizations that provides the dominant coalition with accurate information about what *is* going on out there (Dozier & Ehling, 1992). An important component of environmental scanning is research, because it moves through three phases of problem detection, exploration, and description (Dozier, 1990).

Evaluation.   Cutlip, Center, and Broom (1985) differentiated among the three levels of evaluation: preparation evaluation (includes the quality, appropriateness, and adequacy of information/messages), implementation evaluation (includes measures of messages sent, placed, received, and attended to by publics), and impact evaluation (involves the maintenance or changing of attitudes, opinions, or behaviors).

Feedback.   Broom (1986) developed an open-systems public relations feedback model. This model incorporated organizational adaptation feedback, program adjustment feedback, and performance control feedback.

QUANTITATIVE MODELS OF TWO-WAY SYMMETRICAL RESEARCH

As indicated in the previous section, the amount of quantitative research on two-way symmetrical research is quite limited. The basic format of extant research is more qualitative in nature, based on case study, interview, and focus-group methodology. This finding should not surprise anyone who has been involved with relationship theory and research. Indeed, understanding the specific nature of the relationship(s) and "who says what to whom with what effect" almost always requires researchers to explore the depth and richness of two-way symmetrical, relationship data (hereafter, *relational*). What limited research we do find in relational research—as expressed in the Excellence Project (Grunig, 1992; Grunig, Grunig, & Dozier, 2002)—deals primarily with three triangulated methods: in-depth interview, case study, and survey (the latter being the sole quantitative measure of "excellence").

Variable-Analytic Research

Survey and experimental research, by their very nature, produce variable analytic studies (Hocking, Stacks, & McDermott, 2002; Stacks,

2002). Surveys seek to *understand* how respondents feel or would act toward a particular object (e.g., organization, product, or media), event (e.g., promotion or crisis), or concept (e.g., corporate social responsibility, mission/value statement, or trust). A number of studies (e.g., Coombs & Holladay, 2001; Huang, 2001) have described through survey methodology how different publics or audiences perceive public relationships, primarily through simple correlations between variables or regression models. A few studies (Dozier & Broom, 1995; Heath, Douglas, & Russell, 1995; Kim, 2001; Lauzen, 1992, 1995, 1997; Lauzen & Dozier, 1992) have employed hypothesized models and compared them to actual obtained models (i.e., path analysis) based on survey responses. This body of research, however, is better suited for models that see public relations as a linear model with a pseudocausal path from one variable to the next—hence, it is questionable whether this research is truly symmetrical or is more asymmetrical in nature.

Experimental research, although rare in public relations research—and even rarer in two-way symmetrical research—tests relationships in isolation from the real world to establish the causal relationships between variables free from external contamination. Whether these studies are truly symmetrical or are more asymmetrical is a question that begs answers. Again, these studies predict the relationships to be *linear* combinations of cause-effect correlations. Prototypical experimental studies often employ the same statistical tests of relationships as survey research, simple correlational, simple to complex regressions, path analytical, and sequential equation models (SEM).

Public Relations Variables and Their Measurement

Public relations research presents a number of concerns for two-way symmetrical research. First, the theory does not specify in detail exactly what variables should be measured and how they relate to each other. Second, much of what is studied in two-way symmetrical public relations is perceptual—that is, it is more attitudinal (e.g., reputation, credibility, trust, relationship) than behavioral. Several studies have attempted to explore the attitudinal bases of public relations (e.g., Grunig & Huang, 2000; Hon & Grunig, 1999), creating variables that seek to measure the underlying influences of relationships.

At least two relational variables have received both experimental and practitioner validation. Trust, as defined by various practitioners, was operationalized by Hon and Grunig (1999) and its components validated through experimental research and some descriptive, survey research in the field. The *Edelman Trust Barometer* (Edelman Public Relations, 2005) is an example of a relational variable being used in the practice of public relations. Reputation, also defined in a variety of ways, has been used in the practice to establish a two-way measure of relationship.

SYMMETRY AS A TWO-WAY PROCESS

Symmetrical models of public relations are probably best observed by examining the actual systems in which they operate. General systems theory (GST; von Bertalanffy, 1951, 1966) provides a theoretical framework in which the research can choose the specific system level for analysis. Thus, it can be used from macro- to micro-level analyses, organization to publics, individual unit or worker analysis.

An important element of symmetrical communication is an understanding that, although most systems strive for symmetry, asymmetry is an important feature. Systems theory posits that all systems are bound to fail at some point, and that those systems that merely seek to maintain the status quo will ultimately fail (von Bertalanffy, 1951). This is called *entropy*, and results in a closed system. Closed systems fail. Open systems use the interchange of information (input-throughput-output) to establish disequilbrium or *equifinality*—a state somewhat distant from equality that results in a *negenthrophic* state (e.g., a state that continues to grow, given the system's resources and relationships among its various subsystems). Thus, when we examine public relations from a systems perspective, we're looking for an exchange of information and communication between an organization and its various internal and/or external publics to first maintain homeostasis (stability) and then serve as a way to sustain negenthropic force for growth. (For more on GST and systems theory, see Stacks, Hickson, & Hill, 1991.)

Extremely important in a communication system such as public relations is the process of feedback.[1] From a systems perspective, feedback acts as a control center for system growth and/or death (Monge, 1982). Feedback, then, is the process by which public relations systems grow and prosper—or fail and die. *Feedback may also be redefined as the process of symmetric communication flow between an organization and its publics.* Thus, the practice of symmetric public relations is tied to somewhat equal feedback between and among the organization and its publics.

The problem, however, is that in an organization—unlike a short public relations campaign—the communication process is influenced by and in turn influences time and a fairly homogenous public. *The irony is*

---

[1]Although feedback is an *overused* term, it is employed in this chapter to indicate information input, throughput, and output that is used by the system to maintain a symmetrical relationship within and outside the organization. Feedback—as environmental and internal scanning—is important in the organization's ability to maintain homeostasis, and the public relations functions should be in the forefront of the process.

that effective symmetric public relations requires some form of asymmetric public relations to achieve its goal of mutual satisfaction and simultaneously moving the organization to its next level (i.e., achieving a goal, meeting return on investment [ROI] expectations, surviving a crisis).

The study of organizational feedback stresses the uses of information within communication networks. Monge (1982) called this "Structional-Functional-Systems," or SFS. Figure 4.4 demonstrates three forms of SFS feedback: mutually causal loops, indirect loops, and the self-loop. Of the three feedback loops, mutually causal loops are symmetrical, whereas the indirect and self-loops tend to stray from symmetry toward asymmetry. The indirect loops could represent some form of hierarchical asymmetry, in which one person, department, or subsidiary has more information than others and requests information from one group that, in turn, requires additional input from another, which reports back to the initial requester. Self-loops could represent an internal form of dissent, an influential clique group, or even rumor for internal publics; for external publics, the self-loop might represent regulatory agencies or NGOs that impact on an organization or its product.

Thus, a systems approach to public relations provides practitioners with the ability to observe symmetrical/asymmetrical relationships based on the type of feedback observed. The obvious advantage is the ability to map out the flow of communication at whatever level of the system; the disadvantage is that it is basically descriptive, in that it merely demonstrates the flow of communication via the feedback systems employed. There are ways,

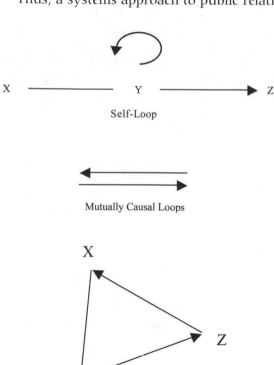

Self-Loop

Mutually Causal Loops

Indirect Loops

FIG. 4.4. Types of loops.

however, to go beyond the descriptive and begin to look at what is being communicated within a system's various feedback/feedforward (feedback about the feedback) systems.

Networks

The analysis of a system's information—communication—networks ranges from a simple social network reflecting the first part of Lasswell's (1948) model of communication—"Who says what in which channel to whom"—to a complex network analysis that adds the final "with what effect." Monge and Contractor (2003) offered a readable, complete primer for communication network research that takes in a number of different theories that may be of use to public relations researchers who are interested in the concepts laid out in this chapter.

Simple Networks. The examples of feedback loops are representative of simple networks. They describe who is speaking to whom or who is speaking about what to whom. In effect, they describe the social network and provide important information about not only the flow of communication, but also the amount of information in various communication networks. They can be graphed as *sociograms* (see Fig. 4.5) and reflect simple linkages indicating who is speaking to whom about a particular subject with or without any directional (feedback) loop indications. From a quantitative perspective, the data gathered is categorical—simple counts of the relationship (usually 1 or 0 binary)—or more complex relationships (could be binary or actual counts that can be analyzed as frequencies, percentages, or proportions of the individual to other relationships).

Social network analysis (Scott, 2000) can be used to establish a number of network indexes to analyze an organization's public relations. From simple paths (directional or nondirectional) to density (the level of information or linkages) to centrality (positions within the communi-

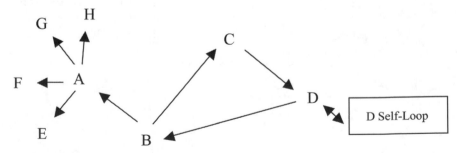

FIG. 4.5. Sample network.

cation network), a number of variables can be examined to establish who is communicating to whom about what.

The data can be analyzed via traditional statistical methods. Simple network analyses are typically correlational in nature, with binary data transformed into simple correlations. When multidimensional scaling (MDS) is used, simple network analysis can produce some rather complex findings—especially when the data are representative of a number of underlying dimensions (usually verified by factor analysis)—that are then displayed by computer in the form of sociograms.

The problem, however, is that the data are binary in nature and may lead to network misdiagnosis (Scott, 2000). Fortunately, a more complex network analysis is available, one that involves nonmetric analyses.

Complex Networks.   Complex network analysis employs nonmetric methods such as small space analysis (SSA)—nonmetric MDS—or Markov probability analysis of linkages or loops. In these cases, inferential statistical probabilities can be calculated and various network properties can be tested. Figure 4.5 depicted communication flow, but did not indicate differences in network information such as centrality, density, and other network properties that are beyond the scope of the current chapter. (For more information on complex network analysis, see Monge & Contractor, 2003; for an example of its use, see Valente, 1995).

NETWORK MODEL OF PUBLIC RELATIONS PROCESS

For two-way symmetrical public relations to occur, feedback must, by definition, occur. At its most symmetrical, a network must possess mutually causal feedback and network connectedness, and information density should be high. There are a number of variables, however, that have been demonstrated to alter the degree of network feedback. Trust, reputation, perceptions of relationship, credibility, and reward are probably the most important antecedent variables leading to two-way symmetrical public relations. The causal criteria for two-way symmetrical public relations are open to debate and will probably be dependent on the nature of the public relations problem.

Two "Network" Models

The following models are, for the purposes of this chapter, representative of what researchers might work with, but are necessarily simplified. The first represents a simple descriptive bivariate systems metric analysis. The second displays a more complex nonmetric analysis, one that goes beyond simple descriptive analyses and includes inferential analyses of flow, density, and centrality.

Metric.   There are two basic analyses that can be made based on metric analyses. A simple metric analysis employs simple binary data (either does or does not communicate) with or about an incidence. The data, of course can be more complex, but must be reduced to a simple 1 or 0 dichotomy through median or mean splits. Suppose we have a 3 × 3 matrix in which the columns represent information being sent and the rows information being sent between three organizations:

	A	B	C
A	-	1	0
B	0	-	1
C	1	1	-

Note that all individuals talk across companies, but not all individuals talk to each other. The simple sociogram that merely describes communication looks like:

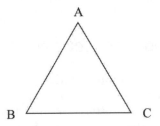

where A, B, and C are communicating. The problem is that the diagram fails to indicate specifically who is communicating to whom.

A more complex sociogram would provide information as to direction and would tell us both direction of communication and relative density of the information within the network:

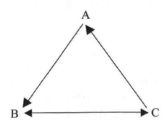

We now see that B and C are symmetrically related, whereas A and B and A and C are asymmetrically related. Furthermore, C's network is twice as dense (providing more information) than is A's or B's.

More complex analyses might look for system bridges (people or organizations that interconnect to different system networks), isolates (those people or organizations that are left out of a network or only connect via one other member), or where cliques may be forming by creating their own internal networks within the larger network and may constitute a "loop" in the network.

Figure 4.6 depicts an organization and several key publics—with unions as a separate stakeholder group that has a self-loop muddying the scanning process. In this example, there is symmetrical communication with regulatory groups, stockholders, and unions. Potential problems may be found in network flow between other stakeholders, and NGOs with no return communication with NGOs and stakeholders (e.g., information is one way for both groups, with the direction indicating NGOs input and stakeholders output).

Making sense of the networks and establishing the probabilities that the information flow is statistically different for various network paths has been made easier with the creation of computer programs, such as UCINET5 (Borgatti, Everett, & Freeman, 1999) and GRADAP (Stokman & Sprenger, 1989), that initially provided simple "tree" dendograms of who communicates to whom in a network and then use the output to produce reproducible quality network sociograms and associated inferential statistics in programs such as NETDRAW (Borgatti, 2002).

Nonmetric. Nonmetric analysis moves from the use of binary or categorical data to continuous interval or ratio data. Although beyond the scope of this chapter, nonmetric analyses produce both the sociograms and indicators of simple associations and density associated with metric analysis, and also provide ways to graph out such networks

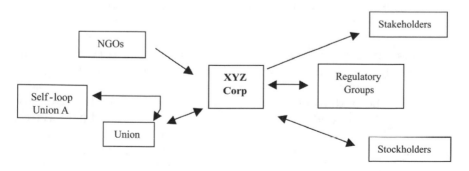

FIG. 4.6 Sample sociogram.

in multidimensional space. One such analysis was presented by Valente (1995) in examining network models of the diffusion of innovations from both structural (metric) and relational (nonmetric) perspectives. His reanalysis of previously recorded datasets on how information flows, to whom it flows, and with what impact is quite informative and demonstrates the potential for this research. However, given the relative immature nature of public relations measurement today, nonmetric analyses are difficult to conduct.

CHALLENGES FOR RESEARCHERS

The challenges for future research in two-way symmetrical public relations are many. First and foremost are the current difficulties in relational public relations measurement:

- What are the relational variables that affect public relations?
- How is it best way to operationalize such measures?
- Can data appropriate for public relations research be obtained from a nonexperimental public?

Second, what do communication networks look like?

- Are there networks—and network flow—that can be expected across the variety of public relations practiced today?
- If so, what do they look like? What kind of information flow do they employ?
- Is truly symmetrical public relations practice actually more effective than asymmetrical practice or, in specific situations, is a combination of asymmetrical and symmetrical public relations most effective? If so, in what type of public relations practice would this be the case?

Third, does social network theory actually benefit the practice of public relations from symmetrical theory?

- Can the descriptive nature of social network theory truly comment on and advance public relations theory?

It is our belief that social network analysis—especially in the corporate context—can and should be studied from a relational perspective. The knowledge gained about who is speaking to whom, through which channels, and with what effect is particularly important in understanding how public relations professionals can manage the flow of information—communication—from a systemic perspective of input, throughput, and output established by a better understanding of when and where to use symmetrical public relations. Based on experience, where environmental scanning for feedback on reputation, trust, or relational variables should be common practice, the ability to establish who is communicating with whom (or, conversely, who is *not* communicating to whom) should be a basic operating principle. Social network analysis should provide the practitioner with an additional tool to manage the flow of communication across a variety of situations.

REFERENCES

Borgatti. S. P. (2002). *Netdraw*. Retrieved August 5, 2005, from http://www.analytictech.com/netdraw.htm

Borgatti, S. P., Everett, M. G., & Freeman, L. C. (1999). *UCINET 5.0 version 1*. Natick, MA: Analytic Technologies.

Broom, G. M. (1986, June). *Public relations roles and systems theory: Functional and historicist causal models*. Paper presented at the International Communication Association Conference, Chicago, IL.

Campbell, K. (2002). *Desperately seeking feedback: A model of feedback-seeking based on the leader–member exchange and communication antecedents*. Unpublished doctoral dissertation, University of Miami, Coral Gables, FL.

Coombs, W. T., & Holladay, S. J. (2001). An extended examination of the crisis situations: A fusion of the relational management and symbolic approaches. *Journal of Public Relations Research, 13*, 321–340.

Cutlip, S. M., & Center, A. H. (1952). *Effective public relations*. Englewood Cliffs, NJ: Prentice-Hall.

Cutlip, S. M., Center, A. H., & Broom, G. M. (1985). *Effective public relations* (6th ed.). Englewood Cliffs, NJ: Prentice-Hall.

Dozier, D. M. (1990). The innovation of research in public relations practice: Review of a program of studies. *Public Relations Research Annual, 2*, 3–23.

Dozier, D. M., & Broom, G. M. (1995). Evolution of the manager role in public relations practice. *Journal of Public Relations Research, 7*, 3–26.

Dozier, D. M., & Ehling, W. P. (1992). Evaluation of public relations programs: What the literature tells us about their effects. In J. E. Grunig & L. A. Grunig (Eds.), *Excellence in public relations and communication management* (pp. 159–184). Hillsdale, NJ: Lawrence Erlbaum Associates.

Edelman Public Relations. (2005). *The sixth annual Edelman Trust Barometer: A global study of opinion leaders*. Retrieved August 5, 2005, from http://www.edelman.com/image/insights/content/

French, R. P., & Raven, B. (1968). The bases of social power. In D. Cartwright & A. Zander (Eds.), *Group dynamics* (3rd ed., pp. 259–629). New York: Harper & Row.

Goldman, E. F. (1948). *Two-way street: The emergence of the public relations counsel*. Boston: Bellman.

Grunig, J. E. (1976). Organizations and public relations: Testing a communication theory. *Journalism Monographs, 46*.

Grunig, J. E. (1984). Organizations, environments, and models of public relations. *Public Relations Research and Education, 1*(1), 6–29.

Grunig, J. E. (1989). Symmetrical presuppositions as a framework for public relations theory. In C. H. Bolton & V. Hazleton, Jr. (Eds.), *Public relations theory* (pp. 17–44). Hillsdale, NJ: Lawrence Erlbaum Associates.

Grunig, J. E. (1992). *Excellence in public relations and communication management*. Hillsdale, NJ: Lawrence Erlbaum Associates.

Grunig, J. E., & Grunig, L.A. (1989). Toward a theory of the public relations behavior of organizations: Review of a program of research. In J. E. Grunig & L. A. Grunig (Eds.), *Public relations research annual* (Vol. 1, pp. 27–63). Hillsdale, NJ: Lawrence Erlbaum Associates.

Grunig, J. E., & Grunig, L. A. (1992). Models of public relations and communication. In J. E. Grunig (Ed.), *Excellence in public relations and communication management* (pp. 285–325). Hillsdale, NJ: Lawrence Erlbaum Associates.

Grunig, J. E., & Huang, Y. H. (2000). From organizational effectiveness to relationship indicators: Antecedents of relationships, public relations strategies, and relationship outcomes. In J. A. Ledingham & S. D. Bruning (Eds.), *Public relations as relationship management: A relational approach to the study and practice of public relations* (pp. 23–53). Mahwah, NJ: Lawrence Erlbaum Associates.

Grunig, J. E., & Hunt, T. (1984). *Managing public relations*. New York: CBS College Publishing.

Grunig, L. A., Grunig, J. E., & Dozier, D. M. (2002). *Excellent public relations and effective organizations: A study of communication management in three countries*. Mahwah, NJ: Lawrence Erlbaum Associates.

Heath, R. L., Douglas, W., & Russell, M. (1995). Constituency building: Determining employees' willingness to participate in corporate political activities. *Journal of Public Relations Research, 7*, 273–288.

Hocking, J. E., Stacks, D. W., & McDermott, S. T. (2002). *Communication research* (3rd ed.). Boston: Allyn & Bacon.

Hon, L., & Grunig, J. E. (1999). *Guidelines for measuring relationships in public relations*. Gainesville, FL: Institute for Public Relations.

Huang, Y. H. (2001). Values of public relations: Effects on organization–public relationships mediating conflict resolution. *Journal of Public Relations Research, 13*, 265–302.

Kim, Y. (2001). Measuring the economic value of public relations. *Journal of Public Relations Research, 13*(1), 3–26.

Lasswell, H. (1948). The structure and function of communication in society. In L. Bryson (Ed.), *The communication of ideas* (pp. 32–51). New York: Harper.

Lauzen, M. M. (1992). Public relations roles, intraorganizational power, and encroachment. *Journal of Public Relations Research, 4*, 61–80.

Lauzen, M. M. (1995). Toward a model of environmental scanning. *Journal of Public Relations Research, 7*, 187–203.

Lauzen, M. M. (1997). Understanding the relation between public relations and issues management. *Journal of Public Relations Research, 9*, 65–82.

Lauzen, M. M.., & Dozier, D. M. (1992). The missing link: The public relations manager role as mediator of organizational environments and power consequences for the function. *Journal of Public Relations Research, 4*, 205–220.

Monge, P. R. (1982). Systems theory and research in the study of organizational communication: The correspondence problem. *Human Communication Research, 8*, 250.

Monge, P. R., & Contractor, N. S. (2003). *Theories of communication networks*. New York: Oxford University Press.

Scott, J. (2000). *Social network analysis: A handbook* (2nd ed.). Thousand Oaks, CA: Sage.

Stacks, D. W. (2002). *Primer of public relations research*. New York: Guilford.

Stacks, D. W., Hickson, M., & Hill, S. R. (1991). *Introduction to communication theory*. Fort Worth, TX: Holt, Rinehart & Winston.

Stokman, F. N., & Sprenger, C. J. A. (1989). *GRADAP: Graph definition and analysis package, Version 2*. Groningen, The Netherlands: iec ProGAMMA.

Thayer, L. (1968). *Communication and communication systems*. Homewood, IL: Irwin.

Tompkins, P. K. (1984). The functions of human communication in organization. In C. C. Arnold & J. W. Bowers (Eds.), *Handbook of rhetorical and communication theory* (pp. 659–719). Boston: Allyn & Bacon.

Valente, T. W. (1995). *Network models of the diffusion of innovations*. Cresskill, NJ: Hampton Press.

von Bertalanffy, L. (1951). Problems on general systems theory, *Human Biology, 23*, 302–312.

von Bertalanffy, L. (1966). General systems theory and psychiatry. In S. Arieti (Ed.), *American handbook of psychiatry* (3rd ed.). New York: Basic Books.

Chapter 5

Public Relations, Conflict Resolution, and Mediation

Kenneth D. Plowman
Brigham Young University

Perhaps it is time for *mediation* to be addressed more fully in the body of literature for public relations, specifically in the evolution of public relations together with conflict resolution. The topics that this chapter addresses, then, that relate to both the characteristics of excellence in public relations programs from the original 1992 study and conflict resolution are: managing strategically, interest-based stakeholders or key publics; the two-way models; and mixed motives. This chapter also covers the contingency model of conflict, international implications, multiple-party negotiations, public relations and mediation, and an updated version of the conflict resolution model of public relations.

Managing public relations strategically involves a long-term perspective. In conflict resolution terms, a win/win by all parties involved in an issue is better predicted if the parties or stakeholders have a long-term relationship. Stakeholders are more likely to support a win/win in any given short-term involvement if they know they are going to have to deal with one another again and again in the future. Another aspect of managing strategically is the environmental scanning role of public relations. The public relations manager is practically the only individual in an organization who constantly scans both internal and external stakeholders to preempt or predict potential conflicts or crises that may arise among the organization and stakeholders in the future.

These interest-based stakeholders can be defined from the conflict resolution literature as those underlying, broader, and more abstract values that individuals and organizations may have in common (Fisher, Ury, & Patton, 1991). Self-interests, from the public relations literature, are not necessarily selfish interests but rather those interests that have intrinsic value for the survival of an entity (e.g., quality of life, needs of family and friends, and even economic well-being; Wilson & Ogden, 2004). These self-interests motivate individuals and organizations to act and to change behavior. Taken one step further, enlightened self-interests assist relationships to be mutually satisfactory. There are inevitable effects in a public relations system of one stakeholder on another. This is inherently two-way symmetrical, as in the models literature, because stakeholders have a constraining effect—they have consequences for each other. The basic survival of an organization in the long term depends on the relationship of self-interests and enlightened self-interests between it and its stakeholders (Plowman, 2005). Grunig, Grunig, and Dozier (2002) posited "that using the two-way symmetrical model or the combination of the two-way symmetrical and the two-way asymmetrical models that we then called the *mixed-motive model* could almost always increase the contribution of public relations to organizational effectiveness" (p. 309).

TWO-WAY MODELS

Conflict resolution in public relations, in essence, evolved from the four models of public relations. The most sophisticated of the four models are the two-way asymmetrical and the two-way symmetrical models. As these two models of public relations evolved, James Grunig (1989) described the two-way symmetrical model as "public relations efforts which are based on research and evaluation and that use communication to manage conflict and to improve understanding with strategic publics" (p. 17). In 1995, the new model of symmetry as two-way practices was developed, by which the win/win zone uses negotiation and compromise to allow organizations to find common ground among their separate and sometimes conflicting self-interests. By doing so, it did not exclude the use of asymmetrical means to achieve symmetrical ends (Dozier, Grunig, & Grunig, 1995).

Pursuing self-interests of stakeholders, even asymmetrically, can lead to mutual benefit for all parties or stakeholders. This also relates to mixed motives in public relations, in which situations and issues are not resolved at the extremes in a pure asymmetrical or symmetrical manner, but rather there are trade-offs, compromise, and so on that lead to both parties being mutually satisfied in their self-interests. (Note that those enlightened self-interests are not necessarily identical.)

MIXED MOTIVES

Although the two-way symmetrical model would seem to be the ideal for conflict management, it is difficult to determine the exact point for appropriate behavior on a continuous scale between two-way asymmetrical and two-way symmetrical communication. Murphy (1991) suggested that a *mixed-motive* version of the two-way symmetrical model might better describe what is happening in the actual practice of public relations, because it incorporates both asymmetrical and symmetrical strategies. More recent studies acknowledge that this mixed-motive model is the more frequently practiced one.

In mixed motives, each side in a stakeholder relationship retains a strong sense of its own self-interests, yet each is motivated to cooperate to attain at least some resolution of the conflict. They may be on opposite sides of an issue, but it is in their best interests to cooperate with each other. Mixed-motive games provide a broad third category that describes behavior as most public relations people experience it: a multidirectional scale of competition and cooperation in which organizational needs must be balanced against constituents' needs. These parties are really cooperative protagonists in the struggle to satisfy their own interests, with the knowledge that satisfaction is best accomplished through satisfying each other's interests as well. In the context of this discussion, protagonists are the main characters in the play of negotiation who seek their own values or self-interests. The question is not one of mixed motives for which short-term asymmetrical tactics are combined with long-term symmetrical tactics, as advocated by Dozier et al. (1995), but rather one of discovering the priority level of importance for the common self-interests of the strategic parties.

More recently, Plowman, Briggs, and Huang (2001) established a number of negotiation strategies that fit into what Plowman called a mixed-motive model for public relations that encompassed the entire spectrum between the two-way asymmetrical and the two-way symmetrical models. It included the strategies of contention, avoidance, accommodation, compromise, cooperation, unconditionally constructive, win/win or no deal, principled, and mediated or cultural. Note the emphasis on the word *strategies*. In 2004, Plowman began to see that there are multitudinous individual tactics that can fit under exclusive strategies above or even across these categories. That is what Glen Cameron did with the 86 factors of his contingency model.

CONTINGENCY MODEL OF CONFLICT

Since 1997, Glen Cameron and his colleagues have been developing a continuum stretching from advocacy (two-way asymmetrical) to accommodation (two-way symmetrical) as the basis for a contingency model of organization–public relationships. Accommodation is not viewed in the classic sense, as giving in to the other party, or as the trend in the conflict literature defines it, as giving in on issues not important while retaining those that are important. Rather, Cameron and colleagues defined it as "the degree of willingness to entertain change for the benefit of others" (Shin, Jin, Cheng, & Cameron, 2003, p. 9). Extending that definition to include change on the part of the opposing party or balance among the self-interests of the two parties would be closer to the two-way symmetrical definition. Research by Shin on conflicts played out in the media showed that an organization uses the advocate strategy more when its key stakeholder advocates are in an escalating spiral, indicating that the media may be a separate, power-brokering party. As the field of conflict resolution and public relations becomes more developed, so too do strategies, factors, and tactics become more complex. This is evidenced by the 86 factors developed for the contingency theory of public relations. Strategies, as mentioned earlier, refer to broad techniques to address organization–public issues. Tactics are relatively isolated tools used.

IMPLICATIONS AT THE INTERNATIONAL LEVEL

Culture is a powerful force that shapes thoughts, perceptions, behavior, and communication. By its very complexity, culture initiates the negotiation strategies of contention or principled in many instances. In the future, the ability to successfully navigate and negotiate cross-culturally will be the key to successful public relations practice on the global scale. Cultural diversity makes communication more difficult. Because knowledge is culture-specific, the more a communicator understands cross-cultural differences, the easier the communication task becomes. Paradoxically, although communication cross-culturally is often more difficult, creating mutually beneficial options can become easier. If negotiators can overcome communication barriers, mutually beneficial solutions—the cooperative strategies and win–win solutions—may become easier. Differences, rather than similarities, can form the basis of mutually beneficial solutions. Obviously, in a multicultural environment, the differences are increased. Thus, the opportunities for mutual gain are also increased (Huang, 1997).

MULTIPLE-PARTY NEGOTIATIONS

Complexity also is a major factor in multiparty negotiations, which may be the next step in this type of public relations research. In 2004, Plowman undertook a qualitative quasi-experimental design with 11 graduate students taking on different roles in the issue regarding disposing of nuclear or hot waste in Utah. These students framed the issue, defined their self-interests as stakeholders, and then conducted a series of five role plays on the issue. All nine strategies were paired against each other in different combinations. Preliminary findings revealed that contention was the most used strategy, but was most often combined with the principled strategy. If those strategies were not successful, then roles players turned to avoidance. During the third round, role players started using cooperation and compromise. Using these two strategies created a less confrontational atmosphere, and the role players were more inclined to discuss alternatives. The most useful strategy, however, was mediation in resolving the hot waste issue.

Most research in conflict resolution has involved only two-party disputes, but in practicality, and especially for public relations, there is most often more than one stakeholder involved. Lawrence Susskind, from the Harvard Program on Negotiation, addressed public relations and conflict resolution in public disputes in 1996 (Susskind & Field, 1996). His book described public relations using terms that essentially equated to one-way and asymmetrical models, and then used a version of Roger Fisher and William Ury's (Fisher, Ury, & Patton,1991) mutual gains approach to resolve public disputes in a symmetrical manner. The field of conflict resolution has realized that more work needs to be done in the area of multiparty disputes, and now public relations is beginning to address it.

A multiparty dispute can be defined as a simultaneous negotiation among three or more parties over multiple issues. In 1989, Saadia Touval (2002) laid out a prescriptive multiparty approach. In such negotiations, the most important work takes place before negotiations and in the prenegotiation phase. Issues that should be addressed about the negotiation itself include the identity and number of parties involved, possible coalitions among them, different possible roles, and an acceptable agenda to follow. The larger the number of participants in these multiple-party conflicts, the more difficulty there will be in defining the problem and agreeing on what an acceptable solution will be. There will be more likelihood of complexity in conflicting positions, the underlying self-interests, and the relationships (e.g., public relationships among the various parties involved). Mediation seems to be a common strategic direction for this part of the field. In multiparty settings, mediators are usually a part of the negotiation. Their intervention does not alter the structure of the negotiation, and mediation is not difficult for the parties involved to accept. Mediators can come from outside the dispute or there can be several, with some acting from their roles inside the dispute.

In 2003 and 2005, several single-embedded cases (Yin, 2003) were conducted that evaluated those new strategies named earlier as well as defined where mediation belongs in the conflict model for public relations. As a result, the model has been reconstructed; mediation now plays a background role for all the nine public relations strategies, because it can be applied to all nine strategies. A new strategy, termed *perseverance*, supplants the terms *aggressive meekness* or *assertive pacifism* in the *Encyclopedia of Public Relations* (2005). Before examining this, however, the concept of public relations taking on an advocacy mediator role to assist stakeholders in resolving issues with a specific organization should be addressed.

PUBLIC RELATIONS AND MEDIATION

Traditionally, a mediator is thought of as a noninterested, neutral third party to any dispute. That is what gives the mediator his or her credibility. A mediator also does not typically suggest alternatives or solutions to a particular problem. The beginnings of thought in this direction occurred in the author's dissertation of 1995 (Plowman, 1995).

The director of corporate communications of the holding company interviewed for the dissertation proposed training opposition publics in negotiation tactics and mediation techniques. He was involved in one proposal in which a dispute resolution process was incorporated in the campaign presentation to the client, "because there [were] going to be major hassles about where this project was going to be put." Even though there might not be trust among the parties in a dispute, it is better when:

> [Y]ou're dealing with common terms, on common ground, and when you know what you're both seeking to do.... And anytime you [the other party] don't think I'm being honest and fair, you cut it off. It's in my best interest that you negotiate well.... You train them how to act in a mediation because the worst thing possible, even worse than having organizations pop up out of the woodwork that don' t agree, is for a trained mediator is to have to deal with someone that's not trained in mediation.

In other words, this public relations manager said that if there is a dispute between two groups, there does not have to be trust, but there does need to be a set of common negotiating or mediation skills. If any resolution of the problem between the groups occurs, it is because they have a common knowledge of how to negotiate with one another.

In 1997, Huang's research in public relations adopted Nicotera, Rodriguez, Hall, and Jackson's (1995) and Putnam and Wilson's (1982) suggestions and used three components as a framework for the examination of conflict management strategies (i.e., integrative, distributive, and avoidance/nonconfrontational strategy). The fourth subscale, third-party mediation, also showed its adequate reliability and validity. Furthermore, Huang added third-party mediation as the fourth factor for examination because mediation has played a critical role in Chinese techniques of conflict resolution and even has integrated itself within the society (Sohn & Wall, 1993; Wall & Blum, 1991).

In the conflict resolution literature, scholars are beginning to see the advantages of *peer mediation*—mediation conducted by peers in an organization who have a vested interest in that organization. Typically, co-mediators (meaning two) independently meet separately with the parties involved within the organization to investigate issues, so as to find possible solutions to raise in a joint session (Cloke & Goldsmith, 2000). In the author's view, there is no reason that public relations, seen as an advocate or one organization, cannot take on that peer mediation role with stakeholders both inside and outside the organization. From the initiation of the mediation, the stakeholders know the advocacy position of the public relations manager. The advantages of peer-based mediation are "numerous and well-documented":

> Peer mediation systems dramatically increase communication skills and understanding regarding organizational conflicts.... Through training and practice, staff members internalize conflict resolution behaviors and strategies.... Results also include a higher rate of resolution of disputes, greater participant satisfaction with the process, reduced likelihood of expensive litigation, lower attorney fees, and increased employee trust in traditional processes. (Cloke & Goldsmith, p. 31)

Mark Sherman (2003) debunked some of the myths of mediators as neutral third parties, much the same way that the field of mass communications generally decries the myth of objectivity among journalists. It is impossible to remove the internal frames of reference of any one individual. This can occur specifically when a mediator meets privately with parties in a dispute, and is evidence of a mediator's style as much as anything else. In such meetings, a mediator may express sympathy with a position or even offer alternatives for a solution to the problem. Such behavior is directed and not neutral, but it helps the parties involved to see possible solutions to their issue. Such behavior is considered inevitable by a significant number of mediators to successfully do their job (Wall, Stark, & Standifer, 2001). One set of authors—Conlon, Carnevale, and Murnighan (1994)—went so far as to call these types of mediators *intravenors*.

Another evolving phenomenon in the field, according to Sherman (2003), is whether it is absolutely essential for the mediator to be independent in order to be effective. In this emerging practice, a professional (e.g., a public relations manager) is an affiliated party who is an inside facilitator and acts as an informal mediator empowered to help resolve conflicts before more formalized, external, and neutral conflict resolution processes occur. Affiliated third parties are often trained in win/win or two-way symmetrical and interest-based stakeholder conflict resolution, as well as in basic mediation skills. The successful use of these public relations managers could mean that positive mediation does not always have to be conducted by a third party who is unaffiliated with any side in a dispute. This individual can offer valuable advice and even settlement options through evaluation of the different parties' positions (Rome, 2002–2003).

A third approach to a public relations manager as mediator is viewed from the advantage of *insight*—which employs a knowledgeable third party, an informal person who contributes some of the knowledge excellence factors. (These could include level of education, intelligence, training, and experience.) There are few studies, besides the Excellence Study, that examine the link between information about the conflict and mediation (Holzworth, 1983). There are even fewer studies that link the stakeholders' perceptions of third-party insight about their enlightened self-interests to processes and outcomes in mediation. Research, however, does show that perceptions of mediator characteristics (e.g., expertise, bias) can have a strong impact on stakeholders' reactions and behaviors in mediation (Arnold & O'Connor, 1999; Conlon & Ross, 1993; Pruitt & Carnevale, 1993).

As field studies have documented, mediators believe that managing disputants' perceptions of how much insight they possess about the dispute is important (Kolb, 1985; Kressel, 1972). Yet, it is not why and to what extent these perceptions affect disputants' judgments of the mediator. A mediator's ability to cultivate disputants' perceptions that he/she has insight into the conflict may lead disputants to view the mediator as credible. *Credibility* refers to a mediator's believability and is the basic principle of mediation (O'Keefe, 2002; Tome, 1992). In fact, many models of mediation place establishing credibility at the forefront of the mediation process (Moore, 1986). In order to be effective and influential, mediators must be seen as credible (Bercovitch, 1996; Gadlin & Pino, 1997; Kolb, 1985).

Despite the importance of credibility in mediation and negotiation, there is comparatively little empirical research on the credibility construct (Lewicki, Saunders, Minton, & Barry, 2003). Much of the research has been adapted from the persuasion and attitude-change literature (Birnbaum & Stegner, 1979; Cooper & Croyle, 1984; McGinnies & Ward, 1980; McGuire, 1985; O'Keefe, 2002). Little research, however, has linked the persuasion and mediation literatures, and almost none comes from the public relations literature (Huang, 1997). Arnold and O'Connor (1999) and Arnold (2000) did show that mediator insight (i.e., information about disputants' interests and needs) will influence stakeholder perceptions of the mediator's competence and, thus, credibility. Perceptions of mediator credibility, in turn, were found to influence how favorably stakeholders responded to third parties (e.g., confidence, acceptability, fairness, satisfaction). Third parties, such as public relations managers, who are seen as having greater insight into the various stakeholders' interests, may be considered more credible and better able to craft recommendations that suit those interests.

CONFLICT RESOLUTION MODEL FOR PUBLIC RELATIONS

Now that mediation has been established as a viable strategy for public relations, the model should be traced for its beginnings. In 1995, Plowman et al. developed the two-way negotiation model for public relations. It was adapted from a number of sources that originated with Thomas' most complete version in 1976. In this model for public relations, dimensions were defined for *contending, cooperating, avoiding, accommodating,* and *compromising.* In 1995, Plowman added two negotiation tactics: what Fisher and Brown (1988) termed as *unconditionally constructive* and what Covey (1990) called *win/win or no deal.*

Unconditionally Constructive

In Plowman's study (1995), problems arose when the opposition or a strategic public refused to come to agreement, even when both parties used cooperative tactics. The alternative action for getting around this impasse was the negotiating tactic of being unconditionally constructive. Being unconditionally constructive was used in the positive sense of Fisher and Brown (1988); that is, guidelines that "will be both good for the relationship and good for me, whether or not you follow the same guidelines" (p. 37). Even if the other party in the conflict does not reciprocate, the organization acts in reconciling the strategic interests of both the organization and its strategic public. Even though the decision to take this altruistic strategy is unilateral, it remains two-way because the organization must have done research to determine the interests of its strategic public. It also is a win/win situation, because both parties mutually benefit from the result of the strategy. The key lies in both parties' common interests. One party cannot be unconditionally constructive if the interests of the other party are not affected positively. Those common interests allow for a limited set of options to be unconditionally constructive (Schelling, personal communication, November 8, 1995). Covey (1991) might have called this condition "principle-centered leadership."

Win/Win or No Deal

The second additional negotiation strategy in Plowman's study (1995) seemed to develop as an alternative beyond unconditionally constructive in order to avoid a stalemate in a negotiation. To get past a stalemate in a positive way for both parties, at least one party's best alternative to a negotiated agreement was the option of no deal at all. The only options in this situation were for either both parties to collaborate in mutually beneficial circumstances or to hold off on any agreement until both parties were ready for a win/win deal to be struck.

In 1990, Covey adapted the game theory terms of Deutsch (1973) into what he called "six paradigms of human interaction." Participants in this study (Plowman, 1995) did not mention the first five but instead emphasized directly the sixth strategy—win/win or no deal. Covey noted, "If these individuals had not come up with a synergistic solution—one that is agreeable to both—they could have gone for an even higher expression of Win/Win—Win/Win or no deal" (p. 213). The *no-deal* addition to the term *win/win* means that if the parties cannot find a solution that would benefit both, then they would agree to disagree—no deal.

Principled.   This tactic spans most of the other tactics already mentioned and is based on a term developed by Covey (1991) in *Principle-Centered Leadership*. The emphasis is on the word *principle*, and the term is *principled*. The basis for this term arose during a session of the April 1998 Southern Communication Association Conference. *Principled* means to hold to higher ethics that cannot be compromised. If a party takes a principled stance, it is unilateral but may be beneficial or detrimental to the other party in the negotiation. Unlike unconditionally constructive, principled does not do necessarily what is best for the relationship. In fact, the principle could even have a negative effect on the originating party. That party could simply "stand on principle" and not be moved from this position because it is a long-held core value or interest.

In a related discussion, Huang (1997) wrote of ethical communication in public relations, referring to two extremes. One related to good or evil consequences that an action brings about, and the other considered the intrinsic features of intent or mental aspect of a contemplated action (Grcic, 1989). Grunig and Grunig (1996) termed these extremes *consequentialist* theories and *nonconsequentialist* theories. In other words, public relations practitioners first should consider the impact of their communication behaviors on their strategic publics; then, they should follow nonconsequentialist rules to be honest, truthful, and sincere when communicating (Reinsch, 1990).

These concepts of ethics in public relations lead to both an asymmetrical and a symmetrical view of principled negotiation. Symmetrical negotiation is one that considers consequences and the effect that they have on a relationship. It encapsulates social responsibility, in that pub-

lic relations managers incorporate the effects their organizations' behavior may have on their stakeholders or publics. Ethics could be
asymmetrical if disclosure was involved and unilateral; that is, one-
sided and nonconsequentialist, in that one party could be honest and
truthful without consideration for the consequences affecting the other
party in a negotiation situation. *Disclosure* refers to advocacy in public
relations—acting in the client organization's best interest. Bivins (1987)
suggested that revealing the reasons for asymmetrical actions could secure ethical standards. Using this rationale means principled negotiation could be either asymmetrical or symmetrical.

These negotiation strategies represent the state of theory in public relations as informed by or discovered through its practice. These are tools
that practitioners can use to develop relationships with both internal
and external strategic publics or stakeholders.

Figure 5.1 represents all of the independent, complementary, and
common interests for both the organization and its strategic publics.
The box also encompasses the alternatives of conflict resolution strategies as well as mediation that can be applied to all the other strategies.
The arrows through the dotted line extending through the win/win
zone shows that these alternatives can flow both ways through the
win/win zone to less desirable alternatives.

Note the absence of the terms *asymmetrical* and *symmetrical*. That is
because the definition of mixed motives is a combination of asymmetrical and symmetrical communication. This model deals with degrees
of each over the spectrum of asymmetrical and symmetrical communication. The only way to represent two ends on either side of the
model would be to represent the one-way models of press agentry and
public information. The two-way models would extend to the begin-

FIG. 5.1.   Conflict resolution model of public relations.

ning of the one-way model. Two-way symmetrical communication is not entirely win/win; it can include elements of compromise, accommodation, and even avoidance, because part of avoidance is unconditional, or win/win or no deal. Likewise, two-way asymmetrical is not entirely contending, but can include elements of all the other negotiation tactics.

A REFORMULATION AND A NEW STRATEGY

Although studies conducted in 2003 and 2005 exhibited almost an impossibility to separate tactics and strategies of conflict resolution, the 2003 study showed the viability of using mediation across all nine strategies. Mediation or the use of a third party, whether neutral or not, is a broader strategy, style, or what have you that mediators or the stakeholders involved in an issue can apply using any of the other eight strategies. However, in six case studies conducted in 2005 (including topics like the U.S. hockey association, the Legacy Highway proposal in northern Utah, starting up an Internet radio station, how Democrats can negotiate their way back into the White House etc.), a new strategy emerged that has been mentioned briefly in the conflict resolution literature as *assertive pacifism* (Keiser, 1988).

The author construed assertive pacifism to a new word, *humwillity*— a strategy that combines *humility* and *strength of will. Humility* is not a term normally associated with business, because business typically epitomizes strength and aggressiveness. Strength would seem to directly oppose humility. In definitions of *humility* posted on the Web, "not everyone regards humility as a virtue" (wordnet.princeton.edu). It is also defined as complete willing surrender, having a lowly opinion of oneself, meekness, and lowliness, the opposite of pride. Humility is generally not taught in management or leadership courses. Organizations usually want their leaders to be visionary and authoritative (Baldoni, 2005), instead of being abject, ignoble, or of poor condition, or not worth much.

In his use of assertive *pacifism*, Keiser (1988) said the best overall strategy for dealing with an aggressive stakeholder is a kind of assertive pacifism—not *passive aggressive*, by which subtle subterfuge is used to sabotage results. Rather, assertive pacifism is a refusal to fight directly, but also a refusal to let the stakeholder take advantage of the situation: "Don't cave in, just don't counterattack. Duck, dodge, parry, but hold your ground. Never close a door; keep opening new ones" (p. 30). This is a strategy to draw stakeholders into creative partnerships to work together and use the options of Fisher et al. (1991). Keiser outlined eight steps to utilizing this assertive pacifism or humwillity:

1. Prepare by knowing your walk away alternatives, that point at which you are better off not negotiating, and by building the number of common self-interests.
2. When under attack, listen—collect as much information as possible from the other stakeholders involved.
3. Keep track of the issues requiring discussion.
4. Assert your organization's interests.
5. Commit to a solution only after it is certain to work for both parties.
6. Save the hardest issues for last.
7. Start high and concede slowly.
8. Finally, don't be trapped by emotional blackmail, meaning anger. (pp. 30–34)

From some of the tactics mentioned in these eight steps there is a combination of the nine or 10 strategies taking place from Fig. 5.1, this author's model. This approach mixes parts of the strategies contention and cooperation, but not just in splitting the difference, as in the strategy of compromise. Numbers 6 and 7 lean toward contention, whereas most of the rest lean toward cooperation. That is why humwillity or perseverance is placed under accommodation and compromise in the model in Fig. 5.1.

This humwillity can be interpreted to mean a quiet strength of resolve, not showy or prideful, but rather having confidence as a public relations manager practicing excellent public relations should—having a depth of knowledge of the field. He or she knows how to survey stakeholder sentiment and knows how to reach those stakeholders to represent the organization. Al Golin, a founder of the worldwide public relations firm Golin/ Harris, devoted a whole chapter to humility in his 2003 book *Trust or Consequences*. He maintained that the public's trust is better gained and maintained from a company that portrays a true image of itself through public relations rather than one that is false through arrogance. He commented: "Humility doesn't mean passive or weak willed" (p. 110). He reminded his readers of the expression, "If you've got it, flaunt it," but maintained that he would change that to, "If you've got it, you don't need to flaunt it" (p. 110).

Golin (2003) cited a number of symptoms of arrogance and lack of humility that apply to public relations and conflict resolution. Among them were running advertising that denigrates competitors as *inferior*, refusing reporters' requests for interviews or information, knowingly structuring win/lose deals (in which your company makes out great and your partner gets the short end of the stick), and using power and leadership positions to push people around (such as the media, suppliers, etc.).

One of Golin's steps (2003) to overcome a perception of arrogance was to use public relations, in part, to communicate a company's humility. The communication could not be a token of "management by walking around" in which the CEO was clearly uncomfortable, but rather should be derived from the mission and goals of the organization. An example would be the CEO who abolished all walls between offices of a company. It was not done just for the sake of positive public relations, but instead because good public relations was a natural outgrowth of a change in management thinking about the work environment of the company.

Another author in the management field, Jim Collins, included a version of humility as good leadership in his book *Good to Great* (2001). In a 5-year study, Collins and his team of researchers found 11 *great* companies. As part of his definition of great, Collins described great leadership essentially as humwillity, as defined in this chapter. He cited Darwin Smith, Chief Executive of Kimberly Clark from 1971 to 1991. Smith turned this aging paper company into the leading paper-based consumer products company in the world. Yet, Collins said that few people, even students of management and corporate history, knew of Smith. That was because Smith never cultivated executive celebrity status, as do many CEOs or turnaround artists of today. However, Collins noted, "[I]f you were to think of Darwin Smith as somehow being meek or soft, you would be terribly mistaken. His awkward shyness and lack of pretense was coupled with a fierce, even stoic, resolve toward life." (p. 18). Collins went on to state that humility plus will equals leadership.

Because most readers of this chapter will not go out and start using the word *humwillity*, a term more commonly used that should fit well as the ninth conflict resolution strategy of public relations is *perseverance*. A definition adapted from Collins (2001) and from Internet postings could include a combination of humility, will power, persistent determination, theologically, to endure to the end—meaning, as Winston Churchill once said, "Never give up." The alternative to perseverance is to totally accede—the lose side of the win/lose definition of the contention strategy. Perseverance is persistence in some task undertaken in spite of difficulty and obstacles. However, combined with humility, it is a quiet strength, a quiet persistence. It acts in the background, like so much of public relations. Credit goes to the CEOs, not the public relations manager. It is the organization, the CEO, the industry—others who usually get the credit. Perseverance can include many of the Excellence Study factors. Perseverance is organized and uses time wisely. It is hard work. It is leadership skills, knowledge, and interpersonal skills. It respects those in authority, and it is humility.

FUTURE RESEARCH

Several directions, then, for future research suggest themselves in the intersection of the conflict resolution and public relations fields. International and cultural aspects, of course, should be included. Also, consideration of public relations and the media's involvement in a conflict should be further explored, as suggested by Susskind and Field (1996) and later by Shin et al. (2003). Plowman (2005) has also been currently conducting research of conflicts played out in the media. Do the media play a third-party mediator role, or is it another party escalating the conflict? Do certain parties gain power through the media to equalize their role in a conflict? What about comparing the notion of community negotiation (meaning negotiation with special interest and citizen groups) in the conflict resolution literature with the activist and segmentation of publics' literature in public relations? Such negotiation implicitly includes multiparty negotiations. It also overlaps into a newer trend in journalism—public or civic journalism—in which reporters have a responsibility to help the public understand the context of the news or conflict. This is very similar to the goal of media relations within public relations—to provide information to the media to ensure balanced coverage. What about the role of the public relations manager in such a public dispute? Is he or she an advocate, a mediator, a third party, or an ombudsman? And, finally, there is the whole concept of relationships among stakeholders in a conflict. How are relationships perceived differently or alike between the two fields? A new strategy is beginning to reveal itself in public relations, as well, that should be investigated. That is the strategy of *humwillity*, or the more commonly known *perseverance*.

REFERENCES

Arnold, J. A. (2000). Mediator insight: Disputants' perceptions of third parties' knowledge and its effect on mediated negotiation. *International Journal of Conflict Management, 11*(4), 318–337.

Arnold, J. A., & O'Connor, K. M. (1999). Ombudspersons or peers? The effects of third party expertise and recommendations on negotiation. *Journal of Applied Social Psychology, 84*, 776–785.

Baldoni, J. (2005). Great motivation secrets of great leaders. New York: McGraw-Hill.

Bercovitch, J. (1996). Understanding mediation's role in preventive diplomacy. *Negotiation Journal, 12*, 241–258.

Birnbaum, M. H., & Stegner, S. E. (1979). Source credibility in social judgment: Bias, expertise, and the judge's point of view. *Journal of Personality and Social Psychology, 37*, 48–74.

Bivins, T. H. (1987). Applying ethical theory to public relations. *Journal of Business Ethics, 6*, 195–200.

Bureau of Labor Statistics. (2004–2005). *Occupational outlook handbook*. Washington, DC: U.S. Department of Labor.

Cloke, K., & Goldsmith, J. (2000). Conflict resolution that reaps great rewards. *The Journal of Quality and Participation, 23*(3), 27–31.

Collins, J. C. (2001). *Good to great: Why some companies make the leap to … and others don't*. New York: HarperCollins.

Conlon, D. E., Carnevale, P. J., & Murnighan, J.K. (1994). Intravention: Third-party intervention with clout. *Organizational Behavior and Human Decision Processes 57*, 387–410.

Conlon, D. E., & Ross, W. R. (1993). The effects of partisan third parties on negotiator behavior and outcome perceptions. *Journal of Applied Psychology, 78*, 1–11.

Cooper, J., & Croyle, R. T. (1984). Attitudes and attitude change. *Annual Review of Psychology, 24*, 395–426.

Covey, S. R. (1990). *The seven habits of highly effective people: Restoring the character ethic*. New York: Fireside.

Covey, S. R. (1991). *Principle-centered leadership*. New York: Fireside.

Deutsch, M. (1973). *The resolution of conflict*. New Haven, CT: Yale University Press.

Dozier, D. M., Grunig, L. A., & Grunig, J. E. (1995). *Manager's guide to excellence in public relations and communication management*. Mahwah, NJ: Lawrence Erlbaum Associates.

Fisher, R., & Brown, S. (1988). *Getting together: Building relationships as we negotiate*. New York: Penguin.

Fisher, R., Ury, W., & Patton, B. (1991). *Getting to yes: Negotiating agreement without giving in*. (2nd ed.). New York: Penguin.

Gadlin, H., & Pino, E. W. (1997). Neutrality, A guide for the organizational ombudsperson. *Negotiation Journal, 13*, 17–37.

Golin, A. (2003). *Trust or consequences: Build trust today or lose your market tomorrow*. New York: American Management Association.

Grcic, J. (1989). *Moral choices: Ethical theories and problems*. St. Paul, MN: West.

Grunig, J. E. (1989). Symmetrical presuppositions as a framework for public relations theory. In C. H. Botan & V. Hazleton, Jr. (Eds.), *Public relations theory* (pp. 17–44). Hillsdale, NJ: Lawrence Erlbaum Associates.

Grunig, J. E. (Ed.). (1992). *Excellence in public relations and communications management: Contributions to effective organizations*. Hillsdale, NJ: Lawrence Erlbaum Associates.

Grunig, J. E., & Grunig, L. A. (1989). Toward a theory of the public relations behavior of organizations: Review of a program of research. *Public Relations Research Annual, 1*, 27–63.

Grunig, J. E., & Grunig, L. A. (1996, May). *Implications of symmetry for a theory of ethics and social responsibility in public relations*. Paper presented to the Public Relations Interest Group, International Communication Association, Chicago.

Grunig, L. A., Grunig, J. E., & Dozier, D. M. (2002). *Excellent public relations and effective organizations: A study of communication management in three countries*. Mahwah, NJ: Lawrence Erlbaum Associates.

Holzworth, J. (1983). Intervention in a cognitive conflict. *Organizational Behavior and Human Performance, 32*, 216–231.

Huang, Y. (1997). *Public relations strategies, relational outcomes, and conflict management strategies*. Unpublished doctoral dissertation. University of Maryland, College Park.

Keiser, T. C. (1988, November–December). Negotiating with a customer you can't afford to lose. *Harvard Business Review*, pp. 30–34.

Kolb, D. M. (1985). To be a mediator: Expressive tactics in mediation. *Journal of Social Issues, 41*(2), 11–26.

Kressel, K. (1972). *Labor mediation: An exploratory survey*. Albany, NY: Association of Labor Mediation Agencies.

Lewicki, R. J., Saunders, D. M., Minton, J. W., & Barry, B. (2003). *Negotiation: Readings, exercises and cases*. (3rd ed.). New York: McGraw-Hill.

McGinnies, E., & Ward, C. D. (1980). Better liked that right: Trustworthiness and expertise as factors in credibility. *Personality and Social Psychology Bulletin, 6*, 467–472.

McGuire, W. J. (1985). Attitudes and attitude change. In G. Lindzey & E. Aronson (Eds.), *Handbook of social psychology* (3rd ed., pp. 223–346). New York: Random House.

Moore, C. W. (1986). *The mediation process*. San Francisco: Jossey-Bass.

Murphy, P. (1991). The limits of symmetry: A game theory approach to symmetric and asymmetric public relations. *Public Relations Research Annual, 3*, 115–131.

Nicotera, A. M., Rodriguez, A. J., Hall, M., & Jackson, R. L. (1995). A history of the study of communication and conflict. In A. M. Nicotera (Ed.), *Conflict and organizations: Communicative processes* (pp. 17–44). Albany: State University of New York.

O'Keefe, D. J. (2002). *Persuasion: Theory and research* (2nd ed.). Newbury Park, CA: Sage.

Plowman, K. D. (1995). *Congruence between public relations and conflict resolution: Negotiation power in the organization*. Unpublished doctoral dissertation, University of Maryland, College Park.

Plowman, K. D. (2004). Multiparty conflict and public relations. In *Proceedings of 7th International Public Relations Research Conference* (pp. 44–45). Miami, Florida.

Plowman, K. D. (2005). Conflict resolution. In R.L. Heath (Ed.), *Encyclopedia of public relations* (pp. 181–184). Thousand Oaks, CA: Sage.

Plowman, K. D., Briggs, W. G., & Huang, Y. H. (2001). Public relations and conflict resolution. In R. L. Heath (Ed.), *Handbook of public relations* (pp. 301–310). Thousand Oaks, CA: Sage.

Pruitt, D. G., & Carnevale, P. J. (1993). *Negotiation in social conflict*. Pacific Grove, CA: Brooks/Cole.

Public relations education for the 21st century: A port of entry. (1999). New York: Public Relations Society of America.

Putnam, L. L., & Wilson, C. E. (1982). Communication strategies in organizational conflict: Reliability and validity of a measurement scale. In M. Burgoon (Ed.), *Communication Yearbook, 6* (pp. 629–652). Beverly Hills, CA: Sage.

Reinsch, N. L. (1990). Ethics research in business communication: The state of the art. *Journal of Business Communication, 27*(3), 251–272.

Rome, D. L. (2002–2003). A guide to business mediation. *Dispute Resolution Journal, 57*(4), 50–60.

Sherman, M. (2003). Mediation hype & hyperbole: How much should we believe? *Dispute Resolution Journal, 58*(3), 43–51.

Shin, J.-H., Jin, Y., Cheng, I.-H., & Cameron, G. T. (2003, November). *Exploring the contingency of conflict management in organization-public conflicts*. Unpublished paper presented at the Public Relations Division of the National Communication Association, Miami Beach, FL.

Sohn, D., & Wall, Jr., J. A. (1993). Community mediation in South Korea: A city–village comparison. *Journal of Conflict Resolution, 37*(3), 536–543.

Susskind, L., & Field, P. (1996). *Dealing with an angry public. The mutual gains approach to resolving disputes*. New York: Free Press.

Thomas, K. (1976). Conflict and conflict management. In M. Dunnette (Ed.), *Handbook of industrial and organizational psychology* (pp. 889–935). Chicago: Rand-McNally.

Tome, V. (1992). Maintaining credibility as a partial mediator: United States mediation in Southern Africa, 1981–1988. *Negotiation Journal, 8*, 273–289.

Touval, S. (2002). *Mediation in the Yugoslav wars*. New York: Palgrave Macmillan.

Wall, J. A., Jr., & Blum, M. (1991). Community mediation in the People's Republic of China. *Journal of Conflict Resolution, 35*(1), 3–20.

Wall, J. A., Stark, J. B., & Standifer, R. L. (2001). Mediation: A current review and theory development. *The Journal of Conflict Resolution, 45*(3), 370–392.

Wilson, L. J., & Ogden, J. D. (2004). *Strategic communications planning for effective public relations and marketing* (4th ed.). Dubuque, IA: Kendall/Hunt.

Yin, R. K. (2003). *Case study research: Design and methods* (3rd ed.). Thousand Oaks, CA: Sage.

Chapter 6

Interpersonal Communication as an Element of Symmetrical Public Relations: A Case Study[1]

Yunna Rhee
Hankuk University of Foreign Studies

Interpersonal communication can be defined in many different ways. According to Adler, Rosenfeld, and Proctor (2004), interpersonal communication refers to "any interaction between two people" (p. 14). Verderber and Verderber (2004) defined interpersonal communication as "the process through which people create and manage their relationships, exercising mutual responsibility in creating meaning" (p. 3). For Trenholm and Jensen (2000), interpersonal communication is "communication between two people, generally in face-to-face interaction" (p. 24).

Despite the variety, most of the definitions include two elements. First, the notion of relationship is discussed as a core concept that dictates interpersonal communication process. Second, definitions refer to the form of communication between people, which is usually face-to-face. The link between public relations and interpersonal communication can be discussed along these two elements.

As Thomlison (2000) explained, relationships are at the core of both public relations and interpersonal communication. Within the interpersonal communication scholarship, relationships between the individual communicators have long been of key research interest. In public relations, relationships between organizations and their key publics have emerged as the focal concept in recent research and practice. Public rela-

---

[1]This study was a part of a larger doctoral dissertation project.

tions scholars reviewed and adopted interpersonal communication concepts in order to explore organization–public relationships (Bruning, 2001). More specifically, public relations scholars looked into how the interpersonal relationship dimensions operate in organization–public relationships. For example, Ledingham and Bruning (1998) identified five dimensions of relationships in interpersonal communication that are applicable to organization–public relationships: trust, openness, involvement, investment, and commitment. Grunig and Huang (2000) also reviewed interpersonal communication theories and proposed trust, control-mutuality, commitment, and satisfaction as relevant dimensions of organization–public relationships.

The second element of interpersonal communication has been mainly linked to the models of public relations. According to Grunig, Grunig, and Dozier (2002), interpersonal communication was identified as an element of public relations practice first in the personal influence model (Grunig, Grunig, Sriramesh, Lyra, & Huang, 1995). In the personal influence model, interpersonal face-to-face communication methods are used to develop personal relationships "with key individuals in the media, government, or political and activist groups" (p. 181). Grunig et al. (1995) found the practice of personal influence model in India, Taiwan, Greece, and the United States.

In the Excellence Study, interpersonal communication was also discussed as an element of symmetrical public relations practice. According to Grunig et al. (2002), excellent public relations functions adopt two-way symmetrical models. In the two-way symmetrical model, communication is balanced, in that it adjusts the relationships between the organization and its publics through negotiation and compromise. The practitioner of this model uses planned communication to manage conflict and to improve understanding with publics. The practitioner uses research to facilitate understanding and communication, rather than to identify messages most likely to motivate or persuade publics. In the symmetrical model, understanding, rather than persuasion, is the principal objective of public relations (Grunig & Grunig, 1992, p. 289). Grunig et al. (2002) explained that although all models of public relations can be practiced using either mediated or interpersonal communication, two-way symmetrical public relations employ interpersonal communication more than mediated communication.

In their work, Grunig and Grunig (1992) delimited interpersonal communication as face-to-face communication. According to the excellence team, forms of interpersonal communication include meetings between government officials and public relations practitioners, or personal meetings between senior managers and various publics or stakeholder groups, which are often differentiated from mass-mediated communication (Grunig et al., 2002).

In this chapter, I expand on the excellence team's research and explore the use of the interpersonal, face-to-face communication method in public relations. More specifically, the best-practice case study introduced herein explores how an organization employed interpersonal communication methods in their symmetrical public relations program to develop positive relationships with their surrounding communities.

BACKGROUND

Brookhaven National Laboratory (BNL) is a multidisciplinary research laboratory focusing on nondefense, basic, and applied research in a variety of fields. In the early 1990s, BNL encountered series of events that led to major public relations crises. In 1997, the lab discovered and announced that there was radioactive tritium in groundwater at the lab. Tritium is a naturally occurring, radioactive form of hydrogen, which also can be artificially produced in nuclear reactors. The surrounding community was outraged, environmental activists enacted protests, and the lab made headlines in the news media almost every day.

In order to calm down the inflamed community and build better relationships with other nearby communities, the lab implemented various community outreach programs. In 2001, the lab reached a point at which it received the Organization of the Year Award from the International Association for Public Participation[2] for its excellent community relations programs. Out of the various programs implemented, the Community Advisory Council (CAC) program is of specific interest in this study.

Community Advisory Council (CAC)

The CAC is a program developed shortly after the environmental scandal that took place during 1997 and 1998. BNL developed CAC as a forum for it to interact with the community on a regular basis. During and after the crisis, the CAC meetings served to create relationships between the lab and the different community groups.

CAC is comprised of a crosscut of stakeholder groups, including local activist groups, civic associations, and employees. The CAC convenes every month at the lab to discuss issues pertaining to the community. For the lab employees and CAC members, this program represents the way the lab and the community approach relationship building with various

---

[2]Details of the award can be found at http://www.iap2.org/corevalues/cvawards-2001.htm

members of the community. The draft charter written in 1998 states the purpose of CAC as follows:

> The purpose of the Brookhaven Community Advisory Council (CAC) is to ensure that the ideas, interests, and concerns of Brookhaven National Laboratory's communities are considered by the Laboratory in its decision-making processes. The CAC's mission is to address concerns about the Laboratory's policies and operations, explicitly those related to environment and public health issues. (Brookhaven National Laboratory, 1998, p. 1)

The CAC also assists the lab in identifying effective mechanisms for consulting with the community to ensure that the interests of community are represented.

THEORETICAL FRAMEWORK

Researchers of the Excellence Study suggested early on that in order for an organization to achieve its goals, building long-term, positive relationships with strategic publics is important (Grunig, Grunig, & Ehling, 1992). The excellence team also explained that in order to produce better long-term relationships with publics, organizations would use two-way symmetrical public relations models, in which interpersonal communication methods are employed (Grunig et al., 2002). However, as Toth (2000) pointed out, research that explored the interpersonal communication processes in public relations has been scarce. In this regard, Hon and Grunig's (1999) research was exceptional, because they adopted interpersonal communication strategies for the development of organization–public relationships.

Based on the results of the Excellence Study and extensive review of relevant literature, Hon and Grunig (1999) developed specific communication strategies for relationship management in public relations. They referred to their communication strategies as "maintenance strategies," and defined them as follows: "communication methods that public relations people use to develop new relationships with publics and to deal with the stresses and conflicts that occur in all relationships" (p. 5). Most recently, Grunig (2002) renamed the maintenance strategies as *cultivation strategies*. Much of the cultivation strategies are drawn from the interpersonal communication and conflict resolution theories.

Hon and Grunig (1999) proposed a selective set of symmetrical communication strategies that are likely to produce relationship outcomes:

> **Access**—members of publics or opinion leaders provide access to public relations people. Public relations representatives or senior managers provide representatives of publics similar access to orga-

nizational decision-making processes. Either party will answer telephone calls or read letters or e-mail messages from the other. Either party is willing to go to the other when they have complaints or queries, rather than taking negative reactions to third parties.

Positivity—anything the organization or public does to make the relationship more enjoyable for the parties involved.

Openness—of thoughts and feelings among parties involved.

Assurances—attempts by parties in the relationship to assure the other parties that they and their concerns are legitimate. This strategy also might involve attempts by the parties in the relationship to demonstrate they are committed to maintaining the relationship.

Networking—organizations' building networks or coalitions with the same groups that their publics do, such as environmentalists, unions, or community groups.

Sharing of tasks—organizations' and publics' sharing in solving joint or separate problems. Examples of such tactics are managing community issues, providing employment, making a profit, and staying in business, which are in the interest of either the organization, the public, or both. (pp. 14–15)

From the conflict management theories, the following strategies were adopted:

Integrative—These approaches are symmetrical because all parties in a relationship benefit by searching out common or complementary interests and solving problems together through open discussion and joint decision making. The goal is a win–win solution that values the integrity of a long-term relationship between an organization and its publics.

Dual Concern—These strategies have particular relevance for public relations because they take into consideration the dual role of balancing the interests of publics with the interests of the organization. These strategies also can be called mixed-motive or collaborative advocacy … Several other dual concern strategies are symmetrical and are the most effective at building and maintaining a relationship in the long term:

Cooperating—Both the organization and the public work together to reconcile their interests and to reach a mutually beneficial relationship.

Being unconditionally constructive—The organization does whatever it thinks is best for the relationship, even if it means giving up some of its positions and even if the public does not reciprocate.

Saying win-win or no deal—If the organization and public cannot find a solution that benefits both, they agree to disagree—no deal. A strategy of no deal is symmetrical because it leaves open the potential to reach a win-win solution at a later date. (pp. 16–17)

Hon and Grunig's strategies prompted active discussions about effective communication strategies for relationship management. However, there are few empirical research studies that have explored Hon and Grunig's cultivation strategies. Based on the literature review, the following research question is posited:

What forms of communication do the participants use, see as important, or find effective in the development of positive organization-public relationships (OPR)?

METHOD

Case study strategy was used in this research. According to Stake (1995), when one has a research question and wants to get insight into the question by studying a particular case, instrumental case study is conducted. Because this study sought to answer questions that arose from a conceptual review of theories and tried to understand the theoretical framework within a specific setting, it could be considered as an instrumental case study.

Interview was my primary data collection method. I interviewed nine CAC members, three public relations managers responsible for the program, and two top managers who participated in the CAC meetings. I conducted participant observation of a 3-hour CAC meeting. I recruited interviewees at this meeting by circulating a notepad on which they could sign up on a voluntary basis for an interview. Most members recruited had been involved in the CAC for at least 3 years. Relevant documents—including meeting minutes, transcripts of CAC meetings for the previous 3 years, policy statements, and newsletters—were collected and reviewed.

RESULTS AND DISCUSSION

In my interviews, most participants described a transition of relationship quality from hostility to respect between the lab and the community members. I asked the participants what communication methods or strategies they thought contributed most to the state of their current relationship.

Management and PR Practitioners' Perspectives

In general, the participants considered face-to-face, one-on-one communication to be vital in building relationships with the community. According to the participants, the group communication setting of the CAC effectively personified the lab. Practitioners and top management found mediated communication vehicles, such as print media or online communication, to be limiting. Public relations practitioners said that interpersonal communication made it possible to observe behavior, facial expressions, and vocal tonality. At community meetings, the lab director also tried to get a sense of the "community's collective emotional state."

Practitioners were able to make meaningful connections with community members through face-to-face communication. The practitioners found that when the lab made a meaningful connection with someone, that person became more aware of the lab's activities and would "at least give a cursory look" to the lab's messages in the mass media. One practitioner referred to this process as "putting a face on the lab."

Community council members' responses indicated that face-to-face communication was having the desired effect. One council member told me, "Depending upon the issue and what's going on, you are going to have a different person each time; so I don't see the lab as necessarily 'they.'" Another member said that, when considering a certain project presented by the lab, she could "visualize the person's face." Face-to-face communication allowed the lab to dispel the mysteriousness of "the lab," and to eliminate past perceptions of it as an impersonal organization that created misunderstandings and speculations. Several of Hon and Grunig's cultivation strategies were also considered effective in developing positive relationships.

Openness. Hon and Grunig (1999) identified several key strategies for relationship building, including honesty and the open sharing of information and decisions with the community. The management and practitioners repeatedly emphasized these same strategies. The top public relations manager said, "We do not convince the public, we do not sell the public. That has not been the reason why we have the programs we do. We involve them, we explain their decision space, and we are honest about it." Another manager explained the lab's strategy this way: "I am not saying that the community gets to steer the boat for us. I'm saying that they get to put their core values on the table and [those values] are heard and respected. There is transparency."

Both managers stressed the importance of providing relevant information, whether good or bad, so the community could make its own judgments about the lab's decisions. In any case, engaging the community in the decision-making process was critical, so that the community could be heard in all matters.

Networking. In Hon and Grunig's (1999) terms, the lab used a networking strategy to build relationships with various groups through the CAC forum. Furthermore, the lab provided an opportunity not only for the community to communicate about the lab's activities, but also to develop understanding among different interest groups within the community.

Development of the CAC was a wise strategy, one practitioner explained. Had the lab approached each community group separately to build a relationship, more manpower and time would have been expended. In this sense, the community council itself was an effective strategy for the lab to cultivate relationships with multiple publics at once. In the interviews, I also found some new cultivation strategies that were different from what Hon and Grunig (1999) suggested.

Visible Leadership. In relation to the personification of the lab, visible leadership was also considered important. Practitioners referred to this strategy as the "top-down approach," which was successful because community members were "hearing from the horse's mouth," as one practitioner put it. As a result, the community was reassured of the management's commitment to the relationship. Most practitioners mentioned that the presence of the key decision makers from the lab at community meetings was crucial, and that directors and deputies needed to be sitting at the table with the community. One manager said, "If you don't have that, it ain't going to work."

Listening. "Listening" was a term often mentioned by the public relations practitioners. The public relations director said that anger directed at the lab during the crisis was "not at the tritium, but the anger was at a lab that wouldn't listen and wouldn't engage. That was it!" She emphasized the importance of listening by saying:

> You know, if you are willing to listen, it's amazing what you can get. If you are willing to listen to people and try not to prejudge, and that's not always easy. It's easy with people you like or agree with most of the time. In fact, we've learned, I have personally learned, probably more from the activist community than I did from our friends. Because they would pick at your weaknesses. It took a long time for me to get to this point, but I [now] look at it as feedback. This is not just a guidepost; it is a way for us to clean up our act to become more careful.

Another community relations practitioner told me that "listening is 80%" of her job. CAC meetings were the main mechanism for listening, one in which different community groups are able to openly share their values and opinions.

Responsiveness.   Timely response to community requests or potential issues was a key strategy for the lab's risk management. When asked to identify key communication strategies for effective community relations, one practitioner explained:

> [When] you are timely in providing the information and responsive to their [communities'] concerns, it doesn't mean that you have to agree with them, but you are responsive and you are acknowledging their issues and recognizing their value and telling them whether or not you've been able to incorporate their input, and if so, how you did it or didn't. If you do those things, you are going to do O.K....

Another practitioner described CAC meetings as a forum for being responsive: "So the CAC gives us feedback, and the end of that is that we have the responsibility to tell them how that feedback was used. To actually go back to the council and say this is what was done with it." She referred to this as "closing the loop." Practitioners' responses made it clear that they were consciously employing two-way models in their communication with the community.

Continued Dialogue/Patience.   Based on their experience with the CAC, most of the management and public relations practitioners suggested "continued dialogue" as an important cultivation strategy. "The biggest thing [for relationship management] is to continue the dialogues" with the community, a top manager stated. Some described continued dialogue as having "patience." Despite difficulties in the beginning, BNL and CAC learned to maintain open communication and, as a result, now have a mutually respectful relationship.

"We [the lab] knew if we started the CAC, it was going to be a long-term commitment," said one practitioner. Another practitioner noted, "It [a positive community relationship] doesn't happen right away. It is painful, it takes time, it is extremely expensive, but it is the right thing to do. You have to wait for the group to mature." The organization saw "investment of time" as a key strategy in their relationship-building process. Employees spent significant time coordinating the 3- to 4-hour CAC meetings that were held after work. One top manager commented that the cost of community relations was "more in time than money." These managers all referred to a temporal aspect of the cultivation strategy that was not included in Hon and Grunig's (1999) theory.

Community Members' Perspectives

Community members also regarded interpersonal interaction as an effective cultivation strategy. One CAC member described why he thought interpersonal interaction was effective:

> People are more likely to believe when they have a one-on-one conversation with somebody and it may be semi-officially, or it might be an informal phone call, might not be a part of a meeting, but that person becomes a human being, less of a representative or a part of a large organization. When you see them as a human being and you hear what they are saying, you tend to believe them more.

Another CAC member said having "people [community] come [to the lab] and speak one on one with people [at the lab]" is one reason the lab has been able to build positive relationships with the community. Because lab employees are present at CAC meetings, one member knows that when he has questions or issues to raise, "dialogue can be done right there [at the CAC meeting]." As one member mentioned, interpersonal communication has helped by "giving a face" to the lab: "It is no longer 'the lab.' You need that personal attachment. Not only do I know about the project, but I can also visualize the person's face. You are taking away some of the scariness."

An interesting theme discerned in interviews with community members was their skepticism about what they see or hear in the mass media. "I don't know if I trust the press," a community member told me while explaining the value of having direct access to a lab employee. Another community member also tended to be "a little cautious and not too hasty in making judgments" about messages she got from the media. She told me that the press can be "misguided" and that she tries to get all the facts before making judgments.

However, community members also exercised constructive skepticism toward the lab, even when they felt they had positive relationships with the lab. They did not take what the lab told them to be the whole truth, but instead looked to other sources for verification. As one member put it, "I can see several sides of all things. I have checked out what they have said as well, just to make sure I have all sides. I also talk to other environmental groups as well."

Interview data suggested that the participation in the CAC made it possible for community members to gather balanced information about issues or problems related to the lab. To some extent, the lab was able to counteract negative bias in mass media coverage through their face-to-face interactions at CAC meetings with the community members. When asked about effective communication strategies, CAC members also talked about the cultivation strategies suggested by Hon and Grunig.

Access.   Hon and Grunig (1999) discussed access as an effective cultivation strategy that provides opinion leaders or members of publics with access to public relations practitioners. Practitioners and management at BNL responded directly to telephone calls from council members, rather than delegating the collection of negative reactions or opinions to third parties.

"I know I can call people who work at the facility and I will get a response. They'll give me information that I want," a CAC member told me. Another member said he knew the lab was "a phone call away" when he needed information. Current lab management has provided more access than in the past, one CAC member said. Another member found that "[in the past] if you wanted information, you could set [an] appointment and go on the lab site to use the library. But it [gaining access to information] was up to you to initiate. Now, the lab has initiated it by forming and hosting CAC."

Respect.   Community council members saw respect as a key to a good communication strategy. They used words such as "sincerity" and "genuineness" to describe it. The council members' description of respect matches what Hon and Grunig (1999) called "assurance," a strategy in which a party "attempts to assure the other parties that they and their concerns are legitimate" (p. 15). For CAC members, understanding the different communication styles of groups was another form of respect displayed at CAC meetings. As one council member commented, "There are different ways of communicating. You and I get the same end result, [but] it's just different processes and mechanisms. If you can respect that, if you can be patient about that, [you can work together]." It is critical, therefore, that public relations practitioners learn to communicate effectively and adapt their communication strategies to each of their publics.

Sharing of Tasks.   Task sharing was another cultivation strategy suggested by Hon and Grunig (1999). In this strategy, organizations and publics solve common or individual problems together. For example, the organization and/or the public interest may be served by managing community issues, providing employment, making a profit, and staying in business. The following anecdote, demonstrates that the lab and community council members employed this task-sharing strategy.

When the lab was under budgetary constraints to carry out an accelerated cleanup of a river in the community, council members lobbied for more money by writing letters to Congress and by placing stories in the media. Environmentalists wanted to achieve greater environmental safety and protection. Civic associations represented residents wishing for a clean environment in which to live. Political coalitions hoped to make elected officials accountable, and employees simply wanted to do the right thing. The groups' motivation to accelerate the river cleanup effort may not have been the same, but the result would serve all interests. As one CAC member put it, the lab and the community were both cognizant of the "utility of collaboration" to solve a collective problem. Interviews with the CAC members also revealed a cultivation strategy different from Hon and Grunig's (1999) suggestions.

Responsiveness.   CAC members also regarded responsiveness as an effective strategy used by the lab. For most members, responsiveness meant that the lab would follow up on issues or requests made by community members. "They always call back," a member told me. "They are pretty responsive to comments," another member said when asked about the lab's most effective strategies.

"They [the lab employees] always ask, 'What do you want,' 'What do you need,' 'What more information can we get for you?'" a member explained. She felt her community's concerns were "being heard and if it's at all possible they will scientifically or physically try to accommodate any concerns that the community may have." CAC members often discussed access and responsiveness together, suggesting the importance of direct communication from both sides.

Summary

Overall, the participants considered interpersonal communication methods to be crucial in the development of positive relationships. More specifically, Hon and Grunig's (1999) openness, networking, access, assurance, and sharing of tasks strategies were found to be effective. In addition, the interview data revealed new cultivation strategies. For instance, the lab emphasized its own temporal strategy, which entailed a patient, ongoing dialogue to cultivate a relationship with the community. Listening and responsiveness were factors critical to a successful community relations program at BNL. Visible leadership helped create a positive relationship with the community by personifying the lab. Community members agreed that the lab successfully employed interpersonal communication strategies to create positive relationships with the public.

IMPLICATIONS AND DIRECTIONS FOR FUTURE RESEARCH

This study has several implications for public relations theory. One contribution this study makes to theory is that it successfully synthesized the excellence and relationship management theories. This case study demonstrated that interpersonal communication methods were, in fact, effective in building positive relationships, as was suggested by the Excellence Study.

Furthermore, new cultivation strategies were also identified, including visible leadership, listening, responsiveness, and continued dialogue/patience. Table 6.1 summarizes the findings on cultivation strategies.

Participants felt the communication behavior of the organization's leadership affected the evaluation of organization–public relationship. To this point, the public relations field has not extensively studied the communication behavior of leadership and its impact on relationship outcomes. Results of this study indicated the need for further exploration of leadership's role in relationship management. BNL used ongoing communication and patience as key public relations strategies. Positive relationships can only be expected to evolve when long-term efforts are in place. For instance, the CAC program existed for over 4 years.

Another course of research would be to conduct a quantitative study to explore the interrelations between the symmetrical interpersonal communication methods and resulting relationship outcomes. Result of such study could provide public relations professionals with guidance for the development of effective communications programs to build and maintain positive organization–public relationships.

As the study showed, interpersonal communication facilitated the implementation of symmetrical principles and to some extent addressed shortcomings of mediated communication. If public relations professionals wish to develop long-term, experiential relationships with their publics, they should incorporate interpersonal communication methods into their program planning, rather than focusing solely on the use of mass-mediated communication and the production of well-refined messages.

However, in exploring the cultivation strategies, practitioners must carefully consider the type and context of the organization. The case organization was a government lab in which profit making was not a major concern. Interpersonal communication methods may have different implications in for-profit settings. Exploration of other areas such as consumer relations or investor relations may provide further knowledge regarding effective interpersonal communication strategies.

TABLE 6.1

Effective Cultivation Strategies for Organization–Public Relationships

	Management and PR Practitioners	*CAC Members*
Newly identified	Visible leadership Listening Responsiveness Continued dialogue/patience	Responsiveness
Hon and Grunig (1999)	Openness Networking	Access Respect (assurance) Sharing of tasks

This case study was confined to a U.S. organization. Cross-cultural replications of the study could elicit valuable insights about interpersonal communication methods. According to Grunig et al. (1995) the culture and political system in which the organization exists is one of the determinants of whether interpersonal methods will be used in public relations. Grunig et al. (1995) explained that when a political system is more authoritarian and a culture is more rigid, reliance on interpersonal communication methods increases. In this regard, exploration of the interpersonal communication methods in a non-U.S. country may elicit interesting comparative results.

REFERENCES

Adler, R. B., Rosenfeld, L. B., & Proctor, R. F. (2004). *Interplay: The process of interpersonal communication* (9th ed.). New York: Oxford University Press.

Brookhaven National Laboratory. (1998). *Draft charter for Community Advisory Committee*. Upton, NY: Author.

Bruning, S. D. (2001). Axioms of relationship management: Applying interpersonal communication principles to the public relations context. *Journal of Promotion Management, 7*, 3–15.

Grunig, J. E. (2002). *Qualitative methods for assessing relationships between organizations and publics*. Gainesville, FL: Institute for Public Relations, Commission on PR Measurement and Evaluation.

Grunig, J. E., & Grunig, L. A. (1992). Models of public relations and communication. In J. E. Grunig (Ed.), *Excellence in public relations and communication management* (pp. 285–326). Hillsdale, NJ: Lawrence Erlbaum Associates.

Grunig, L., Grunig, J., & Dozier, D. (2002). *Excellent public relations and effective organizations: A study of communication management in three countries*. Mahwah, NJ: Lawrence Erlbaum Associates.

Grunig, J. E., Grunig, L. A., & Ehling, W. P. (1992). What is an effective organization? In J. E. Grunig (Ed.), *Excellence in public relations and communication management* (pp. 65–90). Hillsdale, NJ: Lawrence Erlbaum Associates.

Grunig, J., Grunig, L., Sriramesh, K., Lyra, A., & Huang, Y. H. (1995). Models of public relations in an international setting. *Journal of Public Relations Research, 7*(3), 163–186.

Grunig, J. E., & Huang, Y. H. (2000). From organizational effectiveness to relationship indicators: Antecedents of relationships, public relations strategies, and relationship outcomes. In J. A. Ledingham & S. D. Bruning (Eds.), *Public relations as relationship management: A relational approach to the study and practice of public relations* (pp. 23–53). Mahwah, NJ: Lawrence Erlbaum Associates.

Hon, L. C., & Grunig, J. E. (1999). *Guidelines for measuring relationships in public relations*. Gainesville, FL: Institute for Public Relations, Commission on PR Measurement and Evaluation.

Ledingham, J. A., & Bruning, S. D. (1998). Relationship management in public relations: Dimensions of an organization–public relationship. *Public Relations Review, 24*(1), 55–65.

Stake, R. (1995). *The art of case study*. Thousand Oaks, CA: Sage.

Thomlison, T. (2000). An interpersonal primer with implications for public relations. In J. A. Ledingham & S. D. Bruning (Eds.), *Public relations as relationship management: A relational approach to the study and practice of public relations* (pp. 177–202). Mahwah, NJ: Lawrence Erlbaum Associates.

Toth, E. (2000). From personal influence to interpersonal influence: A model for relationship management. In J. A. Ledingham & S. D. Bruning (Eds.), *Public relations as relationship management* (pp. 205–220). Mahwah, NJ: Lawrence Erlbaum Associates.

Trenholm, S., & Jensen, A. (2000). *Interpersonal communication* (4th ed.). Belmont, CA: Wadsworth.

Verderber, K. S., & Verderber, R. F. (2004). *Inter-act: Interpersonal communication concepts, skills, and contexts* (10th ed.). New York: Oxford University Press.

Chapter 7

Coping With an Uncertain World: The Relationship Between Excellence and Complexity Theories

Priscilla Murphy
Temple University

One of the cornerstones of James and Larissa Grunig's Excellence Theory is the role of public relations in helping organizations to deal with an uncertain, and often threatening, environment. Anticipating issues, identifying key publics, building and maintaining relationships that lessen conflict, acquiring the internal power to implement needed changes—all these tasks form the core of public relations that is truly "strategic" (Grunig & Grunig, 2000). Many of these public relations tasks are rooted in the need to establish some stability and control over a world that appears increasingly "heterogeneous, unstable, dispersed, and turbulent" (Grunig, 1984; quoted in Grunig, 1992, p. 475).

This vision is shared by another body of theory: that of complex adaptive systems (CAS). Both excellence and complexity theories are concerned with uncertainty and change, and with the questions of control that these issues raise. Both bodies of theory complement or extend each other; in some respects, they have different aspirations and different emphases. In this chapter, I discuss the commonalities and divergences between excellence and CAS theories in an effort to show how they evolve from similar preoccupations and, in effect, comment on and enlarge each other. In doing so, I am considering both theories as related responses, part of a general trend in current social science thinking: an increasing awareness of contingency and change.

Mainly, my discussion focuses on the themes of interaction, stability, mutual adaptation, prediction, and control. Many more public relations scholars are familiar with excellence than with complexity theory, and so the basic complexity ideas are explicated in the course of discussion. A good starting point is the triad of concepts that the Grunigs and their associates designated as underlying organizational effectiveness: autonomy, interdependence, and relationships (Grunig, Grunig, & Ehling, 1992). These three concepts motivate most interactions among an organization, its environment, and particularly its publics, which are fundamental to both excellence and complexity theories.

RELATIONSHIPS AND INTERACTIONS

Both excellence and complexity-based thinking begin from a view of the world as a shifting, often unpredictable, environment. This sense of flux and uncertainty situate both theories within a contemporary context. As the Grunigs have often argued, "[O]rganizations no longer function as the rational machines depicted in the organizational theories of the 1930s and 1940s—if, indeed, they ever functioned in that way" (Grunig et al., 1992, p. 68). Instead, organizations are "political," in the sense that they represent arenas in which diverse groups, internal and external, compete for power. Many of these groups hold different interpretations of organizational priorities and different goals. Acknowledging the multifariousness of these stakeholders, the Excellence Theory draws on Weick (1976), March and Olsen (1976), and others to create a view of the organization as developing goals from "negotiations among shifting coalitions of powerful managers" and organizations composed of "autonomous subsystems capable of pursuing inconsistent objectives" (Grunig et al., 1992, pp. 78, 79). A major issue for excellent public relations, then, is steering these diverse groups into some form of harmonious existence.

Like Excellence Theory, the theory of complex systems begins with a view of multiple individual agents or subgroups from whose interplay emerges large-scale organizational, or even societal, patterns. Hence, a complex system is defined as "many individual actors who interact locally in an effort to adapt to their immediate situation. These local adaptations, however, accumulate to form large-scale patterns that affect the greater society, often in ways that could not have been anticipated" (Murphy, 2001, p. 450).

The dynamics of the relationships among individual agents in a complex system has peculiar properties that distinguish such a system from a merely "complicated" system. For example, a computer is a complicated system containing a large number of interacting parts, but the relationship among these parts is wholly specifiable and predictable. In contrast, when a system is truly complex, its components are irrevers-ibly (sometimes unpredictably) transformed during its interactions. To use an organizational analogy, a public relations department is not like an assembly line. By pooling their vantage points, public relations staff may generate novel ways to address the organization's goals so that the final public relations strategy may be quite different from what the staff members expected at the beginning of the brainstorming process—a truly "complex" interaction. In contrast, individuals working on a "complicated" assembly line interact to create a predesigned product and unanticipated outcomes constitute defective goods.

Thus, an important feature of a complex system is that its agents in-teract in ways that alter the system itself over time. These interactions are local and cumulative. They have a relatively short range, primarily affecting neighboring agents. No individual agent has complete knowl-edge of the behavior of the system as a whole, only the information re-ceived locally. Kaufmann (2000) termed this local exploration "the adjacent possible" (p. 142), emphasizing that change transpires step by step, as a local interaction creates an "enlarged actual" that then diffuses into a new "adjacent possible" (Mitleton-Kelly, 2003, pp. 36–37). By on-going expansion of the adjacent possible, large-scale changes emerge over time.

In a complex adaptive system, individual agents are both interdepen-dent and autonomous. They do not merely follow fixed rules dictated by a separate force (e.g., senior management or public relations). Rather, the "rules" for interaction are dynamically developed by the agents themselves in the course of their interaction. Furthermore, the agents' actions are nonlinear, and thus the results of individual interactions are unpredictable: Small causes can have a profound impact on the system, and large events may have minimal effect. At the same time, the context of the interaction—organizational, economic, cultural—provides some constraints on the local interactions. Thus, rules for interaction are developed on the micro level with interaction between agents as a situa-tion unfolds, but are patterned by macrolevel expectations and con-text—in other words, by organizational culture.

This concept of constraint and influence is comparable to the Grunigs' observations about the environment in which organizations try to be effective—that is, try to meet their goals and satisfy their mis-sion. Limitations on autonomy come largely from interdependence among agents who share an environment. Hence, Grunig et al. (1992) cited an observation by Pfeffer and Salancik (1978) that "organizations are involved in a constant struggle for autonomy and discretion, con-fronted with constraint and external control," and that "interdepen-dence exists whenever one actor does not entirely control all the conditions necessary" to complete its mission (p. 68). If it is strategic, public relations optimizes the organization's ability to work within the context of this imperfect control: "Managers who manage strategically do so by balancing the mission of the organization—what it is, what it wants to be and what it wants to do—with what the environment will allow or encourage it to do" (Grunig & Grunig, 2000, pp. 308–309).

As this focus on the environment suggests, many of the compatibilities between excellence and complexity viewpoints can be traced to their origins in general systems theories. Showing its own roots in biology, systems thinking emphasizes the goal of homeostasis, or a state of stable equilibrium. The system boundaries are permeable for interaction with the environment to the extent necessary to maintain stability, and the role of managers is task definition and boundary control, as a means of taking timely action to correct for change and preserve equilibrium. In other words, such entities are "self-regulating, goal-directed systems adapting to their environment" (Stacey, Griffin, & Shaw, 2000, p. 65). These adaptations allow the appearance of previously untapped potential that already exists within the organization; thus, managers who base their intervention on systems thinking are also concerned with reaching this potential and drawing it out in service of the organization. For this reason, the concept of control is central to systems theory, as is efficient, linear causality that allows managers to intervene at "leverage points" to manage the dynamics within the system (Gilpin & Murphy, 2005).

In keeping with many of these systems ideas, Grunig et al. (1992) offered a definition of strategic public relations management in terms of interpretation and adaptation to the external environment: "If public relations can identify the strategic publics in the environment and manage the organization's response to these interdependencies,... public relations can help the organization reduce uncertainty and reduce conflict by stabilizing relationships with key publics on which the organization depends" (p. 81). Specifically, Grunig (1989) identified four presuppositions about symmetrical communication as coming from systems theories: holism, interdependence, open system, and moving equilibrium.

Similarly, one can see the stamp of general systems theories on complexity, in its focus on interaction with a changeable environment, on stabilizing (or destabilizing) feedback, on internal control (or lack of control), and on the relationship between history and innovation. However, in a complex system, adaptation is necessarily mutual, transformative, and multifaceted. That means the system does not simply accommodate an outside environment, as general systems theory contends; nor can an organization simply proceed to do what it wishes. As Grunig et al. (1992) pointed out, in this complex environment, it "can adapt to ..., cooperate with ..., or interact with ..., groups that limit its autonomy" (p. 68). Similarly, in a complex system the parts of the whole—including staff, technologies, cultural norms, and institutional and legal structures—adapt to one another in an ongoing process.

Overall, general systems theories' emphasis on interaction and adaptation clearly has proved useful to both excellence and complexity theories. However, both bodies of theory have gone beyond strict systems theory parameters. Grunig and Grunig (2000) found that systems theories, with their emphasis on mere survival in their environment, offered "an extremely weak goal" for measuring organizational effectiveness (p. 306). They drew on manifold other theories—including coorientation, interest group liberalism, conflict resolution, goal attainment, strategic constituencies, and competing values—to define excellence (Grunig, 1989; Grunig & Grunig, 2000).

The shortcomings of general systems theories similarly curtail their usefulness for understanding complex systems. General systems theories propose an essentially passive model in which the system reacts to outside stimuli but does not produce innovation within itself unprompted—it cannot capture the vagaries of human interaction. In addition, general systems theories assume a set of rational rules and procedures that are designed by managers and followed by other organization members (Gilpin & Murphy, 2005). General systems theories encourage a situation that often appears—and is a source for concern—in the Grunigs' work, whereby the "dominant coalition" dictates organizational culture and mission, as well as public relations' role.

In a complex system, mutual adaptation is often spoken of in terms of "fitness landscapes." This concept originated in studies of evolution within biological systems undertaken by Stuart Kauffman (1993, 2000) at the Santa Fe Institute, a practice community that studies complexity in a variety of natural and social sciences. To model evolutionary processes, Kauffman envisioned species as located in a "landscape," or environment, populated by other species whose needs impinge on each others' survival. Each species simultaneously attempts to maximize its fitness—its survivability—and thereby constantly shifts the fitness landscape shared by others, who likewise respond, creating an ongoing series of interactions and adaptations interspersed with temporary periods of stability.

Although this brief synopsis does not begin to do justice to Kauffman's work, it may suggest why his model has been adopted by organizational theorists, particularly those who work in business strategy. Based on network theory, Kauffman created several types of "fitness landscapes" that are used increasingly to model organizations' success within their own environments. Organizational theorists have described this world "as a discernible set of alternative possibilities that can be responded to but which require a repertoire of flexible responses.

Contingencies can be managed but rarely optimally" (Boisot & Child, 1999, p. 244).

This mutual, constrained adaptation proposed by complexity theory provides an additional perspective on relationships, especially the Grunigs' concepts of asymmetrical and symmetrical relationships. Two-way asymmetrical communication, the "dominant view in public relations," is "a way of getting what an organization wants without changing its behavior or without compromising." It presupposes that "the organization knows best and that publics benefit from 'cooperating' with it" (Grunig & White, 1992, pp. 39, 40). The Grunigs and their associates argued that such efforts at dominance are "unethical, socially irresponsible, and ineffective" (Grunig & White, 1992, p. 40). Complexity theory adds dimension to why these efforts are not successful: They are based on a dynamic that is foreign to the world of complex adaptive systems. Because complex adaptive systems are driven by properties of self-organization, it is not possible to permanently dominate publics' opinions and perceptions. Power is inescapably shared in such an environment.

Roos (1997) pointed out that the principle of self-organization is founded on strong organizational identity. He drew an analogy between self-organizing systems and living cells, "which are *open* to energy but *closed* to information and control." In the same way, complex adaptive systems "are open to receive signals.... However, these signals only occasionally lead the system to change its internal rules or norms of operation—the part of the system which is *closed*" (emphasis in original). In fact, the system's internal rules "only change when the external signals stimulate processes that already exist within the system." Roos made an analogy between "embodied knowledge and internal rules" and the system's "identity," which he defined as "the complete set of internal rules, both formal and informal, that guides the behaviour of individuals within the firm as well as the organization as a whole." This view of identity essentially restates accepted definitions of organizational culture, summarized by Sriramesh, Grunig, and Buffington (1992) as "the sum total of shared values, symbols, meanings, beliefs, assumptions, and expectations that organize and integrate a group of people who work together" (p. 591). This complexity-based thinking offers a rich explanation of why asymmetrical attempts to dominate publics in the environment seldom work over the long haul. Like the organizations that attempt to influence them, publics should be conceptualized as complex adaptive systems in their own right: They can be open to data from the environment, but they incorporate those data as their internal rules—their cultures—prescribe. In other words, they self-organize new information around their existing identities.

Complexity-based thinking supports the Grunigs' observations about the inexpedience of an asymmetrical worldview, but casts a somewhat different motivation on this inefficacy. Because it views power as always, inescapably, shared, complexity theory does not look at asymmetry in ethical terms; intractability to influence is simply viewed as a condition of the environment in which multiple complex adaptive systems cohabit. Absent ethical concerns, Grunig's (2001) basic description of the organization/public interface describes an environment very close to that envisaged by complex systems:

> Symmetrical public relations does not take place in an ideal situation where competing interests come together with goodwill to resolve their differences because they share a goal of social equilibrium and harmony. Rather, it take place in situations where groups come together to protect and enhance their self-interests. (p. 18)

For similar reasons, complexity theory also suggests why the Grunigs' symmetrical model of communication can be effective. In contrast to the asymmetrical model, symmetry-based thinking views public relations as ongoing communication in the course of which "the public should be just as likely to persuade the organization's management to change attitudes or behavior as the organization is likely to change the publics' attitudes or behavior" (Grunig & Hunt, 1984, p. 23). This conception sounds very much like a description of a complex adaptive system such as Kauffman's (1993) fitness landscape, in which the behavior of one entity inevitably changes the environment and stimulates different behavior from other entities that cohabit the same space.

However, the difference—and it is significant here—between excellence and complexity theories is that complexity does not assume that power is given up voluntarily or opinions revised self-consciously. Complexity theory takes an ethically neutral position with respect to mutual influence. Because of their focus on ethics, the Grunigs' models of asymmetry and symmetry have sometimes been labeled normative or idealistic, rather than reflecting true conditions in the world where public relations operates (e.g., Leichty, 1997; L'Etang, 1996). Complexity-based thinking offers support for the excellence models' end results but does not require a sense of fair play or a willingness to cede power to the weaker groups that some scholars have found problematical in this normative approach. Grunig et al. (1992) observed that "the reality of interdependence means that organizations have relationships with outside stakeholders ... whether they want such relationships or not" (p. 69). They agreed with the assessment of Pfeffer and Salancik (1978) that "the price for inclusion in any collective structure is the loss of discretion and control over one's activities. Ironically, to gain some control over the activities of another organization, the focal organization must surrender some of its own autonomy" (p. 16). It may be ethical to do so, but from the standpoint of complexity, the norm of reciprocity is not an ethical or voluntary principle as much as it is an incontestable statement of a reality: the inevitable limits of power.

STABILITY AND CHANGE

The lack of stability in a complex adaptive system brings out an aspect of symmetry that is not often discussed: the degree of permanence of a symmetrical relationship. Grunig described symmetry as a process that constantly aspires to balance—generally, balance between listening and arguing, collaboration and advocacy, "self-interest and concern for the interests of others" (2001, p. 28). This continuous aspiration toward a state of balance has been interpreted in terms of equilibrium as stasis (Grunig, 2001). From a complexity standpoint, the only systems that achieve complete and permanent stability are no longer alive.

However, Grunig emphasized that balance does not imply stasis— that "symmetrical public relations refers more to a process than to an outcome." In order to accentuate the ongoing, processual nature of symmetrical communication, he "used the term *moving equilibrium* ... rather than *equilibrium, social harmony,* or *consensus*" (2001, p. 28; emphasis in original). Earlier, he described "moving equilibrium" as an attempt to achieve balance with a mutable and uncertain environment:

> Systems strive toward an equilibrium with other systems, although they seldom actually achieve it. The desired equilibrium state constantly moves as the environment changes. Systems may attempt to establish equilibrium by controlling other systems, by adapting themselves to other systems, or by making mutual, cooperative adjustments. (Grunig, 1989, p. 38)

Again, the concept of moving equilibrium places symmetry theory in the same general realm as complexity theory. Both acknowledge that organizations must try to optimize their position in a constantly shifting fitness landscape in which their options are limited by the interests of others. However, the two theories differ in their aspirations toward balance. Even though it must operate in an uncertain and changeable world, symmetry theory seeks to establish and maintain balance; it accepts, but does not particularly celebrate or seek to increase, the turbulence of its environment. Rather, public relations professionals work to subdue conflict "when they identify the publics that are most likely to limit or enhance their ability to pursue the mission of the organization and design communication programs that help the organization manage its interdependence with them" (Grunig & Grunig, 2000, p. 310). Organizations may have conditions that are "far from equilibrium" imposed on them involuntarily, through crises, activism, or unwanted regulation, but they do not go out and seek turbulence.

In contrast, many organizational theorists who advocate complexity-based thinking actively strive to create a shifting and uncertain environment in order to foster innovation and renewal. For example, Stacey (1996) viewed organizations as being most creative when operating under conditions that are far from equilibrium—that is, far from conditions in which everyday norms apply predictably. He recommended that managers enhance (but also contain) the uncertainties and anxieties of employees or create intentional "fluctuation" (Nonaka & Takeuchi, 1995) to shake up the existing order and force employees to invent new modes of coping with problems. Similarly, Lewin and Regine (2003) applied complexity theory's far-from-equilibrium conditions to a study of St. Luke's advertising agency in London, which was structured around a number of nontraditional properties: Equity was equally distributed among employees; there were common spaces for work, rather than individual offices; and clients and agency staff worked simultaneously on campaigns rather than following the traditional linear process of passing the work from specialist to specialist. The agency became so successful that it had to stop taking clients even after it tripled in size. For at least some types of organizations, changing to far-from-equilibrium conditions can be highly productive.

The concept of symmetry, with its requirements for cooperation as well as advocacy, raises difficult issues about organizational change. Excellence Theory gives primacy to strategic public relations as a change agent; for example, persuading client organizations and publics to adopt symmetrical relationships (Grunig, 2001). In fact, one mark of "less excellent" public relations is its insensitivity to change:

> [A]t some point in their history, most organizations probably develop their public relations programs strategically—that is, the presence of a strategic public probably provides the motivation for initiating public relations programs. As time passes, however, organizations forget the initial reason for the programs and continue communication programs for publics that no longer are strategic. Public relations then becomes routine and ineffective because it does little to help organizations adapt to dynamic environments. (Grunig, 1993, pp. 166–167)

However, Excellence Theory emphasizes that it is very difficult to initiate change in the face of organizational institutionalization. Like complexity theory, it asserts that an organization's present situation is best understood in terms of its past history: "Cultures specific to an organization evolve over time and influence the way in which individuals in the organization interact and react to the challenges posed by the environment" (Sriramesh et al., 1992, p. 584). Similar to complexity theory, excellence emphasizes that organizations, like all complex systems, can be intractable to change. Therefore, public relations managers do not have wide power to initiate change. They can position themselves favorably by doing research, acquiring control over important resources, and becoming central in the dominant coalition (Sriramesh et al., 1992). However, public relations must wait for "windows of opportunity" to implement organizational change, and those opportunities essentially originate elsewhere: "Public relations managers will be most likely to change the model of public relations practiced in an organization when organizational culture is changing," as "when a founder passes from the scene, when an organization's culture is misaligned with its environment, when the environment changes, when the organization performs poorly, or when the organization expands, grows rapidly, or is divested" (Sriramesh et al., 1992, p. 592).

Despite these constraints on changing organizational culture, the Grunigs and their associates have argued that culture can indeed be "managed" or changed and that public relations can be the change agent. They followed Berg (1985) in defining their position as "pragmatist," in contrast to the "purist" position that "an organization's culture develops, not with the conscious effort of a CEO or the dominant coalition, but rather from unconscious evolution among a majority of members in an organization" (Sriramesh, Grunig, & Dozier, 1996, p. 236). Complexity-based thinking, however, tends to favor the "purist" rubric. For example, Anderson (1999) described the role of management as indirect and contextual:

> In environments far from equilibrium,… adaptation must be evolved, not planned. Adaptation is the passage of an organization through an endless series of organizational microstates that emerge from local interactions among agents trying to improve their local payoffs. The task of those responsible for the strategic direction of an organization is not to foresee the future or to implement enterprise-wide adaptation programs, because nonlinear systems react to direction in ways that are difficult to predict or control. Rather, such managers establish and modify the direction and the boundaries within which effective, improvised, self-organized solutions can evolve.… They set constraints upon local actions, observe outcomes, and tune the system by altering the constraints. (p. 228)

As Anderson implied, a public relations professional would manage change not by planned, linear, or direct influence but rather by adjusting the parameters of local interactions in the "adjacent possible," knowing that what might ensue could be quite different from the anticipated or desired effects. Complexity-based thinking thus requires higher tolerance for uncertainty than is advocated by Excellence Theory. However, as in other respects, both theories start with different assumptions to reach compatible goals: By giving up control, public relations' ability to elicit change may actually be enhanced.

PREDICTION AND CONTROL

The strategic management of change is closely connected with questions of prediction and control. These are the areas in which excellence and complexity theories are least alike, although their contrast points to ways in which they complement one another.

The pragmatism of Excellence Theory incorporates a results-oriented approach to public relations. Using environmental scanning and cost-benefit analysis, public relations managers can identify stakeholder categories and segment them into active and passive publics (Grunig & Grunig, 2000). Then "communication programs can be evaluated by identifying the public for which a program is intended, specifying the objectives of the program, and measuring those objectives to determine if the program accomplished them" (Grunig et al., 1992, p. 66). Although symmetry theory opposes attempts to dominate or control stakeholders, it does take the position that specific results can be targeted and measurably achieved with specific communication programs.

Complexity-based thinking requires a considerably looser approach to prediction and control. In a complex system, interactions between agents are repeated in a recursive and reflexive manner that allows variations to build up over time. These subtle variations may produce unforeseen consequences, positive or negative. Change may take place gradually or in a sudden, discontinuous manner (Gilpin & Murphy, 2005). An additional consequence of the nonlinear, interconnected relationships within complex systems is that cause-and-effect connections become difficult, even impossible, to isolate (van Uden, Richardson, & Cilliers, 2001). That is why "rather than shaping the pattern that constitutes a strategy ..., managers [in complex systems] shape the context within which it emerges" (Anderson, 1999, p. 229).

The holistic nature of complex adaptive systems also makes sampling and segmentation far more problematical than in the excellence approach. Looking at strategic constituencies, for example, Grunig et al. (1992) noted that their approach "focuses on interdependencies. However, it concentrates on the segments within the environment that most threaten the organization rather than on the total environment" (p. 76). However, when organizations are seen as complex systems, segmentation becomes difficult. If a system may be accurately and completely described by reducing it to its component parts, then it is merely complicated; but if a system is truly complex, it is more than the sum of its parts. Therefore, in order to understand a complex system, many scholars say it is necessary to trace out the entire history of the system;

it is not possible to reduce the system to its component parts or to allow a sample to stand in for the whole (Stacey, 1996). Less "purist" scholars have noted that CAS models are "not forcing scholars to understand all the parts of a complex system in a holistic way"; rather, they "allow investigators to focus on an agent in its local environment" (Anderson, 1999, p. 220). In any case, excellence and complexity theories approach organizational behavior with different assumptions about the whole versus the parts that cause them to ask slightly different questions: "Instead of asking which ... variables seem to be significantly and causally related to the outcome, [complexity-based thinking] will ask what model of interacting might lead to the observed outcome in dynamic equilibrium, and what other outcomes would be predicted from such a model" (Anderson, 1999, p. 227).

THE COMPLEMENTARITY OF EXCELLENCE AND COMPLEXITY THEORIES

The preceding discussion makes it clear that excellence and complexity theories share central concerns and often envisage the world in similar ways. Both focus on interaction between an organization and its environment, particularly the pressures imposed by other agents who occupy the same space. Both focus on issues of stability and uncertainty. Both raise questions as to how change can be produced, and controlled, in a system that often resists external influences.

Despite these fundamental commonalities, the two bodies of theory diverge in their recommendations for coping with the impinging, unstable, uncertain environment. This divergence can be conceptualized in terms of overall approach to a complex universe: complexity reduction on the one hand, and complexity absorption on the other. Given the premise of bounded rationality—that humans can deal with only so much complexity at once (Simon, 1976)—organizations tend to choose one of these two paths for coping. Complexity reduction "entails getting to understand the complexity and acting on it directly, including attempts at environmental enactment" (Boisot & Child, 1999, p. 237); it is often associated with Western businesses' approach to complex environments, in which there may be little sustained or face-to-face communication and trust between agents.

Conversely, complexity absorption "entails creating options and risk-hedging strategies"; it is often associated with non-Western societies in which trust is ensured by family and clan relationships (Boisot & Child, 1999, p. 237). Complex adaptive systems "have to match ... the complexity of their environment ..., either to achieve an appropriate measure of fit with it or to secure for themselves a degree of autonomy with respect to whatever constraints it might impose" (Boisot & Child, 1999, pp. 237–238). Thus, complex adaptive systems require "requisite variety" (Ashby, 1954), keeping in play a variety of possible responses or strategies depending on the mix of attributes in the fitness landscape.

Both excellence and complexity theories incorporate elements of complexity reduction and complexity absorption, but each tends to favor a different balance of the two approaches. For example, Excellence Theory has elements of complexity absorption: It views relationships as central, sees trust building as a fundamental goal, and identifies face-to-face communication as one of four sets of variables that underlie public relations models (Grunig, 2001). However, the activities that Excellence Theory recommends to achieve this vision favor the techniques of complexity reduction. For instance, Grunig et al. (1992) saw strategic public relations management as a process of winnowing down strategic constituencies and negotiating to increase stability and reduce uncertainty:

> If public relations can identify the strategic publics in the environment and manage the organization's response to these interdependencies,… public relations can help the organization reduce uncertainty and reduce conflict by stabilizing relationships with key publics on which the organization depends. (p. 81)

Similarly, the strategic management approach of Excellence Theory recommends that public relations employ linear, targeted communication techniques: first, environmental scanning and issues management; followed by the development of "formal objectives," "formal programs and campaigns" to accomplish the objectives; implementation; and finally, "evaluat[ing] the effectiveness of programs in meeting their objectives" (Grunig & Repper, 1992, p. 124). Thus, one way in which excellence deals with an uncertain environment is to organize, clarify, and reduce its uncertainty so that it can be dealt with in a programmatic fashion.

In contrast, complexity absorption tends to utilize indirect measures and entertain multiple possibilities for which the outcome is less predictable. According to Boisot and Child (1999), organizations that practice complexity absorption "can hold multiple and sometimes conflicting representations of environmental variety, retaining in their behavioural repertoire a range of responses" (p. 238). This "behavioural plasticity" means there may be "less goodness of fit between any given response and the state of nature to which it needs to be matched, but the range of environmental contingencies that an [organization] can deal with in this way is greater than in a regime of specialization" (Boisot & Child, 1999, p. 238).

Another way of looking at this contrast between excellence and complexity theories is in terms of variance-based and process-based approaches to change. As noted by Poole, Van de Ven, Dooley, and Holmes (2000), variance-based theories require researchers to operationalize phenomena in terms of discrete variables, which may constrain meaning or leave out phenomena that are less amenable to expression as variables. In addition, variance-driven approaches assume that the operation of "efficient causality" drives interaction among variables. In contrast, process-based theories of change take a holistic approach; they require post hoc study of an entire phenomenon, with particular attention to "context and to the particular confluence of forces that influences the developing entity" (p. 48). Both approaches have advantages: Variance-based approaches offer clarity and precision, and they enable powerful statistical analyses; process-based approaches preserve subtle distinctions, and enable a more complete depiction of many organizational behaviors. Causal theories and variance-based approaches "identify important aggregate regularities and factors that help create them. CAS models build on this foundation, explaining observed regularities as the product of structured, evolving interactions" (Anderson, 1999, p. 220).Therefore, the two approaches are "complementary" and "each approach is richer for the other" (Poole et al., 2000, pp. 48–49). For example, the ethical neutrality of complexity theory is addressed by excellence theory; the directedness of excellence is augmented by complexity's incorporation of rich context.

As Grunig has emphasized, particularly in a more recent work (2001), no single approach to public relations is invariably best; his contingency view requires symmetrical behavior in some situations and asymmetrical behavior in others. Similarly, Grunig pointed out that scholars need to move beyond typology, to consider phenomena not by their classification but rather by their mixture of attributes. He was speaking of models of public relations, but in the future we might do the same with excellence and complexity theories, not just taking advantage of their overlaps but also, where they differ, seizing the opportunity to apply both worldviews to public relations situations.

REFERENCES

Anderson, P. (1999). Complexity theory and organization science. *Organization Science, 10*(3), 216–232.

Ashby, W. R. (1954). *An introduction to cybernetics*. London: Methuen.

Berg, P. (1985). Organization change as a symbolic transformation process. In P. J. Frost, L. F. Moore, M. R. Louis, C. C. Lundberg, & J. M. Martin (Eds.), *Organizational culture* (pp. 281–299). Beverly Hills, CA: Sage.

Boisot, M., & Child, J. (1999). Organizations as adaptive systems in complex environments: The case of China. *Organization Science, 10*(3), 237–252.

Gilpin, D., & Murphy, P. (2005). *Crisis management in a complex world: Complexity theory as a new approach to recognizing and dealing with crises*. Unpublished manuscript.

Grunig, J. E. (1984). Organizations, environments, and models of public relations. *Public Relations Research and Education, 1*(1), 6–29.

Grunig, J. E. (1989). Symmetrical presuppositions as a framework for public relations theory. In C. H. Botan & V. Hazleton, Jr. (Eds.), *Public relations theory* (pp. 17–44). Hillsdale, NJ: Lawrence Erlbaum Associates.

Grunig, J. E. (1993). Implications of public relations for other domains of communication. *Journal of Communication, 43*(3), 164–173.

Grunig, J. E. (2001). Two-way symmetrical public relations: Past, present, and future. In Robert L. Heath (Ed.), *Handbook of public relations* (pp. 11–30). Thousand Oaks, CA: Sage.

Grunig, J. E., & Grunig, L. A. (2000). Public relations in strategic management and strategic management of public relations: Theory and evidence from the IABC excellence project. *Journalism Studies, 1*(2), 303–321.

Grunig, J. E., & Hunt, T. (1984). *Managing public relations*. New York: Holt, Rinehart & Winston.

Grunig, J. E., & Repper, F. C. (1992). Strategic management, publics, and issues. In J. E. Grunig (Ed.), *Excellence in public relations and communication management* (pp. 117–157). Hillsdale, NJ: Lawrence Erlbaum Associates.

Grunig, J. E., & White, J. (1992). The effect of worldviews on public relations theory and practice. In J. E. Grunig (Ed.), *Excellence in public relations and communication management* (pp. 31–64). Hillsdale, NJ: Lawrence Erlbaum Associates.

Grunig, L. A. (1992). How public relations/communication departments should adapt to the structure and environment of an organization … and what they actually do. In J. E. Grunig (Ed.), *Excellence in public relations and communication management* (pp. 467–481). Hillsdale, NJ: Lawrence Erlbaum Associates.

Grunig, L. A., Grunig, J. E., & Ehling, W. P. (1992). What is an effective organization? In J. E. Grunig (Ed.), *Excellence in public relations and communication management* (pp. 65–90). Hillsdale, NJ: Lawrence Erlbaum Associates.

Kauffman, S. (1993). *The origins of order: Self-organization and selection in evolution*. New York: Oxford University Press.

Kauffman, S. (2000). *Investigations*. New York: Oxford University Press.

Leichty, G. (1997). The limits of collaboration. *Public Relations Review, 23*(1), 47–56.

L'Etang, J. (1996). Corporate responsibility and public relations ethics. In J. L'Etang & M. Pieczka (Eds.), *Critical perspectives in public relations* (pp. 106–123). London: International Thomson Business.

Lewin, R., & Regine, B. (2003). The core of adaptive organizations. In E. Mitleton-Kelly (Ed.), *Complex systems and evolutionary perspectives on organizations: The application of complexity theory to organizations* (pp. 167–183). New York: Pergamon.

March, J. G., & Olsen, J. P. (1976). *Ambiguity and choice in organizations*. Bergen, Norway: Universitetsforlaget.

Mitleton-Kelly, E. (2003). Ten principles of complexity and enabling infrastructures. In E. Mitleton-Kelly (Ed.), *Complex systems and evolutionary perspectives on organizations: The application of complexity theory to organizations* (pp. 23–50). New York: Pergamon.

Murphy, P. (2001). Symmetry, contingency, complexity: Accommodating uncertainty in public relations theory. *Public Relations Review, 26*(4), 447–462.

Nonaka, I., & Takeuchi, H. (1995). *The knowledge-creating company*. New York: Oxford University Press.

Pfeffer, J., & Salancik, G. R. (1978). *The external control of organizations: A resource dependence model*. New York: Harper & Row.

Poole, M. S., Van de Ven, A. H., Dooley, K., & Holmes, M. E. (2000). *Organizational change and innovation processes: Theory and methods for research*. New York: Oxford University Press.

Roos, J. (1997). *The poised organisation: Navigating effectively on knowledge landscapes*. Retrieved June 20, 2005, from http://www.imd.ch/fac/roos/paper_po.html

Simon, H. A. (1976). *Administrative behavior* (3rd ed.). New York: Free Press.

Sriramesh, K., Grunig, J. E., & Buffington, J. (1992). Corporate culture and public relations. In J. E. Grunig (Ed.), *Excellence in public relations and communication management* (pp. 577–595). Hillsdale, NJ: Lawrence Erlbaum Associates.

Sriramesh, K., Grunig, J. E., & Dozier, D. M. (1996). Observation and measurement of two dimensions of organizational culture and their relationship to public relations. *Journal of Public Relations Research, 8*(4), 229–261.

Stacey, R. D. (1996). *Complexity and creativity in organizations*. San Francisco: Berrett Koehler.

Stacey, R. D., Griffin, D., & Shaw, P. (2000). *Complexity and management*. London: Routledge.

van Uden, J., Richardson, K. A., & Cilliers, P. (2001). Postmodernism revisited? Complexity science and the study of organisations. *Tamara: Journal of Critical Postmodern Organization Science, 1*(3), 53–67.

Weick, K. E. (1976). Educational organizations as loosely coupled systems. *Administrative Science Quarterly, 21*(1), 1–19.

III

Advances
in Understanding
Excellence
and Management

Chapter 8

Contribution of Public Relations to Organizational Strategy Formulation

Benita Steyn
Cape Peninsula University of Technology

A RESEARCH PROGRAM IN STRATEGIC PUBLIC RELATIONS MANAGEMENT IN SOUTH AFRICA

A research program in strategic public relations (PR) management was conducted at the Department of Marketing and Communication Management at the University of Pretoria (UP) between 1997 and 2003. Its first project was intended to replicate the IABC Excellence Study (Dozier, Grunig, & Grunig, 1995), an idea obtained during a presentation by Professor Larissa Grunig on the occasion of her visit to South Africa (SA) in 1996. However, after initial discussions, it was decided to rather build on the Excellence Study findings by using it as a theoretical base for the conceptualization of research aimed at investigating and finding solutions to practical PR problems in the local context. Empirical research on the knowledge base of South African PR managers and their shared expectations with top management was practically nonexistent.

Phase 1 of the UP research program investigated the knowledge base of the PR manager. Groenewald (1998) conducted a national study on the skills that PR managers deemed important in their managerial positions. Significant findings were that PR managers in South African organizations perceived management skills, strategic communication skills, and management communication skills to be significantly more important than technical communication skills. However, the effectiveness of their training in these skills was significantly lower than in technical communication skills. Based on her findings, Groenewald (1998)

137

suggested further research on a strategic role for the PR manager, investigating the nature and activities of such a role.

Steyn (2000a, 2000d) addressed the lack of strategic communication skills among PR managers by conceptualizing public relations strategy. In a longitudinal action research project, she developed a model for the formulation of PR strategy.

Phase 2 of the UP research program, also consisting of two separate studies, focused on the shared expectations between top management and the PR manager. In the first, De Beer (2001) investigated PR managers' perceptions of senior management's expectations with regard to excellent communication in South African organizations. Findings with regards to top communicator perceptions were the following: Senior management expects top communicators to make a strategic contribution to organizational decision making; reporting lines to the chief executive officer (CEO) or another senior manager are not a good indicator of top communicators' strategic contribution to decision making; and, they can make a bigger strategic contribution in large PR departments where technical tasks can be delegated.

The second study in Phase 2 was conducted by Steyn (2000a, 2000b, 2000c, 2000d). This research touched on both prerequisites of excellent communication (Dozier et al, 1995). First, it explored the practitioner's knowledge base in conceptualizing the role of the PR strategist and redefining the historic roles of PR manager and PR technician (Steyn, 2000a). Second, by means of a quantitative study, it addressed shared expectations by measuring and empirically verifying these three PR roles according to CEO normative role expectations for a practitioner heading the PR function (Steyn, 2000a, 2000b, 2000c), as well as CEO perceptions of the role performance of the organization's most senior PR practitioner. Determining whether top management (role sender) perceives the same role for the PR practitioner as the practitioner does (role receiver) is an essential but neglected perspective in the study of PR roles (Johnson, 1989).

Together with *Excellence in Public Relations and Communication Management* (Grunig, 1992), the findings of these studies have recently guided teaching at UP's Department of Marketing and Communication Management. In particular, the author's research on the PR strategist role and public relations strategy formed the core of the subject Strategic Communication Management taught to senior public relations students.

The PR strategist role, the conceptualization of PR strategy, and a model for the development thereof form the major topics of discussion in this chapter. The author acknowledges the major influence that the Excellence Study, and particularly the work of Jim and Lauri Grunig, has had on her research in South Africa.

DEFINITION OF TERMS

Strategic Public Relations Management

Differing from the *Encyclopedia of Public Relations* (Heath, 2005), the author does not equate *communication management* to *strategic communication*. Strategic public relations management (strategic communication management) assumes public relations to be a strategic management function with a mandate to function at the strategic (macro or societal) level of an organization. Grunig, Grunig, and Dozier (2002) called this the full-participation approach to strategic public relations, in which the PR function is empowered (i.e., involved before strategic decisions are made). This approach is based on Knight's postmodern view (cited in Grunig et al., p. 143) of strategic management as "a subjective process in which the participants from different management disciplines ... assert their disciplinary identities." The author agrees with the European scholars Verçic, Van Ruler, Bütschi, and Flodin (2001), who stated that the unique contribution of public relations to an organization's strategic decision-making process is to provide a societal view—showing concern for broader societal issues, approaching any problem with a concern for the implications of organizational behavior toward and in the public sphere. "It is first of all a strategic process of viewing an organisation from an 'outside' perspective" (p. 382).

In its strategic role, public relations thus assists an organization (or institution) to adapt to its societal and stakeholder environment by feeding into the organization's strategy formulation process intelligence with regards to strategic stakeholders (and their concerns or expectations), societal issues, and the publics that emerge around the issues. Public relations influences organizational leaders to address the reputation risks and other strategic issues identified in this process by aligning organizational goals and strategies to societal/stakeholder values and norms—serving both the organizational and the public interest. By acting socially responsible and building mutually beneficial relationships with the organization's stakeholders and other interest groups in society on whom it depends to meet its goals, an organization obtains legitimacy, garners trust, and builds a good reputation. Public relations also influences organizational leaders to state the organization's position on, and practice two-way communication with, external and internal stakeholders about issues of strategic importance. This process constitutes public relations' contribution to strategic decision making and especially to the formulation of an organization's enterprise strategy (i.e., a contribution to the organization's triple bottom line, focused on its "people" and "planet" rather than "profit" components).

Public Relations Management (Communication Management)

This term is defined as the management of communication between an organization (or institution) and its internal and external stakeholders/other societal interest groups. It is performed at the functional level of an organization. In the PR management process (in addition to its role at the top management level), a PR function empowered with a strategic mandate manages all the activities as set out in points 1 and 2 in the list that follows. A PR function without a strategic mandate has no role in strategic decision making at the top management level, does not formulate PR strategy, and manages only the activities outlined under point 2.

1. The functional responsibilities of PR as a function *with a strategic mandate* includes:
   a. Developing PR strategy that addresses the organization's key strategic goals and positions, culminating in public relations goals and themes that are aligned to organizational goals and positions. This does not refer to ad hoc communication planning where public relations communicates when requested to do so by others in the organization, but a concerted effort to study organizational strategies and goals, identifying strategic goals and positions that need to be communicated and advising organizational leaders accordingly. PR strategy in this instance could be classified as deliberate or prescriptive strategy, a well-known concept in the strategic management literature (Lynch, 1997). PR goals developed to implement deliberate PR strategy are referred to as deliberate PR goals by Digital Management (n.d.).
   b. Developing PR strategy that addresses constantly emerging societal and stakeholder issues that are identified in the organization's issues and stakeholder management processes. PR strategy in this instance could be classified as emergent strategy, a concept developed in the strategic management domain by Mintzberg (1987, 1990). PR goals developed to implement emergent PR strategy are referred to as emergent PR goals by Digital Management (n.d.).
   c. Formulating a strategic PR plan to achieve PR goals.
   d. Developing, implementing, and evaluating communication plans in support of the PR function's deliberate and emergent strategies.
   e. Counseling organizational leaders/managers/supervisors on their communication responsibility toward their employees (how to be a communicating leader).

    f. Managing the activities of a support function, as outlined next.

2. The functional responsibilities of PR *as a support function* includes:

    a. Developing, implementing and evaluating communication plans in support of strategies developed at different organizational levels (e.g., enterprise/corporate/business unit).

    b. Developing, implementing, and evaluating communication plans in support of the strategies of other organizational functions (e.g., marketing, human resources).

    c. Developing, implementing, and evaluating communication plans in support of the top management/organizational leadership's communication to employees (so-called management/leadership communication) or other stakeholders.

Public Relations (Corporate Communication) Strategist

A practitioner in the role of the PR strategist functions at the top management level of an organization and has the responsibility for strategic PR management, as outlined previously. By means of environmental scanning, the PR strategist gathers information regarding stakeholder concerns and expectations, identifies societal issues and the publics that arise around the issues, interprets the information with respect to consequences for organizational strategies (pointing out reputation risks and other strategic issues), and feeds this intelligence into the enterprise and/or other organizational strategies.

    The PR strategist thus also advises other top-level managers on strategic goals and positions that need to be communicated and on reputation risks inherent in the business intelligence they obtain through their own functions/business units. It is a strategic decision taken at the top management level as to which risks/issues are managed through the strategies of the public relations function, and which ones through the strategies of other functions/business units. (The PR function might, however, be requested at the communication planning stage to develop communication plans in support of the strategies of other functions/units in order to achieve functional integration and the alignment of organizational messages.)

(Redefined) Public Relations Manager

A practitioner in the (redefined) manager role performs the duties normally associated with any middle management position—namely, planning, organizing, leading, controlling, staffing, budgeting, and so on. Specific functional responsibilities of public relations/communication managers are first the formulation of deliberate and emergent PR strategy; second, the development of the strategic PR plan in conjunction with section heads responsible for developing, implementing, and evaluating ongoing communication programs or time-limited communication campaigns; third, to counsel organizational leaders/managers/supervisors on their communication responsibility toward their employees; and fourth, to oversee the support provided by the PR function to other organizational functions/strategies/units.

Enterprise Strategy

The enterprise strategy focuses on the achievement of an organization's nonfinancial goals, such as obtaining legitimacy, garnering trust, earning a good reputation, being a good corporate citizen, and building sound relationships and partnerships with stakeholders. It portrays the organization's societal role, its stakeholder and communication approach, and its values and standards for socially responsible behavior /ethical conduct (Steyn, 2003b), and its principles for corporate governance.

Public Relations (Corporate Communication) Strategy

PR strategy provides the focus and direction for an organization's communication with its stakeholders and other interest groups in society. Deliberate PR strategy outlines the communication needed to assist in achieving strategic organizational goals, to express organizational positions, to influence organizational managers to become communicating leaders and change agents, to assist them to obtain the loyalty and support of employees for organizational strategies and positions, and to act socially responsibly. Emergent PR strategy outlines the communication needed to address constantly emerging societal and stakeholder issues, and crisis situations. The development of PR strategy makes the PR function relevant in the organization's strategic management process and implies a strategic contribution to decision making.

Strategy Communication

The strategic management literature often portrays the role of PR as merely facilitating the strategy process. Grunig et al. (2002) called this the "message-only" approach to strategic PR, by which practitioners have little involvement in strategic decision making but align messages with organizational goals. Moss & Warnaby (1998) termed this strategy communication and explained it as the need of the organization's management/leadership to communicate the organization's strategic direction to both internal and external stakeholders, ensuring a wide understanding and acceptance of their strategic vision. This includes the role of communication in facilitating the implementation of cultural change within organizations, helping to build a climate of mutual trust and understanding between managers and employees.

In the strategic management literature, communication is thus regarded as an enabling function, facilitating the successful implementation of strategic decisions. By itself, it is not seen as a key element in the strategic decision-making process (as implied in the earlier definition of PR strategy). There are also authors in the PR literature who hold this view. D'Aprix (1996) described strategic communication as the deliberate design of a communication strategy to interpret an organization's vision, values, goals, and intentions to its audiences. The author regards strategy communication as a support function of PR to top management if PR is requested to communicate strategy, or as deliberate PR strategy when the PR function is actively included in decisions on what should be communicated about.

A GRAPHIC PRESENTATION OF THE CONCEPTUALIZATION OF THE STRATEGIC MANAGEMENT OF PUBLIC RELATIONS

As presented in Fig. 8.1, the strategic management of PR rests on two pillars:

- PR role—specifically, the PR strategist role at top management level, the redefined PR manager role at functional level, and the PR technician role at implementation level.
- The levels of strategy formulation—specifically, the development of enterprise strategy at the top management level, the development of PR strategy at the functional level, and the development of implementation strategy at the operational level.

A CONCEPTUALIZATION OF THREE ROLES FOR PUBLIC RELATIONS

In her masters' research, the author (Steyn, 2000a) conceptualized the PR strategist role and redefined the historic PR manager and PR technician roles based on the excellence approach (from the PR domain) as well as on the ecological perspective (from the strategic management domain). The extended conceptualization as presented in Fig. 8.1 has been fully discussed in Steyn (2003a). It is summarized next as a conceptual base for the explication of the contribution of PR to strategy formulation in the remainder of this chapter.

The role of the PR strategist:

DOMAIN	Public relations (PR)		Strategic management (SM)	
METATHEORETICAL APPROACH	→ EXCELLENCE APPROACH PR's contribution to org. effectiveness: • **Focus on strategic constituencies** Prerequisites for excellent communication: • **PR practised at the *macro* level** • **PR practised at the *meso* level** • **PR practised at the *micro* level**		→ ECOLOGICAL PERSPECTIVE (ADAPTATION)	
PARADIGM	→ Public relations role		→ Strategy Formulation	
THEORIES	→ Public relations roles theory • **Public relations manager** • **Public relations technician** Public relations functions in organizational goal achievement • **Mirror function** • **Window function**		→ Context of strategy formulation (environment): • **Boundary spanning roles theory** • **Environmental scanning theory** • **Stakeholder and issues theory** Content of strategies (organizational level): • **Enterprise** • **Corporate** • **Business unit** • **Functional** • **Operational** Process of strategic management: • **Strategic thinking** • **Strategic and operational planning** • **Implementation and control**	

CONCEPT (FROM PR DOMAIN)	(PR) ROLE		
CONSTRUCTS: PR functions	Mirror function	Window function	Window function
CONSTRUCTS: PR levels	Macro organizational level	Meso organizational level	Micro organizational level
CONSTRUCTS: PR roles	Role of public relations strategist ↓	Role of public relations manager ↓	Role of public relations technician ↓
CONCEPT (from SM DOMAIN)	(BOUNDARY SPANNING) ROLE ↓		
CONSTRUCTS: Boundary spanning	Information gathering/processing (information acquisition) in stakeholder and societal environment ↓	External representation (information disposal) in the stakeholder and societal environment ↓	External representation (information disposal) in the stakeholder and societal environment ↓
CONCEPT (from SM DOMAIN)	ENVIRONMENTAL SCANNING ↓		
CONSTRUCTS: Environmental scanning approaches	Outside-in approach (to stakeholders and issues in the societal environment) ↓	Inside-out approach (to stakeholders and issues in the societal environment) ↓	Inside-out approach (to stakeholders and issues in the societal environment) ↓
CONCEPT (from SM DOMAIN)	LEVELS OF STRATEGY FORMULATION ↓		
CONSTRUCTS: Strategic management levels	Inputs into top level organizational strategy formulation processes ↓	Inputs into the PR function's strategy formulation processes	Inputs into PR/communication planning ↓
CONSTRUCTS: Strategy levels	Developing enterprise/institutional strategy ↓	Developing PR/corporate communication strategy ↓	Developing implementation strategy and functional tactics ↓
CONSTRUCTS: Organizational roles in SM process	Strategic role at top management (macro/societal) level	Middle management role at functional (meso/organizational) level	Tactical role at implementation (micro) level

Source: Adapted from Steyn (2000a; 2003a)

FIG. 8.1.   Metatheoretical and conceptual framework for the strategic management of PR (adapted from Steyn, 2000a, 2003a).

145

- Is regarded as a strategic role at the top management/societal/environmental level. (In the strategic management literature, this is referred to as the macro or strategic level.)
- Is based on the outside-in approach to strategic management, conducting environmental scanning to gather information on stakeholders, publics, and issues from the environment.
- Is the information acquisition role of the boundary spanner, being part of the strategic team that adapts the organization to the future.
- Is the information processing role of the boundary spanner, which entails strategic thinking by interpreting information gathered with regards to its consequences for organizational strategies and stakeholders.
- Is to perform the mirror function of PR, consisting of scanning/monitoring relevant environmental developments/societal issues and anticipating their consequences for the organization's policies and strategies, especially with regard to the stakeholder and societal environment.
- Constitutes PR's inputs into the organization's strategy formulation processes—resulting in a strategic contribution mainly toward enterprise strategy, but also assisting corporate, business-unit, and functional strategies in the identification of reputation risks and other strategic issues that need to be communicated about.

The (redefined) role of the PR manager is:

- A role at the organizational or meso level. (In the strategic management literature, this is referred to as the functional or middle management level.)
- Based on the inside-out approach to strategic management, contributing to strategic thinking/planning by identifying core messages (themes) to be communicated to the stakeholders and societal environment.
- Part of the information disposal/external representation role of the boundary spanner, portraying the organization's identity and values to the external environment.
- Part of the window function of public relations, developing PR policy and strategy that results in messages portraying all facets of the organization.
- To make strategic inputs by considering the consequences of societal issues/organizational strategies and behavior on the stakeholders, and deciding what must be communicated to solve the problems/capitalize on the opportunities presented. This strategic information provides the content of the functional (PR) strategy.

The corporate, business-unit, and other functional strategies are also supported.

The role of the PR technician is:

- An implementation role at the micro or program level of the organization. (In the strategic management literature, this is referred to as the operational level.)
- Based on the inside-out approach to strategic management, contributing to PR planning by deciding how messages should be communicated to reach the strategic stakeholders/publics/societal interest groups.
- Part of the window function of PR, developing implementation strategy and communication plans that result in portraying all facets of the organization to the stakeholder and societal environment.
- Part of the information disposal/external representation role of the boundary spanner, in developing and implementing unique PR activities that portray the organization's identity and values to the stakeholder and societal environment.
- To support the enterprise, corporate, business-unit, and functional strategies by aligning communication activities to the organizational mission and goals.

ORGANIZATIONAL STRATEGY FORMULATION

The Concept of Strategy

The term *strategy* is derived from the Greek word *strategia*, which means "office of the general." Strategy is a multidimensional concept and many different definitions of it are to be found in the strategic management literature.

Most authors affirm that the heart of strategy making lies in the conceptual work done by the leaders of an organization. Where there is no clear concept of strategy, decisions rest on either subjective or intuitive assessment and are made without regard to other decisions (Jain, 1997). This view was exemplified by the legendary Chinese general, Sun Tzu, who provided the following reasons for a general's success: "The general who wins a battle makes many calculations in his temple before the battle is fought. The general who loses a battle makes but few calculations beforehand" (Narayanan & Nath, 1993, p. 248).

Management philosopher Drucker (1954) viewed strategy as an indication of the organization's positioning for the future—the "what" rather than the "how." It is more important to do the right thing (improving effectiveness) than to do things right (improving efficiency).

Harvard Business School scholars Christensen and Andrews considered the focus of strategy as the linking of an organization with its environment (Narayanan & Nath, 1993). A strategy could also be seen as an approach, design, or system that directs the course of action in a specific situation (Grunig & Repper, cited in Grunig, 1992). It is the means to achieve the ends (Narayanan & Nath, 1993). Strategy is the thinking, the logic behind the actions (Robert, 1997)—the primary determinant of success or failure in fulfilling the mission and achieving the organization's goals and objectives (Digman, 1990).

Chaffee (1985) clustered strategy definitions in the literature into three groups: linear strategy, focusing on planning; adaptive strategy, in which the environment is seen to consist of trends, events, competitors, and stakeholders to which the organization must adapt; and interpretive strategy, focusing on desired relationships, symbolic actions, and communication. (The latter corresponds to the stakeholder approach to strategic management.)

Mintzberg (2001) suggests five related definitions of strategy: strategy as a plan (intended course of action), a ploy (maneuver to outwit an opponent), a pattern (stream of consistent actions), a position (match between organization and environment), and a perspective (concept that becomes ingrained as shared values among organizational members). Two other well-known approaches to strategy formulation are the prescriptive (deliberate) and the emergent approaches (Lynch, 1997). Supporters of the prescriptive approach view strategy to be a linear and rational process, with objectives being defined in advance and the main elements developed before the strategy commences. Strategy in this view is seen to be formulated. Mintzberg (1987) developed the emergent approach (strategy formation rather than strategy formulation) in which the final strategy is formed and the objective of the strategy is unclear and elements still develop as the strategy proceeds, continuously adapting. More recent approaches to emergent strategy (Mintzberg, 1990; Pettigrew, 1985) have emphasized that people, politics, and culture of organizations all need to be taken into account, whereas Senge (1990) focused on the learning approach to strategy—a process of trial and error.

In developing strategy, Lynch (1997) distinguished between the process, context, and content of strategy formulation. These concepts are shortly explicated, with the author indicating their relevance to PR. (For a more comprehensive discussion, see Steyn, 2002, 2003b.)

The Process of Strategic Management

Process is the method by which strategies are derived, referring to specific phases through which strategies are formulated/implemented: environmental analysis, strategic thinking, strategic planning, operational/tactical planning, and control. The strategic management process indicates how the actions link together/interact as the strategy unfolds against a (changing) environment—the different phases being interactive, and not necessarily occurring in a strict order.

Fahey and Narayanan (1986) defined *environmental analysis* as consisting of four analytical stages: scanning to detect warning signals, monitoring to gather/interpret sufficient data on trends to discern patterns, forecasting future directions of changes, and assessing current/future changes with regard to their organizational implications. The PR strategist scans and monitors the stakeholder and societal environment, interprets the strategic information obtained, assesses its implications for the organization, and feeds this intelligence into the organizational strategy formulation process.

Strategic thinking is both introspective and externally focused, a process in which senior managers set direction and articulate their vision: "A strategist's job is to see the company not as it is ... but as it can become" (Teets, cited in David, 1997, p. 77). Management thinks through the qualitative aspects of the business (opinion, judgments, even feelings of stakeholders) and the environment it faces. The outcome of this process is strategic decisions that deal with the determination of strategy (i.e., what the organization should look like in the future and where it wants to be). Strategic thinking is therefore not the same as strategic planning, but provides the framework for it (Mintzberg, 1987; Robert, 1997). The PR strategist interprets and synthesizes information with regards to stakeholders and societal issues and informs top management of the consequences for organizational strategies and policies, as well as the consequences of management's behavior on stakeholders/society. This information is considered in formulating the enterprise and/or other organizational strategies. The PR manager (with inputs from the strategist) develops deliberate and emergent PR strategy by means of a strategic thinking process, indicating what should be communicated to whom.

Strategic planning is the intermediate step between direction setting (strategy formulation) and budgeting or resource allocation (operational planning). It is required to put strategic decisions into practice (i.e., to operationalize strategies already created by other means). The selected strategy is created for each division or business unit, and specific time-phased actions are required to support the strategy. The result is the strategic, long-range master plan for each division or section (Digman, 1990). Once the deliberate PR strategy has been developed with inputs from the PR strategist, the PR manager (and the heads of PR divisions or sections) formulate a strategic communication plan—expressing the deliberate strategy in terms sufficiently clear to render it formally operational, breaking it down into substrategies and plans (e.g., media plans, employee relations plans, and financial communication plans), and specifying how it is to be implemented. As emergent strategy forms and emergent PR goals are set, the latter are implemented within the existing strategic PR plan.

Operational/tactical planning deals with the implementation/support of strategic plans. Specific actions devised allow realization of targeted priorities. Action plans incorporate four elements (Pearce & Robinson, 1997): specific unique activities (functional tactics/actions) undertaken in the next week/month/quarter; each activity has one or more specific, immediate (short-term) objectives or targets identified as outcomes; a clear time frame for completion; and accountability, identifying persons responsible for actions. PR technicians set objectives for communication (action) plans based on deliberate and emergent PR goals that have been identified in the PR strategy phase by the PR manager/strategist. (The plans are sometimes grouped into programs/campaigns.) The technician decides on implementation strategy (channels to be used), selects communication activities (e.g., media releases, articles for publications, events, audiovisuals, etc.), and implements them.

Control ensures that the chosen strategy is implemented properly and produces desired results. Control is exercised by the PR manager (through evaluation of communication plans) and the PR strategist, who feeds evaluation information into the top management process.

The Context of Strategy Formulation

Context refers to the environment within which the organization operates and develops its strategies. Grunig and Repper (cited in Grunig, 1992) saw a lack of a definite interpretation of the term *environment*, even though it is a key concept in the strategic management process.

When managers make decisions, they do so based on a set of shared perceptions of the organization and its environment, which can be conceptualized in different ways. Some depict the external environment as a set of general components (technological, economic, or social) called the remote/macro/societal environment (Pearce & Robinson, 1997). Others portray it as a set of cognitive maps (Duncan, 1972; Weick, 1969). Lenz and Engledow (1986) viewed the environment as a patterning of strategic issues. Van Wyk (cited in Spies, 1994) called the macro, task, and micro environment the decision-making environment. Mitroff (cited in Spies, 1994) as well as Pearce and Robinson (1997) included the stakeholder environment.

With reference to strategic PR management, the author conceptualizes the environment as the product of the decisions/behavior of strategic stakeholders and the publics/activists that arise around strategic and societal issues—that is, as a collection of stakeholders, publics, and activists, and a patterning of strategic, social, political, environmental, and ethical issues.

The Levels of Strategy Formulation

The levels of strategy typically refer to the *content* or *focus* of strategies (Lynch, 1997). Although separating strategy into levels is more conceptual than real (Bower, 1982), it assists in understanding that different people participate in strategy development at different organizational levels (Digman, 1990), and that different stakeholders are addressed by different levels of strategy (Narayanan & Nath, 1993). This is especially relevant to PR practitioners, criticized by top management for focusing on implementation strategy and tactics at micro level rather than addressing key strategic issues and reputation risks at macro level (Steyn, 2000b). The five levels of strategy as discussed in Steyn (2002) are the following: enterprise strategy, corporate strategy, business-unit strategy, functional strategy, and operational strategy. They have been summarized in Table 8.1 and are not discussed here in detail, except for the functional strategy (relevant to the conceptualization of PR strategy.)

Although the term is not well known in academia or in practice, all organizations have an *enterprise strategy*, whether formally developed or not. Highly relevant to the new business paradigm with its triple bottom line concept (planet, people, profit), the author regards enterprise strategy as an important concept to describe the level of strategy that deals with the achievement of nonfinancial goals such as sound corporate governance, good stakeholder relations, socially responsible behavior, good corporate citizenship, good reputation, and so on. The triple bottom line focus of enterprise strategy is thus "people" and "planet" rather than "profit."

A manifestation of enterprise strategy, for example, is a mission statement; code of conduct; open, sensitive communication approach to crisis communication (or stakeholders in general); identification and interpretation of social/ethical issues, and the use of that intelligence in top-level strategy formulation; and committees on social audits and corporate social responsibility. In the opinion of the author, strategies at the enterprise level are oriented toward society and stakeholders—legitimizing the organization's role in society, building trust in its relationships with stakeholders/other interest groups, and safeguarding its reputation (Steyn, 2003b).

With regards to the PR function, the author proposes that its contribution to organizational effectiveness is maximized (via the triple bottom line concept) when granted a strategic mandate by the organization's top management. With such a mandate, a practitioner in

TABLE 8.1

Summary of the Levels of Strategy Formulation

Level of Strategy	Enterprise Strategy (Conceptualized by Ansoff, 1977)	Corporate Strategy	Business-Unit Strategy	Functional Strategy	Operational Strategy
Responsibility	• Board of directors • Top management	• CEO/top management (and board of directors)	• General manager of a business unit	• Functional managers	• Program managers or project leaders
Goals to be achieved	Mainly nonfinancial goals (e.g., good reputation, sound corporate governance, legitimacy, good corporate citizen, trust, socially responsible behavior, ethical conduct, and good relationships with stakeholders)	• Financial goals (making a profit)	• Financial and business (competitive) goals	Functional goals—indicating what each of the key functional areas needs to do to implement the organization's strategy	• Objectives

Content or focus of strategy	• Outlines organization's mission/role in society/purpose • Influences organization's relationships with its environment • Focus is on the social, political, and environmental component of the triple bottom line (people and planet) • Spells out organization's obligations to society at large • Addresses political and social legitimacy of the organization • Integrates ethical and strategic thinking about the organization • Not always formally stated in the organization • Manifested by mission statements, codes of conduct, and communication approach to crises/stakeholders	• Defines set of businesses that should form the organization's overall profile • Takes strategic decisions re-mergers/acquisitions, strategic alliances, etc. • Selects tactics for diversification and growth • Focus is on the financial/economic component of the triple bottom line (profit) • Manages corporate resources and capabilities • Takes responsibility for the organization's financial performance	• Domain direction and navigation • Single product or a group of related products • Determines the organization's approach to competing in the product/market/industry segment • Takes responsibility for the organization's competitive performance • Focus is on the financial component of the triple bottom line (profit)	• Support of the enterprise, corporate, and business level strategies • Unique contribution of each function to strategy formulation • Maximizes the productivity of resources • Capitalizes on possible synergies and distinctive competencies that the organization may possess • Triple bottom line focus of PR = people and planet; of marketing = profit	• Translation of strategies into action • Management of business units in a cost-effective manner • Maximization of productivity of resources

(continued)

TABLE 8.1 *(continued)*

Level of Strategy	Enterprise Strategy (Conceptualized by Ansoff, 1977)	Corporate Strategy	Business-Unit Strategy	Functional Strategy	Operational Strategy
Orientation	• Societal and stakeholder orientation	• Financial orientation	• Competitive • Market oriented • Marketing oriented	• Support of organizational strategies • Functional coordination	• Productivity • Cost-effectiveness
Information sought	• Social intelligence	• Financial intelligence	• Competitive intelligence	• PR = social • Marketing = competitive/market	Tactical information
Stakeholders addressed	• Nonfinancial stakeholders (e.g., media, communities, activist groups, government, the common good, and society at large)	• Financial stakeholders (e.g., investors and financial analysts)	• Stakeholders in the value chain (e.g., distributors, suppliers, regulators, competitors, and customers)	• Each functional area has its own primary stakeholders (e.g., customers for marketing)	• e.g., for PR, the specific stakeholders targeted by the different communication plans

Source: Vertical classification and table format by Worrall (2005), based mainly on Steyn (2002, 2003b), Steyn and Puth (2000), Digman (1990), and Jain (1997). Reproduced with permission of Diane Worrall, Pretoria, South Africa.

154

the role of the PR strategist assists the organization or institution to adapt to its external environment by delivering intelligence with regards to strategic stakeholders and societal issues primarily for use in enterprise strategy formulation.

Corporate strategy can best be described as the responsibility of the board/top management for financial performance, i.e., strategies are financially oriented (Digman, 1990). The triple bottom line focus is "profit." PR has a support role to corporate (financial) strategy when it provides assistance with producing the annual report, arranging shareholders' meetings, and so on. When, for example, investor relations falls under PR, the latter could make a strategic contribution to corporate (financial) strategy.

Business-unit strategy defines an organization's approach to competing in its chosen market/product/industry segment. At the business-unit level, strategies are often marketing oriented (Digman, 1990) in support of the organization's financial goals and objectives. The triple bottom line focus is "profit." PR mostly has a support role with regards to the business-unit strategy, for instance, when requested to develop and implement communication plans to support it.

Functional strategy describes the unique contribution of a specific functional area to strategy formulation. It involves what should be done in each of the key functional areas (Harrison & St. John, 1998) and contains details on how functional areas should work together.

The marketing function often has the greatest degree of contact with the external environment, gathering and processing information on strategic stakeholders such as customers. With its strategic mandate, marketing plays a pivotal role in higher-level strategy development (Harrison & St. John, 1998)—focusing on the support of business-level strategy and the achievement of financial goals. Marketing strategy evolves from the cumulative pattern of decisions made by employees who interact with customers and perform marketing activities. It is oriented toward exchange relationships (Koekemoer, 1998), mainly with stakeholders in the task (operating) environment.

Other value-adding functions are, for example, human resources (HR), information systems, finance and accounting, and research and development. Until fairly recent, HR activities were considered to be more administrative than strategic. Although some HR departments are still primarily concerned with avoiding strikes, turnover, lawsuits, and unions, others are actively involved in the formulation of strategies (Fulmer, cited in Harrison & St. John, 1998). They serve a coordinating role between management and employees, and between the organization and external stakeholder groups, including labor unions and government regulators. The pattern of decisions about selection, training, rewards, and benefits creates a human resources strategy (Harrison & St. John, 1998).

The role of information systems in organizations has also changed fundamentally since the early 1980s. Computer technology revolutionized the way organizations do business. In some organizations, an information systems department plans computer use organization-wide. The pattern of decisions about how to make use of information systems creates an information systems strategy (Harrison & St. John, 1998).

Concerning the PR function, coordinating with the PR strategist, a practitioner in the (redefined) role of the PR manager, develops emergent and deliberate PR strategy—a pattern of decisions on using communication to solve organizational or communication problems, or using communication as a strategic opportunity in organizational goal achievement. A strategic goal of PR is to build communal relationships with nonfinancial stakeholders (e.g., employees, the media, government, communities, activist/interest groups).

Operational strategy translates strategies into action. Program managers/project leaders establish short-term objectives and implementation strategies that contribute to the achievement of organizational goals (Pearce & Robinson, 1997).

Based on the discussion of the different strategy levels, it seems that the term strategy, as generally applied in the PR process, refers mostly to strategy at the operational level—the level at which PR technicians develop communication plans, programs, and campaigns.

A LACK OF STRATEGIC APPROACHES FOR INTEGRATING SOCIAL INTELLIGENCE WITHIN ORGANIZATIONAL STRATEGY FORMULATION

The strategic management literature points strongly to the lack of integrated approaches for incorporating stakeholder and societal concerns into the strategic decision-making process (Scholes & James, 1997). A strategy should be in place for each stakeholder and interest group—not only for stockholders, but also for groups such as consumer advocates, environmentalists, the media, or any other group affected by the organization's decisions. Their values and expectations, key issues, and willingness to expend resources helping or hurting the organization on these issues must be understood.

An organization therefore needs concepts and processes that provide integrated, strategic approaches for dealing with multiple stakeholders/publics on multiple issues. For each major strategic issue, an organization must think through the effects on its stakeholders/societal interest groups. For each major stakeholder group, managers responsible for that stakeholder relationship must identify the strategic issues that affect the stakeholder, and must understand how to formulate, implement, and monitor strategies for dealing with it. Many organizations do it well with one stakeholder group (e.g., the marketing function with customers). Few, however, have the processes needed to integrate a number of stakeholder concerns (Freeman, 1984) and the issues raised by societal interest/activist groups.

THE CONCEPT OF STRATEGY IN THE PUBLIC RELATIONS LITERATURE

Lack of Clarity on the Concept of Strategy in a Public Relations Context

"Strategy is one of the more mysterious areas of public relations practice" (Lukaszewski, 2001a, p. 13). Tibble (1997) was of the opinion that "use of the strategy word is so sloppy" (p. 358) and is "bandied around like a mantra," (p. 357) but contains little substance. Likely (2002) agrees that few practitioners understand the meaning of strategy, although it is a familiar, uncomplicated concept to those acquainted with management theory. Tibble (1997) further noted:

> Strategy and the communications world, and particularly the PR part of that world, just do not seem to go together. It is certainly unusual to come across a memorable, cogent, sustained, and effective communications strategy. Not a brand strategy. Not a marketing strategy. Not an advertising strategy—a communication strategy. (p. 356)

After conducting a study on the professional views of PR practitioners in the Netherlands, Van Ruler (cited in Moss, MacManus, & Vercic, 1997) concluded that practitioners are not able to cope with abstract strategic planning practices. Grunig et al. (2002) are also of the view that many practitioners do not truly understand the role of PR in strategic management. The author is of the opinion that the key problem seems to lie in the application of strategy to PR/communication issues. Tibble (1997) stated that PR practitioners often use *strategy* incorrectly by using the term describing something important (e.g., strategic messages, strategic direction) or activities (e.g., PR strategy). It is also used mistakenly to describe a PR aim, objective, or tactic. This is not surprising when one considers that there is hardly any theory to guide practitioners on its use. For example, the author found no entry for the term *public relations strategy* in the first edition of the *Encyclopedia of Public Relations* (Heath, 2005). Prominent practitioners, however, refer to strategy in the strategic sense of the word. Lukaszewski (2001b) regards strategy as a "big-picture activity. It is always outcome focused ... is virtually always about the future" (p. 10). Likely (2005) also sheds light on the subject of strategy in suggesting that "the common professional wisdom of linking PR/communication (PR/C) strategy and goals to deliberate corporate strategy and goals is flawed." He inter alia proposes that "PR/C, potentially, can contribute more to emergent strategy than to deliberate strategy development" … (p. 1). The author agrees to some extent with the latter statement, but thinks that PR also has a strategic role to play in developing deliberate PR strategy (as previously referred to).

Strategy as Referred to in Textbooks on the Public Relations Process

According to Steyn (2000a, 2002, 2003b), PR textbooks are mostly seen to emphasize operational planning, rather than strategy formulation in the true sense of the word (Cutlip, Center, & Broom, 1994; Seitel, 1995; Wilcox, Ault, & Agee, 1986; Windahl, Signitzer, & Olson, 1993). This view was supported by Moss and Warnaby (1997) and Moss (in Heath, 2005) who regarded the dominant view of strategy in PR to be planning, portraying the strategic planning process as logical and sequential. More recent strategy approaches—such as emergent strategy (Mintzberg, 1987), adaptive and interpretive strategy (Chaffee, 1985)— as well as the different organizational levels at which strategy is formulated (Ansoff, 1977; Digman, 1990; Freeman, 1984; Harrison & St. John, 1998; Jain, 1997; Narayanan & Nath, 1993; Pearce & Robinson, 1997) have largely been ignored. So has more recent approaches to emergent strategy (Mintzberg, 1990) and Senge's (1990) learning approach to strategy.

The emphasis is on the PR process at the micro or operational level of strategic management, developing implementation strategy as a framework for communication tactics. This emphasis on the tactical level also seems true for PR practice should the following definition of *public relations strategy* in the PRSA's *Accreditation Sourcebook* (Swanston & Kendall, 1995) be taken as a measure: "A general, well-thought out tactical plan. Strategies do not indicate specific actions to achieve objectives. There can be multiple strategies for each objective" (p. 166).

Public Relations Strategy: A Conceptualization

Within the framework of the previous discussion on strategy in the strategic management and PR literature, PR strategy is conceptualized based mainly on Steyn (2000a, 2002, 2003b); Steyn and Puth (2000); and Digital Management (n.d.).

The concept of PR strategy is based on the assumption that public relations/corporate communication is practiced as a strategic management function with a unique disciplinary identity, assisting an organization to adapt to its environment by achieving a balance between the organization's commercial imperatives and socially acceptable behavior. (For this purpose, the environment is conceptualized as a collection of stakeholders, publics and activists, and a patterning of strategic, social, political, environmental, and ethical issues.) This balance is brought about, inter alia, through identifying and responding to issues and stakeholder concerns by ensuring that organizational and communication goals are aligned to societal and stakeholder values, norms, and expectations. Furthermore, by building relationships through communication with those on whom the organization depends to meet its economic and sociopolitical goals.

PR strategy provides the focus and direction for an organization's communication with its stakeholders and other interest groups in society. It is an organization or institution's pro-active response to a fast-changing environment, an approach that directs its course of action and provides an indication of its positioning for the future regarding two-way communication with societal and strategic stakeholders. It is developed within the context of the organization's vision, mission, corporate culture, policies, goals, and objectives (the internal environment), but focuses on an assessment of the external environment.

PR strategy is thus first and foremost a position to match an organization to the concerns, expectations, values, and norms of its societal and stakeholder environment—a pro-active capability to adapt the organization to changes identified through environmental-scanning and boundary-spanning activities. It creates a competitive advantage for the organization through the early detection and management of societal and stakeholder issues and expectations, involving strategic stakeholders in decision making, determining what should be communicated to avoid conflict and obtain win–win solutions—thereby stabilizing societal and stakeholder relationships, giving the organization the autonomy to concentrate on achieving its mission.

PR strategy is not based on the traditional linear approach to strategy formulation. By adapting the organization to values, trends, events, issues, and stakeholders in the environment, it can be regarded as adaptive strategy. It also focuses on relationships, symbolic actions, and communication, emphasizing attitudinal and cognitive complexity among diverse stakeholders and societal interest groups, which is the essence of interpretive strategy.

Based on Mintzberg's (1987) views on deliberate strategy formulation and emergent strategy formation, PR strategy is conceptualized as consisting of both deliberate and emergent components:

1. PR strategy as *deliberate strategy* is a pattern of decisions for using communication as a strategic opportunity in organizational goal

achievement (e.g., building relationships with strategic stakeholders, portraying the organization as a good corporate citizen, maintaining a good reputation, or communicating change initiatives).

Deliberate PR strategy is formulated in the context of the organization's vision, mission, corporate strategies, policies, and strategic goals. It can therefore be considered a mid-term strategy (2 years or more). The organization's key strategic priorities are reviewed to select strategic organizational positions and goals to be communicated to internal and external stakeholders (Digital Management, n.d.). A key focus is therefore the organization's strategies that have already been formulated as part of the regular cycle of strategy development or budgeting process.

2. PR strategy as *emergent strategy* is a pattern in important decisions on using communication to solve organizational or communication problems in unstructured situations, or to capitalize on opportunities presented. In emergent PR strategy, the final objective is unclear and elements are still developing as the strategy proceeds, continuously adapting to events and people (i.e., external and internal stakeholders, societal issues, and the interest/activist groups that emerge around issues). Emergent PR strategy thus outlines the communication needed to address constantly emerging societal and stakeholder issues, and crisis situations. In this sense, emergent strategy is a shorter term strategy (i.e., less than 2 years). The rationale is that should an issue continue for a longer period, it will become part of deliberate strategy.

Emergent PR strategy is in accordance with Grunig and Repper's view (cited in Grunig, 1992) that managing communication strategically entails analyzing the environment to make an organization or institution aware of stakeholders, publics, and issues as they evolve, and developing communication programs that can help resolve such issues. Stakeholder and issues management thus form a core focus of emerging PR strategy.

Deliberate and emergent PR strategy thus produce a profile that can be used to determine which stakeholders or issues should receive more or less emphasis (within PR strategy's triple bottom line focus of people and planet rather than profit).

The process of formulating deliberate PR strategy to communicate organizational positions and assist in achieving organizational goals, and recognizing the issues and possible communication solutions that form emergent PR strategy, entails strategic thinking to prioritize key organizational goals and positions and interpret information gathered mainly in the social, political, and environmental sectors of the macro environment with a view to identifying consequences for organizational stakeholders and other societal interest groups. To put deliberate PR strategy into action, a strategic PR plan is developed for each PR division (i.e., expressing PR strategy in terms sufficiently clear to render it formally operational, breaking it down into substrategies). (It is on the grounds of this strategic PR plan that the PR function lobbies for organizational resources.) Control is exercised to ensure that the chosen strategy is implemented properly and cost-efficiently, and produces the desired results. Emergent PR strategy is turned into action within the framework and structures of this strategic PR plan.

Deliberate and emergent PR strategy is more than "strategy communication." Public relations is not simply an enabling function, facilitating the successful implementation of strategic decisions. In itself, it is a contributor to the strategic decision-making process.

The level with responsibility for formulating deliberate PR strategy is the functional or middle management level. While stakeholder concerns and issues can emerge both internal and external to the organization and be recognized by PR practitioners or employees on any organizational level, it is the responsibility of the PR manager to make a concerted effort to develop emergent PR goals to address stakeholder concerns and issues, by recognizing communication solutions. PR strategy is, however, optimally developed by a PR function with a strategic mandate where the PR strategist:

1. Scans the environment for issues, stakeholder concerns, and reputation risks (the core source of emergent PR strategy).
2. Makes inputs in this regard into the organization's deliberate strategy processes at the strategic level.
3. Facilitates the development of functional PR strategy.

PR strategy thus makes the PR function relevant in the strategic management process by providing the vital link between enterprise/corporate/business strategy and the PR function, aligning PR/communication goals to organizational goals. The deliberate PR strategy indicates what the PR function needs to do (communicate) to implement higher-level deliberate organizational strategies—first and foremost the enterprise strategy, but also the corporate and business-unit strategies, as well as other functional strategies such as marketing and HR. Emergent PR strategy indicates what the PR function needs to do and communicate with regards to emergent issues and stakeholder concerns (i.e., how to use communication to solve organizational problems or capitalize on opportunities presented).

The heart of PR strategy formulation and formation lies in the conceptual work done by senior PR practitioners and the strategic decisions taken in cooperation with other organizational leaders. PR strategy can be seen as the thinking, the logic behind the PR function's actions—the "what" rather than the "how." Implementing PR strategy results in doing the right things, rather than only doing things right. It focuses first on impact and outcomes (effectiveness), and then on process (efficiency). PR strategy is not the same as communication plans, but rather provides the framework for the strategic and operational PR/communication plans necessary to carry out the strategy. PR strategy thus provides a new way of thinking about, defining, and studying organizational and communication problems, and of evaluating the efforts of PR practitioners.

In conclusion, the development of PR strategy makes the PR function relevant in the strategic management process by providing the link between the communication plan/activities and achievement of the organization's mission and top-level strategies. It provides an integrated, strategic approach needed by organizations for dealing with multiple stakeholders on multiple issues.

Models and Frameworks in the PR Literature for Developing PR Strategy

In the PR literature, there are only a few references to conceptual frameworks and models (empirically tested frameworks) for PR strategy formulation at the functional level, implying/referring to PR participation in strategy formulation at the top management (enterprise or corporate) level (Steyn, 2002), among them the conceptual framework of Grunig and Repper (cited in Grunig, 1992) on the stakeholder, public, and issue stages in the strategic management of PR—improved by Grunig et al (2002). Likely (2005) commented that the latter model provides little detail on actual strategic management (i.e., the development and execution of corporate and business level strategy) or on strategy formulation and formation. It therefore required further conceptualization.

The conceptual framework of Moss and Warnaby (1997), linked PR strategy (as functional strategy) to the corporate and competitive levels of strategy formulation and conceptualized PR strategy as adaptive and/or interpretive strategy. In elaborating on the Moss and Warnaby framework, Vercic and Grunig commented that building symbolic relationships with stakeholders/publics by means of communication programs on the micro (implementation) level is not sufficient for a contribution toward organizational effectiveness. Rather, behavioral relationships must be built on the institutional (enterprise or macro) level. "The institutional level obviously is the substance of public relations" (Vercic & Grunig, 2000, p. 40).

Oliver (1997) applied the Johnson and Scholes strategic management model to public relations. Oliver's (2001) reference to this framework included a valuable differentiation between *ordinary* PR management (the need to keep the overall corporate message consistent) and *extraordinary* PR management (the need to monitor changes in stakeholder perceptions that could impact corporate goals, which could in turn lead to changes in the message). The author regarded ordinary PR management as referring to deliberate PR strategy formulation, whereas extraordinary PR management could be seen as emergent strategy formation.

Likely (2003) illustrated the strategic management role of PR by means of a generic strategic management model. He sees a strategic role for PR in all seven stages, notably in deliberate (intended) strategy formulation, strategy execution, emergent strategy formation, and actual realized strategy. Although there are differences, there are also similarities to the author's conceptualization of deliberate and emergent PR strategy in a previous section.

The educational model of Steyn (2000a; Steyn & Puth, 2000) is an empirical model—the outcome of a longitudinal action research project in which the hypothesized framework was implemented among 94 nonprofit organizations, 48 national and provincial government institutions, and 68 small-to-medium-sized companies in South Africa. Basic premises of the model is that different individuals/groups take part in strategy formulation at different organizational levels, and that lower-level strategies and goals support and are developed within the context of higher-level strategies and/or issues. Furthermore, PR strategy is developed on the functional level by a practitioner in the (redefined) role of a PR manager (Steyn, 2000a, 2000d), based on the enterprise strategy but also on ad hoc issues. Functioning at the top management level, a practitioner in the role of the PR strategist (Steyn, 2000a, 2000b) contributes to the development of enterprise strategy. (In smaller organizations, the roles of PR strategist and manager will of necessity be played by one practitioner.)

Complementing the PR strategy model is a model for developing PR plans (Steyn & Puth, 2000), explaining the process for a PR technician to develop implementation strategy and PR activities that are linked to (functional) PR strategy by means of the PR goals identified during the PR strategy formulation phase.

Steyn's (2003c) adapted model for formulating PR strategy, applied in the development of a prototype software solution (Steyn & Bütschi, 2004), clearly differentiates between enterprise and functional level strategy formulation (i.e., PR strategist and manager roles). This model is depicted in Fig. 8.2.

In his master's research, Prinsloo (2005) explored the viability of Steyn's (2003c) adapted model for PR strategy formulation among the dominant coalition of one of South Africa's major banks. Based on the

STRATEGIC LEVEL: Role of the *PR Strategist* in Developing Enterprise Strategy

ANALYSE THE ORGANIZATION'S/INSTITUTION'S INTERNAL ENVIRONMENT
Corporate profile/vision/mission/corporate culture/values/policies
Enterprise/corporate/business unit/functional strategies and internal stakeholder concerns

↑↓

SCAN AND ANALYSE THE EXTERNAL ENVIRONMENT (INCLUDING SOCIETAL VALUES, NORMS, AND EXPECTATIONS)

↓

Identify and prioritize strategic external stakeholders
Determine the consequences of their behavior/expectations/concerns for the organization

↑↓

Identify and prioritize key strategic, social, political and societal issues
Determine their consequences/reputation risks for the organization

↑↓

Identify the publics and activists that emerge around key issues
Determine the consequences of their behavior/reputation risks for the organization

↓

FEED THIS SOCIAL INTELLIGENCE INTO THE *ENTERPRISE* STRATEGY FORMULATED AT THE TOP MANAGEMENT/BOARD LEVEL

↑↓

FUNCTIONAL LEVEL: Role of the *PR Manager* in Developing PR Strategy

DESCRIBE, DIFFERENTIATE AND PRIORITIZE KEY STRATEGIC ISSUES IDENTIFIED IN THE ENTERPRISE STRATEGY, AS WELL AS AD HOC ISSUES

↓

Identify the implications of each issue for each of the strategic stakeholders, publics, activist groups, and society at large

↓

Formulate the key communication themes for each issue
(Decide *what* must be *communicated* to solve the problem/capitalize on the opportunity)

↑↓

Set communication goals, based on the implications of the issues/opportunities
(Decide *what* must be *achieved with the communication*)

Set communication goals in support of other organizational strategies (functional, business unit, corporate)
Integrate communication goals of all the strategies

↑↓

CONDUCT AN OVERALL PR CHANNEL ANALYSIS (which kinds of channels are best suited to the organization)	DEVELOP COMMUNICATION POLICY (who is allowed to communicate *what* to *whom*)

↑↓

DEVELOP STRATEGIC COMMUNICATION PLAN FOR ALL DIVISIONS (e.g. employee/media/community/investor/customer relations)

↑↓

IMPLEMENTATION/OPERATIONAL LEVEL:

Role of the *PR Technician* in Developing Implementation Strategy

Develop and implement communication programs/campaigns/plans

Source: Adapted from Steyn & Puth (2000, p.63); Steyn (2003c). (Reproduced with permission of Heinemann, Sandown, South Africa).

FIG. 8.2.   Model for developing public relations strategy, linked to the enterprise strategy.

findings of the empirical research, Prinsloo proposed a framework for formulating enterprise strategy, differentiating it from corporate (financial) strategy. He also adapted Steyn's (2003c) model to a financial institution.

Public Relations Strategy: An Operationalization

The operationalization of PR strategy that follows next is based mainly on the author's research program on public relations strategy. However, all the models mentioned in the previous section have elements that are also contained in this operationalization. The most important similarities were highlighted in the discussion of each model.

PR strategy consists of both deliberate and emergent components. The process outlined below is not linear and does not necessarily follow this order, but it points out important activities in the development of PR strategy.

Formulating *deliberate* PR strategy can be seen as a process of:

- Analyzing/reviewing the organization's top-level strategies/strategic goals/strategic intent/key priorities that result from the formal strategy development process and budget cycle.
- Scanning and monitoring the environment to identify key strategic stakeholders and their concerns, societal issues, and the publics/activists who express a concern or interest in these issues.
- Drawing the organization's stakeholder map.
- Identifying/selecting those strategic organizational goals, priorities, and positions with consequences for internal and/or external stakeholders, other societal interest groups, and the organization's reputation (i.e., prioritizing what should be communicated *about*).
- Thinking through the implications/consequences/impact of the selected organizational goals, priorities, and positions on each of the stakeholders and publics/societal interest groups.
- Addressing these implications by deciding what should be *communicated* (selecting key communication themes) and what should be *achieved* by this communication (setting deliberate PR goals).
- Developing a strategic communication plan for the PR department's divisions/sections/units to implement the deliberate PR strategy.

Emergent PR strategy unfolds (is formed rather than formulated) in the process of:

- Scanning, monitoring, and analyzing the organization's internal and external environment.

- Identifying strategic/societal issues and the behavior/concerns of those publics and interest groups who emerge around them, as well as those strategic stakeholders whose behavior/concerns have consequences/implications for the organization's strategies, other stakeholders, and reputation (i.e., prioritizing what should be communicated *about*).
- Thinking through the implications/consequences/impact of the concerns/behavior of stakeholders/publics/interest groups for the organization's goals and priorities, other strategic stakeholders, and interest groups.
- Refining the stakeholder map.
- Addressing these implications/concerns by recognizing what must be *communicated* to strategic stakeholders/publics/interest groups to solve the problem or capitalize on the opportunity presented (selecting key communication themes) and the outcomes to be *achieved* with the communication (developing emergent PR goals).
- Achieving these emergent PR goals within the existing strategic communication plan, taking into account available human and financial resources. If need be, deliberate and emergent PR goals must be prioritized.

THEORETICAL CONCLUSION

The PR function is in need of a new paradigm—a new pattern of thinking about and studying organizational and communication problems, and of evaluating PR practice (Steyn & Bütschi, 2004). PR strategy is a core concept of a strategic approach to public relations in which the PR function is empowered with a strategic mandate and PR actions are driven by, and linked to, the enterprise and PR strategies. However, this will necessitate both a strategic role for PR at the top management level (the conceptualized role of the PR strategist), as well as a middle management role at the functional level (the redefined role of the PR manager). The latter develops PR strategy and a strategic communication plan, ensuring the alignment of deliberate and emergent PR goals to key organizational priorities/goals, issues and opportunities.

To develop PR strategy and contribute to enterprise (and other) strategy formulation, senior practitioners will need to understand the business and societal issues that the organization faces. Rather than trying to move communication further up top management's agenda, they should try to link communication with what is already at the top of that agenda. By thinking and talking only in terms of communication processes and activities without identifying the underlying business problems, practitioners risk imposing inappropriate solutions.

Top management is interested in solutions to business problems, not in communication problems. If the PR function is to make a real contribution to organizational effectiveness, they will have to become expert in using communication to help remove the barriers to organizational success (Quirke, 1996).

PRACTICAL CONCLUSION: HOW THE FINDINGS OF THE EXCELLENCE STUDY AND THE RESEARCH IT GENERATED CAN ENTER PRACTICE

A central mission of scholars and educators is to conduct research that contributes knowledge to a scientific discipline on the one hand, and to apply that knowledge to the practice of the discipline on the other hand (Van de Ven, 1989). Such a view is in accordance with a stated purpose of this book—namely, to discover how to build bridges between theory and practice, a contentious issue in the field of PR at present. The Dutch scholar Van Ruler (2004, p. 1) referred to PR professionals as being "from Venus" whereas scholars are "from Mars," and Fawkes and Tench (2004) found traces of anti-intellectualism among PR practitioners/employers in their research study. An editorial in a leading international communication journal (Wood, 2004) challenged academics to communicate their research more effectively rather than "languishing comfortably in an ivory tower" (p. 6).

It is a further aim of this volume to describe advances based on the Excellence Study and to test its findings with more recent theory and findings; to provide explanations for how PR practice can best achieve standards of excellence; to assist students, scholars, and practitioners to gain knowledge about how to institute excellent practices in organizations; and to determine how this knowledge can be gained on a global scale.

It is the contention of the author that problems in practice should not only be the inspiration for new theories, but practice should also be the testing ground of such theories. For this reason, in 2002, she pooled her research with Gerhard Bütschi (Swiss academic turned PR consultant). In his doctoral research, Bütschi (1996, 1997) designed a heuristic method for the development of a PR planning concept. (The empirical study was conducted in the United States, at which time Jim Grunig provided the Excellence Study findings to Bütschi.) In a subsequent consultancy project with Swisscom, Bütschi transformed his doctoral research findings into the first prototype of a software solution for the management of the PR function.

Based on the author's model for developing public relations strategy as theoretical foundation (Steyn, 2000a, 2000d; Steyn & Puth, 2000), Bütschi developed a second software prototype in 2003. South African

PR professional Retha Groenewald, who contributed to the South African excellence research program in 1998, now joined the development team, and a third prototype was developed (Steyn, 2003c; Steyn & Bütschi, 2004). Subsequent developments included a framework for enterprise strategy formulation, outlining the essence of the contribution that a practitioner in the role of the PR strategist makes to enterprise strategy formulation, as well as a framework for PR strategy formulation, to be developed by a practitioner in the role of the PR manager. Both frameworks consist of six steps and have been incorporated in the software (Digital Management, n.d.). Currently a framework for PR evaluation and performance management is being developed, to be added to the software.

Theories should be constructed in order to do something useful with them (i.e., to facilitate practice; Corman, Banks, Bantz, & Mayer, 1995). The software solution referred to earlier is one example of an effort to apply the principles of excellent communication in practice—that is, a suggested solution to some of the efficiency and effectiveness problems increasingly referred to by prominent PR practitioners (Muzi Falconi, 2004; UK Institute of PR, 2004).

However, the issues regarding PR efficiency and effectiveness, and the problems between academics and practitioners referred to earlier, might well be the tip of an iceberg. The real survival issue became apparent in a statement by the Secretary General of the International Communications Consultancy Organization (ICCO): "The PR industry—including both in-house and agency practitioners—is possibly now at the furthest point of divergence from the rest of the organization and must re-align so as to win the respect of senior management" (Quarendon, 2003, p. 3).

With public relations clearly in need of a new paradigm, maybe the time has come for its scholars and practitioners to realize that they are not each other's enemy. The real challenge faced by both is the fast-changing business, social, and technological environment that is making many PR practices outdated. In the spirit of searching for excellence, PR practitioners and scholars should make efforts to work together to develop excellent communication theory and test it in practice, and to develop best practices to increase the triple bottom line contribution of PR to organizations. This is the real survival issue in the field.

REFERENCES

Ansoff, H. I. (1977, May). *The changing shape of the strategic problem.* Paper presented at a special conference on Business Policy and Planning Research: The State of the Art, Pittsburgh.

Bower, J. L. (1982). Business policy in the 1980s. *Academy of Management Review, 7*(4), 630–638.

Bütschi, W. G. (1996). *PR-Metaplanning: The development of a heuristic model for the construction of a public relations planning concept*. Unpublished doctoral dissertation, University of Bern, Switzerland.

Bütschi, W. G. (1997). *PR-Metaplanung: Die entwicklung einer heuristischen entscheidungsmethode zur bestimmung der grundsätze einer PR-planungskonzeption* [PR-Metaplanning: The development of a heuristic method for the development of a public relations planning concept]. Bern, Switzerland: Haupt.

Chaffee, E. E. (1985). Three models of strategy. *Academy of Management Review, 10*(1): 89–98.

Corman, S. R., Banks, S. P., Bantz, C. R., & Mayer, M. E. (1995). *Foundations of organizational communication: A reader* (2nd ed.). New York: Longman.

Cutlip, S. M., Center, A. H., & Broom, G. M. (1994). *Effective public relations* (7th ed.). Englewood Cliffs, NJ: Prentice-Hall.

D'Aprix, R. (1996). *Communicating for change—connecting the workplace with the marketplace*. San Francisco: Jossey-Bass.

David, F. R. (1997). *Concepts of strategic management* (p. 77). Upper Saddle River, NJ: Prentice Hall.

De Beer, E. (2001). *The perception of top communicators of senior management's expectations of excellent communication in South African organizations*. Unpublished master's thesis, University of Pretoria, South Africa.

Digital Management. (n.d.). *Gateway to strategy development*. Retrieved January 13, 2006, from http://www.globalpr.org/knowledge/compro.asp

Digman, L. A. (1990). *Strategic management* (2nd ed.). Homewood, IL: BPI/Irwin.

Dozier, D. M., Grunig, L. A., & Grunig, J. E. (1995). *Manager's guide to excellence in public relations and communication management*. Mahwah, NJ: Lawrence Erlbaum Associates.

Drucker, P. (1954). *The practice of management*. New York: Harper & Row.

Duncan, R. B. (1972). Characteristics of organizational environments and perceived environmental uncertainty. *Administrative Science Quarterly, 17,* 313–327.

Fahey, L., & Narayanan, V. K. (1986). *Microenvironmental analysis for strategic management*. St. Paul, MN: West Publishing.

Fawkes, J., & Tench, R. (2004, July). *Does practitioner resistance to theory jeopardise the future of public relations in the UK?* Paper delivered at BledCom 2004, 11th International PR Research Symposium, Lake Bled, Slovenia.

Freeman, R. E. (1984). *Strategic management: A stakeholder approach*. Boston: Pitman.

Groenewald, J. M. (1998). *Die ontwikkeling van 'n model vir kommunikasiebestuursopleiding*. [The development of a model for communication management training]. Unpublished master's research script (Communication Management), University of Pretoria, South Africa.

Grunig, J. E. (Ed.). (1992). *Excellence in public relations and communication management*. Hillsdale, NJ: Lawrence Erlbaum Associates.

Grunig, L. A., Grunig, J. E., & Dozier, D. M. (2002). *Excellent public relations and effective organizations. A study of communication management in three countries*. Mahwah, NJ: Lawrence Erlbaum Associates.

Harrison, J. S., & St. John, C. H. (1998). *Strategic management of organizations and stakeholders: Concepts and cases*. Cincinnati, OH: South-Western College.

Heath, R. L. (Ed.). (2005). *Encyclopedia of public relations* (Vols. 1 and 2). Thousand Oaks/London: Sage.

Jain, S. C. (1997). *Marketing planning and strategy* (5th ed.). Cincinnati, OH: South-Western College.

Johnson, D. J. (1989). The co-orientation model and consultant roles. In C. H. Botan & V. Hazleton, Jr. (Eds.), *Public relations theory* (pp. 243–265). Hillsdale, NJ: Lawrence Erlbaum Associates.

Koekemoer, L. (Ed.). (1998). *Promotional strategy*. Kenwyn, South Africa: Juta & Co.

Lenz, R. T., & Engledow, J. L. (1986). Environmental analysis: The applicability of current theory. *Strategic Management Journal, 7*(4), 329–346.

Likely, F. (2002). What it takes to be a communication strategist. *Strategic Communication Management, 6*(3), 26–29.

Likely, F. (2003). PR/communication—key player in strategic management processes. *Strategic Communication Management, 7*(6), 18–22.

Likely, F. (2005, March). *Describing the strategic and performance management of the public relations/communication (PR/C) department in the context of the strategic management of the organization and the department.* Paper delivered at the 8th International PR Research Conference, South Miami, FL.

Lukaszewski, J. E. (2001a). How to develop the mind of a strategist. Part 1. *IABC Communication World, 18*(3), 13–15.

Lukaszewski, J. E. (2001b). How to develop the mind of a strategist. Part 3. *IABC Communication World, 18*(5), 9–11.

Lynch, R. (1997). *Corporate strategy*. London: Financial Times Pitman.

Mintzberg, H. (1987, July/August). Crafting strategy. *Harvard Business Review*, pp. 66–75.

Mintzberg, H. (1990). The design school: Reconsidering the basic premises of strategic management. *Strategic Management Journal, 11*, 176–195.

Mintzberg, H. (2001, Fall). The strategy concept I: Five P's for strategy. *California Management Review*, pp. 11–24.

Moss, D., & Warnaby, G. (1997). A strategic perspective for public relations. In P. J. Kitchen (Ed.), *Public relations: Principles and practice* (pp. 43–73). London: International Thomson Business Press.

Moss, D., & Warnaby, G. (1998). Communications strategy? Strategy communication? Integrating different perspectives. *Journal of Marketing Communication, 4*, 131–140.

Muzi Falconi, T. (2004). *Stormy prospects ahead for public relations.* Retrieved January 13, 2006, from http://www.globalpr.org/knowledge/stormypr-Jan-04.pdf

Narayanan, V. K., & Nath, R. (1993). *Organization theory: A strategic approach*. Homewood, IL: Irwin.

Oliver, S. (1997). *Corporate communication: Principles, techniques and strategies*. London: Kogan Page.

Oliver, S. (2001). *Public relations strategy*. London: Kogan Page.

Pearce, J. A., II, & Robinson, R. B., Jr. (1997). *Strategic management: Formulation, implementation, and control* (6th ed.). Chicago: Irwin.

Pettigrew, A. (1985). *The awakening giant: Continuity and change at ICI*. Oxford, England: Blackwell.

Prinsloo, P. W. F. (2005). *A framework for the formulation of corporate communication strategy in a financial services organization—a case study*. Unpublished master's research script (Communication Management), University of Pretoria, South Africa. (Confidential).

Quarendon, S. (2003). PR must "realign" with rest of business to seize on economic recovery. *The Gauge Delahaye Newsletter, 16*(5), 3.

Quirke, B. (1996). Putting communication on management's agenda. *Journal of Communication Management, 1*(1), 67–79.

Robert, M. (1997). *Strategy pure and simple II* (Rev. ed.). New York: McGraw-Hill.

Scholes, E., & James, D. (1997). Planning stakeholder communication. *Journal of Communication Management, 2*(3), 277–285.

Seitel, F. P. (1995). *The practice of public relations* (6th ed.). Englewood Cliffs, NJ: Prentice-Hall.

Senge, P. M. (1990, Fall). The leader's new work: Building learning organizations. *Sloan Management Review*, pp. 7–22.

Spies, P. (1994). A review of some long-term trends in South Africa. Experience with futures research in South Africa. *Futures, 26*(9), 964–979.

Steyn, B. (2000a). *Strategic management roles of the corporate communication function.* Unpublished master's research script (Communication Management), University of Pretoria, South Africa.

Steyn, B. (2000b). CEO expectations in terms of PR roles. *Communicare, 19*(1), 20–43.

Steyn, B. (2000c, March–April). *The South African CEO's role expectations for a public relations manager.* Paper delivered at PRSA Educators Academy PR International Research Conference, Miami.

Steyn, B. (2000d). Model for developing corporate communication strategy. *Communicare, 19*(2), 1–33.

Steyn, B. (2002, July). *From strategy to corporate communication strategy: A conceptualisation.* Paper delivered at the 9th International PR Research Symposium, Lake Bled, Slovenia.

Steyn, B. (2003a, July). *A conceptualisation and empirical verification of the "strategist," (redefined) "manager" and "technician" roles of public relations.* Paper delivered at BledCom 2003, 10th International PR Research Symposium, Lake Bled, Slovenia.

Steyn, B. (2003b). From strategy to corporate communication strategy: A conceptualisation. *Journal of Communication Management, 8*(2), 168–183.

Steyn, B. (2003c). *An adapted model for the formulation of corporate communication strategy.* [Working paper for the development of a software solution]. Gerlafingen, Switzerland: Digital Management AG.

Steyn, B., & Bütschi, G. (2004, July). *A model for developing corporate communication/public relations strategy—an online application.* Paper delivered at BledCom 2005, 11th International PR Research Symposium, Lake Bled, Slovenia.

Steyn, B., & Puth, G. (2000). *Corporate communication strategy.* Sandown, South Africa: Heinemann.

Swanston, D., & Kendall, R. (Eds.). (1995). *Accreditation sourcebook.* New York: PRSA.

Tibble, S. (1997). Developing communications strategy. *Journal of Communication Management, 1*(4), 356–361.

UK Institute of Public Relations. (2004). *Unlocking the potential of public relations.* [Research survey]. Retrieved January 14, 2006, from http://www.ipr.org.uk/unlockpr/index.asp

Van de Ven, A. H. (1989). Nothing is quite so practical as a good theory. *Academy of Management Review, 14*(4), 486–489.

Van Ruler, B. (1997). Communication: Magical mystery or scientific concept? Professional views of public relations practitioners in the Netherlands. In D. Moss, T. MacManus, & D. Vercic (Eds.), *Public relations research: An international perspective* (pp. 247–263). London: International Thomson Business Press.

Van Ruler, B. (2004, May). *Public relations professionals are from Venus, scholars are from Mars.* Paper delivered at the ICA Conference on Communication Research in the Public Interest, New Orleans.

Vercic, D., & Grunig, J. E. (2000). The origins of public relations theory in economics and strategic management. In D. Moss, D. Vercic, & G. Warnaby (Eds.), *Perspectives on public relations research* (pp. 9–58). London/New York: Routledge.

Vercic, D., Van Ruler, B., Bütschi, G., & Flodin, B. (2001). On the definition of public relations: A European view. *Public Relations Review, 27,* 373–387.

Weick, K. (1969). *The social psychology of organizing.* Reading, MA: Addison-Wesley.

Wilcox, D. L., Ault, P. H., & Agee, W. E. (1986). *Public relations: Strategies and tactics.* New York: Harper.

Windahl, S., Signitzer, B. H., & Olson, J. T. (1993). *Using communication theory: An introduction to planned communication.* London: Sage.

Wood, E. (2004). Editorial. *Journal of Communication Management, 9*(1), 6–9.

Worrall, D. N. (2005). *The contribution of the corporate communication and marketing functions to strategy formulation: A case study within a financial services institution.* Unpublished master's research script (Communication Management), University of Pretoria, South Africa. (Confidential).

Chapter 9

Toward a Model of Scenario Building From a Public Relations Perspective

MinJung Sung
Chung-Ang University

Among many organizations in the world, only a small number have persisted for hundreds of years. Even large, successful companies hardly hold out longer than an average of 40 years; long-living organizations try to anticipate what is going to happen and avoid crises (De Geus, 2002; Georgantzas & Acar, 1995). With growing socioeconomic, political, and technological challenges, organizations have recognized that how well and promptly they adapt has become a source of competitive advantage, and have reoriented their goals and missions from making profits to staying in harmony with the environment (Aldrich, 1979; De Geus, 2002; Govindarajan & Gupta, 2001; Mintzberg, 1989, 1990).

Strategic public relations has become a catchphrase in public relations (Grunig & Grunig, 2000a). The scholars and practitioners in the discipline increasingly maintain that public relations should move beyond its technician role to one that contributes to strategic management (Dozier, Grunig, & Grunig, 1995; Grunig, Grunig, & Dozier, 2002; Lauzen, 1995a, 1995b; White & Dozier, 1992). Organizations should make more efforts to discover problems and provide proactive responses in their initial stages, *before* the problems affect the organization. As the eyes and ears of an organization, public relations practitioners enable the management to understand and remain sensitive to different perspectives of publics (Grunig & Repper, 1992; Stoffels, 1994).

However, what specific role can public relations practitioners play in the strategic management of an organization? What should they do after identifying and detecting problems? What kind of tools can public relations personnel use to be part of strategic management? This study attempts to provide answers to these questions through scenario building, which projects multiple environmental situations based on the analysis of a variety of environmental factors (Ratcliffe, 2000). Although the term *strategic public relations* has been frequently used in the discipline, few people have provided the step-by-step guidelines for "strategic" modes of public relations. For example, not much has been discussed about how and with which tool communicators can get into a boardroom to show the influence and value of communication on an organization.

This chapter examines the role of public relations in strategic management and explores how public relations can employ the scenario-planning process as a part of a strategic management function. It first reviews the theories and principles of public relations, specifically the Excellence Theory and strategic management of public relations (Grunig et al., 2002). Second, it proposes a conceptual model of scenario building from a public relations perspective and presents the scenario-building process through a case study. Finally, it attempts to expand the Excellence Theory and suggests a future direction for further development by discussing the theoretical as well as practical implications of scenario building for effective public relations.

CONCEPTUAL BACKGROUND

Public Relations: Strategic Communication

Strategic Management of Public Relations.   How do organizations plan for their future when they do not know what will happen? According to Schwartz (1991), managers can build a profound and realistic confidence for their choices when they have a good understanding of uncertainty in the unpredictable world. They should look ahead and think about uncertainties by asking questions such as what challenges they could encounter or how others would respond to their actions. However, managers often react to uncertainty with wait-and-see attitudes or spend much time on a question like "What will happen to us?" De Geus (2002) argued that this question is relatively useless, because it is impossible to know accurately what would happen in the future. Rather, forward-looking managers should seek answers for questions such as "What will we do if a particular event happens?" Managers and their organization ought to be prepared to make fundamental changes to match the outside world.

Knights (1992) regarded strategic management as a "transformation of subjectivity" (p. 523) that should reflect various subdisciplines such as marketing and finance. In that sense, public relations finds its niche in strategic management by bringing distinctive problems and solutions (Grunig & Grunig, 2000b). As boundary spanners, communicators monitor the environment and bring an outside perspective into the decision-making process so that the organization can choose appropriate goals. As White and Dozier (1992) argued, strategic decisions involve organizations' adequate understanding of the environment; organizations construct meanings about themselves and the environment based on the points of view (Vercic & Grunig, 2000).

Strategic public relations benefits the organization because the members of the dominant coalition often do not see the organization's environment with an objective viewpoint (Grunig et al., 2002). According to Weick (1979), managers enact their environment: They define and view the environment within the scope of their perception, and make decisions based on those perceptions. Consequently, functions that monitor the environment must assist their organizations in enacting the strategic aspects of the environment. Public relations can contribute to strategic management by helping managers and the organization enact the environment, of which they may not be aware. It can also help strategic decision makers understand who are the publics that have consequence to the organization. The functions or departments that monitor the environment must assist their organizations in enacting the strategic aspects of the environment.

Excellence Theory and Public Relations.   The IABC "excellence project" (Grunig, 1992) answered the question "[H]ow, why, and to what extent communication affects the achievement of organizational objectives" (Grunig et al., 2002, p. ix). In an attempt to find answers for the question, the research team maintained that public relations is a unique management function that helps an organization maintain the balance between the organization and its environment through communication. Excellent public relations departments contribute to organizational effectiveness as they help the dominant coalition's decision making, by identifying strategic constituencies, providing information about strategic publics, and building good relationships with them. Participation in strategic management is integral for the public relations function to contribute to achieving the goals of an organization (Grunig & Grunig, 2000a; Grunig et al., 2002; Vercic & Grunig, 2000). Moreover, the value of public relations will be more appreciated if it helps managers identify uncertainties in the future and be prepared (White & Dozier, 1992).

Based on the Excellence Study, the researchers identified characteristics of excellent public relations programs—an "excellence factor" (Grunig et al., 2002, p. 56)—and generated 10 normative, generic principles of excellent public relations (Vercic, Grunig, & Grunig,

1996). The following five keywords summarize the Excellence Theory: *managerial, strategic, symmetrical, diverse,* and *ethical* (Grunig et al., 2002). Excellent public relations departments are two-way and symmetrical in interacting with publics, and balance the interests of organizations with those of publics. Their practice is also ethical with knowledge and professionalism. Strategically managed communication programs make an organization build good relationships with strategic publics.

In a recent publication based on the Excellence Study, the researchers identified a few critical areas that needed to be further researched (Grunig et al., 2002). One of the areas is strategic management of public relations, in that not many studies examined how public relations professionals should detect problems, gather information, and use that information in their practice. In the area of strategic management, the study showed that an organization would be more effective when public relations personnel identified strategic publics and when they developed relationships with those publics through symmetrical communication. However, more study is needed to explain how to conduct public relations environmental scanning and how to use scenarios to explore the outcomes of possible decisions made by an organization.

Environmental Scanning. Uncertainties in the environment influence an organization in various ways. Organizations should be sensitive to their environment and pay attention to issues at every stage, from emergence to dissipation. Excellent public relations emphasizes "monitoring the external environment and altering the organization's mission to it" (Grunig & Repper, 1992, p. 120).

Environmental scanning is "a methodology for coping with external competitive, social, economic and technical issues that may be difficult to observe or diagnose but that cannot be ignored and will not go away" (Stoffels, 1994, p. 1), or a way to obtain the map of the organization's future (Aguilar, 1967). This information-gathering and -processing activity allows organizations to detect problems and issues from emergence to dissipation and "remain sensitive to what's going on out there" (Dozier & Ehling, 1992, p. 176). It helps an organization "monitor, interpret, and respond to the myriad issues that both threaten and enhance survival and growth" (Lauzen, 1995a, p. 187), and connects the organization with its external environment. Therefore, organizations with formal environmental scanning systems monitor more issues in the environment than do those with informal systems. Through this activity, public relations personnel obtain a chance to participate in strategic decision making (Lauzen, 1997; White & Dozier, 1992).

As Chang (2000) found, environmental scanning is not widely conducted in public relations. According to her study of senior public relations managers in U.S. corporations, only a few participating organizations had an advanced environmental scanning system in their public relations departments. Furthermore, most participants were unconvinced about their communicators' ability to conduct environmental scanning.

Grunig and Grunig (2000a) recommended the following methods for early issues identification: qualitative research on activists and personal contacts, monitoring of discussion groups or listservs, systematic analysis of media monitoring, and research based on the situational theory of publics, to name a few. Stoffels (1994) suggested a three-stage process of environmental scanning: gathering inputs and generating information, synthesizing and evaluating emerging issues, and communicating environmental insights. As a premise for the scanning process, those who conduct scanning need to have a basic knowledge of the industry and the environment.

The Situational Theory of Publics. By definition, the concept of a public is imperative to understanding of public relations. J. Grunig's situational theory of publics provides a useful tool for public relations managers to segment a population into publics based on the extent of active and passive communication. A public is a homogeneous group of people who face and recognize a similar problem and organize for action (Grunig, 1997; Grunig & Hunt, 1984; Grunig & Repper, 1992).

Consisting of three independent variables—problem recognition, constraint recognition, and level of involvement—and two dependent variables—information seeking and processing—the theory forecasts the differential responses from publics to important issues. These variables are situational in that they explain the cognitions, attitudes, and behaviors that individuals have of specific situations. Information seeking is an active pursuit of information to understand a problem. On the other hand, people who communicate passively do not look for information but rather process information that is provided. The theory segments publics into four categories: active, aware, latent, and nonpublics. Publics who seek information become aware publics more easily than do those who do not seek information (Grunig, 1997; Grunig & Hunt, 1984).

Public relations practitioners can identify the kind of publics regarding particular issues and understand their attitudes and behaviors. Moreover, predictions on the publics' future behaviors help generate strategic public relations programs for different publics.[1]

---

[1] See Grunig and Hunt (1984) and Grunig (1997) for more information regarding the theory.

Scenario Building

As Schoemaker (1995, 2002) noted, life is inherently uncertain; it is impossible to know accurately what will happen in the future. Yet, managers consider the intrinsic uncertainty in the future as an obstacle and often react with wait-and-see attitudes. Managers can build a realistic confidence on their choices by having a good understanding of uncertainty (Schwartz, 1991).

The essence of strategy is to understand how to reinvent and develop an organization in the future. Scenario building is a strategic planning technique that identifies "possible alternative futures" (Georgantzas & Acar, 1995, p. 40) for an organization. It allows decision makers to examine potential uncertainties and refine present actions "by providing a context for planning and programming, lowering the level of uncertainty and raising the level of knowledge in relation to the consequences of actions which have been taken, or are going to be taken, in the present" (Ratcliffe, 2000, p. 130). It also is a process intended to interpret the future based on the patterns occurring over the course of an organization's history and build a database for future strategies (Fahey & Randall, 1998; Godet, 1987; Lukaszewski, 2002; Schoemaker, 1995; White & Dozier, 1992).

By definition, scenarios challenge the frame of mind of managers and extend planning horizons by looking at beliefs and assumptions from multiple perspectives (Georgantzas & Acar, 1995; Mercer, 1995; Wack, 1985a, 1985b). Fahey and Randall (1998) identified three roles of scenarios: augmenting understanding, producing new decisions, and reframing existing decisions. Scenario building is a learning process that shares and explores different perspectives. It attempts to identify driving forces that often seem obvious to one person but hidden to another (Ringland, 1998; Schoemaker & van der Heijden, 1992; Von Reibnitz, 1988). In that, it is inevitably a team-based process; only when working as a team can individuals recognize what each individual has missed. Schwartz (1991) advised to form a scenario team with individuals who have competence to select most appropriate scenarios and to communicate the outcomes to others. Knowledge and experience in the subjects, in addition to a wide range of expertise, are important. Diversity in age, social class, specializations, and qualifications are some components to consider (Von Reibnitz, 1988).

Little research has been done on scenario building in public relations. As it has aided other fields, scenario building can be a useful tool to enlarge public relations' contribution. By using it, public relations managers can generate possible futures for an organization based on issues detected from scientific research on the environment. Through these research activities, public relations can bring in environmental factors that decision makers often overlook.

A Conceptual Model of Scenario Building

Although there are no rigorous formulas for building scenarios, typical scenario-building processes are based on observation of external influencing factors and their relationships. The conceptual process of scenario building from a public relations perspective includes a "key public identification" step based on the situational theory of publics, which will improve accuracy and plausibility of scenarios as it identifies the types of publics and their future behaviors (Grunig et al., 2002; Schoemaker, 1995; Schwartz, 1991; Von Reibnitz, 1988). The review of literature leads to the following process:[2]

1. Task analysis—define the scope, such as time frame and geographic ranges, and analyze the present situation (corporate identity, goal, strategies, and the strengths and weaknesses). Team discussion is appropriate for scenario building in that it creates a shared language and compiles collective meanings and opinions (Ringland, 1998, Wack, 1985b).
2. Environmental influence analysis—identify external influencers such as major stakeholders and basic trends, and analyze their interrelationships through environmental scanning and review of document.
3. Issue selection and analysis—select the most critical issues from the comprehensive review of the environment based on overall strategic plans and external environmental changes.
4. Key uncertainty identification—classify key uncertainties as well as strategic stakeholders by combining driving forces in areas such as politics, economy, society, and technology.
5. Key public identification—identify and segment strategic publics among multiple uncertainties and stakeholders based on the situational theory of publics (Grunig, 1997).
6. Scenario plot and component identification–derive scenario components from the outcome of environmental scanning and interviews with publics, and combine them into scenario plots.
7. Scenario development and interpretation—develop a draft of scenarios based on the plots and receive feedback in the areas such as consistency, plausibility, and sense making.

---

[2]See Sung (2004) for a more detailed process of scenario building.

8. Final scenario scenarios—check consistency, plausibility, and clarity of scenarios based on the anticipation of reactions from major stakeholders.
9. Consequence analysis and strategies development—evaluate the scenarios and derive possible opportunities and risks for an organization to develop communication strategies.

Figure 9.1 provides a slightly condensed version of this process, which is the version employed in the case study discussed later in this chapter.

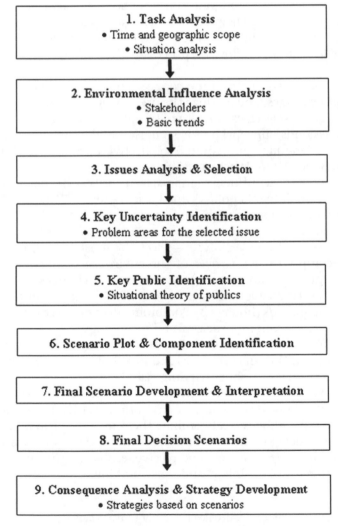

FIG. 9.1.   Scenario building process for strategic management of public relations.

CASE STUDY

Overview of the Organization

Insurance X was one of the largest insurance companies in the United States. Consisting of two business units—protection and financial—the company employed about 40,000 employees and thousands of agents and financial specialists across the country. At the corporate level, "the senior management team"—a group of executives such as the chairman, the presidents of business operations, and executive officials—made strategic decisions.

The company's public relations was managed by a communication department at the home office and field communicators from regional offices. The central public relations department consisted of several teams and two vice presidents who shared departmental responsibilities. These two vice presidents had no presence in the dominant coalition, but had a direct reporting relationship to a member of the dominant coalition, who oversaw administration, human resources, and law and regulation. This person had a general understanding of communication and might "put up a red flag" if he saw that some decisions might be problematic.

Public Relations Practice

Public relations was involved in the organization's strategic management on an issue-by-issue basis. Top communicators would be brought to the table if the management saw the need for advice from a communication perspective. Often they were called in at the last minute, after decisions were made or issues had evolved into crises. However, although not necessarily in a formal manner, the top communicators had an access to the dominant coalition, including the CEO, when they wanted. One of the vice presidents said, "The solid-line reporting relationship is nice to have, but not a must have." On the other hand, one manager said, "It would be better if [we] report directly to the chairman," because it would "add credibility and recognition" of public relations. "It is a totally different dynamic when you have somebody in between," another person said.

The company did not have any issues management function or system; issues were managed by ad hoc committees as they occurred. The public relations department's involvement in the process was decided by clients or the heads of these committees. Although communicators tried to run a "reputation filter"[3] for major issues, it often resulted in aggra-

---

[3]"Reputation filter" is a model that measures the impact of decisions in terms of issues management and reputation management. Communicators would run the filter for major business decisions to determine their implication or ramification on reputation. Based on the result, clients would alter decisions or at least consider their ramifications.

vation from the people who thought it slowed down decision making. These people, who had "tunnel vision" or "silos," did not understand the dollar value attached to public relations and sometimes asked communicators to simply deliver messages.

Public relations' informal involvement in strategic management indicated that its role as a strategic advisor was not enacted within the dominant coalition. Therefore, as Grunig et al. (2002) argued, public relations often remained a technical function. With a narrow perception about public relations, the dominant coalition tended to define it as media relations or community relations, which made it challenging for public relations personnel to contribute to strategic management. Public relations did not always have symmetrical relationships with other functions. Because of the organization's emphasis on government affairs and regulatory matters, the public relations department was often considered as a support function for the legal or the marketing departments.

Even though communicators identified themselves as strategic counselors who would advise on the ramifications of decisions on external audiences, their own focus was often limited to media relations. Public relations personnel's environmental scanning focused on media, such as monitoring media coverage or contacting reporters. In addition, they did not have a formal system to scan the environment or to share information. They typically conducted informal and "seat-of-the-pants" (Grunig et al., 2002, p. 394) research with occasional formal research. Although communicators understood the importance of the monitoring activity, they treated it as a secondary priority due to their lack of time and resources. They also did not precede other functions in detecting or obtaining information about emerging issues; frequently, issues management was led by functions such as law and regulation or marketing.

Insurance X's public relations department was in the process of transformation toward excellence. Public relations' involvement in strategic decision-making processes had recently increased because of continuous effort such as professional designation with knowledge and expertise in communication. It increasingly underscored the importance of "strategic minds" and public relations competence. It tried to hire people with good communication skills and knowledge, and came to receive more respect from other functions than before. The department used to be considered as a "fuzzy area" or simply a delivery function. The relationship with other departments improved with this increased respect. The public relations department also tried to introduce strategic approaches and scientific processes, such as reputation filter. Communicators' business knowledge and understanding helped move the department closer to strategic management. One manager pointed out "a mile wide and an inch deep" knowledge outside the insurance industry as a significant asset to enable this transition and to demonstrate the dominant coalition in the link between communication and success.

The Public Relations Scenario-Building Process

Step 1: Task Analysis. Public relations practitioners examined the environmental situation and defined the time and geographic scope, which was a 3- to 5-year timeframe in the United States. They pointed out that Insurance X was not rightfully positioned as good a company as it actually was because of negative consumer perceptions about insurance.[4] Heavy regulatory constraint and intensive market competition were obstacles as well. The company's long-term strategy was to grow; one of the strategies was to obtain high-value customers who have relatively lower loss cost.

Step 2: Environmental Influence Analysis. Public relations practitioners identified 12 stakeholders, or environmental influencers. Through environmental scanning[5] and document review, I identified general social trends, such as economics, consumers, competition, legislation, regulation, and demographics trends.

Step 3: Issues Analysis and Selection. Participants named several issues, such as class action lawsuits, global sourcing, and insurance regulatory reform. The areas of interest and the level of knowledge varied with their clients and responsibility. Several people mentioned the difficulty of selecting one issue. Forty issues were identified through environmental scanning, document review, and interviews. Most issues were related to one another and involved a broad review of the environment.

Several communicators chose the use of credit scoring for insurance rating as a critical issue because of its currency and impact on business from several aspects. Many insurers employed credit scores as one of rating tools, because actuarial studies demonstrated strong correlation between an individual's credit score and the risk for an insurance claim. However, as insurers admitted, it had not been explained why this correlation existed. As one of the Insurance X's communicators said, "We

---

[4]Consumers do not appreciate insurance due to the nature of the product—insurance is needed only when something bad happens. The company tried to send the message that insurance mechanism was an indispensable function to society.

[5]A variety of documents, such as internal reports or media clippings, were analyzed; the coverage from 19 newspapers and journals and 14 industry publications was monitored via electronic databases such as Lexis-Nexus and Factiva. Using search engines, I also identified a total of 22 discussion groups and activist Web sites and regularly visited them during the entire research period to record and analyze their content.

can't tell you why this works…. The problem is that people cannot intuitively make that link."

The lack of clear explanation has resulted in consumer and legislative opposition. Opponents have argued that correlation was not sufficient to explain causality, and accordingly, it might wrongfully discriminate people with lower incomes or with specific racial or ethnic backgrounds. For some consumers, bad credit scores resulted in insurance premium increase. Consumer advocates and regulators have asked for access to insurers' rating formulas and data for further analysis; however, insurers have been reluctant to disclose the information because they consider them a trade secret, or proprietary. In some states, legislators have tried to restrict or ban use of such information.

Step 4: Key Uncertainty Identification. I analyzed the issue by reviewing sources such as newspapers, journals, trade publications, and a variety of Web sites, as well as interviewing communicators. I first identified major influencers and the environmental factors in the scenario environment, such as politics, economy, society, and technology. With 45 influencing factors, I identified 13 driving forces[6] that were most relevant to the three influencers: regulators, consumers, and consumer activists.

Step 5: Key Public Identification. Twelve consumer advocates were interviewed to examine their perceptions and behaviors based on the situational theory of publics (Grunig, 1997). Participants had *high problem recognition* because they thought about the issue frequently, such as "every day" or "several times a week." They had an extremely negative view on the issue, which was partially based on their deep distrust in the insurance industry. They described it as an unfair apparatus that was "full of mistakes" with possible redlining or profiling. The fact that insurance companies denied consumer organizations' request to access rating data raised skepticism. Participants had *high level of involvement* in the issue as individual policyholders as well as consumer advocates. They also had *low constraint recognition* in that they believed that they could do something about the issue. They were working actively to pressure state legislatures to ban the use of credit scoring: lobbying, writing letters, offering testimony, publishing newsletters, posting information online, conducting research, and contacting media. However, participants also recognized their limits in influencing the insurance industry, which exercised political power on regulators and legislators.

---

[6]Ringland (2002) defined *driving forces* as "forces in the macro-environment that will affect the key factors" (p. 131). These major forces drive the development of a specific issue and result in uncertainties or possible problems.

Participants were the members of an activist public who actively sought information by searching the Internet, tracking news, and talking to experts through interpersonal networks. Thus, they were highly likely to communicate about this issue (Grunig, 1997). They generated and disseminated information to persuade and educate consumers through e-mail action alerts, Web sites, and newsletters. They urged consumers to shop around for better insurers. Furthermore, several consumer groups developed a coalition with diverse interest groups against the industry. They were also all-issue publics who were interested in any consumer issues. Consequently, consumer advocates were a strategic public who could pressure the industry by mobilizing constituencies or appealing to regulators, legislators, the courts, and the media.

Participants said that they would continue, and even increase, their action in the future. Although the increasing use of credit scores in the U.S. society left limited alternatives for consumers, the participants would do anything to ban insurance credit scoring. However, they were willing to communicate with insurers. Some activists anticipated that the bill to ban credit scoring would pass soon in their states. Others expected that ongoing litigations and court rulings would add more restriction on the use of insurance credit scoring. Participants also said that Congress would play a critical role in development of this issue.

Step 6: Scenario Plot and Component Identification.   Primary scenario topics and initial themes were developed from the result of environmental scanning and the interviews with publics. I combined uncertainties, trends, driving forces, environmental influencers, and the public's behavior, and identified four possible developments: the status quo, moderate regulatory changes with increasing consumer complaints, continuous use of credit scoring with stricter regulation, and complete ban on credit scoring.

Step 7: Scenario Development and Interpretation.   A draft of scenarios was developed from the plots. I asked Insurance X's communicators to read the scenarios and provide feedback. Overall, participants evaluated that the scenarios were accurately depicting the situation with thorough review of components. A few participants pointed out the small number of scenarios as a possible weakness; they believed that two scenarios were too few to capture subtle meanings and that multiple scenarios would increase accuracy.

Step 8: Final Decision Scenarios.   I revised the scenarios based on the feedback from Insurance X's communicators and checked their consistency and plausibility. The final scenarios are attached in the appendix to this chapter.

Step 9: Consequence Analysis and Strategy Development.   Two scenarios led to the conclusion that Insurance X needed to examine the issue not only within the insurance industry, but also in the broader U.S. economy and society. It also needed to remain sensitive to the actions of consumers and activists as well as state regulators and legislators. Consumer advocates were strategic publics who could pressure the organization by exercising influence on regulators and legislators through lobbying and grassroots mobilization.

Consequently, it was first advised that Insurance X's communicators generate a comprehensive list of stakeholders and continuously monitor the "broader" environment in addition to media. The company did not consider consumer advocates to be critical stakeholders, even though they were strategic publics. Second, the company needed to consider direct communication with these strategic publics to understand what they have to say. The public had a firm, negative position and a clear direction of action toward the issue, much of which resulted from insurers' defensive attitude and responses to the public's concern. The company may have needed to employ open communication strategies to rectify any unnecessary misunderstanding and distrust, such as giving opponents permission to study the data with a strict confidentiality agreement. Otherwise, activists would continuously use denial of disclosure to undermine the legitimacy and fairness of each company's credit scoring apparatus, which could possibly involve regulatory intervention. Finally, Insurance X needed to establish a system to reinforce frequent reporting and seamless communication between the headquarters and the field offices. Environmental scanning activity within the public relations function had been neither regularly nor rigorously conducted.

Influence of Scenario Building on Public Relations

Most participants were positive about adopting scenario-building technique as part of their actual public relations practice. If the top communicators saw the need, according to participants, the scenario-building project had a high chance of employment.

One of the primary values of scenarios was providing a chance to look at the situation from long-term perspectives. One communicator said the scenario-building process would be "absolutely useful for longer-term public relations"; she explained that people tended to project what would happen based on what they would like to see. Participants pointed out the need for a uniform model, such as scenario building, which would enforce thinking about what it would take for the company to achieve its goal. "It's very useful ... that you can help provide more formal structure in terms of how to do [forward thinking] better," one manager expatiated. A rigorous process would prevent recklessly sitting down and assuming positive futures. Communicators also expected that scenario building would initiate cross-functional conversation with people from other functions, such as law and marketing.

When asked to discuss issues they believed to be important to the organization, participants tended to name the issues that were mostly concerned with their own clients. Therefore, some participants who were not directly responsible for the issue of credit scoring were unfamiliar with it. After reading the scenarios, participants said that they provided a good opportunity to learn about the issue. "I learned so much from your scenarios," one mid-level manager said.

A few participants pointed out that the scenarios were only "half the discussions." They said that the next step should be to discuss strategies derived from the scenarios, such as how Insurance X would react to the ban. It was pointed out that a deeper examination and discussion would lead to more rigorous scenarios with more subtle nuances, which would provide interesting subjects for further discussions and education in the form of a 1- or 2-day workshop. However, some participants pointed out that having public relations practitioners lead this process might be difficult, although possible, because they had overwhelmingly busy everyday schedules and lacked resources. Often, long-term strategic thinking was considered "nice to have," but not critical for the moment.

Excellent Public Relations and Scenario Building

Although not trying to forecast the exact future, scenario building helps an organization understand its environment and make more strategic decisions. Scenario building from a public relations perspective considers a critical factor that was overlooked in general scenario-building processes: publics. It also has much in common with the Excellence Theory in that it emphasizes the role of public relations in conducting research, monitoring the environment, bringing in external information, and helping the management make strategic decisions based on that information. The case study shows that it is hard to develop scenarios without proper understanding of publics. It also demonstrates why decision makers need to understand publics. In the following section, I examine the characteristics of scenario building and compare them with the excellence principles.

According to the Excellence Study (Grunig et al., 2002), public relations' involvement in strategic management can be examined by observing how it is represented among the dominant coalition. To be considered "excellent," top communicators must be a part of the dominant coalition and have access to or a direct reporting relationship. Excellent public relations professionals are empowered either by having top communicators as part of the dominant coalition or by having immediate access to other managers. The dominant coalition and communicators need to share expectations for public relations' role and contribution.

At the core of excellent public relations is the practitioners' professionalism and knowledge for a managerial, strategic, symmetrical, and ethical role. Public relations expertise and research competence are vital components in the scenario-building process. Scenarios are developed based on a great deal of information derived from research, such as public surveys, interviews, and environmental scanning, which identifies basic trends and uncertainties. For example, the knowledge of the situational theory of publics allows public relations practitioners to segment publics and anticipate patterns of behaviors. Therefore, it improves communicators' strategic problem-solving power and cultivates strategy-embedded culture. In addition, with the set of knowledge and skills, public relations managers can generate scenarios that help their organizations stay knowledgeable and sensitive about the external environment and get prepared for possible futures. By doing so, they can broaden the perspectives of decision makers.

The study shows that scenario building could help Insurance X's public relations function move toward the management function. It enables communicators to participate in a decision-making process as sources of information regarding the organization's environment, such as strategic issues and publics. Communicators can present the specific outcome of this process—public relations scenarios—to the dominant coalition and provide advice on communication ramification and implication of certain decisions based on logical development of an issue. Public relations' unique contribution as a boundary spanner—comprehensive monitoring of the environment and communication with strategic publics—distinguishes it from other management functions and eventually leads it to the decision-making table. Through the scenario-building process, the value of public relations and the research capacity of public relations practitioners can be better recognized within the organization. They can use scenario building along with the reputation filter that they already employed. The combined use of these two tools will generate more persuasive outcome to explain "why" and "why not" of certain decisions. By working with several departments, it can show the value of two-way communication and understanding the publics in management decisions. As Dozier et al. (1995) pointed out, excellence in public relations is based on a "partnership" (p. 14) between public relations practitioners and the dominant coalition.

Organizations with excellent public relations disclose relevant information to publics and listen to publics through research. They maintain the balance between their organizations' interests with those of publics through symmetrical communicating. They attempt to develop and maintain good relationships with publics through dialogue. Good scenarios are based on two-way communication because they involve listening to and understanding publics' interest and behavior. The case study shows that an organization that employs two-way communication is more likely to generate plausible scenarios.

In turn, an organization that adopts scenario building will recognize the value of two-way communication. The presented scenario-building process shows the value of two-way symmetrical communication, which will help the organization understand its environment and publics accurately. By understanding the publics' perceptions and attitudes, the organization can have a realistic expectation about their future behavior. Although the accuracy of scenarios is not the primary goal of scenario building, accuracy will certainly help public relations practitioners come up with workable strategies when a similar situation happens in the future. Hence, it will increase the value of scenario building and add to public relations' credibility. In addition, this type of information sharing and collection will add to the organization's database.

Furthermore, public relations scenario building can show the value of two-way symmetrical communication to the people from other management functions. By projecting multiple situations and the ramifications resulting from choosing different strategic options—approaches based on different models of public relations—communicators can show the long-term benefit of two-way symmetrical communication and good relationships for the organization.

Finally, scenario building encourages an organization to obtain diverse perspectives in decision making and problem solving. The goal of scenario building is to project multiple developments of a situation, not a linear development of an issue. Therefore, the scenario-building process requires entailing possible, multiple perspectives and opinions, not the most likely and reasonable projection. Several scenario scholars advise to organize the scenario team with people who have diverse experiences and backgrounds. External experts might be invited to deal with particular topics (Ringland, 1998; Schwartz, 1991; Von Reibnitz, 1988).

Further Benefit of Scenario Building for Public Relations

Scenario building is a dynamic process to gain access to strategy development. The overview of theories in public relations, environmental scanning, and scenario building shows that public relations can participate in and contribute to strategic management through scenario building in many ways. Moreover, scenario building from a public relations perspective further expands the Excellence Theory in that it induces a formal environmental scanning system, cultivates strategic thinking among communicators, facilitates organizational learning, and helps public relations practitioners play the role of integrators across the organization.

Institutionalization of Environmental Scanning. Environmental scanning, one of the most important activities of public relations, is identical to the step that identifies environmental factors and uncertainties in the process. Scenario building inherently involves regular and rigorous monitoring of the "broader" environment and understanding of publics in several steps. If an organization regularly conducts environmental scanning, it already has much information that is needed for scenario building and, consequently, can employ and develop scenarios with less extra effort. Therefore, an organization with a formal environmental scanning function is more likely to employ scenario building and use it more effectively than is an organization that does not conduct environmental scanning.

In the case study's organization, the public relations department needs to establish a formal environmental scanning function and share the results with other functions and the dominant coalition on a regular basis. It is also necessary to broaden the scope of environmental scanning activities. Insurance X hardly identified or considered other publics, such as general consumers and consumer activists. The company was not able to proactively identify diverse publics unless they raised problems and were covered by the media.

An organization with formal issues management will enjoy similar benefits, in that the scenario-building process identifies, analyzes, and draws strategy options. Whereas scenarios examine multiple possible situations in the future, issues management focuses on handling the issue in a strategic way (Chase, 1984; Jones & Chase, 1979; Lauzen, 1997). The proposed model of scenario building incorporates a large part of issues management. To lead this process, the public relations department needs to establish a system that would reinforce research, including identification and segmentation of publics.

Facilitating Strategic Thinking and Conversation. As Insurance X's communicators pointed out, scenario building entails and facilitates longer-term strategic thinking and conversation among communicators. Although public relations practitioners expected and desired to have more involvement in strategic decision making, most of them tended to remain narrow and shortsighted. They did not consider the discussions about long-term (more than 3 to 5 years)—strategies critical for them. Often, they viewed long-term thinking and strategies as insignificant, because of busy everyday work. Scenario building can function as a formal and compulsory process that forces public relations practitioners to think more strategically and have a wider perspective, which cannot be achieved through individual initiatives only. It would compel scenario planners and their audiences to think about what would take for the organization to achieve its goal in the future. It naturally extends the horizon of planning and thinking to the defined timeframe.

As Mintzberg (1983) maintained, government intervention can make the situation serious because it leads to more control. Consumer activists try to involve the government in addition to the media in their activities to work against organizations. Consequently, management of the issue requires collaboration among several functions and well-crafted strategy. Activists encourage communication and other action through multiple channels. I also found a similar situation to what Anderson (1992) noted in her study of activists. Because the organization fails to identify consumer activists as people with whom to communicate, activists try to find information through their own networks and increase pressure through lobbying. Insurance X needed to be sensitive to these activists, identify them early, and develop communication strategies to cultivate mutual understanding with them.

Scenario building can be particularly useful for highly diversified and decentralized organizations to obtain integration and common understanding among managers. The scenario-building process can initiate and facilitate strategic conversation among people with different focuses or across different functions. Insurance X's public relations had a relatively limited domain because several areas of public relations were managed by other functions. Individual communicators focused on the areas that were directly related to their daily responsibility, and frequently said, "It's not my area," or "That's not my issue"; however, longer-term strategies need broader perspectives, such as understanding of the interrelationships among different issues. In order to generate consistent and plausible scenarios, public relations departments need to work with others, such as the strategic planning department or the dominant coalition. By adopting scenario building, public relations can invite input from other departments and work together in developing scenarios.

Organizational Learning.   An organization benefits from scenario building because it is a collective and learning process. The scenario-building process, which entails extensive review of issues and the environment, can provide an opportunity to educate the organization's managers about the environment and issues. The process can offer a uniform model to examine and analyze an issue. Final scenarios also present succinct but quick overviews of the situation to those who are not familiar with specific issues or areas.

Furthermore, as Fahey (2000) argued, learning through scenario building shifts the emphasis from developing and refining the outcome to assessing the scenarios for strategy development from unexpected directions. In the case study, this educational effect was detected during the situation analysis stage as well. Participants exchanged new information in their areas or expertise, such as employee relations, public affairs, or regulation; some participants asked the others about new policies or economic trends with which they were unfamiliar.

CONCLUSION

Good scenarios facilitate careful examination of the environment and recognize what may happen out of anticipation. They also help develop organizational goals and strategies and broaden managers' viewpoints (Georgantzas & Acar, 1995; Mercer, 1995). Scenario building from a public relations angle allows a new perspective to the management of uncertainty (van der Heijden, 1996). Using the situational theory of publics, which is employed as a part of the process, public relations practitioners obtain proper understanding of the publics and generate more plausible and accurate scenarios. The topics and components of scenarios are also derived from the outcomes of research by communicators, such as public surveys, interviews, and environmental scanning. Consequently, scenarios allow an organization's management to consider behaviors and attitudes of publics in its decision making. By doing so, the management will be able to broaden the perspectives of decision makers and make them responsive to the external environment. The case study shows that the more an organization's public relations is excellent, the more it is likely to accept, appreciate, and use scenario building in its public relations practice.

Strategic management of public relations requires more than communication and public relations expertise. To be fully involved in strategic decision making, public relations managers need to have adequate business knowledge and information beyond the public relations realm. They must understand the organization's business, the industry, and the environment in general, in addition to the knowledge and expertise in public relations. Scenario building helps communicators, because it implicitly as well as explicitly forces them to conduct research and broaden understanding of the environment. It is more useful for an organization in a complex environment to systematize environmental scanning and communication-strategy development. This can also be incorporated with issues management and engage cross-functional managers.

Finally, scenario building benefits public relations practitioners not only as a strategy-building technique, but also as a device for internal educational and organizational learning. Furthermore, not having public relations at the decision-making table is likely to result in an information shortage among members of the dominant coalition about the organization's environment and its publics. The information that the public relations practitioners collect as boundary spanners may not be communicated to the dominant coalition when it is needed; thus, public relations may not be able to play the role of strategic advisor or the source of information in decision-making processes. In turn, the organization's dominant coalition may fail to make strategic decisions that maintain balance with the external environment.

As one of the first that uses scenario building in public relations research, this study calls for additional research based on the similar conceptual framework. First, future research needs to include actual strategy development and evaluation as part of scenario building. Applying this model to other organizations with different structures and environments will help improve this model as well as the theory of strategic management of public relations. Second, it is necessary to explore the role of communicators in the decision-making process in relation to scenario building and strategy development. The educational aspect of scenario building motivates to further investigate using it for organizational learning. Third, later studies could be conducted to reflect more diverse perspectives and situations. Collaboration with cross-functional managers other than public relations practitioners, such as lawyers and marketers, may expand the use of this method and theory. Finally, although this study is based on qualitative methods, future research may include quantitative methods to obtain a different perspective.

APPENDIX: FINAL SCENARIOS

Scenario 1: "Insured, but Not Scored": Complete Ban on Credit Scoring

As the labor market—the payroll market in particular—remains weak, the unemployment rate increases and levels of household income stay low. More and more consumers experience financial difficulty. Meanwhile, the minority population of the United States grows as a result of immigration. Most minorities and recent immigrants have low incomes. As many insurance policyholders experience rate hikes or are rejected because of low insurance scores—regardless of their driving records—public awareness of the issue of credit scoring increases. A majority of those who are affected are low-income minorities and people living in poor neighborhoods. Thus, factions such as consumer groups, minority groups, and ethnic organizations are concerned about the issue. The bad credit problem becomes a social issue and draws attention from federal and state governments. In addition, Hispanics live in a largely cash society and their nonuse or limited use of credit has a deleterious impact on their credit rates.

Consumer groups try to ban the use of credit scoring for insurance. The groups publicize it as "redlining" that discriminates against consumers. They build a coalition with a variety of groups, such as religious or ethnic organizations, and obtain support from state insurance commissioners and insurance agents who are against credit scoring. Because of the coalition's education efforts, consumers may change their insurance-shopping behavior. The media covers negative stories related to insurance scoring. An investigative news program reports the lack of "scientific evidence" of credit scoring and questions previous studies. Some studies reveal that credit reports have a high rate of error, and many consumers have been disadvantaged by the errors. A significant number of Insurance X's policyholders, especially those who do not have good credit scores, file complaints to their state insurance commissioners and write and call state representatives. The lobbying efforts and grassroots activism of consumer advocates influence state legislators. States such as Texas and California decide to ban credit scoring for insurance. Even in the states where credit scoring is allowed, the state governments develop stricter regulation and require insurers to disclose their scoring data and formula, which Insurance X has kept as a trade secret. Insurance X refuses to compromise or resolve any credit-related disputes. It comes to face more consumer lawsuits.

Scenario 2: "Credit Rules"—Continuous Use of Credit Scoring

The U.S. economy stays robust and healthy with the end of the war in Iraq. The insurance price drops in some instances because of heavy competition, the use of technology, and the reform of distribution channels (e.g., direct marketing or Web-based marketing). The use of credit scoring proliferates as a critical evaluative tool in several industries other than the insurance industry; consumers become fatalistic about the trend. Credit score management is considered the personal responsibility of each individual in U.S. society. Because a large number of complainers are minorities or people with low incomes, they have little social and political influence. The development of new technology enables individuals to access their credit reports easily. A number of "lower-value" Insurance X policyholders, especially those who do not have good credit scores, move to competitors with better rates or who do not use credit scoring. However, the company's strategic "high-value" customers remain loyal. Consumer groups' efforts to form public opinion against credit scoring has little effect because of their limited resources. The media do not pay attention until something "bigger" happens. Most insurance consumers have little information and understanding of credit scoring and do not consider it when buying insurance. As the opponents increasingly request an independent, credible study for credit scoring, the insurance industry decides to cooperate and open the data. In most states, insurance companies succeed in persuading state legislatures to their thinking and continue to use credit scoring.

This research makes a contribution to the body of knowledge of public relations by articulating a theoretical foundation to develop the process of scenario building, and providing a practical model. Public relations practitioners have been told to think and act strategically, often without knowing how to do so. A scenario will be a helpful instrument to examine comprehensive future options and develop optimal strategies for decision making. Practitioners who want to try this method may use the proposed model in their practice. This study demonstrates why it is necessary for public relations to have a longer-term, broader perspective beyond being specialists with technical expertise. In addition, the scenario-building process will empower practitioners by helping them discover novel and valuable ways for involvement in decision-making processes.

REFERENCES

Aguilar, F. (1967). *Scanning the business environment*. New York: Macmillan.

Aldrich, H. E. (1979). *Organizations and environments*. Englewood Cliffs, NJ: Prentice-Hall.

Anderson, D. S. (1992). Identifying and responding to activist publics: A case study. *Journal of Public Relations Research 4*(3), 151–165.

Chang, Y. C. (2000). *A normative exploration into environmental scanning in public relations*. Unpublished master's thesis, University of Maryland, College Park.

Chase, W. H. (1984). *Issue management: Origins of the future*. Stamford, CT: Issue Action.

De Geus, A. (2002). *The living company*. Cambridge, MA: Harvard Business School Press.

Dozier, D. M., & Ehling, W. P. (1992). Evaluation of public relations programs: What the literature tells us about their effects. In J. E. Grunig (Ed.), *Excellence in public relations and communication management* (pp. 159–184). Hillsdale, NJ: Lawrence Erlbaum Associates.

Dozier, D., Grunig, L. A., & Grunig, J. E. (1995). *Manager's guide to excellence in public relations and communication management*. Mahwah, NJ: Lawrence Erlbaum Associates.

Fahey, L. (2000). Scenario learning. *Management Review, 89*(3), 29–34.

Fahey, L., & Randall, R. M. (1998). *Learning from the future*. New York: Wiley.

Georgantzas, N. C., & Acar, W. (1995). *Scenario-driven planning: Learning to manage strategic uncertainty*. Westport, CT: Quorum.

Godet, M. (1987). *Scenarios and strategic management*. London: Butterworths.

Govindarajan, V., & Gupta, A. K. (2001,). Strategic innovation: A conceptual roadmap. *Business Horizons, 4*(4), 3–12.

Grunig, J. E. (Ed.). (1992). *Excellence in public relations and communication management*. Hillsdale, NJ: Lawrence Erlbaum Associates.

Grunig, J. E. (1997). A situational theory of publics: Conceptual history, recent challenges and new research. In D. Moss, T. MacManus, & D. Vercic (Eds.), *Public relations research: An international perspective* (pp. 3–48). Boston: International Thomson Business Press.

Grunig, J. E., & Grunig, L. A. (2000a). Research methods for environmental scanning. *Jim and Lauri Grunig's research: A supplement of pr reporter, 7*, pp. 4–7.

Grunig, J. E., & Grunig, L. A. (2000b). Public relations in strategic management and strategic management of public relations: Theory and evidence from the IABC excellence project. *Journalism Studies, 1*(2), 303–323.

Grunig, J. E., & Hunt, T. (1984). *Managing public relations*. New York: Holt, Rinehart & Winston.

Grunig, J. E., & Repper, F. C. (1992). Strategic management, publics, and issues. In J. E. Grunig (Ed.), *Excellence in public relations and communication management* (pp. 91–108). Hillsdale, NJ: Lawrence Erlbaum Associates.

Grunig, L. A., Grunig, J. E., & Dozier, D. (2002). *Excellent public relations and effective organizations: A study of communication management in three countries*. Mahwah, NJ: Lawrence Erlbaum Associates.

Jones, B. L., & Chase, W. H. (1979). Managing public policy issues. *Public Relations Review, 5*(2), 3–23.

Knights, D. (1992). Changing spaces: The disruptive impact of a new epistemological location for the study of management. *Academy of Management Review, 17*, 514–536.

Lauzen, M. M. (1995a). Public relations manager involvement in strategic issue diagnosis. *Public Relations Review, 21*(4), 287–304.

Lauzen, M. M. (1995b). Toward a model of environmental scanning. *Journal of Public Relations Research, 7*, 187–204.

Lauzen, M. M. (1997). Understanding the relation between public relations and issues management. *Journal of Public Relations Research, 9*, 65–82.

Lukaszewski, J. (2002). Jim Lukaszewski's strategy. *Pr reporter, 18*(Suppl.), 1–4.

Mercer, D. (1995). Scenarios made easy. *Long-Range Planning, 28*(4), 81–86.

Mintzberg, H. (1983). *Power in and around organizations*. Englewood Cliffs, NJ: Prentice-Hall.

Mintzberg, H. (1989). *Mintzberg on management*. New York: Free Press.

Mintzberg, H. (1990). The design school: Reconsidering the basic premises of strategic management. *Strategic Management Journal, 11*, 171–195.

Ratcliffe, J. (2000). Scenario building: A suitable method for strategic property planning? *Property Management, 18*(2), 127–135.

Ringland, G. (1998). *Scenario planning: Managing the future*. Chichester, England: John Wiley & Sons.

Ringland, G. (2002). *Scenario in business*. Chichester, England: John Wiles & Sons.

Schoemaker, P. J. H. (1995). Scenario planning: A tool for strategic thinking. *Sloan Management Review, 36*(2), 25–40.

Schoemaker, P. J. H. (2002). *Profiting from uncertainty: Strategies for succeeding no matter what the future brings*. New York: Free Press.

Schoemaker, P. J. H., & van der Heijden, C. A. J. M. (1992). Integrating scenarios into strategic planning at Royal Dutch/Shell. *Planning Review, 20*, 41–46.

Schwartz, P. (1991). *The art of the long view: Paths to strategic insight for yourself and your company.* New York: Currency Doubleday.

Stoffels, J. (1994). *Strategic issues management.* Thousand Oaks, CA: Sage.

Sung, M. (2004). *Toward a model of strategic management of public relations: Scenario building from a public relations perspective.* Unpublished doctoral dissertation, University of Maryland, College Park.

van der Heijden, K. (1996). *Scenarios: The art of strategic conversation.* Chichester, England: Wiley.

Vercic, D., & Grunig, J. E. (2000). The origins of public relations theory in economics and strategic management. In D. Moss, D. Vercic, & G. Warnaby (Eds.), *Perspectives on public relations research* (pp. 9–58). London: Routledge.

Vercic, D., Grunig, L. A., & Grunig, J. E. (1996). Global and specific principles of public relations: Evidence from Slovenia. In H. M. Culbertson & N. Chen (Eds.), *International public relations: A comparative analysis* (pp. 31–65). Mahwah, NJ: Lawrence Erlbaum Associates.

Von Reibnitz, U. (1988). *Scenario techniques.* Hamburg: McGraw-Hill.

Wack, P. (1985a). Scenarios: Shooting the rapids. *Harvard Business Review,* pp. 139–150.

Wack, P. (1985 b, Sep./Oct.). Scenarios: Uncharted waters ahead. *Harvard Business Review,* pp. 72–89.

Weick, K. E. (1979) *The social psychology of organizing* (2nd ed.). Reading, MA: Addison-Wesley.

White, J., & Dozier, D. M. (1992). Public relations and management decision making. In J. E. Grunig (Ed.), *Excellence in public relations and communication management* (pp. 91–108). Hillsdale, NJ: Lawrence Erlbaum Associates.

Chapter 10

An Alternative Postmodern Approach to Corporate Communication Strategy

Ursula Ströh
University of Technology, Sydney, Australia

Probably the most important finding of the Excellence Study—a research project funded through a grant from the International Association of Business Communicators (IABC) Research Foundation—was that strategic management represents the greatest differentiator between excellent and mediocre public relations (Grunig, Grunig, & Dozier, 2002). Both the quantitative and qualitative results confirmed that the function of public relations should be empowered to play a prominent role in the strategic managerial function of effective organizations. This important contribution of the study set the benchmark for the practice of public relations in terms of strategic planning, research, networking, and approaches to gathering information.

On the other hand the Excellence Study (Grunig et al., 2002) also suggested that the concepts of strategic management and planning are rather vague, and can be understood in many different ways. The study most commonly reflected that *strategic* means that public relations messages are aligned with organizational goals already decided by the dominant coalitions. Practitioners and students in the field of public relations are therefore not always clear on how to design a proper communication management strategy that will both be accepted by top management structures in organizations, and reflect the contribution this function makes to the overall success of the organization. They often look for a step-by-step guide to follow. Many textbooks suggest detailed methods of long-term strategic planning and communication programs that are derived from strategic management theory (Broom, Casey, & Ritchey, 1997; Cutlip, Center, & Broom, 1994; D'Aprix, 1996; Ferguson, 1999; Kendall, 1992; Oliver, 2001; Smith, 2002; Steyn & Puth, 2000). Software programs are even being developed to enable corporate communicators to create strategies and communication plans that include budgeting and research aspects—a very worthwhile contribution to traditional corporate communication theory (Bütschi, 2004).

New theoretical approaches to management and corporate communication have, however, extended the thoughts surrounding strategic planning, and these new developments are what I put forward in this chapter. I suggest a new approach to corporate communication strategy in line with postmodern approaches of chaos and complexity theories. I argue for a more participative and nonlinear approach, rather than the structured approaches suggested by current corporate communication theorists. Because of the vast bodies of knowledge and literature associated with the labels of *postmodernism*, *chaos*, and *complexity*, I run the danger of drowning in the rhetoric regarding these headings, or, because of limited space, I could do them an injustice by discussing them superficially. However, striving to understand the unique contribution of these approaches to strategic corporate communication management is important. I attempt to explain some of the basic ideas behind the general emergent projects relevant to public relations strategy. I start this chapter by explaining the basic principles of the traditional approaches to public relations strategy. I then discuss alternative postmodern ideas and explain how they contribute to emergent views of management philosophies and application. These approaches all accentuate the importance of interaction, relationships, and self-regulation. The final part of the chapter explores the implications of the emergent approaches on strategic public relations.

TRADITIONAL APPROACHES TO STRATEGIC MANAGEMENT AND CORPORATE COMMUNICATION STRATEGY

The traditional ontology of management science relies heavily on strategic planning and strategic thinking. Within this paradigm, the role of management is to set goals and objectives, plan actions, and remove any obstacles that may hinder the achievement of these objectives. This is done in an ordered, controlled fashion, and all conflict is quickly eradicated. All processes are simplified so that the environment can be simplified. As goals and objectives are set, possible outcomes are predicted and alternatives for action are planned. These are communicated throughout the organization. The traditional approach to strategic management describes it as a process of analysis in which the strengths, weaknesses, opportunities, and threats to the organization are used to develop the mission, goals, and objectives of the organization (Harrison, 2003). The management of tactics for plans and programs are short term and adaptive, whereas the management of strategy is continuous, and changes are geared toward broader goals as well as to the vision of the organization.

Structured and planned approaches to strategic management imply fixed patterns, procedures, and positions that influence the way the organization is managed and controlled. As Graetz, Rimmer, Lawrence, and Smith (2002) observe, "For most people, strategy is generally perceived as a plan—a consciously intended course of action that is premeditated and deliberate, with strategies realized as intended" (p. 51). Here, strategy and management are constantly referred to as the ways to provide a framework for planning and decision making that control and manage influences from the environment. Although flexibility is mentioned, it is still within the paradigm of a strong order and firm position.

The planned approach to strategic management is a current overarching paradigm in management literature—especially from the perspective of change and transformation (Genus, 1998; examples can also be seen in Burnes, 1996; Cummings & Worley, 2001; Ghoshal & Bartlett, 2000; Gouillart & Kelly, 1995; Head, 1997; Hill & Jones, 2004; Mintzberg & Quinn, 1996; Sanchez & Aime, 2004; Senior, 1997). With this approach, the importance of strong leadership and strategic management teams is emphasized. This paradigm is tightly linked to strategy and on identifying and managing processes designed to make organizations more successful and competitive (Sanders, 1998). All these processes are focused on providing solutions to help management attain improved productivity and competitive advantage. Strategic planning makes the results tangible, helps control the processes, guides decision making, and provides security around uncertainties.

Current public relations theories that deal with management and corporate communication strategy are much in line with the previously mentioned general strategic management views of structured planning and decision making. Public relations literature portrays a rather traditional view of strategic communication management because emphasis is placed on the planning process of campaigns and communication plans, which, in other words, is a tactical and technical view of the communication management process. The planning process is usually described as well-defined steps or stages that follow one another, comprised broadly of research (formative and environmental scanning), planning (sometimes called the "strategy stage"), implementation (or "tactics stage") and evaluation (Cutlip et al., 1994; Kendall, 1992; Oliver, 2001; Smith, 2002). Steyn and Puth (2000), Grunig and Repper (1992), and White and Dozier (1992) called this process "communication management planning," which is distinct from "corporate communication strategy." One of the leading theorists in current views of corporate communication strategy, Steyn (2000), pointed out that "[W]here strategic thinking determines the strategy (i.e., what the organization should be doing), strategic, long-term and operational planning helps to choose how to get there by programming the strategies, making them operational" (p. 38). Plans should be linked to strategies, but a strategy is the outcome of strategic thinking and has external, long-term focus.

Steyn (2002) described the corporate communication process of strategic thinking as "senior communicators and top managers taking strategic decisions with regard to the identification and management of, and communication with, strategic stakeholders" (p. 126). Furthermore, corporate communication strategy should be viewed on a functional level, where each functional unit of the organization will contribute to the higher-level strategies associated with strategy implementation. Grunig et al. (2002) supported this in pointing out that the Grunig and Repper's model (1992) was developed to adjust to the postmodern view; that is, in which the participation from all management disciplines amalgamates resources to create and implement a strategy.

Again, Steyn and Puth (2000) suggested that the contribution of the corporate communication function should be the provision of information about stakeholder interests through research. Proposed here was a model for the development of a corporate communication strategy in which a series of steps provides guidelines to follow. The same basic model was also proposed by Ferguson (1999), and started with an analysis of the internal environment of the organization in terms of the mission, culture, vision, and the like. The most important step is to establish the organizational goals and objectives, because the communication strategy should support and flow from these macrolevels. The next step is the identification of the strategic stakeholders and publics of the organization through an environmental analysis (Ferguson, 1999; Grunig & Repper, 1992; Grunig et al., 2002; Smith, 2002; Steyn & Puth, 2000). This is followed by the "issues stage," in which problems are identified that could have an impact on the organization or the stakeholders. The issue stage would then lead to the setting of communication strategies, goals, and objectives out of which communication plans are developed. All of these newer and sophisticated approaches to strategic communication management emphasize the importance of relationships as the core principle around which these strategies have to operate.

Grunig, Grunig, and Ehling (1992) referred to the terms *manage* and *strategy* as "thinking ahead or planning rather than manipulation and control" (p. 123). Strategic management is a symmetrical process in which the organization considers its strategic interest, and changes its behavior in order to accommodate stakeholders in its environment.

Grunig et al. (1992) further described it as "an approach, design, scheme, or system" (p. 123). This view of strategic management, which has only just emerged in the past 2 decades together with postmodern approaches to strategic management, coincides with the strategic management perspective of the organization as a network of relationships with stakeholders (Harrison, 2003; Steyn & Puth, 2000).

I have a few concerns with these perspectives, and I address them with reference to the postmodern approaches, namely, the chaos and complexity applications to strategic communication management. Some of these problems relate to the fact that the previously cited models still follow deterministic, logical, causal, linear steps and processes. The improved model by Grunig & Repper (L. A. Grunig et al., 2002) suggests a more interactive and cyclical approach, but the "three stages" still emphasize chronological inputs and consequences. The systems theory is used often as a basic approach on which public relations efforts and strategies are based (Angelopulo, 1994; L. A. Grunig et al., 2002; Steyn, De Beer, Steyn, & Schreiner, 2004). Stacey (2003) explained that a system within this paradigm is a spatial notion of "inside" and "outside" with borders, hierarchical levels, and rationalist causality. In contrast, chaos and complexity theories suggest that systems are temporal notions of process based on paradoxical causality in perpetual transformation.

A further issue that I wish to address is top management strategic decision making, which suggests a top-down approach. That is, although the necessity of the corporate communication function as part of the dominant coalition is emphasized throughout (Grunig et al., 2002), I question the initial assumption that strategy lies with the upper levels in the organization. If communication managers then become part of the decision-making process, they become part of the problem. As McKie (2001) aptly asked, "Whose strategy is being planned? Is it the strategy of the board of directors, the chief executive officer, the key stakeholders, or the customers? And the level of participation in the production of strategy arises as well" (p. 77). I also question whether relationships can be managed by formulating corporate communication strategies. This statement and the related questions warrant further explanation. Therefore, I discuss the basic principles of relevant postmodern approaches that form the conceptual framework and guiding paradigm of my approach to strategic relationship management.

EMERGENT APPROACHES TO STRATEGY AND MANAGEMENT

Modernist approaches seem to have ceased to contribute to the development of strategic management theory, and postmodernism has stripped modernist concepts of its rational objectivity (Chia, 1995; Jackson &

Carter, 1992). From a management perspective, postmodernism has emerged out of postindustrialism as a way to question and criticize the relevance of business thinking during the Industrial Age (Sherman & Schultz, 1998). The whole paradigm has shifted from a mechanistic view to a more organic worldview of science, management, and basic thinking methodologies. Organizations are now seen as organisms submitting to natural laws of evolution, transformation, and process. Kreiner (1992), for instance, noted that in postmodernism the frames of reference of management and organizational theory is blurred, because of the improbability to identifying a common theoretical paradigm. In other words, it is difficult to distinguish basic assumptions with well-defined methodological borders. The use of scientific methods to create and understand organizational epistemology is ignored to the extent that even popular literature on organizational experience has been accepted as valid depictions of reality.

Chaos theory and, to a greater extent, complexity theory are relevant postmodern approaches that contribute to emergent views of management philosophies and applications. They both accentuate the importance of interaction, relationships, and self-regulation—concepts that are explored in more depth in this discussion relevant to communication management and strategic management in organizations.

Postmodernism

Postmodernism spreads over different fields of study and domains and offers a reconceptualization of how we view the world around us (Chia, 1995; Cova, 1996). Postmodernism underwrites a worldview that relies on constructivism, in which knowledge is created through the process of interaction, making communication central to the social construction of truth and reality (Littlejohn, 1992). Although there can be no unified postmodern theory or collective set of approaches to mark postmodernism (Kilduff & Mehra, 1997), it is possible to say that there are countervailing trends of postmodernism. The more academic definition of postmodernism is "incredulity towards meta-narratives" (Cilliers, 1998, p. 114), which in comparison to modernism implies an appeal to metanarratives. In organizational terms, this suggests that an organization ought to challenge what it traditionally holds as sacrosanct, such as its culture, legends, strategic intent, how it creates meaning—its metanarratives (Kreiner, 1992; Sherman & Schultz, 1998).

Postmodernism is considered a response to the failure or natural consequence of the shortcomings of modernism, which implies an underlying question about the rationality of the scientific approach to strategic management theory (Chia, 1995; Cova, 1996; Jackson & Carter, 1992). Singh and Singh (2002) went as far as suggesting that postmodern approaches provide explanations of why strategic planning will not work, and that these approaches throw strategy formulation out the window. Cova (1996) described postmodernism as the integration of new models into a "generic perspective on life and human condition" (p. 15) and an epochal swing from modernity, breaking free from functionality and rational thinking. These authors stated that postmodernism rejects epistemological postulations, contends methodologies, refutes accepted theories, and contrasts the modernist realities in almost every sense.

It is important to point out nevertheless that postmodernism is inexplicably connected to modernism in that postmodernism is the modern in an embryonic state. It can only be articulated through the modern, whereas the modern can only be expressed as a passing image of the postmodern (Chia, 1995; Cilliers, 1998; Cova, 1996). This also applies to strategic management theory, so the comments on the applications of chaos and complexity to strategic corporate communication expressed in this chapter should be seen against the background of modernist strategic planning. For this reason, I do not argue to discard strategic planning altogether. Instead, I appeal for it to be less positivistic, controlled, linear, and planned; that is, for it to be more flexible, emotional, participative, and understanding.

Chaos and complexity theories can both be described as postmodern approaches. According to Cilliers (1998), postmodernism has an implicit sensitivity to complexity, and acknowledges the importance of philosophical perspectives such as self-organization and connectionism, which are important factors influencing the way in which chaos and complexity theories are approached. These approaches all accentuate the importance of interaction, relationships, and self-regulation. More specific similarities between postmodernism and the chaos and complexity theories include: The view of the organization is organic and flexible; structure and linearity are considered impossible because of the unpredictability of the environment; diversity is a common feature and conformity is criticized; change and transformation are inevitable and uncontrolled; relationships are essential and the crux of all interactions; conflict is natural and necessary, and is seen as growth and creativity; perspectives, ideas, and views are contradictory and irrational; knowledge is a process of learning—it is not linear, but rather is borne out of discourse and debate; systems should not regulate people or values; and the concepts of self-regulation through interaction and relationships apply.

Paradoxes and discourses characterize postmodern approaches, and complex relationships and networks interlink in postmodern organizations and structures (Cova, 1996; Holtzhausen, 2000). Meaning is created through constant interaction, participation, change, and self-organizing growth. Boundaries are challenged, and there are no structures or hierarchies. Diversity brings about creative information processes that become knowledge. Although there are differences between postmodernism, chaos and complexity theories, they share the same emphasis on participation and relationships through connectionism (Ströh, 2004). These approaches all justify an ontology of interactions and non-linear self-organization.

Complexity and Chaos Theories—Connectionism, Self-organization, Strange Attractors, and Participation

Complexity refers to the fact that in a system "there are more possibilities than can be actualized" (Luhmann, 1985, p. 25). The distinction between "complicated" and "complex," according to Cilliers (1998) is this: In a complicated system, the components (e.g., computers and jets) can be clearly identified; in a complex system, the interaction among the components of a system, and among systems and the environment, are so intricate that it is impossible to completely understand the system simply by studying its components. Some examples of complex systems are societies, the brain, organizations, and language (Laszlo & Laugel, 2000). A further important characteristic that makes these systems complex is that their relationships and interactions shift, change, and transform, which make them even more difficult to study. As Cilliers (1998) pointed out, "A complex system is not constituted merely by the sum of its components, but also by the intricate relationships between these components" (p. 2). It is not merely a linguistic occurrence—that is, in the way we describe systems—that make them simple or complex; rather, that complexity results because of the interactions and connections among subsystems.

According to Cilliers (1998), the interaction of all the entities of a complex system, the role of the relationships formed, and the creation of information and knowledge through these interactions form the basis of the complexity approach. In societal terms, this implies that a person or groups of people derive meaning from the relationships they have with other individuals or groups in their environment (Stacey, 2003).

Structure, in complexity terms, relates to the internal device developed by a system to receive, encode, change, and store information, while the system reacts to such information through some form of output. Cilliers (1998) maintained that these internal devices can transform and evolve without the interference of any external creator or some centralized form of internal control. Furthermore, a system will develop a self-organizing process as a result of complex interaction among the environment, the current state of the system, and the history of the system. Cilliers (1998) noted that this self-organization process refers to a "spontaneous emergence of order and structure" (p. 89), and is "a property of complex systems which enables them to develop or change internal structure spontaneously and adaptively in order to cope with, or manipulate, their environment" (p. 90). Stacey (2003) added to this by describing self-organization as the process when evolution happens out of selection through dialectic forces of competition and co-operation. The overall behavior of the system is thus paradoxical.

Some attributes of self-organizing systems relevant to this discussion are as follows (Cilliers, 1998): Structure of a system is the result of interaction between the system and the environment, not of a predetermined design, plan, or external conditions; a complex system can adapt in a flexible way to unpredictable changes in the environment; self-organization is not caused by linear processes of feedback or control, but rather involves higher-order, nonlinear processes; and because of the self-organization process not being guided or regulated by prespecified goals, one cannot talk about a "function" of a system. A system's function can only be described in terms of the context within which it exists—self-organizing systems cannot be reduced to simple levels or units, because all the levels are intertwined.

Because organizations characteristically resemble the preconditions for self-organization in complex systems, it can be derived that self-organization also occurs in organizations and between organizations and its different stakeholders in macrosocietal systems. The implications of the process of self-organization on organizational ethics directly affect public relations. Ethics is described as "normative science of human conduct" (Beck, 1975, p. 563) and ethical conduct is described as wisdom, virtuous character, and goodwill (Griffin, 2002; Shaw, 1999). However, Cilliers (1998) suggested that it is not merely a "nicety" to have values in a system, but that they are essential for the survival and growth of a system. A flexible system increases its survival by decentralizing control, and self-organizes in order to adjust to changes in the environment. It is reasonable to speculate teleologically that the consequences of unethical behavior of a system might ultimately lead to its collapse. From a public relations perspective, ethical behavior is advocating the building and maintenance of healthy relationships within and outside organizations, and ultimately working toward harmony in society (Seib & Fitzpatrick, 1995).

The chaos and complexity approaches described and followed in this chapter are similar to the complex responsive processes of Stacey (2003), who suggested an alternative to the systems perspective used to understand strategy and organizational change. Stacey (2003) warned that many theorists who apply chaos and complexity theories do it from a systematic and cognitivist psychological perspective, and in so doing lose the valuable insights that these two perspectives may offer. He argued that many theorists apply these approaches from a static systems thinking paradigm embedded in cybernetics. Within this paradigm, organizations are approached from the perspective of powerful autonomous individuals who become external observers during change. System theorists often apply the mathematical and modeling techniques derived from the natural sciences. These techniques enable forecasting models and provide simple rules taken from living systems in nature, to conform and submit to harmonious wholes.

Such approaches, Stacey (2003) argued, alienate people because they do not feel that they are part of a larger whole and therefore have no influence on outcomes. In other words, they do not take responsibilities for their actions. When a small group of powerful people claim to predict the behavioral outcomes of an organization, they are actually trying to manipulate and control. According to Stacey (2003), organizations are not living systems, but rather are processes of communication and joint action. In this sense, organizations are complex responsive processes of relating. The key concepts of these complex responsive processes are communication, relationships, and the processes (as apposed to systems) that maintain the communication and relationships.

A relevant characteristic of the chaos approach to complex responsive processes is what is called a *strange attractor*. This is a deep structure within any system that has a natural order behind the seeming disorder, and this order is taken from an attractor that traces a path in a regular pattern (Evans, 1996). According to Murphy (1996), "An attractor is an organizing principle, an inherent shape or state of affairs to which a phenomenon will always tend to return as it evolves, no matter how random each single moment may seem" (p. 98). Chaos systems are contained within a shape with a strange attractor holding it together (Wheatley, 1994). Briggs and Peat (1989) referred to systems being constantly pulled apart and iterated toward change, transformation, and disintegration, while at the same time some magnetic powers draw these systems into order and shapes so that "eventually all orderly systems will feel the wild, seductive pull of the strange chaotic attractor" (p. 77).

Both chaos and complexity theories refer to relationships between different elements in complex adaptable processes as the strange attractors that hold them together (Stacey, 2003). It is also these strange attractors that guide the self organization of a complex responsive process.

IMPLICATIONS OF THE EMERGENT APPROACHES ON RELATIONSHIPS AND PARTICIPATION OF CORPORATE COMMUNICATION STRATEGY

In all of the models mentioned in the first part of this chapter, the emphasis is still on communication management and communication strategy, and not on the management of relationships, as is seen here in Steyn and Bütschi's (2003) definition of public relations strategy:

> Public Relations strategy provides the focus and direction for an organization's communication with its stakeholders, determining what should be communicated to assist in achieving organizational goals. These core messages are derived by identifying the organization's key strategic issues (including social, political and ethical issues) and determining their impact on the stakeholders/other interest groups in society. Thereafter, determining what should be communicated internally and/or externally to solve the problem or capitalize on the opportunity presented by the issue. (p. 4)

This definition demonstrates clearly that the focus is not on relationships or on the process of relationships, but rather on communication, particularly with a major focus on determining what should be communicated, placing the control in the hands of the communication manager in terms of the content of the message. The control within this view of communication is not totally symmetrical or participative, with reference to the stakeholders at whom the communication is aimed. There is no implication of participation in the formation of the messages, or much mention of the application of relationship management in order to achieve strategic goals. One could compare the involvement and participation raised by Steyn and Puth's (2000) model to the involvement principle in the critical theory of Deetz (Griffin, 2003), in which stakeholders are involved by making themselves heard, but they do not have any true participation in the decision-making processes. Admittedly, Steyn and Puth (2000) did argue for more participation in which:

> [R]esearch must shift from explaining the organization's position or point of view, to listening with a view to taking different actions. Create forums for stakeholders to share expectations, invite them to comment, to help create values and to take part in auditing to see how the organization adheres to its policies and values. (p. 197)

Yet, the approach is about agreement and the resolution of conflicts, and the relationship is still controlled by the strategic managers of the organizations. The public relations manager is prompted to improve research and strategic skills in order to become part of top management and be allowed into the boardroom—much the same as one of the suggestions from the findings of the Excellence Study (Grunig et al., 2002). In contrast, critical postmodern approaches call for ongoing negotiations (Deetz, 1995), that is, for the public relations managers to be activists and not conform to management principles and power practices (Holtzhausen & Voto, 2002).

For true participation to take place, all decision-making processes should be codetermined by all being influenced and by a decision outcome. The only way for decision outcomes to be ethical and moral is by equable participation (Deetz, 1995). Answers lie in ongoing negotiation processes, not in the outcome of negotiations (i.e., especially if the negotiation processes are governed by strategy put together by powerful dominant groups).

The problem with most of these corporate communication, or public relations strategies, is the lack of emphasis on participation and relationships. Many have processes of two-way communication and involvement, but whether they incorporate true participation, as put forward by the critical theories (postmodernism, chaos, and complexity) is to be questioned. The importance of involvement or participation of publics is mentioned but not discussed in detail, and without clear guidelines of how this would be included in the strategic processes proposed (Steyn, 2002; Steyn & Puth, 2000). Many communication managers are beginning to understand the idea of attending to stakeholder needs and building relationships with them, but few recognize the fundamental difference between being involved and being given a voice (Deetz, 2001). Loyalty and commitment is encouraged through involving stakeholders, and most strategic communication managers are co-opted into top management structures to form relationships that decrease resistance and resolve conflict. However, communication managers should rather play the role of organizational activist (Holtzhausen & Voto, 2002), in which collaborative decision making results from genuine decisional inputs from stakeholders. In order to improve the positions of management, stakeholders, and the environment, communication managers ought to take the role of relationship managers by seeking alternative viewpoints to debate, providing forums for those conflicts, and contributing to meaning making through continuous negotiations.

Publics need to become part of the organization and the creation of meaning through two way symmetrical communication and participation. They do not merely want to be identified, described, researched, and communicated to (as suggested by most models of strategic corporate communication management); instead, they want to be part of strategy formulation. Research findings show that a higher degree of participation in organizations will lead to significantly more positive overall relationships between an organization and its internal publics, than with lower degrees of participation and planned approaches to strategic management and change (Ströh, 2002). Participation also increases work satisfaction and employee productivity (Pfeffer, 1995). Again, this participation does not merely suggest interaction (communication) with stakeholders, but rather participation (negotiation, discourse) by all stakeholders in the creation of the strategic process itself—a bottom-up approach to strategic management. Steyn (2000) alluded to this notion when she referred to participation of and partnering with stakeholders of an organization, although the rhetoric used in her suggestions still indicate traditional management ontology—such as the mention of "appointment to board of directors," "management," "control," and "included in major decisions"—which implies that the processes are still managed and manipulated by the organization. A postmodern perspective would suggest taking a step back, to where diverse stakeholders are part of a network of relationships, and decisions resolve and flow naturally out of discourse and constant change. The emphasis is on the relationships, not on the decision-making processes. If the relationships are strong, the outcomes of decisions ought not matter because whatever they are, their consequences should work out to the benefit of the organization in the long run.

Corporate Communication Strategy—an Alternative?

Relationships have previously been studied from the systems theory perspective (Angelopulo, 1994; Broom, Casey, & Ritchey, 2000; Grunig & Hunt, 1984; Grunig et al., 2002; Steyn & Puth, 2000), in which mutually influential interactions exist between an organization and other systems in the environment because of the interdependence of subsystems. This is a clear indication of the modernist perspectives to many of the current theories and approaches to strategic communication management and public relations. Spicer (1997) is one of many theorists who have criticized the systems approach, particularly in terms of the lack of recognition of the power differences between subsystems. Furthermore, the systems theory has an inherent bias toward management, and that asymmetry seeks consensus, custom, and conformity to culture. In this respect, Spicer (1997) predicted that as the field of public relations matures, emphasis will shift beyond the organizational and managerial bias toward the societal role and a broader interconnectedness with the environment.

This chapter aims to contribute to the strategic managerial approach of public relations on a broader sphere, from a *process* perspective. Within the paradigm of complex responsive processes, practitioners do not set out strategies and agendas beforehand, but instead become participants in self-organized ongoing processes of strategic thinking. They do not play the role of facilitators who take notes, summarize, structure, or call for feedback, but rather listen, guide articulation, link themes, reflect, and thus become part of the narrative and conversation of the organization. As Stacey (2003) envisioned:

> It is these shifts in communicative patterning that constitute organizational change. This means that unlike the systems practitioner, the practitioner from a complex responsive processes perspective is not concerned with any whole or system at all but with the detail of the local interactions between people in the living present. (p. 403)

One of the problems with the approach that excellent public relations should be part of strategic decision making is that the emphasis is on the communication manager becoming part of the top management function in order to have decision-making and influencing powers in strategy (Grunig et al., 2002; Steyn & Puth, 2000). The main issue lies with the power differences between the then dominant coalition, of which the public relations practitioner is a part of, and the internal and external publics of the organization.

Another problem with the formulation of corporate communication strategies is the question of whether relationships can be managed this way. Postmodern theorists and corporate communication managers are starting to move away from models of strategic planning, objective setting, and positivistic measurement. New approaches support environmental scanning as an important starting point to identifying stakeholders who might be affected by organizational actions. Conflict management, discourse, and participation are emphasized. However, while an organization's success within the modernist paradigm depends on its ability to process information of appropriate richness, reduce uncertainty, and clarify ambiguity (Spicer, 1997), emergent approaches focus attention on anxiety, diversity, conflict, unpredictability, and paradox (Stacey, 2003). In highly complex environments and processes with emergent long-term outcomes, the control and linearity associated with strategic management—as suggested by theorists such as Steyn and Puth (2000), Harrison (2003), Smith (2002), and Ferguson (1999)—are impossible. Postmodern approaches support contradiction, ambiguity, and uncertainty (Stacey, 2003). In this sense, managers ought to learn, for example, how to take action while experiencing the anxiety of unpredictability, and use the anxiety as energy for creativity.

Stacey (2003) further suggested that complex interactions between people and groups make it impossible for strategic processes to be governed by top management through designed procedure. Interestingly, Stacey also made it clear that it is not that management cannot, or should not, make decisions or choices, but rather that strategy should be an emerging process of relationship building. That is, "Strategic management is the process of actively participating in the conversations around important emerging issues. Strategic direction is not set in advance but understood in hindsight as it is emerging or after it has emerged" (Stacey, 2003, p. 423).

Measuring as Part of Strategy

McKie (2001) postulated that public relations is too concerned with quantitative measuring and the need to demonstrate measurable goals and objectives. In the postmodern era, true long-term value for an organization is in focusing on the process of relationship building rather than on the outcomes of those relationships (Sheth & Parvatiyar, 1995). As is revealed in relationship marketing, the shift in focus—that is, from outcomes of an exchange (transaction) to process of relationship engagement and enhancement—means that boundaries in organizations are broken down and the roles of the marketing actors are enmeshed and blurred. These co-operative relationships eventually have little to do with the exchange of products, services, or even values, but instead become "a process of value creation through co-operative and collaborative effort" (Sheth & Parvatiyar, 1995, p. 414).

As Sheth and Parvatiyar (1995) noted, this is clearly an example of an evolution toward a postmodern approach. It would therefore be to the benefit of the field of public relations to shift the focus from measuring outputs (or even behavioral outcomes) to the relationship processes; that is, of engagement and enrichment through constant dialogue, debate, and discourse. This is the making of true values, not only for the organization, but also its environment and, ultimately, society as a whole. The well-known business philosopher Charles Handy (2002) asserted that running an organization should be a moral issue. This is because many organizations have lost the trust of their stakeholders because the stakeholders suspect that corporations serve only themselves. By focusing too much on measurable outcomes, and too little on building democratic proceses and healthy two-way relationships could also cost an organization dearly. In this sense, an organization becomes good by doing good (Ledingham, 2003; Shaw, 1999).

Measurement, from the emergent perspective, focuses on qualitative methodologies, participative action research, and ethnographic research. Organizations can maintain strong relationships with stakeholders by conducting action research with full participation of all involved, constantly sharing open and honest information, and getting involved in discussions and discourse regarding shared interests. The answer is not to be fixated on measurement, but rather to be more flexible in the acceptance of less positivistic approaches, and to use participative research to achieve a deeper understanding of contexts and behavior.

Specifically, participatory action research methodologies will be much better suited to further research on relationship management within complex environments. Participatory action research (PAR) involves the participants to the extent that these participants help to set the research agenda, participate in data gathering and processing, and share in decisions about the use of outcomes (Babbie & Mouton, 2001). In other words, participants share ownership of the total strategic and research process. Furthermore, PAR has a strong emphasis on power sharing between the researcher and the researched. Action research can thus become a valuable tool in creating strategy. As Babbie and Mouton (2001) pointed out, "PAR aims towards social change or transformation" (p. 64); that is, where actions toward the upliftment and empowerment of people are the outcomes.

Scenario Planning

No business can expect to survive if it negatively affects any significant group of people or interest. Stakeholders provide an organization with a "license to operate," and they only truly benefit if the organizational goals are devoid of harm through pollution or unwelcome cultural influences, reduction of risk, or creation of offsetting benefits (Post, Preston, & Sachs, 2002). Although this seems obvious, most organizations still place a large emphasis on ensuring investor and share-owner gain, and bottom-line results. However, as environments become more turbulent, it becomes increasingly difficult to plan for specific outcomes, as Sherman and Schultz (1998) observed: "Planning doesn't work well in relation to unanticipated behaviors because it is essentially linear" (p. 22).

The new sciences emphasize limitless possibilities and the "process of everlasting becoming" (Sherman & Schultz, 1998, p. 23), thus encouraging the practice of scenario planning and consideration of all possibilities for outcomes. Similarly, Costin (1998, p. xii) suggested that a differentiation of scenarios may be a solution to the debates about normative and descriptive approaches to strategy. In other words, whether a strategy should be analytical, structured, planned, or rational—or whether it should be intuitive, unplanned, chaotic, or flexible—ought to be determined by various factors appropriate to the strategic scenarios. Factors such as the number of actors involved, the information available, or the timing of decision making may all have various implications and effects. In order to consider all possibilities, it is necessary to have as much information from the environment as possible. Scenario planning has become highly regarded in strategic management thinking because it provides solutions "far beyond the traditional financial and forecast-based planning approaches" (Graetz et al., 2002). Scenario planning has become a communication tool for managers in aiding their decision making during chaotic times of high uncertainty and complexity (Graetz et al., 2002; Ströh & Jaatinen, 2001). It is thinking outside the box, challenging the status quo, and stimulating lateral thinking. Furthermore, scenario planning is about finding a balance between overpredicting the outcomes of strategic thinking and change, and falling over the edge of chaos into total disintegration.

CONCLUSION

Traditional and conventional strategic management approaches are linear in methodology, but the unpredictability of the business environment is so acute that managers are unable to control the implementation of strategies and strategic plans. Long-term planning, therefore, becomes impractical and impossible (Singh & Singh, 2002). As the chaos and complexity approaches demonstrate, strategic management should be more about facilitation than management, which means that corporate communication managers should be more concerned with the building of relationships with stakeholders through the facilitation of participation than with strategic planning and strategic management. Therefore, the role of the communication manager should not be one of facilitator between management and stakeholders, or internal problem solver, or for that matter being part of top management. Instead, it should be one of organizational activist (Holtzhausen, 2000)—a fourth role to be added to the strategist, manager, or technician roles, as identified by Steyn (2003). Furthermore, they should be involved with the facilitation of conflicts rather than the resolution of conflicts, thereby instigating dynamic instability. Communication managers should create and maintain channels for discourse by opening all information systems to allow self-regulation of communication. They should not seek unanimous control and equality, but rather should work toward allowing for diversity and different voices in order to keep the system creative and on the edge of chaos. Instead of measuring, they should try to understand the complexity of the environment and the interaction of all the different components of the organization by being involved in the day-to-day conversations and arguments in the organization.

If we think about the concept of relationship, and return to some of the basic relational theories, we find some alternatives to linear strategic management processes. People are in relationships because they have a need to share and create something better for themselves than what they could accomplish on their own. Handy (2002) referred to the reason for the existence of an organization as not being simply for profit. Similarly, Dave Packard (cited in Handy, 2002) maintained that an organization is a group of people who get together "to accomplish something collectively that they could not accomplish separately—they make a contribution to society, a phrase which sounds trite but is fundamental" (cited in Handy, 2002, p. 36). More important still is that people enter into relationships without planned strategies of how they are going to achieve success in those relationships. Healthy relationships tend to be self-organizing. They exist when a new entity is formed out of the togetherness of individuals, and the relationship becomes more important than these individual units.

Grunig and Huang (2000) referred to Ferguson's focus on the relationships in public relations, in which the emphasis is not on the organization nor the public, but instead on the relationship between them, which amounts to a kind of third party or entity in the relationship that takes a higher priority than do the two individual parties. If an organization can put the relationships with stakeholders first rather than focusing on its own bottom line, the relationship will give back a lot more, and the bottom line will look after itself. In essence, respect for the environment and for the stakeholders creates exponential returns.

Another element of good interpersonal relationships from which organizations can learn is the principle of trust, which develops out of moral and ethical behavior between two parties. In this sense, running an organization is about ethics (Handy, 2002; Shaw, 1999). Organizations can have healthy relationships by being good citizens and by leading in areas such as "environmental and social sustainability" (Handy, 2002, p. 53). We do not constantly measure or plan our personal relationships, yet they happen and go well if we are good partners in those relationships. If we are ethical and moral, and if we share the same visions and values, we become part of growing, loving, and trusting relationships. As Handy (2002) consoled, if we apply this concept to organizations, "[D]oing good does not necessarily rule out making a reasonable profit" (p. 55).

As mentioned before, my idea is not to reject linear and logical strategic methodologies. Neither do I propose that practitioners should not strive to be part of the top management structures of the organization. That would not be acceptable within most current organizational structures, because public relations departments seem to still be battling to justify and measure their contribution to the bottom line. I am merely suggesting that there are different worldviews to consider that could be complementary and enhance strategic thinking. The challenge for scholars and practitioners will be to research and experiment with these somewhat esoteric ideas and find the practical value in them. I suggest that action research could be the most relevant methodology to explore the strategic contribution of relationship management. One of the greatest tests would be to find organizations that will be open-minded enough to try out these ideas and learn through the process.

The postmodern ontology proposed in this chapter recognizes that an organization is not a unit of analysis, physical object, or resource, but instead consists of complex relationships among the entities that make up the organization. Postmodern communication management therefore ought to play an important role in empowering marginalized groups through participation. Furthermore, it ought to create dialogue and recognize differences and dissension between the organization and its publics. I therefore argue for a more participative approach with high ethical and moral meaning creation through action science and research, rather than the emphasis on structured approaches practiced by current corporate communication scholars and practitioners. This participative and ethical approach will ensure a positive reputation for the organization through socially responsible strategy making, which will have relational influences on the larger societal community structure.

REFERENCES

Angelopulo, G. (1994). A systems approach to public relations. In B. Lubbe & G. Puth (Eds.), *Public relations in South Africa: A management reader* (pp. 40–57). Durban, South Africa: Butterworths.

Babbie, E., & Mouton, J. (2001). *The practice of social research*. Cape Town, South Africa: Oxford University Press.

Beck, R. N. (1975). *Perspectives in philosophy: A book of readings*. New York: Holt, Rinehart & Winston.

Briggs, J., & Peat, D. F. (1989). *Turbulent mirror: An illustrated guide to chaos theory and the science of wholeness*. New York: Harper & Row.

Broom, G. M., Casey, S., & Ritchey, J. (1997). Toward a concept and theory of organization–public relationships. *Journal of Public Relations Research, 9*(2), 83–98.

Broom, G. M., Casey, S., & Ritchey, J. (2000). Concept and theory of organization–public relationships. In J. A. Ledingham & S. D. Bruning (Eds.), *Public relations as relationship management: A relational approach to the study and practice of public relations* (pp. 3–22). Mahwah, NJ: Lawrence Erlbaum Associates.

Burnes, B. (1996). *Managing change: A strategic approach to organizational dynamics*. London: Pitman.

Bütschi, G. (2004). *Digital management software solutions*. Retrieved December 21, 2004, from http://www.digitalmgmt.com

Chia, R. (1995). From modern to postmodern organizational analysis. *Organizational Studies, 16*(4), 579–605.

Cilliers, P. (1998). *Complexity and postmodernism: Understanding complex systems*. London: Routledge.

Costin, H. (Ed.). (1998). *Readings in strategy and strategic planning*. Orlando, FL: Dryden.

Cova, B. (1996). The postmodern explained to managers: Implications for marketing. *Business Horizons, 39*(6), 15–23.

Cummings, T. G., & Worley, C. G. (2001). *Organization development and change* (7th ed.). Mason, OH: South-Western.

Cutlip, S. M., Center, A. H., & Broom, G. M. (1994). *Effective public relations* (7th ed.). Englewood Cliffs, NJ: Prentice-Hall.

D'Aprix, R. (1996). *Communicating for change*. San Francisco: Jossey-Bass.

Deetz, S. (1995). *Transforming communication, transforming business: Building responsive and responsible workplaces*. Cresskill, NJ: Hampton.

Deetz, S. (2001). Conceptual foundations. In F. M. Jablin & L. L. Putnam (Eds.), *The new handbook of organizational communication: Advances in theory, research, and methods* (pp. 3–46). Thousand Oaks, CA: Sage.

Evans, K. G. (1996). Chaos as opportunity: Grounding a positive vision of management and society in the new physics. *Public Administration Review, 56*(5), 491–494.

Ferguson, S. D. (1999). *Communication planning: An integrated approach.* London: Sage.

Genus, A. (1998). *The management of change: Perspectives and practice.* London: International Thomson Business Press.

Ghoshal, S., & Bartlett, C. A. (2000). Rebuilding behavioural context: A blueprint for corporate renewal. In M. Beer & N. Nohria (Eds.), *Breaking the code of change* (pp. 195–222). Cambridge, MA: Harvard Business School Press.

Gouillart, F. J., & Kelly, J. N. (1995). *Transforming the organization.* New York: McGraw-Hill.

Graetz, F., Rimmer, M., Lawrence, A., & Smith, A. (2002). *Managing organisational change.* Milton, Australia: Wiley.

Grunig, J. E., Grunig, L. A., & Ehling, W. P. (1992). What is an effective organization? In J. E. Grunig (Ed.), *Excellence in public relations and communication management* (pp. 65–90). Hillsdale, NJ: Lawrence Erlbaum Associates.

Grunig, J. E., & Huang, Y. (2000). From organization effectiveness to relationship indicators: Antecedents of relationships, public relations strategies, and relationship outcomes. In J. A. Ledingham & S. D. Brunig (Eds.), *Public relations as relationship management: A relational approach to the study and practice of public relations* (pp. 23–53). Mahwah, NJ: Lawrence Erlbaum Associates.

Grunig, J. E., & Hunt, T. (1984). *Managing public relations.* New York: Holt, Rinehart and Winston.

Grunig, J. E., & Repper, F. C. (1992). Strategic management, publics, and issues. In J. E. Grunig (Ed.), *Excellence in public relations and communication management* (pp. 117–157). Hillsdale, NJ: Lawrence Erlbaum Associates.

Grunig, L. A., Grunig, J. E., & Dozier, D. M. (2002). *Excellent public relations and effective organizations: The study of communication management in three countries.* Mahwah, NJ: Lawrence Erlbaum Associates.

Handy, C. (2002). What's a business for? *Harvard Business Review, 80,* 49.

Harrison, J. S. (2003). *Strategic management of resources and relationships.* New York: Wiley.

Head, C. W. (1997). *Beyond corporate transformation: A whole systems approach to creating and sustaining high performance.* Portland, OR: Productivity Press.

Hill, C. W. L., & Jones, G. R. (2004). *Strategic management theory: An integrated approach.* Boston: Houghton Mifflin.

Holtzhausen, D. R. (2000). Postmodern values in public relations. *Journal of Public Relations Research, 12*(1), 93–114.

Holtzhausen, D. R., & Voto, R. (2002). Resistance from the margins: The postmodern public relations practitioner as organizational activist. *Journal of Public Relations Research, 14*(1), 57–85.

Jackson, N., & Carter, P. (1992). Postmodern management: Past-perfect or future-imperfect? *International Studies of Management and Organizational Studies, 22*(3), 11–17.

Kendall, R. (1992). *Public relations campaign strategies.* New York: HarperCollins.

Kilduff, M., & Mehra, A. (1997). Postmodernism and organizational research. *Academy of Management Review, 22*(2), 453–241.

Kreiner, K. (1992). The postmodern epoch of organization theory. *International Studies of Management and Organizational Studies, 22*(2), 37–43.

Laszlo, C., & Laugel, J. (2000). *Large-scale organizational change: An executive's guide*. Woburn, MA: Butterworth-Heinemann.

Ledingham, J. A. (2003). Explicating relationship management as a general theory of public relations. *Journal of Public Relations Research, 15*(2), 181–198.

Littlejohn, S. W. (1992). *Theories of human communication* (4th ed.). Belmont, CA: Wadsworth.

Luhmann, N. (1985). *A sociological theory of law*. London: Routledge & Kegan Paul.

McKie, D. (2001). Updating public relations: "New science," research paradigms, and uneven developments. In R. L. Heath (Ed.), *Handbook of public relations* (pp. 75–91). Thousand Oaks, CA: Sage.

Mintzberg, H., & Quinn, J. B. (1996). *The strategy process: Concepts, contexts and cases*. Englewood Cliffs, NJ: Prentice-Hall.

Murphy, P. (1996). Chaos theory as a model for managing issues and crises. *Public Relations Review, 22*(2), 95–113.

Oliver, S. (2001). *Public relations strategy*. London: Kogan Page.

Pfeffer, J. (1995, February). Producing sustainable competitive advantage through the effective management of people. *Academy of Management Executive, 9*(1), 55–69.

Post, J. E., Preston, L. E., & Sachs, S. (2002). *Redefining the corporation: Stakeholder management and organizational wealth*. Stanford, CA: Stanford University Press.

Sanchez, R., & Aime, H. (2004). *The new strategic management*. New York: Wiley.

Sanders, I. T. (1998). *Strategic thinking and the new science*. New York: Free Press.

Seib, P., & Fitzpatrick, K. (1995). *Public relations ethics*. Fort Worth, TX: Harcourt Brace College Publishers.

Senior, B. (1997). *Organizational change*. London: Pitman.

Shaw, W. H. (1999). *Business ethics*. Belmont, CA: Wadsworth.

Sherman, H., & Schultz, R. (1998). *Open boundaries: Creating business innovation through complexity*. Reading, MA: Perseus.

Sheth, J. N., & Parvatiyar, A. (1995). The evolution of relationship marketing. *International Business Review, 4*(4), 397–418.

Singh, H., & Singh, A. (2002). Principles of complexity and chaos theory in project execution: A new approach to management. *Cost Engineering, 44*(12), 23–28.

Smith, R. D. (2002). *Strategic planning for public relations*. Mahwah, NJ: Lawrence Erlbaum Associates.

Spicer, C. (1997). *Organizational public relations: A political perspective*. Mahwah, NJ: Lawrence Erlbaum Associates.

Stacey, R. D. (2003). *Strategic management and organisational dynamics: The challenge of complexity*. Harlow, England: Prentice-Hall.

Steyn, B. (2002). *From "strategy" to "corporate communication strategy": A conceptualisation*. Paper presented at the conference on the Status of Public Relations Knowledge in Europe and Around the World, Bled, Slovenia.

Steyn, B. (2003). *A conceptualisation and empirical verification of the "Strategist," (redefined) "manager" and "technician" roles of public relations*. Paper presented at the 10th International PR Research Symposium, Lake Bled, Slovenia.

Steyn, B., & Bütschi, G. (2003). *Reflective public relations: A commentary on conceptual and empirical similarities and differences between South African roles research and European reflective research*. Paper presented at the conference on Reflections as a Key Concept in Communication Management, Bled, Slovenia.

Steyn, B., & Puth, G. (2000). *Corporate communication strategy*. Sandown, South Africa: Heinemann.

Steyn, E., De Beer, A., Steyn, T. F. J., & Schreiner, W. N. (2004). Enron and Saambou Bank in South Africa: A case study of insufficient relationship management. *Public Relations Review, 30*, 75–86.

Ströh, U. (2002). *An experimental study on the impact of change communication management on relationships with employees*. Retrieved December 13, 2002, from http://www.iabc.com/fdtnweb/pdf/Stroh_paper2002.pdf

Ströh, U. M. (2004). *An experimental study of organisational change and communication management*. Retrieved May 5, 2006, from http:// upetd.up.ac.za/ thesis/available/etd-05092005-123748/unrestricted/04chapter4.pdf (p. 105).

Ströh, U., & Jaatinen, M. (2001). New approaches to communication management for transformation and change in organisations. *Journal of Communication Management, 6*(2), 148–165.

Wheatley, M. J. (1994). *Leadership and the new science: Learning about organization from an orderly universe*. San Francisco: Berrett-Koehler.

White, J., & Dozier, D. M. (1992). Public relations and management decision making. In J. E. Grunig (Ed.), *Excellence in public relations and communication management* (pp. 91–108). Hillsdale, NJ: Lawrence Erlbaum Associates.

Chapter 11

Public Relations
and Organizational Power

Bruce K. Berger
University of Alabama

Organizational power is sometimes naked. Several years ago, as a consultant I visited a company's European headquarters in northern Italy. The office building, located on the shores of a beautiful lake, vividly depicted structural power in the organization. The lavish lakeside offices, replete with chandeliers and marble floors, housed high-level executives. Offices for mid-level managers were stationed on the opposite side of the building and looked out, through far smaller windows, onto a congested avenue. The cramped offices for low-level managers and technicians were located in the windowless basement. High-level executives also enjoyed privileged parking spaces for their chauffeurs, exclusive use of an ornate espresso bar on site, and a private dining room in which an eminent Italian chef prepared delightful luncheons and dinners. Other administrative personnel took their meals in a nearby factory cantina.

Organizational power isn't always quite so visible, but it is ever present in and around the practice of public relations. Power in many forms shapes what practitioners do, how they are perceived, and what public relations is and might be. Professionals often encounter relations of power from their first moments in practice, and these relations attach to them like shadows as they march through assignments and years.

This chapter focuses on organizational power and some of its implications for public relations practice. I first review the significant contributions of Professors James and Larissa Grunig and their colleagues, who have highlighted several crucial concepts and issues regarding organizational power and public relations in their excellence research and theorizing. I then outline some other work in the area and suggest several pathways for future research that may lead us to better understand how to empower the profession.

POWER CONCEPTIONS IN EXCELLENCE THEORY

Power and *influence* are closely related terms. *Power* is often described as a capacity, or something possessed, that allows one to get things done or get others to do what you want them to do (Grunig, 1992; Lauzen & Dozier, 1992). Barbalet (1985) defined power as "getting things done, or getting others to do them.... If it means anything, social power is the generative force through which social relations and institutions are directed" (p. 538).

If power is the capacity or potential to get things done, then *influence* is the use, expression, or realization of power (Mintzberg, 1983; Salancik & Pfeffer, 1977). Influence is the process through which power is used to get things done, or to accomplish something, for some purpose in organizations (Kanter, 1977; Mintzberg, 1983; Pfeffer, 1992).

The relative absence of power, or lack of empowerment, in strategic decision making in organizations has long been a contentious issue in public relations. Practitioners know that power and influence are crucial to getting things done inside organizations. They need a seat at the table, or at least the attention of organizational leaders, when important decisions are being made or implemented. Yet, they are often absent during these strategic moments. Grunig, Grunig, and Dozier (2002) summarized the issue this way:

> Although expertise in public relations may seem essential for organizations, organizations and their managers vary greatly in the extent to which they recognize and empower the function. Two reasons seem to explain why: (a) Senior managers with the most power in an organization—the dominant coalition—often fail to recognize and appreciate their dependency on the public relations function, and (b) public relations practitioners often lack the expertise needed to meet that dependency even if the dominant coalition recognizes it (p. 3).

The Grunigs and their colleagues in the excellence project and in subsequent research explored these two rationale and related power issues. The resulting body of research has advanced our understanding of such power-related concepts and issues as power-control theory, the dominant coalition, empowerment, and the managerial role.

Power control theory argues that organizational choices and actions grow out of decisions made by those with most power in the organization (Grunig, 1992). Power holders compete with each other, as well as through coalitions they form to strengthen their power bases, to shape organizational decisions, actions, and interpretations. These ongoing conflicts produce organizational structure (Grunig et al., 2002; Lauzen & Dozier, 1992).

The *dominant coalition* is that inner circle of organizational members, often executives, who hold the greatest power. They make strategic choices, allocate resources, influence organizational values, and shape organizational ideologies (Grunig, 1992). Public relations professionals often remain outside this inner circle, or do not hold seats at decision-making tables, and thus are not in a position to affect strategic discussions and choices.

This lack of *empowerment of the profession* is detrimental to the organization, its stakeholders, and society because the communication and policy expertise of public relations professionals is ignored or muted. An empowered profession can help plan, execute, and evaluate an organization's communications with its publics, which can favorably affect the organization's ability to meet its goals and acquire social legitimacy (Grunig, 1992; Grunig et al., 2002).

The Dominant Coalition

According to Grunig et al. (2002), "The essence of the Excellence Theory is that effective communication helps manage an organization's interdependencies with its strategic constituencies—the publics that either support or constrain organizations through their activism, litigation, or pressuring for government regulation" (p. 140). To provide such effective communication and management, however, public relations professionals must be in a position to interact with strategic decision makers, and this highlights the pivotal nature of the dominant coalition in Excellence Theory.

Schneider (a.k.a. L. Grunig, 1985) first incorporated this concept and the power-control perspective into public relations research by linking the function to an organization's external publics and its internal decision making (Lauzen & Dozier, 1992). Dozier, Grunig, and Grunig (1995) found that decisions of the dominant coalition not only shaped organizational actions and ideologies, but also influenced the practice of public relations. Public relations is practiced the way it is in organizations "because the people who have power in an organization choose that behavior" (Grunig, 1992, p. 23).

To produce effective (two-way symmetrical) communication in and for organizations, then, and to realize the potential of public relations to help organizations manage their crucial interdependencies, practitioners require a seat at the decision-making table: "Only as part of the dominant coalition could public relations professionals be influential enough to shape the organization's ideology" (Grunig, 1992, p. 491).

This perspective was subsequently modified to equate power in public relations to the empowerment of everyone in the organization, as well as external stakeholders affected by the organization's decisions and actions. Excellence Theory explained that empowered public relations professionals must be members of the dominant coalition not to influence organizational decisions, but rather to "allow the organization to benefit from the expertise of the public relations profession—something that is most likely to happen when the public relations function is involved in the strategic management of the organization" (Grunig et al., 2002, pp. 142–143).

Others have pointed out that being a member of the dominant coalition or inner circle is no guarantee of influence (Berger, 2005), and membership also carries the risk of co-optation of professional voice and values (Holtzhausen, 2000; Holtzhausen & Voto, 2002). Nevertheless, membership in organizational power circles provides important advantages. It signifies that some formal authority has been granted to the public relations professional. In addition, membership in the dominant coalition provides regular access to key decision makers and to more strategic information for use (Kanter, 1977). Being present in strategic circles also provides professionals with opportunities to speak, advocate, debate, resist, and actively participate in strategic decision making.

Whither Empowerment?

The excellence project and Excellence Theory highlight some of the important factors that impede or advance empowerment in public relations (Dozier et al., 1995; J. Grunig, 1992; Grunig, 2001; J. Grunig & L. Grunig, 1989; L. Grunig, 1992; Grunig, 1997; L. Grunig et al., 2002). These include personal characteristics, professional roles, and structural and cultural factors.

Some characteristics of public relations professionals themselves are problematic, including lack of business or organizational knowledge, inadequate education or professional expertise, passivity, and inexperience or naiveté about organizational politics and power relations (L. Grunig, 1992). Gender and longevity are also important issues with respect to determining roles and power in organizations (Grunig et al., 2002; Grunig, Toth, & Hon, 2001; Hon, Grunig, & Dozier, 1992; Toth & Cline, 1989).

Perceptions of public relations roles by both practitioners and organizational executives are another issue. Research in this area has differentiated the technical versus managerial role (Broom & Dozier, 1986; Dozier, 1992; Dozier & Broom, 1995). As technicians, practitioners carry out production activities (e.g., writing, design, and communication distribution tasks) but are not engaged in policy decision making. Managers possess similar technical skills but also have research, problem-solving, and strategic-thinking capabilities and are accountable for results. Dozier and Broom (1995) claimed that "knowledge to enact the manager role was the single most powerful correlate of excellence in public relations and communication management" (p. 4). Public relations professionals who possess such managerial skills, sufficient experience, and a managerial perspective are therefore more likely to ascend to the dominant coalition (J. Grunig, 1992; Grunig et al., 2002).

Findings in the Excellence Project suggested that structural and cultural factors also may impede or advance empowerment and excellence of public relations in organizations (Grunig, 1997; Grunig et al., 2002). Important structural factors for the public relations function include participation of the senior public relations executive in strategic management processes of the organization; representation of the senior public relations executive in the dominant coalition, or a direct reporting relationship to a senior leader who is a member of the dominant coalition; and an integrated communication function that is separated structurally from other functions in the organization.

Cultural factors are equally significant and include a supportive organizational context, or a "culture for communication"; the support of top management in words and deeds; and equal opportunities for women, men, and practitioners of diverse ethnic, cultural, and racial backgrounds to lead the public relations function and carry out the roles and activities of the function.

OTHER RESEARCH INTO POWER AND PUBLIC RELATIONS

Insights and concepts regarding power in Excellence Theory have stimulated other public relations scholars to explore power in and around the practice. Some scholars have embraced and sought to advance the concepts of empowerment, the dominant coalition, and the managerial role, whereas other scholars have rejected them or approached them from different perspectives. A few of these approaches are briefly outlined here.

Spicer (1997), for example, argued that a political system metaphor is the best way to understand relationships between public relations power and organizational power. In his view, practitioners need to become more politically astute to serve as effective players in the organization's political infrastructure. Increased political astuteness, a strong track record of accomplishments, and especially a managerial perspective will help practitioners better serve their organizations and the public good.

Building on role theory and the importance of worldviews in professionals, Lauzen (1992) claimed that there are four keys to strengthening the power of public relations departments. She suggested that practitioners must aspire to the managerial role in practice and possess the requisite skills and competencies to carry out that role. In addition, the most senior leader in the function must enact the managerial role and "believe that public relations is a powerful organizational function" (p. 77).

Some critical theorists have challenged the notion of symmetrical communication and argued that the power of public relations directly reflects the power that it gains through its instrumental service *to* the dominant coalition or the dominating interests of particular groups (German, 1995; Motion & Leitch, 1996; Weaver, 2001). In this view, the goal of public relations is asymmetrical because it seeks to protect those interests and existing power bases. Motion and Leitch (1996) and Motion and Weaver (2005) asserted that public relations practitioners play the role of experienced and strategic technicians—"discourse technologists" who shape discourse and culture inside and outside organizations through the production and dissemination of texts.

In his study of power relations inside the dominant coalition, Berger (2005) discovered a matrix of constraints on public relations that render it difficult for practitioners to get things done and to do the "right things" in organizations even when they want to do so. These impediments include the presence of multiple power coalitions, shifting coalition venues and roles, multiple checkpoints on public relations power through review processes, and pressures for organizational compliance. He also suggested that a gendered dialectic in dominant coalitions undermined the role and legitimacy of public relations.

Postmodern scholars (Holtzhausen, 2000; Holtzhausen & Voto, 2002) underscore the web of power relations surrounding public relations work and warn practitioners against being co-opted by the dominant coalition or other dominant power structures in organizations. They contend that professionals, even without authoritative or structural power, can exert influence by developing strong relationships, using expertise, gaining access to powerful individuals, and relying on their biopower (or personal inner power). By taking on the role of organizational activists, public relations professionals have the potential to help emancipate organizations and the profession and to institutionalize ethics into practice.

EXPANDING OUR VOCABULARY OF POWER

Excellence Theory emphasizes a relational orientation characterized by two-way symmetrical communication; that is, dialogue, compromise, and shared power. It acknowledges primacy of the dominant coalition in taking organizational decisions and influencing public relations practices. It emphasizes the importance of an empowered public relations function that participates in the dominant coalition and other strategic decision-making arenas so that the practice can help organizations solve problems, become more socially responsible, and acquire and maintain social legitimacy. It argues that public relations professionals are more likely to be so empowered if they possess managerial skills and a managerial worldview and subsequently enact the managerial role.

On the occasion of this special book, then, two things seem clear regarding Excellence Theory and organizational power. First, the concepts of the dominant coalition, empowerment within and for the profession, and the public relations managerial role remain central issues in the field. This doesn't mean there aren't other power issues or perspectives in the field (e.g., chaos theory, contingency theory, rhetorical criticism, and political economy approaches). Rather, it suggests that whether researchers seek to advance our understanding of these concepts within a relational and symmetrical perspective, or approach them or other power issues from alternative perspectives, the concepts themselves continue to be crucial terms in our vocabulary of public relations power.

Second, there is more work to do. Excellence Theory has illuminated a crucial pathway to power discussions about the practice, and revealed some of the breaks and disruptions that the profession must navigate along this pathway. We must continue to research and to reflect on how to do so even as we discover other breaks or disruptions. Further research is essential to expand our vocabulary of power and to better understand organizational power in its many forms, as well as its corresponding implications for teaching and practice.

Pedagogical Considerations

Recently I asked five former public relations students to identify the biggest surprise that they had discovered on the job. One said it was the long work hours; the other four said it was organizational politics and all the "power stuff" they encountered in their organizations. They wondered why we didn't teach more of the power stuff at the university. It's a good question. A related question is, how do we do so? What kind of "power training" do we provide to our students for entering organizations in which power intersects and influences daily practice?

So far as I know, there are no undergraduate textbooks that focus on power issues in practice, and few chapters or passages in books that attempt to do so. Yet, power is a central issue for academics and practitioners. Is it enough to provide students with the technical and managerial skills for the job? Is it enough to define and lecture about the dominant coalition, empowerment issues, and the importance of the managerial role? Are the use of case studies, guest speakers, and class exercises sufficient? Do we need to do more to arm students with conflict-resolution and negotiation skills? Alternatively, do we need to prepare them to be capable activists as well as competent advocates? More research into teaching and power issues is sorely needed if we believe that power relations substantively shape the practice of public relations.

Is Dissensus in the Field a Constraint on Professional Power?

Public relations is characterized by historical dissensus in the field about what the practice is, who it serves, and what its roles and responsibilities are. Of course, individual practitioners know what they do and can explain their role on a microlevel. However, to others in organizations and the public at large, what the profession is and does is less clear because it has come to mean and to be named so many things. Film publicist, lobbyist, reputation manager, special events coordinator, social responsibility director, marketing consultant, speech writer, senior counselor, thought partner—none of these actual titles include the words *public relations*, but all of the individuals who bear the titles claim they are public relations professionals.

To what extent does systemic dissensus within the profession contribute to its power shortages and overall image? Is it possible that how public relations professionals see, understand, and engage in power relations is closely linked to how they see, understand, and practice public relations? Is it possible to conceive of "a public relations profession" outside of its long-standing functional mode, perhaps as a power system, a community, a text, or a powerful social actor?

Alternatively, is dissensus in the field perhaps not a debilitating but rather healthy condition, even a potential source of power? Does the steady churn and anxiety produced by dissensus yield a kind of intellectual or professional stimulus—a form of energy that can be somehow harnessed within the profession? Research that probes types of dissension in the field and their relationships to power and to excellence in practice surely may help us better understand these relationships and provide insights to ameliorating or capitalizing on them.

At the Table, Inside of Power Relations

One of the strengths of Excellence Theory is the extent to which it has explained the value of public relations to the dominant coalition and to organizations generally. Public relations can help solve environmental problems that organizations confront because it is a boundary-spanning function. Professionals understand publics, they know how to scan the environment, they can conduct research, they possess negotiation and conflict-resolution skills, and they can formulate ethical strategic approaches and tactical plans to help organizations resolve stakeholder issues and acquire necessary social legitimacy.

However, Excellence Theory tells us less about how practitioners can accomplish these things or how things work inside the dominant coalition, and these represent important areas of questioning for further research. What happens at the table, for example, and how does it happen? What opportunities and constraints do public relations managers confront? What communication tactics and strategies are brought to bear as decision makers debate, posture, exchange, and attempt to advance their ideas in this power-control center? What influence resources do public relations managers mobilize and use, and what influence tactics work best in various conditions? When and how do public relations managers dissent or embrace activist approaches in their organizations?

HOW DOES PUBLIC RELATIONS ACQUIRE POWER AND LEGITIMACY?

Acquiring greater power and professional legitimacy remain central issues in the field, and knowing how best to do so continues to be frustratingly elusive. Excellence Theory suggests that more education, experience, and expertise, along with a strong ethical orientation and enactment of the managerial role, will help empower the profession, and there is some evidence to support this contention (Grunig et al., 2002). However, widespread empowerment of professionals has been slow to come, and we must consider other approaches through which the profession may gain power.

Over the past few years, a colleague and I have taken an alternative approach that examines issues of professional empowerment and legitimacy through the lens of power relations (Berger & Reber, 2006). Through interviews with nearly 200 professionals, and survey responses from more than 1,000 others, we explored perceptions of power; influence resources and tactics; professional roles; constraints on practice; organizational politics; and advocacy, dissent, and activist approaches in practice.

Our practical-critical approach makes a counterintuitive argument that professionals can increase their influence and legitimacy with organizational decision makers by engaging in resistance activities (forms of advocacy, dissent, and activism) against the forces that constrain them. Long-time approaches to legitimate the profession—we call them *Alpha approaches*—have relied on case studies, accreditation and measurement initiatives, and repeated claims about the value and crucial role of the practice, among others. Despite such efforts to induce support from top decision makers—and there have been some successes— many professionals still do not hold a seat at the table, and the public image of the profession remains tarnished.

We contend that practitioners have many power and influence resources available for use, and they can benefit from developing and mobilizing more of these resources. They also may increase their influence by supplementing traditional Alpha approaches with Omega approaches, which are forms of dissent, professional activism, and more controversial influence tactics that represent potentially rich but largely untapped power sources. To gain influence and increase their legitimacy, then, public relations professionals must better understand power relations and develop and effectively use a wider range of influence resources and approaches. Above all, they must possess the political will to engage in the often-confrontational power relations that occur in organizational decision-making arenas.

Supportive Findings in the Research Projects

Some findings in our research projects confirm insights from previous studies or support Excellence Theory propositions. For example, although practitioners in our influence interviews ($n = 65$) defined influence in practice in diverse ways, most equated professional influence and empowerment with membership in the dominant coalition and participation in strategic decision making. Also, most of the professionals in our PR success interviews ($n = 97$) defined public relations practice as a strategic management function that can help organizations solve problems and achieve success. Nearly half of the participants in this study also said that the biggest impediment to empowerment of public relations in their organizations was the inaccurate or narrow perceptions of the function's role and value by other organizational executives.

In the combined interviews for three projects ($n = 186$), most practitioners agreed that lack of empowerment in the profession was due to (a) CEOs who "just don't get it" about public relations, and (b) public relations professionals who "just don't have it" in terms of professional expertise, experience, leadership skills, and managerial capabilities. These results resonate with both the summary statement of Grunig et al. (2002) regarding empowerment issues (quoted earlier in this chapter) and previous findings that support the importance of the managerial role.

Findings That Lead in Other Directions

Conceptualizing a resistance role for public relations in our research provided a way to abstract power relations out of practice and closely examine them in terms of influence resources, tactics, and political decision-making arenas, among other factors. This approach also led us to explore some related subfields that often lie within the shadows of power studies in the field; that is, forms of dissent in public relations, professional activism, and the use of Omega approaches or unsanctioned influence tactics in practice (e.g., planting information in the grapevine, selectively using data, constructing counternarratives to explain organizational decisions, and leaking information).

Additional research in these areas of practice is important because, as Barbalet (1985) reminded us, any attempt to theorize or explain organizational power must include the concept of resistance, because resistance to prevailing power influences the outcomes of power relations themselves. Our own research regarding resistance practices (Berger & Reber, 2006) includes the interviews referenced earlier, an in-depth case study of public relations influence strategies and tactics used to win support for a major communication project in one company, and the first comprehensive survey ($n = 808$) of dissent practices in public relations. Based on these studies, we developed a number of propositions for further testing and research. Three of the propositions are briefly discussed here by way of suggesting other approaches to examining and advancing empowerment in public relations.

Proposition 1: Public relations professionals can increase their power in practice by developing, mobilizing, and wisely using a greater number and more diverse range of influence resources and tactics.

Practitioners across diverse organizations told us that (a) they draw primarily from personal and relational sources of power, (b) structural power is in short supply in the profession, and (c) systemic power sources are underutilized or underdeveloped. *Systemic resources* refer to professional organizations and associated codes, standards, established measures of professional value, reputation, collective actions, and so forth. Practitioners also indicated that they rely heavily on just three types of influence tactics—rational advocacy, coalitions, and pressure—and use consultation, legitimation, exchange, and emotional and inspirational appeals far less often.

Recognizing, mobilizing, and using more influence resources and more diverse influence tactics increases potential power in practice. Yet, our research suggested that many professionals overlook a number of power sources and develop and use only a narrow range of influence resources and tactics, despite the fact that repeated use of these same resources and approaches over the years has not yielded greater empowerment. More research into public relations influence resources, strategies, and tactics may help us better understand how practitioners can become more capable, active, and savvy participants inside the dominant coalition and other decision-making arenas.

Proposition 2: Public relations practitioners have greater allegiance to their organizations than to stakeholders or society, but they draw the devotion line to their organizations at legal or moral wrongdoing and embrace assertive behaviors in these situations.

Although public relations practitioners serve multiple interests and "masters," two thirds of the practitioners in the influence interviews (*n* = 65) said that their primary allegiance was to their organization. Only a handful of professionals responded that they primarily served other stakeholders or society, and a similar number commented that they tried to balance the interests of their organization and its stakeholders. Nevertheless, most of the participants in the dissent survey (*n* = 808) said that their allegiance to the organization stopped at legal or moral wrongdoing. At such times, most practitioners said they would assertively confront management to try to overturn illegal, immoral, or unethical decisions, or to prevent their implementation. On the other hand, about 10% of the respondents indicated that they would never dissent or challenge such decisions or actions, no matter how egregious.

These findings suggest that most practitioners value and embrace organizational and professional codes of conduct and societal laws and norms when faced with legal or moral wrongdoing in their organizations. The findings also bear pedagogical implications; there is a need to empower practitioners to engage in constructive conflict, and assertive confrontation may be addressed to a greater extent in both classrooms and professional workshops.

Proposition 3: The extent to which public relations may influence results in organizational political arenas is linked to the professional, managerial, and political skills—and especially to the political will—of the public relations leader(s) in the organization.

Lauzen (1992) argued that public relations managers possess more strategic power than they imagine, and PR departments can indeed become more powerful. She said that the key to this power was that "the most senior practitioner in the organization must believe that PR is a powerful organizational function" (p. 77). This suggests that power is already present in various sources and forms and can be taken and actualized; public relations leaders can increase their power by believing in the power of the function and possessing the will to act on these beliefs.

Analysis of the Whirlpool case study (Berger & Reber, 2006) led to a similar conclusion and underscored the importance of political willpower in the public relations leader. Winning support for a $21 million communication change program in the company was achieved in part because of the leadership team's political influence skills, its belief that the change program was the right thing to do and could be done, and its tenacious political will in trying to make it happen.

Management theorists Mintzberg (1983) and Pfeffer (1981, 1992) contended that political willpower is a crucial factor in exerting influence in often messy and confrontational decision-making arenas in organizations. Yet, we know little about political willpower in public relations practice. This individual power source is likely an important dimension of a managerial role, or an activist role, and further research is needed to learn more about political will and its role in empowerment, along with its implications for teaching and practice.

In addition to many other contributions to public relations, Excellence Theory has spurred research into power issues in the profession and provided an important vocabulary of terms and concepts. Nevertheless, any number of areas of power research—from pedagogical and professional dissensus concerns, to influence tactics and forms of resistance—require attention by the next generation of public relations scholars. If how professionals see, understand, and engage power in organizations is linked to how they see, understand, and practice public relations, then there is more work to do on a number of research fronts, and great urgency in getting on with it.

REFERENCES

Barbalet, J. M. (1985). Power and resistance. *The British Journal of Sociology, 36*(4), 531–548.

Berger, B. K. (2005). Power over, power with, and power to relations: Critical reflections on public relations, the dominant coalition, and activism. *Journal of Public Relations Research, 17*(1), 5–27.

Berger, B., K., & Reber, B. H. (2006). *Gaining influence in public relations: The role of resistance in practice*. Mahwah, NJ: Lawrence Erlbaum Associates.

Broom, G. M., & Dozier, D. M. (1986). Advancement for public relations role models. *Public Relations Review, 12*(1), 37–56.

Dozier, D. M. (1992). The organizational roles of communications and public relations practitioners. In J. E. Grunig (Ed.), *Excellence in public relations and communication management* (pp. 327–356). Hillsdale, NJ: Lawrence Erlbaum Associates.

Dozier, D. M., & Broom, G. M. (1995). Evolution of the manager role in public relations practice. *Journal of Public Relations Research, 7*(1), 3–26.

Dozier, D. M., Grunig, L. A., & Grunig, J. E. (1995). *Manager's guide to excellence in public relations and communication management*. Mahwah, NJ: Lawrence Erlbaum Associates.

German, K. M. (1995). Critical theory in public relations inquiry. In W. N. Elwood (Ed.), *Public relations inquiry as rhetorical criticism* (pp. 279–294). Westport, CT: Praeger.

Grunig, J. E. (Ed.). (1992). *Excellence in public relations and communication management: Contributions to effective organizations*. Hillsdale, NJ: Lawrence Erlbaum Associates.

Grunig, J. E. (2001). Two-way symmetrical public relations: Past, present and future. In R. L. Heath (Ed.), *Handbook of public relations* (pp. 11–30). Thousand Oaks, CA: Sage.

Grunig, J. E., & Grunig, L. A. (1989). Toward a theory of the public relations behavior of organizations: Review of a program of research. *Public Relations Research Annual, 1,* 27–63.

Grunig, L. A. (1992). Power in the public relations department. In J. E. Grunig (Ed.), *Excellence in public relations and communication management* (pp. 483–502). Hillsdale, NJ: Lawrence Erlbaum Associates.

Grunig, L. A. (1997). Excellence in public relations. In C. L. Caywood (Ed.), *The handbook of strategic public relations and integrated communications* (pp. 286–300). New York: McGraw-Hill.

Grunig, L. A., Grunig, J. E., & Dozier, D. M. (2002). *Excellent public relations and effective organizations.* Mahwah, NJ: Lawrence Erlbaum Associates.

Grunig, L. A., Toth, E. L., & Hon, L. C. (2001). *Women in public relations: How gender influences practice.* New York: Guilford.

Holtzhausen, D. R. (2000). Postmodern values in public relations. *Journal of Public Relations Research, 12,* 93–114.

Holtzhausen, D. R., & Voto, R. (2002). Resistance from the margins: The postmodern public relations practitioner as organizational activist. *Journal of Public Relations Research,14*(1), 57–84.

Hon, L. C., Grunig, L. A., & Dozier, D. M. (1992). Women in public relations: Problems and opportunities. In J. E. Grunig (Ed.), *Excellence in public relations and communication management* (pp. 419–438). Hillsdale, NJ: Lawrence Erlbaum Associates.

Kanter, R. M. (1977). *Men and women of the corporation.* New York: Basic Books.

Lauzen, M. M. (1992). Public relations roles, intraorganizational power, and encroachment. *Journal of Public Relations Research, 4*(2), 61–80.

Lauzen, M. M., & Dozier, D. M. (1992). The missing link: The public relations manager role as mediator of organizational environments and power consequences for the function. *Journal of Public Relations Research, 4*(4), 205–220.

Mintzberg, H. (1983). *Power in and around organizations.* Englewood Cliffs, NJ: Prentice-Hall.

Motion, J., & Leitch, S. (1996). A discursive perspective from New Zealand: Another world view. *Public Relations Review, 22*(3), 297–309.

Motion, J., & Weaver, C. K. (2005). A discourse perspective for critical public relations research: Life sciences network and the battle for truth. *Journal of Public Relations Research, 17*(1), 49–67.

Pfeffer, J. (1981). *Power in organizations.* Marshfield, MA: Pitman.

Pfeffer, J. (1992). *Managing with power: Politics and influence in organizations.* Cambridge, MA: Harvard Business School Press.

Salancik, G. R., & Pfeffer, J. (1977). Who gets power—and how they hold on to it: A strategic-contingency model of power. *Organizational Dynamics, 5,* 3–21.

Schneider (a.k.a. Grunig), L. A. (1985). The role of public relations in four organizational types. *Journalism Quarterly, 62,* 567–576, 594.

Spicer, C. (1997). *Organizational public relations: A political perspective.* Mahwah, NJ: Lawrence Erlbaum Associates.

Toth, E. L., & Cline, C. G. (Eds.). (1989). *Beyond the velvet ghetto.* San Francisco: IABC Research Foundation.

Weaver, C. K. (2001). Dressing for battle in the new global economy. *Management Communication Quarterly, 15*(2), 279–288.

Chapter 12

A Revisit of Symmetrical Communication From an International Perspective: Status, Effect, and Future Research Directions

Yi-Hui Huang
National ChengChi University

In the early 1990s, J. Grunig, L. Grunig, and associates developed a generic theory of global public relations using data derived from a decade-long study by the International Association of Business Communications. The Excellence Study included more than 300 organizations throughout the United Kingdom, Canada, and the United States, and had begun in 1984 (J. Grunig, 1992; Grunig, Grunig & Dozier, 2002; Grunig, Grunig, & Vercic, 1998). An organization's use of symmetrical communication, encompassing a generic to excellent public relations worldview, was the focus, specifically in terms of social and ethical responsibilities (Lauzen & Dozier, 1994).

Grunig (2000) noted that symmetrical public relations is a type of practice that "attempts to balance the interests of client organizations with those of publics they affect" (p. 24). Symmetrical communication is conceptualized by emphasizing the organization's intent to initiate changes, in contrast to merely trying to change the cognitions, attitudes, or behaviors of the publics. Organizations with an asymmetrical worldview see communication as a tool that they use to change the cognitions, attitudes, or behaviors of another person, organization, or similar system. Symmetrical communication, however, is balanced; it adjusts the relationship between the organization and public.

Grunig, Grunig, Sriramesh, Huang, and Lyra (1995), examining the practice of public relations beyond the Anglo countries, focused on India, Taiwan, and Greece. The study showed that craft public relations (i.e., press agentry) predominates in these countries. Grunig et al. (1995) also revealed that although a few knowledgeable public relations managers practice the two-way symmetrical model, for most practitioners this model serves as a normative ideal. Grunig et al. noted that most of the conditions that foster professional public relations—such as societal culture, political systems, and knowledge for practicing symmetrical communication—may not exist in most organizations in other countries.

Replication of the Excellence Theory, following Grunig et al.'s study (1995), has been extensive and internationally applied (Holtzhausen, Petersen, & Tindall, 2003; Rhee, 2002; Sriramesh, Kim, & Takasaki, 1999). Debate about the theory centers on symmetrical communication and in three areas in particular. First, is symmetrical communication more idealistic than reflective of reality? Critics claim that symmetrical communication is too utopian to be practiced in the real world (Kersten, 1994; L'Etang, 1996) and that the two-way symmetrical model doesn't reflect reality but simply suggests the path an organization should take (Van der Meiden, 1993). Murphy (1991) held that symmetrical communication is hard to find in practice, and likened the two-way symmetrical communication model to a model of pure cooperation in game theory. Second, is the "one best style"—an organization's practice of repeatedly using the same public relations practices—truly an effective course of action? Leichty and Springston (1993) suggested that rather than being aggregated "across public and relations stages and globally characterized as an organization's overall public relations practice" (p. 334), public relations models should be assessed relationally. Third, are an organization's interests favorably supported by symmetrical communication? Ignoring the needs of a client's organization comes as a result of symmetrical communication, some critics say (quoted in Grunig, 2000).

Grunig et al. (1995) emphasized the pressing need to "know much more about strategies that practitioners can and do use at different points" (p. 23). A decade later, the purpose of this chapter is to respond to the this debate and extend the current research by examining the practice of public relations in Taiwan in two respects. First, does symmetrical communication currently exist in Taiwan? If yes, to what extent, in what form, and under what conditions does it exist? Second, does symmetrical communication serve organizations' interests? In what respects can symmetrical communication be effective?

The method adopted in this study is first introduced, followed by contextual factors of global public relations and specific situations in Taiwan. Then, two research questions are explored. Last, the paper concludes with a framework that proposes suggestions for future research.

METHOD

I chose to examine the case of Taiwan as a basis for exploring symmetrical communication for three reasons. First, the unique political climate, societal culture, and economic makeup of Taiwan, and its transformations during the past 50 years with respect to these contextual factors, promise a productive basis for the generic theory of global public relations in general and symmetrical communication in particular. As a study that uses a Western public relations theory as a theoretical foundation and explores its application to a Far Eastern country, I believe the case of Taiwan can contribute to the theoretical development of global public relations.

Second, in economic and political terms, Taiwan differs greatly from mainland China. As a result of its shift to a democracy, Taiwan, which considers itself the successor of Chinese traditions and culture (Clough, 1978), presents Chinese public relations practitioners with a host of controversial issues. This mix of traditional and modern cultures makes Taiwan an ideal case.

Third, following Dozier and Lauzen's (2000) suggestion, this study analyzed public relations at the societal level. There have been a sufficient number of published works focusing on public relations practice in Taiwan. A meta-analysis of these works within Taiwan's societal and cultural context not only can provide answers to the research questions posed earlier, individually or jointly, but also can control possible extraneous variations due to contextual or infrastructure influences (see Sriramesh & Vercic, 2001) in order to allow cross-study comparisons to be made.

Various indexes (PsycInfor, CommInex) were examined to locate studies containing suitable data to include in this analysis. A study had to have the following characteristics to be included in this study: investigate models of public relations in general and/or symmetrical communication in particular, and the effects of symmetrical communication; be published in English or Chinese journals between 1996 and 2005; and contain empirical data collected in Taiwan, either quantitative or qualitative. A total of nine independent studies in seven published works were identified. The results of the meta-analysis should provide sufficient empirical evidence for the purpose of cross-validation, because the relevant studies reported differ considerably in their respondents' demographics, organization's type, issues examined, and in their goal-attainment and strategic-constituency perspectives.

Rather than conducting further statistical analysis across these published works, this study reports the results derived from each published work with respect to two research questions posited in this study. Depending on the situation, the researcher contacted the authors for raw data and conducted necessary computations, such as the means of models of public relations, if they were not shown in the original publications.

Then, the considerations that should factor into the practice of symmetrical public relations [for relevant discussions, see Heath, 2001; see Toth & Pavlik, 2000; and a special issue of the *Journal of Public Relations*, *12*(1)] are used as a conduit of discussion and analysis. For example, Cheney and Christensen (2001) posited that the role of public relations struggles for democracy in cultures that are dominated by, or at least largely biased toward, corporatism. Likewise, Spicer (2000) questioned, "[D]oes public relations serve moneyed interests to the exclusion of groups without substantial resources?" (p. 124). Leitch and Neilson (2001) then advocated that the practice of discipline can be enriched by developing a public-centered view of the practice rather than looking essentially at organizations. Last, Dozier and Lauzen (2000) suggested examining moral and ethical contradiction in public relations practices. Based on this literature, the following factors serve as analytical framework for cross-study comparison: (a) Is the investigation reflecting an organization's or public's perspective? (b) Is the organization examined a for-profit or a nonprofit? (c) Is the issue investigated related to corporatism and moneyed interest, or not?

CONTEXTUAL FACTORS OF GLOBAL PUBLIC RELATIONS AND THE SPECIFIC SITUATION IN TAIWAN

Five Contextual Factors of Global Public Relations

The contextual or infrastructure variables and their specific influences on public relations, which are identified in the theory of global public relations, include societal culture, political-economic system, media, activism, and level of development (Grunig et al., 1998; Sriramesh & Vercic, 2001).

First, Grunig et al. (1998) and Sriramesh and White (1992) correlated the relationship between Hofstede's (1980) four cultural dimensions with the generic principle of public relations. The first cultural dimension is individualism or collectivism, which refers to how individuals relate to larger groups such as extended families, tribes, or organizations. The propositions are that symmetrical communication and social responsibility would seem more likely to be adopted in collectivist cultures. Second, Grunig et al. (1998) predicted that the greater the power distance—which describes how cultures deal with inequality—the more difficult it would be to practice the generic principles of public relations. Third, when uncertainty avoidance (which suggests the extent to which people in a society can tolerate uncertain or ambiguous situations) is high, people tend to be more dogmatic and hence make application of generic principles more difficult. The fourth cultural dimension is masculinity. In general, masculine cultures value aggressiveness, assertiveness, and acquisition. Feminine cultures, on the contrary, value relationships, concerns for others, and quality of life. Again, the generic principles such as symmetrical communication, diversity, and social responsibility fit better with feminine cultures than with masculine ones.

The second contextual factor is political system. Grunig et al. (1998) maintained that a two-way symmetrical communication model would be impossible in a totalitarian and an authoritarian system, whose propaganda often is used to coerce people and keep the elite in power. An organization in a democratic state, on the other hand, would be more likely to practice the two-way symmetrical model. Culbertson (1995) also supported the theoretical proposition that authoritarianism limits the development of public relations, much as it shackles the press. The third contextual factor concerns media system. Grunig et al. (1998) suggested that only the Western media reflects the traditional idea of media relations, as placement and brokerage of news stories. In the other system, to some extent, media are employed as public relations vehicles for the government or some certain organizations. Fourth, Grunig et al. correlated level of development and public relations, and posited that the generic principles of excellent communications are difficult to apply in a less-developed country, inasmuch as less-developed countries are more likely than developed countries to have cultures that emphasize power distance, uncertainty avoidance, and masculinity. Last, in view of the powerful pressure that an activist group can place on an organization, Grunig et al. maintained that activism ultimately forces organizations to pay attention to and communicate with strategic publics. Pattakos (1989) argued that during the last 20 years, there has been notable growth in the number of activist groups that focus attention on the perceived lack of socially responsible behavior by business.

Taiwan as a Specific Case With Respect to the Five Contextual Factors

Taiwan's history, as it relates to the media, its culture, the existence of activist groups, and the development of the economic and political systems, is similar to the evolution of the field of public relations (see Sha & Huang, 2003). Politically, Taiwan has emerged as a democracy over the past 50 years from its roots as an authoritarian regime. When the Nationalist government began losing ground to the Communists in the Chinese Civil War (1945–1949), it moved the government to Taipei at the end of the war. The ROC then used "emergency decrees" and "temporary provisions" to place Taiwan under martial law (Tien, 1989), essentially acting as an authoritarian regime until martial law was lifted in 1987.

The rise of the media in Taiwan came after the government lifted restrictions on daily newspaper production, including how long each paper was allowed to be, in 1988. More than 300 newspapers were being published just 9 years later. Only four public relations companies existed in 1987, a number that grew to approximately 45 companies in 1992 (Huang, 1993) and reaches almost 60 today. This explosion came as a result of the "free" media, which public and private organizations discovered they could try to influence. Today's socially minded, activist Taiwan was fostered by the increasingly liberal media. This activism allowed for the growth of several groups and social movements that organizations now need strategies with which to deal. Following the lifting of martial law in 1987, the capitalist, industrial Taiwan that exists today emerged from a government-run and heavily agricultural economy of the 1950s. Today, Taiwan is economically vibrant and has a stock exchange (*Taiwan*, 2000).

Last, with respect to societal culture, in Hofstede's 1980 study, Taiwan was rated as low in "individualism," moderate in "power distance," moderate in "uncertainty avoidance," and moderately low in "masculinity." However, as Fernandez, Carlson, Stepina, and Nicholson (1997) noted, societal changes such as economic growth, education, and democracy may affect cultural dimensions. For example, Wu, Taylor, and Chen (2001) showed the public relations practitioners to be moderately high on individualism and collectivism, in the middle of the power distance index, a little higher than average on uncertainty avoidance, and very high on femininity and masculinity. Compared with Hofstede's (1980) and Wu et al.'s (2001) studies on four cultural dimensions of Taiwan, for the past 20 years, although the dimensions of power distance and uncertainty avoidance have remained at a moderate level, the other two dimensions that stood at one extreme 20 years ago (i.e., collectivism and femininity) have moved toward two ends in each dimension (i.e., the co-existence of individualism and collectivism as well as masculinity and femininity).

Summing up the previous discussion, examining Taiwan as a case should generate valuable insights into relevant theoretical arenas. All of the contextual factors identified in the theory of global public relations not only have their unique influences on Taiwan's public relations practice, but they also have experienced transformations over the past 50 years. Namely, most of the conditions that foster professional or excellent public relations that did not exist prior to 50 years ago should exist in Taiwan by now.

Chinese Culture, Confucianism, and Relational Orientation

Among the five contextual factors, Chinese social culture is distinct from that of Western countries and worthy of further exploration to better understand the background involving the extent and the effect of symmetrical communication in Taiwan, which can be discussed from two aspects. On the one hand, the characteristics of Confucian traditions—which emphasize authority, harmony, order, and relationships—help in explaining the nuances and complexities of public relations practice in Taiwan. On the other hand, Chinese culture also exerts compounding challenges to applying a generic principle of global public relations in an Oriental society. The challenges have four facets.

First, understanding public relations from the *guanxi* perspective (interpersonal relationships) is essential. Relationship, or *guanxi*, has long been considered a key to understanding Chinese behavior in political (Jacob, 1979), organizational (Walder, 1983), and social contexts (Chang, 2001; Chen & Chung, 1994; Fried, 1969; Hwang, 1987; King, 1985; Leung, Wong, & Wong, 1996). Three important aspects help convey the role of relationships in Chinese society: "1) People exist through, and are defined by, their relationships to others; 2) these relationships are structured hierarchically; 3) social order is ensured through each party's honoring the requirements in the role of relationships" (Bond & Hwang, 1986, p. 216).

Hwang's model of face and favor in Chinese society categorized human relationships into three types on the basis of their expressive and instrumental components. The first category is expressive tie, which basically denotes the relationship among members in a family or other congenial groups. According to Hwang, the governing rule in this tie is the *need* rule: People have the responsibility to strive for resources to satisfy the legitimate needs of each member. The second category, *mixed tie*, characterizes the *guanxi* outside an individual's immediate family. In the mixed tie relationship, people often share some commonality with others, such as relatives, neighbors, classmates, colleagues, teachers, or students. Hwang maintained that the rules of *renqing* (favor) and *mianzi* (face) are the means that people use the most in this tie to expand their human network and obtain resources from resource allocators. The third category is *instrumental ties*, in which an individual establishes temporary and anonymous relationships with people such as customers, salesperson, taxi drivers, and so on. The rule of thumb for a Chinese interacting with a person in an instrumental relationship is the equity rule. Hwang suggested that in an instrumental relationship, a person often uses social exchange theory as a rule of thumb.

Today's public relations and communication problems may stem from Confucianism's asymmetrical view of the world, especially given the favorable influence that Confucian teachings have on the Chinese. A unique cultural feature that emerged in Chinese culture—a culture that has a well-defined relationship structure—is *gao guanxi*, a way that a minority class can associate itself with power, thus creating a negative connotation that one is exploiting a personal relationship or connection (Bond & Hwang, 1986). When competing for resources such as status, information, money, and other goods, one way in which a person might hope to strengthen *guanxi* with the allocator, as described in Hwang's (1987) model of face and favor in Chinese society, is to find more opportunities to interact with the allocator, thus increasing one's influence.

Second, relational orientation,[1] which refers to the ways in which an individual relates himself or herself to a larger group as a member of various relationships, also helps in understanding how Chinese people relate with others. In essence, Confucius' Five Cardinal Relations set rules for interpersonal relationships, but did not specify rules for organization–public relationships. In response to the social relationships beyond the *wu-lun* or the Five Cardinal Relations, Yang (1992) noted that Chinese people adopt familism in families and panfamilism outside families. For organizations outside families, the Chinese people tend to follow familism to apply the following three tenets (Yang, 1992): family structures and principles based on which families operate, ethics and roles related to family hierarchy, and learning of interpersonal and social skills from families. Basically, only when a relation is identified as expressive tie (Huang, 2000; Hwang, 1987), or within family, could the *need* rule (Huang, 2000), symmetrical communication, or communal relationship (see Grunig, 2000, for discussion on communal relationship) occur.

First, relational fatalism notes the Chinese people's concepts of karma. It emphasizes that, prior to the inception of a relationship, karma dictates the occurrence of certain patterns of interpersonal relationships and even "the duration and outcomes of such a relationship." Second, relational determinism refers to the characteristics of the degree of intimacy in differential order (Yang, 1992). Such characteristics categorize interpersonal or social relationships into relationships with family members, acquaintances, and strangers (Hwang, 1987). Differential order also dictates how a person deals with others and the affairs related to others. Third, relational role assumption refers to the phe-

---

[1]The theory of relational orientation (Yang, 1992) is illuminating and pertinent, because of its indigenous nature in one aspect, and its sound theoretical base in another. Given the theoretical pertinence, it also faces various challenges from the trends of Westernization and globalization. Among the theories of Chinese relationalism, Yang's theory of relational orientation is particularly pertinent to the subject of intercultural relationship. Yang (1992) stressed five core concepts representing relational orientation in Chinese society, which provide a better understanding of intercultural relationship from a Chinese perspective.

nomena that interpersonal interactions primarily hinge on roles assumed in a given relationship, in which roles and related behaviors to a great extent are predesignated and fixed (e.g., the Five Cardinal Relations, the related roles, and corresponding behaviors; Yang, 1992). Fourth, relational interdependence (reciprocity) notes that corresponding roles in social relationships are supplementary and reciprocal. Basically, they are not on equal ground; as a result, "they become interdependent" (Yang, 1992, p. 101). Yang maintained that reward is the concept most closely associated with reciprocity and interdependence, and that the implementation of a reward system employs "face" and "favor," which are important resources in social exchanges in the traditional society. Fifth, relational harmony stresses that harmony and naturalness are pursued in interactions amongst the Chinese people. Yang noted that traditional Chinese people pursued interpersonal harmony to an extent of "harmony for the sake of harmony," and that there are even cases of "anxiety about disharmony" and "fear of conflicts" (p. 103).

Third, one area that deserves special attention concerns the level or units in organization–public relationships. In theory, public relations practitioners serve the function of boundary spanners for an organization (i.e., an organizational role). In essence, what regulates Western ethics in public relations is professional ethics, which are of universal and absolute natures that are not contingent on different issues, people, places, and/or time. Chinese ethics, on the other hand, are regulated by Confucian norms associated with relational orientation, which is essentially oriented from interpersonal relationships and amounts to situational ethics and particularistic ethics (Huang, 2000). Thus, the different normative natures could bring about moral and ethical challenges for the implementation of symmetrical communication.

The last challenge concerns the differences in the fundamental purpose and nature of communication between Asian and Western cultures (Scollon & Scollon, 1994). Scollon and Scollon (1994) suggested that, in Western cultures, the purpose of communication is information exchange. By contrast, people in Asian cultures communicate for the purpose of relationship building and maintenance; they emphasize relationships over communication.

In summary, traditional Chinese society is asymmetrically structured, holds different perspectives toward communication than does Western society, and emphasizes interpersonal relationships. The cultural assumption of relationship and communication is different from Western countries. The extent to which symmetrical communication is practiced is worthy of further exploration.

RESULTS

Research Question 1: Does Symmetrical Communication Currently Exist in Taiwan? If Yes, to What Extent, in What Form, and Under What Conditions Does It Exist?

Four models of public relations have been widely examined in public relations theory: the press agentry model, the public information model, the two-way symmetrical model, and the two-way asymmetrical model. Huang (2001b, 2004b) responded to the debates concerning public relations strategies conceptualized in terms of typology or "four boxes" (Grunig, 2000, 2001) and used five dimensions of public relations (i.e., symmetrical communication, two-way communication, interpersonal communication, mediated communication, and social activity) as an analytical framework[2] to ensure the flexibility of variation when a variety of models exist in practice. Using four models and five continua of public relations as a discussion conduit, Research Question 1 investigates the extent to which symmetrical communication is practiced in Taiwan.

Table 12.1 reported the means of four models of public relations for those studies adopting a quantitative approach (e.g., Liu, 2003; Wu et al., 2001) and general pattern of using models of public relations for those adopting a qualitative approach (e.g., Hung, 2004; Shu, Yang, & Liu, 1998; Sun, 1998). Table 12.2 depicts four studies using Huang's

---

[2]Huang (2001b, 2004b) suggested four essential continuum be taken into account from the Western literature and one from the Chinese culture to characterize public relations practice and strategies. The four Western dimensions are as follows. First, two-way communication—the distinguishing factor between one-way communication and two-way communication is whether there is feedback in the communication process. Feedback, which may originate from either party, can exist in various forms, such as conducting research or an interview. Second, interpersonal communication, and third, mediated communication—the key to distinguishing interpersonal communication from mass-mediated communication is the channel—whether these public relations activities occur face-to-face or via mass media. Interpersonal communication is conceptualized as face-to-face communication behavior, whereas mediated communication occurs via a mass medium (Huang, 2004b). Fourth, symmetrical communication—the definition has been noted earlier. The fifth and new dimension, social activity, which reflects Oriental culture, was added later into the instrument based on interview findings in the first survey of the current paper. Social activities and interpersonal communication are regarded as intercorrelated but separate dimensions. In Huang (2004b), interpersonal communication was conceptualized as a public relations practice occurring in a face-to-face yet information-oriented sense. In contrast, social activities were conceptualized in terms of the socially or *guanxi*-oriented nature, although social activity may be highly dependent on face-to-face interaction. Based on previous discussions, social activity may be conceptualized from the perspective of *guanxi*- and *renqing*-oriented strategies, such as holding dinners, gift giving, and ceremonial occasion invitations such as weddings, funerals, birthday parties, or festivals in one's hometown, which are different from the notion of interpersonal communications as typically defined.

TABLE 12.1

Mean and General Pattern Uses of Four Models of Public Relations in Taiwan*

Published Works	Research Method/Respondent Samples	Organization's or Public's Perspective	For-Profit or Nonprofit Organization	The Nature of the Issues Examined	Press Agentry	Public Information	Two-Way Asymmetrical	Two-way Symmetrical
Wu et al. (2001)	Survey to 40 PR practitioners from corporations and PR agencies (scale 1–7)	Organization's perspective	For-profit	Corporate PR and agency PR	5.23	4.29	4.82	5.09
Shu et al. (1998)	Case studies on three nonprofit foundations	Organization's perspective	Nonprofit	Nonmoneyed interest		v	v	v
Sun (1997)	Interviews with members of the telecommunication industries	Organization's perspective	For-profit	Community relations/moneyed interest		v		
Liu (2003)	Survey to 340 univer-sity students about their perceptions to-ward the university's Internet-based PR practice	Public's perspective	Nonprofit	Education relations/nonmoneyed interest	v	n/a	n/a	v 2.80 (more effective for satisfaction)
Hung (2004)	A case study that includes interviews with three persons in Taipei city government and an activist group	Both organization's and public's perspective	Nonprofit	Activist relations (on the issue of termination of licensed prostitution)	v	n/a	n/a	v

*v = the adoption of the particular model of public relations in qualitative research.

245

TABLE 12.2
Means of Five Continua of Public Relations Strategies in Taiwan

Published Works	Research Method/ Respondent Samples	Organization's or Public's Perspective	For-Profit or Nonprofit Organization	The Nature of the Issues Examined	Mediated Communication	Social Activity	Interpersonal Communication	Two-way Communication	Symmetrical Communication
Huang (2001b, Study 2)	A survey to 235 congressional liaisons (scale 1–4)	Organization's perspective	Nonprofit	Congressional relations, legislative–executive relations	2.54	2.19	3.70	3.58	3.45
Huang (2004b, Study 3)	A survey to 326 PR practitioners (scale 1–4)	Organization's perspective	For-profit	Corporate PR/agency PR	3.17	2.65	3.36	3.46	3.66
Huang (2004b, Study 1)	A survey to 235 legislative members and assistants (scale 1–4)	Public's perspective	Nonprofit	Congressional relations/Legislative – executive relations	2.21	1.99	3.22	2.40	2.11
Huang (2004a, Study 2)	A survey to 1,087 Taiwan residents (scale 1–4)	Public's perspective	A mixture of governmental, institutional, and for-profit	Nuclear issue (on the Taipower Company's PR practice involving the construction of the fourth nuclear power plant/a mixture of moneyed interests and non-moneyed interests)	n/a	n/a	n/a	n/a	2.16

(2004) five continua of public relations strategies. These two tables also noted the following three characteristics of the studies: whether an organization's or public's perspective was adopted, whether a for-profit or nonprofit organization was involved, and the nature of the issues examined.

The analyses of Tables 12.1 and 12.2 revealed the following results. All four models of public relations and five continua of public relations exist in Taiwan to some extent. The patterns of symmetrical communication, however, are inconclusive in two respects—different patterns exist in different contexts, issues, and groups' perspectives with respect to organization's perspective. Two points merit further exploration.

First, symmetrical communication was reported more frequently from an organization's perspective, although it was perceived less from the public's viewpoint. For example, in Huang (2001b, Study 2), Huang (2004b, Study 3), Wu et al. (2001) and Shu et al. (1998), which adopted organizations' perspective for investigation, symmetrical communication were reported as the first (mean = 3.66 on a 1–4 scale in Huang, 2004b, Study 3), second (mean = 5.09 on a 1–7 scale in Wu et al., 2001), or the least, third frequently used strategies (mean = 3.45 on a 1–4 scale in Huang, 2004a, Study 1). In contrast, Huang (2004a, Study 2) and Huang (2004b, Study 1), examined from stakeholders' viewpoints, revealed that symmetrical communication was "seldom" practiced, that is, the mean being 2.11 (in Huang, 2004b, Study 1) and 2.16 (in Huang, 2004a, Study 2) on a 1–4 scale.

Second, symmetrical communication seems to have higher correlations with nonprofit organizations and nonmoneyed issues than with for-profit organizations and moneyed interests. Liu (2003), examining a university's public relations, was the only study that adopted the stakeholders' perspective (i.e., students' viewpoints) and found symmetrical communication to be the most frequently used strategy. The reason that might factor in could be related to its nonprofit or nonmoneyed nature. Likewise, Shu et al. (1998), adopting an organization's perspective, noted the existence of two-way symmetrical communication in a nonprofit foundation.

Moreover, the results revealed two common patterns involving two-way communication and the press agentry model. First, except for Wu et al. (2001), two-way communication was practiced more frequently than was the one-way model, regardless of issue, organization, or perspective. For example, in Shu et al. (1998), Sun (1998), Liu (2003), and Hung (2004a), two-way communication was more frequently used than was the one-way model. Moreover, Huang (2004a, Study 2) demonstrated that the mean of two-way communication is about 3.5, much higher than the average of 2.5. Second, the press agentry model was reported to exist more often related to for-profit organizations than to nonprofit organizations. For example, in Wu et al. (2001), press agentry was rated as the most frequently used model (mean = 5.23 in a 1–7 scale) by public relations practitioners from corporations and PR agencies, whereas in Shu et al. (1998), none of the three nonprofit foundations interviewed self-reported use of press agentry.

Beyond four models of public relations, the following findings related to the five continua of public relations strategies merit discussion. First, a common self-reported pattern of uses by organizations across two studies (Huang, 2001b, Study 2; Huang, 2004b, Study 3) was that two-way communication, symmetrical communication, and interpersonal communication are the first three frequently used strategies, followed by mediated communication and social activities.

Second, conducing factor analyses on five public relations dimensions, Huang (2004b, Studies 1, 2, & 3), across three studies, found three distinct, or disconnected, patterns of strategies: two-way, interpersonal symmetrical communication; social activities; and mediated communication. The first pattern is that the correlations among interpersonal communication, two-way communication, and symmetrical communication are consistently high across three independent survey samples (Huang, 2004b, Studies 1, 2, & 3). The second pattern concerns the distinctiveness of social activity. Social activity was reported as the least frequently used strategy, but it was also found to be barely correlative with symmetrical communication across Huang's three studies (2004b, Studies 1, 2, 3). Third, mediated communication was also found to be barely correlated with symmetrical communication. Huang (2000) discerned that the correlation between mediated communication and symmetrical communication was low from the constituencies' perspective, whereas moderate from the public relations practitioners' perspective. Moreover, the correlations between mediated communication and social activities were consistently low across three studies. The results suggest that all respondents, regardless of organizations' or constituencies' perspectives, reserved the possibility of co-existence between social activities and mediated communication.

Synthesis

Compared with Grunig's et al. (1995) finding that the press agentry model predominates in three non-Anglo countries, this study found two distinctive differences. First, two-way communication was practiced more frequently than was the one-way model, across different groups' perspectives, and different natures of organizations and issues. The results suggest that conducting research and obtaining feedback from the publics or stakeholders have become a common practice of public relations in Taiwan. Second, the press agentry model seems to be more likely to correlate with for-profit organizations than with nonprofit ones. On other hand, the practice of symmetrical communication indeed exists in Taiwan, although the pattern of its existence is contingent on organization, issue, and perspective of perception. Specifically, symmetrical communication seems to be more correlative with organizations' perspective, nonprofit organizations, and nonmoneyed interest issues.

Moreover, the relationship between symmetrical communication and other practices of public relations sheds light on the extent to which, and the form of which, symmetrical communication is practiced. First, symmetrical communication often co-exists with, or appears in the form of, two-way communication and interpersonal communication, in both government and for-profit corporations in Taiwan. Second, two-way, interpersonal, symmetrical communication is barely correlated with mediated communication, at least from the public's perspective. Third, social activity—a *guanxi-*, *face-*, and *favor-*exchanged but not *information-*focused strategy—is a culturally oriented pattern. Both organizations and stakeholders, however, do not perceive social activity parallels with symmetrical communication. Namely, social activity seldom is practiced in a symmetrical manner. The co-existing patterns among various practices of public relations not only echo Grunig and Hunt's (1984) advocacy of the two-way symmetrical model and Grunig et al.'s proposition (1998) that symmetric communication with publics is difficult through the media, but also further extends this stream of research by illuminating that two-way symmetrical communication might indeed occur in an interpersonal or face-to-face manner.

Research Question 2: Does Symmetrical Communication Serve Organizations' Interests? In What Respects Can Symmetrical Communication Be Effective?

Grunig et al. (1995) suggested that public relations practices containing at least elements of the two-way symmetrical model may be generic to effective practice in all countries. Responding to this proposition, critics held that symmetrical communication does not serve the client organization's interests or even could abandon the clients' interests in favor of accommodating the interests of its publics (Grunig, 2000).

This study attempted to extend the line of research by further specifying the aspects of "effective practice." Consulting Heath (2001), Huang (2004b) assessed public relations effectiveness from three aspects: (a) public relations effectiveness with respect to direct-effect values—that is, organization–public relationships; Grunig & Huang, 2000; Huang, 2001b), organizational reputation (Grunig, 1993; Hon, 1997; Kim, 2001), and media exposure (Bissland, 1990; Dozier & Ehling, 1992; Lindenmann, 1988, 1993, 1995); (b) organizational effectiveness with respect to revenue-generation effects of public relations value, which include market input (Kim, 2001) and specific organizational goal (Huang, 2001a, 2001b; Kim, 2001); and (c) organizational effectiveness with respect to cost-reduction effects of public relations value, which includes conflict resolution (Anderson, 1992; L. Grunig, 1992; Huang, 1994, 1997, 2001a; Pavlik, 1987) and crisis management (Benoit & Brinson, 1999; Hearit, 1996; Marra, 1998).

Using the aforementioned measures as an analytical framework, Fig. 12.1 depicts the causal or correlation relationship shown in the published works among three types of effect indexes (i.e., direct effect of public relations effectives, cost-reduction paradigm, and revenue-generating paradigms of organizational effectiveness) and three aforementioned major public relations strategies found in Taiwan (i.e., two-way, interpersonal symmetrical communication, mediated communication, and social activity). Because the existing published works on the effects of symmetrical communication are mainly found in Huang (2001b, 2004b) and Liu (2003), as shown in the arrows connecting relevant variables, discussions are mainly based on these works.

The first analysis is to respond to Dozier and Lauzen (2000), which suggested examining moral and ethical contradiction in public relations practices. The results revealed that symmetrical communication, across four studies (Huang, 2001b, Studies 1 & 2; Huang, 2004a, Study 2; Huang, 2004b, Study 3), is inherently perceived as and executed in an ethical manner, regardless of legislative-administrative, nuclear, or general for-profit public relations issues. Specifically, factor analyses in Huang (2004a, Studies 1, 2, & 3) showed that the focal notions underlying the items in the factor "symmetrical/ethical communication" include symmetrical worldview and teleology.

Second, Fig. 12.1 indicated that symmetrical communication contributes to almost all of the indexes of public relations effectiveness and organizational effectiveness, indirectly or directly. First of all, a consistent pattern exists across two studies (Huang, 2004b, Studies 2 & 3), from both an organization's or a public's perspectives (i.e., symmetrical communication has the highest predictive power or correlation relationship with respect to two cost-reduction indexes—conflict resolution and crisis management— followed by two revenue-generating indexes—market input and overall organizational effectiveness).

Second, symmetrical communication positively contributed to the entire five outcome variables identified as relational characteristics of organization–public relationships. Three of the five relational characteristics (i.e., trust, control mutuality, and face and favor) then lead symmetrical communication to conflict resolution (Huang, 2001b, Study 2). Similarly, Liu (2003) demonstrated the causal relationship between symmetrical communication and satisfaction. Moreover, Huang

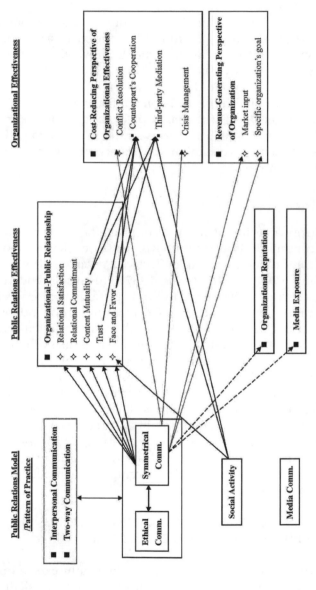

Figure 1: Effects of Symmetrical Communication and Other Relevant Public Relations Patterns *

*1: Three main patters of public relations practices in Taiwan, i.e., symmetrical communication, social activity, and mediated communication were investigated.

*2: Various arrow signs stand for the references the empirical support derived from.

→ Huang (2001b, study 2)
➔ Huang (2004a, study 2 & 3)
⇢ Huang (2004b, study 3)

FIG. 12.1.   Effects of symmetrical communication and other relevant public relations patterns.*†

251

(2004a, Study 3) also found statistically significant, positive correlations between symmetrical communication and organizational reputation and favorable media exposure. It should be noted, however, that this significant correlation only exists from organizations', but not stakeholders', viewpoints.

Third, it is worth noting that Huang (2004a, Studies 2 & 3) compared the effect sizes of all regression tests and found that the effect sizes from constituencies' perspective (Study 2) were higher than were those from organizations' perspective (Study 3). Fourth, Huang (2001b, Study 2) showed that social activities, among the five public relations strategies, exert distinctive, direct and indirect effects on conflict resolution. The study revealed that, mediated by the exchange of face and favor, the employment of social activities as public relations strategies can inspire the counterpublic to search for creative and mutually acceptable solutions or seek third-party mediation.

Synthesis

Moving beyond the previous literature that endorsed the need for two-way symmetrical communication primarily using the evidence showing that the other three models seemed ineffective (Anderson, 1992; L. Grunig, 1992; Huang, 1994, 2001a; Pavlik, 1987), this study rendered the support by demonstrating direct and indirect relationships between symmetrical communication and various effect measures from both organizations' and publics' perspectives. The result first suggested that symmetrical communication is inherently ethical, regardless of perspective, issue, or organization. Then, symmetrical communication was shown to not only *not* abandon client organizations' interests, but indeed to contribute to several performance measures of public relations effectiveness and organizational effectiveness. However, it should be noted that the effect size of the influences was in the order of cost-reduction indexes (crisis management and conflict resolution), revenue-generating indexes (overall organizational goal and market input), and mediating indexes (organization reputation, organization–public relationships, and media exposure).

DISCUSSIONS AND PROVISIONS OF SUGGESTIONS FOR FUTURE RESEARCH DIRECTIONS

This study found that a symmetrical worldview not only exists, but that its influence can be applied to different cultures, is universal, and upholds moral and ethical expectations. The latter allows an organization to meet its goals while being effective overall. Moreover, this study discerned that a new addition to the public relations model—social activity—considered along with the four Western models, has emerged as a result of taking into account Chinese culture when applying a Western theory.

This section provides a theoretical framework (Fig. 12.2) that suggests future research directions. The basic premise of this framework is that suggestions should be preceded by and rooted in a sound conceptual specification of global theory and local societal culture. Specifically, research should not only establish discourses with relevant Western theories, but should also factor in an indigenous cultural perspective of public relations. The framework is extended based on a conceptual model of Factors influencing the choice of a model of public relations, originated by Grunig and White (1992). The direction for future research as depicted in Fig. 12.2 includes three areas: antecedents—context and condition factors, symmetrical communication and other relevant public relations patterns, and the effects and consequence.

Antecedents

Contextual Factors and Specific Societal Culture.   The five contextual factors identified in the global theory of public relations and the four cultural dimensions in Hofstede's theory should serve as viable theoretical frameworks. Nevertheless, when applying a Western theory to an area rooted in a different culture, in addition to exploring these areas suggested in general theories, an international researcher should also be sensitive to the discrepancies embedded in theoretical and cultural assumptions between cultures. For example, when investigating public relations in Chinese society, the cultural characteristics such as *guanxi*, face, favor, Confucian's teaching, interpersonal relations, and relational orientation (Huang, 2004c; Yang, 1992) should be explored for investigation and explanation.

For instance, relational orientation could help us to better understand the reasons why and the extent to which symmetrical communication is practiced the way that it is. As previously suggested, only under a relation identified as within expressive tie and family could need rule (Hwang, 1987), symmetrical communication, or communal relationship occur. This proposition explains why symmetrical communication is more likely to occur in a nonprofit organization, inasmuch as a nonprofit organization is more likely to treat its publics as family members. Moreover, relational orientation also helps explain why symmetrical communication often co-exists with interpersonal communication rather than social activity. Interpersonal communication and need rule are applied in expressive tie. Social activity, mainly using *guanxi*, face, and favor as a medium of exchange, however, often occur in instrumental tie, and thus it would be hardly associated with symmetry. Further-

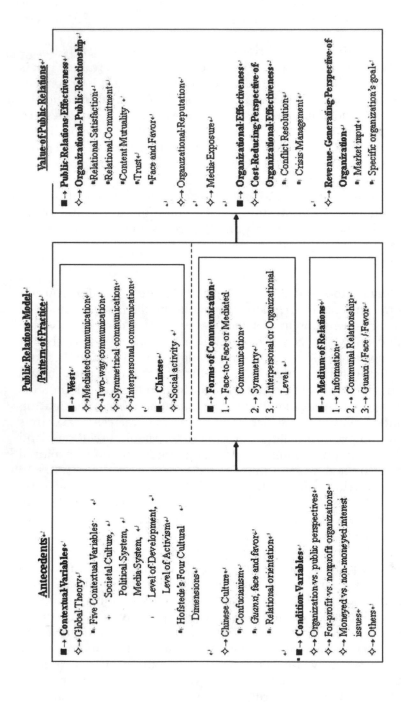

FIG. 12.2. A causal sequential model of international public relations.

more, due to the instrumental nature of social activity, its implementation often could bring about moral and ethical issues and challenges. Last, that mediated communication was rated as the second from the last frequently used strategy across three studies (Huang, 2004a, Studies 1, 2, 3) also suggested that typical Chinese might tend to adopt face-to-face communication rather than the mediated method for their public relations practice. This finding also echoes a Chinese cultural feature that emphasizes interpersonal rather than paper interaction.

In summary, an international researcher should look in depth into his or her culture and adopt a more indigenous perspective for investigation and interpretation. Thus, the body of knowledge can be enriched by bridging global application and local phenomenon.

Condition Variables.   This study showed that the extent to which symmetrical communication exists and is effective is contingent on the nature of perspective, issue, and organization. Thus, a critical next step should be to explore the relationships between symmetrical communication and the germane condition variables in order to better understand what variables moderate the existence and effects of symmetrical communication. For example, discrepant assessment of the value of symmetrical communication exists between an organization's and a public's perspectives. Some questions may deserve special attention in future research: Is symmetrical communication always more valued by the constituencies than by the organizations themselves? Could it be contingent on some certain condition factor, such as a normal versus a crisis situation? Could symmetrical communication be undervalued from a goal-attainment perspective? Taking a step further, under a condition that involves the interaction between and among different natures of organizations, issues, and perspectives, to what extent will the symmetrical communication be effective? Finally, what are the other pertinent condition variables that could factor into the practice and effects of symmetrical communication?

Symmetrical Communication and Other Relevant of Public Relations Patterns

The relevant theory should be enriched by developing an interpersonal-focused view of symmetrical communication, when taking into account the findings that two-way symmetrical communication might indeed occur in an interpersonal or face-to-face manner and that symmetric communication with publics is difficult through the media. The direction of future research, from an international or, more specifically, Chinese perspective, should focus on investigating symmetrical communication not only from an organizational level, but also from an interpersonal level, or at least a mixture of interpersonal and interorganizational approaches.

Moreover, to advance the research on symmetrical communication, scholars should look beyond the principles of mass communication as the rationale for defining the discipline (see also Coombs, 2001). Namely, the paradigm should shift from a linear mass communication approach to interpersonal communication perspective and to the integration of these two approaches. Thus, the interplay of the five continua of public relations strategies (Huang, 2004a) is worth of further investigation. Moreover, as shown in Fig. 12.2, the interplay between three forms of communication—face-to-face or mediated communication, symmetrical communication, and interpersonal or the organizational level of communication—and the three mediums of relations—information, communal relationship, and *guanxi*, face, or favor—is another direction worthy of examination. From an interdisciplinary perspective, incorporating other germane bodies of knowledge, such as negotiation, relationship, and conflict resolution, which are also interpersonal—or a mixture of interpersonal and interorganizational focused—into conceptualization and investigation of public relations theory is also critical. Thus, the concepts embedded in symmetrical communication, such as dialogue (Heath, 2000; Spicer, 2000) and collaboration (Grunig, 2000), would be more likely to occur and be effective.

Given the previously discussed paradigm shift, the relationship between mediated communication and symmetrical communication is still worth noting. The findings showed the disconnection between mediated communication and symmetrical communication, although organizations tend to consider the co-existence to a moderate extent whereas the stakeholder hardly perceives the concurrence. Comparing the findings and reality, the paradox is that public relations has long been regarded as a practice using mediated communication. Thus, on the one hand, the results urge public relations practitioners to strive for enhancing mediated communication in a symmetrical manner. On the other hand, it also should call for public relations scholars' special attention to explore related philosophical problems and practical solutions with respect to the contradiction. For example, Heath (1992) responded to the debate on when persuasion is unethical, and suggested that persuasion could be ethical if it meets three rhetorical principles: standards of truth and knowledge, good reasons, and perspectives criticism. Grunig (2000) and Spicer (2000) held collaborative advocacy as a pertinent argument. In summary, by extending the domain in this direction, the logical paradox involving symmetrical communication and mediated communication may be resolved through rigorous explication.

Last, this study demonstrated that in addition to the four Western public relations strategies, "social activity" indeed stands out as the fifth strategy salient in the cultural dimension. However, social activity, although it is barely practiced in a symmetrical manner, was also found to be effective in relationship building and conflict resolution. Thus, a critical next step would be to investigate in depth the form, the condition, and the consequences of using social activity at the individual, organization, and industry levels.

Although Grunig and Huang (2000) have examined the relationship strategy from the perspective of symmetry, it is limited with respect to interpersonal relationship compared to *guanxi-* and *favor-*associated activities. Steidlemeier (1999) investigated the double effects of gift giving in Chinese society, and found that people's respect for another person can be positively affected by it. Conversely, negative effects of a social activity like gift giving could include the appearance of bribery and the ensuing unethical consequences. Steidlemeier (1999) explained that in Chinese literature, there are examples condemning such gift giving as indications of corruption or extortion.

Given the potential dual nature of gift giving, the following questions could be examined: What are the rules of engaging in a social activity such as giving or receiving a gift? What expectations come as a result of gift giving? Could resource transfers such as tips, consulting fees, or commissions be interpreted as bribes in a culture that routinely employs such practices?

Another logical next step would be to further explore the relationships among these three patterns of public relations and their relative effects on various performance measures. Exploring the relationships and comparing relative effects could help answer questions such as: Under what kind of conditions can symmetrical, interpersonal communication prevail in its effects over social activity?

Effects and Consequences

The effect and consequence of symmetrical communication is another issue worthy of in-depth exploration in two aspects. The first concerns the ethical, moral concerns, or unintended consequence (Dozier & Lauzen, 2000) of symmetrical communication, which has been examined in the existing literature and should continue to be explored.

The second aspect suggests exploring the effects of symmetrical communication from a broader scope than those of the traditional measures. The study reviewed in this chapter demonstrated that the effects of symmetrical communication seem to be stronger on cost-reduction indexes (crisis management and conflict resolution) than on revenue-generating measures (overall organizational goal and market input) and mediating indexes (organization reputation, organization–public relationships, and media exposure). The findings, in essence, challenge two conventional wisdoms. The first challenges the effect of traditional measures of public relations values, such as media exposure (Lindenmann, 1988, 1993, 1995) and organization reputation (Kim, 2001), which were found to have the weakest effects in the current study. The second concerns the "cost" of symmetrical communication (Grunig, 2000). Grunig maintained that organizations would be motivated to develop exchange (asymmetrical) relationships more than communal relationships because of the cost of the latter. The results of this study were at least in contrast to, though not contrary to, to Grunig's argument, in that it found that symmetrical communication contributes to cost-reduction indexes to a great extent, compared to other measures.

Thus, the study reviewed here suggested an assessment of the value of public relations from the cost-reduction perspective or paradigm. Heath (2001) noted, "[T]he underpinning assumption is that public relations is a relationship-building professional activity that adds value to organizations because it increase the willingness of markets, audiences, and publics to support them rather than to oppose their effects" (p. 8). Parallel to Heath's argument, this chapter suggested that the underpinning assumption of symmetrical communication not only lives up to the moral and ethical expectation, but is also an effective professional activity that adds value to organizations because it mainly reduces the costs that result from crisis and conflict, then increases the willingness of publics to support them rather than oppose their efforts, and obtains positive media exposure and organizational reputation. Based on this chapter's discussion, the theory would be enriched by close analysis of the effects of symmetrical communication, along with other patterns of public relations, on cost-reduction, revenue-generation, and mediating variables.

REFERENCES

Anderson, D. S. (1992). Identifying and responding to activist publics: A case study. *Journal of Public Relations Research, 4,* 151-165.

Benoit, W. L., & Brinson, S. L. (1999). Queen Elizabeth's image repair discourse: Insensitive royal or compassionate queen. *Public Relations Review, 25*(2), 145–156.

Bissland, J. H. (1990). Accountability gap: Evaluation practices show improvement. *Public Relations Review, 10,* 3–12.

Bond, M. H., & Hwang, K. K. (1986). The social psychology of Chinese people. In M. H. Bond (Ed.), *The psychology of Chinese people* (pp. 213–266). New York: Oxford University Press.

Chang, H.-C. (2001). Harmony as performance: The turbulence under Chinese interpersonal communication. *Discourse Studies, 3*(2), 155–179.

Chen, G.-M., & Chung, J. (1994). The impact of Confucianism on organizational communication. *Communication Quarterly, 42*(2), 93–105.

Cheney, G., & Christensen, L. T. (2001). Public relations as contested terrain: A critical response. In R. L. Heath (Ed.), *Handbook of public relations* (pp. 167–182). Thousand Oaks, CA: Sage.

Clough, R. (1978). *Island China.* Cambridge, MA: Harvard University Press.

Coombs, W. T. (2001). Interpersonal communication and public relations. In R. L. Heath (Ed.), *Handbook of public relations* (pp. 105–114). Thousand Oaks, CA: Sage.

Culbertson, H. (1995). Introduction. In H. Culbertson & N. Chen (Eds.), *International public relations: A comparative analysis* (pp. 1–13). Mahwah, NJ: Lawrence Erlbaum Associates.

Dozier, D. M., & Ehling, W. P. (1992). Evaluation of public relations programs: What the literature tells us about their effects. In J. E. Grunig (Ed.), *Excellence in public relations and communications management* (pp. 159–185). Hillsdale, NJ: Lawrence Erlbaum Associates.

Dozier, D. M., & Lauzen, M. M. (2000). Liberating the intellectual domain from the practice: Public relations, activism, and the role of the scholar. *Journal of Public Relations Research, 12*(1), 3–23.

Fernandez, D. R., Carlson, D., Stepina, L. P., & Nicholson, J. D. (1997). Hofstede's country classification 25 years later, *Journal of Social Psychology, 137*(1), 43–54.

Fried, M. H. (1969). *The fabric of Chinese society: A study of the social life of a Chinese county seat.* New York: Octagon.

Grunig, J. E. (1992). *Excellence in public relations and communication management.* Hillsdale, NJ: Lawrence Erlbaum Associates.

Grunig, J. E. (1993). Image and substance from symbolic to behavioral relationships. *Public Relations Review, 19*(2), 121–139.

Grunig, J. E. (2000). Collectivism, collaboration, and societal corporatism as core professional values in public relations. *Journal of Public Relations Research, 12*(1), 23–49.

Grunig, J. E. (2001). Two-way symmetrical public relations: Past, present, and future. In R. L. Heath (Ed.), *Handbook of public relations* (pp. 11–30). Thousand Oaks, CA: Sage.

Grunig, J. E., Grunig, L. A., Sriramesh, K., Huang, Y. H., & Lyra, A. (1995). Models of public relations in an international setting. *Journal of Public Relations Research, 7*(3), 163–187.

Grunig, J. E., & Huang, Y. H. (2000). From organizational effectiveness to relationship indicators: Antecedents of relationships, public relations strategies, and relationship outcomes. In J. Ledingham & S. D. Bruning (Eds.), *Public relations as relationship management: A relational approach to the study and practice of public relations* (pp. 23–53). Mahwah, NJ: Lawrence Erlbaum Associates.

Grunig, J. E., & Hunt, T. (1984). *Managing public relations.* New York: CBS College Publishing.

Grunig, J. E., & White, J. (1992). The effect of worldviews on public relations theory and practice. In J. E. Grunig (Ed.), *Excellence in public relations and communication management* (pp. 31–64). Hillsdale, NJ: Lawrence Erlbaum Associates.

Grunig, L. A. (1992). Toward the philosophy of public relations. In E. L. Toth & R. L. Heath (Eds.), *Rhetorical and critical approaches to public relations* (pp. 65–91). Hillsdale, NJ: Lawrence Erlbaum Associates.

Grunig, L. A., Grunig, J. E., & Dozier, D. M. (2002). *Excellent public relations and effective organizations: A study of communication management in three countries.* Mahwah, NJ: Lawrence Erlbaum Associates.

Grunig, L. A., Grunig, J. E., & Vercic, D. (1998). Are the IABC's excellence principles generic? Comparing Slovenia and the United States, the United Kingdom and Canada. *Journal of Communication Management, 2,* 335–356.

Hearit, K. M. (1996). The use of counter-attack in apologetic public relations crises: The case of General Motors vs. Dateline NBC. *Public Relations Review, 22*(3), 233–248.

Heath, R. L. (1992). Critical perspectives on public relations. In E. L. Toth & R. L. Heath (Eds.), *Rhetorical and critical approaches to public relations* (pp. 37–64). Hillsdale, NJ: Lawrence Erlbaum Associates.

Heath, R. L. (2000). A rhetorical perspective on the values of public relations: Crossroads and pathways toward concurrence. *Journal of Public Relations Research, 12*(1), 69–92.

Heath, R. L. (2001). A rhetorical enactment rationale for public relations: The good organization communicating well. In R. L. Heath (Ed.), *Handbook of public relations* (pp. 31–50). Thousand Oaks, CA: Sage.

Hofstede, G. (1980). *Culture's consequences: International differences in work-related values.* Newbury Park, CA: Sage.

Holtzhausen, D. R., Petersen, B. K., & Tindall, N. T. J. (2003). Exploding the myth of the symmetrical/asymmetrical dichotomy: Public relations models in the new South Africa. *Public Relations Research, 15*(4), 305–343.

Hon, L. C. (1997). What have you done for me lately? Exploring effectiveness in public relations. *Journal of Public Relations Research, 9*(1), 1–30.

Huang, Y. H. (1993). Revision and prospect of public relations in Taiwan. *ROC Advertising Yearbook, 1992–1993,* pp. 91–102.

Huang, Y. H. (1994). *Ke chi feng hsien yu huan pao kang cheng: Tai-wan min chung feng hsien jen chih ke an yen chiu* [Technological risk and environmental activism: Case studies of public risk perception in Taiwan]. Taipei: Wu-nan Tsung Shu.

Huang, Y. H. (1997). *Public relations, organization–public relationships, and conflict management.* Unpublished doctoral dissertation, University of Maryland, College Park.

Huang, Y. H. (2000). The personal influence model and gao guanxi in Taiwan Chinese public relations. *Public Relations Review, 26*(2), 216–239.

Huang, Y. H. (2001a). OPRA: A cross-cultural, multiple-item scale for measuring organization–public relationships. *Journal of Public Relations Research, 13*(1), 61–91.

Huang, Y. H. (2001b). Value of public relations: Effects on organization–public relationships mediating conflict resolution. *Journal of Public Relations Research, 13*(4), 265–301.

Huang, Y. H. (2004a). PRSA: Scale development for exploring the cross-cultural impetus of public relations strategies. *Journalism and Mass Communication Quarterly, 81*(2), 307–326.

Huang, Y. H. (2004b). Is symmetrical communication ethical and effective? *Journal of Business Ethics, 53*(4), 333–352.

Huang, Y. H. (2004c). A Chinese perspective of intercultural organization–public relationship. *Intercultural Communication Studies, 12*(4), 151–176.

Hung, C. J. F. (2004). Relationship building, activism, and conflict resolution: A case study on the termination of licensed prostitution in Taipei City. *Asian Journal of Communication, 13*(2), 21–49.

Hwang, K. K. (1987). Face and favor: The Chinese power game. *American Journal of Sociology, 92,* 944–974.

Jacob, B. J. (1979). A preliminary model of particularistic ties in Chinese political alliances: *Ran-ching* and *kuan-hsi* in a rural Taiwanese township. *China Quarterly, 78,* 237–273.

Kersten, A. (1994). The ethics and ideology of public relations; A critical examination of American theory and practice. In W. Armberecht & U. Zabel (Eds.), *Normative aspekte der public relations* (pp. 109–130). Opladen, Germany: Westdeutscher Verlag.

Kim, Y. (2001). Measuring the economic value of public relations. *Journal of Public Relations Research, 13*(1), 3–26.

King, A. Y. C. (1985). The individual and group in Confucianism: A relational perspective. In D. E. Munro (Ed.), *Individualism and Holism: Studies in Confucian and Taoist values.* Ann Arbor: Center of Chinese Studies, University of Michigan.

Lauzen, L., & Dozier, D. M. (1994). Issues management mediation of linkages between environmental complexity and management of the public relations function. *Journal of Public Relations Research, 6,* 163–184.

Leichty, G., & Springston, J. (1993). Reconsidering public relations models. *Public Relations Review, 19*(4), 327–339.

Leitch, S., & Neilson, D. (2001). Bringing publics into public relations: New theoretical frameworks for practice. In R. L. Heath (Ed.), *Handbook of public relations* (pp. 127–138). Thousand Oaks, CA: Sage.

L'Etang, J. (1996). Public relations and rhetoric. In J. L'Etang & M. Pieczka (Eds.), *Critical perspective in public relations* (pp. 106–123). London: International Thomson Business Press.

Leung, T. K. P., Wong, Y. H., & Wong, S. (1996). A study of Hong Kong business's perception of the role of *guanxie* in the People's Republic of China. *Journal of Business Ethics, 15,* 749–758.

Lindenmann, W. K. (1988). Beyond the clipbook. *Public Relations Journal, 44*(12), 22–26.

Lindenmann, W. K. (1993). An effectiveness yardstick to measure public relations success. *Public Relations Quarterly, 38*(1), 7–9.

Lindenmann, W. K. (1995, April 25). *Measurement: It's the hottest thing these days in PR.* Speech given to the PRSA Counselors Academy, Key West, FL.

Liu, C. D. (2003). University's internet-based public relations strategy: An analysis of internet users' perception and their interactive satisfaction. *Journal of Advertising & Public Relations, 20,* 13–50.

Marra, F. J. (1998). Crisis communication plans: Poor predictors of excellence crisis public relations. *Journal of Management Studies, 34*(5), 769–791.

Murphy, P. (1991). The limits of symmetry: A game theory approach to symmetric and asymmetric public relations. In L. A. Grunig & J. E. Grunig (Eds.), *Public relations research annual* (Vol. 3, pp. 115–131). Hillsdale, NJ: Lawrence Erlbaum Associates.

Pattakos, A. K. (1989). Growth in activist groups: How can business cope? *Long-Range Planning, 22,* 98–104.

Pavlik, J. V. (1987). *Public relations: What research tells us.* Newbury Park, CA: Sage.

Republic of China Yearbook 1998. (1998). Taipei, Taiwan: Government Information Office.

Scollon, R., & Scollon. S. W. (1994). Face parameters in East-West discourse. In S. Ting-Toomey (Ed.), *The challenge of facework* (pp. 1–14). Albany: State University of New York Press.

Sha, B., & Huang, Y. H. (2003). Public relations in Taiwan: Evolving with the infrastructure. In K. Sriramesh (Ed.), *Public relations in Asia* (pp. 161–185). Singapore: Thomson Learning.

Shu, M. L., Yang, C. C., & Liu, C. C. (1998). Public relations strategies in nonprofit organizations. *Public Opinion, 204*, 1–25.

Spicer, C. H. (2000). Public relations in a democratic society: Value and values. *Journal of Public Relations Research, 12*(1), 115–130.

Sriramesh, K., Kim, Y., & Takasaki, M. (1999). ??Public relations in three Asian cultures: An analysis. *Public Relations Research, 11*(4), 271–292.

Sriramesh, K., & Vercic, D. (2001). International public relations: A framework for future research. *Journal of Communication Management, 6*(2), 103–117.

Sriramesh, K., & White, J. (1992). Societal culture and public relations. In J. E. Grunig (Ed.), *Excellence in public relations and communication management* (pp. 531–575). Hillsdale, NJ: Lawrence Erlbaum Associates.

Steidlemeier, P. (1999). Gift giving, bribery and corruption: Ethical management of business relationships in China. *Journal of Business Ethics, 20*, 121–131.

Sun, H. H. (1998). Has the paradigm shifted? An analysis of cable television system's community relations strategies. *Journal of Advertising and Public Relations, 3*, 159–185.

Taiwan: World of Information Business Intelligence Report. (2000). Essex, England: Walden Publishing.

Tien, H. M. (1989). *The great transition: Political and social change in the Republic of China.* Taipei, Taiwan: SMC Publishing.

Toth, E., & Pavlik, L. (2000). Public relations values in the new millennium. *Journal of Public Relations Research, 12*(1), 1–2.

Van der Meiden, A. (1993). Public relations and "other" modalities of professional communication: Asymmetric presuppositions for a new theoretical discussion. *International Public Relations Review, 16*(3), 8–11.

Walder, A. G. (1983). Organized dependency and cultures of authority in Chinese industry. *Journal of Asian Studies, 63*, 51–75.

Wu, M. Y., Taylor, M., & Chen, M. J. (2001). Exploring societal and cultural influences on Taiwanese public relations. *Public Relations Review, 27*, 317–336.

Yang, K. S. (1992). Zhong guo ren de she hui qu xiangù she hui hu dong de guan dian [Chinese social orientation: A social-interaction approach]. In K. S. Yang & A. B. Yu (Eds.), *Zhong guo ren de xin li yu xing wenùli nian yu fang fa pian [Chinese psychology and behavior: Methodological and conceptual considerations].* Taipei, Taiwan: Gue-Gyuan Book Co.

Chapter 13

Relationship Measures Applied to Practice

Jennifer Scott
Ogilvy PR Worldwide

Over the past 2 years, StrategyOne—the specialist research agency owned by Daniel J. Edelman, Inc.—has been applying the Relationship Index on behalf of corporate clients. This research, which has included Fortune 500 companies across three continents, has provided valuable insights into how the index functions to serve the needs of communications professionals and the goals of organizations.

The Relationship Index itself was developed by Dr. James Grunig as a means of measuring and managing an organization's relationships with its most strategic publics (key stakeholders). It is based on the assumption that the establishment and maintenance of long-terms relationships will allow organizations to be effective by helping them achieve their goals. These goals are numerous and can include objectives relating to organizational structure, executive leadership, labor force management, supply system efficiency, product development and marketing, infrastructure, financial operations, patents, legislative environment, and community relations.

The Relationship Index itself is comprised of a series of standardized and validated agree/disagree statements. Respondents are asked to rate the degree to which they think each statement describes a corporation or organization on a scale of 1 to 9 (where 1 is "does not describe at all" and 9 is "describes very well"). The index measures the quality of relationships across four key dimensions: trust (including integrity, dependability, and competence), commitment (the extent to which each party believes that the relationship is worth spending energy to maintain and promote), control mutuality (the degree to which parties agree on who has the rightful power to influence the other), and satisfaction (the ex-

263

tent to which positive expectations about the other are reinforced). The index generates scores on a scale of 1 to 9 for each of these dimensions. As such, it establishes a new standard for evaluating and informing public relations strategy and the role of PR in business outcomes.

StrategyOne has worked with Dr. Grunig on applying the Relationship Index in the corporate environment. These have not been pilot studies, but rather fully realized applications of the instrument for clients who have been willing to invest in obtaining a better understanding of their stakeholder relationships. The fact that we have—over the past 2 years—had the opportunity to implement six major and several minor Relationship Index studies indicates that this tool does have resonance and value for major corporations. This chapter contains highlights from the past 2 years of real-world index application. These can be segmented into three broad categories: perceived value, methodological application, and outcomes. Each contains interesting and perhaps surprising findings, which speak to the larger role of relationship management in organizations.

PERCEIVED VALUE

In our experience, the Relationship Index has been most valued as a stakeholder management tool, rather than as a means of understanding and engaging the general public. This is due to its focus on diagnosing the dimensions of what are, in fact, quite complex and "committed" relationships. The questions that make up the index are not best applied to the casual observer of a corporate entity. Instead, they tap into emotions and values that are evoked only as the result of a reasonably detailed understanding of an organization and a set of important intersecting interests. Thus, we have found that the most nuanced, consistent, and detailed index data comes from studies that are implemented among interested stakeholder groups, including non-government organization (NGO) representatives, journalists, investors, analysts, employees, regulators, legislators, and industry peers and competitors. This focus on engaged elites rather than regular consumers is not only driven by the fact that the index is best suited to diagnose more sophisticated relationships; it is also because the most effective relationship building tends to take place in a two-way, personalized, often one-to-one environment. This is high-investment engagement and, as a result, is generally only applied to important stakeholders. Thus, both PR professionals and their clients in corporate communications groups tend to value the index most for what it can tell them about how to engage with these elites. Our observations that follow are thus confined to our work on applying the index to stakeholder groups.

The value of the Relationship Index is most deeply understood and appreciated by PR professionals on the agency side, as well as by their counterparts inside of corporations. In the case of the latter, this is partly because these executives are often tasked by the C-suite with fulfilling stakeholder management programs, but—at the same time—are not provided with the most basic of forecasting tools common to other departments within the company. Thus, whereas the IT department has access to detailed information on the cost and capabilities of various operational systems for its planning purposes, and the sales group can easily obtain retail data for the past year against which to plot new goals for the forthcoming cycle, the vice president of communications is often expected to deliver against an undefined target (Who exactly *are* the stakeholders?), on undefined goals (What, exactly, are we supposed to *do* with them?), and using ad hoc techniques (How are we supposed to *achieve* this?). In this world of intangibles and educated guesses, the Relationship Index is valued as a means of concretely mapping the universe of stakeholders to prioritize which groups are most in need of engagement, understanding the most appropriate terms of that engagement, and providing a benchmark against which to track the impact of a communications program over time. The numeric nature of the index is an important element of its perceived value. Being able to apply a score to the various dimensions of stakeholder relationships allows PR executives to speak in quantitative terms about what has always been seen as a notoriously "soft" variable. This, in turn, can engender a deeper appreciation for the relevance of good stakeholder relationships to business success.

We have also found that the Relationship Index is highly valued on the agency side. For the PR professional tasked with applying an outreach program, the Relationship Index is an important validation of the overall strategy because of its ability to prioritize stakeholder groups according to the quality of their existing relationships with an organization. Thus, the index helps the PR professional decide which stakeholder relationships are healthy and need only ongoing maintenance, which are vulnerable and need increased engagement, and which are weak, and require new efforts at relationship building. The Relationship Index also helps agency professionals determine where to invest campaign resources because of its ability to concretely demonstrate the importance of engaging with various groups. Thus, if the Relationship Index scores show that a powerful stakeholder group has a deeply antagonistic relationship with a client, this helps reinforce a decision to put greater resources against outreach to this constituency. Finally, the Relationship Index is a valuable source of tactical insight because of its ability to score across numerous dimensions of a relationship. This latter attribute has proved to be perhaps the most valuable for agency professionals. Tasked with crafting messages and engagement techniques, these professionals value the ability to mine the "nuts and bolts" of index scores to determine which dimensions of each stakeholder relationship are weakest, and to address these directly in the campaign.

The quantitative nature of the Relationship Index naturally raises the question of whether it is possible to establish norms or benchmarks against which to measure and track a company's index scores. Client requests for industry or sector norms against which to assess their own scores can be difficult to respond to, especially when dealing with elite stakeholder groups. There are a number of reasons for this. For example, elite stakeholders, by their nature, have very specific and often specialized relationships with corporations. We have found that the same groups tend to engage very differently with corporations depending on variables that include where they are located geographically, the pressing issues of the moment, their own specific areas of concern, and the presence of other players in the space. For example, we have found that environmental NGOs tend to mobilize around local issues, and that these range across a wide spectrum—from wetlands preservation, to air pollution, to deforestation, to sustainable agriculture. Over time, these issues can change from minor to major issues of concern. Thus, any large corporation wanting to measure its index scores from environmental NGOs against those for other companies in its sector is faced with a difficult and somewhat unreliable comparison. The company may be involved in operations that tap into timely, very specific, local environmental concerns of a few important NGOs, making its scores on the index unique. Counseling clients against relying too heavily on comparisons with other companies' scores on the index can be difficult because—naturally—they want to evaluate their scores in a larger industry context.

Having said this, StrategyOne has developed a very workable methodological solution to the question of benchmarking: Incorporating peer/competitor relationship diagnostics into the stakeholder audit. Thus, researchers obtain scores for one to two of our client's direct competitors or industry peers on the index in the course of the research. This provides a specific, time-sensitive point of comparison. It also offers a very helpful profiling of the other players in the space, who are likely to be actively engaged in relationship building with the same organizations and directly impacting their perceptions. For this solution to work methodologically, it can only be applied to one—or at most two—other organizations. This is due to the lack of tolerance among elite respondents for completing multiple runs of the Relationship Index battery. Thus, we tend to obtain an index reading for our client first and then to follow up with one or two peers in rotation in case respondents show fatigue or resistance after the second run through the index.

METHODOLOGICAL APPLICATION

Application of the index has raised various methodological challenges and opportunities that are apparent only once an instrument is in the field. Most of these, if anticipated and managed, have little impact on the reliability and value of the index.

There is a very important methodological approach to our application of the index, which we believe allows the instrument to yield its most valuable data. We always situate the battery of index questions within a larger qualitative instrument that allows us to probe for insights into *why* respondents give our clients the scores they do. Thus, we usually schedule 30- to 45-minute in-depth interviews with our respondents, administered in person or by phone. After some initial discussion about the general context (understanding the respondent's professional priorities, probing their perceptions of important issues in general, etc.), we conventionally administer the index for our client and up to two peers. This delivers a fairly fresh and uninfluenced read and takes about 10 minutes. Following this, we probe more deeply into why the respondent has given the scores they have. This qualitative "shell" around the index obviously provides valuable data for corporations and agencies wanting to develop more meaningful and effective engagement strategies. However,, from a research perspective, it also helps to validate the index scores and to compensate for occasions when the total number of elite respondents in our sample is limited. Hence, we aim to come out of every stakeholder audit with an integrated profile of each group, in which the index scores fit logically into the bigger picture of the company–stakeholder dynamic.

Perhaps the most interesting methodological challenge surrounding the application of the index results from the fact that—in our experience—it is most useful when applied to elites who have relatively close relationships with the organization in question. This automatically reduces the sample size to fewer than 50 respondents per interest group in many cases. The difficulty of conducting research with these respondents (recruiting, scheduling, incentivizing, etc.), also depresses sample size, as does the cost- and time-prohibitive nature of interviewing them in larger numbers. The quantitative, standardized nature of the index would seem to demand large, statistically robust sample sizes to ensure a workable margin of error in the analysis. However, the nature of the target constituency and the actual purpose of the audit argue against this. First, elites—be they financial analysts, journalists, directors of nonprofits, or legislators—have complex and dynamic relationships with organizations in which they have an interest. Together, they make up a profile of opinion and behavior, but, in many ways, they also have a significant impact when they operate in small groups or even as individuals. This fact tends to diminish the importance of securing a large sample size—even though a large sample seems methodologically appropriate for a quantitative instrument.

Second, the value of stakeholder audits to communications derives primarily from their ability to discern how elites are likely to react to corporations going forward, based on the quality of their existing relationships. The index—because it taps into the drivers of future behaviors by examining their relational underpinnings—is the ideal tool for this enterprise. Again, this means that more importance is placed on building a detailed profile of key relational drivers and motivations within elite groups, rather than on ensuring a large enough sample to achieve highly reliable statistical projections. In practice, we have found that only a relatively small number of elite respondents per group are required to yield scores on the index that add up to a cohesive, logical picture of the key drivers of that group's relationship with the company. Thus, after about 10 interviews with carefully selected elites in each stakeholder category, we begin to notice clear, consistent patterns developing in the index scores. If this is not the case, and the data appears disjointed and contradictory, we would suggest increasing the number of respondents. We have not encountered this circumstance as of yet. Another caveat must be applied to the small sample sizes used in our approach. Because our use of the index is relatively new, we have not yet had the opportunity to track stakeholder relationships over longer time frames such as a year or two (although we do have tracking studies scheduled). Thus, we are not in a position to report on whether modest sample sizes support reliable longitudinal tracking.

The use of relatively small sample sizes in stakeholder studies begs the question of whether the number of respondents is robust enough to discern differences *within* stakeholder groups. Are studies with fewer than 50 respondents able to provide the level of detail that will allow us to develop relationship profiles within the media, NGOs, business partners, and so on? What we have found, in practice, is that our ability to do this kind of analysis is primarily contingent on the care we take in building up our list of potential respondents. Thus, if a client is interested in learning more about its relationship with directors of Washington think tanks, we are careful to obtain interviews with a good cross-section of this group of influencers—ranging across the political spectrum and including both small and large organizations.

Likewise, we aim to conduct interviews with journalists from local, major regional, and national media who cover issues relevant to our clients. In this case, we have often found that, for companies whose operations not located in the major media centers (e.g., New York, Washington, Los Angeles), relationships with the local press are generally healthier than with the national press. This often reflects the fact that local press is more aware of a corporation's involvement with local communities, including its value as an employer. This immediacy helps enrich relationships. However, national press is at a critical remove and requires a more deliberate engagement to build a healthy relationship. Further to this, we are particularly careful to include smaller, local NGOs in any study that includes this stakeholder group, because we have found that much NGO activity is driven by local concerns. Interestingly, these are often the groups who "fly under the radar" of the corporation and with whom they have the least healthy relationships. This can be problematic because of the ability of local NGOs to build local alliances and mobilize community sentiment. At this point, it is a short step to national media involvement, and the issue—which could likely have been resolved at the local level—becomes much more loaded and the parties more intractably divided.

We have also been able to engage in limited applications of the index across various Anglophone countries, and have found that, in places like the United Kingdom and Australia, the index appears to "translate" well. We have also piloted the index across countries in the European Union and South America, as well as in Russia, and have found that it does seem to deliver consistent and cohesive data within various stakeholder groups that broadly corresponds to findings from other qualitative and quantitative studies. In a few cases, clients have noted that the index scores appear to correlate with existing data on other measures of business success, such as share of market, legislative climate, and stock price. Although this is anecdotal evidence at this stage, it argues for a more deliberated study of the correspondence between Relationship Index scores and other, more traditional measures of corporate success.

An interesting methodological challenge has also arisen based on the actual diagnostic thrust of the index—namely, that it investigates the quality of relationships. It appears that the concept of having a "relationship" with an organization (rather than with an individual) is not always a comfortable one for respondents to entertain. Thus, we have found that a small minority of elite stakeholder respondents can be resistant to the instrument. These respondents do not overtly think of themselves as having a personal relationship with a corporate entity; rather, they think of themselves as engaging with that corporation in a very dispassionate and rational way as representatives of their organization's interests, rather than their own. Hence, when they are asked about relational elements that include emotional content around trust, shared values, mutual respect, and so on, they are challenged to think in this way about themselves.

In these cases, the respondent will often ask the researcher, "Am I supposed to answer this from a professional or personal perspective?" or "Do you want me to speak for my organization or for myself?" When this question is posed, standard practice is to ask the respondent to react from a personal perspective. In most cases, respondents are able and willing to do so. Analytically, we must bear in mind that organizational imperatives and agendas always influence relationships and outcomes. However, we have found that the index gives valuable insight into the relational dimensions of an organization's dealings with our clients, allowing them to engage with these groups more appropriately and productively. For example, we found that NGO respondents regarded one of our clients as inaccessible and arrogant (low commitment and control mutuality scores). This was clearly reflected in wariness on the part of their organizations toward engaging constructively and openly with our client. On the basis of the index data, our client was able to examine and understand these attitudes among the NGOs. This insight also enabled our client to reflect on how its own suspicion of these same groups was contributing to the standoff between them.

To a lesser extent, we have noticed that a minority of respondents prefer not to complete the full index because they base their sense of their own professional integrity on their ability to be dispassionate about organizations. Journalists, who sometimes see any form of "relationship" with the organizations they write about to be a breach of their professional ethics, tend to fall into this category. In these cases, we do not attempt to complete the index if the respondent is resistant.

To get the best out of the index, we have found it necessary to develop a narrative introduction to the battery of questions that our researchers review prior to administering the battery. This introduction is designed to prepare the respondent for a standardized battery, on which they might find some of the statements not directly relevant to their situation or slightly unusual in their phrasing. It is also intended to put elite respondents—who are used to answering very specific, tailored questions—at ease with the more generic-sounding phraseology of the index. Most understand the value and purpose of standardized batteries and are willing to co-operate to the best of their ability.

OUTCOMES

All of our index applications have been proprietary investigations for paying clients and, as such, we cannot use any of them as case studies. However, we would like to speak very generally about some insights the index has given us on relationships between organizations and their most important stakeholder constituencies.

First, we have found that one of the most valuable outcomes of the application of the index has been that it enables PR professionals and their clients to integrate communications management more effectively into the overall business decision making of the organization. Critically, it helps PR departments gain the ear of the CEO and the opportunity to be seen as a key variable in the effective management of the company. It helps elevate the PR function to a level where it can lay claim to a place at the table at which major management decisions are being made. Because the index maps the matrix of relationships surrounding a company, it also helps make transparent the potential for those relationships to impact a company's ability to achieve its business goals. Thus, if the index demonstrates poor scores on the critical dimension of trust, it becomes clear to the company that its statements (financial, operational, organizational) are less likely to be well received, that its business goals (financial forecasts, forward-looking business plans, etc.) are less likely to be taken at face value, and that its ability to deliver on business goals is less likely to be viewed confidently. In this case, a poor trust score clearly has the potential to impact the bottom line by depressing investor confidence, inhibiting goodwill, weakening alliances with third parties or business partners, allowing for competitive incursions, and possibly removing the willingness of others to give the organization a fair hearing in a time of crisis. By helping demonstrate the link between good relationships and the bottom line, the index helps focus the C-suite on the importance of the communications function. This means that communication comes to be seen as a variable that needs to be taken into account when making business decisions, and not only brought into play once those decisions have been made and require implementation.

A number of general insights regarding the relationships between organizations and their stakeholders have emerged as a result of applying the index. Among the metatrends exposed by repeated applications of the instrument is a phenomenon related to the dimension of trust. Trust is divided into three components: integrity, dependability, and competence. In analyzing trust scores for large corporations, we have often found that the overall score on this dimension is elevated by the competence element and depressed by the integrity and dependability elements. Qualitative questioning around respondents' reasons for giving these scores has revealed that large corporations—because of their huge resources—are usually expected to be able to deliver on their goals (competence). However, they are not as often trusted to be telling the truth about what those goals are (integrity), or to necessarily have the willingness to deliver on them (dependability).

Because of this split in scores for the different elements of trust, we mandate that our researchers always separate out this dimension into its component parts in the analytic phase. We want to ensure that our clients are not misled by a fairly robust trust score into thinking that they are doing well on reliability and credibility, when the good score is being driven by competence ratings. Having said this, it has been very helpful to the practice of organizational communications and outreach to be able to dissect trust into its three component parts. This is because good scores on competency mean that our clients have one critical element of the trust dimension intact and can use this as a foundation for creating a relationship that works to reinforce the other two. In many cases, we counsel our clients to leverage their perceived competency (i.e., their significant resources) to initiate outreach to less resourced stakeholders. Thus perceived, competence becomes the foundation on which companies can build an appreciation for the fact that they are also credible and reliable. The strong competency dimension often brings to the table third parties that would otherwise be resistant to engaging with the company. Furthermore, once a healthy level of trust is established, the other relationship dimensions become easier to address and improve. Without the foundational element of trust, there are limits to how healthy perceptions of satisfaction, commitment, control mutuality, and shared values can become.

Another general finding from the application of the index relates to the dimension of commitment. We have found at times a sharp difference between the commitment scores a company receives from more business-orientated stakeholder groups (analysts, journalists, peers/competitors, business partners, etc.) and those from NGOs representatives. For many companies, NGOs comprise a relatively undefined stakeholder group, one that is often thought to be hostile, and for which there seem to be few rules of engagement. This is particularly concerning given evidence of the rise in the stature of NGOs globally. The Edelman Trust Barometer (an annual survey of trust among influencers across eight countries) has tracked the steady rise in trust in NGOs in the United States. The 2005 Barometer showed NGOs to be the most trusted type of institution in the United States (compared to business, media, and government), putting them on a par with NGOs in the United Kingdom, France, and Germany.

The low commitment scores that NGO representatives so often give corporations on the Relationship Index are an indicator of the need for companies to revise their attitudes toward these groups and to be more deliberate about establishing processes for relationship building with them. Interestingly, when we have probed into reasons for poor commitment scores on the index, we have inevitably found that the most pressing issues for NGO representatives is that they believe that the corporation does not want to have a relationship with them at all. They neither expect the company to hold a similar agenda, nor to agree with them on key issues. What they do want is for the company to at least show goodwill in engaging with them. This means that, in many cases, all a company needs to do to elevate its commitment scores is to establish contact and perhaps a means of engaging in dialogue with NGOs.

The company does not have to agree with the NGO's agenda or give in to its requests. This reaching out often requires relatively little commitment in terms of resources on the part of companies. What it does require is a shift in corporate attitude toward these groups, which is often more difficult than it seems.

Finally, repeated applications of the index have shown that control mutuality scores are usually depressed relative to those for the other dimensions. This is particularly the case for large Fortune 500 companies. Our qualitative probing indicates that stakeholders perceive that large corporations have a significant power advantage over them. This assumption appears to hold across almost all stakeholder groups, but especially among journalists, NGO representatives, legislators, regulators, and employees. We can speculate that large companies are, by their very nature, challenged to convince external stakeholder groups of their willingness to cede a degree of control over the management of issues of mutual concern. These companies are assumed to hold virtually all the cards—and, in fact, this may well be true. However, it behooves these companies to make a particular effort to be magnanimous. Surrender of a relatively small degree of control is likely to have significant value in terms of building healthy stakeholder relationships. This earned relationship equity will stand the company in good stead, particularly during those times when it may not—for some reason—hold all the cards.

CONCLUSION

Application of the Relationship Index in the real world of PR has validated its enormous value as an instrument that elevates the status of the practice of communications, provides strategic insights and tactical direction, and contributes significantly to the general reserve of knowledge about how to facilitate healthy relationships between corporations and their stakeholders. Application of the index has also affirmed the value of relationships to corporate health and success, and contributes significantly to the integration of the PR and communications function into the highest decision-making structures of major corporations.

Chapter 14

The Extent of Ethics

Shannon A. Bowen
University of Maryland

One that desires to excel should endeavor it in those things that are in themselves most excellent.
—Epictetus (Goodman, 1997, p. 258)

Epictetus would, no doubt, consider ethics one of those excellent endeavors in and of itself. Philosophers such as Aristotle and Kant declared ethics to be the most pure of all intellectual pursuits, worthy of contemplation by its very nature, as opposed to being dependent on its outcomes. Therefore, it is a natural progression of the *Excellence in Public Relations and Communication Management* (Grunig, 1992c) study to consider the ethical, the moral, and the good to be essential components of excellence. Scholars such as this author argue that ethics is the most crucial of all excellence factors because it unifies and promulgates all of the other factors of excellence. Ethics is a single excellence factor and the common underpinning of *all* factors that predict excellent public relations. This chapter discusses the unification of ethics and the principles of excellence as an advancement toward the future of Excellence Theory.

Readers of this volume are presumed to be somewhat conversant with Excellence Theory. This exploration focuses on the generic or universally applicable principles of excellence and their linkages to ethics: the extent of ethics in Excellence Theory. None of the principles of excellence can be studied without, at the least, an admonition to implement them ethically in practice. Moral philosophy is the theory of ethics, and it is used to reinforce the understanding and applicability of ethics in public relations theory and practice. As suggested in Grunig, Grunig, and Dozier (2002), this research picks up the challenge of locating "the role of public relations in the ethical decision making of organizations" (p. 554). Ethics permeates the excellence factor and is inseparable from much of the theory in the Excellence Study, as explained in the following discussion. By applying moral philosophy and a deeper conceptualization in ethics, the Excellence Theory is extended and enriched in both theoretical and practical explanatory and predictive power. This chapter emphasizes the central role of ethics in the future of the public relations discipline.

THE OVERALL VALUE OF PUBLIC RELATIONS

As the Excellence Study demonstrated, the value of public relations can be studied at four levels: the level of a specific public relations program, the level of the public relations function, the level of contributing to organizational effectiveness, and the societal level. Ethical considerations can be applied to all four of these levels, but perhaps hold the most impact at the organizational and societal levels.

Ethical communication enhances the value that excellent public relations adds to an organization. Research has found that an organization can maintain more trusting long-term relationships with publics if those publics know to expect consistently ethical decisions (Bowen, 2004b; Huang, 2001, 2004). In this respect, ethical communication results in effectiveness in both cost-reduction paradigms and the revenue- generation paradigms favored by practitioners, as identified by Heath (2001). Although there are many approaches to measuring organizational effectiveness, the Excellence Study (Grunig et al., 2002) concluded, "[W]e show that the value of public relations comes from the relationships that communicators develop and maintain with publics" (p. xi).

Furthermore, when relationships are maintained, the organization experiences a greater level of autonomy free from externally imposed regulations or strictures. Moral philosophy has a long tradition of supporting autonomy as a basis for ethical decision making. In fact, Kant (1785/1964) argued that a moral decision is an impossibility without the necessary condition of autonomy, which supports a rational and impartial moral analysis. Excellence Theory researchers argued for autonomy on the basis of creating value to the organization and enhancing organizational effectiveness, but again an ethical basis extends this principle of public relations excellence.

The value of ethics in public relations is arguably most significant at the societal level. Public relations can help organizations be socially responsible and good citizens of the communities in which they operate. However, a broader view of ethical communication reveals that public relations functions as an important facilitator of communication in a society. Public relations performs the ethically responsible role of exchanging information with publics, so that an informed society can make reasoned judgments.

AN ETHICAL IMPERATIVE OF COMMUNICATION

Public relations makes information available both inside and outside of organizations that would not otherwise be free flowing, contributes to understanding in various publics of organizational policy and issues, and helps in problem solving between organizations and their publics (including other organizations, governments, and cultures). This expansive function, when performed ethically, upholds the moral responsibility of facilitating dialogue (Habermas, 1984; Pearson, 1989a) as an ethical imperative. Therefore, public relations holds the enormous moral obligation of facilitating dialogue and maintaining relationships on a social level. Public relations—in the ethical role of facilitating communication among systems, subsystems, organizations, and publics in the environment—is the proverbial oil that greases the wheels of society. The implications of this societal level impact are enormous: Public relations communicates on levels of public policy, activism, and social norms, and even values on a global level in multinational organizations. As an organizational function, public relations is undoubtedly influential at the societal level. Public relations even surpasses the research and development function of an organization in spurring social impact, because without communication, diffusion theory shows that new innovations are rarely adopted.

Following the logic of this argument one step further allows the revelation that public relations is indeed responsible for the betterment of society. Through the facilitation of open communication and maintenance of symmetrical relationships with publics, the ethical obligation of dialogue is furthered, and society is improved by the open flow of communication. An informed marketplace of ideas would be almost impossible without public relations to provide information and to engage in dialogue, debate, and policy formation. The social role of public relations is to communicate in the public interest and for the good of society. Facilitating a free and open flow of information is ethically sound, and this responsibility belongs to public relations practitioners, whether they work in the corporate world, the government, nonprofit, education, activism, and so on. Public relations fills an important role in the structure of society by providing information flow between disparate groups and organizations. Public policy is made from the debate surrounding issues of interest, and it is public relations practitioners who lead communication on those issues. They define the issues of concern, delineate options for resolution, and champion preferred outcomes. Social change is the result of this process, and an outcome with such far-reaching implications must be handled with a great sense of moral responsibility. Therefore, it is imperative that public relations practitioners are grounded in moral analysis and use ethical techniques to facilitate understanding through communication.

A STRUCTURAL-FUNCTIONALIST RATIONALE FOR PUBLIC RELATIONS' SOCIAL ROLE

Systems theory contributes to the concept of the responsible social role for public relations in helping society function, but this perspective is highly based on structural-functionalist (Durkheim, 1893/1984) sociology. The structural-functionalist school of sociology maintains that society is held together by the structural relationships between social institutions (Collins, 1985). Public relations is one of these social functions that serves to hold society together by maintaining relationships through communication.

The professional communicators of society are responsible for maintaining relationships and functional linkages, resolving conflicts in the public arena, advancing ideals, helping the informed marketplace of ideas exist, and facilitating greater knowledge and understanding among publics. In today's complex and fragmented society, it is difficult to envision an informed public without the existence of public relations. As the disassociation that structural-functionalists termed "anomie" (Durkheim, 1897/1951) increases, people might become confused and lost in the social world without communication to contextualize and create meaning as well as order. Most people would have a difficult time receiving messages they cared about without the communication and context provided by public relations professionals. A world without public relations would run contrary to the ideals of a free marketplace and an informed public, and would create social disorder and increased anomie.

This social role must be viewed with respect and discipline because of the enormous impact that public relations efforts can have in changing society. Lobbying efforts, social acceptance campaigns, and even war or peace can be informed and influenced by the communication of public relations. The news media is also heavily influenced by public relations' communication, with some researchers (Cutlip, Center, & Broom, 2000) finding that about three fourths of news stories originate from a public relations source. The impact of defining issues, advancing causes and issues, determining who communicates and what is communicated (and what is not), and what is worthy of communication (and what is not) are functions of public relations that hold tremendous impact. Furthermore, consider the responsibilities that public relations practitioners hold not only to an employer or client, or even to a profession, but also to society as a whole. The macro, societal-level impact of public relations is hard to accurately pinpoint because of its pervasive nature, but the social role of public relations is indeed enormous.

By combining moral philosophy and sociology's structural-functionalist perspective, theory can be extended from the Excellence Study to include an enlarged social role for public relations. Public relations is serving a larger and more ethically responsible role by communicating for the good of society, both for the benefit of specific groups and for the maintenance of society itself. Civilization has grown to the point of becoming a global information society. With this increase in information, the public relations function holds responsibility for helping to create meaning, clarify issues, provide access to pertinent information, cut through information overload with strategically targeted messages, and facilitate problem-solving communication. The creation and maintenance of positive social linkages—relationships—is perhaps the most vital and ethical function of public relations that exists in the context of serving parts of a larger social system. All of these responsibilities are crucial to the maintenance of a larger social order, and these arguments illustrate that public relations exists to and for the benefit of society.

EMPOWERMENT OF THE PUBLIC RELATIONS FUNCTION

Excellence Study researchers (Dozier, Grunig, & Grunig, 1995; Grunig, 1992c; Grunig et al., 2002) argued that the public relations function should be empowered within the organization, and discerned strong empirical support for their contention. Empowerment included two primary variables: being invited into the strategic planning process, and being a part of the dominant coalition of an organization, as well as supporting factors such as having the respect of the CEO along with credibility and a shared worldview of symmetrical public relations (Grunig et al., 2002). All of these components of the excellence factor can be reinforced and supported by the extension of ethics to this area. Because of space limitations, this chapter focuses on the primary variables of inclusion in strategic management and membership in the dominant coalition.

Moral philosophy provides powerful means of analysis of moral dilemmas, and if the public relations function is responsible for this analysis, it is likely to be integral to strategic management of the organization. Often this responsibility is the domain of issues management or even crisis management as parts of public relations. Scholars (Bowen, 2002; Grunig & Repper, 1992; Heath, 1997; Lauzen & Dozier, 1994) asserted that issues management should guide the complex decisions facing management on problematic issues, potential crises, or moral dilemmas. Using deontological moral philosophy to analyze ethical dilemmas allows a thorough consideration of all publics involved in or affected by the decision (see Fig. 14.1; note that the arrows at each corner in the schema represent two-way communication).

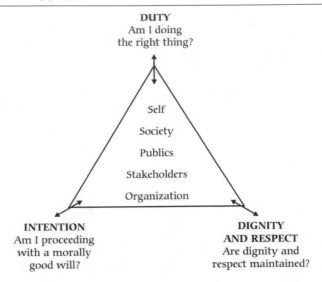

DUTY
Am I doing
the right thing?

Self

Society

Publics

Stakeholders

Organization

INTENTION
Am I proceeding
with a morally
good will?

DIGNITY
AND RESPECT
Are dignity and
respect maintained?

FIG. 14.1.   Ethical consideration triangle. Reprinted by permission. Bowen, S. A. (2000). *A theory of ethical issues management: Contributions of Kantian deontology to public relations' ethics and decision making.* Unpublished doctoral dissertation, University of Maryland, College Park, MD.

Applying the concepts of ethics to the Excellence Theory allows the argument for inclusion in the dominant coalition to counsel on ethical issues to be strengthened. Public relations is the only organizational function with extensive knowledge of publics—and in many cases has existing relationships with those publics—who can accurately conduct a moral analysis and include the values of those publics in that analysis. The linkages to publics provided by public relations' boundary-spanning role make it a natural location for consideration of the values of those publics and how they will interpret an organization's actions. This input can be provided to the dominant coalition and the CEO in times of strategic decision making. Such counsel proved invaluable to the CEO in research conducted by Bowen (2002), and reinforced the value of including public relations in the dominant coalition.

Congruent with moral philosophy, decisions with consequences affecting publics should include the viewpoints of those publics. The Kantian argument for autonomy in moral analysis strongly advocates the independent analysis of moral dilemmas by public relations; then, the role of counsel to the CEO and dominant coalition can be enacted giving the viewpoint of that independent moral analysis. The relationships maintained by the public relations function should prove invaluable in conducting a thorough moral analysis that weighs many points of view. The information resulting from these relationships can be viewed as a commodity that public relations brings to the management table. This unique commodity, combined with the skill of moral analysis, should help public relations earn credibility in counseling the CEO and becoming a part of the dominant coalition. This credibility can be used to further the social responsibility of the organization by advising the CEO on ethical actions, and can also benefit the public relations function by placing it in a respected and in-demand position in the organization.

Membership of public relations in the dominant coalition is strongly correlated with organizational effectiveness. Grunig et al. (2002) explained, "[N]early two thirds of top communicators in the top 10% of our organizations were in that powerful group, compared to about 45% in the overall sample" (pp. 191–192). The fact that the best organizations include public relations in the dominant coalition indicates that they desire counsel from the public relations function regarding issues, the external environment, public opinion, and management concerns that impact the organization. Including a public relations perspective in the strategic management function is ethical, because it uses the boundary-spanning role of practitioners to include the views of diverse publics in organizational decision making. These publics are both internal and external, but they would not have appreciable input into organizational decision making without the public relations function providing a critical linkage and communication input to the organization. Ethics is maintained in this variable by the inclusion of many voices in strategy and the consideration of the impact of the organization on publics, rather than implementing unilateral, self-interested decisions.

Deontological ethics requires that the respect and dignity of others be maintained in ethical decision making. Through using this mode of input into the organization publics, can have some voice in organizational decisions. Their ideas must still be meritorious and worthy of concern rather than simply being taken at face value due to their source, but they have the opportunity to be included in the strategic management process of the organization. The organization should be open to input from publics in the environment; bringing information into the organization was proclaimed in the Excellence Study (Grunig et al., 2002) to be one of the most valuable contributions of public relations. Ethical aspects of equal responsibility to both publics and organization are seen in this boundary-spanning role. Again, the Excellence Theory is congruent with the ethical tenets of moral philosophers.

The ethical aspects of the Excellence Theory extend to include acting in the process of strategic management on behalf of both the organization and its publics. A sense of rationality and mutual benefit should be maintained when considering ethical decisions, and the public relations function has the responsibility of conducting this analysis, incorporating it into strategic management, and communicating with publics regarding the situation. Although true objectivity is not possible in the human condition, one can strive to be objective in evaluating the ethics of decisions. Objectivity can be augmented with rationality, which can compensate for many of the biases and subjective concerns that enter the ethical decision-making process. Public relations acting as the rational ethical counsel is a valuable part of the social role of the function that serves society, and also plays a pivotal role in enhancing organizational efficacy.

COMMUNICATOR ROLES

Roles, or the activities people do in their daily work, show what duties a practitioner generally performs within the public relations function. In general, there are communication technicians, who are writers performing skills-based roles, and communication managers, who are held accountable for results and making policy decisions. The technician role requires a specific skill set for creating communication tactics, whereas the manager role is based in experience, strategy, and knowledge (Dozier & Broom, 1995). Despite prior controversy over the reliability of the public relations roles, factor analysis in the Excellence Study revealed the distinct emergence of both manager and technician roles (Dozier et al., 1995). The Excellence Study showed clearly and without a doubt that public relations needs to be more than a technical function of communication implementation, and must be led by public relations officers who are managers (Grunig et al., 2002). Public relations managers should play a strategic management role within the organization and in leading the public relations department.

Part of the management role is decisional autonomy, or the freedom to analyze situations and implement decisions as the managers' judgment dictates (Daft & Weick, 1984). In deontological moral philosophy, the autonomy to conduct an independent moral analysis is a prerequisite for making an ethical choice. The manager role is congruent with moral philosophy in allowing public relations managers the decisional autonomy needed to arrive at an ethical outcome. If public relations managers are accorded a role in the strategic planning function of the organization, their responsibility level is increased. With this strategic management responsibility also comes increased autonomy in their decision making. Although these levels of responsibility generally decide organizational policy, the public relations technician also has ethical decisions to make. Technicians are often responsible for deciding which vendors to use for a campaign, how to word the communication about a client, the points to emphasize in the CEO's speech, and so on. These types of decisions can be fraught with ethical dilemmas and also require a degree of moral autonomy and scrutiny demanded of professionals. Many technicians face ethical decisions just as often as do their counterparts in management. The ethical role that technicians play might be, at times, overlooked. However, the word choice in a speech written by a technician has made national headlines on more than one occasion. Therefore, the management and technical roles must work together to be ethically responsible.

As rational, moral beings, technicians and managers have equal responsibility under deontological philosophy to analyze the ethics of their decisions. Those in the manager role should consult with, encourage, and train technicians to recognize and deal with ethically problematic situations (Sims, 1994). Managers should have the added knowledge of how to generate, interpret, and use research in public relations (Grunig et al., 2002), and this research can also shed light on the values of publics and how to maintain an ethically appropriate consideration for them. The knowledge of research and the symmetrical model used for dialogue with publics required in the manager role is upheld as an ethical approach by deontological philosophy. The manager performs his or her duty to consider others and the universal implications of an issue before making a decision. These arguments are congruent with those in the Excellence Study regarding roles in the public relations function. In conclusion, both the manager and technician roles in the public relations function require ethical sensitivity and moral analysis. The manager role, as stressed in the Excellence Study research, must lead the way in these considerations.

INTRAORGANIZATIONAL STRUCTURE OF THE PUBLIC RELATIONS FUNCTION

Public relations must be valued in itself as an important part of the management team of an organization (Grunig & Grunig, 2000), in terms of both Excellence Theory and moral philosophy. When the public relations function is encroached upon or subsumed by other organizational functions, its potential for excellence is drastically diminished (Grunig & Grunig, 1998). Public relations can add the greatest value in an organization when it provides an independent viewpoint in counseling the dominant coalition or in strategic planning and decision making. The ability to provide an independent viewpoint is taken away when public relations is subsumed by marketing, legal, human resources, or other organizational functions. Encroachment is ethically problematic because it places the voices of publics in a position from which they might never reach the ears of decision makers. Through applying moral philosophy, we have already discussed that denying the dignity and respect owed to others by considering them in decisions conflicts with the pursuit of ethics. It is the moral duty of the organization to consider those whom it affects; not including public relations in the decision-making core of the organization makes it exceptionally difficult or impossible to know and consider the views of those publics. Organizations fail this moral test when they exclude public relations from decision making involving those whom the decisions will affect.

Better decisions arise from considering a multiplicity of views and options, and this ability is constricted if public relations is not included in the dominant coalition and unable to bring in the views of publics because it is subsumed by another organizational function (Dozier & Grunig, 1992). This author's (Bowen, 2002) research also found that a reporting structure in which public relations was included in the dominant coalition resulted in more effectiveness in dealing with organizational issues than did a structure in which public relations reported to the legal department. Organizational structures in which public relations is not a member of the dominant coalition have less potential of being excellent than do those in which public relations is, at least most of the time, a part of that decision-making core. They also have less of a chance of being ethical. To make ethical decisions, the senior public relations executive should have the authority and autonomy to provide his or her analysis and input into organizational decisions. Because of the difficulty in gaining membership in or access to the dominant coalition, many organizations exclude the counsel of public relations and thereby do not maximize their ethical potential.

Most often, when encroachment occurs, public relations is subsumed by the marketing function of an organization (Lauzen, 1992). The marketing function is well versed in communication with consumer publics, but often the other, nonconsumer publics of an organization are not communicated with in such a scenario. When public relations is subsumed by marketing, the focus of the function shifts from maintaining mutually beneficial relationships with all types of publics to a limited scope of product publicity. Community groups, government legislators, activists, government regulators, and many other important publics are then ignored or forgotten in decision making, and little or no efforts are made at maintaining relationships with nonconsumer publics. Again, this scenario is ethically unacceptable because it fails the obligation of dialogue and it does not maintain the inherent dignity and respect of these publics who are worthy of consideration but are ignored in favor of consumer publics. Encroachment or subsumption of the public relations function in an organization clearly hinders and threatens the ability of that organization's management to make ethically sound decisions.

MODELS AND DIMENSIONS OF PUBLIC RELATIONS

Public relations can be accurately described by the classic four models—public information, press agentry, two-way asymmetrical, and two-way symmetrical (Grunig & Hunt, 1984)—and those models are both normative and positive (Grunig, 2001). Despite the skepticism of some scholars (Deatherage & Hazleton, 1998; L'Etang & Pieczka, 1996), the excellence research found that even the most normative model, the two-way symmetrical model, existed in practice and was regularly used by public relations practitioners (Grunig et al., 2002). The models of public relations are indeed linked with ethical considerations. Intention drives the ultimate determination of the moral worth of an action, and thus the use of any of the models can be argued to be ethical if the intention driving it is ethical. However, only the symmetrical model withstands moral scrutiny as ethical in a *prima facie* sense. Grunig and Grunig (1996) argued the symmetrical model to be ethical in that it provided dialogue and contributed to the social responsibility of the public relations function. Deontological philosophy can also be used to reinforce the inherent ethical nature of the symmetrical model by applying the categorical imperative. Intention or a morally good, pure will holds the highest place in deontological philosophy. Intention is the ultimate arbiter of the moral worth of an action.

Kant's (1785/1964, 1793/1974) deontological moral approach was based on the duty of upholding universal moral principles. In deontological philosophy, the decision maker has the duty to analyze the situation with regard to respecting the dignity of others. Only in the dialogue for the purposes of understanding found in the two-way symmetrical model is the dignity of the other maintained. The two-way asymmetrical model also uses dialogue (Grunig, Grunig, & Dozier, 1999), but the motive in that model is not to understand but rather to persuade, manipulate, or change; these motives are not deemed morally worthy in a prima facie sense in deontological philosophy. Of course, there are exceptions (in which persuasion is undertaken out of good intention), but on the whole, the asymmetrical model fails the ethical test because it is not based on respecting the dignity of the other to make up his or her mind free of influence. The press agentry model clearly fails the ethical test because of its persuasive or manipulative intent, and the public information model fails the ethical test because it ignores the moral obligation of dialogue. That leaves the symmetrical model as the only approach that consistently passes the rigorous moral tests of Kantian philosophy. A symmetrical approach maintains the obligation of dialogue and respects the dignity of others by engaging them in discussion that is aimed at mutual understanding, rather than applying persuasion. Using the symmetrical model for purposes of mutual understanding and dialogue is consistent with the "good will" (Kant, 1785/1993, p. 154) or morally good intention required in deontological philosophy.

Excellence Study researchers (Grunig et al., 2002) clarified the components of excellence in relation to the four models of public relations, concluding that four "underlying dimensions" (p. 378) provided keys to excellence. These underlying dimensions were: two-way communication, meaning that public relations was based on research; mediated or interpersonal communication with publics, and a symmetrical approach (often contending with asymmetrical approaches). The researchers explained that two-way communication included the symmetrical model, the asymmetrical, mixed-motive, or contingency model, because little conceptual difference existed. The researchers suggested a fourth dimension of excellence: ethics, although they noted it was not originally included in the study. Grunig et al. (2002) concluded, "Further research, we predict, will establish ethics as a crucial component of excellent public relations" (p. 378). Research in this vein has already begun (Bowen, 2000, 2004a, 2005b; Huang, 2004), and this chapter promises to extend that conceptualization further by illustrating how ethics works in synergy with and buttresses the other factors of excellence.

CULTIVATING, BUILDING, AND MAINTAINING RELATIONSHIPS WITH PUBLICS

According to Ledingham and Bruning (2000), relationship management as the core function of public relations (rather than simply a functionary communication role) was first advocated by Ferguson in 1984. Ferguson (as cited in Grunig & Huang, 2000) wrote, "The unit of study should not be the organization, nor the public, nor the communication process. Rather the unit of study should be the relationships between organizations and their publics" (p. 23). As discussed in an earlier section of this chapter, engaging in dialogue with publics is an ethically responsible course of action and is the moral obligation or duty of an organization that makes decisions affecting those publics. Now we turn to the maintenance of relationships with those publics for discussion and ethical analyses.

The Excellence Study placed relationships at the center of the purpose of the public relations function. Grunig (1992a) explained, "The major purpose of public relations is to save money for the organization by building relationships with publics that constrain or enhance the ability of the organization to meet its mission" (p. 20). Excellence Study research (Grunig et al., 2002) noted that organizations that used two-way communication to build relationships with publics held a more long-term view than did those who did not, but expected a return on their investment in the long run. The researchers (Grunig et al., 2002) explained that participants were aware that two-way communication built and maintained relationships over the long term: "Top communicators and their CEOs tended to agree that two-way programs of communication could result in long-term gains that were critically important to the organization" (p. 467).

In terms of moral philosophy, the maintenance of relationships is ethical and preferable to an organization not making efforts at relationships maintenance. Deontology sees the duty of the organization to consider the perspective of publics as one driving force behind the ethical imperative of relationship maintenance. The other ethical consideration is that relationships are to be built in order to maintain the dignity and respect of publics in contact with the organization. To ignore these publics or not make efforts to build relationships would fail the second test of the categorical imperative regarding maintaining the dignity and respect of those affected or involved with a decision. Furthermore, research (Bowen, 2000) has shown that publics can grow to trust the organization when its decisions are consistently ethical, rational, and consider the perspective or values of the publics they affect. Trust and credibility arising from this type of ethical consistency enhanced the relationship between organization and publics (Bowen, 2004b), and were found to be antecedents of relationships between organizations and publics (Grunig & Huang, 2000). Excellence Study researchers (Grunig et al., 2002) concluded, "Relationships based on trust or credibility ... help organizations weather crises in the short term and survive—even prosper—in the long term" (p. 460). Trust and credibility are enhanced by relationship building and maintenance, and this paradigm results in an ethical approach according to analysis through deontological moral philosophy.

ACTIVISM

Activism challenges organizations to remain in touch with publics in its environment, specifically with the demands of those publics who become active on one or more issues. These groups can be small or large, formal or informal, regular or episodic, and so on (Murphy & Dee, 1992). As discussed in the excellence research (Grunig, 1992), activists are highly effective at disrupting the target organization. The disruption can take the form of the need to handle a major initiative (e.g., a boycott or class action suit) or it can simply mean that the organization must redirect some resources to address the activist issue. Organizations are often thrown into turmoil or even crisis when they are targeted by activists; however, the Excellence Study found that this need not be the case (Grunig et al., 2002).

Activism can indicate pressures to change from the environment, so that the organization maintains a policy consistent with those of the publics it serves. The empirical research conducted in the Excellence Study found that the two-way symmetrical model exists in practice and is regularly used by public relations practitioners, even though it is a highly normative model (Grunig et al., 2002). A two-way approach, using elements of asymmetrical in an overall symmetrical paradigm, is particularly useful when an organization exists in a turbulent environment, is a target of government regulation, or is approached by activist groups. When symmetrical approaches of relationship maintenance are employed by an organization, it is less likely to be a target for activist groups than if it ignores or antagonizes them. In fact, incorporating the ideas of activist groups might promote the interests of the organization and its ultimate success, as found in Bowen's (2005b) research. Risk management research (Heath, Seshadri, & Lee, 1998) also advised the monitoring and inclusion of activist and community publics whenever possible as a method of stabilizing a turbulent environment and sharing risk.

The ethical aspects of communication with activists are perhaps more complicated than are readily apparent. One complicating factor is that the dominant coalition rarely realizes the importance of maintaining relationships with activists unless the public relations practitioner has made valiant efforts in that area. Power-control theory (Hage, 1980) explains the matter: Those holding power in the organization (the dominant coalition) will make decisions that serve their own interests. This theory is positive but lacks philosophical appeal because it is based on self-interest alone, a morally unsound method of decision analysis according to deontologists (Habermas, 1979; Kant, 1790/1952). Public relations professionals must struggle to impress on the power elite in the organization the crucial nature of communication with activists before they create problems for the organization that are often difficult and expensive to solve.

The ethical basis for the inclusion of activist perspectives can be viewed as a deontological obligation to equally and objectively consider the interests of each party affected by a decision, as well as to maintain respect and dialogue. However, this rationale might not be as successful in countering the insular power-control mindset of the dominant coalition as would be pointing out the negative consequences caused by activism. Self-interested decision making is dangerous in its insular nature; systems theory also advises the organization to incorporate the input and feedback of publics into its strategic management. To ignore activists is not only to risk missing valuable input from the environment, but also to court disaster in the form of expensive strikes, boycotts, and other activities that lead to a tarnished reputation for the organization.

Ethically, both a systems approach and a symmetrical paradigm are moral ways in which to communicate with publics. Excellence researchers (Grunig et al., 2002) advised that accepting the input of activist groups could enhance the equilibrium between an organization and its environment, giving it a competitive advantage over organizations that do not maintain relationships with activist groups. The Excellence Theory is again congruent with moral philosophy; advice based on the empirical findings of the study is not only ethical but also wise from a business management perspective.

INTERNAL COMMUNICATION AND ORGANIZATIONAL CULTURE

Internal factors of organizational culture and systems of internal communication allow the organization to function as a system operating toward self-defined goals. Effective internal communication and a supportive organizational culture are important components of excellence because employee publics are arguably those most important to the success or failure of an organization (Bowen, 2005d). Scholars (Grunig, 1992b; Sriramesh, Grunig, & Buffington, 1992; Wright, 1995) have posited that organizations can maximize human resource potential by instituting an effective system of two-way communication inside the organization. When assessed through deontology, the ethical nature of communication with internal and employee publics is essentially the same as for other publics of an organization: obligations of dignity and respect, as well as dialogue. A Kantian universal norm to treat others as you would wish to be treated, and would want all others treated in an ideal world, appears especially appropriate in the internal communication of an organization, where stakes are high for employees who trust the organization with their retirement and other interests (Bowen & Heath, 2005; Sims & Brinkman, 2003).

Much of the responsibility for ethical internal communication rests with the dominant coalition, who should lead by example in matters of open, honest communication, and should reinforce an organizational culture that values and rewards ethical behavior. Research (Bowen, 2004b) based on the Excellence Study discerned that ethical communication should also be rewarded and trained internally. The qualitative findings of the Excellence Study (Grunig et al., 2002) also discussed the importance of the CEO in fostering an emphasis on internal communication, and moreover quantitatively identified a significant relationship between the excellence factor and participatory organizational cultures. Excellent organizations were also noted to be more likely to foster the careers of women and, to a lesser degree, minorities (Grunig et al., 2002). These findings are congruent with what would be ethically demanded through considerations of autonomy, moral equality, dignity, and respect.

DIRECTIONS FOR FUTURE RESEARCH

Dewey (1916) argued that democracy and social responsibility are predicated by an education grounded through experience, reflection, and awareness. We must strive to educate ourselves as public relations scholars and practitioners in ethics, through reflection, awareness, and experience with using modes of moral analysis. Much work remains to be done in the area of public relations ethics, both academically and in practice. This section explores and suggests but a few directions of many for future research and reflection.

One of the primary avenues of research to explore is the actual components of excellent public relations ethics. Although this author has undertaken some exploratory research in the area (Bowen, 2004b), future research should address the organizational and individual characteristics that foster ethical decision making in public relations. Research in business ethics identified organizational characteristics(Chun, 2005; Grojean, Resick, Dickson, & Smith, 2004; Sauser, 2005) encouraging ethical decisions, whereas other scholars focused on the individual characteristics, such as integrity (Dudzinski, 2004; Koehn, 2005) or honesty (Quinn, Reed, Browne, & Hiers, 1997; Smith, 2003), that support ethical behavior. Public relations scholars should build on these findings and apply them to the public relations discipline. We need to learn more about how and to what extent public relations practitioners understand and use ethics before we can improve on their ability to act as ethics counselors. Studying the component factors of excellent and ethical public relations would give us the knowledge necessary to address deficiencies and extend competencies in the field.

Another area of future ethical study is to apply more types of philosophy to public relations ethics. Excellence Theory also has significant ideological overlap with the teleological school of moral philosophy in its consideration of the actions of an organization and their consequences on publics and relationships with those publics. Huang's (2004) factor analysis found that symmetrical communication included the concept of teleology. Theoretical explication and practical application of teleological frameworks to Excellence Theory and symmetrical versus asymmetrical communication would prove valuable in ascertaining the parameters of ethical public relations. The work of neo-Kantian philosophers, such as Jurgen Habermas, would also enrich our conceptualization of ethics and add to the deontological approach studied by this author. For example, Pearson (1989b) applied Habermas' ideal communication situation to public relations in discussing dialogue and coorientation, but the theory is rich enough to support further application in public relations ethics.

Research on ethics conducted by this author and colleagues for a grant supported by the IABC Research Foundation offered more questions regarding ethics in the public relations practice. The data (Bowen, 2005c) confirmed earlier findings (Wright, 1985) of large and significant disparities between men and women on ethical issues, preferred modes of moral deliberation, and ethics training. We do not know why the gender differences among public relations practitioners regarding ethical issues exist, how they form, what role they play in the profession, or even if they have an impact on the ethical counselor function. For instance, differing rates of moral development between males and females (Kohlberg, 1969) seem to hold some implication for these findings, but what that means for public relations is still speculative (Bowen, 2005a). We do know that these disparities are found in various studies of ethics in public relations, and that they warrant further study by scholars who specialize in feminization of the field, public relations ethics, or both.

Research also needs to address the question of how to best teach and train public relations ethics. Findings of the Excellence Study and scholars who have made advances in public relations ethics must be relayed to professionals in the practice of public relations. Without communication of the knowledge generated by research, scholarship becomes impotent and the profession stagnates. However, many impediments to this communication exist. Codes of ethics used by the professional associations in the discipline are routinely criticized for their lack of ability to support moral reasoning (Parkinson, 2001) or their irrelevance (Wright, 1993). Certification programs (such as ABC or APR) are difficult to uniformly implement and costly for members to maintain; with a small number of public relations practitioners overall as accredited members, these might not be the best avenues of ethical study and training. How, then, are we to make sure that public relations professionals are educated in ethics, trained in moral reasoning, and ready to act as an ethics counsel if or when the need arises?

Finally, many scholars have concluded that a pervasive negative connotation surrounds the discipline (Baskin, 1989; Ehling, 1992), study (Bowen, 2003; Stacks, Botan, & Turk, 1999), and practice of public relations (Belz, Talbott, & Starck, 1989; Kopenhaver, 1985; Spicer, 1993). Confusion among promotion, press agentry, propaganda, and public relations exacerbates the controversy. The negative connotation of public relations is often found to be perpetuated by the mass media through entertainment or news, but also has an academic quarter with some critical theorists and skeptical journalism professors. Grunig et al. (2002) wrote that to many critical theorists, "the symmetrical model represents a utopian attempt to make an inherently evil practice look good" (p. 317). Therefore, the challenge public relations ethics faces is one of legitimacy. Despite the arguments for inclusion of publics in management decision making and its dedication to corporate responsibility, many critics believe that public relations acting as an ethical conscience is akin to "letting the fox guard the hen house." For public relations ethics to progress, scholars must grapple with the difficult questions arising from the sometimes dubious history of public relations, and issues such as hypocrisy, qualifications to debate matters of ethics, divided loyalties, and the role of acting as a conscience counselor in an organization. These issues are connected to the legitimacy of the public relations function, and are arguably the most pressing concerns facing the discipline as a whole.

PUBLIC RELATIONS: THE MORAL LOCUS AND VOICE OF AN ORGANIZATION

One of the most important issues facing public relations is to determine if it is to be responsible for ethical considerations in an organization. This issue is far from settled, as many scholars have noted that public relations does not even have a consistent theory of ethics to guide the discipline. Danner and Mitrook (2005) observed, "Until public relations can come to grips with the reasons that public relations, as a profession, ought to act ethically, public relations will not achieve a normative theory of public relations ethics" (p. 19). Although the Excellence Study did not specifically measure the role of ethics in public relations and communication management, it is clear that ethical considerations support the main theoretical contentions of the excellence principles.

The excellence research provided a solid foundation on which a theory of public relations ethics has now begun to build. Empirical study revealed that the many principles that loaded into the excellence factor had a sound ethical basis; this chapter has attempted to link those factors with moral philosophy. Ethics is its own consideration when assessing what makes public relations excellent (Bowen, 2001). However, as this review has demonstrated, the factors of excellence are each based on moral principles that also make ethics a part of their administration. Ethics is both a single consideration among many that leads to public relations excellence, and the ultimate unifying factor that predicts excellent communication. The ethical basis of the individual principles of excellence, present in each factor, makes ethical communication a thing worthy in and of itself.

If one accepts the argument that public relations has a duty to society to facilitate dialogue and conflict resolution between disparate groups, then it is also a valid argument that public relations is the moral conscience and voice of an organization. Systems theory illustrated how public relations provides linkages with other systems in the environment, and it was argued that it is the obligation of an organization to consider and interact with those whom it affects.

Therefore, one can conclude that public relations exists as the enactment of a moral obligation to consider others—to make decisions meeting a universal test of morality in the form of deontological considerations of dignity, respect, dialogue, and autonomy. Public relations gives physical location, form, and voice to the moral obligations of an organization. An organization must consider its impact on society, publics, and stakeholders—as well as itself, internal publics, and its industry—in order to earn the right to exist and thrive. Many scholars have noted that an organization exists by permission of society, but the vehicle of communication used to negotiate that permission as an ethical obligation has been little studied.

Public relations is the communication liaison between organizations and their societies, publics, government, competitors, and stakeholders that provides essential information and resolves conflict. Public relations also serves in the role of internal decision maker for many organizations in terms of analyzing and resolving ethical issues, as well as communicating about those issues in a two-way manner with publics. When conceptualized as facilitating the flow of open communication in society, conducting ethical analyses, and operating by the principles of excellence based on moral norms, public relations fulfills a positive and necessary social role.

Epictetus' advice to consider the things that are excellent in themselves would then include excellent public relations and communication as a *prima facie* good, existent for the betterment of society, for providing socially necessary communication, and thereby improving the world in which we live. Excellence Theory and ethical communication are unified in the concept that public relations is—and should be—the ethical locus and voice of the organization.

REFERENCES

Baskin, O. W. (1989, Spring). Business schools and the study of public relations. *Public Relations Review*, pp. 25–37.

Belz, A., Talbott, A. D., & Starck, K. (1989). Using role theory to study cross-perceptions of journalists and public relations practitioners. In J. E. Grunig & L. A. Grunig (Eds.), *Public relations research annual* (Vol. 1, pp. 125–140). Hillsdale, NJ: Lawrence Erlbaum Associates.

Bowen, S. A. (2000, June). *A theory of ethical issues management: Contributions of Kantian deontology to public relations' ethics and decision making.* Unpublished doctoral dissertation, University of Maryland, College Park, MD.

Bowen, S. A. (2001, May). *A theory of ethical issues management: Expansion of ethics as the tenth generic principle of public relations excellence.* Paper presented at the meeting of the International Communication Association, Washington, DC.

Bowen, S. A. (2002). Elite executives in issues management: The role of ethical paradigms in decision making. *Journal of Public Affairs, 2*(4), 270–283.

Bowen, S. A. (2003). "I thought it would be more glamorous": Preconceptions and misconceptions of public relations among students in the principles course. *Public Relations Review, 29*, 199–214.

Bowen, S. A. (2004a). Expansion of ethics as the tenth generic principle of public relations excellence: A Kantian theory and model for managing ethical issues. *Journal of Public Relations Research, 16*(1), 65–92.

Bowen, S. A. (2004b). Organizational factors encouraging ethical decision making: An exploration into the case of an exemplar. *Journal of Business Ethics, 52*(4), 311–324.

Bowen, S. A. (2005a). Moral development. In R. L. Heath (Ed.), *Encyclopedia of public relations* (Vol. 2, pp. 540–542). Thousand Oaks, CA: Sage.

Bowen, S. A. (2005b). A practical model for ethical decision making in issues management and public relations. *Journal of Public Relations Research, 17*(3), 191–216.

Bowen, S. A. (2005c, June). *Schism in public relations ethics: Overview of grant research findings.* Paper presented at the meeting of the International Association of Business Communicators, Washington, DC.

Bowen, S. A. (2005d). Internal relations and employee communication. In S. M. Cutlip, A. H. Center, & G. M. Broom (Eds.), *Effective public relations* (pp. 222–250). Upper Saddle River, NJ: Pearson Prentice-Hall.

Bowen, S. A., & Heath, R. L. (2005). Issues management, systems, and rhetoric: Exploring the distinction between ethical and legal guidelines at Enron. *Journal of Public Affairs, 5*, 84–98.

Chun, R. (2005). Ethical character and virtue in organizations: An empirical assessment and strategic implications. *Journal of Business Ethics, 57*(3), 269–284.

Collins, R. (1985). *Three sociological traditions.* New York: Oxford University Press.

Cutlip, S. M., Center, A. H., & Broom, G. M. (2000). *Effective public relations* (8th ed.). Upper Saddle River, NJ: Prentice-Hall.

Daft, R., & Weick, K. (1984). Toward a model of organizations as interpretations systems. *Academy of Management Review, 9*, 284–295.

Danner, B., & Mitrook, M. A. (2005, August). *Ethical discussion in peer reviewed public relations journals: A content analysis.* Paper presented at the meeting of the Association for Education in Journalism and Mass Communication, San Antonio, TX.

Deatherage, C. P., & Hazleton, V. (1998). Effects of organizational worldviews on the practice of public relations: A test of the theory of public relations excellence. *Journal of Public Relations Research, 10*(1), 57–71.

Dewey, J. (1916). *Democracy and education.* New York: Free Press.

Dozier, D. M., & Broom, G. M. (1995). Evolution of the manager role in public relations practice. *Journal of Public Relations Research, 7*(1), 3–26.

Dozier, D. M., & Grunig, L. A. (1992). The organization of the public relations function. In J. E. Grunig (Ed.), *Excellence in public relations and communication management* (pp. 395–417). Hillsdale, NJ: Lawrence Erlbaum Associates.

Dozier, D. M., Grunig, L. A., & Grunig, J. E. (1995). *Manager's guide to excellence in public relations and communication management.* Hillsdale, NJ: Lawrence Erlbaum Associates.

Dudzinski, D. M. (2004). Integrity: Principled coherence, virtue, or both? *Journal of Value Inquiry, 38*(3), 299–313.

Durkheim, E. (1893/1984). *The division of labor in society* (W. D. Halls, Trans.). New York: Free Press.

Durkheim, E. (1897/1951). *Suicide: A study in sociology* (J. A. S. G. Simpson, Trans.). New York: Free Press of Glencoe.

Ehling, W. P. (1992). Public relations education and professionalism. In J. E. Grunig (Ed.), *Excellence in public relations and communication management* (pp. 439–464). Hillsdale, NJ: Lawrence Erlbaum Associates.

Goodman, E. C. (Ed.). (1997). *The Forbes book of business quotations.* New York: Black Dog & Leventhal.

Grojean, M. W., Resick, C. J., Dickson, M. W., & Smith, D. B. (2004). Leaders, values, and organizational climate: Examining leadership strategies for establishing an organizational climate regarding ethics. *Journal of Business Ethics, 55*(3), 223–241.

Grunig, J. E. (1992a). Communication, public relations, and effective organizations: An overview of the book. In J. E. Grunig (Ed.), *Excellence in public relations and communication management* (pp. 1–30). Hillsdale, NJ: Lawrence Erlbaum Associates.

Grunig, J. E. (1992b). Symmetrical systems of internal communication. In J. E. Grunig (Ed.), *Excellence in public relations and communication management* (pp. 531–575). Hillsdale, NJ: Lawrence Erlbaum Associates.

Grunig, J. E. (Ed.). (1992c). *Excellence in public relations and communication management.* Hillsdale, NJ: Lawrence Erlbaum Associates.

Grunig, J. E. (2001). Two-way symmetrical public relations: Past, present, and future. In R. L. Heath (Ed.), *Handbook of public relations* (pp. 11–30). Thousand Oaks, CA: Sage.

Grunig, J. E., & Grunig, L. A. (1996, May). *Implications of symmetry for a theory of ethics and social responsibility in public relations.* Paper presented at the meeting of the International Communication Association, Chicago.

Grunig, J. E., & Grunig, L. A. (1998). The relationship between public relations and marketing in excellent organizations: Evidence from the IABC study. *Journal of Marketing Communications, 4,* 141–162.

Grunig, J. E., & Grunig, L. A. (2000). Public relations in strategic management and strategic management of public relations: Theory and research from the IABC excellence project. *Journalism Studies, 1,* 303–321.

Grunig, J. E., Grunig, L. A., & Dozier, D. M. (1999, May). *Combining the two-way symmetrical and asymmetrical models into a contingency model of excellent public relations.* Paper presented at the meeting of the International Communication Association, San Francisco.

Grunig, J. E., & Huang, Y. H. (2000). From organizational effectiveness to relationship indicators: Antecedents of relationships, public relations strategies, and relationship outcomes. In J. Ledingham & S. Bruning (Eds.), *Public relations as relationship management: A relational approach to the study and practice of public relations* (pp. 23–53). Mahwah, NJ: Lawrence Erlbaum Associates.

Grunig, J. E., & Hunt, T. (1984). *Managing public relations.* New York: Holt, Rinehart & Winston.

Grunig, J. E., & Repper, F. C. (1992). Strategic management, publics, and issues. In J. E. Grunig (Ed.), *Excellence in public relations and communication management* (pp. 117–157). Hillsdale, NJ: Lawrence Erlbaum Associates.

Grunig, L. A. (1992). Activism: How it limits the effectiveness of organizations and how excellent public relations departments respond. In J. E. Grunig (Ed.), *Excellence in public relations and communication management* (pp. 503–530). Hillsdale, NJ: Lawrence Erlbaum Associates.

Grunig, L. A., Grunig, J. E., & Dozier, D. M. (2002). *Excellent public relations and effective organizations: A study of communication management in three countries*. Mahwah, NJ: Lawrence Erlbaum Associates.

Habermas, J. (1979). *Communication and the evolution of society* (T. McCarthy, Trans.). Boston: Beacon Press.

Habermas, J. (1984). *The theory of communicative action: Reason and the rationalization of society* (T. McCarthy, Trans. Vol. 1). Boston: Beacon Press.

Hage, J. (1980). *Theories of organizations: Form, processes, and transformation*. New York: Wiley.

Heath, R. L. (1997). *Strategic issues management: Organizations and public policy challenges*. Thousand Oaks, CA: Sage.

Heath, R. L. (2001). Shifting foundations: Public relations as relationship building. In R. L. Heath (Ed.), *Handbook of public relations* (pp. 1–10). Thousand Oaks, CA: Sage.

Heath, R. L., Seshadri, S., & Lee, J. (1998). Risk communication: A two-community analysis of proximity, dread, trust, involvement, uncertainty, openness/accessibility, and knowledge on support/opposition toward chemical companies. *Journal of Public Relations Research, 10*(1), 35–56.

Huang, Y. H. (2001). Opra: A cross-cultural, multiple-item scale for measuring organization–public relationships. *Journal of Public Relations Research, 13*(1), 61–90.

Huang, Y. H. (2004). Is symmetrical communication ethical and effective? *Journal of Business Ethics, 53*(4), 333–352.

Kant, I. (1952). *Critique of judgment* (J. C. Meredith, Trans.). Oxford, England: Oxford University Press. (Original work published 1790)

Kant, I. (1964). *Groundwork of the metaphysic of morals* (H. J. Paton, Trans.). New York: Harper & Row. (Original work published 1785)

Kant, I. (1974). *On the old saw: That may be right in theory but it won't work in practice* (E. B. Ashton, Trans.). Philadelphia: University of Pennsylvania Press. (Original work published 1793)

Kant, I. (1993). Metaphysical foundations of morals (C. J. Friedrich, Trans.). In C. J. Friedrich (Ed.), *The philosophy of Kant: Immanuel Kant's moral and political writings* (pp. 154–229). New York: Modern Library. (Original work published 1785)

Koehn, D. (2005). Integrity as a business asset. *Journal of Business Ethics, 58*(1), 125–136.

Kohlberg, L. (1969). Stage and sequence: The cognitive developmental approach to socialization. In D. A. Goslin (Ed.), *Handbook of socialization theory of research* (pp. 347–480). Chicago: Rand McNally.

Kopenhaver, L. L. (1985). Aligning values of practitioners and journalists. *Public Relations Review, 11*(1), 34–42.

Lauzen, M. M. (1992). Public relations roles, intraorganizational power, and encroachment. *Journal of Public Relations Research, 4*, 61–80.

Lauzen, M. M., & Dozier, D. M. (1994). Issues management mediation of linkages between environmental complexity and management of the public relations function. *Journal of Public Relations Research, 6*(3), 163–184.

Ledingham, J., & Bruning, S. (2000). Introduction: Background and current trends in the study of relationship management. In J. Ledingham & S. Bruning (Eds.), *Public relations as relationship management: A relational approach to the study and practice of public relations* (pp. xi–xvii). Mahwah, NJ: Lawrence Erlbaum Associates.

L'Etang, J., & Pieczka, M. (Eds.). (1996). *Critical perspectives in public relations.* London: International Thomson Business Press.

Murphy, P., & Dee, J. (1992). DuPont and Greenpeace: The dynamics of conflict between corporations and activist groups. *Journal of Public Relations Research, 4*(1), 3–20.

Parkinson, M. (2001). The PRSA code of professional standards and member code of ethics: Why they are neither professional or ethical. *Public Relations Quarterly, 46*(3), 27–31.

Pearson, R. (1989a). Business ethics as communication ethics: Public relations practice and the idea of dialogue. In C. H. Botan & V. Hazleton, Jr. (Eds.), *Public relations theory* (pp. 111–131). Hillsdale, NJ: Lawrence Erlbaum Associates.

Pearson, R. (1989b). *A theory of public relations ethics.* Unpublished doctoral dissertation, Ohio University, Athens.

Quinn, J. K., Reed, J. D., Browne, M. N., & Hiers, W. J. (1997). Honesty, individualism, and pragmatic business ethics: Implications for corporate hierarchy. *Journal of Business Ethics, 16*(13), 1419–1430.

Sauser, W. I., Jr. (2005). Business ethics: Answering the call. *Journal of Business Ethics, 58*(4), 345–357.

Sims, R. R. (1994). *Ethics and organizational decision making: A call for renewal.* Westport, CT: Quorum.

Sims, R. R., & Brinkman, J. (2003). Enron ethics (or, culture matters more than codes). *Journal of Business Ethics, 45*(3), 243–256.

Smith, T. (2003). The metaphysical case for honesty. *Journal of Value Inquiry, 37*(4), 517–531.

Spicer, C. (1993). Images of PR in the print media. *Journal of Public Relations Research, 5*(1), 47–61.

Sriramesh, K., Grunig, J. E., & Buffington, J. (1992). Corporate culture and public relations. In J. E. Grunig (Ed.), *Excellence in public relations and communication management* (pp. 577–595). Hillsdale, NJ: Lawrence Erlbaum Associates.

Stacks, D. W., Botan, C., & Turk, J. V. (1999). Perceptions of pubic relations education. *Public Relations Review, 25,* 9–29.

Wright, D. K. (1985). Can age predict the moral values of public relations practitioners? *Public Relations Review, 11*(1), 51–60.

Wright, D. K. (1993). Enforcement dilemma: Voluntary nature of public relations codes. *Public Relations Review, 19*(1), 13–20.

Wright, D. K. (1995). The role of corporate public relations executives in the future of employee communications. *Public Relations Review, 21*(3), 181–198.

Chapter 15

Integrated Communication: Implications for Public Relations Beyond Excellence

Kirk Hallahan
Colorado State University

Two tenets of Excellence Theory are that public relations should be situated in a single or integrated unit and that is should be a separate function from marketing. Today, these propositions are being challenged with the advent of integrated communication. This chapter traces the evolution of these propositions and analyzes the findings of the Excellence Study in light of subsequent theory and research. In particular, it examines a) the definition of integrated communication, b) the overlap between PR and IC theory, and c) alternative arrangements for organizing the public relations function. Although Excellence Theory considers integration within public relations and between public relations and marketing, the author argues that integration also must be addressed as an organizationwide phenomenon.

When the original Excellence Study report was published in 1992, public relations scholars and practitioners were embroiled in a heated debate about the concept of communication integration and the relationship between public relations and marketing. For a variety of reasons, the traditional marketing paradigm that placed advertising at the center of promotional activities by organizations had come under siege (e.g. McKenna, 1986). The late 1980s had seen the rise of *integrated marketing communications* (IMC) as a moniker to describe the coordinated use of a variety of different promotional communications tools toward a single objective. IMC was not a particularly new idea; *total marketing* had been advocated in the early 1970s (Thorman, 1970). However, advertising agencies were attracted to the concept as a defensive move to recapture client spending that was being siphoned off into direct response, trade and consumer promotions, sponsorships, and cooperative cause-related marketing (Atler, 1990; Duncan & Caywood, 1996; "It's All Advertising," 1991; Magrath, 1991, Promotion Marketing Association, 1993; Rice, 1991). Many ad agencies or their holding companies quickly acquired specialty firms (including PR agencies) and touted their ability to orchestrate integrated campaigns for clients (Novelli, 1989–1990).

The use of publicity and public relations for marketing purposes had thrived for nearly a century (Bernays, 1965; Tye, 1998). However, few early agencies practiced marketing public relations in the strategic way it is practiced today (Goldman, 1990; Harris 1991, 1993), and many ad agencies proudly kept separate rosters of advertising and PR clients (Koelle, 1991; Novelli, 1989–1990).

Developments in Marketing

Marketing theorists and practitioners had recognized the value of product publicity for a long time (Conley, 1954; Lightcap, 1984; Murray 1976). In a seminal marketing textbook, McCarthy (1960) outlined the 4 Ps of marketing—product design, product pricing, product placement (distribution), and product promotion. Publicity, along with advertising, sales promotion, and personal selling were part of McCarthy's promotion mix (Waterschoot & Van den Bulte, 1992). By the early 1970s, marketing theorists also had recognized that marketing principles could be applied to the promotion of ideas—what was termed *generic marketing* and later *social marketing* (Kotler, 1972; Kotler & Levy, 1969a, 1969b; Luck, 1969).

During the 1980s, a variety of marketing theorists shifted their focus from a microeconomic to a macroeconomic perspective, and recognized the potential contributions of public relations. Arndt (1983) drew attention to the political economy in which marketers operated. Zeithaml and Zeithaml (1984) theorized about marketing's external environment and identified public relations as one of 16 environmental management strategies. Then, Kotler (1986) coined the term *megamarketing* and added 2 Ps to McCarthy's marketing mix: political power and public relations. Two veteran PR educators quickly pointed out that megamarketing was actually nothing more than an integrated communication campaign. They also expressed relief that a leading market educator had become "enlightened about the positive interaction of public relations and marketing" (Newsom & Carrell, 1986, p. 170).

Further changes in marketing theory recognized the increased complexity, knowledge richness, and turbulence in which marketing organizations operated—manifested in new organizational forms such as alliances, strategic partnerships, franchises, and networks. These changes demanded increased attention to norms-driven systems involving shared benefits and burdens, cooperative (vs. competitive) internal cultures, power sharing, commitment, and trust (Achrol, 1991; Achrol & Kotler, 1999). More broadly, marketers had placed strong emphasis on social responsibility (the societal marketing concept; Kotler, 2000) and had shifted from a focus on exchanges to relationships based on satisfaction, value, and quality performance as key strategic resources of the business (Kotler, 2000; Webster, 1992, 1994).

Controversy in Public Relations

The debate among public relations scholars began in earnest when the relationship between publics and marketing—already a hot topic in professional circles (Broom & Tucker, 1989; Dilenschneider, 1991; Finn, 1989; Novelli, 1989–1990)—was the focus of a 1989 symposium at San Diego State University. Although participants acknowledged integrated communication, its benefits were described mostly in terms of a convenience for clients. (Broom, Lauzen, & Tucker, 1991). Symposium participants concluded that marketing and public relations had distinct missions, philosophies, theories, and turfs: "Marketing builds and maintains a market for an organization's goods and services, whereas public relations builds and maintains hospitable social and political environments" (Broom et al., 1991, p. 225). Both were essential to organizational survival and success.

Ehling (1989) introduced the notion of marketing imperialism at the event, and Lauzen (1990, 1991, 1992; Dozier & Lauzen, 1990) later provided empirical evidence for encroachment by marketers in the absence of top communicators enacting a manager role. Similar evidence was soon found within the fundraising field (Kelly, 1993; see discussion in Grunig, Grunig, & Dozier, 2002, p. 213). Separately, in a move to enhance the stature of the marketing-support function, Harris (1991) called for differentiating marketing public relations from corporate public relations.

Public relations' relationship to marketing became the topic of a special issue of *Public Relations Review* (Van Leuven, 1991a), and IMC was the focus of a special issue of *Public Relations Quarterly* (Nakra, 1991; Niederquell, 1991; Stanton, 1991; Strenski, 1991; Totorici, 1991). Heated debates ensued at three meetings of the Public Relations Division of the Association for Education in Journalism and Mass Communication (Newsom & Carrell, 1992) and in the Public Relations Section (now Educators Academy) of the Public Relations Society of America. A study on IMC commissioned by AEJMC's Public Relations Division (Duncan,

Caywood ,& Newsom, 1991, 1993) was strongly opposed by PRSA's Educational Affairs Committee (Ferguson & Van Slyke Turk, 1993) and ultimately rejected by the AEJMC membership ("Educators Address Tension," 1995; "Educators Reject IMC ...," 1993; Kendall, 1994). The sentiment of the time was captured by J. Grunig, who was quoted as saying, "I perceive integrated communication as a threat to my profession" (cited in Gronstedt, 1994, p. 29). In part, Grunig's opposition was based on a fear that public relations would lose its ability to communicate with groups other than consumers (Lauer, 1995). Meanwhile, the debate continued for more than a decade (Adams, 2001; Drobis, 1997–1998; Gayeski & Woodward, 1996; Gonring, 1994; Kozikowski, 1993, 1995; Lee, 2002; Lepley, 2000; Miller & Rose, 1994; Turney, 2001).

THE EXCELLENCE STUDY AND INTEGRATED COMMUNICATIONS

Against this backdrop, Excellence Theory posited the need for public relations to maintain its distinct role in organizations. To put the evolving arguments into perspective, it is useful to review five key publications produced under the auspices of the Excellence Study between 1991 and 2002. Key propositions were introduced in the special marketing issue of *Public Relations Review* (Grunig & Grunig, 1991) and codified in *Excellence in Public Relations and Communication Management* (J. Grunig, 1992a). Three years later, a brief commentary appeared in the *Manager's Guide to Excellence in Public Relations and Communication Management* (Dozier, Grunig, & Grunig, 1995). The argument was renewed in a major review of Excellence Study findings in the *Journal of Marketing Communications* (Grunig & Grunig, 1998) and in chapter 7 of *Excellent Public Relations and Effective Organizations* (Grunig et al., 2002). The chapter drew heavily from the 1998 article.

Public Relations Review (1991)

In previewing the Excellence Study, Grunig and Grunig (1991) laid out their theoretical distinction between marketing and public relations by stating, "[T]he marketing function is concerned with products, services and customer markets. Public relations, in contrast, is concerned with all relevant publics of that organization" (p. 263). The authors argued, "Whereas marketing's purpose is to make money, public relations strives to save money for the organization by managing threats to its mission or mobilizing support for it" (p. 263). According to the Grunigs:

> Both processes begin with the mission of the organization. The role of public relations, however, is to identify the consequences of the mission on people outside the decision structure. Marketing also begins with the

mission, but marketing selects the segment of the environment that will make it possible to implement its mission. Public relations, in contrast, tries to change the mission to avoid confrontations with publics that make implementation of the mission costly or impossible. (Grunig & Grunig, 1991, p. 265)

They summarized the argument by saying:

> Without public relations, organizations will be *diverted from their missions*. Without marketing, they would miss an essential mechanism for implementing their missions. Both functions are essential to an organization. When one function is sublimated to the other, it follows, we believe, the organization will not be likely to practice the sublimated function as completely as the dominant function. (Grunig & Grunig, 1991, p. 266; italics in original)

Whereas the Grunigs described marketing as largely proactive, they characterized public relations as interactive (vs. reactive). The authors lamented that too many PR practitioners had adopted marketing segmentation strategies rather than public relations segmentation strategies (based on J. Grunig's ideas about active and passive publics). This, they suggested, was an example of how public relations was being sublimated by marketing. Although recognizing that strategic management is a characteristic that can be found in both marketing and public relations, the Grunigs asserted that "a public relations program organized strategically by marketing theory could not achieve the same effect as a program organized by public relations theory" (p. 267). They explained:

> Sublimation of the public relations function ... results in a more asymmetrical approach to public relations, even though public relations may be practiced according to a strategic model of marketing. As a result, organizations lose the valuable function that public relations provides—of managing interdependencies with publics that constrain the autonomy of organizations to pursue and meet their goals. (p. 275)

Excellence Report (1992)

The original excellence report codified the two key issues relevant to integrated communication as the second and third of 17 characteristics of excellent public relations. According the report, public relations operates as (#2) "a single or integrated public relations department" that is (#3) "a separate function from marketing" (J. Grunig, 1992b, p. 28).

The discussion about the structure of the public relations department was centered in chapter 14, where David Dozier and Larissa Grunig summarized the argument this way:

> The public relations function must be integrated within a single department. Only within such a structure does the practitioner have the autonomy and mandate to define publics and channels of communication dynamically. Only in such a setting can the practitioner focus on genuine strategic problem solving, rather than routinized communicating. (Dozier & Grunig, 1992, p. 402)

The authors made their case by drawing on a combination of systems theory and power-control theory perspectives—with a heavy emphasis on the latter. The arguments rooted in systems theory were that public relations must have access to management decision making and must be located in an integrated unit in order to work effectively as part of the adaptive (boundary spanning) subsystem of the organization. Dozier and L. Grunig (1992) began by stating, "There is no organizational structure for the public relations function that will be ideal for all organizations and all environments" (Dozier & Grunig, 1992, pp. 402–403). But they then argued systems theory *required* access to management, integration within a single department, and a flexible horizontal structure. Their power-control theory argument focused on the fact that dominant coalitions determine organizational structures to satisfice organizational needs and their own interests, preferring centralization, formalization, and simplicity. They noted, however, that particular structures also persist in organizations because of historical inertia, routinization, and costs sunk into units (Dozier & Grunig, 1992). Elsewhere, L. Grunig (1992a) argued that "Excellent departments practice public relations appropriately for their environment in part because the structure of their organizations places the head of public relations in a position to monitor that environment and to interact with the dominant coalition internally" (p. 479).

The relationship between marketing and public relations was detailed in chapter 13, in which excellence team members William Ehling, Jon White, and James Grunig formally summarized the proposition that public relations function of an excellent organization exists separately from and is not subsumed into marketing (Ehling, White, & J. Grunig, 1992).

Interestingly, this chapter did not discuss integrated communications or integrated marketing communications. Instead, the chapter expanded the argument that marketing and public relations have important but different missions to fulfill, and rely on different paradigms or models of the organization's social environment. The authors warned against the uncritical acceptance of the dominance of marketing and maintained that the roles of the two functions were "murky, often overlapping and frequently conflicting." (p. 358). Ehling, White, and Grunig summed up the differences in approaches as follows:

In short, the communication system developed under public relations management is interpersonally focused, bilaterally designed, bidirectionally oriented, and organized in two stages. These attributes set up public relations communication apart from, and sometimes in opposition to, marketing communication. In contrast to public relations, marketing communication is characterized by unilateral design, unidirectional message flow, and one-stage operation—with an aim of persuasion to boost sales or increase a company's market share. (p. 389)

The authors argued vehemently against equating public relations to product publicity and rebutted efforts by marketers such as Philip Kotler to position marketing as the central activity of an organization. Both moves would relegate public relations to an inferior technical role and divest public relations of any significant administrative responsibilities. What's more, questionable and unscrupulous marketing practices had been largely responsible for the rise of the consumerism movement and for the hostile environment in which businesses operated. As evidence, Ehling et al. drew extensively on Peter Drucker's *Managing in Turbulent Times* (1980), which the authors contended "provided clear justification for the establishment and departmentalization of the public relations function" (p. 366), even though Drucker never mentioned public relations (Ehling et al., 1992).

Managers Guide (1995)

Surprisingly little attention was paid to the question of integration in the *Managers Guide to Excellence in Public Relations and Communication Management*, which was published in 1995 to share the findings of the Excellence Study with practitioners. The limited discussion focused on the curricular question of whether public relations ought to be taught in schools of business rather than in college communications programs. Dozier et al. (1995) expressed little support for moving public relations education to business because, in their view, such a move would do little to advance public relations excellence: "Our concern is that educators in business schools will share many of the same misconceptions about communications and public relations as do dominant coalitions in less-than-excellent organizations" (p. 71). Although aspiring PR professionals would benefit from cross-training in marketing and advertising, the authors contended that an integrated communications curriculum would "destroy the core of communication excellence" and again "relegate communicators to the kind of technical support roles they now play in less-than-excellent organizations" (p. 72). For discussions of IC educational proposals, see Caywood and Ewing (1991), Rose and Miller (1994), Lauer (1995), and Farrelly, Luxton, and Brace-Govan (2001).

Journal of Marketing Communications (1998)

Grunig and Grunig (1998) introduced the topic of integrated communication in an early article reporting empirical evidence from the Excellence Study. Taking a somewhat more tempered stance, they elaborated on their philosophical approach to public relations—a practice that they recognized played a dual role in organizations by providing marketing support and by helping organizations cope with their external environments.

The authors provided a useful review of historical precedents (Tedlow, 1979), strategic considerations (White & Mazur, 1995), and models from the marketing literature related to the relationship between public relations and marketing (Hallahan, 1992; Kotler & Mindak, 1978). They also cited research by Hunter (1997, 1999a), who had found little evidence of sublimation of public relations among U.S. corporations. Instead, organizational predominance of marketing versus public relations depended on the relative importance of key stakeholders in organizations (Grunig & Grunig, 1992). The Grunigs thus suggested that the key questions for examination was "not whether public relations and marketing should be integrated or merged but how they work together most truthfully in successful, well-managed organizations" (1998, p. 144).

Grunig and Grunig defined IMC as combining marketing public relations with advertising, but repeated their earlier observation that marketing theorists and IMC adherents viewed public relations as primarily a technical support (vs. management) function. They suggested that the M in IMC had been largely dropped in the nomenclature in favor of *integrated communication*—a possibly misleading observation in light of the continued widespread use of the IMC nomenclature (e.g., Duncan & Mulhern, 2004). They suggested that IMC's definition had been expanded to include attention to stakeholders other than consumers in order to make the concept more palatable to public relations and advertising professionals. In criticizing approaches to IMC suggested by authors such as Gronstedt (1996a) and Duncan and Caywood (1996), Grunig and Grunig roundly rejected efforts to implement integration through marketing communications. Instead, they proposed "beginning at the highest level of integration and then pulling marketing communication and communication programs for other stakeholders into the public relations function" (1998, p. 147).

The Grunigs outlined four principles of excellence that should specify the relationship between public relations to strategic management and to other management functions such as marketing:

1. The public relations should be located in the organizational structure so that it has ready access to the key decision makers of the organization—the dominant coalition—and so that it can contribute to the strategic management processes of the organization.

2. All communication programs should be integrated into or coordinated by the public relations department.
3. Public relations should not be subordinated to other departments, such as marketing, human resources, or finance.
4. Public relations departments should be structured horizontally to reflect strategic publics so that it is possible to reassign people and resources to new programs as new strategic publics emerge and other publics cease to be strategic (Grunig & Grunig, 1998; see also Grunig et al., 2002).

In reporting evidence from the excellence research (see Grunig et al., 2002), the Grunigs explained that top communicators in the study were asked about the existence of separate "marketing public relations" and "public affairs" functions, the budgets allocated to each, and the level of support received by each from the organization's dominant coalition. Among 323 organizations studied in the United States, Canada, and the United Kingdom, 75 organizations reported greater support for marketing public relations units, 104 reported greater support for public affairs-oriented units, and 137 reported equal levels of support.

Practitioners' excellence index scores were below average when marketing public relations received greater support, average when public affairs received greater support, and above average when the two received approximately equal support. The Grunigs' conclusion: Public relations was most likely to be excellent when marketing communication does not dominate the communication function. Public relations had greatest value when the public relations and marketing functions were treated as equal partners.

Findings reported in 1998 from second-phase, in-depth interviews with CEOs from organizations identified as having excellent public relations departments suggested that chief executives were better prepared to make informed decisions when they relied on the distinct perspectives of both marketing and public relations. However, to be successful relative to their peers in marketing, PR practitioners had to be "peer professionals"—that is, equivalent in terms of expertise, brains, respect, and salary.

Grunig and Grunig (1998) concluded that the Excellence Study "seems to provide compelling evidence in support of separate marketing and public relations functions and of integrating communications programs—not just marketing communication programs—through the public relations department or by coordinating a set of public relations departments" (p. 157). They added, "Although we prefer our conceptual approach to that of an advertising or marketing approach, we recognize the value of different approaches and conceptual world views" (p. 157). They identified seven characteristics of marketing communication theory that differed from their public relations approach (Grunig & Grunig, 1998; compare to Grunig et al., 2002).

Effective Organizations (2002)

In chapter 7 of their final analysis of the excellence results, Grunig et al. (2002) repeated their call for the integration of all communications functions within a single public relations department. The authors also expressed continued frustration that, despite the fact that IC theorists had moved toward ideas comparable to Excellence Theory, their rationale continued to be based on marketing communication theory and not public relations theory (see also Grunig & Grunig, 1998).

In reviewing research that supported their arguments, the authors cited an article by Pettegrew (2000–2001), who questioned why IMC had not been implemented more extensively. Meanwhile, a survey of 76 Fortune 300 companies by Hunter (1999b) continued the call for integrating communications within communications (vs. marketing) departments (cited in Grunig, Grunig, & Dozier, 2002, p. 277). *Effective Organizations* also went out of its way to argue against the conceptualizations of integration by authors such as Duncan and Moriarty (1997) and Gronstedt (2000), but nonetheless admitted that these affirmed key concepts of excellent public relations.

The additional quantitative findings reported in 2002 (not in the 1998 article) revealed that only 28 public relations department heads out of 370 in the Excellence Study actually reported to a non-PR unit. Most important, however, the authors reported *no statistically significance differences* in practitioners' excellence scores based on whether the practitioner worked in a central department (166 organizations) or in specialized departments (176 organizations). Similarly, whether practitioners worked in a department that combined marketing and public affairs or in separate units resulted in no statistically significant difference in practitioners' excellence scores. Finally, budget allocations—that is, spending more on marketing support versus public affairs activities—appeared to have no impact on excellence scores. These nonsignificant results applied whether all organizations or only for-profit corporations were considered. Although the excellence researchers had made no predictions, the data reported in *Effective Organizations* suggested that a variety of excellence scores were higher among organizations that used outside public relations firms.

CRITIQUE AND DISCUSSION

From this review, it is clear that integration is a key consideration in Excellence Theory. Yet, the key empirical evidence provided is fragmentary, and hardly conclusive to support for the argument favoring a single public relations department or the necessity to avoid sublimation by marketing. Three key challenges confront researchers seeking to better understand the question of integration as it applies to and extends beyond Excellence Theory: better defining integrated communication; reconciling the emerging theoretical overlap between PR and IC; and recognizing alternative, latter-day structures for organizing public relations.

Defining Integrated Communication

Perhaps the most important challenge is to define precisely what is meant by *integration*. The excellence researchers stated, "[W]e advocate integrated marketing communication of advertising and marketing public relations" (Grunig & Grunig, 1998, p. 141). However, they also addressed the integration of the corporate (public affairs) and marketing public relations functions and the integration of all public relations activities, which can be centralized, specialized, or sometimes delegated to other units in an organization (Grunig, Grunig, & Dozier, 2002; Grunig & Grunig, 1998).

In *Effective Organizations*, the authors appeared to accept the definition of integration provided by Gronstedt (2000), who observed that integration is "commonly defined as the process of achieving unity of effort in *various organizational subsystems*" and is "the stuff that profitable relationships are built on" (cited in Grunig et al., 2002, p. 274; emphasis added).

Today, no single definition of IMC or IC is generally accepted (for recent reviews, see Copley, 2004; Duncan & Mulhern, 2004; Kliatchko, 2005). However, several useful models of stages of integration have been proposed (Caywood, 1997a, 1997b; Duncan & Caywood, 1996; Pickton & Hartley, 1998; Schultz & Kitchen, 2000). Some critics would argue that IMC does not differ much from earlier marketing theories (Spotts, Lambert, & Joyce, 1998). Others contend that, similar to Excellence Theory, IMC merely serves as a rhetorical and teleological construct (Cornelissen, 2001; Cornelissen & Lock, 2001; Massie & Anderson, 2003) that envisions how communication *ought* to be approached normatively—rather than how communications are *actually* conducted.

The term *integrated communication* can be applied in public relations in at least three different ways, following a typology suggested by Nowak and Phelps (1994). First, the one voice/one look communications approach suggests that an organization must develop a single *persona* and voice and communicate as an organization consistently. Few practitioners would argue with the value of consistency (Finn, 1990; Hutton, 1996, 2001; Miyamoto, 1997). Although not explicitly stated by excellence theorists, this form of integration provides a strong justification for single or integrated public relations departments and for dynamic and flexible horizontal structures within public relations units (Dozier & Grunig, 1992).

Second, the coordinated marketing campaigns approach is the sense of the term generally used in the Excellence Study, and calls for the orchestrated use of public relations together with other marketing tools to promote an organization's products, services, candidates, or causes. Importantly, publicity and public relations can achieve outcomes not possible through advertising, sales promotion, direct response, and so on (Duncan & Moriarty, 1997; Hallahan, 1996; Harris, 1993).

Third, the integrated communications approach was originally conceptualized by Nowak and Phelps (1994) as the effort to both develop an image and directly influence consumer behavior in a traditional communications program. More generally, however, the concept can be applied to an organization communicating purposefully (i.e., to establish an image and/or influence behavior) at all levels of contact or "touch points" with key stakeholders (Gronstedt, 1994, 1996b, 2000; Hartley & Pickton, 1999). This approach suggests that integration is not limited to activities conducted by communications specialists at the headquarters level, but instead involves everyone in the organization (Stewart, 1996).

Reconciling the Emerging Theoretical Overlap Between PR and IC

A second challenge involves the growing convergence of public relations and integrated communication theory. Grunig and Grunig (1998) commented:

> One major hurdle remains, however, before communications can be fully integrated: public relations theorists and marketing communication theorists—particularly advertising scholars—conceptualize communication in very different ways. Many marketing communications programs apply marketing communication rather than public relations theory to communication management … in ways that we believe do not result in effective communication. (p. 157)

However, a careful reading of the most recent IMC literature suggests the two fields, in fact, are more similar than different.

Since 1991, advocates of integrated communications such as Don Schultz, Clarke Caywood, Philip Kitchen, and Tom Duncan have spearheaded robust programs of research and publication that advocate the convergence of communication activities in contemporary organizations. Their work has extended beyond just a marketing perspective to include concepts and approaches that have traditionally been the province of public relations. Varey (1998), for example, called on marketers to consider how marketing fits within the broader context of corporate communications and how marketers could work with public relations.

Although *Effective Organizations* (Grunig et al., 2002) suggested that IMC theory has moved in the direction espoused by Excellence Theory, few IMC theorists acknowledge or even imply that excellence principles per se informed their work. At best, the evidence suggests that they have embraced general public relations concepts (Hutton, 1996, 2001; Moriarty, 1994; Varey 1988), although some of the principles of Excellence Theory are actually challenged directly (Cornelissen, 2003; Cornelissen & Thorpe, 2001; Moss, Warnaby, & Thame, 1996; Varey, 2001).

Examples of this theoretical convergence with public relations include IMC's emphasis on dialogue and interactivity, which are direct analogs to two-way communication (Duncan & Moriarty, 1997; Duncan & Mulhern, 2004). Similarly, IC adherents incorporate stakeholders and publics—not merely consumers and markets—in their theorizing (Greenley & Foxall, 1996; Hartley & Pickton, 1999; Kitchen & Schultz, 2003; Schultz & Kitchen, 2000, 2003). Finally, marketing theorists in general and IMC adherents in particular emphasize establishing and maintaining relationships with people and institutions in an organization's value-creation chain (Gronstedt, 2000; Pelton, Strutton & Lumpkin, 2002; Schultz & Kitchen 2000). In this regard, Varey (2001) observed, "If an overarching motive of establishing, maintaining and enhancing relationships is adopted, the two fields [marketing and public relations] can become one. Relationships are the necessary focus of contemporary management" (p. 78).

The increasingly enlightened approach in the marketing and IMC literature largely contradicts the assumptions made in the early 1990s by the Excellence Study (Ehling, White, & Grunig, 1992) and by others (e.g., Brody, 1994; Ferguson & Van Slyke Turk, 1993; Miyamoto, 1997) that marketing only focuses on short-term, profit-oriented product/service promotion. Rather, as it has come of age, IMC/IC provides a viable, paradigmatic alternative to public relations. Importantly, nothing in the latter-day literature suggests that IMC/IC theorists are attempting to intentionally encroach on or co-opt public relations. If anything, writers such as Moriarty (1994; Duncan & Moriarty, 1997) call for drawing on the unique perspectives and abilities of public relations professionals.

Over the coming years, clarifying the theoretical domains of the two fields will become increasingly important. Whereas marketing and IMC theorists have been open to developing linkages to other disciplines, public relations researchers have remained incredibly insular. As a result, they are possibly missing out on opportunities to expand their sphere of influence and their ability to serve organizations strategically (Moriarty, 1994). This problem is particularly evident in the United States, where virtually no research has been published in the past decade to bridge public relations to other professional communications disciplines. Such insularity, this author believes, can be attributed to the slavish emphasis found in Excellence Theory on preserving public relations as a distinct function in organizations and as a separate discipline in academia.

Alternative Structures for Organizing Public Relations

Beyond the definitional and theoretical issues, a third major challenge involves untangling the structural/organizational imperatives advocated in the Excellence Study. J. Grunig and his colleagues have been unyielding in their position that public relations must be a distinct management function and is uniquely capable of helping organizations manage external interdependencies. However, this raises the important philosophical question of whether public relations theory and research should study the activities of specific functional units or public relations as it might be practiced anywhere within an organization.

Findings from the Excellence Study showed that the public relations function can be organized in a centralized or decentralized way (see also Argenti, 2003; Argenti & Forman, 2002). Although the anecdotal qualitative findings are informative, the quantitative evidence easily leads readers to the conclusion that structure does not matter. The principal significant differences reported in practitioners' excellence scores were based on a confound to the central hypothesis (i.e., perceptions by practitioners), not actual levels of support given by senior managers to units primarily involved in marketing versus public affairs (Grunig & Grunig, 1998; Grunig et al., 2002). The evidence did not support the expectations that practitioners who work in units that are not centralized or integrated or that emphasize marketing (vs. public affairs) are less likely to exhibit excellence characteristics.

In sharp contrast to tenets of Excellence Theory, few IMC adherents are concerned about creating or maintaining particular organizational structures (Prensky, McCarty, & Lucas, 1996; Ruekert & Walker, 1987; Ruekert, Walker, & Roering, 1985). Most readily recognize the organizational and other barriers to structural integration (Copley, 2004; Hartley & Pickton, 1999; Koelle, 1991; Petrison & Wang, 1996). At best, Duncan and Moriarty (1997) suggested that a possible benefit of IMC is to cure overdepartmentalized companies.

In a valuable literature review covering 20 published studies over the previous decade, Cornelissen (2003) corroborated the Excellence Study's conclusion that there is little evidence of communication disciplines being combined into single departments. Instead, Cornelissen concluded that integrated communications today is characterized by high levels of collaboration among separate communications disciplines.

Separately, Cornelissen and Thorpe (2001) challenged the Excellence Study's call for reliance on perceptual data (Grunig, 1989) to assess interdepartmental cooperation. Instead, the authors provided empirical evidence of a high level of cooperation between corporate communications and marketing among U.K. companies. Measures included transactions (exchanges of work, resources, and technical assistance), the amount of communication, and the use of information provided by the other department. The researchers found support for 18 propositions related to internal and external environmental conditions that facilitate effective cooperation. In contrast to the power-control emphasis found in the Excellence Study, the authors concluded that organizations are highly capable of installing appropriate coordinating procedures to achieve desired or required levels of interaction between communications departments (Cornelissen & Thorpe, 2001). Units are not dependent on structures imposed by an organization's dominant coalition.

Modernist Versus Postmodernist Approaches to Structure. Excellence Theory is squarely based in modern management thought that is grounded in the division of labor and structural-functionalism (Grunig, 1976; L. Grunig, 1992a; Grunig et al., 1992). Thus, it argues that the public relations is a specialized function uniquely capable of managing external exigencies facing an organization, whereas senior officers and other units are less capable of assuming such specialized responsibilities. However, the latter argument was roundly refuted by practitioners at the time it was proffered (e.g., Harris, 1993) and contradicts the evidence readily available at the time about marketers' concern with the external environments in which clients operate.

The arguments set forth in the Excellence Study and by others (e.g., Cook, 1972; Hunter, 1997; Wrightman, 1999) that communications of an organization ought to be consolidated into a single public relations function stems from structural-functional thinking that flies in face of how organizations communicate today (Amiso, 2000; Deighton, 1996; Gronstedt, 1994, 2000). For more than 2 decades, modern management theorists such as Kanter (1983) have warned against segmentalism and called for integrative management techniques involving teams, empowerment, delegation, open systems, and holistic problem solving. Ironically, Excellence Theory recognizes the value of these principles at the organizational level (Grunig et al., 2002), but appears to ignore them when theorizing about the how the public relations function itself ought to operate and relate with other units within organizations.

Many of these ideas have morphed into postmodern management theories that reject mechanistic specialization, bureaucracy, and hierarchy in favor of dedifferentiation, democracy, and flexible, organic organizational structures (Calton & Kurland, 1996; Clegg, 1990; Hassard,

1996; Hatch, 1997; Vibert, 2004; Wallace, 1998). In an era of flattened, decentralized, divisionalized, and special-purpose organizational structures, postmodern management theory would reject the idea that an organization's single dominant coalition, along with the head of the communications department, should determine the most strategic publics for an organization. Instead, multiple coalitions would be expected to be at work, and decision making would be expected to be delegated and shared.

In this vein, Fleisher (1998; Fleisher & Hoewing, 1992) pointed out that corporate communications might eventually become more of a line management function and that, it in order to be most effective, will need to be diffused throughout the organization's line executives and units.

By contrast, Varey (2001) called for a more collaborative alternative to the centralized control model suggested in Excellence Theory. Varey claimed that communications departments are powerful because of their strategic contributions to organizations based on their organizational knowledge and technical expertise (evidence supporting this argument was provided by Grunig et al., 2002). Varey argued that emphasizing control and ownership is counter to responsive and responsible management. He called on public relations managers to focus in relationship management instead of object management within the organization. He based this alternative perspective on the same systems theory (but not power-control theory) that provided a basis for Excellence Theory:

> As organizations re-engineer business processes, they should re-engineer their communication management into a truly corporate (sub) system for managing. Departments should not be allowed to seek independence, and the concern of managers should not be encroachment, but how to remove barriers to real cooperative working so that "communicating" can add value to the business enterprise. The integrated approach does not promote the engagement of non-specialists in competition to manage traditional communication departments. Rather it seeks to foster greater recognition of corporate dependence and the need for wider interaction and participation in constructing meanings, identity and knowledge.... A value-creation perspective (of managing) on the departmentalization issue is required if the power-control assumptions and desires of the traditional manager (enacting constraining managerialism) are to be overcome for the benefit of the corporate community. This will require that managers recognize communications as central to the work of the entire community. (p. 69)

Instead of centering public relations in a single or integrated department, as suggested in Excellence Theory, Varey advocated deployment of a coherent stakeholder management system using a "wiring diagram" involving various units within the organization. His integrated approach calls for organizing communications based on clearly defined objectives, relationships, rules, task definitions, and allocations and connections to key publics and markets, rather than components or activities: "The question would then not be concerning who owns particular groupings of tasks, but who can work together to effectively and efficiently manage specific relationships with key stakeholders" (p. 73). This requires a shift from functions to communicative activities.

Grunig et al. (2002) made it clear that their call for concentrating authority in a single public relations unit was not based on a quest for power per se:

> The Excellence Theory emphasizes the empowerment of public relations in the dominant coalition, not because that would allow public relations to help dictate organizational decisions but because empowerment allows the organization to benefit from the expertise of the public relations profession—something that is most likely to happen when the public relations function is involved in the strategic management of the organization. (pp. 142–143)

The distinction between power and empowerment is a fine one, undoubtedly. Giving up authority is difficult and few practitioners would agree that the sole reason for being placed high in the organization is merely to empower the public relations function (see the discussion about power, power sharing by the dominant coalition, and power enhancement by public relations in L. Grunig, 1992b).

Except for several general references to the use of matrix structures (Grunig et al., 2002), Excellence Theory doesn't address collaboration or power sharing *by* public relations with others in the organization. This includes how public relations managers ought to interact with units across the organization—including senior managers of divisions and managers of functional units such as marketing, finance, or law—to jointly formulate organizational policies. Instead, the Excellence Theory places a premium on the discipline maintaining autonomy (Dozier & Grunig, 1992; L. Grunig, 1992a, 1992b).

Future researchers need to reconsider the assumptions of Excellence Theory on how power, control, and autonomy influence the restructuring of public relations. More emphasis needs to be placed on how public relations is involved in multiple coalitions, how the management of external interdependencies must be shared, and how public relations must enable (empower) colleagues to collaborate in setting public relations policies. Although collaboration opportunities are frequently limited in public relations work generally (Leichty, 1997), the contingency model of public relations has recognized the importance of decentralization of decision making and the important role of line managers in formulating public relations practices (Cancel, Mitrook, & Cameron, 1999).

FUTURE DIRECTIONS FOR RESEARCH

Based on this discussion, a broad array of research questions about communication integration awaits investigation by the next generation of public relations scholars. These relate to integration within public relations, integration between public relations and marketing activities, and integration of communication by the entire organization. A few key issues are briefly summarized here; an inventory of more specific research questions appears in the appendix.

Integration Within Public Relations

Two key questions emerging from the Excellence Study particularly merit attention.

Organization of the Public Relations Function. In the absence of compelling quantitative evidence favoring excellence among practitioners working in centralized and integrated (vs. decentralized and specialized) units, more needs to known about alternative schemes for organizing public relations and its relationship to professional values and performance. Little attention has paid to this issue (see Cornelissen, 2003; Holtzhausen, 2002; Varey, 2001). Future investigations need to examine the benefits, trade-offs, and challenges of alternative organizational schemes. If public relations concepts are viable and valuable to organizations, it could be argued that particular organizational schemes are neither sufficient nor necessary for success.

Differences Between Specialties. Perhaps the more provocative question is whether there is actually a difference between marketing- and public affairs-oriented public relations. Grunig (1984) referred to this as an organization's product/service environment versus political/regulatory environment. Excellence Theory suggests that public relations should concentrate on the later because disgruntled publics can cost organizations money, whereas customers (distributors and consumers) merely enable organizations to make money (Grunig & Grunig, 1991). In fact, both environments are strategically important to most organizations. In situations in which risks from noncustomer publics are low, an emphasis on marketing support might be entirely appropriate. Future research needs to examine this dichotomy, including actual and perceived differences in the nature, value, organization, and management support of these specialties.

Integration Between Public Relations and Marketing

Assuming that the encroachment and sublimation are moot points, future research needs to examine more closely the working relationship between public relations and marketers, as suggested by the Grunigs (1998).

Place and Value of Public Relations in the IMC Mix.   A nearly untapped avenue for research lies in looking at the application of public relations theories in marketing. IMC is a young and undeveloped subdiscipline of marketing (Duncan & Mulhern, 2004) that has barely examined the adoption of IMC and only touched on the specific role of public relations. More also needs to be done to examine the degree to which public relations practitioners themselves perceive their involvement in IMC and integration processes.

Collaborative Strategies.   With the emphasis on collaboration suggested earlier, a second major avenue for research focuses on the structural and functional relationships between public relations and marketing. Organizations can deal with their environments using either control or adaptation strategies (Grunig, 1984). In keeping with the research by others summarized in *Effective Organizations*, various adaptive mechanisms are now being employed by organizations to encourage collaboration and cooperation. Future research needs to examine the collaboration process, including how it is shaped by organizational culture, general management styles, and strategy-making modes (Moss & Warnaby, 1998).

Mutual Emphasis on Relationship Management.   In light of the shared focus on relationship management found in the literature, it is becoming increasingly necessary to understand the parallels between how public relations and marketing approach building and maintaining relationships. To what extent are their approaches complementary? Then, the question involves the degree to which marketing and public relations practitioners actually embrace the relationship focus.

Integration Involving Organizationwide Communications

Finally, understanding integrated communications in diversified and decentralized organizations requires looking beyond corporate-level activities involving communications specialists to understanding how organizations communicate integratively with key stakeholders across the organization. Indeed, strategic communication cannot be entrusted to specialists in public relations and marketing alone, but must involve the entire organization as it learns and continuously improves itself (Stewart, 1996).

Integration of Experiences.   Today, people's knowledge, attitudes, and behaviors about organizations, products, and services reflects the sum of their interactions and experiences with an organization. These cannot be handily partitioned into activities labeled "public relations" or "advertising" because people rarely differentiate between these functional activities (Schultz & Kitchen, 2000). Understanding a person's total experience with an organization includes examining the role of cognitive constructs such as organizational identity, image, brand, and reputation (Argenti, 2003; Argenti & Forman, 2002; Barich & Kotler, 1991; Fombrun, 1996). These are ideas dismissed in Excellence Theory in favor of behaviorally based measures of relationships (Grunig, 1993a, 1993b; Grunig & Grunig, 1998; Grunig et al., 2002).

Integration of Organizational Communication Channels. Truly integrated organizational communications call for the use of media neutral planning (MNP), the abandonment of traditional mass-mediated models of communication, and overcoming channel choice biases based on historical precedents, political imperatives, and managers' personal experience and preconceptions (Cornelissen, 2003). This issue is particularly important in an era when public relations and personalized approaches have garnered favor vis-à-vis advertising (Dilenschneider, 1991; Jo, 2004; Koelle, 1991; McKenna, 1986; Ries & Ries, 2002; Zyman, 2002). Similarly, hybrid messages—product placements, advertorials, sponsored events and sponsored media, and cause-related marketing—have been widely accepted (Balasubramanian, 1991; Cameron & Curtin, 1995; Cameron, Ju-Pak, & Kim, 1996; Gupta & Gould, 1997; Jaffe, 2005; Karth, 1998; Pardun & McKee 1999; Sandler & Secunda, 1993; Zinkham & Watson, 1996). More research is needed to consider how organizations ought to take advantage of the full range of communications available to them (Hallahan, 2001). Why? As Zyman (2002) aptly put it, "everything communicates!" (p. 219).

Integration of Organizational Communication Messages. An obvious consequence of organizationwide integration is the increased importance of honing organizational objectives and key messages or themes that the organization wants to share consistently with stakeholders. This is an area in which PR and IC professionals can provide valuable counsel. More research is needed to better understand the nature and implementation of the one voice/one look approach and how these core ideas should be determined and implemented. This involves a more thorough research related to message consistency, coordination, synergy, and complementarity.

Interactivity. Whereas Excellence Theory focuses on two-way communications, IC adherents focus on interactivity in the broadest sense—that is, all the ways in which people engage with an organization. Conventional wisdom suggests that the more ways a stakeholder positively interacts with an organization, the better (e.g., Roman, Mass, & Nisenholtz, 2003). Interactivity is particularly important in light of new technologies—a topic addressed in one short paragraph in the conclusion to *Effective Organizations* (Grunig et al., 2002). Rust and Varki (1996) argued that interactive media will functionally displace mass media, and the importance of new technology is widely recognized by IC advocates. Research needs to address the impact of the Internet (Hallahan, in press), self-service technologies (SSTs) that automate all stakeholder contacts (Barnes, Dunne, & Glynn, 2000; Meuter, Ostrom, Roundtree, & Bitner, 2000), and integrated customer relations management (CRM) systems that utilize combinations of telephone, mail, and computer interfaces at a distance (Buttle, 2004; Cooper, 2001).

CONCLUSION

By addressing communication integration, the Excellence Study provided a valuable launching point for investigating two of the most important issues confronting public relations theory and research in the future: how public relations ought to be organized within the organization, and how public relations communication fits within an organization's overall communications scheme. As Buer (2002) observed, communication integration might not only become a necessity, but also an imperative.

Future research must look beyond public relations as a specialty function to consider how public relations activities—including relationship building and strategic communication—are undertaken by the entire organization. Stated another way, the level of the analysis used in studying public relations management needs to expand from the department level to the organization level, and must recognize that public relations activities are not carried out only by people who call themselves public relations practitioners.

For researchers concerned with public relations as a function, the challenge will be to reconsider the tenets of Excellence Theory in the light of the changed environment in which organizations operate today and the alternative perspectives outlined here. Importantly, this can involve extending—not discarding—excellence model principles. Many valuable principles found in Excellence Theory can be applied to re-examining additional dimensions of how public relations interacts with units in an organization beyond the dominant coalition. These include ideas related to systems theory, interdependencies, and internal relationships; participation in decision making; organizational culture; and the engagement of others in two-way symmetrical communication when formulating public relations policies and strategies.

One of the shortcomings of the excellence model is its failure to focus sufficient attention on what constitutes excellent public relations communications beyond the rarified concepts of symmetrical versus asymmetrical two-way communication (Grunig, 1992c). In the future, more emphasis needs to be placed on excellent (best) communication strategies, practices, and techniques. Such efforts are critical if the discipline is to avoid a threat far greater than encroachment: *implosion*, based on an inability to sustain itself as a distinct discipline. Beyond enacting roles as managers, public relations professionals must be excellent strategic communicators who contribute collaboratively to the fulfillment of an organization's mission and goals.

APPENDIX: AN INVENTORY OF RESEARCH QUESTIONS RELATED TO INTEGRATED COMMUNICATION

Topics are organized according to the outline of key issues topics outlined in the article. References draw primarily from the excellence and integrated communication literature. Use these in tandem with sources that can be found in public relations literature to provide a launching point for further exploration.

Integration Within Public Relations

Organizational Structure

Benefits/problems of centralized versus specialized units (Argenti, 2003; Argenti & Forman, 2002; Dozier & Grunig, 1992; L. Grunig, 1992a, 1992b; Hunter, 1997, 1999a, 1999b).

Effects of organizational size, complexity focus, geographic diversity, and structure on organizing the PR function (Grunig, 1989; Holtzhausen, 2002; Van Leuven, 1991b).

Impact of postmodern management theory on organization of the PR function (Carlton & Kurland, 1996; Clegg, 1990; Hassard, 1996; Hatch, 1997; Holtzhausen, 2002; Vibert, 2004; Wallace, 1998)

Alternatives to Excellence Theory (Cornelissen, 2003; Cornelissen & Thorpe, 2001; Varey, 1998, 2001).

Structural approaches in IMC/marketing (Prensky et al., 1996; Ruekert, Walker, & Roering, 1985).

Public Affairs Versus Marketing Public Relations

Validity of distinguishing between an organization's product/service environment and political/regulatory environment (Buer, 2002; Grunig, 1984)

Effects of separating marketing and public affairs functions, including practitioners' performance, self-perceptions, and self-efficacy (Grunig, Grunig, & Dozier, 2002).

Influence of senior management's perceptions—based on their understanding, experience, and assessment of the contribution to the organization.

Integration Between Public Relations and Marketing

General Use of IMC by Organizations

Overviews (Conley, 1954; Duncan, 2001; Duncan & Mulhern, 2004; Kitchen & Schultz, 2001; Schultz & Kitchen, 2000; Schultz & Schultz, 2004; Schultz, Tannenbaum, & Lauterhorn, 1993; Thorson & Moore, 1996).

Extent of adoption of IMC by organizations (Caywood, 1994; Caywood, Schultz, & Wang, 1991; Duncan & Everett, 1993; Eagle, Kitchen, Hyde, Fourie, & Padisetti, 1999; Kim, Han, & Schultz, 2004; McArthur, 1997; Pettegrew, 2000; Phelps, Harris, & Johnson, 1996; Rose,1996; Schultz, 1996; Schultz & Kitchen, 1997).

Adoption of IMC based on industry, organization, and type (Low, 2000); by consumer products companies (Reid, Johnson, Ratcliffe, Skrip, & Wilson, 2001); by consumer services organizations (Carlson, Grove, Laczniak, & Kangan, 1996; Carlson, Grove, & Dorsch, 2003; Grove, Carlson, & Dorsch, 2002); by retail organizations (Barnes, 2001; Moss, Warnaby, & Thame, 1996, 1997; Mulhern, 1997; Nowak, Cameron, & Delorme, 1996); and by business-to-business organizations (Garber & Dotson, 2002; Stewart, Frazier, & Martin, 1996).

Barriers/contributors to adoption (Duncan & Moriarty, 1997; Koelle, 1991; Petrison & Wang, 1996; Prensky et al., 1996; Schultz, 1993, 1994).

Definitions/Stages of IMC development (Caywood, 1997, 1997a, 1997b; Duncan & Caywood, 1996; Duncan & Mulhern, 2004; Kliatchko, 2005; Nowak & Phelps, 1994; Schultz & Kitchen, 2000).

Planning concerns (Moore & Thorson, 1996; Petrison & Wang, 1996; Raulus & Vepsalainen, 2001).

Assessment and evaluation (Jones, 1996; Keller, 1996; Pickton & Hartley, 1998; Schultz & Kitchen, 2000; Wang & Schultz, 1993).

Place of Public Relations in the IMC/Marketing Mix

Role/place of public relations in IMC programs/marketing (Broom & Tucker, 1989; Caywood, 1997; Duncan & Everett, 1993; Goldman, 1990; Hallahan, 1996; Harris, 1991, 1993; Hutton, 1996, 2001;

Kitchen & Schultz, 2001a, 2001b; Kotler & Mindak, 1978; McArthur, 1997; Reid et al., 2001).

Opinions about IMC among PR practitioners (Eicholz, 1995; Kitchen & Li, 2005; Miller & Rose, 1994).

Examples/case studies of integration in communications messages (Amiso, 2000; Carlson, Grove, Lawler, & Tourelle, 2002; Haytko, 1996; Deighton, 1996; Laczniak & Kangan, 1996).

Practitioners' preparedness to assume a role in IMC: (Hunter, 1997; Wrightman, 1999).

Collaborative Strategies

Structural models about relationships between PR and marketing (Hallahan, 1992; Hutton, 1996, 2001; Kotler & Mindak, 1978).

Division of labor, skills of PR versus marketing personnel (Spicer, 1991).

Mechanisms used to coordinate activities (Cornelissen, 2003; Cornelissen & Thorpe, 2001; Gronstedt, 1994, 1996b, 2000; Hunter, 1997; Moss, Warnaby, & Thame, 1996, 1997; van Riel, 1995; Varey, 2001).

Conflict and encroachment (Ehling, 1989; Kelly, 1993; Lauzen, 1991, 1992, 1993).

Impact on client-agency relations and roles (Beard, 1996, 1997; Gould, Grein, & Lehrman, 1996; Gronstedt, 1996c; Gronstedt & Thorson, 1996; Ruekert, Walker & Roaring, 1985; Schultz & Kitchen, 1997).

Integration of public relations and advertising education (Caywood & Ewing, 1991; Dozier et al., 1995; Duncan, Caywood, & Newsom, 1991, 1993; Farrelly, Luxton, & Brace-Govan, 2001; Ferguson & Van Slyke Turk, 1993; Lauer, 1995; Newsom & Carroll, 1992; Rose & Miller, 1994).

Mutual Emphasis on Relationship Management

Comparative emphasis on relationship building among marketing versus PR practitioners; how organization size and culture influence relationship orientation (Webster, 1992, 1994).

Understanding, appreciation of tenets of Excellence Theory among marketers.

Integration of Organizationwide Communications

Integration of Stakeholder Experiences

Integrated perceptions of organizations by audiences (Englis & Solomon, 1996; Fill, 2001; Schultz & Kitchen, 2000; Solomon & Englis, 1996).

Managing organizational experiences (Schmitt, 1999, 2003; Schmitt, Rogers, & Vrotsos, 2004).

Role of corporate identity, image and reputation versus behavioral measures of organizational-public relationships (Argenti, 2003; Argenti & Forman, 2002; Barich & Kotler, 1991; Fombrun, 1996; J. Grunig, 1993, 1993a, 1993b).

Adapting organization structure to audiences; role of organizational learning and continuous improvement/KAIZEN (Stewart, 1996).

Integration of Communication Channels

Zero-based media planning (Garber & Dotson, 2002; Grounds, 2003; Hallahan, 2001; Lloyd, 1996; Moran, 1992; Phelps et al., 1996; Schimmel & Nicholls, 2005; Shannon, 1996; Sissors & Bumba, 1992; Zinkham & Watson, 1996).

Audience understanding of hybrid messages, differentiation of genres (Balasubramanian, 1991; Cameron & Curtin, 1995; Cameron et al., 1996; Gupta & Gould, 1997; Hallahan, 1996, 1999a, 1999b; Jo, 2004; Karth, 1998; Pardun & McKee, 1999; Sandler & Secunda, 1993; Zinkham & Watson, 1996).

Integration of Messages

Developing an organizational persona and voice (Stern, 1996).

Characteristics of strong messages (Duncan & Moriarty, 1997; Roman et al., 2003; van Riel, 1995).

Role of message consistency, coordination, synergy and complementarity (Edell & Keller, 1989; Haytko, 1996; Keller, 1996, 2001; Moriarty, 1996; Schumann, Dyer, & Petkus, 1996; Solomon & Englis, 1994).

Impact of adverse/negative/unplanned messages (Duncan & Moriarty, 1997; Moriarty, 1994).

Interactivity

Role of interactive media (Holtzblatt, 2001; Kitchen & Schultz, 2001a, 2001b; Mueller-Heumann, 1992; Peltier, Schibrowsky & Schultz, 2003; Rust & Varki, 1996; Schultz, 1996; Schultz & Kitchen, 2000, 2001; Stewart et al., 1996).

Integration and relationship building online (Hallahan, in press).

Integration of self-service technologies (Barnes, Dunn, & Glynn, 2000; Meuter, Ostrom, Roundtree, & Bitner, 2000).

Integration and role of customer relationship management (Buttle, 2004).

REFERENCES

Achrol, R. S. (1991, October). Evolution of the marketing organization: New forms for turbulent environments. *Journal of Marketing, 55,* 77–83.

Achrol, R. S. & Kotler, P. (1999). Marketing in the network economy [Special issue]. *Journal of Marketing, 63,* 146–163.

Adams, B. (2001). Talking about integrated communications. *Public Relations Tactics, 8*(2), 26.

Amiso, G. M. (2000). The new public relations: Integrating marketing and public relations strategies for student recruitment and institutional image building—a case study of the University of Texas at San Antonio. *Journal of Nonprofit & Public Sector Marketing, 7*(4), 17–31.

Argenti, P. A. (2003). *Corporate communication* (3rd ed.) Boston: McGraw Hill Irwin.

Argenti, P. A., & Forman, J. (2002). *The power of corporate communication. Crafting the voice and image of your business.* New York: McGraw-Hill.

Arndt, J. (1983, Fall). The political economy paradigm: Foundation for theory building in marketing. *Journal of Marketing, 47,* 44–54.

Atler, S. (1990, March 19). Now, try all-new advertising! *Adweek,* p. 50.

Balasubramanian, S. K. (1991). *Beyond advertising and publicity: The domain of hybrid messages* (Report No. 91-131). Cambridge, MA: Marketing Science Institute.

Barich, H., & Kotler, P. (1991). A framework for marketing image management. *Slogan Management Review, 32*(2), 94–104.

Barnes, B. E. (2001). Integrated brand communication planning: Retail applications. *Journal of Marketing Communications, 7*(1), 11–18.

Barnes, J. G., Dunne, P. A., & Glynn, W. J. (2000). Self-service and technology. In T. A. Swartz & D. Iacobucci (Eds.), *Handbook of services marketing & management* (pp. 89–102). Thousand Oaks, CA: Sage.

Beard, F. (1996). Integrated marketing communications: New role expectations and performance issues in the client–ad agency relationship. *Journal of Business Research, 37*(3), 207–216.

Beard, F. K. (1997). IMC use and client–ad agency relationships. *Journal of Marketing Communications, 3*(4), 217–230.

Bernays, E. L. (1965). *Biography of an idea. Memoirs of public relations counsel Edward L. Bernays.* New York: Crown.

Brody, E. W. (1994, Summer). PR is to experience what marketing is to expectations. *Public Relations Quarterly, 39*(2), 20–22.

Broom, G. M., Lauzen, M. M., & Tucker, K. (1991). Dividing the public relations and marketing conceptual domain and operational turf. *Public Relations Review, 17*(3), 219–226.

Broom, G. M. & Tucker, K. (1989, November). An essential double helix. *Public Relations Journal, 45*(11), 40, 39.

Buer, L. (2002). What have public affairs and advertising got in common? *Journal of Public Affairs, 2*(4), 293–295.

Buttle, F. (2004). *Customer relationship management: Concepts and tools.* Oxford, England: Elsevier/Butterworth-Heinemann.

Calton, J. M., & Kurland, N. B. (1996). A theory of stakeholder enabling: Giving voice to an emerging postmodern praxis of organizational discourse. In D. M. Boje, R. P. Gephart, Jr., & T. J. Thatchenkery (Eds.), *Postmodern management and organization theory* (pp. 154–180). Thousand Oaks, CA: Sage.

Cameron, G. T., & Curtin, P. A. (1995). Tracing sources of information pollution: A survey and experimental test of labeling policy for feature advertising. *Journalism & Mass Communications Quarterly, 72*(1), 178–189.

Cameron, G. T., Ju-Pak, H., & Kim, B. (1996). Advertorials in magazines: Current use and compliance with industry guidelines. *Journalism & Mass Communication Quarterly, 73*(3), 722–733.

Cancel, A. E., Mitrook, M. A., & Cameron, G. T. (1999). Testing the contingency theory of accommodation in public relations. *Public Relations Review, 25*(2), 171–198.

Carlson, L., Grove, S. J. & Dorsch, M. J. (2003). Services advertising and integrated marketing communications: An empirical examination. *Journal of Current Issues and Research in Advertising, 25*(2), 69–82.

Carlson, L., Grove, S. J., Laczniak, R. N., & Kangun, N. (1996). Does environmental advertising reflect integrated marketing communications? An empirical investigation. *Journal of Business Research, 37*, 225–232.

Caywood, C. L. (1994, August). *The evolving management of marcom and corpcom: An exploratory essay on an integrated approach.* Paper presented to the Advertising and Public Relations Divisions, Association for Education in Journalism and Mass Communication, Atlanta.

Caywood, C. L. (1997a). The future of integrated communications and public relations. In C. L. Caywood (Ed.), *The handbook of strategic public relations and integrated communications* (pp. 564–566). New York: McGraw-Hill.

Caywood, C. L. (1997b). Twenty-first century public relations: The strategic stages of integrated communications. In C. L. Caywood (Ed.), *The handbook of strategic public relations and integrated communications* (pp. xi–xxvi). New York: McGraw-Hill.

Caywood, C. L., & Ewing, R. (1991). Integrated marketing communications: A new master's degree concept. *Public Relations Review, 17*(3), 237–244.

Caywood, C., Schultz D. E. & Wang, P. (1991). *Integrated marketing communications: A survey of national consumer goods advertisers.* Evanston, IL: Northwestern University Press.

Clegg, S. (1990). *Modern organizations. Organization studies in the postmodern world.* London: Sage.

Conley, C. (1954). *Publicity and its relation to selling* [Brochure]. New York: Know-How Publishing.

Cook, J. (1972, September). Consolidating the communication function. *Public Relations Journal, 26*(9), 6–8, 28.

Cooper, K. C. (2001). *The relational enterprise: Moving beyond CRM to maximize all your business relationships.* New York: AMACOM.

Copley, P. (2004). *Marketing communications management: Concepts, theories, cases and practices.* Amsterdam: Elsevier Butterworth Heinemann.

Cornelissen, J. P. (2001). Integrated marketing communications and the language of marketing development. *International Journal of Advertising, 20*, 483–498.

Cornelissen, J. P. (2003). Change, continuity and progress: The concept of marketing communications and marketing communications practice. *Journal of Strategic Marketing, 11*, 217–234.

Cornelissen, J. P. & Lock, A. R. (2000, September/October). Theoretical concept or management fashion? Examining the significance of IMC. *Journal of Advertising Research, 40*(5), 7–15.

Cornelissen, J. P., & Thorpe, A. R. (2001). The organization of external communications disciplines in UK companies: A conceptual and empirical analysis of dimensions and determinants. *Journal of Business Communications, 38*(4), 413–438.

Deighton, J. (1996). Features of good integration: Two cases and some generalizations. In E. Thorson & J. Moore (Eds.), *Integrated communication. Synergy of persuasive voices* (pp. 243–259). Mahwah, NJ: Lawrence Erlbaum Associates.

Dilenschneider, R. L. (1991). Marketing communications in the post-advertising era. *Public Relations Review, 17*(3), 227–236.

Dozier, D. M., & Grunig, L. A. (1992). The organization of the public relations function. In J. E. Grunig (Ed.), *Excellence in public relations and communication management* (pp. 395–417). Hillsdale, NJ: Lawrence Erlbaum Associates.

Dozier, D. M., Grunig, L. A., & Grunig, J. E. (1995). *Managers guide to excellence in public relations and communication management.* Hillsdale, NJ: Lawrence Erlbaum Associates.

Dozier, D. M., & Lauzen, M. M. (1990, August). *Antecedents and consequences of marketing imperialism on the public relations function.* Paper presented to the Public Relations Division, Association for Education in Journalism and Mass Communication, Minneapolis, MN.

Drobis, D. R. (1997–1998). Integrated marketing communications redefined. *Journal of Integrated Communications, 8*, 6–10.

Drucker, P. (1980). *Managing in turbulent times.* New York: Harper & Row.

Duncan, T., & Caywood, C. (1996). The concept, process and evolution of integrated marketing communication. In E. Thorson & J. Moore (Eds.), *Integrated communication: Synergy of persuasive voices* (pp. 13–34). Mahwah, NJ: Lawrence Erlbaum Associates.

Duncan, T., Caywood, C., & Newsom, D. (1991, July). *Preparing advertising and public relations students for the communication industry in the 21st century. Report for the Task Force on Integrated Communications.* Paper presented to the Annual Convention of the Association for Education in Journalism and Mass Communication, Kansas City. MO.

Duncan, T., Caywood, C., & Newsom, D. (1993, December). *Preparing advertising and public relations students for the communications industry in the 21st century. Report of the Task Force on Integrated Communications.* Evanston, IL: Northwestern University Press.

Duncan, T., & Everett, S. (1993). Client perceptions of integrated marketing communications. *Journal of Advertising Research, 33*(3), 30–39.

Duncan, T., & Moriarty, S. (1997). *Driving brand value: Using integrated marketing to manage profitable stakeholder relationships.* New York: McGraw-Hill.

Duncan, T., & Mulhern F. (Eds.). (2004, March). *A white paper on the status scope and future of IMC.* Denver: University of Denver Daniels School of Business; Evanston, IL: Northwestern University Medill School of Journalism.

Eagle, L., Kitchen, P., & Hyde, K. (1999). Perceptions of integrated marketing communications among marketers and ad agency executives in New Zealand. *International Journal of Advertising, 18*(1), 89–119.

Edell, J. A., & Keller, K. L. (1989. The information processing of coordinated media campaigns. *Journal of Marketing Research, 26*, 149–163.

Educators address tension between IMC and PR. (1995, May 29). *PR News*, p. 3.

Educators reject IMC task force proposals; charge report based on "spurious consensus." (1993, Winter). *PRSA Educators Section Quarterly Newsletter*, pp. 1–2

Ehling, W. P. (1989, January). *Public relations management and marketing management: Different paradigms and different missions.* Paper presented to A Challenge to the Calling: Public Relations Colloquium 1989, San Diego.

Ehling, W. P., White, J., & Grunig, J. E. (1992). Public relations and marketing practices. In J. E. Grunig (Ed.), *Excellence in public relations and communication management* (pp. 357–394). Hillsdale, NJ: Lawrence Erlbaum Associates.

Eicholz, M. (1995). *Integrated marketing communications: Integration or cooperation?* Unpublished paper, Syracuse University.

Englis, B. G., & Solomon, M. R. (1996). Using consumption constellations to develop integrated communications strategies. *Journal of Business Research, 37,* 183–191.

Farrelly, F., Luxton, S., & Brace-Govan, J. (2001, May). Critical issues to understanding IMC in the future—an academic and practitioner developed marketing communication curriculum for the 21st century. *Marketing Bulletin, 12.* Retrieved June 15, 2005; from http://marketing-bulletin.massey.ac.az

Ferguson, D., & Van Slyke Turk, J. (1993, August 11). *Position statement: Preparing advertising and public relations students for the communications industry in the 21st century.* New York: Public Relations Society of America Educational Affairs Committee.

Fill, C. (2001). Essentially a matter of consistency: Integrated marketing communications. *The Marketing Review, 1,* 409–425.

Finn, D. (1990). An integrated approach is best in any communications effort. *Marketing News 24*(15), 13–14.

Fleisher, C. S. (1998). A benchmarked assessment of the strategic management of corporate communications. *Journal of Marketing Communications, 4,* 163–176.

Fleisher, C. S., & Hoewing, R. (1992). Strategically managing public affairs: New challenges and opportunities. *Journal of Strategic Change, 1*(5), 89–96.

Fombrun, C. J. (1996). *Reputation: Realizing value from the corporate image.* Boston: Harvard Business School Press.

Garber, L. L., Jr., & Dotson, M. J. (2002). A method for the selection of appropriate business-to-business integrated marketing communications mixes. *Journal of Marketing Communications, 8*(1), 1–17.

Gayeski, D. M., & Woodward, B. E. (1996, June). *Integrated communication: From theory to performance.* Paper presented to the International Association of Business Communicators.

Goldman, J. (1990). *Public relations in the marketing mix.* Chicago: Crain.

Gonring, M. P. (1994). Putting integrated marketing communications to work today. *Public Relations Quarterly, 39*(3), 45–48.

Gould, S. J., Grein, A. F. & Lerman, D. W. (1999). The role of agency–client integration in integrated marketing communications: A complementary agency theory-interorganizational perspective. *Journal of Current Issues & Research in Advertising, 21*(1), 1–12.

Greenley, G. E., & Foxall, G. R. (1996). Consumer and nonconsumer stakeholder orientation in U.K. companies. *Journal of Business Research, 37,* 105–116.

Gronstedt, A. (1994). *Integrated communications at America's leading total quality management corporations.* Unpublished doctoral dissertation, University of Wisconsin–Madison.

Gronstedt, A. (1996a). Integrating marketing communication and public relations: A stakeholder public relations model. In E. Thorson & J. Moore (Eds.), *Integrated communication; Synergy of persuasive voices* (pp. 287–304). Mahwah, NJ: Lawrence Erlbaum Associates.

Gronstedt, A. (1996b). Integrated communications at America's leading total quality management corporations. *Public Relations Review, 22*(1), 25–42.

Gronstedt, A. (1996c). How agencies can support integrated communications. *Journal of Business Research, 37*(3), 201–206.

Gronstedt, A. (2000). *The customer century: Lessons from world class companies in integrated marketing communication.* New York: Routledge.

Gronstedt, A., & Thorson, E. (1996, March/April). Five approaches to organize an integrated marketing communications agency. *Journal of Advertising Research*, *36*(2), 48–58.

Grounds, J. (2003). Media neutral planning and evaluation: The chicken and egg of integrated communication. *International Journal of Nonprofit & Voluntary Sector Marketing*, *8*(3), 202–206.

Grove, S. J., Carlson, L., & Dorsch, M. J. (2002). Addressing services' intangibility through integrated marketing communication: An exploratory study. *Journal of Services Marketing*, *16*(5), 393–412.

Grunig, J. E. (1976). Organizations and public relations: Testing a communication theory. *Journalism Monographs*, *46*.

Grunig, J. E. (1984). Organizations, environments and models of public relations. *Public Relations Research and Education*, *1*(1), 6–29.

Grunig, J. E. (Ed.). (1992a). *Excellence in public relations and communication management*. Hillsdale, NJ: Lawrence Erlbaum Associates.

Grunig, J. E. (1992b). Communication, public relations and effective organizations: An overview of the book. In J. E. Grunig (Ed.), *Excellence in public relations and communication management* (pp. 1–30). Hillsdale, NJ: Lawrence Erlbaum Associates.

Grunig, J. E. (1992c). Symmetrical systems of internal communication. In J. E. Grunig (Ed.), *Excellence in public relations and communication management* (pp. 531–576). Hillsdale, NJ: Lawrence Erlbaum Associates.

Grunig, J. E. (1993a). Image and substance: From symbolic to behavioral relationships. *Public Relations Review*, *19*(2), 121–139.

Grunig, J. E. (1993b). On the effects of marketing, media relations and public relations: Images, agendas and relationships. In. W. Armbecht, H. Avenarius, & U. Zabel (Eds.), *Image and PR* (pp. 263–295). Opladen, Germany: Westdeutscher Verlag.

Grunig, J. E., & Grunig, L. A. (1991). Conceptual differences in public relations and marketing: The case of health-care organizations. *Public Relations Review*, *17*(3), 257–278.

Grunig, J. E., & Grunig, L. A. (1998). The relationship between public relations and marketing in excellent organizations: Evidence from the IABC study. *Journal of Marketing Communications*, *4*, 141–162.

Grunig, J. E., Grunig, L. A., & Ehling, W. P. (1992). What is an effective organization? In J. E. Grunig (Ed.), *Excellence in public relations and communication management* (pp. 65–90). Hillsdale, NJ: Lawrence Erlbaum Associates.

Grunig, L. A. (1989). Horizontal structure in public relations: An exploratory study of departmental differentiation. *Public Relations Research Annual*, *1*, 175–196.

Grunig, L. A. (1992a). How public relations/communications departments should adapt to the structure and environment of an organization... and what they actually do. In J. E. Grunig (Ed.), *Excellence in public relations and communication management* (pp. 467–482). Hillsdale, NJ: Lawrence Erlbaum Associates.

Grunig, L. A. (1992b). Power in the public relations department. In J. E. Grunig (Ed.), *Excellence in public relations and communication management* (pp. 484–501). Hillsdale, NJ: Lawrence Erlbaum Associates.

Grunig, L. A., Grunig, J. E., & Dozier, D. M. (2002). *Excellent public relations and effective organizations: A study of communication management in three nations*. Mahwah, NJ: Lawrence Erlbaum Associates.

Gupta, P. B., & Gould, S. J. (1997). Consumers' perceptions of the ethics and acceptability of product placements in movies: Product category and individual differences. *Journal of Current Issues and Research in Advertising, 19*(1), 37.

Hallahan, K. (1992, August). *A typology of organizational relationships between public relations and marketing.* Paper presented to Public Relations Division, Association for Education in Journalism and Mass Communication, Montreal.

Hallahan, K. (1996). Product publicity: An orphan of marketing research. In E. Thorson & J. Moore (Eds.), *Integrated communication: Synergy of persuasive voices* (pp. 305–330). Mahwah, NJ: Lawrence Erlbaum Associates.

Hallahan, K. (1999a). No, Virginia, it's not true what they say about publicity's third-party endorsement effect. *Public Relations Review, 25*(4), 331–350.

Hallahan, K. (1999b). Content class as heuristic cue in the processing of news versus advertising. *Journal of Public Relations Research, 11*(4), 293–320.

Hallahan, K. (2001). Strategic media planning: Toward an integrated public relations media model. In R. L. Health (Ed.), *Handbook of public relations* (pp. 461–470). Thousand Oaks, CA: Sage.

Hallahan, K. (in press). Organizational–public relationships in cyberspace. In T. Hansen-Horn & B. D. Neff (Eds.), *Public relations from theory to practice.* Boston: Allyn & Bacon.

Harris, T. L. (1991). *The marketer's guide to public relations.* New York: Wiley.

Harris, T. L. (1993). How MPR adds value to integrated marketing communications. *Public Relations Quarterly, 38*(2), 13–18.

Hartley, B., & Pickton, D. (1999). Integrated marketing communications requires a new way of thinking. *Journal of Marketing Communications, 5*, 97–106.

Hassard, J. (1996). Exploring the terrain of modernism and postmodernism in organization theory. In D. M. Boje, R. P. Gephart, Jr., & T. J. Thatchenkery (Eds.) *Postmodern management and organization theory* (pp. 45–59). Thousand Oaks, CA: Sage.

Hatch, M. J. (1997). *Organization theory: Modern, symbolic, and postmodern perspectives.* Oxford, England: Oxford University Press.

Haytko, D. L. (1996). Integrated marketing communication context: The Indiana middle grades reading program. In E. Thorson & J. Moore (Eds.), *Integrated communication: Synergy of persuasive voices* (pp. 233–243). Mahwah, NJ: Lawrence Erlbaum Associates.

Holtzblatt, K. (2001). Inventing the future. *Communications of the ACM, 44*(3), 108–110.

Holtzhausen, D. R. (2002). The effects of a divisionalized and decentralized organizational structure on a formal internal communication function in a South African organization. *Journal of Communication Management, 6*(4), 323–339.

Hunter, T. (1997). *The relationship of public relations and marketing against the background of integrated communications: A theoretical analysis and empirical study at US–American corporations.* Unpublished master's thesis, University of Salzburg, Austria.

Hunter, T. (1999a). The relationship between public relations and marketing. *Integrated Marketing Communications Journal, 5*(1), 41–44.

Hunter, T. (1999b). *Integrated communication: Current and future developments in integrated communication and brand management, with a focus on direct communication and new information and communication technologies, such as the Internet and stakeholder databases.* Unpublished doctoral dissertation, University of Salzburg, Austria.

Hutton, J. G. (1996). Integrated marketing communications and the evolution of marketing thought. *Journal of Business Research, 37,* 155–162.

Hutton, J. G. (2001). Defining the relationship between public relations and marketing: Public relations' most important challenge. In R. L. Heath (Ed.), *Handbook of public relations* (pp. 205–214). Thousand Oaks, CA: Sage.

It's all advertising. (1991, October). *Promo: The International Magazine for Promotion Marketing,* p. 1.

Jaffe, J. (2005). *Life after the 30-second spot: Energize your brand with a bold mix of alternatives to traditional advertising.* Hoboken, NJ: Wiley.

Jo, S. (2004). Effect of content type on impact: Editorial v. advertising. *Public Relations Review, 30*(4), 503–514.

Jones, J. P. (1996). Integrated communications: Some hidden complications. In E. Thorson & J. Moore (Eds.), *Integrated communication: Synergy of persuasive voices* (pp. 217–230). Mahwah, NJ: Lawrence Erlbaum Associates.

Kanter, R. M. (1983). *The change masters.* New York: Simon & Schuster.

Karth, J. (1998). Brand placement: A review. *Journal of Current Issues and Research in Advertising, 20*(2), 31–49.

Keller, K. L. (1996). Brand equity and integrated communications. In E. Thorson & J. Moore (Eds.), *Integrated communication: Synergy of persuasive voices* (pp. 103–132). Mahwah, NJ: Lawrence Erlbaum Associates.

Kelly, K. (1993). Public relations and fund-raising encroachment: Losing control in the nonprofit sector. *Public Relations Review, 19*(4), 349–365.

Keller, K. L. (2001). Mastering the marketing communications mix: Micro and macro perspectives on integrated marketing communication programs. *Journal of Marketing Management, 17,* 810–847.

Kendall, R. (1994, Summer). Beyond "integrated marketing communication." *PR Educator,* pp. 1–2.

Kim, I., Han, D., & Schultz, D. E. (2004). Understanding the diffusion of integrated marketing communications. *Journal of Advertising Research, 44*(1), 31–45.

Kitchen, P. J., & Li, T. (2005). Perceptions of integrated marketing communications: A Chinese ad and PR agency perspective. *International Journal of Advertising, 24*(1), 51–78.

Kitchen, P. J., & Schultz, D. E. (Eds.). (2001a). *Raising the corporate umbrella: Corporate communication in the 21st century.* New York: Palgrave/St. Martin's Press.

Kitchen, P. J., & Schultz, D. E. (2001b). The role of integrated communication in the interactive age. In P. J. Kitchen & D. E. Schultz (Eds.), *Raising the corporate umbrella: Corporate communication in the 21st century* (pp. 82–114). New York: Palgrave/St. Martin's Press.

Kitchen, P. J., & Schultz, D. E. (2003). Integrated corporate and product brand communication. *Advances in Competitiveness Research, 11*(1), 66–86.

Kliatchko, J. (2005). Towards a new definition of integrated marketing communications. *International Journal of Advertising, 24*(1), 7–35.

Koelle, M. I. (1991, June 19). Barriers to the dream. In J. Z. Sissors (Ed.), *Integrated marketing communications: Reprints of talks at the First Annual Symposium on Integrated Marketing Communications at Northwestern University* (pp. 6–10). Evanston, IL: Northwestern University Medill School of Journalism.

Kotler, P. (1972). A generic concept of marketing. *Journal of Marketing, 36,* 45–54.

Kotler, P. (1986). Megamarketing. *Harvard Business Review, 62*(2), 117–124.

Kotler, P. (2000). *Marketing management. The millennium edition.* Upper Saddle River, NJ: Prentice-Hall.

Kotler, P., & Levy, S. J. (1969a). Broadening the concept of marketing. *Journal of Marketing, 33*(1), 10–15.

Kotler, P., & Levy, S. J. (1969b). A new form of marketing myopia: Rejoinder to Professor Luck. *Journal of Marketing, 33*(3), 55–57.

Kotler, P., & Mindak, W. (1978). Marketing and public relations: Should they be partners or rivals? *Journal of Marketing, 42*, 41–44.

Kozikowski, M. (1993, December). IMC: A process whose time has come. In *Dialogue*, pp. 1–2. Flemington, NJ: Author.

Kozikowski, M. (1995, November). *The role of public relations in integrated marketing communication.* Presentation to Public Relations Society of America, Orlando, FL.

Lauer, D. (1995). Integrated communication. *Communication World, 12*(7), 26–27.

Lauzen, M. M. (1990, August). *Losing control: An examination of the management function in public relations.* Paper presented to Public Relations Division, Association for Education in Journalism and Mass Communication, Minneapolis, MN.

Lauzen, M. M. (1991). Imperialism and encroachment in public relations. *Public Relations Review, 17*(3), 245–2l56.

Lauzen, M. M. (1992). Public relations roles, interorganizational power and encroachment. *Journal of Public Relations Research, 4*, 61–80.

Lauzen, M. M. (1993). When marketing involvement matters at the manager level. *Public Relations Review, 19*(3), 247–260.

Lawler, A., & Tourelle, G. (2002). Public relations: The integrated communication tool in the launch of a new software operating system—a case study. *Journal of Communication Management, 7*(2), 156–159.

Lee, T. J. (2002, August/September). Integration, say hello to integrity. *Strategic Communication Management, 6*(5), 11.

Leichty, G. (1997). The limits of collaboration. *Public Relations Review, 23*(1), 47–59.

Lepley, P. (2000). Integrated communications: Is it real or a hackneyed phrase? *Public Relations Tactics, 7*(11), 14.

Lightcap, K. (1984). Marketing support. In B. Cantor (Ed.), *Experts in action: Inside public relations* (pp. 124–129). White Plains, NY: Longman.

Lloyd, C. V. (1996). How leading advertising agency media directors view integrated communication: A qualitative study of integrated communications and the media planning process. In E. Thorson & J. Moore (Eds.), *Integrated communication: Synergy of persuasive voices* (pp. 35–48). Hillsdale, NJ: Lawrence Erlbaum Associates.

Low, G. S. (2000, May/June). Correlates of integrated marketing communications. *Journal of Advertising Research, 40*(3), 27–39.

Luck, D. (1969, Spring). Broadening the concept of marketing—too far. *Journal of Marketing, 33*(3), 53–55.

Magrath, A. J. (1991, September). Collaborative marketing comes of age again. *Sales & Marketing Management*, p. 1.

Massie, L., & Anderson, C. L. (2003). Integrating communications: Is the ideal achievable? *Corporate Communications: An International Journal, 8*(4), 223–228.

McArthur, D. N. (1997). A marketing management view of integrated marketing communications. *Journal of Advertising Research, 57*(35), 19–26.

McCarthy, E. J. (1960). *Basic marketing. A managerial approach.* Burr Ridge, IL: Irwin.

McKenna, R. (1986). *Relationship marketing. Successful strategies for the age of the customer.* Reading, MA: Addison-Wesley.

Meuter, M. L., Ostrom, A. L., Roundtree, R. I., & Bitner, M. J. (2000). Self-service technologies: Understanding customer satisfaction with technology-based service encounters. *Journal of Marketing, 64*(3), 50–64.

Miller, D. A., & Rose, P. B. (1994). Integrated communications: A look at reality instead of theory. *Public Relations Quarterly, 39*(1), 13–16.

Miyamoto, C. (1997). *Integrated communication: A concept so old that it's new.* Retrieved June 1, 2005, from http://www.geocities.com/WallStreet/8925/integcom.htm

Moore, J., & Thorson, E. (1996). Strategic planning for integrated marketing communications programs: An approach for moving from chaotic to systematic. In E. Thorson & J. Moore (Eds.), *Integrated communication: Synergy of persuasive voices* (pp. 135–152). Mahwah, NJ: Lawrence Erlbaum Associates.

Moran, W. T. (1999). Brand presence and the perceptual frame. *Journal of Advertising Research, 30,* 9–16.

Moriarty, S. E. (1994). PR and IMC: The benefits of integration. *Public Relations Quarterly, 39*(3), 38–44.

Moriarty, S. E. (1996). The circle of synergy: Theoretical perspectives and an evolving IMC research agenda. In E. Thorson & J. Moore (Eds.), *Integrated communication: Synergy of persuasive voices* (pp. 333–354). Hillsdale, NJ: Lawrence Erlbaum Associates.

Moss, D. A., & Warnaby, G. (1998). Communications strategy? Strategy communication? Integrating different perspectives. *Journal of Marketing Communications, 4*(3), 131–140.

Moss, D. A., Warnaby, G., & Thame, L. (1996). Tactical publicity or strategic relationship management? An exploratory investigation of the role of public relations in the UK retail sector. *European Journal of Marketing, 30*(12), 69–84.

Moss, D., Warnaby, G., & Thame, L. (1997). Public relations or simply product publicity? An exploration of the role of public relations in the UK retail sector. In D. Moss, T. MacManus, & D. Vercic (Eds.), *Public relations research: An international perspective* (pp. 135–158). London: International Thomson Business Press.

Mueller-Heumann, G. (1992). Market and technology shifts in the 1990s: Market fragmentation and mass customization. *Journal of Marketing Management 8,* 303–314.

Mulhern, F. J. (1997). Retail marketing: From distribution to integration. *International Journal of Research in Marketing, 14*(2), 103–124.

Murray, L. (1976). Corporate communications: Management's new marketing skill. *Public Relations Quarterly, 21*(1), 18–28.

Nakra, P. (1991). The changing role of public relations in marketing communications. *Public Relations Quarterly, 36*(1), 42–46.

Newsom, D., & Carrell, B. (1986). Megamarketing [Letter to editor]. *Harvard Business Review, 64*(5), 170.

Newsom, D. A., & Carrell, B. (1992, August). *The tower of babel: A descriptive report on attitudes toward the idea of integrated communication programs.* Paper presented at the meeting of the Association for Education in Journalism and Mass Communication, Montreal.

Niederquell, M. O. (1991). Integrating the strategic benefits of PR into the marketing mix. *Public Relations Quarterly, 36*(1), 23–25.

Novelli, W. (1989–1990). One-stop shopping: Some thoughts on integrated marketing communications. *Public Relations Quarterly 34,* 4, 7–9.

Nowak, G. J., Cameron, G. T., & Delorme, D. (1996). Beyond the world of packaged goods: Assessing the relevance of integrated marketing communications for retail and consumer service marketing. *Journal of Marketing Communications, 2,* 173–190.

Nowak, G. J., & Phelps, J. (1994). Conceptualizing the integrated marketing communications' phenomenon: An examination of its impact on advertising practices and its implications for advertising research. *Journal of Current Issues and Research in Advertising, 16*(1), 49–66.

Pardun, C. J., & McKee, K. B. (1999). Product placement as public relations: An exploratory study of the role of public relations firms. *Public Relations Review, 25*(4), 481–494.

Peltier, J. W., Schibrowsky, J. A., & Schultz, D. E. (2003). Interactive integrated marketing communication: Combining the power of IMC, the new media and database marketing. *International Journal of Advertising, 22,* 93–115.

Pelton, L. E., Strutton, D., & Lumpkin, J. R. (2002). *Marketing channels. A relationship management approach.* Boston: McGraw-Hill Irwin.

Petrison, L. A., & Wang, P. (1996). Integrated marketing communication: Examining planing and executional considerations. In E. Thorson & J. Moore (Eds.), *Integrated communication: Synergy of persuasive voices* (pp. 153–166). Mahwah, NJ: Lawrence Erlbaum Associates.

Pettegrew, L. S. (2000–2001). If IMC is so good, why isn't it being implemented? Barriers to IMC adoption in corporate America. *Journal of Integrated Communications, 10,* 29–37.

Phelps, J. E., Harris, T. E., & Johnson, E. (1996). Exploring decision-making approaches and responsibility for developing marketing communications strategy. *Journal of Business Research, 37,* 317–223.

Pickton, D., & Hartley, B. (1998). Measuring integration: An assessment of quality of integrated marketing communications. *International Journal of Advertising, 17*(4), 447–465.

Prensky, D., McCarty, J. A., & Lucas, J. (1996). Integrated marketing communication: An organizational perspective. In E. Thorson & J. Moore (Eds.), *Integrated communication: Synergy of persuasive voices* (pp. 167–184). Mahwah, NJ: Lawrence Erlbaum Associates.

Promotion Marketing Association of America. (1993). *Factors influencing marketing strategies* [report]. New York: Author.

Raulus, M., & Vepsalainen, A. (2001). Integrated marketing communications management—a promotion process portfolio approach: Abstract. *European Journal of Marketing, 29*(5), 36–37.

Reid, M., Johnson, T., Ratcliffe, M., Skrip, K., & Wilson, J. (2001). Integrating marketing communications in the Australian and New Zealand wine industry. *International Journal of Advertising, 20,* 239–262.

Rice, F. (1991, December 16). A cure for what ails advertising? *Fortune,* pp. 119–122.

Ries, A., & Ries, L. (2002). *The fall of advertising and the rise of public relations.* New York: HarperBusiness.

Roman, K., Mass, J., & Nisenholtz, M. (2003). *How to advertise* (3rd ed.) New York: Thomas Dunne/St. Martin's Press.

Rose, P. B. (1996). Practitioners' opinions and interests regarding integrated marketing communications in selected Latin American countries. *Journal of Marketing Communications, 2*(1), 125–139.

Rose, P. B., & Miller, D. A. (1994). Merging advertising and PR: Integrated marketing communications. *Journalism Educator, 48,* 52–63.

Ruekert, R.W., & Walker, O. C., Jr.(1987, January). Marketing interaction with other functional units: A conceptual framework and empirical evidence. *Journal of Marketing, 51*(1), 1–19.

Ruekert, R.W., Walker, O. C. , Jr., & Roering, K. J. (1985). The organization of marketing activities: A contingency theory of structure and performance. *Journal of Marketing, 49*(1), 13–25.

Rust, R. T., & Varki, S. (1996). Rising from the ashes of advertising. *Journal of Business Research, 37,* 173–181.

Sandler, D. M., & Secunda, E. (1993). Point of view: Blurred boundaries—where does editorial end and advertising begin? *Journal of Advertising Research, 33,* 73–80.

Schimmel, K., & Nicholls, J. (2005, Spring). Segmentation based on media consumption: A better way to plan integrated marketing communications media. *Journal of Applied Business Research, 21*(2), 24–36.

Schmitt, B. H. (1999). *Experiential marketing.* New York: Free Press.

Schmitt, B. H. (2003). *Customer experience management.* Hoboken, NJ: Wiley.

Schmitt, B. H., Rogers, D. L., & Vrotsos, K. (2004). *There's no business that's not show business: Marketing in an experience culture.* Upper Saddle River, NJ: Prentice-Hall Financial Times.

Schultz, D. E. (1993, July 19). How to overcome the barriers to integration. *Marketing News,* p. 16.

Schultz, D. E. (1994). The IMC process. In *Transcript of Third Integrated Marketing Communications Symposium* (pp. 6–13). Evanston, IL: Northwestern Medill School of Journalism.

Schultz, D. E. (1996). The inevitability of integrated communications. *Journal of Business Research, 37*(3), 139–147.

Schultz, D. E., & Kitchen, P. J. (1997). Integrating marketing communications in U.S. advertising agencies: An exploratory study. *Journal of Advertising Research, 37*(5), 7–18.

Schultz, D., & Kitchen, P. J. (2000). *Communicating globally: An integrated marketing approach.* Lincolnwood, IL: NTC Business Books.

Schultz, D., & Kitchen, P. J. (2001). The role of integrated communications in the interactive age. In P. J. Kitchen & D. E. Schultz (Eds.), *Raising the corporate umbrella: Corporate communications in the 21st century* (pp. 82–114). New York: Palgrave/St. Martin's Press.

Schultz, D. & Schultz, H. (2004). *IMC: The next generation. Five steps for delivering value and measuring returns using marketing communication.* New York: McGraw-Hill.

Schultz, D. E., Tannenbaum, S. I., & Lauterhorn, R. F. (1993). *Integrated marketing communications.* Lincolnwood, IL: NTC Business Books.

Schumann, D. W., Dyer, B., & Petkus, E., Jr. (1996). The vulnerability of integrated marketing communication: The potential for boomerang effects. In E. Thorson & J. Moore (Eds.), *Integrated communication: Synergy of persuasive voices* (pp. 51–65). Mahwah, NJ: Lawrence Erlbaum Associates.

Shannon, J. R. (1996). The new promotions mix: A proposed paradigm, process and application. *Journal of Marketing—Theory and Practice, 4*(1), 56–69.

Sissors, J. Z. & Bumba, L. (1992). *Advertising media planning* (4th ed.) Lincolnwood, IL: NTC Business Books.

Solomon, M. R., & Englis, B. G. (1994). Observations: The big picture product complementarity and integrated communications. *Journal of Advertising Research, 34*(1), 57–63.

Solomon, M. R., & Englis, B. G. (1996). Consumption constellations: Implications for integrated communication strategies. In E. Thorson & J. Moore (Eds.), *Integrated communication: Synergy of persuasive voices* (pp. 65–86). Mahwah, NJ: Lawrence Erlbaum Associates.

Spicer, C. H. (1991). Communication functions performed by public relations and marketing practitioners. *Public Relations Review, 17*(3), 293–306.

Spotts, H. E., Lambert, D. R., & Joyce, M. L. (1998). Marketing déjà vu: The discovery of integrated marketing communications. *Journal of Marketing Education, 20*(3), 210–208.

Stanton, E. M. (1991). PR's future is here: Worldwide, integrated communications. *Public Relations Quarterly, 36*(1), 46–47.

Stein, B. F. (1996). Integrated communication: The company "voice" and the advertising persona. In E. Thorson & J. Moore (Eds.), *Integrated communication: Synergy of persuasive voices* (pp. 87–102). Mahwah, NJ: Lawrence Erlbaum Associates.

Stewart, D. W. (1996). Market-back approach to the design of integrated communications programs: A change in paradigm and a focus on determinants of success. *Journal of Business Research, 37*(3), 147–153.

Stewart, D. W., Frazier, G. L., & Martin, I. (1996). Integrated channel management: Merging the communication and distribution functions of the firm. In E. Thorson & J. Moore (Eds.), *Integrated communication: Synergy of persuasive voices* (pp. 185–216). Mahwah, NJ: Lawrence Erlbaum Associates.

Strenski, J. B. (1991). Marketing public relations sells: Case studies prove it. *Public Relations Quarterly, 36*(1), 25–27.

Tedlow, J. P. (1979). Keeping the corporate image. In *Public Relations and business, 1900–1950*. Greenwich, CT: JAI.

Thorman, D. J. (1970). Survival in the seventies depends on total marketing. *Public Relations Journal, 26*(9), 93–100.

Thorson, E., & Moore, J. (Eds.). (1996). *Integrated communications: Synergy of persuasive voices*. Mahwah, NJ: Lawrence Erlbaum Associates.

Tortorici, A. J. (1991). Maximizing marketing communications through horizontal and vertical orchestration. *Public Relations Quarterly, 36*(1), 20–23.

Turney, M. (2001). *On the way to integrated marketing communication? Online readings in public relations by Michael Turney*. Retrieved June 1, 2005, from http://www.nku.edu/prclass/readings/mkting3.html

Tye, L. (1998). *The father of spin: Edward L. Bernays and the birth of public relations*. New York: Crown.

Van Leuven, J. (1991a). Public relations and marketing: An overview. *Public Relations Review, 17*(3), 215–217.

Van Leuven, J. (1991b). Corporate organization strategies and the scope of public relations departments. *Public Relations Review, 17*(3), 279–293.

Van Riel, C. B. M. (1995). *Principles of corporate communication*. London: Prentice-Hall.

Varey, R. J. (1998). Locating marketing within the corporate communication managing system. *Journal of Marketing Communication, 4*(3), 177–190.

Varey, R. J. (2001). Responsive and responsible communication practices: A pluralistic perspective. In P. J. Kitchen & D. E. Schultz (Eds.), *Raising the corporate umbrella: Corporate communication in the 21st century* (pp. 62–81). New York: Palgrave/St. Martin's Press.

Vibert, C. (2004). *Theories of macro organizational behavior*. Amonk, NY: M.E. Sharpe.

Wallace, W. D. (1998). *Postmodern management. The emerging partnership between employees and stockholders*. Westport, CT: Quorum.

Wang, P., & Schultz, D. E. (1993, August). *Measuring the return on investment for advertising and other forms of marketing communications using an integrated marketing communications approach*. Paper presented to Advertising Division, Association for Education in Journalism and Mass Communication, Kansas City, MO.

Waterschoot, W., & Van den Bulte, C. (1992). The 4P classification of the marketing mix revisited. *Journal of Marketing, 56,* 83–93.

Webster, F. E., Jr. (1992). The changing role of marketing in the corporation. *Journal of Marketing, 56,* 1–17.

Webster, F. E. (1994). *Market-driven management.* New York: Wiley.

White, J., & Mazur, L. (1995). *Strategic communications management: Making public relations work.* Workingham, England: Addison-Wesley.

Wrightman, B. (1999). Integrated communications: Organization and education. *Public Relations Quarterly, 44*(2), 18–22.

Zeithaml, C. P., & Zeithaml, V. A. (1984, Spring). Environmental management: Revising the marketing perspective. *Journal of Marketing, 48*(1), 56–53.

Zinkham, G. M., & Watson, R. T. (1996). Advertising trends: Innovation and the process of creative destruction. *Journal of Business Research, 37*(3), 163–171.

Zyman, S. (2002). *The end of advertising as we know it.* Hoboken, NJ: Wiley.

IV

Advances in Program Planning and Its Evolutions in the New Century

The Situational Theory of Publics: Practical Applications, Methodological Challenges, and Theoretical Horizons

Linda Aldoory
University of Maryland

Bey-Ling Sha
San Diego State University

The situational theory of publics is a highly regarded, well-tested theory that has been integrated into the Excellence Theory (Dozier, L. A. Grunig, & J. E. Grunig, 1995; J. E. Grunig, 1992; L. A. Grunig, J. E. Grunig, & Dozier, 2002). Credited by public relations scholars as being the first "deep theory" in public relations (cf. Zoch & Collins, 2002), the situational theory may also be one of the most useful theories for understanding why publics communicate and when they are most likely to do so. The theory was first developed in 1968 by James E. Grunig, who spent the following 3 decades testing the theory in various professional settings, ultimately refining and expanding it (J. E. Grunig, 1978, 1983, 1987, 1989, 1992; J. E. Grunig & Hunt, 1984). J. E. Grunig (1997) offered a detailed and extensive overview of the history and development of the situational theory and a critique of the research that created variations of the variables and their relationships.

In this chapter, we move forward from J. E. Grunig's 1997 piece by posing methodological and theoretical challenges to readers in order to further the development and the practical use of the situational theory in public relations. We argue that the situational theory of publics can be particularly valuable for the next generation of public relations practitioners and scholars if current methodological operationalizations and

339

theoretical understandings are problematized and reconstituted to reflect the diverse and complex nature of today's publics and organizations. To support this claim, we begin this chapter with a brief overview of the original theory and then examine both theoretical elaborations and practical applications of the theory. We conclude with a critical consideration of methodological challenges to the situational theory and a call for future work in specific theoretical areas.

OVERVIEW OF THE SITUATIONAL THEORY

Theoretical Origins

Public relations scholars have defined members of a public as having something in common—they are affected by the same problem or issue, and behave similarly toward a problem (Cutlip, Center, & Broom, 2000; J. E. Grunig & Hunt, 1984; Van Leuven & Slater, 1991). Hallahan (1999) defined a public as a group of people who relate to an organization, demonstrate varying degrees of activity or passivity, and might or might not interact with others concerning their relationship. The situational theory of publics was formed from these notions of publics and uses three factors, or independent variables, to predict communication behavior, attitude change, and behavior change (J. E. Grunig, 1978, 1983, 1997; J. E. Grunig & Hunt, 1984; J. E. Grunig & Ipes, 1983; J. E. Grunig & Stamm, 1979). The three independent variables are problem recognition, constraint recognition, and level of involvement.

The first and perhaps most important independent variable is level of involvement, a measure of how personally relevant a problem can be for an individual (J. E. Grunig & Hunt, 1984). Also defined as perceived emotional connection or relevance, involvement increases the likelihood of individuals attending to and comprehending messages (Pavlik, 1988). If someone personally connects to an issue or message, they will more likely attend to and comprehend it (J. E. Grunig & Hunt, 1984; Pavlik, 1988). Persons with high levels of involvement analyze issues more often, prefer messages that contain more and better arguments (Heath, Liao, & Douglas, 1995), and attain greater knowledge levels (Chaffee & Roser, 1986; Engelberg, Flora, & Nass, 1995). In addition, high involvement can lead to active information seeking. According to Hallahan (1999), involvement has "generated robust findings among researchers as a molar construct" (p. 12).

A second independent variable is problem recognition—the extent to which individuals recognize a problem facing them. As J. E. Grunig and Hunt (1984) explained, people do not stop to think about situations unless they perceive that something needs to be done to improve the situation. Major (1993) found that the likelihood of communication is increased by problem recognition, such that, among people facing problems, information seeking and processing are likely to occur even under low-involvement conditions. However, Hamilton (1992) noted that problem recognition did not account for active media use and that other variables played a greater role.

Finally, constraint recognition is the extent to which individuals perceive factors that inhibit their ability to move to action or change behavior. Perceived high constraints tend to reduce communication. In studying the effects of a drunken driving campaign, J. E. Grunig and Ipes (1983) showed that the campaign made the least impact on constraint recognition. J. E. Grunig and Ipes (1983) concluded, "For a campaign to move people to develop organized cognitions and perhaps to change their behavior, it must show people how they can remove constraints to their personally doing anything about the problem" (p. 51).

Originally, the situational theory of publics included a fourth independent variable (cf. J. E. Grunig, 1997), the referent criterion, which was "defined as a solution carried from previous situations to a new situation" (p. 11). Studies examining the impact of this variable on communication behavior were inconclusive, and by the mid-1980s the variable had been dropped from research using the situational theory.

The three surviving independent variables have repeatedly been shown to affect whether and how much an individual engages in information processing and information seeking, two forms of communication behavior (J. E. Grunig, 1997; J. E. Grunig, Clifford, Richburg, & White, 1988; J. E. Grunig & Hunt, 1984; J. E. Grunig & Ipes, 1983). More recent research has also found the variables that affect attitude change and behavior change (J. E. Grunig, 1997). Information processing occurs when people pay attention to a message and absorb some of it, even when not intentionally doing so (Slater, Chipman, Auld, Keefe, & Kendall, 1992). Information seeking, on the other hand, is the deliberate search for information on a particular issue. This active communication leads people to develop more organized cognitions, hold attitudes about a situation, and engage in behaviors to do something about the situation. An active public often seeks information through a variety of media, interpersonal contacts, and specialized channels, whereas a passive public more likely processes information from only mass media (J. E. Grunig, 1980; Heath et al., 1995).

Based on the relationships among the independent and dependent variables, J. E. Grunig (1997) formulated different publics and their likelihood of active communication and potential behavior change. Active publics have low constraint recognition and high problem recognition and involvement; these publics are actively seeking information about a problem and are potentially sharing information and becoming activists about it. Aware publics have high problem recognition and involvement, but due to higher levels of constraint recognition, do not move to action. Once aware publics perceive constraints to be removed, they are more likely to become active. Latent publics have low problem recognition, but their level of involvement is still moderate to high. Latent publics are often designated as targets of campaign messages (J. E. Grunig, 1989; J. E. Grunig et al., 1988).

There have been additional conceptualizations for levels and types of active publics. The situational theory generally has been used to separate active publics (i.e., single-issue publics and all-issue publics) from apathetic publics arising around a set of related issues, such as environmental or health issues. J. E. Grunig (1997) also defined a hot-issue public, one that is "active only on a single problem that involves nearly everyone in the population and that has received extensive media coverage" (p. 13).

Theoretical Elaborations

Antecedent Factors.   A few studies have examined antecedent factors of the situational theory's independent variables (Aldoory, 2001; Hallahan, 1999; Sha, 1995, 1998, 2006; Sha & Lundy, 2005). Sha (1995, 1998, 2006), for example, discerned that differences in identification with racioethnic groups predicted differences in problem recognition, level of involvement, information processing, and information seeking. Consequently, she suggested that the original concept of referent criterion be revived and examined in the context of cultural identities (Sha, 1995). Drawing on the Elaboration Likelihood Model (cf. Petty & Cacioppo, 1981), Sha and Lundy (2005) hypothesized that other antecedent variables affecting information processing and seeking could include individual factors (e.g., need for cognition and motivation to process), as well as constraining factors (e.g., distraction, message comprehensibility, issue familiarity, and appropriate schema). These authors also noted that message factors such as argument quality, argument strength, and source credibility may affect information processing and seeking (Sha & Lundy, 2005).

Hallahan (1999) also looked at antecedent factors to what he termed *motivation*, which he equated with involvement. His factors, derived from marketing and consumer research, focused solely on the content of media messages. Factors included attractive and interesting messages, novel stimuli, moderately complex messages, and sources who were credible, attractive, or similar to the audience. In a related vein, Aldoory (2001) found a set of factors that influenced women's involvement with health messages, including a consciousness of everyday life (e.g., motherhood, pregnancy, employment, housing arrangements, neighborhood, sexual identity), media source credibility, self-identity, and a consciousness of personal health (whether health sensitive, perceived healthful, or perceived invulnerability).

Reconceptualizing the Independent Variables.   A few studies have examined the usefulness of dividing and detailing the three independent variables into six or more variables. For example, personal and impersonal dimensions of the independent variables have been created and tested (Cameron & Yang, 1991; Dorner & Coombs, 1994; Heath & Douglas, 1990). Researchers argued that the independent variables, such as involvement, were driven by either egoistic concerns (personal) or altruistic concerns (impersonal) (Dorner & Coombs, 1994). Results of these studies indicated that distinguishing situations by personal and impersonal dimensions resulted in a useful extension of the situational theory, because of the dimensions' improvement in segmenting publics (Cameron & Yang, 1991; Dorner & Coombs, 1994).

Similarly, J. E. Grunig and Childers (1988) examined internal and external dimensions of the three independent variables, distinguishing, for example, between internal involvement being in the mind of the person and external involvement being in the person's real-world environment. However, these authors noted that internal and external dimensions of involvement and of constraint recognition did not explain communication behavior as well as internal and external problem recognition. They also found that people most often recognized problems (external problem recognition) that are related to their self-identity or to their worldview (internal involvement).

PRACTICAL APPLICATIONS OF THE THEORY

There have been several studies and essays that have supported the situational theory's utility in professional public relations practice. Authors have examined environmental publics, investor relations, health campaigns, activist groups, and educational settings (Berkowitz & Turnmire, 1994; Cameron, 1992; J. E. Grunig, 1989; J. E. Grunig et al., 1988; J. E. Grunig & Childers, a.k.a., Hon, 1988; Major, 1993). Studies have shown the practical benefits of segmenting publics according to their active engagement with an issue, for purposes of message development and campaign design (Werder, 2005). Much of this vein of research has applied the situational theory to public health and education efforts (e.g., Cameron & Yang, 1991; Dorner & Coombs, 1994; Pavlik, 1988; Sha & Pine, 2004).

The situational theory has helped identify the different publics that health messages could be targeted to, according to level of involvement, problem recognition, and constraint recognition. In studying the effects of a drunk-driving campaign, for example, J. E. Grunig and Ipes (1983) supported the role that constraint recognition played in limiting the effects of a campaign. Pavlik (1988) measured the role of involvement and constraint recognition in heart health as contingent conditions between mediated heart health messages and increased complexity of heart health knowledge.

More recently, Aldoory (2001) used the situational theory to examine women's level of involvement with health campaigns. The data indicated several factors that could be used in developing campaign messages for women from different ethnic, racial, sexual, and economic backgrounds. Similarly, Sha and Pine used the situational theory to identify which publics would be best to target for an education campaign on prevention of childhood sexual abuse. These publics were then targeted in a national educational effort, headlined by a special event marathon called *Race to Stop the Silence* (Pine & Sha, 2004; Sha & Pine, 2004). The situational theory also was useful in determining which issues could best be integrated with childhood sexual abuse in terms of campaign messaging, so that the more sensitive problem of child abuse prevention—with its potential to turn off target publics—would not be left alone to attract attention by itself (Sha & Pine, 2004).

Applications for Pedagogy

Although we located no published work that explicitly applied the situational theory to the teaching of public relations, Sha has been developing a program of research with undergraduate and graduate students that highlights the strengths of using the situational theory as a pedagogical tool. Like many teachers in public relations, Sha has engaged with her students in service-learning projects for nonprofit clients. These projects included phone or in-person administrations of a survey instrument to measure levels of problem recognition, involvement, and constraint recognition, as well as levels of information processing and information seeking.

Students then used the survey results to design public relations campaigns in such areas as environmental protection, tobacco use prevention, child sexual abuse prevention, listening, parent–school communication, and sexual assault awareness and prevention. Table 16.1 summarizes these studies, which were conducted with student researchers from the University of Maryland, College Park, and from San Diego State University. From the work performed and the findings, it was clear that the situational theory of publics offered several pedagogical advantages.

From a teaching standpoint, the existence of an extensively validated survey instrument facilitates data collection by students, as well as timely approval of research projects by university institutional review

TABLE 16.1

Educational and Practical Applications

Service-Learning Client (Campaign Area)	Data Collection Method and Time Frame	Number of Students Involved
Promoting Awareness, Victim Empowerment (sexual assault education and prevention)	In-person group-administered surveys in spring 2005	52
International Listening Association (the importance of listening as a quality-of-life issue)	Phone surveys in spring 2004	32
Montgomery County Business Roundtable for Education (parent–school communication)	Phone surveys in fall 2003	17
Chesapeake Bay Foundation (environmental protection)	Phone surveys in spring 2003	23
Futures Institute for Sustainable Development (child sexual abuse prevention)	Phone surveys in spring 2003	22
Maryland Department of Health and Mental Hygiene, Center for Health Promotion, Education & Tobacco Use Prevention (tobacco use prevention)	In-person individually administered surveys in fall 2002	20

boards. Furthermore, the situational theory is useful for showing students ways to segment publics that go beyond mere demographics, because survey results enable students to correlate situational theory variables with demographic and psychographic information.

Obtaining quantitative benchmarks of levels of problem recognition, involvement, constraint recognition, and communication behaviors also permits students to set measurable objectives for their campaigns, which in turn facilitates the development of realistic campaign evaluation plans. In Sha's classes, the students were able to turn the data into actual campaign tools and messages specifically targeting different publics, and all of the service-learning clients used at least parts of the student-designed campaigns in their ongoing public relations activities.

Whereas textbooks often tout the importance of tailoring messages and targeting publics for public relations efforts, students here experienced firsthand the ways to target publics and the usefulness of theory in doing so. The situational theory, therefore, makes the connection among theory, research, and practice easier to understand, especially for undergraduate students who often have difficulty seeing the value of theory in their everyday work in public relations.

METHODOLOGICAL CHALLENGES

Despite the pedagogical advantages and professional applications of the extant situational theory, recent research also suggests that methodological improvements would greatly benefit both public relations scholars and practitioners. There is ongoing examination of the most popular measuring method for the situational theory, that of survey methodology; there have been few but helpful qualitative explorations that elaborate on situational variables; and there have been attempts at experimental design to support the predictive ability of the situational theory's independent variables.

Survey Operationalization

As indicated in J. E. Grunig (1997), the independent variables of the situational theory traditionally are measured by four items each. The internal reliability of items measuring problem recognition and level of involvement have consistently been near or above the acceptable 0.7 level for Cronbach's alpha (see Table 16.2 for some examples). However, in recent research by Sha, the Cronbach's alpha for items measuring constraint recognition has been problematic, as indicated in Table 16.3. Alpha scores have been lower than expected, and feedback from research

TABLE 16.2
Internal Reliabilities of Independent Variables on the Situational Theory

Issue in Situation Set	Study: Promoting Awareness, Victim Empowerment (Sexual Assault Education and Prevention)		
	Alphas for Problem Recognition	Alphas for Level of Involvement	Alphas for Constraint Recognition
Financial aid	.8272	.8548	.5016
Alcohol abuse	.7375	.7016	.3603
Sexual assault	.7662	.6685	.3857
Racial discrimination	.8221	.7895	.4479
Academic dishonesty	.7594	.6648	.3604
Sexual harassment	.7875	.7040	.3784

Note.   Specific survey items used to measure these variables are found in J. Grunig (1997).

TABLE 16.3
Breakdown of Alphas for Items Measuring Constraint Recognition

Study: Promoting Awareness, Victim Empowerment
(Sexual Assault Education and Prevention)

Issue in Situation Set (Cronbach's Alpha)	Alpha if ECR1* Deleted	Alpha if ICR1 Deleted	Alpha if ICR2 Deleted	Alpha if ECR2* Deleted
Financial aid (.5016)	.3648	.3121	.6028	.4035
Alcohol abuse (.3603)	.1518	.1472	.5441	.2134
Sexual assault (.3857)	.2628	.1714	.5380	.2215
Racial discrimination (.4479)	.2296	.2102	.6301	.3189
Academic dishonesty (.3604)	.1362	.0988	.5670	.2321
Sexual harassment (.3784)	.2402	.1517	.5053	.2816

Notes.   ECR1 = "I believe this issue is a problem that I can do something about"; ICR1 = "I think this problem is too complicated for me to do anything about"; ICR2 = "I would say this problem is more difficult for me to understand than other campus problems"; and ECR2 = "I believe that I could affect the way this problem is eventually solved if I wanted to" (cf. J. Grunig, 1997).
*Indicates that item was reverse-scored.

participants on the items measuring constraint recognition has been critical of their simplicity in measuring the complexity of constraints on people's current everyday lives.

These findings may reflect the operational challenge of measuring a complex and evolving concept such as constraints, which we believe is dependent on a host of other factors, including cultural identity, resource access, and a rich and varied media environment that may influence constraint perceptions regarding social and health issues.

Besides the question of internal reliabilities of the items measuring the independent variables, there is the issue of questionnaire length and how this affects respondent participation in studies testing the situational theory. Of the six studies illustrated in Table 16.1, only the two using in-person survey administration used the full four items for each independent variable. Only one item per variable was used in the phone surveys, because pretest results indicated that phone respondents were unwilling to respond to 12 items compared to 3. Thus, another methodological challenge facing scholars using the situational theory is which of the four items for each independent variable should be used if the researcher must reduce the number of questions in the instrument.

Traditionally, J. E. Grunig operationalized each variable with one questionnaire item, but then developed more items to measure when internal and external dimensions were considered for each independent variable. In more recent, unpublished work by J. E. Grunig and his students, the parsimonious three-item measure for independent variables has been resurrected (personal communication, September 13, 2004). However, this then reduces researchers' ability to examine the complexities and nuances within the factors that influence communication behavior. Although no single easy answer is going to emerge from this chapter or any one study, the concerns raised here call for greater empirical exploration for survey measures that validly and reliably reflect 21st-century publics and the wide variety of issues and media they contend with daily.

Moving now from the independent to the dependent variables of the situational theory, the manner in which the information processing items often are constructed may in fact be yielding confounding results for this variable. Specifically, survey items measuring information processing generally pose a hypothetical news lead that may include the name of an organization that purportedly is releasing the news in question (cf. J. E. Grunig, 1997); for example, "According to researchers at Harvard University, the number of sexual assaults on college campuses is on the rise." The intention behind this operationalization was to determine the extent to which respondents would process information about a particular issue. However, respondents may in fact be more influenced by the source of the news than by the news item itself. For this reason, we suggest some new methodologically oriented studies be conducted, using the same issues and varying the news sources, to gauge whether information processing in the situational theory is in fact issue driven or source driven.

With respect to information seeking, the traditional questionnaire items have asked respondents the extent to which they are likely to "call or send for" free informational brochures about particular issues (J. E. Grunig, 1997). Because the nature of information seeking has changed with new and globalized technologies, scholars using the situational theory should test operationalizations of information seeking that reflect the global media environment. We recommend that researchers compare measures to test whether the nature of information seeking varies by the channel of availability of the information (e.g., phoning for a brochure, using an Internet search engine, or responding to an e-mail query). In particular, ongoing research on uses and users of the Internet suggests that age, gender, and class all have the potential to affect whether people seek information using the Web (*A Nation Online*, 2004).

Quantitative Data Analysis

Another challenge posed by the survey method lies in the statistical method of analysis traditionally used by scholars taking this approach. Following the lead of J. E. Grunig (cf. 1997), researchers typically use canonical correlation, which is an appropriate statistical tool for determining the effects of a set of independent variables on a set of dependent variables (cf. Thompson, 1984). However, this method of data analysis was developed prior to more recent advances in multiple regression techniques, and we would suggest that methodologically oriented studies be undertaken to compare the strengths and weaknesses of canonical correlation against newer multiple regression methods.

There are at least two ongoing challenges to the continued use of canonical correlation for situational theory. First, the Windows version of SPSS does not have "point-and-click" options for this statistical manipulation. Thus, researchers must enter the syntax for each canonical correlation calculation. This may be somewhat intimidating for beginning researchers, as well as time consuming for even seasoned scholars. Second, there are no standard power tables for canonical correlation (cf. Cohen, 1988). This means that, in studies where the Ns are deemed to be too small, no assertions can be made as to the appropriateness of the data set by undertaking a power analysis. Both of these challenges would be resolved by using alternate, multiple regression techniques.

Qualitative Exploration

Qualitative methodology allows for depth and detail into the dimensions and factors that construct the situational theory variables for people within the context of their everyday lives. In addition, focus groups and in-depth interviews assist with operationalizations of variables for further quantitative work that would be more externally valid. Aldoory has conducted several focus groups as part of different studies on the application of the situational theory to health and risk contexts. One study helped determine antecedent factors to level of involvement for women as they make meaning of health communication (Aldoory, 2001), and unpublished research has found that sharing perceptions of involvement in risk situations increases people's likelihood to move to action.

Therefore, as response rates to all kinds of traditional surveys continue to drop (cf. Wimmer & Dominick, 2006), qualitative research offers alternative ways to gauge publics' levels of problem recognition, involvement, and constraint recognition. Although some scholars might be hesitant to use qualitative means to study the situational theory because of limitations on generalizability, researchers need to consider whether the lack of external validity purportedly inherent in qualitative research would be any worse than using quantitative methods with low response rates and small sample sizes.

Experimental Design

An innovative methodological turn in situational theory studies is the use of experimental design for purposes of measuring predictability and control in the relationships among variables. Although we found no published reports of experiments testing the situational theory, there is some current work being conducted by students at the University of Maryland under the advisement of J. E. Grunig and Aldoory. Experiments allow for testing whether proposed antecedent variables are actually predictive of the independent variables. They can also be tools to categorize publics within treatment groups. Although involvement is not easily manipulated, experiments can assist in manipulating problem recognition and constraint recognition to measure their effects on information processing and communication behavior.

We have articulated here some methodological challenges and opportunities facing users of the situational theory of publics. By noting these, we are not suggesting that the theory is irreparably flawed from a methodological standpoint; rather, we believe that, to maintain the relevance of this theory for future generations of public relations scholars and practitioners, we should take a hard look at how we operationalize its variables, so that the theory can only be strengthened as it matures. Perhaps the effort to refine measurements of the variables in the situational theory of publics must begin with a reexamination of those variables themselves, as well as the constructs that underlie them; thus, we turn now to some new theoretical horizons for the situational theory.

THEORETICAL HORIZONS

Although the situational theory is more than 30 years old, empirically tested, and well supported, we believe that the global media environment, the changing cultural landscape of the United States and other countries, and the widespread and diffuse nature of information regarding health and social norms all combine to illuminate gaps in the traditional conceptualizations used in the situational theory of publics. New research has shown the value in being innovative, complex, and sensitive in examining publics' information needs and behaviors. By no means is the following list of theoretical avenues exhaustive; rather, we view it as a draft of initial sites for future research.

Antecedent Factors

Although there has been some research exploring possible antecedent factors to the theory's independent variables, as discussed previously, much more qualitative and quantitative focus needs to be on this area of the theory. There is a significant gap in our understanding of the situational theory regarding any antecedent factors that may help explain the development of involvement, constraint recognition, or problem recognition. In particular, preliminary research has uncovered the potential impact of cultural identity on problem recognition and level of involvement.

Focused Research on Each Independent Variable

Most studies in the past have rightly included an examination of all three independent variables and their influence on communication behaviors. However, now that we have established significant relationships among these factors, more sophisticated and in-depth conceptualizations are needed for each independent variable. Studies should consider focusing on one of the variables—involvement only or constraint recognition only—and delve into the ways the concept has been defined and studied in other disciplines. This may then be used to articulate more nuanced dimensions of each concept, such as measuring whether internal and external dimensions are worthy of exploration.

Greater Understanding of Dependent Variables

Although the situational theory originally was developed to explain communication behaviors, this connection has often become lost in current research, especially with research in health contexts in which physical behavior change is most important. We need clearer articulations of "active communication," given what seems to be the confluence in some scholarship of information seeking behavior and physical actions (i.e., whether someone requested a brochure vs. whether someone walked along a picket line).

Just as active communication should be conceptually clarified, we should examine what is meant by the constructs "passive communication" or "information processing." There are more media outlets now than when the situational theory was first developed, the Internet has become a common source of entertainment and information, and media consumers are far more sophisticated than they were 30 years ago. These factors have played a role in changing the dynamics of information processing. As Chey-Nemeth (2001) argued, "New technologies such as the Internet demonstrate a new form of information accessibility and dissemination that may well transform previously passive publics into active publics" (p. 128).

Analysis of Activist Organizations and Hot Issue Publics

Since 9/11 and the military conflicts in Afghanistan and Iraq, there has been a growing need to understand "special" publics—those that have emerged following these types of crises that have forever changed government and social policies in the United States and in allied countries. Hot-issue publics have been addressed by media scholars, but not from the point of view of being able to influence their communication behavior. The situational theory of publics can address some of these objectives if further research is done on the composition of hot-issue publics.

Similarly, interest in activist publics has been increasing, but it has not kept up with the increasing importance of activists on public policy and advocacy efforts. Activists are not just publics of an organization; they are frequently organizations unto themselves who often know sophisticated public relations strategies and theory. Future research could examine the use of the situational theory among activist organizations and how they negotiate their dual role as public and public communicator.

Breadth of Topics and Issues to be Examined

There are some current examples, by students and the authors of this chapter, of the breadth of applications that the situational theory could have on environmental communication, health communication, activist public relations, and educational efforts. However, there is a wide range of topics that can be addressed within the purview of expanding the situational theory. Government relations, public diplomacy, media relations, and other areas can examine the usefulness of the theory for better predicting attitudes and behaviors of key publics.

CONCLUSION

In this chapter, we posed methodological and theoretical challenges to readers in order to further the development and the practical use of the situational theory in public relations. We have argued that the situational theory of publics can be particularly valuable for the next generation of public relations practitioners and scholars if current methodological approaches and theoretical understandings are problematized and reconstituted to reflect the diverse and complex nature of today's publics and organizations. We hope that readers perceive the theoretical horizons and methodological challenges as calls to action for future research, so that the situational theory will only become stronger and more useful for the public relations profession.

REFERENCES

A Nation Online: Entering the Broadband Age. (2004). Washington, DC: U.S. Dept. of Commerce, Economics and Statistics Administration, National Telecommunications and Information Administration.

Aldoory, L. (2001). Making health communications meaningful for women: Factors that influence involvement and the situational theory of publics. *Journal of Public Relations Research, 13,* 163–185.

Berkowitz, D., & Turnmire, K. (1994). Community relations and issues management: An issue orientation approach to segmenting publics. *Journal of Public Relations Research, 6,* 105–123.

Cameron, G. T. (1992). Memory for investor relations messages: An information-processing study of Grunig's situational theory. *Journal of Public Relations Research, 4,* 45–60.

Cameron, G. T., & Yang, J. (1991). Effect of support and personal distance on the definition of key publics for the issue of AIDS. *Journalism Quarterly, 68,* 620–629.

Chaffee, S., & Roser, C. (1986). Involvement and the consistency of knowledge, attitudes and behaviors. *Communication Research, 13,* 373–399.

Chey-Nemeth, C. (2001). Revisiting publics: A critical archaeology of publics in the Thai HIV/AIDS issue. *Journal of Public Relations Research, 13,* 127–161.

Cohen, J. (1988). *Statistical power analysis for the behavioral sciences* (2nd ed.). Hillsdale, NJ: Lawrence Erlbaum Associates.

Cutlip, S. M., Center, A. H., & Broom, G. M. (2000). *Effective public relations* (8th ed.). Upper Saddle River, NJ: Prentice-Hall.

Dorner, C., & Coombs, W. T. (1994, July). *The addition of the personal dimension to situational theory: A re-examination and extension.* Paper presented to International Communication Association, Sydney, Australia.

Dozier, D. M., Grunig, L. A., & Grunig, J. E. (1995). *Manager's guide to excellence in public relations and communication management.* Hillsdale, NJ: Lawrence Erlbaum Associates.

Engelberg, M., Flora, J. A., & Nass, C. I. (1995). AIDS knowledge: Effects of channel involvement and interpersonal communication. *Health Communication, 7,* 73–91.

Grunig, J. E. (1978). Defining publics in public relations: The case of a suburban hospital. *Journalism Quarterly, 55,* 109–118.

Grunig, J. E. (1980). Communication of scientific information to nonscientists. In B. Dervin & M. J. Voigt (Eds.), *Progress in communication sciences* (Vol. 2, pp. 167–214). Norwood, NJ: Ablex.

Grunig, J. E. (1983). Communication behaviors and attitudes of environmental publics: Two studies. *Journalism Monographs, 81.*

Grunig, J. E. (1987, May). *When active publics become activists: Extending a situational theory of publics.* Paper presented to the International Communication Association, Montreal.

Grunig, J. E. (1989). Sierra Club study shows who become activists. *Public Relations Review, 15,* 3–24.

Grunig, J. E. (1992). *Excellence in public relations and communication management.* Hillsdale, NJ: Lawrence Erlbaum Associates.

Grunig, J. E. (1997). A situational theory of publics: Conceptual history, recent challenges and new research. In D. Moss, T. MacManus, & D. Vercic (Eds.), *Public relations research: An international perspective* (pp. 3–48). London: International Thomson Business Press.

Grunig, J. E., & Childers, L. (1988, July). *Reconstruction of a situational theory of communication: Internal and external concepts as identifiers of publics for AIDS.* Paper presented to Association for Education in Journalism and Mass Communication, Portland, OR.

Grunig, J. E., Clifford, L., Richburg, S. J., & White, T. J. (1988). Communication by agricultural publics: Internal and external orientations. *Journalism Quarterly, 65,* 26–38.

Grunig, J. E., & Hunt, T. (1984). *Managing public relations.* New York: Holt, Rinehart & Winston.

Grunig, J. E., & Ipes, D. A. (1983). The anatomy of a campaign against drunk driving. *Public Relations Review, 9*(1), 36–51.

Grunig, J. E., & Stamm, K. R. (1979). Communication situations and cognitive strategies in resolving environmental issues: A second study. *Journalism Quarterly, 56,* 715–726.

Grunig, L. A., Grunig, J. E., & Dozier, D. M. (2002). *Excellent public relations and effective organizations: A study of communication management in three countries.* Mahwah, NJ: Lawrence Erlbaum Associates.

Hallahan, K. (1999, June). *Communicating with inactive publics: The moderating roles of motivation, ability and opportunity.* Paper presented to PRSA Educators Academy, College Park, MD.

Hamilton, P. K. (1992). Grunig's situational theory: A replication, application, and extension. *Journal of Public Relations Research, 4,* 123–149.

Heath, R. L., & Douglas, W. (1990). Involvement: A key variable in people's reaction to public policy issues. In J. E. Grunig & L. A. Grunig (Eds.), *Public relations research annual* (Vol. 2, pp. 93–204). Hillsdale, NJ: Lawrence Erlbaum Associates.

Heath, R. L., Liao, S., & Douglas, W. (1995). Effects of perceived economic harms and benefits on issue involvement, use of information sources, and actions: A study in risk communication. *Journal of Public Relations Research, 7,* 89–109.

Major, A. M. (1993). Environmental concern and situational communication theory: Implications for communicating with environmental publics. *Journal of Public Relations Research, 5,* 251–268.

Pavlik, J. V. (1988). Audience complexity as a component of campaign planning. *Public Relations Review, 14,* 12–20.

Petty, R. E., & Cacioppo, J. T. (1981). *Attitudes and persuasion: Classic and contemporary approaches.* Dubuque, IA: William C. Brown.

Pine, P., & Sha, B.-L. (2004, September). *The four-step public relations process as a foundation for an effective CSA [child sexual abuse] awareness campaign.* Paper presented to the 9th International Conference on Family Violence, San Diego, CA.

Sha, B.-L. (1995). *Intercultural public relations: Exploring cultural identity as a means of segmenting publics.* Unpublished master's thesis, University of Maryland, College Park.

Sha, B.-L. (1998, August). *Intercultural public relations: Cultural identity and the segmentation of publics.* Paper presented to the Association for Education in Journalism and Mass Communication, Baltimore, MD.

Sha, B.-L. (in press). Cultural identity in the segmentation of publics: An emerging theory of intercultural public relations. *Journal of Public Relations Research.*

Sha, B.-L., & Lundy, L. K. (2005, March). *The power of theoretical integration: Merging the situational theory of publics with the elaboration likelihood model.* Paper presented to the International, Interdisciplinary Public Relations Research Conference, Miami, FL.

Sha, B.-L., & Pine, P. (2004, March). *Using the situational theory of publics to develop an education campaign regarding child sexual abuse.* Paper presented to the International, Interdiscliplinary Public Relations Research Conference, Miami, FL.

Slater, M. D., Chipman, H., Auld, G., Keefe, T., & Kendall, P. (1992). Information processing and situational theory: A cognitive response analysis. *Journal of Public Relations Research, 4,* 189–203.

Thompson, B. (1984). *Canonical correlation analysis: Uses and interpretation.* Newbury Park, CA: Sage.

Van Leuven, J. K., & Slater, M. D. (1991). How publics, public relations, and the media shape the public opinion process. In L. A. Grunig & J. E. Grunig (Eds.), *Public relations research annual* (Volume 3, pp. 165–178). Hillsdale, NJ: Lawrence Erlbaum Associates.

Werder, K. P. (2005). An empirical analysis of the influence of perceived attributes of publics on public relations strategy use and effectiveness. *Journal of Public Relations Research, 17,* 217–266.

Wimmer, R. D., & Dominick, J. R. (2006). *Mass media research: An introduction* (8th ed.). Belmont, CA: Thomson Wadsworth.

Zoch, L. M., & Collins, E. L. (2002, August). *PR educators—"the second generation": Measuring and achieving consensus.* Paper presented to the Association for Education in Journalism and Mass Communication, Miami, FL.

Chapter 17

Activism

Derina R. Holtzhausen
University of South Florida

It is not surprising that activism has become such an inherent part of the Excellence Theory, because it touches on and incorporates several theoretical traditions of this research program. In fact, the Excellence Theory holds that of the six contextual conditions that affect public relations, "activism might be the most important" (L. Grunig, J. Grunig, & Dozier, 2002, p. 546). The others are culture and language, political, economic, and media systems, and level of development.

Because of the impact of activism on public relations theory, particularly as generated through the Excellence project, it is also not surprising that this research program has laid the foundation for additional, and sometimes alternative, perspectives on public relations practice as a form of activism. This chapter reviews the theoretical foundations of activism in the Excellence Study, looks at other studies on activism spawned from this study, and offers some perspectives on possible future research in this area.

THEORETICAL FOUNDATIONS OF ACTIVISM AS A DRIVER OF EXCELLENT PUBLIC RELATIONS

The Excellence Theory maintains that activism "pushes organizations toward excellence" and is the "second greatest determinant" for top management to value public relations (L. Grunig et al., 2002, p. 442). Research into the impact of activism on public relations practice has made a major contribution to the development of public relations theory, because it focused the attention of scholars on a number of factors to consider when evaluating successful public relations practices. This section reviews each of these factors, which are:

- The impact of organizational environments on public relations practice.
- The role of power in activist relations as it relates to the structural position of the public relations function.
- The importance of knowledge for public relations practitioners.
- The need for two-way symmetrical communication to success- fully communicate with activists.

Organizations and Their Environments

Activists are "people who join small activist groups [and] are character- ized by their motivation, even fervor." An activist public is "a group of two or more individuals who organize in order to influence another pub- lic or publics through action that may include education, compromise, persuasion, pressure tactics, or force" (L. Grunig et al., 2002, p. 446).

Activism emphasizes the importance of studying the impact of orga- nizational environments on public relations practice. L. Grunig (1986a, 1986b) laid the earliest foundations for this kind of research through analyses of case studies of how organizations used public relations to deal with activist publics and how activist publics communicated. Her studies were informed by Olson's (1982) radical theory of pressure groups, based in economic theory, to understand why people join activ- ist groups and why small groups are more effective than are large groups. Olson proposed that members join a group because it enables them to reach their goals without having to bear the costs. The research also drew on Mintzberg (1983), who maintained that special interest groups are formed outside the organization in an effort to control orga- nizational behavior. Mintzberg argued that it is important for organiza- tions to retain their autonomy in dealing with powerful external publics—namely, mass media, governments, and special interest groups. L. Grunig's (1986a, 1986b, 1992) findings indicated that most organizations take a closed rather than an open stance toward activist groups. Most activists have social and/or economic goals when dealing with organizations. Their actions pose a real threat to organizations, and, among others things, might lead to government regulation. The analysis indicated that the lack of success in dealing with activist groups might be ascribed to a lack of knowledge among practitioners in apply- ing two-way symmetrical communication.

L. Grunig's (1992) focus on activism also laid the foundation for the theoretical conceptualization of activism as part of the Excellence Study. As mentioned, earlier organizational theorists were driven by a fear that activists might affect the organization's autonomy. Advocating a sys- tems approach to deal with activists, Jones and Chase (1979) best artic- ulated this fear: "The overwhelming important challenge faced by professional senior management is how to develop and establish the systems approach to the management of public policy issues in order not to surrender corporate autonomy and efficiency to the whims of bureaucrats and activist groups" (p. 8). However, the notion of organizational autonomy is increasingly being questioned. The Excellence Study argued that organizational environments are, by their very nature, turbulent (Ehling, White, & J. Grunig, 1992). Activists are an inevitable part of that turbulence and "the effective organization exists in an environment more characterized by dynamism and even hostility than stability" (L. Grunig et al., 2002, p. 477). This suggests that organizations are less autonomous than they desire or perceive, and it is therefore inevitable for organizations to deal with elements in their environment. Turbulent environments thus do not only necessitate communication with elements in that environment, but also require excellent practitioners to perform the function.

Furthermore, the Excellence Study found some support for the assumption that activist pressure promotes excellence in public relations. Research results pointed to a relatively weak but nonetheless statistically significant correlation between activist pressure exerted on an organization and the "Excellence Index" (L. Grunig et al., 2002, p. 448). The practitioners participating in this study experienced more activist pressure than did their CEOs, which might be an indication that practitioners are more likely to enact their role professionally and are more aware of activist groups when they are educated.

Power and Activist Relations

One of the most consistent critiques of the Excellence Theory is that it promotes the interests of organizations over those of activists (e.g., Leitch & Neilson, 2001). Although the Excellence Theory undoubtedly is slanted toward both for- and nonprofit institutions, one also has to acknowledge that the Excellence Study has always recognized the legitimacy of activist groups. Since the conceptualization of the study, activist pressure on government and organizations has been viewed as "a legitimate method of communication" (L. Grunig, 1992, p. 527). Nonetheless, the Excellence Theory does not address the inevitable power imbalance between organizations, which often have unlimited resources, and activist groups, which have to essentially rely on the media to realize their goals. It maintains that activists often have the upper hand over organizations in terms of media coverage, and often use government pressure to force change on organizations. However, there is increasing evidence that this is changing, as is discussed later.

There have been increased efforts to make the Excellence Theory more inclusive of activists. Following the calls of Karlberg (1996) and Dozier and Lauzen (2000) to develop public relations theories for activists, L. Grunig et al. (2002) suggested additional research on activism "would help make the theory of excellent public relations more applicable in all kinds of organizations—those that apply activist pressure as well as those that experience the pressure in a democratic society" (p. 547). J. Grunig (2000; 2001) argued that the same principles of symmetrical communication, relationship building, and ethical behavior would also benefit activist groups. He proposed the development of a normative theory for activists based on a five-step process developed by J. Grunig and L. Grunig (1997), which includes using the situational theory of publics, enlarging and empowering the group through strategic alliances with other activist groups, using symmetrical communication at the initial stages of the campaign, switching to asymmetrical communication if the organization does not respond, and finally returning to symmetrical communication and conflict resolution when the organization has been forced to consider the problem.

The Excellence Theory indirectly addressed the issue of power in dealing with activists by arguing that public relations managers are more likely to successfully deal with activists when they are part of the dominant coalition. Mintzberg (1996) believed that the role of managers in the "strategic apex" is, among others, "to serve the needs of those people who control or otherwise have the power over the organization (such as owners, government agencies, unions of the employees, pressure groups)" (p. 237). Mintzberg's model does not include public relations in the strategic apex, but the Excellence Theory has consistently argued that public relations is practiced most effectively when the public relations professional is "part of the power elite" (L. Grunig et al., 2002, p. 469). In this position of power, the practitioner would have more autonomy and would be better able to influence communication with activists. The results of the Excellence Study, however, did not necessarily support this assumption. The only statistically significant correlation between success with activist groups and practitioner involvement in the dominant coalition was reported by practitioners themselves, and those relationships were weak. Instead, the results of the study pointed to a reversal in cause and effect, namely, that "CEOs who experience activism are more likely to include public relations in the dominant coalition" (L. Grunig et al., 2002; p. 471). Inclusion in the dominant coalition was not found to be a prerequisite for dealing with activists. Practitioners' knowledge rather than their reporting levels determined an organization's success with activists.

Despite this discussion, the impact of power on public relations practice remains undertheorized in the Excellence Theory and is addressed more thoroughly later, in a review of alternative approaches to activism.

Practitioner Knowledge and the Ability to Deal With Activists

The importance of public relations knowledge for excellent public relations practice is a cornerstone of the Excellence Theory. Since the conceptualization of the study, it also was argued that knowledgeable practitioners would be more successful in dealing with activists than would those who do not have the necessary knowledge. Specifically, knowledge of two-way symmetrical communication, expertise in negotiation and research, and issues and crisis management skills were deemed crucial (L. Grunig, 1992). Indeed, of all the theoretical propositions regarding activism and the Excellence Study, the research results provided the most support for this assumption (L. Grunig et al., 2002). Despite this, not many participants in the study actually have "sophisticated, ongoing, systematic ways of evaluating the effectiveness of those programs" (p. 477).

In addition to research skills the Excellence Study also has consistently argued that issues management—that is, the ability "to scan the environment and help the dominant coalition prepare for contingencies in a proactive way"—is crucial to the organization's success in dealing with activist groups (L. Grunig et al., 2002, p. 467). The ability to practice risk and crisis communication and the subsequent effects on communication with activists were not directly tested in this study, but qualitative data supported the notion that expertise in these areas is important for successfully dealing with activists. If public relations practitioners have the ability to scan the environment, perform a boundary-spanning function, and practice two-way communication with activist publics, top management will value public relations. This particularly will be the case when practitioners have the knowledge to practice issues, risk, and crisis management.

Although knowledge of the situational theory was not directly evaluated in the Excellence project, a discussion of activism as part of the Excellence Theory cannot be complete without a brief review of this theory. When the Excellence Study was conceptualized, the situational theory was deemed a necessary part of the strategic management of public relations, which included issues management (J. Grunig & Repper, 1992). Knowledge of the situational theory is important in the segmentation of the most important publics for an organization, because it predicts both communication behavior and activism (Dozier & Ehling, 1992). The situational theory holds that people will become active publics and seek information from organizations when they recognize a problem, are highly involved in the issue, and believe they can actually do something about it. Active publics are more likely to affect organizations than are passive publics because they are more likely to either openly oppose or support organizations and join activist groups.

Active publics also are more likely to display information-seeking behavior, but less likely to be persuaded to adopt another viewpoint. They also are more likely to seek and process information that supports their viewpoints. Passive publics are more likely to merely process information and not act on that information (J. Grunig, 1997).

A fourth area of knowledge deemed crucial for dealing with activists is that of two-way symmetrical communication, which is discussed in the next section.

Activism and Communication Models

Since its conceptualization, the Excellence Theory has held that identifying activist issues early, and communicating openly and honestly with those activists, will offer the best opportunity for success (L. Grunig, 1992). The research results largely supported this proposition (L. Grunig et al., 2002). Listening to constituencies—even when they are hostile—and engaging them through the development of special programs, informal conversation, or special committee, are ways in which excellent organizations involved activists. However, communication methods are the same for both excellent and average organizations, involving "(d)ialogue and dispute resolution, position papers and communication strategies, and media relations" (p. 457).

Although two-way symmetrical communication was originally theorized to be the most effective way to communicate with activist groups, the research results indicated that both two-way symmetrical and two-way asymmetrical communication serve as indicators of excellent public relations. There was little difference in correlation statistics between these two models and how CEOs experienced activist pressure, how they perceived activist success, and how successful they thought their organizations were in dealing with activists (L. Grunig et al., 2002). It was also largely the case for participating public relations practitioners, who showed slightly higher correlations between knowledge of two-way symmetrical communication and the success of the organization in dealing with activists. There were some indications that activists would be more successful when practitioners used the two-way asymmetrical and one-way models, but the relationships were weak.

Arguing that three of the items in the two-way asymmetrical index related to research and thus represented more symmetrical rather than asymmetrical behavior, the researchers concluded that two-way communication would be better explained as a "two-way contingency model" (L. Grunig et al., 2002, p. 472). More recently, the researchers have gone to great lengths to clarify the concept of symmetrical communication and acknowledged "the criticisms of the models of public relations and, in particular, of the two-way symmetrical model have identified conceptual ambiguities in the theory that need to be addressed" (J. Grunig, 2001, p. 20). Criticism of the symmetrical model in particular seemed to center around two areas: that it is a too idealistic (normative) model to be practical, and that advocacy rather than two-way symmetrical communication is the main purpose of public relations. These issues also are discussed in other chapters in this text but both these arguments also pertain to organizations' reaction to activists.

Building on Murphy's (1991) mixed-motive model and Spicer's (1997) model of collaborative advocacy, the researchers argued that both the qualitative and quantitative results of the Excellence Study found "no organization and no communication program to be exclusively symmetrical or asymmetrical" (L. Grunig et al., 2002, p. 472). In pursuing "enlightened self-interest" (p. 472), practitioners make decisions contingent on who most needs to be persuaded in particular situations. The Excellence Study thus concluded that practitioners use both advocacy and symmetrical communication in the form of collaboration when dealing with activists. At the same time, the study discerned little evidence that activists change their stance toward organizations, and practitioners admitted that some issues could not be resolved. Furthermore, L. Grunig et al. argued that the results of the study confirm that two-way symmetry was not a purely normative theory but that both qualitative and quantitative results showed practitioners indeed apply two-way symmetry in practice. Collaborating with activists did not imply that organizations had to abandon their self-interests but would instead create a strategic advantage for organizations (Vercic & J. Grunig, 2000).

ALTERNATIVE PERSPECTIVES ON ACTIVISM

The amount of discourse the Excellence project has generated is indeed an indication of its importance and contribution to the field of public relations. In actual fact, before the Excellence Theory there was no theoretical benchmark in the field of public relations against which theory development could take place. The current theoretical discussions are healthy for the field of public relations because a science cannot be practiced without a continuous and critical debate about every aspect of that science. A dedicated group of scientists must diligently and dogmatically work in their field and must not give in to criticism too easily. Criticism should stimulate scientists working in the field to explore new theories and lines of thought (Holtzhausen, 1995). Discussion about tenets of the Excellence project should be viewed against this perspective; in this case, particularly regarding activism.

In the realm of activism, the most pervasive criticism against the Excellence project is its privileging of institutional perspectives over the interests of activists. In the previous overview much of this critique was addressed, but there is no doubt that when the Excellence Study was conceptualized it was informed by the work of organizational theorists of the time, who viewed activists as real threats to organizations. Those perspectives have indeed changed, and more efforts have been exerted to make the Excellence Theory also relevant to activist groups. Despite those efforts, one has to agree that activists' needs, organizational structures, financial structures, and access to management and public relations expertise are vastly different from those of organizations, and therefore in significant ways the Excellence Theory is not quite appropriate for activist groups.

Activist groups are increasingly viewed as the true voices of democracy (Holtzhausen, 2000). As institutional theory argues, organizations only exist when they adhere to the value systems of their environment (Scott, 1987; Selznick, 1957). Activists advocating for their different causes play an important role in guiding organizations through this process (Holtzhausen, 2005). As the results of the Excellence project indicated, organizations that listen to and communicate with activist groups can obtain institutional legitimacy that make their survival more likely. Nonetheless, despite the notion that excellent organizations are prepared to modify some of their behavior to accommodate activists, activists still are viewed as presenting "an enormous problem in the typical organization" (L. Grunig et al., 2002, p. 450). For many organizations it remains a must-win situation. It might behoove public relations practitioners to understand that instead of shying away from activists, engaging them could make an important contribution to democracy. By communicating about issues, even when advocating on behalf of one party, public relations practitioners place issues on the agenda and invoke reaction and discussion. It might even be that practitioners attract activism through the communication process and in this way stimulate democratic discourse.

The ongoing hostility toward activist groups remains problematic. One has to wonder why activists have been so set apart for organizational hostility, because there is evidence that other stakeholders such as shareholders and government agencies could have a more devastating effect on organizational autonomy. One might also argue that organizations' insistence on autonomy prevents them from seeking alliances that might make it easier for them to reach their goals. One recent example is the battle over saving the Old Mining Battlefield in West Virginia (Dao, 2005). The individual coal mining companies and even the coal workers' union was no match for the alliance of historians, environmentalists, and state agencies who wished to preserve the battlefield.

If activists are the true voices of democracy in democratic societies, their behavior in some ways could serve as a model for public relations practice. This notion led to the exploration of public relations practice as activism, rooted in postmodern theory, which is discussed next.

Public Relations as Activism

The quest to determine why it often is so difficult to practice symmetrical communication led Holtzhausen (2000) to explore alternative explanations for the position and role of public relations in organizations. Mostly informed by an analysis of public relations theory and practice from a postmodern perspective, Holtzhausen concluded that power in the public relations environment plays an important role in shaping practice. Power, however, can be resisted, which creates a space for public relations practitioners to take on the role of organizational and social activists who advocate against abusive power. A postmodern analysis takes a dialectic approach "that sees human reality as evolving and conflict ridden." Instead of "idealizing society as one only of cooperation and harmony," a postmodern approach focuses on "how social relations today are shaped principally by competition, conflict, struggle, and domination" (Best & Kellner, 2001, p. 14). Best and Kellner also commented that the aim of a dialectic approach to public relations is the ability "to make connections that were not hitherto apparent" (p. 27). Thus, a postmodern approach departs from the Excellence project in a small but not unimportant way; namely, that it is much more focused on conflict and resistance than on collaboration and symmetry.

Public relations as activism is philosophically informed by postmodernism and guided by the postmodernization of society. Postmodernism is best articulated as a response to modernism, which is accused of having created a bureaucratized society that is extremely differentiated, e.g., between work and home, men and women, professional and artisan, manager and technician (Holtzhausen, 2002). In modern society, urbanization has broken down the traditional sense of community and its members are controlled through intense levels of surveillance. The focus is on senseless consumerism rather than necessary consumption, and certain classes of conformist citizens are viewed as normal whereas the "other" is regarded as deviant (Best & Kellner, 2001).

Power and Public Relations Practice. Postmodernists argue that this society is shaped through unseen power networks that control the individual subject through social institutions, discourses, and practices (Foucault, 1982). Public relations practitioners, as part of for- and non-profit institutions, not only form part of these unseen power networks but actively help sustain them (Holtzhausen, 2000, 2002). The best way not to become part of the power grid that promotes the power elites of our societies is to act as social and organizational activists (Holtzhausen, 2000; Holtzhausen & Voto, 2002). This is in line with Karlberg's (1996) and the Excellence project's calls for the development of public relations theories that can help activists reach their goals. Holtzhausen (2000) contended that public relations practitioners, with their ability to communicate and organize, could help activists reach their goals, create alliances, and wage micropolitical struggles that would unleash a powerful force for social change and democracy. In this way, public relations practitioners can support the actions of activists that lead to "social change, through fundamental deconstruction and reconstruction of the social order" (Dozier & Lauzen, 2000, p. 14). Also, practitioners who are so inclined could take leadership roles in social change movements and thus become social activists themselves.

In this focus on power the activist perspective deviates from the Excellence project in that it focuses more on the individual power of practitioners rather than on the power of the function as a part of the dominant coalition. The Excellence Theory focused on the power-control theory to explain the practice of public relations, and incorporated the concept of empowerment of the public relations function, which the researchers defined as the "symmetrical concept of power" that "allows organizations to benefit from the expertise of the public relations profession" (L. Grunig et al., 2002, p. 142).

Postmodern theory argues the power context is particularly relevant to the position of the public relations practitioner in the organization and takes a broader approach to power relations that go beyond the dominant coalition. Foucault (1988a) said the aim of political power is to induce obedience and conformity from within the subject. It is this type of insidious power that subjects the individual and results in an uncritical acceptance of power relations. Power is indeed everywhere: "Every human relationship is to some degree a power relation. We move in a world of perpetual strategic relations" (Foucault, 1988a, p. 168). It is the responsibility of the individual to deal with these power relations reflexively. As Birch (1992) so succinctly put it, "The human being is a subject and not simply an object pushed around by external relations. To be a subject is to be responsive, to constitute oneself purposefully in response to one's environment" (p. 293). It is in this resistance to power that public relations practitioners find their role as organizational activists. Foucault (1988b) said, "[A]s soon as there is a power relation, there is a possibility of resistance. We cannot be ensnared by power: we can always modify its grip in determinate conditions and according to precise strategy" (p. 123).

As a result of this power perspective, communication for public relations activists is more conflict based and confrontational than in the two-way contingency model proposed in the Excellence Study (L. Grunig et al., 2002). Admittedly, in this approach the opportunities for collaboration and consensus might be considerably less. Holtzhausen (2000) argued this explains the problems that practitioners face when they want to communicate symmetrically. Also, the postmodern focus on dissensus and dissymmetry provides an explanation for the fact that organizational environments are dynamic and hostile rather than stable, and illuminates why the researchers "heard little about activists shifting their stance toward the organizations they pressure" (p. 461). One of the reasons for this might be the fear of activists to be co-opted into supporting organizational practices to which they were opposed in the first place. Particularly people who have the fervor of activists will be careful that a discussion does not take place in the frame of reference of the other party, which Lyotard (1988) referred to as the "differend" (p. 9).

Like Foucault, Lyotard (1988) believed that all discourse is political, and that political debates, particularly those with activists, are about persuasion. Lyotard therefore asserted that difference and division are more just than reconciliation. Postmodernists embraced the change and new ideas that emerge from conflict, and believed that dissensus extends thinking (Docherty, 1993). These points of irreconcilable differences are called "tensors" (Lyotard, 1993, p. 54). Holtzhausen (2000) noted, "The role of public relations practitioners is … not to strive for consensus but to identify the tensors between the organization and internal and external publics" (p. 107). The qualitative data from the Excellence Study indicated that collaboration between activists and organizations were the exception rather than the rule.

Public Relations as Organizational Activism.   The aim of the postmodern project is not to predict public relations practice but rather to describe and explain a certain type of practitioner behavior, particularly as it is affected by a changing social dispensation. As mentioned earlier, the postmodern focus is on those social and organizational factors that affect public relations practice and make it difficult for practitioners to follow through with actions such as symmetrical communication practice or ethical decision making. In order to determine whether practitioners actually display postmodern behavior and to explore power relations in the workplace, Holtzhausen and Voto (2002) conducted 16 interviews with public relations practitioners in the Tampa Bay area. The findings indicated that some practitioners are more likely to display postmodern, activist behavior depending on their organizational environments and their individual differences. As suggested in postmodern theory, some practitioners indeed serve as activists by speaking up about unfair treatment and standing up to power. Power is a factor in their practices, and their decisions and ethical stances are often over-ruled by more powerful managers. Activist practitioners are also more likely to be change agents. As boundary spanners, they are more in touch with the changes in the social and cultural environments, and change becomes an inherent part of their practice.

The study also questioned whether practitioners need to be part of the dominant coalition to be effective, as was proposed in the Excellence Study. Several practitioners in the study said they have access to power and being outside of the dominant coalition makes it easier for them to stand up to dominant power and gain credibility with external and internal publics. Activist practitioners practice dissensus and experience dissymmetry, and talked about the tensors in situations where it was impossible to change their own or the opposing side's perspective. The study found support for the following definition of organizational activism:

> The practitioner as organizational activist will serve as a conscience in the organization by resisting dominant power structures, particularly when these structures are not inclusive, will preference employees' and external publics' discourse over that of management, will make the most humane decision in a particular situation, and will promote new ways of thinking and problem solving through dissensus and conflict. These actions will contribute to a culture of emancipation and liberation in the organization. (Holtzhausen & Voto, 2002, p. 64)

Activist Public Relations in Transitional Societies. More empirical support for an activist model of public relations practice came from a descriptive study that Holtzhausen, Petersen, and Tindall (2003) conducted with South African practitioners. In conceptualizing the study, they argued that the South African environment—with its high levels of conflicting social values—would stimulate activist behavior in public relations practitioners, particularly because organizations are under pressure to change and adapt to the new political dispensation in the country. In addition to testing the four historic models of public relations as conceptualized by J. Grunig and Hunt (1984), the researchers also tested the mixed-motive model, which combined items from the two-way asymmetrical and the two-way symmetrical models (Dozier, L. Grunig, & J. Grunig, 1995).

The researchers tested two additional models: a Western dialogic model based on postmodern theory and an African dialogic model based on African communication practices (Holtzhausen et al., 2003). Using the reliability standards set by Stacks (2002), they found that only the mixed-motive and Western dialogic models had acceptable alpha levels of above .70. They subsequently subjected all 24 items measuring practitioner behavior to a factor analysis; again, two models with alpha levels of above .70 emerged. The one factor included three items from the two-way asymmetrical model, one item from the symmetrical model, and one from the Western dialogic model. All these items referred to research methods or situational analyses.

Arguing that these items pointed to professional behavior of environmental analysis rather than symmetrical intent, Holtzhausen et al. (2003) named this the *situational model*. These findings were somewhat similar to the findings of the Excellence Study, which eventually included the three research items from the two-way asymmetrical model in the symmetrical two-way contingency model (L. Grunig et al., 2002). The second model, called the *activist model*, included two items from the two-way symmetrical model and two from the Western dialogic model (Holtzhausen et al., 2003). This indicated that although practitioners believe the purpose of public relations is mutual change and understanding, they also believe they are change agents and have to challenge management when they treat internal or external publics unfairly. Means for using the activist model increased with age and tenure. This study led the researchers to believe that South African practitioners practiced these models for professional rather than symmetrical or asymmetrical motives, although the study did not exclude the existence of the concepts of symmetry and asymmetry. Several of the models described in the study indicated that South African practitioners are willing to work toward "equality, emancipation, and social change in general" (Holtzhausen et al., 2003, p. 337).

Structure and Activist Organizations

In research on activism, public relations scholars quite rightly critique the field for privileging institutional discourse over that of activists. Distinguishing between systems organizations, which "embody the strategic rationality of the systems of state and economy," and lifeworld organizations, which "grow out of the debates that take place within the public sphere," Leitch and Neilson (2001, p. 132) argued that systems organizations are always in the "subject position" (p. 128). It is hard to argue against this critique. Even in the postmodern research discussed earlier, the emphasis largely remained on practitioners in institutional settings. One of the reasons it might be hard to change this situation is that the relatively short lifecycles and "the dynamic nature of activist groups" (Smith & Ferguson, 2001, p. 296) make it hard to study them. One also might argue that activists lose their typical activist attributes as they become institutionalized. Thus, activist organizations such as the Sierra Club and PETA, or any other nonprofit organization, can be studied in the same way as corporations once they have the same structural and organizational attributes. However, there is little doubt that true grassroots activist organizations can use formal public relations help. Using participant observation Burek (2001) worked with an environmental activist group in Tampa Bay for 6 months and found that the infighting, lack of organizational skills, and lack of fundraising and media communication skills contributed significantly to the group's inability to reach its goals. On the other hand, the structured and determined approach of the activists in the Old Mining Battlefield case appeared to have played an important role in their success in reaching their goals (Dao, 2005). It thus appears that some formalization of activities, particularly in the areas of public relations expertise, is crucial to activists' success.

The problem is that there are few studies that investigate the willingness of public relations practitioners who are employed in more formal public relations positions to become involved in activist groups. One might assume that public relations practitioners, like other citizens, would be motivated by the factors as explained in the situational theory of publics (i.e., high problem recognition, high levels of involvement, and low levels of constraint recognition to become activists themselves). It might even be possible that public relations practitioners have lower levels of constraint recognition in general because of their experience in the field.

Environmental Impact on Public Relations Practice

As mentioned before, one of the major contributions of the Excellence project was the focus on the impact of organizations' environments on public relations practice. In applying the two-way contingency model, one might also argue that the environment would probably play the most important role in determining who "most needs to be persuaded in particular situations" (L. Grunig et al., 2002, p. 472).

Although several scholars have suggested that media often give activists power over organizations (L. Grunig, 1992; Holtzhausen, 2000), some more recent trends have indicated that the situation would depend on the particular environment. In public relations, environments have traditionally been studied from organizational theory perspectives. As discussed before, contingency theory argues that environments are particularly influential when they are turbulent, highly dynamic, and fraught with uncertainty (Robbins, 1990). Dynamic and uncertain environments are also particularly vulnerable to political and regulatory changes, which might result in public relations practitioners seeking information from the organization's environment and hence creating the need for communication with that environment (L. Grunig, 1992). Uncertainty about the environment also plays an important role in organizational behavior. When managers feel uncertain, they create organizations that match their perceived complexity of the environment (Aldrich & Mindlin, 1978; Weick, 2001). Institutional theory in particular argued that environments would reward organizations for conforming to the values, norms, rules, and beliefs of society (Scott, 1987; Selznick, 1957).

Although this too would suggest that activists have more power than organizations, it is apparent that it depends on what the environment values. Roper (2005), for instance, noted that no matter how hard governments try to balance the interests of market economies with social concerns, governments "find themselves increasingly obliged to create and protect infrastructure that favors corporations and the financial institutions that support them" because the economy is "in a position to remove its capital readily from one nation to another" (p. 75). If societies value their market economies more than their people and environment, one can assume that activists' interest will also be less valued than those of corporations.

Two recent reports indicated that these trends are already underway in the United States. Van Sickler (2005) commented that environmentalists "find themselves increasingly marginalized" (p. B1) as they become more and more powerless against urban developers. In a report on the loss of employee benefits, particularly pension funds, Gosselin (2005) wrote that "a broadening swath of corporate America successfully is retreating from the safety-net business and wants you to take its place." Because companies only have "room [to] focus on the competition ... working families are left largely on their own" (p. 1).

In contrast, South African practitioners reported that their organizations are under pressure to play an important role in the social uplifting and economic advancement of previously marginalized people. These practitioners feel they make an important contribution to their organizations' survival by bringing such value systems into the organization and giving preference to those important social publics with high symbolic value over the specific interests of the organization (Holtzhausen, 2005). This study supported the notion that political systems affect practice.

The Excellence Theory asserted that public relations practices are more likely to develop in democratic societies and are "less prevalent in countries with collective cultures and authoritarian political systems" (L. Grunig et al., 2002, p. 546). However, it might be particularly turbulent political and even undemocratic environments that inspire excellent practice. The Holtzhausen (2005) study found that the 208 practitioners who participated in the study said the most pervasive impact of the political change in that country on their practice is that it is much more appreciated as a management function and practice itself became more professional. The third most pervasive change is that practice became much more participative and inclusive of community groups, particularly those groups who were marginalized in the previous political dispensation. This also appears to be the case in other transitional societies, among others in South America (Molleda, Athaydes, & Hirsch, 2003) and Eastern Europe (Van Ruler & Vercic, 2004). In actual fact, it is often the actions of civil society—consisting of activist groups, NGOs, and other grassroots movements—that push countries toward democratization. This brings us to the application of chaos and complexity theory to public relations practice.

Perspectives from chaos and complexity theory (Murphy, 2000) imply that the relationship between organizations and their environments is much more seamless than previously argued. Interactions in complex systems are local, nonlinear, dynamic, and rules based. History is essential to complex systems. Densely interconnected relationships lead to intricate networks of cause and effect, which would counter the argument of organizational autonomy. Furthermore, these complex systems are essentially self-organizing, and it appears as if all participants in this complex system have an equal opportunity to shape the system. This indicates that the relationship among organizations, their employees, and their environments is unstable, complex, and susceptible to resistance and continuous change. It is this environment of change that Holtzhausen (2004) maintained requires activist behavior from public relations practitioners. All complex systems are situated within a social context. It would be impossible to separate an organization from the complex systems of power that permeate all levels of society, and from the power relations entrenched in the organization's history. Thus, one might argue that, in all complex systems, the struggle for power that is inherent in the system's environment will be perpetuated within the system. Organizations themselves will become terrains of contested power. If complexity and chaos are to offer the opportunity for organizational renewal and adaptation, it will be important to understand this power dynamic. Displaying activist behavior, public relations practitioners will be able to ensure that the same power relations in organizational environments do not permeate organizations, thus making it impossible for organizations to truly transform themselves.

FUTURE CHALLENGES TO THE STUDY OF ACTIVISM

The future study of activism faces many challenges; among others, to preserve the complexity of the systems that influence the formation of activist groups and the reaction to them. For those scholars who support a postmodern perspective, the challenge will be to watch against

reductivist theories and preserve the "resistance [to] and the abandonment of a linear narrative in favor of a fragmented multiperspectivist
form that examines the evolution of modern Western society from a scientific, technological, economic, political, cultural, journalistic, historical, and mythological standpoint" (Best & Kellner, 2001, p. 25).

The Excellence project has already provided ample proof of this complexity facing scholars. Echoing Best and Kellner (2001), it too called for
studies that better explore the impact of environmental factors on the
formation and success of activists. The two-way contingency model of
communication suggested in the study further complicates communication with and about activists. It will be a future challenge for scholars
to determine under what circumstances practitioners decide to use collaboration or advocacy, and what factors influence those decisions.

The research discussed here implies that power is undertheorized in
public relations literature. As mentioned before, power plays a major
role in both the formation and life cycle of activist groups and organizational responses to it. It also affects public relations practice and decision
making, even when public relations practitioners are part of the dominant coalition (Berger, 2005). Future studies can benefit from how public relations practitioners resist power as proposed in postmodernism
through the work of Foucault (Holtzhausen, 2000; Holtzhausen &
Voto, 2002), and in sociology as proposed through Giddens'
structuration theory (Durham, 2005), which will allow practitioners to
enact an activist role in organizations and society.

The phenomena of dissensus and dissymmetry, as theorized by
Lyotard (1988, 1993), also need further investigation. It appears that
these postmodern phenomena have become entrenched in postmodern
society, with high levels of partisanship in politics and media consumption. It seems that Western society, at least, has adopted the postmodern
understanding that there is no longer a single truth, and that each person's truths are as valid as the next. As Best and Kellner (1991) explained, postmodernists built on the legacy of Nietzsche, who attacked
the philosophical conceptions of Western philosophy and replaced it
with "a perspectivist orientation for which there are no facts, only interpretations, and no objective truth, only the constructs of various individuals or groups" (p. 22). As a result, people are increasingly seeking
and processing only those media that support their own convictions, as
the situational theory predicts. This leads to increased media fragmentation as the media themselves become increasingly partisan, which in
turn feeds an increasingly fragmented society in which people have
drawn lines in the sand.

The Excellence Theory has, quite correctly, asserted that activists often have more power than do organizations. However, changes in the
media environment offer challenges to activists and practitioners alike.

Although the proliferation of alternative media, such as Web sites and Web logs ("blogs"), allow activists and organizations to get their word out in many new ways, this also makes it more difficult to get their messages out to people who do not process those media. For instance, viewership of news broadcasts on network television and readership of traditional newspapers are declining (Fenton, 2005). They are being replaced by a variety of alternative, highly fragmented news options, such as 24/7 cable news stations, online newspapers and magazines, blogs, and even comedy news programs, such as John Stewart's *The Daily Show*, which many have come to view as a credible news commentary outlet. All of this will no doubt contribute to the further fragmentation of social discourse and a breakdown of traditional power systems.

Also, the very nature of activism has changed. As discussed before, in the United States at least, the impact of environmental and even feminist and human rights activists are decreasing, whereas people are becoming more activist about moral and religious issues. As Roper (2005) suggested, this might well be due to the success of market economies and globalization, which are often supported by conservative ideologies. Although these issues point to the complexity and dynamic nature of organizational environments, it also is inevitable that they would spill over into organizations, which will put challenges to public relations practitioners to play an activist role.

A further contribution of the Excellence Theory is that it has highlighted the importance of historical perspectives in the field. The four historic models of public relations as formulated by J. Grunig and Hunt (1984) have arguably become the most taught models in the history of the field. These models have also been tested in virtually every country in which public relations is studied. A future challenge for the field is to expand these historical perspectives to explore public relations' roots in political activism. Cutlip's (1995) history of public relations in the United States includes many examples of public relations in the service of political activism and social change. Nonetheless, these examples have not yet been subjected to a thorough analysis of their contribution to the field's roots. The American history of public relations is viewed as emerging through the use of the term *public relations*. Therefore, the founding fathers of public relations are seen as P. T. Barnum, Ivy Lee, and Edward Bernays, and the histories of these figures are closely tied to the development of American commerce and industry or the development of the industrial/military complex (i.e., the development of American capitalism). This historical perspective ties public relations intimately to the history of journalism, which is why public relations is so often located in schools of journalism or mass communications. One might well ask: What if our history were written by activists and not journalists?

What if our common history emanated from resistance to British colonialism and not from P. T. Barnum, Ivy Lee, and Edward Bernays? What if our heroes were Thomas Jefferson, Margaret Sanger, Alexander Hamilton, members of the Civil Rights Movement, 19th-century British activist Emily Hobhouse, the African National Congress, and Nobel Peace Prize winner Jody Williams? When looking at public relations practice from this historical perspective, the idea of public relations as social and organizational activism is not so far-fetched.

The word *activist* is often bandied about. Activism is no longer the prerogative of civil society. We now have an activist judiciary (Bandow, 2005), activist politicians, and even an activist president ("State of the Union," 2005). Organizations themselves are becoming activist on behalf of ideologies, as the recent cases of Wal-Mart (Sellers, 2005) and the Air Force Academy (Federal News Service, 2005) show. The concept of activism has increasingly come to refer to people who feel strongly about an issue and actively advocate on behalf of that issue, sometimes in a not-too-flattering sense, as Adler (2005) wrote: "As commonly understood, judicial activists are those judges who place their own policy preferences above the law in rendering opinions."

Although this is hardly the type of activism that public relations practitioners should pursue, the question might well be asked why an activist model would be important to public relations and what value this would add to practice. The answer likely lies in both the economic and social contexts of public relations. First, activist public relations practitioners will actively advocate on behalf of the less powerful and will fearlessly stand up to unfair power. In that way, they will help their organizations align with the value systems of their environments, which will ensure their economic survival. As the Excellence Theory holds, these practitioners will set goals that are aligned with those of stakeholders (L. Grunig et al., 2002). Organizational environments are ever changing and dynamic. If organizations wish to keep aligned with value systems in their social environment, they will need to be cognizant of those changes. It will be the role of activist practitioners to continuously push organizations to change and adapt. Second, activist public relations practitioners can also be powerful role players in bringing about social change. In a time in which social change is increasingly brought about through activism, public relations practitioners have all the necessary attributes and skills to lead social change movements.

Finally, future research can benefit from studying the concepts of agency in public relations. Durham (2005) and Holtzhausen (2003) argued that public relations practitioners as agents are not powerless but, like most human beings, will assert themselves reflexively in the face of dominant power. That is exactly what activist public relations practitioners will and should do.

REFERENCES

Adler, J. H. (2005, May 23). Not activist enough. *National Review Online.*. Retrieved June 26, 2005, from www.web.lexis-nexis.com/universe/document

Aldrich, H. E., & Mindlin, S. (1978). Uncertainty and dependence: Two perspectives on environment. In Lucien Karpik (Ed.), *Organization and environment: Theory, issues and reality* (pp. 149–170). London: Sage.

Bandow, D. (2005, March 2). A way to end bitter fights over justices. *Los Angeles Times*, p. B13.

Berger, B. K. (2005). Power over, power with, and power to relations: Critical reflections on public relations, the dominant coalition, and activism. *Journal of Public Relations Research, 17*, 5–28.

Best, S., & Kellner, D. (1991). *Postmodern theory. Critical interrogations.* New York: Guilford.

Best, S., & Kellner, D. (2001). *The postmodern adventure. Science, technology, and cultural studies at the third millennium.* New York: Guilford.

Birch, C. (1992). The postmodern challenge to biology. In C. Jencks (Ed.), *The postmodern reader* (pp. 392–398). London: Academy Editions.

Burek, K. (2001). *Environmental activism and public relations.* Unpublished master's thesis, University of South Florida, Tampa.

Cutlip, S. M. (1995). *Public relations history: From the 17th to the 20th century. The antecedents.* Hillsdale, NJ: Lawrence Erlbaum Associates.

Dao, J. (2005, May 15). A new campaign to preserve an old mining battlefield. *New York Times*, S. 1, p. 22.

Docherty, T. (Ed.). (1993). *Postmodernism: A reader.* New York: Columbia University Press.

Dozier, D. M., & Ehling, W. P. (1992). Evaluation of public relations programs: What the literature tells us about their effects. In. J. E. Grunig (Ed.), *Excellence in public relations and communication management* (pp. 159–184). Hillsdale, NJ: Lawrence Erlbaum Associates.

Dozier, D. M., Grunig, L. A., & Grunig, J. F. (1995). *Manager's guide to excellence in public relations and communication management.* Mahwah, NJ: Lawrence Erlbaum Associates.

Dozier, D. M., & Lauzen, M. M. (2000). Liberating the intellectual domain from the practice: Public relations, activism, and the role of the scholar. *Journal of Public Relations Research, 12*, 3–22.

Durham, F. (2005). A prescriptive critique of the Starlink global food contamination case. *Journal of Public Relations Research, 17*, 29–47.

Ehling, W. P., White, J., & Grunig, J. E. (1992). Public relations and marketing practices. In J. E. Grunig (Ed.), *Excellence in public relations and communication management* (pp. 357–393). Hillsdale, NJ: Lawrence Erlbaum Associates.

Federal News Service. (2005). *The U.S. Air Force Report on the religious climate at the U.S. Air Force Academy.* Retrieved June 26, 2005, from www.web.lexis-nexis.com/universe/document

Fenton, T. (2005). *Bad news: The decline of reporting, the business of news, and the danger to us all.* New York: HarperCollins.

Foucault, M. (1982). The subject and power. In H. L. Dreyfus & P. Rabinow (Eds.), *Michel Foucault: Beyond structuralism and hermeneutics* (pp. 208–226). Chicago: University of Chicago Press.

Foucault, M. (1988a). Social security. In L. D. Kritzman (Ed.), *Michel Foucault: Politics, philosophy culture* (pp. 159–177). New York: Routledge.

Foucault, M. (1988b). Power and sex. In L. D. Kritzman (Ed.), *Michel Foucault: Politics, philosophy culture* (pp. 110–124). New York: Routledge.

Gosselin, P. G. (2005, May 22). Losing ground. *St. Petersburg Times*, p. P1.

Grunig, J. E. (1997). A situation theory of publics: Conceptual history, recent challenges, and new research. In D. Moss, T. MacManus, & D. Vercic (Eds.), *Public relations research: An international perspective* (pp. 3–48). London: International Thomson Business Press.

Grunig, J. E. (2000). Collectivism, collaboration, and societal corporatism as core professional values in public relations. *Journal of Public Relations Research, 12,* 23–48.

Grunig, J. E. (2001). Two-way symmetrical public relations. Past, present and future. In Robert L. Heath (Ed.), *Handbook of public relations.* Thousand Oaks, CA: Sage.

Grunig, J. E., & Grunig, L. A. (1997, July). *Review of a program of research on activism: Incidence in four countries, activist publics, strategies of activist groups, and organizational responses to activism.* Paper presented at the Fourth Public Relations Research Symposium, Bled, Slovenia.

Grunig, J. E., & Hunt, T. (1984). *Managing public relations.* Forth Worth, TX: Holt, Rinehart & Winston.

Grunig, J. E., & Repper, F. C. (1992). Strategic management, publics, and issues. In. J. E. Grunig (Ed.), *Excellence in public relations and communication management* (pp. 117–157). Hillsdale, NJ: Lawrence Erlbaum Associates.

Grunig, L. A. (1986a, August). *Activism and organizational response: Contemporary cases of collective behavior.* Paper presented to the Association for Education in Journalism and Mass Communication, Norman, OK.

Grunig, L. A. (1986b, September). *Environmental and organizational response: Contemporary cases of collective behavior.* Paper presented to the 15th annual conference of the North American Association for Environmental Education, Eugene, OR.

Grunig, L. A. (1992). Activism: How it limits the effectiveness of organizations and how excellent public relations departments respond. In. J. E. Grunig (Ed.), *Excellence in public relations and communication management* (pp. 503–530). Hillsdale, NJ: Lawrence Erlbaum Associates.

Grunig, L. A., Grunig, J. E., & Dozier, D. M. (2002). *Excellent organizations and effective organizations. A study of communication management in three countries.* Mahwah, NJ: Lawrence Erlbaum Associates.

Holtzhausen, D. R. (1995). *The role of public relations theory and research in a postmodern approach to communication management in the organization.* Unpublished doctoral dissertation, Rand Afrikaans University, Johannesburg, South Africa

Holtzhausen, D. R. (2000). Postmodern values in public relations. *Journal of Public Relations Research, 12,* 93–114.

Holtzhausen, D. R. (2002). Towards a postmodern research agenda for public relations. *Public Relations Review, 28,* 251–264.

Holtzhausen, D. R. (2003, July). *The agency of public relations.* Paper presented at BledCom 2003, Golf Hotel, Bled, Slovenia.

Holtzhausen, D. R. (2004, November). *Complexity, postmodern power and public relations.* Paper presented at the Convention of the National Communication Association, Chicago.

Holtzhausen, D. R. (2005). The effects of political change on public relations practice in South Africa. *Public Relations Review, 31*(3), 407–416.

Holtzhausen, D. R., Petersen, B. K., & Tindall, N. T. J. (2003). Exploring the myth of the symmetrical/asymmetrical dichotomy: Public relations models in the New South Africa. *Journal of Public Relations Research, 15,* 305–341.

Holtzhausen, D. R., & Voto, R. (2002). Resistance from the margins: The postmodern public relations practitioner as organizational activist. *Journal of Public Relations Research, 14*(1), 57–84.

Jones, B. L., & Chase, W. H. (1979). Managing public policy issues. *Public Relations Review, 5,* 3–23.

Karlberg, M. (1996). Remembering the public in public relations research: From theoretical to operational symmetry. *Journal of Public Relations Research, 8,* 263–278.

Leitch, S., & Neilson, D. (2001). Bringing publics into public relations. New theoretical frameworks for practice. In Robert L. Heath (Ed.), *Handbook of public relations* (pp. 127–138). Thousand Oaks, CA: Sage.

Lyotard, J.-F. (1988). *The differend: Phrases in dispute. Theory and history of literature* (Vol. 46). Minneapolis: University of Minnesota Press.

Lyotard, J.-F. (1993). *Libidinal economy.* Bloomington: University of Indiana Press.

Mintzberg, H. (1983). *Power in and around organizations.* Englewood Cliffs, NJ: Prentice-Hall.

Mintzberg, H. (1996). The five basic parts of the organization. In J. M. Shafritz & J. S. Ott (Eds.), *Classics of organization theory* (4th ed., pp. 232–244). Fort Worth, TX: Harcourt Brace College.

Molleda, J.-C; Athaydes, A., & Hirsch, V. (2003). Public relations in Brazil: Practice and education in a South American context. In K. Sriramesh & D. Vercic (Eds.), *The global public relations handbook* (pp. 356–377). Mahwah, NJ: Lawrence Erlbaum Associates.

Murphy, P. (1991). The limits of symmetry: A game theory approach to symmetric and asymmetric public relations. In L. A. Grunig & J. E. Grunig (Eds.), *Public relations research annual* (Vol. 3, pp. 115–131). Hillsdale, NJ: Lawrence Erlbaum Associates.

Murphy, P. (2000). Symmetry, contingency, complexity: Accommodating uncertainty in public relations theory. *Public Relations Review, 26,* 447.

Olson, M. (1982). *The logic of collective action: Public goods and the theory of groups.* Cambridge, MA: Harvard University Press.

Robbins, S. P. (1990). *Organization theory: Structure, design, and applications* (3rd ed.). Englewood Cliffs, NJ: Prentice-Hall.

Roper, J. (2005). Symmetrical communication: Excellent public relations or a strategy for hegemony? *Journal of Public Relations Research, 17,* 69–86.

Scott, W. R. (1987). The adolescence of institutional theory. *Administrative Science Quarterly, 32,* 493–511.

Sellers, J. M. (2005, May 29). God & Wal-Mart. *St. Petersburg Times,* p. P1.

Selznick, P. (1957). *Leadership in administration.* New York: Harper & Row.

Smith, M. F., & Ferguson, D. P. (2001). Activism. In R. L. Heath (Ed.), *Handbook of public relations.* Thousand Oaks, CA: Sage.

Spicer, C. (1997). *Organizational public relations: A political perspective.* Mahwah, NJ: Lawrence Erlbaum Associates.

Stacks, D. W. (2002). *Primer of public relations research.* New York: Guilford.

State of the Union; An activist president sets high goals. (2005, February 4). *The Union Leader,* p. A12.

van Ruler, B., & Vercic, D. (2004). Overview of public relations and communication management in Europe. In B. van Ruler and D. Vercic (Eds.), *Public rela-*

tions and communication management in Europe (pp. 1–11). Berlin: Mouton de Gruyter.

Van Sickler, M. (2005, May 15). Will eco-warriors ride again? *St. Petersburg Times*, p. B1.

Vercic, D., & Grunig, J. E. (2000). The origins of public relations theory in economics and strategic management. In D. Moss, D. Vercic, & G. Warnaby (Eds.), *Perspectives on public relations research* (pp. 7–58). London: Routledge.

Weick, K. E. (2001). *Making sense of the organization*. Oxford: Blackwell.

Chapter 18

Redefining "Requisite Variety": The Challenge of Multiple Diversities for the Future of Public Relations Excellence

Bey-Ling Sha
San Diego State University

Rochelle Larkin Ford
Howard University

One of the key characteristics of public relations excellence is diversity (J. Grunig, 1992). As originally examined in the Excellence Study, the concept of diversity was grounded in the principle of requisite variety (cf. Weick, 1979). However, despite its acknowledged importance, diversity and its potential to contribute to excellent public relations remains an underexplored aspect of public relations theory, and discussion of diversity in public relations practice remains limited to descriptions of the experiences of minority practitioners. We believe that, for diversity in public relations to fulfill its potential for excellence, we must bridge this gap and find a way to connect culturally relevant, normative public relations theories with robust empirical evidence on multiple diversities.

In this chapter, we briefly review the concept of diversity as propounded by the Excellence Study, consider scholarship and dialogue in the area of diversity public relations, discuss ways in which our thinking of diversity in public relations can be expanded, and suggest ways in which future scholars and practitioners can maximize the potential of diversity for public relations excellence. The latter section comprises the bulk of this chapter, as we offer suggestions for incorporating considerations of diversity into public relations scholarship, pedagogy, and practice.

Before continuing with our discussion, we feel that it is important for readers to understand the diverse personal backgrounds of the authors. We offer this information not to justify or apologize for our presentation of this chapter, but rather to acknowledge, as did Gunaratnam (2003), that our identities have affected and continue to influence our development as public relations theorists and practitioners. Bey-Ling Sha is a Chinese American woman married to a White Frenchman, and they have two biracial, bicultural, and multilingual children. Rochelle Ford is an African American woman who was raised in a primarily Caucasian American environment, but whose childhood home was culturally African American. A wife and mother of four, she is raising her children in a predominately African American community and teaches students primarily from the Black diaspora. These culturally rich backgrounds at the intersections of race, gender, culture, language, and nationality have given rise to our personal and academic interests in diversity issues in public relations. We both have written about diversity issues in public relations, researched them, practiced multicultural public relations, and made numerous presentations on diversity in public relations.

DIVERSITY AND EXCELLENCE

Our first encounter with the Excellence Study occurred when we were both master's students at the University of Maryland. In classes with James and Larissa Grunig, we learned about the importance of diversity to public relations and about Karl Weick's (1979) theory of requisite variety, or the idea that organizations should be as diverse internally as their environments are externally. The Excellence Study extended Weick's (1979) argument that requisite variety is critical to an organization's ability to resolve organizational problems by placing it in the context of an open systems approach to organizational adaptation to its environment.

After our initial thrill that such an important work in our field as the Excellence Study was in essence validating our long-held personal concerns about diversity, we were disappointed to find, on closer examination, that the original literature review of the study (cf. J. Grunig, 1992) discussed diversity primarily in only two ways, which have continued to dominate scholarly work on diversity public relations in the United States. First, the Excellence Study examined questions of gender equity, as well as valuing, hiring, and promoting women in public relations (cf. L. Grunig, Toth & Hon, 2000, 2001; Hon, L. Grunig, & Dozier, 1992). Second, the study focused on the impact of societal culture on public relations excellence, using Hofstede's

(1980) cultural dimensions (cf. Sriramesh & White, 1992), with little explicit consideration for diversity within those national cultures (cf. Sriramesh, 2004; Sriramesh & Vercic, 2003).

Perhaps the diversity focus taken by the original Excellence Study was the inevitable outcome of a research team comprised of White men and women, except for one non-White, non-U.S. scholar. Yet, we would argue that the study and practice of diversity public relations should not be limited to those with some kind of personal background in a particular area. Just as a minority public relations professional should be qualified to practice "general" public relations or to study "mainstream" public relations issues, so should supposedly "non-diverse" members of the majority be able to question, problematize, research, and engage in diversity issues in public relations.[1] We believe that the qualifications for engaging in diversity public relations go beyond personal background to other characteristics, and we return to this theme in our concluding section on multicultural competence.

Overall, we believe that, for public relations to truly be excellent, all of us must learn to consider multiple diversities as constituting integral and integrated aspects of the field, rather than as "Others" who are somehow different and separate from "mainstream" public relations.[2] Just as a consideration of ethics should permeate all aspects of public relations scholarship and professionalism, so too should a consideration of diversity issues be incorporated into the research and practice of our field. However, the day of that ideal is not yet come; until then, we resign ourselves to the next best alternative—that the relevance of diversity in public relations be highlighted in a separate manner, as a distinct concept of import to our field.

SCHOLARSHIP ON DIVERSITY IN PUBLIC RELATIONS

Before elaborating on alternate ways to think about diversity in public relations, we briefly examine some extant academic and trade literature in this area. We offer this discussion with no claims to its being an exhaustive literature review; rather, we present a small sampling of some of the ways in which diversity is examined by public relations scholars and practitioners.

---

[1]Some Caucasian scholars who have indeed published research on diversity issues in public relations include Hon (1997), Hon and Brunner (2000), Aldoory (2001), and Pompper (2004, 2005).

[2]This subtle shift in perspective could be accomplished in small ways, such as by including entries for "diversity" or "multicultural public relations" in an encyclopedia of the field, rather than Otherizing diversity in an entry titled "minorities in public relations" (cf. Health, 2005).

Public relations diversity scholarship essentially covers three areas: racial and ethnic minority practitioner experiences, communicating with racial and ethnic subcultures, and public relations' role in organizational diversity management. First, despite the increase in the number of studies regarding the experiences of racial and ethnic minority practitioners, there has been no decrease in the racism and discrimination that these practitioners report. Foundational pieces on the experiences of Asian, Latino, African American and Native American practitioners were conducted by Marilyn Kern-Foxworth (1989a, 1989b, 1989d; Kern-Foxworth, Gandy, Hines, & Miller, 1994). A recent publication of Kern-Foxworth's in this area was an encyclopedia entry on "minorities in public relations" (cf. Heath, 2005), in which she noted that "much more work is yet to be done in examining the experiences of minority practitioners" (p. 534).

Second, both trade and academic journals in recent years have published more articles on segmenting and communicating with racial and ethnic subcultures within the United States. For example, Linda Morton regularly publishes a column in *PR Quarterly* explaining how demographics can help practitioners understand psychographic and sociographic characteristics of publics; yet, she cautions practitioners not to stereotype their publics (Morton, 1997, 1998). She also analyzed the segmentation of groups using gender (1999, 2001b, 2002c), age cohorts (2001b, 2001c, 2002a, 2002c, 2003a, 2003b), ethnic groups (2001a, 2002b), education levels (2005), and social class (2004a, 2004b, 2004c).

Similarly, Maria Len-Rios has investigated communications targeting Hispanics (Len-Rios, 2002a, 2002b), finding that presidential candidates communicated strategically with Hispanic voters via the Internet. In January 2004, Rochelle Ford started a regular column in *PR Tactics*, called "Diversity Dimensions," which the PRSA leadership has deemed so relevant to the profession that the column is made available free online, bypassing the regular subscription charge for the publication. These columns have included news items, research findings, and practical tips of interest to professionals in diversity public relations.

Public relations scholars are not the only ones to study the impact of diversity on organizational practices. In recent years, organizational management theory has grown tremendously regarding the business imperative of diversity, with studies demonstrating the impact that diversity has on organizational effectiveness and efficiency. Recent diversity management theorists explain that diversity must take a holistic approach versus a solely human resources approach (Diversity Inc., 2003; Thomas, 1991, 1996). Public relations' role in diversity management is discussed in more depth in the practice section of this chapter.

PROFESSIONAL DIALOGUES ABOUT DIVERSITY

Recognition of the need for greater dialogue about and awareness of diversity in public relations also has been reflected by the leadership of the Public Relations Society of America (PRSA),[3] the largest professional organization in our field in the United States. In the 1970s, PRSA developed a National Minorities Affairs committee to assist with creating more racial and ethnic diversity within the profession and within the association; this committee, at the urging of Marilyn Kern-Foxworth, coined the term ALANA to represent Asian, Latino, African American, and Native American practitioners. This national committee, which reported to the National Board of PRSA, created multiple initiatives, including a scholarship for ALANA students, a multicultural campaign awards program that later became a category of the Silver Anvil competition, the D. Parke Gibson Award to recognize pioneers in multicultural public relations, networking and professional development seminars, and a newsletter. In 1997, these ongoing efforts became part of the National Multicultural Communications Section, in an effort to broaden opportunities for involvement in the committee's activities, with a focus on outreach to ALANAs.

In 2000, the National Board made a renewed commitment to diversity by establishing a Diversity Initiative under the leadership of Ofield Dukes, an African American pioneer in public relations. Those efforts led to a PRSA Chapter Diversity Awards Program. From 2001 to 2004, other professional sections took an interest in the diversity initiative, and in 2004, under the direction of Rosanna Fiske, PRSA released a comprehensive toolkit to aid chapters and individuals in creating diversity initiatives. Although PRSA recognizes the value of a holistic approach to diversity, its diversity initiatives focus on race, ethnicity, gender, and sexual orientation. In 2004, a coalition of public relations professional organizations held a "diversity summit"; however, the focus of the conference became racial and ethnic diversity.

As is obvious from the preceding discussion, public relations scholarship and practice continue to have limited definitions of "diversity," with most attention being paid to racial and ethnic minorities within the United States. Thus, we would like to push the boundaries of "requisite variety" in this chapter by offering some new conceptualizations of diversity.

NEW CONCEPTUALIZATIONS OF DIVERSITY

Frequently, diversity is categorized into primary and secondary dimensions (Loden & Rosener, 1991). The primary dimensions of diversity are

---

[3]For more information about the history of PRSA's diversity efforts, visit http://www.prsa.org

those differences among people that generally cannot be altered, such as age, race, sexual orientation, gender, ethnicity, and physical abilities/qualities[4] (Loden & Rosener, 1991). On the other hand, secondary dimensions of diversity are those aspects over which people generally exert more control, such as language, income, marital status, parental status, hobbies, interests, geography, values, religion, and military experience. Although secondary dimensions of diversity often are considered in the design and execution of public relations programs, they have received scant attention in scholarly work in our field, despite their potential impact on publics' communication behavior.

Besides distinguishing between primary and secondary dimensions of diversity, we would like to point out that the concept of diversity has at least two other dimensions—how we see ourselves and how others perceive of us—two sides of the critical coin of cultural identity. Drawing on literature from intercultural communication, Sha (1995, 1998, 2006) argued that this distinction between our avowed identities (how we see ourselves) and our ascribed identities (how others perceive of us) is relevant to public relations because, in their efforts to communicate with their stakeholders, organizations risk ascribing identities to their publics that those publics may not avow or assert for themselves. For example, a chemical factory located in a primarily Hispanic neighborhood might try to communicate with local residents in Spanish; yet, this effort would backfire if residents are in fact second- or third-generation Hispanics with both a strong command of the English language and a sore spot for being perceived as Spanish-only speakers. Thus, even as we outline in this chapter some of the primary and secondary dimensions of diversity, we urge readers to keep in mind that conducting research on avowed identities is critical to the development of mutually beneficial relationships between organizations and their publics.

Some underexamined aspects of diversity that we feel are important for public relations research and practice today include religion, age, living arrangements, sexual orientation, and military veteran status.[5] Even a decade ago, Huntington (1996) argued that religion would come to constitute one of the major "fault lines" in modern world politics, and events in the United States since 9/11 have supported his claim. Despite being a country founded in the name of religious freedom, the United States has witnessed in recent years an uneasy rise in the relevance of re-

---

[4]We acknowledge that race and ethnicity are sociological or political concepts, rather than biological or natural science constructs (cf. Fish & Schles, 1995; Hall, 1990; Sha, 2006). However, because one generally cannot change his or her race or ethnicity, these remain a primary aspect of diversity.

[5]We acknowledge that our selections are grounded in an American worldview and that other dimensions of diversity may be more relevant outside the United States.

ligion to our quotidian existence, from headlines about the racial profiling of American Muslims by law enforcement officials, to the "browning" of the U.S. Catholic Church with an influx of devout Hispanics, to the "political evangelicalism" of the Protestant Christian right wing as demonstrated in the 2004 presidential elections.

Studies also have shown that members of Generation X are raising their own children with religious values, contrary to the way they themselves were brought up. This difference also underscores the myriad other ways in which membership in an age or generational cohort affects Americans today. For instance, as baby boomers move into their retirement years, marketers increasingly tout products targeting the physical, nutritional, and entertainment needs of seniors. However, seniors in general do not want to be singled out as being different or stereotyped as severely impaired, despondent, curmudgeonly, reclusive, or elitist, nor do they want to be portrayed via overly positive stereotypes like the perfect grandparent, the conservative, the liberal matriarch or patriarch, or the small-town neighbor (Tharp, 2001).

In 2000, the U.S. census recorded 34.9 million Americans 65 years of age or older, and others estimate that, by 2010, one out of every four Americans will be over 55 years old. States with high percentages of mature Americans are not the same states with the largest number of mature Americans, and diversity within the mature American public exists and should be taken into consideration by public relations scholars and practitioners. For example, with the increased scrutiny of senior citizens' lifestyles has emerged another trend, that of grandparents serving as primary caregivers of their grandchildren (Simmons & Dye, 2003). Census 2000 marked the first time that the U.S. Census Bureau was directed by Congress to collect data specifically on grandparents as caregivers, thus fulfilling the directive of the Personal Responsibility and Work Opportunity Reconciliation Act of 1996. These "coresident grandparents" are likely to avow "senior" identities that differ sharply from non-coresident grandparents in their generational cohort, thus making them relevant for organizations seeking to establish relationships with senior citizens.

With 5.8 million coresident grandparents in 2000, the issue of living arrangements is another diversity dimension that should be considered in public relations, as the proportion of "traditional" households of mother-father-two-kids continues to decline. As reported in Simmons and O'Neill (2001), Census 2000 found an increase in the diversity of living arrangements in the United States, of which coresident grandparents was only one arrangement. Others included multigenerational families (3.7% of all U.S. households in 2000, with no data available from the 1990 census), one-person households (26% of all households, up from 25% in 1990), female family households with no husband present (7.2% of all households, up from 6.6%), and unmarried-partner households (5.2% of all households, up from 3.5%). Of the latter household type, the majority were opposite-sex unmarried partners, but about 1 in 9 of these households had same-sex unmarried partners (Simmons & O'Connell, 2003).

Some of those same-sex partners may identify themselves as being part of an LGBT (lesbian, gay, bisexual, and transgendered) community; however, the U.S. Census Bureau is not authorized by Congress to collect data on sexual orientation. In part due to the lack of an official accounting, the size of the LGBT community is disputed; however, estimates range from 2% to 10% of the overall U.S. population, with some estimates as high as 34% of the population in cities with 1 to 3 million people (Tharp, 2001). The difficulty of identifying an LGBT community is compounded by the fact that avowing an LGBT identity can put an individual at personal risk (Eadie, 2006). Thus, many LGBTs never publicly identify themselves and remain "in the closet," whereas others are "openly closeted," meaning their sexual orientation is only known online (cf. Tharp, 2001).

Nevertheless, public awareness of and exposure to LGBT individuals have increased dramatically as a result of representations of LGBTs in the mass media, including on television shows such as *Will and Grace* and *Queer Eye for the Straight Guy*, in movies such as *The Birdcage*, and by public figures like Ru Paul, Ellen DeGeneres, Martina Navratilova, and Greg Louganis. Furthermore, with continued changes and challenges to marital laws, domestic partnerships rights, and holistic diversity initiatives, managing communication with and issues of concern to LGBTs will become increasingly important to public relations scholars and practitioners.

Finally, with the wars in Afghanistan and Iraq dividing U.S. public opinion in sharp echoes of the public controversy over the Vietnam War, we believe that it is appropriate for public relations scholars to consider military veteran status as a relevant diversity dimension. As a result of U.S. military involvement around the world, the United States today has a new generation of veterans of foreign wars. Yet, unlike in past wars where most people in the country had relatives or friends serving in the military, the abolishment of the draft has meant that most Americans today have little personal experience with the military beyond what they see in the mass media (Perry, 2005). For this reason, public relations efforts to communicate with organizational stakeholders should consider whether veteran status is a hidden diversity dimension in specific publics, especially as those recovering from their war experience may be very different from their demographic counterparts who did not serve in the military.

MAXIMIZING THE POTENTIAL OF DIVERSITY FOR PUBLIC RELATIONS EXCELLENCE

Our discussion of new conceptualizations of diversity leads us to our central question: How can we maximize public relations excellence by incorporating multiple diversities into our research, teaching, and practice? The remaining sections of this chapter focus on ways in which we might begin our search for the answer to this important question, and we conclude our suggestions with an articulation of multicultural competence and how this quality can help both scholars and practitioners maximize the potential of diversity for public relations.

Diversity in Scholarship

There are many ways to further the inclusion of diversity in public relations scholarship, including the incorporation of cultural identity as a communication predictor, the development of a culture-general measure of identity, more critical examination of extant public relations theory as hegemonic, and addressing methodological issues in data collection from diverse research participants.

Predicting Communication Behavior. We believe that one way to incorporate diversity considerations in public relations is to examine cultural identity as a way of segmenting organizational publics. As reported in a previous chapter of this book, earlier research has found that racioethnic identification significantly affects four of the five variables in the situational theory of publics: problem recognition, level of involvement, information processing, and information seeking (cf. Sha, 1995, 1998, 2006). Similarly, ReVelle (1995) reported differences between African Americans and Caucasians in problem recognition of and level of involvement with workplace issues related to race.

Moving from avowed racial identity to age identity, Tillery (a.k.a. Ford; 1995) found in a study about health care reform that old-age identification was not a significant indicator of communication behavior, nor did it add to the identification of publics using the situational theory. However, she did find that age identification gave additional insight into the constraint recognition levels of senior citizen publics, with seniors identifying with the "old-old" cohort experiencing and perceiving more internal and external constraints than did their peers. In short, the relevance of cultural identity as a predictor of communication behavior offers tantalizing potential for public relations theory-building efforts.

Operationalizing Cultural Identity.   The relevance of cultural identity in diversity public relations also calls for ways to better operationalize the extent to which people identify with certain groups. Thus, we also call on public relations scholars to work with colleagues in intercultural communication, sociology, educational psychology, and other disciplines to develop a measure of cultural identity that, unlike extant models, would go beyond determining levels of assimilation of "minority" groups into the mainstream of U.S. society, or the extent to which children of immigrant families maintain ties to the parents' homeland. For cultural identity to be treated seriously in public relations scholarship as a variable, it requires a systematic and validated measurement tool.

Problematizing Extant Scholarship.   In addition to including and measuring cultural identity as a construct in models predicting communication behavior, we should problematize extant theoretical constructs and ask whether they are relevant or appropriate for a public relations discipline that incorporates multiple diversities. For example, questions already have been raised about the appropriateness of symmetrical communication for all organization types, with some scholars arguing that certain types of activist organizations (usually those in the minority on some position) simply cannot be symmetrical (Dozier & Lauzen, 2000; Sha, 2004).

In a related spirit of scholarly debate, we would question whether the tenets of public relations Excellence (cf. Dozier, L. Grunig, & J. Gruing, 1995; J. Gruing, 1992; L. Grunig, J. Grunig, & Dozier, 2002) can really serve to accommodate the needs of diverse organizations and their publics, or whether the hegemony created by the prevalence of this theoretical approach in public relations scholarship means that, in fact, the concerns of the oppressed are co-opted rather than truly addressed and resolved. We encourage more rigorous scholarship in public relations that poses these questions in the critical tradition (e.g., Pompper, 2005; Roper, 2005), but recommend that scholars in this area go beyond critiquing extant theories to offering constructive ways of improving them or to offering alternative paradigms altogether.

Resolving Methodological Challenges.   Along similar lines, we suggest a reconsideration of methodological issues in public relations scholarship. Despite the advent of qualitative research methods in our field, the quantitative approach to data collection, analysis, and reporting continues to dominate our journals (cf. Pasadeos & Renfro, 1992), compared to other methods of scholarly inquiry. Understandably, quantitative research often is preferred for its purportedly greater external validity. Yet, if this is true, and public relations scholars continue—as they should—to seek information from understudied populations, then we need to examine the ways in which our quantitative measurements work for collecting data across linguistic, cultural, and physical access barriers. For example, hearing-impaired members of the population are likely to be excluded from phone surveys, as are people whose primary language is not English or those with cultural reservations about giving out personal information.

Another data collection challenge lies in the need to make sure that efforts to translate our data collection tools are undertaken with appropriate scholarly rigor, and that translations into target languages are also independently back-translated to English for validation and verification purposes. Similarly, we should strive for sampling procedures that enable the collection of information from adequate subsets of the population (e.g., disproportionately stratified samples for groups underrepresented in survey research, such as Asian Americans), so that findings can be generalized to the U.S. population as a whole when appropriate. In the absence of such innovations on the sampling end, we would encourage public relations scholars on the analysis end of survey research to engage when feasible in more sophisticated weighting techniques, again to account for traditionally underrepresented groups in our scholarship.

Having suggested some ways to maximize the potential of diversity in public relations by addressing theoretical and methodological challenges, we now offer brief ideas for encouraging diversity in public relations education.

Diversity in Pedagogy

Several commissions on PR education have issued reports on recommended curricula, but until recently diversity has only been mentioned in passing. In 2006, the Commission on PR Education dedicated an entire section to the issue of diversity. Textbooks are beginning to address diversity more seriously, including *International and Intercultural Public Relations: A Campaign Case Approach* by Parkinson and Ekachai (2006). In contrast, prior to 1995, few textbooks even addressed diversity issues from a practitioner or practice perspective (Hannon, 1998; Kern-Foxworth, 1989c, 1990). Today more so than ever before, we need to teach students about the value of workplace diversity and how to incorporate culture and other elements of diversity into public relations campaigns. We thus call for public relations textbooks to give more in-depth treatment to diversity issues in our field, beyond citing numbers of minority practitioners or featuring campaigns targeting minority publics.

In addition to teaching public relations students about multiple diversities in the field, we should teach them to engage in self-awareness and self-reflection. One of the more important competencies necessary to conduct multicultural public relations and manage diversity within public relations is self-awareness of one's own identity, including heritage, culture, gender, race, ethnicity, sexual orientation, and socioeconomic status (Banks, 1995, 2000; Sheng, 1995; Tharp, 2001). Furthermore, basic skills such as research are essential to achieving a better understanding of the avowed identities of diverse publics.

Diversity in Practice

There are at least three aspects to maximizing the potential for diversity in public relations practice: improving the experiences of minority practitioners, using public relations to promote organizational commitment to diversity, and facilitating the development of multicultural competencies in public relations. Maximizing diversity in public relations practice is critical to maximizing diversity in public relations scholarship, because development of the latter often depends on data collected from and about practitioners in our field.

Diversity and the Practitioner. In 2004, the member organizations of the PR Coalition made a verbal commitment to address diversity issues within the public relations workforce (Nolan, 2005), even as the public relations industry continued to struggle with achieving racial and ethnic diversity among its practitioners overall. Furthermore, recent studies of minority practitioners reported high levels of dissatisfaction with the level of diversity in the public relations field, as well as with our efforts at recruitment and retention of minorities (Appelbaum & Ford, 2005; PR Coalition, 2005; Public Relations Society of America, 2003). About 90% of practitioners surveyed for the PR Coalition Survey indicated that more should be done to improve diversity, especially for racial and ethnic minorities in our field (PR Coalition, 2005).

Further, Appelbaum and Ford (2005) found that 40% of the Hispanic and Black practitioners surveyed had experienced overt discrimination and that 53% had experienced subtle discrimination within our industry because of their race or ethnicity. Likewise, 62% felt that they had to be more qualified for positions than their Caucasian American counterparts; 60% believed that multicultural practitioners in general are put on slow-moving career tracks; and 56% asserted that multicultural practitioners are frequently relegated to menial tasks (Appelbaum & Ford, 2005). These findings echo those of earlier studies (e.g., Kern-Foxworth, 1989b; Kern-Foxworth et al., 1994; Len-Rios, 1998, 2002b; Mallette, 1995; Tillery-Larkin, 1999; Wise, 1997; Yamashita, 1992; Zerbinos & Clanton, 1993). Thus, improving the experiences of minority practitioners, as well as increasing their numbers in public relations, is critical for achieving excellence in our field.

Diversity and Intra-Organizational Commitment.   In addition to the challenge of diversifying the public relations workforce, practitioners in general are not engaged in the diversity practices of organizations (Hon & Brunner, 2000). In fact, 62% of the practitioners surveyed by the PR Coalition (2005) indicated that their organizations have "no comprehensive process to ensure all employees are aware of the organization's policy on diversity" (PR Coalition, 2005, p. 6). This is problematic when we consider that multiple diversities must be appreciated and managed within organizations as part of a strategic human resources effort to attract the best talent from diverse backgrounds.

According to Diversity Inc. (2003), corporate communications plays a vital role in the success of organizational diversity initiatives, beginning with the revision of the organizational mission to explain the company's stance on diversity; this effort should be proactive and undertaken as a strategic business effort, rather than solely as a courtesy to key stakeholders. Public relations practitioners should embrace this opportunity to be proactively involved in shaping and communicating the organizational mission, particularly as it applies to diversity. In other words, maximizing diversity within organizations represents an unique opportunity for public relations to participate in the articulation of organizational mission statements.

Diversity and Multicultural Competence.   About a decade ago, Sheng (1995) conducted a foundational study on both the elements of effective multicultural public relations practice and competencies necessary for practitioners of multicultural public relations. Through a two-round Delphi study with public relations scholars and practitioners, she found that effective multicultural public relations campaigns[6] demonstrated interdependence, cultural sensitivity, valuing diversity, and symmetrical communication. First, multicultural public relations campaigns must show respect for the interdependence between cultural publics[7] and the organization, recognizing that these publics can affect the organization and be affected by the organization. Likewise, practi-

---

[6]Sheng (1995) defined multicultural communications campaigns as involving an organization and its target public(s) from more than two primary racial or ethnic cultures. However, in this chapter, in keeping with our previous conceptualization of diversity, we would argue that all public relations can be considered cultural communication: intracultural (within the same cultural group), intercultural (between two cultures or subcultures), and multicultural (among two or more cultural groups; cf Banks, 1995, 2000; Ford, 2004; Tillery-Larkin, Mallette, & Sha, 2002).

[7]We define cultural publics here as organizational stakeholders with salient avowed identities related to a group grounded in a primary or secondary dimension of culture.

tioners must demonstrate cultural sensitivity in each step of their campaign, taking the necessary steps to recognize the cultural dimensions or patterns that can affect the perceptions, attitudes, and behaviors of the organization's cultural publics. Also, before beginning an outreach campaign to cultural publics—especially racial, ethnic, and sexual orientation minority groups—organizations must demonstrate a genuine commitment to and valuing of diversity, which begins with ensuring that the organization's diversity policy is available, publicized, and implemented formally and informally. In the implementation process of a multicultural public relations campaign, practitioners should use symmetrical communication techniques to foster long-term relationships and mutual understanding between the organization and its cultural publics.

Moving from effective campaigns to effective practitioners, Sheng (1995) found that appropriate competencies for individuals practicing multicultural public relations should include self-awareness, multicultural relational skills, multicultural sensitivity, and managerial skills. First, practitioners should be aware of how their own cultural backgrounds might shape their perspectives and influence their decisions, actions, and attitudes. Second, skill in multicultural relations refers to the ability to communicate with people different from one's self, and although this trait might involve knowing languages besides English, it goes beyond language competence to include the ability to be sensitive to cultural subtexts and concerns. In particular, Sheng's (1995) participants argued that multicultural sensitivity was not innate, but rather is learned through education and personal experience, thus also offering support for Banks' (1995, 2000) argument regarding the importance of education and training in preparing practitioners for multicultural public relations. Finally, managerial skills were seen in Sheng's (1995) study as an important competency, because possessing them meant that practitioners could design effective multicultural public relations campaigns without interference from others in the organization.

We would like to emphasize that being a member of a particular cultural group was *not* found by Sheng (1995) to be a prerequisite for becoming a successful practitioner of multicultural public relations. All of the competencies identified by Sheng (1995)—self-awareness, multicultural relational skills, multicultural sensitivity, and managerial skills—are learned and learnable. This means that anyone, regardless of his or her personal background, can become "fluent" in the practice of multicultural public relations. Furthermore, we believe that these same traits would enable researchers of any background to pursue scholarly endeavors in diversity and public relations. In short, for public relations to maximize the potential of diversity in our field, we must facilitate the development of these multicultural competencies in our practitioners, students, and researchers.

CONCLUDING THOUGHTS

By shifting the focus of diversity in public relations from characteristics grounded in primary dimensions of diversity to learnable competencies for multicultural scholarship and practice, we enable the broadening of "requisite variety," as well as the acknowledgment of multiple diversities, the integration of which is absolutely essential for public relations to maximize its potential for excellence. That future is not yet here, and much more work, in both scholarship and practice, remains to be done. Anyone, regardless of his or her own cultural background, can take up this challenge—will you?

REFERENCES

Aldoory, L. (2001). Making health communications meaningful for women: Factors that influence involvement and the situational theory of publics. *Journal of Public Relations Research, 13*, 163–185.

Appelbaum, L., & Ford, R. (2005). *Multicultural public relations practitioner survey*. Retrieved July 1, 2005, from www.ccny.cuny.edu/prsurvey

Banks, S. P. (1995). *Multicultural public relations: A social-interpretive approach*. Thousand Oaks, CA: Sage.

Banks, S. P. (2000). *Multicultural public relations: A social-interpretive approach* (2nd ed.). Ames: Iowa State University.

Diversity, Inc. (2003). *The business case for diversity*. New Brunswick, NJ: Allegiant Media.

Dozier, D. M., Grunig, L. A., & Grunig, J. E. (1995). *Manager's guide to excellence in public relations and communication management*. Mahwah, NJ: Lawrence Erlbaum Associates.

Dozier, D. M., & Lauzen, M. M. (2000). Liberating the intellectual domain from the practice: Public relations, activism, and the role of the scholar. *Journal of Public Relations Research, 12*(1), 3–22.

Eadie, W. F. (2006). In plain sight: Gay and lesbian communication and culture. In L. A. Samovar, R. E. Porter, & E. R. McDaniel (Eds.), *Intercultural communication: A reader* (pp. 198–208). Belmont, CA: Wadsworth.

Fish, J. M., & Schles, K. (1995). Mixed blood. *Psychology Today, 28*(6), 55–63.

Ford, R. L. (2004, January). Understanding multicultural vocabulary. *PR Tactics*, n.p.

Grunig, J. E. (Ed.). (1992). *Excellence in public relations and communication management*. Hillsdale, NJ: Lawrence Erlbaum Associates.

Grunig, L. A., Grunig, J. E., & Dozier, D. M. (2002). *Excellent public relations and effective organizations: A study of communication management in three countries*. Mahwah, NJ: Lawrence Erlbaum Associates.

Grunig, L. A., Toth, E. L., & Hon, L. C. (2000). Feminist values in public relations. *Journal of Public Relations Research, 12*(1), 49–68.

Grunig, L. A., Toth, E. L., & Hon, L. C. (2001). *Women in public relations: How gender influences practice*. New York: Guilford.

Gunaratnam, Y. (2003). *Researching "race" and ethnicity: Methods, knowledge and power*. London: Sage.

Hall, S. (1990). Cultural identity and diaspora. In J. Rutherford (Ed.), *Identity: Community, culture, difference* (pp. 222–237). London: Lawrence and Wishart.

Hannon, S. (1998). A comparative analysis of ethnic inclusion in public relations textbooks and reference books. *Teaching Public Relations, 45*, 1–4.

Heath, R. L. (Ed.). (2005). *Encyclopedia of public relations*. Thousand Oaks, CA: Sage.

Hofstede, G. (1980). *Culture's consequences: International difference in work-related values*. Newbury Park, CA: Sage.

Hon, L. C. (1997). "To redeem the soul of America": Public relations and the civil rights movement. *Journal of Public Relations Research, 9*(3), 163–212.

Hon, L. C., & Brunner, B. (2000). Diversity issues and public relations. *Journal of Public Relations, 12*(4), 309–340.

Hon, L. C., Grunig, L. A., & Dozier, D. M. (1992). Women in public relations: Problems and opportunities. In J. E. Grunig (Ed.), *Excellence in public relations and communication management* (pp. 419–438). Hillsdale, NJ: Lawrence Erlbaum Associates.

Huntington, S. P. (1996). *The clash of civilizations and the remaking of world order*. New York: Simon & Schuster.

Kern-Foxworth, M. (1989a). An assessment of minority female roles and status in public relations: Trying to unlock the acrylic vault and assimilate into the velvet ghetto. In E. L. Toth & C. G. Cline (Eds.), *Beyond the velvet ghetto* (pp. 241–286). San Francisco, CA: International Association of Business Communicators Research Foundation.

Kern-Foxworth, M. (1989b). Minorities 2000: The shape of things to come. *Public Relations Journal, 14–18*, 21–22.

Kern-Foxworth, M. (1989c). Public relations books fail to show women in context. *Journalism Educator, 44*(3), 31–36.

Kern-Foxworth, M. (1989d). Status and roles of minority pr practitioners. *Public Relations Review, 15*(3), 39–47.

Kern-Foxworth, M. (1990). Ethnic inclusiveness in public relations textbooks and reference books. *Howard Journal of Communication, 2*(2), 226–237.

Kern-Foxworth, M., Gandy, O., Hines, B., & Miller, D. A. (1994). Assessing the managerial roles of black female public relations practitioners using individual and organizational discriminants. *Journal of Black Studies, 24*(4), 416–434.

Len-Rios, M. E. (1998). Minority public relations practitioner perceptions. *Public Relations Review, 24*(4), 535–555.

Len-Rios, M. E. (2002a). The Bush and Gore presidential campaign Web sites: Identifying with Hispanic voters during the 2000 Iowa caucuses and New Hampshire primary. *Journalism and Mass Communication Quarterly, 79*(4), 887–904.

Len-Rios, M. E. (2002b). Latino professionals in public relations: More than meets the eye. *Public Relations Quarterly, 47*(1), 22–27.

Loden, M., & Rosener, J. B. (1991). *Workforce America!: Managing employee diversity as a vital resource*. Homewood, IL: McGraw-Hill Trade.

Mallette, W. A. (1995). *African Americans in public relations: Pigeonholed practitioners or cultural interpreter?* Unpublished master's thesis, University of Maryland, College Park.

Morton, L. P. (1997). Targeting minority publics. *Public Relations Quarterly, 42*(2), 23–28.

Morton, L. P. (1998). Segmenting publics: An introduction. *Public Relations Quarterly, 43*(3), 33–34.

Morton, L. P. (1999). Segmenting publics by gender. *Public Relations Quarterly, 44*(4), 41–42.

Morton, L. P. (2001a). Segment to target Arab Americans. *Public Relations Quarterly, 46*(4), 47–48.

Morton, L. P. (2001b). Segment to target professional boomer women. *Public Relations Quarterly, 46*(2), 37–39.

Morton, L. P. (2001c). Segmenting baby boomers. *Public Relations Quarterly, 46*(3), 46–47.

Morton, L. P. (2002a). Targeting generation Y. *Public Relations Quarterly, 47*(2), 46–48.

Morton, L. P. (2002b). Targeting Hispanic Americans. *Public Relations Quarterly, 47*(3), 46–48.

Morton, L. P. (2002c). Targeting mid-life men. *Public Relations Quarterly, 47*(4), 43–45.

Morton, L. P. (2003a). Targeting generation X. *Public Relations Quarterly, 48*(4), 43–45.

Morton, L. P. (2003b). Targeting retirees. *Public Relations Quarterly, 48*(2), 36–38.

Morton, L. P. (2004a). Segmenting social classes: The middle class. *Public Relations Quarterly, 49*(3), 46–47.

Morton, L. P. (2004b). Segmenting social classes: The working class. *Public Relations Quarterly, 49*(2), 45–47.

Morton, L. P. (2004c). Upper or elite class. *Public Relations Quarterly, 49*(4), 30–32.

Morton, L. P. (2005). Education, more than a demographic. *Public Relations Quarterly, 50*(1), 19–20.

Nolan, H. (2005, January 24). Panel explores tactics for industry diversity efforts. *PR Week,* p. 2.

Parkinson, M., & Ekachai, D. (2006). *International and intercultural public relations: A campaign case approach.* Boston: Allyn & Bacon.

Pasadeos, Y., & Renfro, B. (1992). A bibliometric analysis of public relations research. *Journal of Public Relations Research, 4*(3), 167–187.

Perry, T. (2005, May). *Making news in Iraq: How military public affairs officers and embedded journalists brought war news home to America.* Presentation at San Diego State University, CA.

Pompper, D. (2004). Linking ethnic diversity & two-way symmetry: Modeling female African American practitioners' roles. *Journal of Public Relations Research, 16*(3), 269–299.

Pompper, D. (2005). "Difference" in public relations research: A case for introducing critical race theory. *Journal of Public Relations Research, 17*(2), 139–169.

PR Coalition. (2005). *Focus on diversity: Lowering the barriers, raising the bar.* Unpublished white paper, Arthur Page Society, New York.

Public Relations Society of America (PRSA). (2003). *Diversity survey.* Unpublished report, Public Relations Society of America, New York.

ReVelle, C. M. (1995). *Relationship of race and ethnicity to the predictors of communication behavior of employees and managers and to the nature of employee publics in a physical plant.* Unpublished master's thesis, University of Maryland, College Park.

Roper, J. (2005). Symmetrical communication: Excellent public relations or a strategy for hegemony? *Journal of Public Relations Research, 17*(1), 69–86.

Sha, B.-L. (1995). *Intercultural public relations: Exploring cultural identity as a means of segmenting publics.* Unpublished master's thesis, University of Maryland, College Park.

Sha, B.-L. (1998, August). *Intercultural public relations: Cultural identity and the segmentation of publics.* Paper presented to the Association for Education in Journalism and Mass Communication, Baltimore, MD.

Sha, B.-L. (2004). Noether's theorem: The science of symmetry and the law of conservation. *Journal of Public Relations Research, 16*(4), 391–416.

Sha, B.-L. (2006). Cultural identity in the segmentation of publics: An emerging theory of intercultural public relations. *Journal of Public Relations Research, 18*(1), 45–65.

Sheng, V. W. (1995). *Multicultural public relations: A normative approach.* Unpublished master's thesis, University of Maryland, College Park.

Simmons, T., & Dye, J. L. (2003). *Grandparents living with grandchildren: 2000* (Census 2000 Brief, C2KBR-31). Washington, DC: U.S. Census Bureau.

Simmons, T., & O'Connell, M. (2003). *Married-couple and unmarried-partner households: 2000* (Census 2000 Special Reports, CENSR-5). Washington, DC: U.S. Census Bureau.

Simmons, T., & O'Neill, G. (2001). *Households and families: 2000* (Census 2000 Brief, C2KBR/01-8). Washington, DC: U.S. Census Bureau.

Sriramesh, K. (Ed.). (2004). *Public relations in Asia.* Singapore: Thomson Asia.

Sriramesh, K., & Vercic, D. (Eds.). (2003). *The global public relations handbook: Theory, research, and practice.* Mahwah, NJ: Lawrence Erlbaum Associates.

Sriramesh, K., & White, J. (1992). Societal culture and public relations. In J. E. Grunig (Ed.), *Excellence in public relations and communication management* (pp. 597–614). Hillsdale, NJ: Lawrence Erlbaum Associates.

Tharp, M. C. (2001). *Marketing and consumer identity in multicultural America.* Thousand Oaks, CA: Sage.

Thomas, R. (1991). *Beyond race and gender: Unleashing the power of your total work force by managing diversity.* New York: Amacom.

Thomas, R. (1996). *Redefining diversity.* Chicago: American Management Association.

Tillery, R., a.k.a., Ford, R. L. (1995). *Analysis of senior citizen health care reform publics using the situational theory of publics.* Unpublished master's thesis, University of Maryland, College Park.

Tillery-Larkin, R., a.k.a., Ford, R. L. (1999). *Surveying perceived pigeonholing among African American public relations practitioners.* Unpublished dissertation, Southern Illinois University, Carbondale.

Tillery-Larkin, R., a.k.a., Ford, R. L., Mallette, W. A., & Sha, B.-L. (2002, October). *Multicultural public relations competence.* A panel presentation at the International Conference of the Public Relations Society of America, San Francisco, CA.

Weick, K. E. (1979). *The social psychology of organizing* (2nd ed.). Reading, MA: Addison-Wesley.

Wise, N. (1997). *The African American female public relations professional: Gender socialization and career experiences.* Unpublished master's thesis, University of Maryland, College Park.

Yamashita, S. H. (1992). *Examination of the status and roles of Asian–American public relations practitioners in the United States.* Unpublished master's thesis, University of Maryland, College Park.

Zerbinos, E., & Clanton, G. A. (1993). Minority public relations practitioners: Career influences, job satisfaction and discrimination. *Public Relations Review, 19*(1), 75–91.

Chapter 19

Reconceiving Gender for an "Excellent" Future in Public Relations Scholarship

Linda Aldoory
University of Maryland

In the third volume of the series of books on the Excellence Study, (L. A. Grunig, J. E. Grunig, & Dozier, 2002), authors discussed gender and the feminization of public relations throughout the text. In particular, they found that, on the departmental level, gendered public relations contributed to excellent public relations and that female top communicators enacted both technical and managerial tasks significantly more than did male top communicators. On the organizational level, data indicated a positive relationship among support for women and participative culture, symmetrical communication, and employee satisfaction.

Since the release of Grunig et al.'s volume, there have been a small number of studies published that have expanded roles theory and explored in depth the perceptions of women in public relations. However, the extant body of knowledge on gender and public relations is thin and narrowly focused. It is thin, in that overall few pieces have been published in the field that focus on gender or gender theory. It is narrowly focused, in that the majority of work has examined experiences and perceptions of *women* in public relations—there has been limited work on *gender* as a social construction guiding public relations practice, or on *men* as gendered beings that are also affected by the feminization of public relations. Although there have been some attempts to develop theory that can inform public relations scholarship, the efforts, including my own, have not been comprehensive or empirically tested.

In this chapter, therefore, I attempt to extend the present body of knowledge on gender and public relations by highlighting gaps in gender research and suggesting areas of conceptualization for future research. First, I provide a brief overview of the current research on gender. Then, I critique the research and formulate conceptualizations that can be considered for future studies.[1]

RESEARCH ON GENDER (READ WOMEN) AND PUBLIC RELATIONS

Since the late 1980s, there have been several studies and professional literature focusing on the impact of women in public relations. In what is now well known as the benchmark research on gender, Elizabeth Toth, Lauri A. Grunig, and their colleagues addressed topics that were of great concern to the women entering the field or trying to move to management positions. Topics included hiring, salary discrepancies, and promotion (L. A. Grunig, 1989; Toth & Cline, 1991; Toth & L. A. Grunig, 1993), sexual harassment (Serini, Toth, Wright, & Emig, 1998), and job satisfaction (Serini, Toth, Wright, & Emig, 1996). The more well-publicized studies, which cited gender discrepancies and discrimination, were: *The Velvet Ghetto* (Cline et al., 1986); *Beyond the Velvet Ghetto* (Toth & Cline, 1989); a special issue of *Public Relations Review* on women in public relations (L. A. Grunig, 1988); *Under the Glass Ceiling* (Wright, L. A. Grunig, Springston, & Toth, 1991); a Public Relations Society of America (PRSA) audit of gender issues (Toth, Serini, Wright, & Emig, 1998); Hon's (1995) feminist theory of public relations; and a compilation of the literature on how gender influences public relations practice, *Women in Public Relations* (L. A. Grunig, Toth, & Hon, 2001). More recently, there have been some published articles and a few attempts at compiling the literature on gender in public relations for purposes of theory development. (For more comprehensive reviews of gender and feminist literature, see Aldoory, 2003, 2005; Aldoory & Toth, 2002; L. A. Grunig et al., 2001.)

Women currently comprise at least 70% of the field (Toth, 2001), and their impact on the profession has been labeled the "feminization" of public relations. This feminization has sparked serious debate about dramatic changes seen in the profession, its reputation, and its scholarship. On one hand, critics have argued that feminization would negatively affect the profession and its reputation (Lauzen, 1992; Lesly, 1988; Scrimger, 1989). This institutional- and ideological-level sexism would disempower individual women who work in public relations, through lowered salaries and a lack of managerial and decision-making power. On the other hand, feminization might open doors to feminist scholars, feminine ideals, and a desirable transformation of the profession and scholarship (Rakow, 1989). For example, the push for relation-

---

[1]Portions of this chapter derive from two of my previously published articles (Aldoory, 2003, 2005).

ship building with publics is seen as a direct result of feminization—
women are socialized (or misperceived) to be naturally inclined toward
sensitivity, collaboration, and, hence, relationship building (Hon,
Grunig, & Dozier, 1992). Also, Sha (1996) asserted that feminization
makes public relations more ethical, "not merely in appearance, but in
practice" (p. 3). Feminization has offered alternative perspectives and
has introduced more symmetrical management, because women know
both the dominant male reality and their own reality. With this dual
consciousness, women may be more sensitive to the perspectives of different organizational publics, and therefore, be more ethical in their
practice of public relations (Sha, 1996).

The feminization of public relations was the impetus for the early
studies of gender in the field; since then, authors have examined gender
through empirical means, qualitative research, and critical approaches.
In an earlier work of mine (Aldoory, 2003), I categorized the extant literature on gender and public relations into three types of scholarship: descriptive scholarship that marks mostly the earlier years, when scholars
were searching for evidence that discrimination existed; explanatory research that followed, in order to suggest why discrepancies existed; and
critical scholarship that exposed gaps in research and suggested
transformative solutions to the androcentric nature of public relations
that exists even with a majority of women present in it. Each of these
types is briefly described next.

Descriptive Scholarship: Examining the Status of Women

Most of the research on gender and feminism in public relations has focused on describing the status, roles, and perceptions of women as compared to men in public relations (Choi & Hon, 2002; Cline et al., 1986; L.
A. Grunig et al., 2001; Molleda & Ferguson, 2004; Tam, Dozier, Lauzen, &
Real, 1995; Weaver-Lariscy, Sallot, & Cameron, 1996; Wright et al.,
1991). This research has examined the roles that practitioners perform,
salaries, job satisfaction, sexual harassment, racism in the profession
(Kern-Foxworth, 1989a, 1989b; Kern-Foxworth, Gandy, Hines, & Miller,
1994; Zerbinos & Clanton, 1993), education (Creedon, 1989; DeRosa &
Wilcox, 1989; Farmer & Waugh, 1999; L. A. Grunig, 1989; Sha & Toth,
2004), and the historical invisibility of women's contributions (Henry,
1995; Lamme, 2001). The range of methodologies used has included not
only quantitative surveys and qualitative focus groups, but also historical assessment. This is an important area of study because, for the first
time since the feminization of the field, research was used to highlight the
impact of the influx of women on women themselves and on the profession as a whole. Additionally, the research helped to explain communication processes within organizations in which female practitioners

worked. It also examined factors that influenced communication management and production.

Taken as a whole, the body of knowledge reflects a liberal feminist standpoint, for which equality is the implicit goal. From the earliest studies conducted in the 1980s to today, findings consistently show evidence of discrepancies by gender and race, and awareness among research participants of the discrepancies.

Explanatory Scholarship: Moving Ahead to Theory

There is a body of scholarship that has moved beyond description of women's status and has focused on two general goals: (a) to elaborate on mainstream theories in public relations by using women as research participants or by including gender as an intervening variable (Aldoory, 1998, 2001a; L. A. Grunig, 1991; Slater, Chipman, Auld, Keefe, & Kendall, 1992), and (b) to take the earlier descriptive studies and suggest explanations and predictor variables for what was found (Creedon, 1991; L. A. Grunig et al., 2001; Hon, 1995; O'Neil, 2003; Wrigley, 2002). Explanatory research has added intervening variables to mainstream public relations theories, making them more heuristic. It has also contributed a greater understanding to how communication strategies are managed. Although the work here illustrates some liberal feminism, much of it resonates with a radical feminist perspective in its focus on systemic problems.

The mainstream public relations theories that have been extended have included two-way communication (L. A. Grunig, 1991), public relations roles and leadership (Aldoory, 1998; Aldoory & Toth, 2004), and the situational theory of publics (Aldoory, 2001a). Studies found that gender did influence whether two-way communication was practiced, and that women did not necessarily engage in two-way communication more than men did. In addition, research with women as participants have led to a greater understanding of the nature of involvement as a factor in information seeking.

Critical Scholarship: Radical Feminism for Purposes of Change

Although few in number, critical feminist scholars are well publicized due to the controversy of their arguments, the threat to the status quo that they encourage, and their ability to empower younger scholars to follow in their scholarly pursuits. The research reflects a more radical feminist perspective, through which theory, the profession, education, and research are examined.

The critical research conducted in public relations has used radical feminist theory as the lens through which to view roles theory (Aldoory,

2001b; Creedon, 1991; Toth, 1988, 1989, 2001), two-way communication (Creedon, 1993; Toth, 1989), ethics (L. A. Grunig, Toth, & Hon, 2000), education (Grunig, 1988, 1993), and feminists' own research efforts (Aldoory, 2005; L. A. Grunig, 1988). Overarching goals for this body of work include uncovering masculinist ideologies guiding theory and practice, and transforming the institutional systems that drive discriminatory practices. Reforms have been suggested for theoreticians, organizations, higher education curricula, and feminists themselves.

The Excellence Study and Gender Research

In the first excellence text (J. E. Grunig, 1992) that is considered the comprehensive literature review used to develop the Excellence Study, a chapter was devoted to "Women in Public Relations: Problems and Opportunities." Chapter authors Hon, Grunig, and Dozier detailed the descriptive, explanatory, and some of the critical research that had been published by that time. As part of their explanations for gender discrepancies, the authors used feminist theory to critique the liberalism that was guiding the gender research in public relations. They stated that both radical and liberal feminist philosophies are required to understand the gendered nature of the public relations profession:

> The inequities female practitioners face are not exclusively the result of sexist discrimination and sexist socialization. Nor will equity be achieved completely through equalizing access and women's rising above traditional sex-role attitudes and behaviors. As socialist/Marxist and radical feminists have argued, societal and institutional changes are needed to eliminate sexism and its consequences. (p. 433)

Hon et al. did not include formal research propositions that measured gender within organizations, but they did conclude their chapter by arguing that evidence of restructuring will be found in the organizations characterized as "excellent" for their study.

In the second excellence text, which was based on the findings of the Excellence Study (Dozier, Grunig, & Grunig, 1995), researchers did in fact find a link between organizations that valued gender and ethnic diversity and organizations that fostered communication excellence. Instead of focusing on individual perceptions and salary levels—which authors argued had been studied by others in the field—research questions examined policies, climate, and other institutional factors that play a role in gender equity. Mentoring, a supportive climate, and non-discrimination policies were all factors found to be significantly important for the most excellent organizations in the survey.

In the third volume of the series of books on the Excellence Study (L. A. Grunig, et al. 2002), authors addressed gender and the feminization of public relations from both an individual-level and a macro-level perspective. Within public relations departments, they found that female top communicators enacted both technical and managerial tasks significantly more than did male top communicators, even in excellent organizations. They summarized that the gender of the top communicator did not help or hinder communication excellence. On the organizational level, quantitative and qualitative data indicated a positive relationship between support for women and participative culture, symmetrical communication, and employee satisfaction.

RECONCEIVING GENDER

There are several areas of research that can be conducted that will fill gaps in the current body of knowledge on gender and public relations. Following are conceptualizations that not only re-examine some of the primary theoretical and operational concepts used in gender studies, but also allow for opportunities for future research.

Gender Is Socially Constructed

Gender should be studied as a constructed and problematic concept that not only defines women, but also men, the public relations profession itself, and the theories developed for the field. Rakow (1992) defined gender as an organizing principle used to classify and differentiate humans and to offer guidelines for how to interact with others. Wood (2001) similarly defined gender as a social, symbolic creation by which we "learn" how to be "masculine" and "feminine" (p. 22). In a 1994 text, van Zoonen focused on the discursive nature of gender, asserting that gender is a set of overlapping and contradictory cultural descriptions and "prescriptions" referring to sexual difference, which arises from economic, political, and social nondiscursive contexts. Gender as constructed socialization rather than as female/not male emphasizes the fact that everyone is gendered. All actors who work in, are targets of, or study public relations are constrained by gender, and all are bound by certain expectations and stereotypes. This type of gendered vision would allow space for scholarship about men, and about lesbian, gay, bisexual, and transsexual experiences. Viewing gender as a learned social system also helps prohibit essentializing females as naturally skilled public relations practitioners.

Future research could focus on how humans interact and communicate with each other and how men and women interact within gendered organizations. It could examine the discursive meaning making of individuals and how professional roles are played out in organizations. Future studies could account for how male and female professionals and scholars are understood in terms of expectations and frames ascribed to them due to gender socialization.

Reconceiving and Studying Power for a Gendered Profession

For Foucault (1979, 1980), power did not exist as something someone or some group has, but rather in discursive practices. This is the way power should be reconceived and studied in public relations. Mumby (2001) wrote that power was the production and reproduction of, resistance to, or transformation of relatively fixed structures of communication and meaning that support the interests (symbolic, political, and economic) of some organization members or groups over others. Power is exhibited through control over meanings in organizations. The group that is best able to "fix" meaning and articulate it for its own interests is the group best able to maintain and reproduce relations of power—in public relations, this is defined as the dominant coalition. In public relations, managerial status has become the only avenue for success, but reconceiving power as controlling meaning would place power additionally in the hands of technicians. According to Baker Miller (1992), power is the capacity for change, which helps dispel the myth that women are powerless or that power is unimportant for women. She suggested that women may have resisted discussing power or using power because of how it has been conceived and exercised as a masculine form of constraint.

Future scholarship, therefore, could acknowledge power relations and examine the discursive constructions of it in the field. Research could explore groups and organizations that view power differently and practice public relations differently. For example, various activist groups and social movements could become more important for study. These types of groups would no longer be defined as "powerless," but would instead be valued for their contributions to understanding perhaps different forms of public relations.

Work–Life Challenges for Practitioners

In completing surveys and focus groups of women and men in the profession (Aldoory & Toth, 2002; Hon, 1995; Toth et al., 1998), scholars often came across data that indicated a perceived conflict between work roles and home/personal roles. In particular, focus group studies revealed that both women and men struggle with balancing work and "life" pleasures and responsibilities. However, there have not been published works in public relations that focus on this relatively new phenomenon. There is precedence in other communication disciplines. For example, in organizational communication, several feminist scholars have examined how employees talk about and make meaning of work–life balance (Buzzanell, 1997, 2000; Farley-Lucas, 2000; Golden, 2000, 2001, 2002; Jorgenson, 2000; Kirby, 2000; Kirby, Golden, Medved, Jorgenson, & Buzzanell, 2003; Kirby & Krone, 2002; Mallia & Ferris, 2000). Other scholars have examined the perceptions of women in certain careers and these women's conflicts with balancing work and family commitments (Engstrom, 2000; Engstrom & Ferri, 1998).

For public relations, this area of research should be a critical focus for the future. On one level, public relations professionals themselves negotiate between work and family commitments and are potential consumers of their organizations' family-friendly policies. On a second level, they are often responsible for planning and implementing internal communication about organizational policies. Even when they are not specifically responsible for this, they often act as organizational communicators. Therefore, they negotiate their organizational roles as communicators with their personal conflicts between work and family.

Examining how women and men who work in public relations articulate the work–family balance and struggle will help elaborate and strengthen gender theory in the field. It could also offer practical strategies on an individual and organizational level for balancing and negotiating work and family commitments.

Taking Diversity and Inclusiveness Seriously

The public relations profession has encouraged diversity and inclusiveness for purposes of increasing organizational success. However, rarely are these concepts challenged on a theoretical level or applied on an empirical level in research. As mentioned earlier, some studies have described differences between practitioners of color and practitioners who are white in their job roles, salaries, and other job factors (Kern-Foxworth, 1989a, 1989b; Kern-Foxworth et al., 1994). However, these studies did not examine why these differences exist or how practitioners make meaning of these differences.

Diversity should be studied as situated knowledge, which influences the research participant, his/her performance and communication, the researcher, and his/her data collection and interpretations. Haraway (1988) explained that every individual is located at a particular position depending on identity, life experiences, and social, physical, and economic constraints. This situated position creates situated knowledge, in which each individual views a narrow reality depending on his or her own perspective. The only way to achieve a greater understanding of experience and reality is to interconnect different perspectives from different people—this should be an avenue for future research in public relations.

One powerful way to seriously study diversity and inclusiveness in public relations is by making visible the privileges that are ascribed to whiteness. When whiteness is accepted as an invisible norm, differences are ignored, "and white people, their assumptions and ways are empowered" (Grimes, 2002, p. 382). This has been the accepted practice in public relations research. Future research should interrogate the assumptions of whiteness that guide public relations.

The means by which we can interrogate whiteness and interconnect perspectives is via studying communicative acts that construct meaning about diversity and racism in organizations and public relations. Researchers should openly discuss the lack of diversity and the impact that different perspectives may have on the mainstream theories that were developed within implicit and hidden norms of whiteness. Research should also begin to focus on issues and concerns that may be relevant to professionals of color but that may not be issues of current concern. For example, perhaps pigeonholing, mentoring, or marginalization by type of industry may be important to practitioners of color, in addition to the more commonly studied issues of sexual harassment, promotions, and salary.

CONCLUSION: AN "EXCELLENT" FUTURE

The research on gender and public relations hit a peak in the late 1980s, and since then there has not been as much published scholarship. Perhaps this is due to the narrow focus of the extant literature, perhaps it is due to a lessening interest in gender issues, or perhaps there is a backlash to publishing gender research, which I find more prevalent at conferences and in dissertations and theses.

In any case, the purpose of the chapter was to offer reconceptualizations of common concepts in gender research that may spark future research that will extend and elaborate public relations theory and practice. Although not an exhaustive list of future possibilities, the suggestions for future research may be able to reinvigorate gender scholarship and increase the validity of feminist research for public relations. At the minimum, I hope the reconceptualizations spark dialogue among readers and scholars in the field.

The concepts of gender, power, and diversity are central to all research questions asked in public relations scholarship. It is not the domain only of feminists. As suggested in the Excellence Study, greater openness to understanding and supporting gender diversity and feminist values increases the likelihood of excellent public relations. By extension, gender and feminism could also increase the potential for excellent public relations scholarship.

REFERENCES

Aldoory, L. (1998). The language of leadership for women in public relations. *Journal of Public Relations Research, 10*, 73–101.

Aldoory, L. (2001a). Making health communications meaningful for women: Factors that influence involvement and the situational theory of publics. *Journal of Public Relations Research, 13*, 163–185.

Aldoory, L. (2001b). The standard white woman in public relations. In E. L. Toth & L. Aldoory (Eds.), *The gender challenge to media: Diverse voices from the field* (pp. 105–149). Cresskill, NJ: Hampton.

Aldoory, L. (2003). The empowerment of feminist scholarship in public relations and the building of a feminist paradigm. *Communication Yearbook, 27*, 221–255.

Aldoory, L. (2005). A (re)conceived feminist paradigm for public relations: A case for substantial improvement. *Journal of Communication, 55*, 668–684.

Aldoory, L., & Toth, E. L. (2002). Gender discrepancies in a gendered profession: A developing theory for public relations. *Journal of Public Relations Research, 14*, 103–126.

Aldoory, L., & Toth, E. L. (2004). Leadership and gender in public relations: Perceived effectiveness of transformational and transactional leadership styles. *Journal of Public Relations Research, 16*, 157–184.

Baker Miller, J. (1992). Women and power. In T. E. Wartenburg (Ed.), *Rethinking power* (pp. 240–248). Albany: State University of New York.

Buzzanell, P. M. (1997). Toward an emotion-based feminist framework for research on dual career couples. *Women and Language, 20*(2), 40–48.

Buzzanell, P. M. (Ed.). (2000). *Rethinking organizational and managerial communication from feminist perspectives.* Thousand Oaks, CA: Sage.

Choi, Y., & Hon, L. C. (2002). The influence of gender composition in powerful positions on public relations practitioners' gender-related perceptions. *Journal of Public Relations Research, 14*, 229–264.

Cline, C. G., Toth, E. L., Turk, J. V., Walters, L. M., Johnson, N., & Smith, H. (1986). *The velvet ghetto: The impact of the increasing percentage of women in public relations and business communication.* San Francisco: IABC Foundation.

Creedon, P. J. (1989). Public relations history misses "her story." *Journalism Educator, 44*, 26–30.

Creedon, P. J. (1991). Public relations and "women's work": Toward a feminist analysis of public relations roles. *Public Relations Research Annual, 3*, 67–84.

Creedon, P. J. (1993). Acknowledging the infrasystem: A critical feminist analysis of systems theory. *Public Relations Review, 19*, 157–166.

DeRosa, D., & Wilcox, D. L. (1989). Gaps are narrowing between female and male students. *Public Relations Review, 15*, 80–89.

Dozier, D. M., Grunig, L. A., & Grunig, J. E. (1995). *Manager's guide to excellence in public relations and communication management.* Mahwah, NJ: Lawrence Erlbaum Associates.

Engstrom, E. (2000). Looking through a gendered lens: Local U.S. television news anchors' perceived career barriers. *Journal of Broadcasting & Electronic Media, 44*, 614–635.

Engstrom, E., & Ferri, A. J. (1998). From barriers to challenges: Career perceptions of women TV news anchors. *Journalism and Mass Communication Quarterly, 75*, 789–802.

Farley-Lucas, B. S. (2000). Communicating the (in)visibility of motherhood: Family talk and the ties to motherhood with/in the workplace. *Electronic*

Journal of Communication, 10(3/4). Retrieved October 10, 2005, from http://wwwcios.org/www/ejc/v10n3400.htm

Farmer, B., & Waugh, L. (1999). Gender differences in public relations students' career attitudes: A benchmark study. *Public Relations Review, 25,* 235–237.

Foucault, M. (1979). *Discipline and punish: The birth of the prison.* New York: Vintage.

Foucault, M. (1980). *Power/knowledge: Selected interviews and other writings, 1972–1977* (C. Gordon, Trans. & Ed.). New York: Pantheon.

Golden, A. (2000). What we talk about when we talk about work and family: A discourse analysis of parental accounts. *Electronic Journal of Communication, 10,* 3/4, n.p. Retrieved October 10, 2005, from http://www.cios.org/www/ejc/v10n3400htm

Golden, A. (2001). Modernity and the communicative management of multiple roles: The case of the worker-parent. *The Journal of Family Communication, 1,* 233–264.

Golden, A. (2002). Speaking of work and family: Spousal collaboration on defining role-identities and developing shared meanings. *Southern Communication Journal, 67,* 122–141.

Grimes, D. S. (2002). Challenging the status quo? *Management Communication Quarterly, 15,* 381–410.

Grunig, J. E. (Ed.). (1992). *Excellence in public relations and communication management.* Hillsdale, NJ: Lawrence Erlbaum Associates.

Grunig, L. A. (1988). A research agenda for women in public relations. *Public Relations Review, 14,* 48–57.

Grunig, L. A. (1989). Sex discrimination in promotion and tenure in journalism education. *Journalism Quarterly, 66,* 93–100, 229.

Grunig, L. A. (1991). Court-ordered relief from sex discrimination in the foreign service: Implications for women working in development communication. *Public Relations Research Annual, 3,* 85–113.

Grunig, L. A. (1993). The "glass ceiling" effect on mass communications students. In P. J. Creedon (Ed.), *Women in mass communication* (2nd ed., pp. 276–300). Newbury Park, CA: Sage.

Grunig, L. A. (2000). A feminist phase analysis of research on women in postmodern public relations. In D. Moss, D. Vercic, & G. Warnaby (Eds.), *Perspectives on public relations research.* London: Routledge.

Grunig, L. A., Grunig, J. E., & Dozier, D. M. (2002). *Excellent public relations and effective organizations: A study of communication management in three countries.* Mahwah, NJ: Lawrence Erlbaum Associates.

Grunig, L. A., Toth, E. L., & Hon, L. C. (2000). Feminist values in public relations. *Journal of Public Relations Research, 12,* 49–68.

Grunig, L. A., Toth, E. L., & Hon, L. C. (2001). *Women in public relations.* New York: Guilford.

Haraway, D. (1988). Situated knowledges: The science question in feminism and the privilege of partial perspective. *Feminist Studies, 14,* 575–599.

Henry, S. (1995). Dissonant notes of a retiring feminist: Doris E. Fleishman's later years. *Journal of Public Relations Research, 10,* 1–33.

Hon, L. C. (1995). Toward a feminist theory of public relations. *Journal of Public Relations Research, 7,* 27–88.

Hon, L. C., Grunig, L. A., & Dozier, D. M. (1992). Women in public relations: Problems and opportunities. In J. E. Grunig (Ed.), *Excellence in public relations and communication management* (pp. 419–438). Hillsdale, NJ: Lawrence Erlbaum Associates.

Jorgenson, J. (2000). Interpreting the intersections of work and family: Frame conflicts in women's work. *Electronic Journal of Communication, 10*(3/4), n.p. Retrieved October 10, 2005, from http://cios.org/www/ejc/v10n3400.htm

Kern-Foxworth, M. (1989a). An assessment of minority female roles and status in public relations: Trying to unlock the acrylic vault and assimilate into the velvet ghetto. In E. L. Toth & C. G. Cline (Eds.), *Beyond the velvet ghetto* (pp. 241–286). San Francisco, CA: IABC Foundation.

Kern-Foxworth, M. (1989b). Status and roles of minority public relations practitioners. *Public Relations Review, 5,* 14–22.

Kern-Foxworth, M., Gandy, O., Hines, B., & Miller, D. A. (1994). Assessing the managerial roles of black female public relations practitioners using individual and organizational discriminants. *Journal of Black Studies, 24*(4), 416–434.

Kirby, E. L. (2000). Should I do as you say, or do as you do?: Mixed messages about work and family. *Electronic Journal of Communication, 10,* 3/4, n.p. Retrieved October 10, 2005, from http://www.cios.org/www/ejc/v10n3400.htm

Kirby, E. L., Golden, A. G., Medved, C. E., Jorgenson, J., & Buzzanell, P. M. (2003). An organizational communication challenge to the discourse of work and family research: From problematics to empowerment. *Communication Yearbook, 27,* 1–43.

Kirby, E. L., & Krone, K. J. (2002). "The policy exists but you can't really use it": Communication and the structuration of work–family policies. *Journal of Applied Communication Research, 30,* 50–77.

Lamme, M. O. (2001). Furious desires and victorious careers: Doris E. Fleischman, counsel on public relations and advocate for working women. *American Journalism, 18,* 13–33.

Lauzen, M. (1992). Effects of gender on professional encroachment in public relations. *Journalism Quarterly, 69,* 173–180.

Lesly, P. (1988). Public relations numbers are up but stature down. *Public Relations Review, 14,* 3–7.

Mallia, K. L., & Ferris, S. P. (2000). Telework: A consideration of its impact on individuals and organizations. *Electronic Journal of Communication, 10,* 3/4, n.p. Retrieved October 10, 2005, from http://www.cios.org/www/ejc/v10n3400.htm

Molleda, J. C., & Ferguson, M. A. (2004). Public relations roles in Brazil: Hierarchy eclipses gender differences. *Journal of Public Relations Research, 16,* 327–352.

Mumby, D. K. (2001). Power and politics. In F. M. Jablin & L. L. Putnam (Eds.), *The new handbook of organizational communication: Advances in theory, research and methods* (pp. 585–623). Thousand Oaks, CA: Sage.

O'Neil, J. (2003). An analysis of the relationships among structure, influence, and gender: Helping to build a feminist theory of public relations. *Journal of Public Relations Research, 15,* 151–179.

Rakow, L. F. (1989). From the feminization of public relations to the promise of feminism. In E. L. Toth & C. G. Cline (Eds.), *Beyond the velvet ghetto* (pp. 287–298). San Francisco: IABC Foundation.

Rakow, L. F. (1992). The field reconsidered. In L. F. Rakow (Ed.), *Women making meaning: New feminist directions in communication* (pp. 3–17). New York: Routledge.

Scrimger, J. (1989). Women communicators in Canada: A case for optimism. In E. L. Toth & C. G. Cline (Eds.), *Beyond the velvet ghetto* (pp. 219–240). San Francisco: IABC Foundation.

Serini, S. A., Toth, E., Wright, D. K., & Emig, A. (1996). Watch for falling glass … women, men and job satisfaction in public relations: A preliminary analysis. *Journal of Public Relations Research, 9*, 99–118.

Serini, S. A., Toth, E., Wright, D. K., & Emig, A. (1998). Power, gender, and public relations: Sexual harassment as a threat to the practice. *Journal of Public Relations Research, 10*, 193–218.

Sha, B. L. (1996, May). *Does feminization of the field make public relations more ethical?* Paper presented to the International Communication Association, Chicago.

Sha, B. L., & Toth, E. L. (2004). Future professionals' perceptions of work, life, and gender issues in public relations. *Public Relations Review, 31*, 93–100.

Slater, M. D., Chipman, H., Auld, G., Keefe, T., & Kendall, P. (1992). Information processing and situational theory: A cognitive response analysis. *Journal of Public Relations Research, 4*, 189–203.

Tam, S. Y., Dozier, D. M., Lauzen, M. M., & Real, M. R. (1995). The impact of superior–subordinate gender on the career advancement of public relations practitioners. *Journal of Public Relations Research, 7*, 259–272.

Toth, E. L. (1988). Making peace with gender issues in public relations. *Public Relations Review, 14*, 36–47.

Toth, E. L. (1989). Whose freedom and equity in public relations? The gender balance argument. *Mass Comm Review, 16*, 70–76.

Toth, E. L. (2001). How feminist theory advanced the practice of public relations. In R. L. Heath & G. Vasquez (Eds.), *Handbook of public relations* (pp. 237–246). Newbury Park, CA: Sage.

Toth, E. L., & Cline, C. G. (Eds.). (1989). *Beyond the velvet ghetto.* San Francisco: IABC Foundation.

Toth, E. L., & Cline, C. G. (1991). Public relations practitioner attitudes toward gender issues: A benchmark study. *Public Relations Review, 17*, 161–174.

Toth, E. L., & Grunig, L. A. (1993). The missing story of women in public relations. *Journal of Public Relations Research, 5*, 153–175.

Toth, E. L., Serini, S. A., Wright, D. K., & Emig, A. G. (1998). Trends in public relations roles: 1990–1995. *Public Relations Review, 24*, 145–163.

van Zoonen, L. (1994). *Feminist media studies.* Thousand Oaks, CA: Sage.

Wood, J. T. (2001). *Gendered lives: Communication, gender, and culture* (4th ed). Belmont, CA: Wadsworth.

Weaver-Lariscy, R. A., Sallot, L., & Cameron, G. T. (1996). Justice and gender: An instrumental and symbolic explication. *Journal of Public Relations Research, 8*, 107–121.

Wright, D. K., Grunig, L. A., Springston, J. K., & Toth, E. L. (1991). *Under the glass ceiling: An analysis of gender issues in American public relations.* New York: PRSA Foundation.

Wrigley, B. J. (2002). Glass ceiling? What glass ceiling? A qualitative study of how women view the glass ceiling in public relations and communications management. *Journal of Public Relations Research, 14*, 27–55.

Zerbinos, E., & Clanton, G. A. (1993). Minority practitioners: Career influences, job satisfaction, and discrimination. *Public Relations Review, 19*, 75–91.

Chapter 20

For Reputation's Sake: Managing Crisis Communication

Linda M. Hagan
Michigan State University

Product tampering, workplace shootings, management fraud, earthquakes and hurricanes, product recalls, terrorism—the list goes on of crises that challenged the survival, and in some cases the actual existence, of organizations at the outset of the new millennium. The bizarre, the unthinkable, the unlikely, the unexpected, and the unimaginable can bring day-to-day operations to a standstill and cause growth strategies and fiscal plans thrown out. The only certainty is that no organization is immune; every organization is vulnerable to crises. As such, one would think that crisis management would be an ongoing management process in organizations, yet the role of process owner many times remains unnamed.

At the beginning of the 21st Century, there has been a proliferation of books, articles, videos, and Web sites covering case studies on organizational crises and "how to" guides on crisis management. Crisis experts, government agencies, and the Public Relations Society of America (PRSA) offer tips and techniques on crisis management, with PRSA and public relations consultants holding training seminars and workshops around the country. In recent years, many public relations professionals and public relations firms began actively offering lucrative counsel as "crisis communication experts." It seems a natural match—public relations as crisis manager. Corporate executives might say, "Who better to face the scrutiny of the media in times of crisis than the media expert?" However, crisis management means more than media relations, and media relations is only a fraction of what public relations managers should be doing. Although this chapter provides a review of recent studies on crisis communication from a public relations theory building perspective, along with an overview of crisis management tips, it also looks more closely at the role of public relations in strategically planning for crisis communication—a perspective involving assessment and ongoing relationship management with relevant publics. In this chapter, one case in particular is examined. This case involved a safety recall in the automotive industry—the Audi 5000 model during the late 1980s—and its damage to corporate reputation in the aftermath of the recall. This case offers a practical perspective, suggesting a normative theory that the ongoing practice of excellent public relations and the cultivation of relationships with key constituents can favorably affect an organization's reputation and help lessen the negative consequences associated with crises.

DEFINING CRISIS

What is organization crisis? Crisis, by definition, can mean a predicament, emergency, calamity, disaster, or catastrophe. Crisis management expert Kathleen Fearn-Banks, in her book titled *Crisis Communications* (2002), said a crisis is anything that "interrupts the normal flow of business" (p. 2). Although businesspeople, especially public relations professionals, claim every day that they face crises, Fern-Banks stressed that a crisis impacts normal business activity and can even "sometimes threaten the existence of the organization" (p. 2). Fern-Banks enumerated 43 common crises that can affect any size of organization, ranging from fire, floods, and hurricanes to acquisitions, embezzlement, product failures, and workplace violence.

Crisis researcher Otto Lerbinger (1997) classified seven types of organizational crises:

1. *Natural crises*, including crises of the physical world or acts of God, such as tornados, hurricanes, and earthquakes.
2. *Technological crises*, such as the Union Carbide chemical tragedy in Bhopal, India; the world's worst nuclear power plant disaster in Chernobyl, in the former U.S.S.R.; or the U.S. *Challenger* explosion.
3. *Confrontation crises*, involving confrontation, for instance, between organizations and activist publics.
4. *Crises of malevolence*, such as malicious acts and terrorism.
5. *Crises of skewed management failure*.
6. *Crises of deception*.
7. *Crises of management misconduct*.

The U.S. Federal Emergency Management Agency (FEMA) offers on its Web site a systematic guide detailing how business and industry can manage emergencies. In the guide, FEMA classified an emergency as "any unplanned event that can cause deaths or significant injuries to employees, customers or the public; or that can shut down your business, disrupt operations, cause physical or environmental damage, or threaten the facility's financial standing or public image" (p. 5). According to the Institute for Crisis Management (2000), "no warning" or sudden crises such as industrial accidents, oil spills, and bizarre crimes of terrorism are the minority of crises that organizations face. The Institute's findings of business crises since 1990 indicated that the majority of organizational crises are actually "smoldering crises" where management knows about them, or should, before they blow up into a full-blown crisis. Interestingly, the Institute for Crisis Management (2000) Web site noted that "the most newsworthy business crises are the results of management decisions, actions, or inaction."

Results of the Excellence Study (J. Grunig, 1992b) indicated that there are crises that are beyond anyone's control and are "normal accidents." The IABC (International Association of Busi8ness Communicators) Excellence Study researchers, however, determined that many crises are the result of poor relationships with the organization's constituents, and more specifically, poor relationships or lack of relationships with activists (Grunig, Grunig, & Dozier, 2002). The excellence findings indicate how good crisis communication adds value to the role of public relations in the organization.

PUBLIC RELATIONS' VALUE LINKED TO CRISES

Only in recent years have public relations scholars started to research crisis communication from a public relations and reputation management perspective, with mostly case studies offering more of a prescriptive approach to handling postcrisis situations rather than theory. As recently as the 1992 publication of the first Excellence Study book (J. Grunig, 1992b), which was a comprehensive literature review of theory and public relations research, only one entry on "crisis communication" appeared in the index, and in a discussion on conflict and the importance of the issues management process. According to J. Grunig (1992a):

> When conflict occurs, publics "make an issue" out of the problem. Organizations use the process of *issues management* to anticipate issues and resolve conflict before the public makes it an issue. Organizations that wait for issues to occur before managing their communication with strategic publics usually have crises on their hands and have to resort to short-term *crisis communication*. (p. 13)

The two-decade landmark research project on public relations and communication management—led by a team of researchers including James E. Grunig, Larissa A. Grunig, and David M. Dozier—did link public relations' value to crises. At the outset of the project, the excellence researchers set out to study communication, and "how, why, and to what extent" it affects how organizations meet their objectives (Grunig et al., 2002, p. ix). The result extended public relations theory, and more specifically a theory of public relations excellence, but had not looked directly at crisis communication. Yet, according to Dozier, Grunig, and Grunig (1995), in the follow-up book to the excellence study that summarized the research data, crisis management is "one of the effects of excellent communication" (p. 233). This mention of crisis management came under the subheading of the "Softer Benefits of Communication Excellence," although results of the excellence survey found:

> CEOs and communicators mentioned crises again and again as catalysts for changes in management's views of communication; the Bhopal tragedy, the Exxon *Valdez* oil spill, the oil embargo of the 1970s, and activist opposition to nuclear power plants are examples. These events served as wake-up calls to senior managers who previously placed little importance on public relations and communication management. (Dozier et al., 1995, p. 103)

L. Grunig (1992), as one focus in the Excellence Study, extensively examined activism and how the presence of activist groups can create turbulent environments for organizations that, in turn, negatively affect the organization's effectiveness. Grunig concluded that although her research showed no "radical departure from what textbooks recommend for effective practice of public relations" it did support the idea that organizations must be proactive in their dealings with various constituents, and the two-way symmetrical model of public relations, even if it "turns out to be no panacea," holds promise for organizations (p. 528). Based on their continuing research in the Excellence Study, Grunig et al. (2002), cited "environmental turbulence as the catalyst for pushing public relations and communications management to center stage" (p. 434).

CRISIS AS A PR PROBLEM

Unfortunately, public relations may not always be ready to be under the spotlight when pushed to center stage. In a study on automotive recalls, Hagan (2003) found public relations practitioners often forced to handle organizational crises, despite their absence from senior decision-making activity precrisis. Interestingly, Hagan observed that media focus and intensity seemed to shift the crisis from a management issue to a "PR problem." With advancements in technology, a crisis can become a "global PR nightmare" as media scrutiny and coverage can traverse message channels in seconds. The way an organization's spokesperson handles communication during those first few hours and in subsequent days can alter the future of the organization, the management team, and the individual public relations practitioner. For example, soon after the prime-time, investigative news show *60 Minutes* aired features on product recalls at Audi of America and Ford Motor Company, there was a shift in both organizations' top executives and public relations leaders (Hagan, 2003).

External publics form perceptions of organizations through mediated communications. In times of organizational turbulence, an adage to remember is "perception is reality" (Barton, 1994). Crisis consultant Buckley (personal communication, 1998) said external audiences perceive big businesses almost immediately as guilty, and that the court of public opinion is costlier than the court of law. In postcrisis analysis, if perceived outcome (as determined by internal and external publics) is negative for the organization, the blame is on "bad PR," whereas credit goes to other management functions when the outcome is favorable.

PUBLIC RELATIONS AND REPUTATION

Ford Motor Company was notorious for recall actions in 2000/2001, receiving widespread, international media coverage for the recalls of 13.3 million Bridgestone/Firestone tires and 500,000 SUVs (Shreve, 2001). After months of international media scrutiny, in early 2002, in the midst of environmental turbulence, Ford Motor Company announced the need for plant closing, layoffs, changes in management, and a massive restructuring as its sales, income, and stock prices dropped dramatically. Direct and indirect costs of the conflict totaled an estimated $10 billion (Butters, 2002). The media suggested that this was the outcome of the perceived poor handling of the Ford Bridgestone/Firestone tire and SUV situations (Alsop, 2001; Butters, 2002; Child, 2001; Connelly, 2001; Dixon, 2002). One automotive journalist reported on the Ford situation as the company's "nastiest public relations black eye" (Ulrich, 2000, p. 1). To some public relations professionals and corporate executives, there is a distinct correlation between the role of public relations and reputation, especially in times of organizational crisis; others perceive the public relations function as having little impact on reputation.

In *Fortune* magazine's annual ranking of "America's Most Admired Companies," Ford Motor Company fell from the first-place spot in 1998 and 1999 in the Motor Vehicle Industry List to ninth place in 2003 ("Motor Vehicles Industry Snapshot," 2003). Since 1982, *Fortune* magazine has surveyed more than 10,000 executives, directors, and securities analysts annually (Sung & Tkaczyk, 2002) to rank U.S. companies in 55 different industry lists on their corporate reputation. The attributes used to measure organizational effectiveness in the survey were innovativeness; ability to attract, develop, and keep talented people; quality of management; quality of products/services; value as a long-term investment; financial soundness; social responsibility; and use of corporate assets. Companies garnering the most praise based on their performance in the eight attribute categories rank as "America's most admired companies." Interestingly in 1997, *Fortune* cited the key factor contributing to the lowest or *least-admired* ranking (#431 out of 431) in the reputation survey was an airline company's "PR meltdown" during a crisis (Robinson, 1997, p. 69). The magazine, however, did not mention public relations as a criterion contributing to the success of the most admirable of companies.

Public relations textbooks (Baskin, Aronoff, & Lattimore, 1997; Cutlip, Center, & Broom, 2000; Hunt & Grunig, 1994; Seitel, 1998; Wilcox, Ault, & Agee, 1998) have cited the high-profile Tylenol crisis case numerous times as an example of effective public relations. By contrast, at a major business college, a university professor addressing M.B.A. and other graduate students in a course on implementing strategic management directly pointed to Johnson & Johnson's corporate mission statement (i.e., Johnson & Johnson's credo) and internal processes as to why the company survived the 1982 Tylenol tampering crisis.[1] During the discussion, no mention, nor link, was made to public relations. Business schools tend to exclude public relations from discussion and management training curriculums. That trend may soon change as many CEOs and business school deans recognize the need to add crisis communication and reputation management to M.B.A. training (Alsop, 2005).

WHAT IS PUBLIC RELATIONS' ROLE?

Grunig and Hunt (1984) defined public relations as "the management of communication between an organization and its publics" (p. 6). Cutlip et al. (2000) defined public relations as "the management function that establishes and maintains mutually beneficial relationships between an organization and the publics on whom its success or failure depends" (p. 6). Both definitions suggest a management role, even though some people view public relations as solely a technical function (Dozier et al., 1995) whereby the public relations department handles such functions as media relations, product publicity, community affairs, and employee communications. Some organizations subjugate public relations under another department, such as marketing. In those organizations, public

---

[1]This latter point was covered extensively by Professor W. Stefan in a 1997 course he taught at the University of Maryland.

relations serves as a support staff for sales and marketing primarily to get "free advertising" for products and services through media publicity activities. Public relations may also act as the support staff for the legal department to defend the company in the court of public opinion by putting the "right spin" on stories or "just getting the facts out" to the media.

Hagan (2003) noted that the public relations management function has long played a significant role at automotive companies. Henry Ford was said to be a believer in the importance of public relations. Automotive companies have long had public relations representatives as members of a core team of corporate management. In Hagan's study (2003) on automotive recalls, a public relations consultant said that there is an understanding of the importance of public relations. According to the consultant:

> Public relations does have a great standing in the automotive industry. The automotive industry does get it. Mainly because it's an industry that faces so many challenges. It's among the most regulated of all the industries. It has a crisis each day. It has new products all the time. It has a retail base out there that is not owned by the corporation. It impacts the daily lives of everyone. (p. 211)

As such, the automotive industry, especially smaller companies, may view the role of public relations as media relations. Grunig and Repper (1992) wrote that the "conventional wisdom" of many public relations practitioners and CEOs considers public relations as media relations alone (p. 127). However, Hagan (2003) found in the automotive industry that there appears to be an appreciation for effective communication. For example, communication with publics other than the media may fall under an umbrella of corporate communications or within the departments of dealer relations, employee relations or human resources, government relations, legal or the office of the general counsel, factory relations, customer relations or the customer service/service department, manufacturer relations with the parent company, and investor relations. To develop and maintain good relationships with the publics of the organization, the Excellence Theory maintains that communication activities must be coordinated and orchestrated, ideally through one function—the public relations department. Hagan (2003) asserted that the role of public relations within an organization and its strategic management function affect its response capabilities when faced with a crisis and the organization's ability to recover from the crisis.

Over the years scholars, students, and practitioners have continued to conduct research on the Excellence Theory, contributing and strengthening the theoretical foundation that public relations, as a strategic management function, adds value to organizations.

APPLYING KNOWLEDGE LEARNED FROM THE EXCELLENCE STUDY

As mentioned in previous chapters, the Excellence Theory of public relations (Dozier et al., 1995; J. Grunig, 1992b), and the more recent research on the Excellence Theory done by Grunig et al. (2002) and discussed in the book *Excellent Public Relations and Effective Organizations*, conceptualized excellent public relations. The Excellence Study showed that public relations practiced "excellently" can have a positive impact in handling the communications for an organization faced with a crisis. At the core, however, was the notion that in order for public relations to be effective in handling crises, public relations had to have a strategic role within the organization and maintain some of the key principles of good practice.

The findings from the Excellence Study in public relations and communication management showed 10 generic principles found in organizations with excellent practices:

1. The involvement of public relations in strategic communication.
2. The empowerment of public relations in the dominant coalition or a direct reporting relationship to senior management.
3. An integrated public relations function.
4. Public relations as a management function separate from other functions.
5. The public relations unit headed by a manager rather than a technician.
6. The two-way symmetrical or mixed-motive model of public relations in practice.
7. A symmetrical system of internal communication.
8. The knowledge in the department needed to practice the managerial role and symmetrical public relations.
9. Diversity embodied in all public relations practitioner roles.
10. A strong sense of ethics and social responsibility.

Based on these principles, more recently Grunig et al. (2002) list five keywords to describe Excellence Theory: *managerial, strategic, symmetrical, diverse,* and *ethical.* That is, public relations contributes best to organizations when practiced excellently, in which it is managerial, strategic, symmetric, diverse, and ethical.

PUBLIC RELATIONS AND RELATIONSHIPS

Recently, the continued work by some of the original Excellence Study team (Grunig et al., 2002) focused on the value of public relations and the link to relationships. The researchers said, "[T]he value of public relations comes from the relationships that communicators develop and maintain with publics" and "[R]eputation is a product of relationships and that the quality of relationships and reputation result more from the behavior of the organization than from the messages that communicators disseminate" (Grunig et al., 2002, p. xi).

Unarguably, the Excellence Study in the early years focused on the importance of the two-way symmetrical model of communication, and compared and contrasted public relations effectiveness examining an organization's model of communication. In 1984, Grunig and Hunt introduced four models of practice for public relations in their book *Managing Public Relations*. The models, especially the Excellence Study's call for the two-way symmetrical model, underwent intense scrutiny and criticism by scholars who wanted to dispel the prominence of the theory as being misguided. Later Grunig et al. (2002) further clarified the models, adopting Murphy's (1991) mixed-model continuum. Despite the criticisms, the models of public relations continue to remain a reality of practice and worthy of explanation, especially in a discussion of crisis communication.

DIFFERENT MODELS FOR HANDLING CRISIS

1. *Press agentry/publicity model:* In this model,. public relations practitioners—sometimes referred to as "PR flaks," "press agents," "event planners," and "publicists"—try to get attention for their organization any way they can. In 2005, a hit reality TV show on MTV titled *PoweR Girls* glamorized the work of PR flaks at Lizzie Grubman's New York City PR agency. Commonly, the fashion, sports, and entertainment industries practice the press agentry/publicity model, following the notion that any publicity, even bad news, is good publicity. When it comes to crises, publicists may even take an optimistic view, seeing them as opportunities to get their organization's name in the media. Press agents may tantalize tabloid news outlets, Web blogs, and even mainstream media with "bad news" stories on celebrity drug convictions, divorces, scandals, and sordid affairs in order to get coverage for their clients. Managing the crisis indeed becomes managing the reputation.

2. *Public information model:* This model finds practitioners as "journalists-in-residence," distributing accurate and positive information about the organization. Government agencies and educational institutions use the title of PIO, or public information officer, to identify public relations practitioners. In crises, public information officers work with management and emergency personnel, issuing "official" statements of the organization and informing the media, employees, customers, community members, and other key publics

about the situation. The role of public relations becomes the task of getting the word out, with the understanding that if the organization fails to tell its side of the story, others will do it for them, in many cases in a manner that is damaging to the organization's reputation.

3. *Two-way asymmetrical model:* In some ways, this model is similar to developing traditional advertising messages. Practitioners "use research to develop messages that are most likely to persuade strategic publics to behave as the organization wants" (J. Grunig, 1992a, p. 18). Grunig and Hunt (1984) called this "scientific persuasion." In crisis times, practitioners might utilize public opinion research such as polling, focus groups, and Internet surveys to gauge reactions and craft messages to influence public opinion and change perceptions. Planting crafted messages that the publics want to hear—or, in some extreme cases, leaking stories with the intent of discrediting the accusers—may be planned strategies. Following this model, public relations may be criticized as "spin doctoring" with the intent of altering public perceptions in times of crisis. The message, or words, rather than the organization's actions, are of most importance.

4. *Two-way symmetrical model:* This model is similar to the asymmetric model in that it is management focused rather than emphasizing the technical craft of public relations. It, too, is based on research and "uses communication to manage conflict and improve understanding with strategic publics" (J. Grunig, 1992a, p. 18). The focus in the two-way symmetrical model, then, is balanced communication—a give-and-take relationship—between an organization and its publics. In times of crisis, an organization would not only attempt to "say the right thing," but "do the right thing" as well. According to work by Grunig et al. (2002), the researchers refined the symmetrical model to alleviate criticism and confusion that some in public relations had relating to the idea of accommodation. It was not J. Grunig's intention to have the symmetrical model thought of as having either the organization or the public accommodating the other or the giving up of one's own interest. Instead, some people believed that it should be a goal to reach an acceptable "win-win" dynamic for both. Grunig et al. (2002) stated, "The essence of the symmetrical model is that *both* the organization and a public must be willing to accommodate the interests of the other" (p. 315).

5. *The mixed-motive model:* For this model, Grunig et al. (2002) adopted Murphy's (1991) mixed-motive continuum in which one end signifies the dominant coalition's position and the other end the public's position. In the middle of the continuum, both parties reach symmetry in the acceptable "win-win" zone. The opposite ends of the continuum are considered asymmetric zones, representing where the

organization's position dominates or the public's position dominates. During normal activity, practitioners would have an understanding of the organization's publics making it easier to communicate to them openly, honestly, and appropriately when faced with a crisis. During a crisis, public relations departments serve as advocates for the organization as well as for the strategic publics. The dimensions of the mixed-motive model, thus, match that of the symmetrical model. In the third excellence book, the researchers described the two-way symmetrical model as representing both models.

Despite the evolution of public relations, the models still may describe practice. Yet, Grunig et al. (2002) considered it more appropriate that "excellent public relations is research based (two-way), symmetrical (although organizations constantly struggle between symmetry and asymmetry when they make decisions), and based on either mediated or interpersonal communication (depending on the situation and public)" (p. 378).

Public relations in the two-way symmetrical model takes on the role of the "eyes and ears" of the organization, channeling outside perspectives, gathered through systematic research, in with the possibility of changing the organization's behaviors, while channeling out internal perspectives with the possibility of changing publics' attitudes, opinions, and behaviors. In practice, especially in crisis communication, the challenge may be that public relations must at times present contrary views of external publics to a management this is sometimes unwilling to hear and accept them. For this reason, Grunig et al. (2002) indicated that public relations, when practiced based on symmetrical values, adds both diverse perspectives and ethical considerations into organizational decisions and behavior—essential considerations for effective crisis management.

EXPERTISE NEEDED FOR HANDLING CRISIS COMMUNICATION

Crisis case studies and the Excellence Study data indicate public relations practitioners need the "communication expertise to help dominant coalitions manage the environmental challenge" (Grunig et al., 2002, p. 434). In times of crisis, CEOs and senior managers look for a fast "PR fix" and look to public relations professionals as having the expertise to handle crises. Before a crisis, public relations managers may not have an active role in the process of strategic development, but in times of crisis, public relations practitioners typically get the urgent call by senior management "to deal with the crisis" and its aftermath, especially the responsibility of "dealing with" the media. The image becomes one of public relations practitioners as firefighters, coming to the aid of the burning organization and dousing out the flames spurred on by the heat of intense media coverage.

When faced with crisis, sometimes organizations must endure a "trial by the media" (Lerbinger, 1997). One seasoned public relations professional said, "Perverse as it is, media love crises. They make for great TV and they sell newspapers" (McDonald, 2005); yet, in practice, few can truly be prepared for the "onslaught of media coverage" (Hagan, 2003, p. 134) that follows an organizational crisis. As one public relations practitioner faced with a crisis commented, "We were flying by the seat of our pants a lot of the times too, because we had never been exposed to this type of communication crisis" (Hagan, 2003, p. 134).

In reality, public relations professionals may not always be able to put out the fire, but "effective public relations at least can mitigate the damage to the organization" (Grunig et al., 2002, p. 473). For this reason, in recent years there has been a focus on crisis communication training. The Public Relations Society of America (PRSA), for instance, recommends that undergraduate and graduate public relations education include case studies on crisis management strategy and skills training as part of the curriculum. One such case study in the automotive industry concerns the communication of product recalls.

THE CRISIS OF SAFETY-RELATED RECALLS IN THE AUTOMOTIVE INDUSTRY

Product recalls prevail in nearly every industry for a number of safety and performance reasons. The multibillion-dollar automotive industry is the largest global industry in terms of production, sales, revenues, and employment. Although automotive manufacturers make an effort to sell a quality vehicle, product problems occur. In 2004, U.S. automakers recalled a record number 30.6 million cars and trucks (Plungis, 2005), more vehicles than were sold in the country that same year. In the United States, manufacturers recall millions of cars every year to correct safety-related defects for numerous reasons, ranging from faulty windshield wipers to fuel system defects that cause vehicle fires, steering components that cause partial or sudden loss of control, improperly designed or constructed tires that shred or blow out unexpectedly, accelerator controls that stick, air bags that cannot deploy, and passenger restraint systems that cause unreasonable risk or injury (NHTSA, 1998). According to the National Highway Traffic Safety Administration (NHTSA) of the U.S. Department of Transportation (DOT), there are nearly 42,000 lives lost in traffic crashes on the nation's highways every year. It estimated that vehicle crashes cost society more than $150 billion annually in economic loss in terms of medical costs, insurance costs, worker productivity, and so forth (NHTSA, 2005).

The investment one makes in the vehicle (e.g., an average price of approximately $23,000) compounded with the severity of injury or loss of life because of accidents involving the vehicles have a profound effect on society. Just as in other industries, the human toll of safety-related defects in products can be tragic. The costs to manufacturers for safety-related recalls in terms of direct repair and labor costs are great, along with exorbitant expenses associated with research and development, engineering, defending lawsuits, and in litigation, as well as incalculable losses in productivity, employment costs, shareholder value, future sales, and reputation. In the automotive industry, in theory, product quality and the organization–public relationships together directly influence the organization's reputation. Poor product quality, as determined by the number of recalls or repair visits to the dealer, and negative relationships with the organization's constituents as determined by poor customer or dealer satisfaction indicators, together contribute to a manufacturer's unfavorable reputation. Likewise, good product quality and positive organization–public relationships help the organization build and maintain favorable reputation, or at least neutralize or minimize the negative effects on reputation. Product quality satisfaction in automobiles, it is important to note, also includes the price, styling, engineering, and performance of the vehicles as integral factors.

THE AUDI 5000 CASE

Hagan (2003) conducted a case study on the safety-related questions and recalls of the Audi 5000 vehicle during the late 1980s. Employing a triangulation of methods, she conducted qualitative interviews with 18 executives, senior managers, franchised dealers, and journalists; an examination of more than 100 archival documents and 600 newspaper articles and media transcripts; a review of existing data; and an autoethnographic approach that focused on the organization's communication, actions, and relationships with constituents. The study focused on an automotive company's crisis involving the Audi 5000 vehicle, a top-selling, high-line, German-made vehicle noted for its "art of engineering," which sold in the United States from 1978 until the late 1990s (Hagan, 2003). The international automotive and mainstream press praised the Audi 5000 and awarded the vehicle with coveted accolades as being one of the best cars in its class. In the United States, Audi sales reached 74,061 in

1985, but by 1991 had plummeted to a record low of 12,283 units. Rumors had the company considering leaving the U.S. market.

What happened in those few years was a situation that began with a few disgruntled Audi 5000 owners in New York, Audi's largest market accounting for 20% of national sales, who became frustrated with their vehicle problems and angered by the company's response. The customers networked (despite not having the computer technology of today), formed a formidable activist group called the "Audi Victims Network," and connected with some highly media-savvy consumer interest groups. The groups contacted and received the support of the New York attorney general, who called a press conference raising questions about the safety of the Audi 5000 model and urged the U.S. Transportation Department to investigate. Eventually, the story made its way onto the popular CBS primetime news program *60 Minutes*, with a 17-minute segment on the Audi 5000 model and "unintended acceleration." The show's commentator talked about cars "rocketing" out of control, resulting in deaths and severe injuries. Continually through the broadcast, the commentator said that Audi blamed the drivers for the accidents, and used the phrase "driver error" as the company's only explanation as to why there were more incidents in Audis, because the company could find nothing wrong with the vehicles. Audi managers later admitted they regretted the phraseology of "driver error" as a plausible reason. Noteworthy, during the same time many other automakers also were under investigation for similar incidences of sudden or unexpected acceleration but they received little mention by the press.

Overnight, it was Audi at the center of nationwide attention in the auto industry. Some parking garages in New York City and other cities even began banning Audi vehicles from parking in them. Some newspaper editorial cartoons and comedians made jokes of Audi and its excuse of driver error. Audi in the United States and in Germany conducted exhaustive research in laboratory and actual driving simulations trying to replicate "unintended acceleration." It was unexplainable. Audi products were not experiencing unintended acceleration anywhere else in the world where Audi sold the model. The media quoted several different company public relations managers during the height of media attention (1986–1989), remarking that "driver error," "pedal misapplication," "driver unfamiliarity with the vehicle," and even height of drivers ("short women") caused the unintended acceleration. The company insisted there was nothing wrong with the cars. Media coverage scarcely quoted top officials, such as the chief executive, although during the 16-month period, four chief executives for Audi in the United States transitioned through the corner office.

EXONERATED, YET DAMAGE IS DONE

Three years later, however, NHTSA fully and completely exonerated the Audi 5000 model from having any defects and the company from any wrongdoing and closed the case, citing that there was no indication that the product was faulty from a lack of engineering or manufacturing. On July 13, 1989, Volkswagen of America, Audi's parent company in the United States, called a news conference to announce the closure of the federal unintended acceleration probe of the Audi 5000S. Only a few brief articles of Audi's exoneration appeared in the papers. Audi's reputation suffered and sales crashed. There were whispers within the automotive industry that the continual loss of sales and increasing costs of litigation might force Audi AG to withdraw from the U.S. market. The company continued to fight the battle in courts of law and in the court of public opinion. Litigation expenses—combined with loss of revenues, dealers, employees, and reputation—put the company near the edge of retreat. Some industry insiders ventured to say it cost the company *billions* of dollars over the years in terms of lost sales and market share, marketing costs, and litigation expenses (Hagan, 2003).

Despite the vindication, the company stopped manufacturing the Audi 5000 model. As one automotive writer noted, "Even when the facts later exonerated the vehicles, as with the Corvair and the Audi's acceleration allegation, the damage had been done" (Ulrich, 2000, p. 1).

Just as public relations academicians acknowledge the Tylenol case as an example of effective public relations, within the automotive industry (but before the Ford Firestone recall) the handling of the safety-related investigation of the Audi 5000 model is, to some, an example of ineffective public relations (Crain, 1995; Jedlicka, 2002; Ulrich, 2000). For example, one automotive writer (Ulrich, 2000) lumped together "Tylenol's product-tampering case. Audi and unintended acceleration. The Exxon *Valdez* disaster. And now, Ford Motor Company and its suspect Firestone tires" (p. 1) as high-profile corporate crises.

FINDINGS FROM THE AUDI UNINTENDED ACCELERATION CASE ON CRISIS AND REPUTATION

Hagan (2003) discerned a direct link between how an organization responds to crisis with its formed reputation. In her study, a few participants indicated that it takes a crisis or other event that gets attention for a reputation to be favorable or unfavorable. Hagan's findings indicated that relationships with the organization's constituents share an almost equal influence with product quality and company behavior. Public relations scholars (Grunig & Huang, 2000; Grunig & Hung, 2002) have suggested that reputation is a product of the behavioral relationship between and organization and its publics, noting that behavior had the strongest effect on relationships. Hagan's study (2003) furthered that theory into a normative practice and determined that public relations is a highly influential factor, although it is one of many factors that influence reputation. Interestingly, Hagan's research found evidence that reputation is formed from cognitive behaviors (Grunig & Huang, 2000), but noted that an emotional component played a factor in how publics assign reputation. As one research participant remarked, "Reputation? There, again, it's back to rational and emotional and the two of those coming together to create the reputation" (p. 225).

In her study on the automotive industry, Hagan (2003) discovered that there could be different reputations assigned to company, brands, products, dealers, and individuals (i.e., company executives or public relations people). Specifically in the handling of service actions and recalls—essentially, crises for an automotive manufacturer—the organization's actions, product satisfaction, service satisfaction, and relationships (all of which are weighed as actual and perceived behaviors) can affect favorable or unfavorable reputation. Cognitive and emotive components are the basis of corporate reputation formation, with emotion playing a larger role than one might expect. In the automotive industry, when a product fails, publics expect the company to do the right thing, fix the problem quickly, and demonstrate humanness with sincere compassion for constituents (Hagan, 2003).

Data from Hagan's study (2003) reflected that the role of public relations was a factor in influencing the relationships the organization had with constituents, who then assigned a reputation to the company based on that relationship. Grunig and Hung (2002) identified the relationships a person may have directly with an organization and relationships a person may have indirectly or secondhand with an organization as *experiential* versus *reputational*. Experiential relationships are based on what people experience themselves, firsthand with the organization; for example, as an owner and primary driver of an automobile. Hagan retermed reputational relationships as *mediated* relationships because these types of relationships are affected by what people read or hear through mediated channels such as via the media, in advertising, or through word-of-mouth. For example, in times of crisis in the automotive industry, particularly the Audi crisis, the mediated relationships have a significant influence on the reputation of the company and can then affect experiential relationships. According to one participant:

> [In the Audi situation] when you have a bombardment of any kind of media, whether it's a bombardment of good media or it's a bombardment of

bad media, it does, in fact have a significant impact on your ability to have experiential communication. If you are not a brand that is a top of mind brand … [b]ombardments of good publicity and bad publicity can accelerate your opportunity to have experiences. There is no question about that. What has been amazing to me has been the passion with which people who have had good experience with the brands have defended their position of the brand in the face of ridiculous negative media. (Hagan, 2003, pp. 227–228)

Results showed that unfavorable mediated relationships can greatly affect a company's reputation; over time, however, through positive experiences with quality products, service, and relationships, a company can rebuild a positive reputation.

Another participant said emphatically that public relations can influence a reputation.: "It absolutely can. But, public relations can only help to reveal the true nature of the company. Unlike advertising, the public relations is hard to fake" (Hagan, 2003, p. 228). In the Audi 5000 situation, some research study participants commented that people started to believe what they were hearing from the media because the company was not saying anything. The opposite can happen as well. According to the participants in the same study, if people see that the company is trying to do the right thing, there can be a positive "ripple effect."

Public relations should be actively involved (not only having a seat at the decision-making table, but a voice as well) in the decision-making process relating to investigations and potential crises. Excellent public relations can influence the reputation of the organization by recommending actions the company should take. Those actions should include be open, be honest, be responsive, be reliable, "do the right thing," be rational, be emotional, conduct research, be strategic, promote diversity, and take responsibility. For example, when a product fails, customers expect the manufacturer to fix it and make it right. Executives typically weigh their decisions based on "hard" factors such as economic, legal, technical, logistical, and timing concerns. Therefore, too, they need to base decisions on "soft factors" or human factors involving emotion as well. When a product has defects, especially something safety related, a company must act quickly and responsibly. It is public relations' role to communicate those actions to publics and maintain relationships with them.

THE NEED TO KNOW YOUR ORGANIZATION'S PUBLICS

Organizations perhaps need to adopt a relational approach (Coombs, 2000) to crisis management. After all, as retired public relations profes-

sor James Grunig told his students, "We're in the public *relations* business," and that means we need to understand relationships. Ledingham
(2003) suggested a relationship management theory of public relations
with an axiom that "the proper focus of the domain of public relations is
relationships, not communication" (p. 195). Organizations exist in society because of the interdependent relationships (Coombs, 2000;
Ledingham & Bruning, 2000) they have with individuals and different
groups of people. Organizational crises can put stress on the people, and
thus can strain organization–public relationships. Organizational
publics (sometimes also referred to as *stakeholders*, *constituents*, or *target audiences* in public relations literature and practice) include present
employees, retired and former employees, shareholders or donors, customers or clients, media, government regulators, community members, vendors and suppliers, and the competition.

It is essential that organizations know who their publics are and address them appropriately throughout the relationship, but most importantly during a crisis (Barton, 1994; Coombs, 2000). For example,
according to Barton (1994), "[E]mployees can be your greatest resource
or hurt you in a crisis." With their personal stake and possible financial
risk (potential loss of pay), employees need the organization to survive.
Contrary to this, in cases of internal wrongdoing, employees who have
been privy to insider information may become whistleblowers or send
out mixed messages that can negatively affect the organization. Inevitably, every employee becomes a spokesperson for the organization,
whether by word-of-mouth through their circle of friends and family
or as a spokesperson in front of the camera. Consider the TV reporter
who stands outside the factory gate waiting for information about a disaster that ensued inside. As employees leave the scene, they are the ones
confronted by reporters for person-on-the-street-type interviews or
they freely go in front of the camera to offer their perspective. The key to
good crisis communication is understanding how the crisis has affected
all of the organization's relationships, and communicating responsively
and responsibly to those stakeholders.

Coombs (2000) examined stakeholder theory and "neoinstitution-
alism" (organizational legitimacy) and suggested that "relational history affects organization–public relationships when organizations face
crisis. According to Coombs, "[B]oth reputation and relational history
are built from past interactions between the organization and the stakeholder" (p. 76). Initial studies to determine the quality of relationships
(Grunig, Grunig, & Ehling, 1992; Huang, 1997) led Grunig and Huang
(2000) to determine that the four essential indicators of quality of organization–public relationships are trust, control mutuality, relational
commitment, and satisfaction in the relationship. The quality and ex-

tent of precrisis relationships with publics becomes an important factor in crisis management.

Situational Theory of Publics

Organizations should frequently conduct public relations audits to determine whom their key stakeholders are, how those stakeholders stand on various issues, and assess the quality of the relationship. Grunig (1997), developing his situational theory of publics over the past 30 years, identified three independent variables to segment people into active and passive publics. His theory stated that "publics are more likely to be active when the people who make them up perceive that what an organization does *involves them (level of involvement)*, that the consequences of what an organization does is a *problem (problem recognition)*, and that they are *not constrained* from doing something about the problem *(constraint recognition)*" (p. 28). Active publics should be the focus of public relations programs; in times of crisis, active publics should be the focus of communication. Active publics that are ignored soon can become activist publics and create more issues for the organization (Anderson, 1992: L. Grunig, 1992). More recently, Grunig and Hung (2002) found that low-involvement publics could develop reputational relationships with organizations based on negative reputations formed from sources like the media and others. Grunig and Repper (1992) suggested that public relations managers should rank publics by which is "most important—the most strategic" (p. 126) and plan communication programs with them. This should be a must-have element of a crisis communication plan.

Recent public relations studies and practitioners seem to agree on the importance of organizations developing and maintaining open and honest relationships with all of their key constituents. According to the Excellence Study (2002), two-way communication used by excellent organizations communicates to publics about what the organization is doing about both positive and negative situations. According to the researchers, "Openness seems to be the key to both short-term and long-term gains. Candor helps the organization survive the crisis" (Grunig et al., 2002, p. 459). Hagan (2003) identified factors that affect relationships such as honesty, integrity, trust, credibility, caring, listening, mutual respect, mutual understanding, satisfaction, stability, and commitment as expected by constituents, especially when the company faces an unfavorable situation. In times of crisis, open, and honest communication is essential.

CRISIS MANAGEMENT PLANS

When it comes to crisis, organizations need to be prepared. Corporate communications expert Thomas F. McDonald (2005) said, "Ignoring crisis communication planning is like driving without car insurance; for as long as you can get away with it, nobody's the wiser. But the moment disaster strikes, finding yourself woefully unprepared can really leave you in a very undesirable situation."

Public relations planning and management in the 21st century requires formal contingency planning for crises and disasters. Fearn-Banks (2002), along with other crisis experts (Barton, 1994; Caponigro, 1998), offered outlines of crisis management plans (CMPs) and crisis communication plans (CCPs). Experts recommend that writing crisis plans be a group effort, put together with input by a diverse team of managers representing core processes such as public relations, legal, human resources, finance, marketing, operations, and risk management. Although there is some recognition in industry that crisis plans are necessary, few companies take the time (or have the time) to formalize them. Every organization, no matter its size, needs a detailed CMP as a plan B or back-up plan "just in case" business is suddenly interrupted by crisis.

ASSESSING VULNERABILITIES

Crucial to the effectiveness of crisis management plans is the research that is involved in determining an organization's vulnerabilities. Organizations need to assess their vulnerability to crisis. Assessing the risk of crisis involves research that examines internal processes as well as all external influences that could alter the operations of the organization. For example, in the wake of the 9/11 terrorism assault, Wrigley, Salmon, and Park (2003) noted that 70% of Michigan's largest corporations had a crisis plan, but only few had a plan in place for a bioterrorism threat. In the video *Crisis Management: When Disaster Strikes*, Barton (1994) offered the analogy that "geologists learn geology, after the earthquake" when it is too late.

A crisis management plan should include an exhaustive list of every possible scenario of what could go wrong within the organization and in the world that could affect its daily business or possibility threaten the organization's survival. Barton (1994) suggested answering the question "What's the worst that could happen to us?" and drafting a plan of action. Fearn-Banks (2002) recommended that all organizations conduct a "crisis inventory," listing crises that the organization could face and ranking each crisis as far as level of potential damage to the organization.

ENVIRONMENTAL SCANNING RESEARCH AND ISSUES MANAGEMENT

Effective public relations practitioners use research methods to scan the internal and external environments of their organization, engaging in environmental scanning, to detect and anticipate potentially damaging situations. Environmental monitoring/scanning (Grunig & Repper, 1992) is a technique used in issues management (Bowen, 2000; J. Grunig, 1992b; Grunig & Repper, 1992) and is critical to public relations practice. Issues management is a method whereby organizations can detect and anticipate issues and conflict within their organization, or external to the organization in its industry, communities, or globally. The goal is to resolve conflict before the public makes it an issue. By conducting issues management both internally and externally, organizations can identify early warning signals, particularly potential crises involving skewed management practices or breakdowns in organizational processes.

Some methods to alert managers of internal issues include setting up internal chat groups to address rumors and gossip, making available and accessible employee suggestion boxes, conducting employee satisfaction surveys, or hiring a corporate ombudsperson. The Internet and sophisticated research methods allow communication managers "to get a pulse" of external environments quickly. Conducting research by scanning the media—such as "cybersurfing" Internet sites, Web blogs, and chat groups—are effective techniques used in issues management.

Effective communication managers can utilize issues management research as an early warning system for crisis. Organizations should constantly be on the lookout for crisis warning signs, anticipating emergencies and detecting organizational vulnerabilities. Fearn-Banks (2002) recommended having a "detection" strategy as the first of five stages of a crisis, followed by prevention/preparation, containment, recovery, and learning. Hagan (2003) commented that, in the automotive industry, the public relations function should be actively involved in environmental monitoring and issues management as an early warning system to management for issues involving key constituent groups such as employees, customers, dealers, regulatory agencies, unions, suppliers, media, consumer groups, activist organizations, competitors, and so forth.

CRISIS SIMULATION AND ROLE PLAYING

In preparation of crises, organizations should designate a crisis management team and conduct training activities, including mock crisis drills or crisis simulations (Barton, 1994; Caponigro, 1998;

Fearn-Banks, 2002). During these rehearsals, designated managers representing key departments such as legal, human resources, public relations, marketing, and operations role play how they would handle various "what if?" scenarios. What if there is a fire? What if a disgruntled employee becomes violent in the workplace? What if there has been some fraudulent activity approved by the management ranks? What if there is loss of human life? What if there is physical and/or structural damage to a facility? How will we communicate to our employees? Who will be the spokesperson to the media? What will we say to our customers and shareholders? What do we need to handle immediately? Whom can we call on for help? These are just a small number of the questions managers need to address.

Besides periodically conducting mock drills, Barton (1994) recommended that organizations put their crisis management plan in writing and include such details as home and cell phone numbers of senior managers, a media list, public relations background materials, and contact information for emergency personnel, insurance firms, and social workers. The Excellence Study (Grunig et al., 2002) found that organizations ranking in the top percentiles of excellence *managed* crises proactively. Yet, many anecdotal cases studies indicate reactive practices are more typical, especially in responding to the media and media inquiries.

The Public Relations Society of America and various articles and books on crisis management offer prescriptive strategies, citing many tips and techniques on how to handle the communication at the outset, during, and in the aftermath of crisis. Some of the PRSA (2005) tips for the first 24 hours postcrisis included:

- Try to bring the situation under control as quickly as possible. Remember, "protect people first and property second."
- Analyze and anticipate the situation's newsworthiness for media attention. (Some crises seem to be more newsworthy depending on what else is in the news at the time.)
- Conduct fact-finding. Get all the facts—who, what, where, when, why, how, what next—and stick to the facts in your messages. Do not speculate or offer personal perspectives.
- Activate your crisis management team and set up your crisis communication center, if necessary.
- Have your pre-appointed spokespeople (ideally your CEO or another senior manager) address the media. (Speak with the same message in all locations, nationally and internationally.)
- Be open, honest, and responsive.
- Never say, "No comment."
- Provide follow up information as necessary.

POSTCRISIS: RESOLUTION MEANS MENDING RELATIONSHIPS

Nurturing organization-public relationships should be an ongoing process, precrisis and postcrisis as well. In personal relationships, people tend to forgive friends easier than mere acquaintances and forgive those who offer contrition, realizing that people make mistakes and that it is human to err. In other instances, people are willing to move on once the wrongdoer has served time in some way or offered penance. Former American President Bill Clinton at first denied committing adultery while in office and instead offered in his defense that he was the victim of a "right-wing conspiracy." After his impeachment, Clinton publicly apologized and his public rating improved. A few years later, Clinton successfully continued his diplomatic and humanitarian efforts in America and internationally.

In their book *Guide to Media Relations* (2004), Schenkler and Herrling discussed various options for crisis response when communicating to the media. They diagrammed a continuum of mutual problem solving in which organizations may be proactive and choose to respond or reactive at which time they are forced to react. They can also respond in either an aggressive or passive manner. From an aggressive standpoint, organization responses can be "free to attack" or "forced to defend" and from a passive stance can be "free to avoid" or "forced to avoid" (p. 109). Schenkler and Herrling gave examples of message strategies for each.

Ware and Linkugel (1973) and Ihlen (2002) considered apologia from rhetorical literature as an appropriate response strategy in times of crisis. A literature review by Lyon and Cameron (2004) examined various crisis response strategies. Their experimental design study took a relational approach to examining the "interplay of prior reputation and immediate response to crisis" (p. 213) and suggested that "an apology after a crisis can help reinstate an organization back into the 'good graces' of its publics and restore supporting behavioral intentions" (Lyon & Cameron, 2004, p. 231). Findings by Lyon and Cameron (2004) indicated that publics view apologetic response strategies to crises more favorably than defensive strategies, even for organizations that had a poor reputation prior to the crisis. The data showed that publics are more likely to support and invest in an organization that uses accommodative response strategies, especially when it already has a favorable credibility with its constituents, based on its reputation of social responsibility. Lyon and Cameron, however, noted a need for further public relations research in the area of message testing in response to crisis. From a more practical perspective, Emmy-award-winning reporter Jeff Crilley (2003), in his book titled *Free Publicity*, advised that when handling negative news, "No jury award is as expensive as the damage you can do yourself by mishandling a crisis" (p.

77). He added, "Honesty really is the best policy. If you mess up, fess up. Apologize and move on" (p. 80).

In Hagan's (2003) study on automotive recalls, one participant discussed how a company should respond in this way:

> And, in the instance where you are facing lightening decisions, you've got to work with the best information you've got; so the guide to everybody, and I always say this, don't fail quietly. It's absolutely a sin to make, to get ourselves into this situation, we understand that; but it's a much graver sin if we don't put all the facts on the table. Own up. And, you know, people are far more forgiving than you ever, than you think. If you literally come along and say, "You know, we designed this thing and we never thought it would do...." Because people [who design and build the cars] don't do things wrong for a purpose and everybody makes mistakes. So we made it, we designed it, we never thought this set of circumstances would have happened and we screwed up. Everybody's going to say, "Well done for saying that." (p. 220)

Although American society tends to cheer for the underdog, wanting the phoenix to rise, it also can be harsh on people and organizations, especially ones whom public opinion views as not "doing the right thing." Organizations must not only say the right thing but also be doing the right actions. Ultimately, it is the organization's behavior (what it says and what it does) that influences the organization's relationships with its constituents and therefore its reputation. In Hagan (2003), study participants said they thought it takes a crisis, or some other event that gets attention, for an organization's reputation to be favorable or unfavorable. After intense public scrutiny, however, publics can at times forgive, forget, or just move onto the next breaking news story. In mid-2005, for instance, Martha Stewart signed a TV deal for a new show and Exxon oil, Ford Explorers, Audi vehicles, and Bridgestone/Firestone tires were still strong market competitors.

LEARNING FROM CRISES

The final step in crisis management involves learning from the crisis (Fearn-Banks, 2002). Evaluation encourages improvement and growth. Learning comes from assessing whether the organization handled the situation appropriately or mishandled aspects of it. This helps organizations prepare for the next crisis. Case study analysis of other organizational crises also can provide managers with essential tools to anticipate and proactively manage future crises.

ON TO THE NEW CENTURY—FUTURE RESEARCH DIRECTIONS

In the new century, public relations researchers and practitioners must continue to challenge theories and look to strategies to support organizational communication effectiveness. Future researchers should move away from case analysis and explanatory studies offering prescriptions to utilizing quantitative methodology for theory building. If public relations is to become the process owner of crisis communication, then practitioners must speak the language of executives in a convincing manner, which typically must include quantitative arguments more than qualitative data.

Studies have suggested that there is a link among public relations, crisis communication, relationships, and reputation, but there needs to be further examination to determine how much of a link there is. Future research needs to explore whether or not organizations may be perceived as more socially responsible if crises are addressed via symmetrically managed communications with all the organization's publics.

Future research might look at the notion of emotion in times of crisis. Hagan's study (2003) found that publics assign a corporate reputation based on what they experience (actual experiences with the organization) and what is perceived (mediated relationships). Much of what is experienced, especially pre-, during, and postcrisis, involves a high degree of emotion along with cognitive thinking. The concept of emotion offers an interesting perspective on company behavior and actions. Organizations must show emotion and that they care and want to do the right thing. Additional research should determine how a company could show that it cares. Along these lines, additional research is needed on mediated relationships. Proponents of integrated marketing communications may find fruitfulness in testing the impact that advertising messages along with public relations strategies have on restoring organization reputation postcrisis. What carries the most weight in mediated relationships when it comes to restoring or building reputation? Is it public relations activities, advertising, or word-of-mouth?

Because many crises are smoldering more than conflagrant, more research needs to explore ways to make issues management more effective as an early-warning system for organizations. Which function of the organization is best to serve in that role and monitor the internal and external environment? As Lyon and Cameron (2004) suggested, much more research needs to be done on response strategies and message testing. When, and how, is it best to respond to crises?

IN CONCLUSION

Based on the groundbreaking work of the Excellence Study and follow-up studies by other scholars in recent years, evidence indicates that organizations that scan the environment for potential problem areas and maintain positive relationships with the organization's various publics handle and survive crises better than do others. Thus, how well, if at all, an organization endures a crisis factors on its ability to manage it—by managing its relationships and strategically preparing and planning for crises. Crisis management offers an opportunity for skilled public relations professionals to gain credibility as strategic communication advisors. The research team of James and Larissa Grunig paved the way for the field of public relations, advancing it to a strategic management field in the 21st century. The task for future scholars is to further the field by building on theories.

REFERENCES

Alsop, R. (2001, February 7). Survey rates companies' reputations, and many are found wanting. *The Wall Street Journal*, pp. B1, B6.

Alsop, R. (2005, February 8). M.B.A. track. *The Wall Street Journal*, p. B4.

Anderson, D. S. (1992). Identifying and responding to activist publics: A case study. *Journal of Public Relations Research, 4*, 151–165.

Barton, L. (Producer). (1994). *Crisis management: When disaster strikes* [Video]. Cincinnati, OH: South-Western.

Baskin, O., Aronoff, C., & Lattimore, D. (1997). *Public relations. The profession and the practice*. Madison, WI: Brown and Benchmark.

Bowen, S. A. (2000). *A theory of ethical issues management: Contributions of Kantian deontology to public relations' ethics and decision-making*. Unpublished doctoral dissertation, University of Maryland, College Park.

Butters, J. (2002, March 29). Tire impact on Ford up to $10 billion. *Detroit Free Press*, p. C1.

Caponigro, J. R. (1998). *The crisis counselor: The executive's guide to avoiding, managing and thriving on crises that occur in all businesses*. Southfield, MI: Barker Business Books.

Child, C. (2001, June 25). Ford's image slips among consumers. *Automotive News*, p. 1.

Connelly, M. (2001, June 11). Firestone crisis dims Nasser's star. *Automotive News*, pp. 1, 8.

Coombs, T. (2000). Crisis management: Advantages of a relational perspective. In J. A. Ledingham & S. D. Bruning (Eds.), *Public relations as relationship management: A relational approach to public relations* (pp. 73–93). Mahwah, NJ: Lawrence Erlbaum Associates.

Crain, K. E. (Ed.). (1995, April 3). Chrysler accepted the inevitable on minivan latches. *Automotive News*, p. 12.

Crilley, J. (2003). *Free publicity: A tv reporter shares the secrets of getting covered on the news*. Dallas, TX: Great Impressions.

Cutlip, S. M., Center, A. H., & Broom, G. M. (2000). *Effective public relations* (8th ed.). Upper Saddle River, NJ: Prentice-Hall.

Dixon, J. (2002, January 7). Ford, Firestone may resolve spat. *Detroit Free Press*, p. F5.

Dozier, D. M., Grunig, L. A., & Grunig, J. E. (1995). *Manager's guide to excellence in public relations and communication management*. Mahwah, NJ: Lawrence Erlbaum Associates.

Fearn-Banks, K. (2002). *Crisis communications: A casebook approach* (2nd ed.). Mahwah, NJ: Lawrence Erlbaum Associates.

Federal Emergency Management Agency [FEMA]. (n.d.). *The emergency management guide for business & industry*. Retrieved May 29, 2005, from http://www.fema.gov/library/bizindex.shtm

Grunig, J. E. (1992a). Communication, public relations, and effective organizations: An overview of the book. In J. E. Grunig (Ed.), *Excellence in public relations and communication management* (pp. 1–28). Hillsdale, NJ: Lawrence Erlbaum Associates.

Grunig, J. E. (Ed.). (1992b). *Excellence in public relations and communication management*. Hillsdale, NJ: Lawrence Erlbaum Associates.

Grunig, J. E. (1997). A situational theory of publics: Conceptual history, recent challenges, and new research. In D. Moss, T. MacManus, & D. Vercic (Eds.), *Public relations research: An international perspective* (pp. 3–46). London: International Thomson Business Press.

Grunig, J. E., & Huang, Y. (2000). From organizational effectiveness to relationship indicators: Antecedents of relationships, public relations strategies, and relationship outcomes. In J. A. Ledingham & S. D. Bruning (Eds.), *Public relations as relationship management: A relational approach to the study and practice of public relations* (pp. 23–53). Mahwah, NJ: Lawrence Erlbaum Associates.

Grunig, J. E., & Hung, C. F. (2002, March). *The effect of relationships on reputation and reputation on relationships: A cognitive, behavioral study*. Paper presented at the PRSA Educator's Academy 5th Annual International, Interdisciplinary Public Relations Research Conference, Miami.

Grunig, J. E., & Hunt, T. (1984). *Managing public relations*. New York: Holt, Rinehart & Winston.

Grunig, J. E., & Repper, F. C. (1992). Strategic management, publics, and issues. In J. E. Grunig (Ed.), *Excellence in public relations and communication management* (pp. 117–157). Hillsdale, NJ: Lawrence Erlbaum Associates.

Grunig, L. A. (1992). Activism: How it limits the effectiveness of organizations and how excellent public relations respond. In J. E. Grunig (Ed.), *Excellence in public relations and communication management* (pp. 503–530). Hillsdale, NJ: Lawrence Erlbaum Associates.

Grunig, L. A., Grunig, J. E., & Dozier, D. M. (2002). *Excellent public relations and effective organizations*. Mahwah, NJ: Lawrence Erlbaum Associates.

Grunig, L. A., Grunig, J. E., & Ehling, W. P. (1992). What is an effective organization? In J. E. Grunig (Ed.), *Excellence in public relations and communication management* (pp. 65–90). Hillsdale, NJ: Lawrence Erlbaum Associates.

Hagan, L. (2003). *Public relations, relationships, and reputation: A case study of a safety recall in the U.S. automotive industry*. Unpublished doctoral dissertation, University of Maryland, College Park.

Huang, Y. H. (1997). *Public relations, organization–public relationships, and conflict management*. Unpublished doctoral dissertation, University of Maryland, College Park.

Hunt, T., & Grunig, J. E. (1994). *Public relations techniques*. Fort Worth, TX: Harcourt Brace.

Ihlen, O. (2002). Defending the Mercedes A-class: Combining and changing crisis-response strategies. *Journal of Public Relations Research, 14*, 185–206.

Institute for Crisis Management. (2000). *Myths in crisis management*. Retrieved May 29, 2005, from http://www.crisisexperts.com/myths.htm

Jedlicka, D. (2002). 2000 Audi A4. Retrieved January 18, 2003, from http://carpoint.msn.com/VIP/Jedlicka/Audi/A4/2002.asp

Ledingham, J. A. (2003). Explicating relationship management as a general theory of public relations. *Journal of Public Relations Research, 15*(2), 181–198.

Ledingham, J. A., & Bruning, S. D. (Eds.). (2000). *Public relations as relationship management: A relational approach to the study and practice of public relations.* Mahwah, NJ: Lawrence Erlbaum Associates.

Lerbinger, O. (1997). *The crisis manager: Facing risk and responsibility.* Mahwah, NJ: Lawrence Erlbaum Associates.

Lyon, L., & Cameron, G. (2004). A relational approach examining the interplay of prior reputation and immediate response to a crisis. *Journal of Public Relations Research, 16*(3), 213–241.

McDonald, T. F. (2005). *Four pillars for building a solid crisis communications plan.* Unpublished manuscript.

Motor vehicles industry snapshot. (2003, March 3). *Fortune.* Retrieved March 18, 2003, from http://www.fortune.com/fortune/mostadmired/industry snapshot

National Highway Traffic Safety Administration (NHTSA). (1998, October). *Motor vehicle defects and recall campaigns* (DOT HS 808 795). Retrieved July 20, 2005, from http://www.nhtsa.dot.gov/hotline/recallprocess.html.

Murphy, P. (1991). The limits of symmetry: A game theory approach to symmetric and asymmetric public relations. *Public Relations Research Annual, 3,* 115–132.

Public Relations Society of America. (n.d.). *Tips & techniques: Crisis management.* Retrieved April 5, 2005, from http://www.prsa.org/_Resources/resources/crisis.asp?ident=rsrc3

Plungis, J. (2005). *Carmakers staggered by record '04 recalls.* Retrieved July 20, 2005, from http://www.detnews.com/2005/autosinsider/0501/06/A01-48858.htm

Robinson, E. A. (1997, March 3). America's most admired companies. *Fortune,* pp. 68–75.

Schenkler, S., & Herrling, T. (2004). *Guide to media relations.* Upper Saddle River, NJ: Pearson Education.

Seitel, F. P. (1998). *The practice of public relations* (7th ed.). Upper Saddle River, NJ: Prentice-Hall.

Shreve, M. A. (2001). Recalls at record levels. *NADA's Auto Exec, 73*(8), 26–29.

Sung, J., & Tkaczyk, C. (2002, March 4). Who's on top and who flopped. *Fortune,* p. 75.

Ulrich, L. (2000, August 28). *Tires put pressure on Ford: Recall could cut big profits from new Explorer.* Retrieved November 11, 2002, from http://www.auto.com/industry/Ford26_2000826.htm

Ware, B. L., & Linkugel, W. A. (1973). They spoke in defense of themselves: On the generic defense of apologia. *Quarterly Journal of Speech, 59,* 274–283.

Wilcox, D. L., Ault, P. H., & Agee, W. K. (1998). *Public relations' strategies and tactics* (5th ed.). New York: Addison-Wesley.

Wrigley, B. J., Salmon, C. T., & Park, H. S. (2003). Crisis management planning and the threat of bioterrorism. *Public Relations Review, 29,* 281–290.

V

Conditions for Global Excellence in Public Relations and Communication Management

Toward the Theory of Relationship Management in Public Relations: *How* to Cultivate Quality Relationships?[1]

Chun-Ju Flora Hung
Hong Kong Baptist University

Too often communicators focus on creating perceptions and communicating messages. If we are truly to become a boardroom discipline, then we should understand the science of managing stakeholder relationships on behalf of our sponsors. It is relationships that drive outcomes ... not perceptions.

—Alan VanderMolen, President of Asia Pacific, Edelman,
personal communication, April 24, 2005

In this chapter, I intend to articulate the theory of relationship management with the focus on relationship cultivation strategies. I consider that the application of different cultivation strategies is affected by different factors inside and outside an organization. As a result, I have adopted the dialectical perspective to explain the phenomenon. In doing so, I first examine the current studies on organization–public relationships and provide a new perspective on relationship management, which encompasses relationship antecedents, relationship types, relationship cultivation strategies, and relationship outcomes. I then demonstrate the current research on the factors affecting the choice of relationship cultivation strategies and the influence that the cultivation strategies have on relationship outcomes.

[1]The author would like to express her greatest gratitude to her PhD adviser, Dr. James Grunig, for his guidance in the author's study in the University of Maryland. I also want to thank Dr. Larissa Grunig for her teaching and support all the time. Last but not least, I thank Dr. Elizabeth Toth for giving me the opportunity to honor Jim and Lauri.

J. Grunig and his colleagues' Excellence Study on how public relations contribute to an organization's strategic planning and effectiveness has indicated that public relations helps an organization identify its strategic publics and uses symmetrical communication "to develop and maintain quality long-term relationships with these strategic publics" (L. Grunig, J. Grunig, & Dozier, 2002, p. 548). L. Grunig et. al. (2002) and Hon and J. Grunig (1999) posited that organizations should conduct environmental scanning to identify strategic publics that the organization needs, relationships and issues that the organization should develop, and communication plans to communicate with the strategic publics. Toth (2000) considered that public relations is relational communication. Scholars after 1997 have strived to find out how to successfully evaluate the effectiveness of the communication programs by paying attention to the topic of measuring and evaluating organization–public relationship outcomes (Brunner, 2000; Hon & J. Grunig, 1999; Huang, 2001a, 2001b; Kim, 2001; Ledingham & Bruning, 2000). Yet, when discussing this topic, we have to see how we define the terms *organization–public relationships* and *relationship management*.

DEFINITION OF ORGANIZATION–PUBLIC RELATIONSHIPS

Broom, Casey, and Ritchey (1997) called for the need for a definition of organization–public relationships. In response to such call, Ledingham and Bruning (1998) provided the following definition: "[An organization-public relationship is] the state which exists between an organization and its key publics, in which the actions of either can impact the economic, social, cultural or political well being of the other" (p. 62). Broom, Casey, and Ritchey (2000) developed another definition from the exchange perspective:

> Organization–public relationships are represented by the patterns of interaction, transaction, exchange, and linkage between organization and its publics. These relationships have properties that are distinct from the identities, attributes, and perceptions of the individuals and social collectivities in the relationships. Though dynamic in nature, organization–public relationships can be described at a single point in time and tracked over time. (p. 18)

Hon and J. Grunig (1999) pointed out that an organization–public relationship begins when there are consequences created by an organization that affect publics, or when the behaviors of publics have consequences on an organization. From the systems theory and resource theory perspectives, organizations and their publics affect each other with their behaviors. As a result, Hung (2005a) provided another definition: "Organization–public relationships arise when organizations and their strategic publics are interdependent and this interdependence results in consequences to each other that organizations need to manage" (p. 396). Ki and Shin (2005) also contended that there is no consistent definition for the term. For this chapter, I use Hung's definition, inasmuch as this definition not only describes the state of an organization–public relationship but also emphasizes the importance of managing the consequences of an organization's behaviors.

REVIEW OF THE CURRENT STUDY ON ORGANIZATION–PUBLIC RELATIONSHIPS

Following Ferguson's (1984) first call for focusing public relations research on relationships with publics, the first researcher who responded was Ballinger (1991), who did a master's thesis about organization–public relations. However, it was not until 1997 that the research on relationships started to move forward.

Ballinger's (1991) thesis adapted Millar and Roger's (1987) relational communication perspective to propose a model of public–organizational relationships, which was produced using six variables: intimacy, trust, control, perceptions, communication behaviors, and relational outcomes. This thesis later served as a basis for Broom et al.'s (1997, 2000) discussion of organization–public relationships.

Huang (1997) developed a theory integrating public relations strategies (models of public relations), conflict resolution strategies, and relationship outcomes. In her dissertation, Huang identified indicators for evaluating relationships: trust, control mutuality, relational commitment, and relational satisfaction. More recently, she developed two more relationship outcomes from a cultural perspective: face and favor (Huang, 2001a).

J. Grunig and Huang (2000) consulted Stafford and Canary's (1991) cultivation strategies, management theories for organizational effectiveness, and conflict resolution strategies (Plowman, 1995) in order to develop a complete theory of organization–public relationships. In addition, they provided methods for evaluating relationships in each stage: relationship antecedents, cultivation strategies, and relationship outcomes.

Broom et al. (1997, 2000) reviewed literature in interpersonal communication, psychotherapy, interorganizational relationship, and systems theory, and posited a model describing the antecedents and consequences of organization–public relations. In Ledingham and Bruning's (2000) *Public Relations as Relationship Management: A Relational Approach to the Study and Practice of Public Relations*, Broom et al. (2000) reported the results of a pilot study, based on a theoretical framework they had developed.

Ledingham, Bruning, and Wilson (1999) identified time as an indicator of the perceptions and behavior of members of a key public. They reviewed literature on interpersonal relationships, mainly Wood's (1996) concepts of investment, commitment, trust, and comfort.

Bruning and Ledingham (1999) identified the following dimensions of organization–public relations: professional relationships, personal relationships, and community relationships. These dimensions help scholars understand that more than business transactions occur between an organization and its publics. Organizations with social responsibilities need to think about their constituencies' best interests. Cultivating a good community relationship will enable an organization to minimize the risk of protests from activist groups.

Hon and J. Grunig (1999) produced a report on how to measure relationships in public relations. This report contained quantitative measurements of six relationship outcomes: trust, control mutuality, relationship commitment, relationship satisfaction, communal relationships, and exchange relationships. This report—the first document applying the concept of communal and exchange relationships in a survey—has helped scholars understand why the degree of trust one organization gains from its publics is lower or higher than that of other organizations. The indicators of trust, control mutuality, commitment, satisfaction, and communal and exchange relationships were later adopted in Brunner's (2000) and Len-Rios' (2001) research.

Toth (2000) posited that public relations should be conceptualized in terms of interpersonal communication, in which public relations serves as the bridge between an organization and its publics. She also presented a model suggesting that public relations should utilize interpersonal relationships. This highlight concurs with J. Grunig's (2001) notion that public relations practices should include the interpersonal communication dimension, and the idea that the practice of public relations is for building quality, long-term relationships (J. Grunig, 2001, L. Grunig et al., 2002).

Hazelton and Kennan (2000) discussed social capital theory, which provides additional explanation of how a relationship starts. Cited in Hazelton and Kennan (2000), Bourdieu said that social capital is "the aggregate of the actual or potential resources which are linked to possession of a durable network of more or less institutionalized relationships of mutual acquaintance or recognition" (p. 2). Portes (1998) commented that this definition contains two critical elements: (a) the social interactions that provide the participants access to resources from their connections, and (b) the quantity and quality of those resources. Social capital also describes obligation and expectations in interactions. Coleman (1988) noted that if one does something for the other and trusts the other to reciprocate in the future, an expectation is established in this person and an obligation is incurred in the other person.

Hazelton and Kennan (2000) identified the positive outcomes of properly applied social capital: increased and more complex forms of social capital, reduced transaction costs, and organizational advantage. However, the flaw of social capital lies in determining whether parties understand when and in what form such obligations are to be repaid. In addition, parties may also violate the reciprocity expectation. The social capital theory, however, helps to support the theories of communal and exchange relationships, which are the theories I focus on in the latter part of this chapter.

In the application area, Coombs (2000) applied stakeholder theory and attribution theory to examine relationships in crisis management. He contended that early and continuing attention to a relationship could minimize conflicts between an organization and its stakeholders.

Hung (2000a) adopted J. Grunig and Huang's (2000) theory of relationship cultivation strategies and relationship outcomes, and conducted a qualitative pilot study of the relationship between a Taiwanese company and its Chinese publics. Interestingly, the findings showed that none of the cultivation strategies contributed to trust between the company and its publics. However, the results also showed that legitimacy plays a significant role in relationship building, especially for control mutuality, relational commitment, and relational satisfaction.

Len-Rios (2001) conducted two online surveys to test the reliability and validity of using a rules–appropriate testing evaluation scale (RATES) for diagnosing the health and strength of online organization–public relationships. This online research made use of the rule theory, which states that specific rules usually influence interpersonal relationship formation and dissolution. Yet, Len-Rios left open several important questions: How are the rules defined by different users on the Internet? What are the rules defined by organizations? Is there any consensus between the organization and its publics on the Internet, so that they can "play by rules"?

The six-dimension scale of measurement developed by Hon and J. Grunig (1999) was soon adopted by Hon and Brunner (2002) and Jo, Hon, and Brunner (2004) in studying university–student relationships. It was regarded as a conceptually and operationally meaningful depiction of an organization–public relationship that should be useful for understanding and measuring public relationships.

Huang (2001a, 2001b) presented a cross-cultural, multi-item scale for measuring organization–public relations, so as to establish the measurement with standards of reliability and validity as well as capability in cross-cultural comparability. She included the items of face and favor in addition to trust, control mutuality, commitment, and satisfaction, and found that control mutuality was the most critical factor in predicting overall relationships (Huang, 2001a).

J. Grunig and Hung (2002) studied the effect of relationship on an organization's reputation. After surveying Internet users on their evaluation of relationships with five different organizations (General Electrics, American Red Cross, Microsoft, National Rifle Association, and Social Security), they concluded that recall of good and bad behaviors had the greatest effect on the evaluation of relationships, and that our measure of reputation can be used for publics who mostly have a *reputational* relationship with an organization as well as for those who also have an *experiential* relationship.

Y. Kim (2001) used the same items that Hon and J. Grunig (2001) developed for measuring relationships and items from interpersonal, relationship marketing, and public relations literature, and constructed four relationship dimensions: trust, commitment, local and community involvement, and reputation.

Bruning and Galloway (2003) explored the role that structural and personal commitment plays in organization–public relationships. Employing personal relationship commitment and structural commitment as approaches to commitment, they refined and redefined three dimensions of relationship: the professional benefit/expectation dimension, the personal commitment dimension, and the community improvement dimension.

Jo and Y. Kim (2003) examined the effect of Web characteristics on the building of organization–public relationships. Their research findings suggested that a corporation's Web interactivity had significant effects on relationship building.

Ki (2004) did a content analysis from the Web sites of the 286 corporations on the 2002 Fortune 500 list in exploring how these companies used the relationship maintenance strategies through their Web sites, and also whether different industry types applied different levels of relationship maintenance strategies. Her findings demonstrated that openness is the most common strategy for corporate Web sites, and the strategies of positivity, openness, and access showed significant results in differentiating industry types.

H. Kim (2005) argued that the research on organization–public relationships does not address the exploration of the antecedents of relationships—the first stage of relationship management. She examined and confirmed that organizational structure and the system of internal communication play the role of the antecedents of internal relationships on employee–organization relationships.

After reviewing about 40 scholastic works in organization–public relationships, Ki and Shin (2005) summarized the status of research and identified satisfaction, commitment, trust, mutual understanding, control mutuality, and benefit as outcomes of organization–public relationship. Satisfaction was the most frequently adopted outcome variable.

PERSPECTIVES IN STUDYING RELATIONSHIPS

Social Exchange Approach

Drawing from the current studies on organization–public relationships, scholars mostly have accepted the social exchange perspective. Social exchange theory has been widely used to explain when and why relationships begin, are maintained, and terminated (Hinde, 1997; Thibaut & Kelley, 1959; Thomlison, 2000). This approach assumes that people are more willing to develop relationships when their profits are maximized, which equals rewards minus costs. Social exchange theory posits that social relationships involve the exchange of resources, such as status, information, goods, services, money, intimacy, friendship, social acceptance, and so on (U. Foa, Converse, Törnblom, & E. Foa, 1993; Hinde, 1997). According to Canary and Zelley (2000), social exchange involves several approaches. Interdependence theory and equity theory represent this perspective.

Acknowledged by Dindia and Canary (1993), interdependence theory is the most influential perspective in studying relationships. Interdependence theorists (e.g., Kelley & Thibaut, 1978) believe that people find relationships satisfactory when their rewards are commensurate to their cost. Interdependence theory also emphasizes that people control each other in terms of their unilateral or bilateral dependence (Kelley, 1979). As a result, two types of relationships can be described: whether one person dominates the other, or whether the relationship is defined by its interdependence. To sum up, interdependence theory portrays the nature and structure of people's reliance on each other (Canary & Zelley, 2000).

Extending from interdependence theory, Rusbult and other scholars developed the investment model, which tests one's level of commitment. Rusbult, Drigotas, and Verette (1994) asserted that commitment reflects the effects of interdependence in the cultivation process.

The equity theory has been a traditional explanation of people's use of communication strategies. For Deutsch (1985), equity is based on the principle of distributive justice, which suggests that rewards should be distributed according to who provides the most inputs to the dyadic or group system. Similar to other theories in the social exchange approach, equity theory contends that people prefer to maximize their rewards and minimize their cost. Yet, apart from the rational theory discussed earlier, equity theorists believe that people seek equity in a fair manner and that they look to restore equity in case their relationships with others become unequal (Hatfield, Traupmann, Sprecher, Utne, & Hay, 1985).

Canary and Stafford (1992, 1993, 1994, 1997; Stafford & Canary, 1991) adopted equity theory to develop the relationship maintenance (cultivation) strategies that one uses and relationship outcomes that one receives. J. Grunig and Huang (2000) and Hon and J. Grunig (1999) applied some of their relationship cultivation strategies and relationship outcomes; these two concepts are discussed in the latter part of the chapter.

The Dialectical Perspective in Studying Relationships

As J. Grunig and Huang (2000) explained, social exchange theory lacks the ability to describe "change pressures" from the environment, which usually have little or nothing to do with resource exchange. They further argued, "[P]ublics come and go and change as situations change" (p. 35). Accordingly, I decided to disregard the traditional view of evaluating relationships—that is, the degrees of relationship outcomes perceived by publics. Researchers must look into the whole context of relationships so that they understand how to manage relationships. Hence, in order to observe the dynamic aspect of relationships, I combined another approach with social exchange theory in studying relationships—the dialectical approach.

The dialectical approach, primarily developed by Baxter and Montgomery (Baxter & Montgomery, 1996; Montgomery & Baxter, 1998), is considered a new approach in researching relationships. Dialectics is not a theory. Rather, it is a perspective or a metatheory, which is a series of assumptions (Baxter & Montgomery, 1996; Canary & Zelley, 2000). Dindia and Canary (1993) posited that relationships are differentiated by "opposite but interrelated forces" (p. 168). Scholars using this approach consider opposing tensions—for example, love and hate, peace and war—as facts of life. Baxter (1988) pointed out that the three major oppositional forces are autonomy versus connection, novelty versus predictability, and closedness versus openness. These major forces, as a result, create constant changes in the relationships.

The dialectical perspective attempts to emphasize the dynamics of relationships, seeking to find out how relationships operate in the midst of parties "being drawn together as well as pushed apart" (Canary & Zelley, 2000; p. 323). This dialectical approach also calls attention to a holistic evaluation of relationships: to the idea that a relational entity cannot exist without the fluctuating interactions between its opposing parts, or between the opposing parties of a relationship. Acknowledged by Rawlins (1989), this approach provides a full understanding of the whole relationship process. As a result, the dialectical approach can be adopted to explain how external factors, such as an organization's interactions with other units in the environment, influence the nature of the relationships that the organization maintains with different publics (Hung, 2005b).

A Dialectical Approach to Study Relationships: Examining the Dynamics

Baxter and Mongomery have been the two major scholars applying this approach to the study of relationships (Baxter, 1988, 1990, 1993, 1994; Baxter & Montgomery, 1996; Montgomery & Baxter, 1998a). People in relationships seek both autonomy and connection, openness and closeness. In addition, Ball (1979) pointed out that researchers studying relationship cultivation usually favor logic, functionalism, or formal cause as an appropriate explanation for human behavior. He further elaborated that researchers have long ignored the opposing tensions in relationships and the fact that social interactions sometimes do not follow a logical pattern.

A dialectical approach hypothesizes that people spiral between communicative behaviors. Aside from a linear or cyclical approach, a spiraling model suggests that relationships often move forward in time; thus, context and situations that relationship parties experience are not the same. Fundamentally, people in relationships act and react as relationships spiral forward and reshape reality (Baxter & Montgomery, 1996, 1998; Montgomery & Baxter, 1998a, 1998b; Canary & Zelley, 2000).

Ball (1979) indicated that Marx and Freud acknowledged dialectical methods as means of discussing tensions and contradictions within a capitalist economy, social hierarchy, and population growth, respectively. In discussing the historical roots of dialectics, Baxter and Montgomery (1996) said that dialectics usually encompasses two broad types of meanings: epistemology and ontology. In philosophy, epistemology is the study of knowledge, whereas ontology is the study of the nature of reality. Dialectics-as-epistemology means a method of reasoning by going through the clash of opposing arguments, as rooted in rhetoric. Dialectics-as-ontology, however, focuses more on the dynamic interplay of opposing tensions in reality. In discussing relationships, I follow Baxter and Montgomery's choice of concentrating on the ontological view of dialectics.

The Russian social theorist Mikhail Bakhtin extended and reshaped Marx's idea of dialectic to coin "dialogism," by which he meant an understanding of "a contradiction-ridden, tension-filled unity of two embattled tendencies" (Bakhtin, 1981, p. 272). He called these tendencies centripetal (the intention to draw together) and centrifugal (the intention to seek differentiation). More specifically, Bakhtin (1981) pointed out that these contradicting tendencies mostly show up in communication behavior (e.g., dialogues) found in a relationship.

Acknowledged by Canary and Zelley (2000), Baxter is the scholar who has systematically adapted Bakhtin's dialogism to interpersonal relationships. She has extended the centripetal and centrifugal concepts and identified the characteristics of a dialectical approach: contradiction, change, praxis, and totality.

   Contradiction.   Contradiction refers to the dynamic interaction between united opposites. This perspective assumes that, in relationships, interdependent yet opposing tensions regularly exist; therefore, they pull people together and push them apart. Hence, these interdependent but mutually negative tendencies cannot be fulfilled completely at the same time. However, Baxter and Montgomery (1996; Montgomery & Baxter, 1998a) pointed out that contradiction in relationships is not considered as negative. In a healthy relationship, as elaborated by these authors, contradiction is viewed as necessary to some degree. Three primary points of contradiction are: integration/separation, stability/change, and expression/privacy (Baxter, 1993). These three points reflect Bakhtin's centripetal/centrifugal thinking, in which the three kinds of contradiction are legitimate and essential in relationships.

   Change.   One of the most important characteristics of the dialectical approach is contradiction, which serves as an agent of change. For example, if one tendency is fulfilled, the contradicting side is unfulfilled. Therefore, there arises an intention to fulfill this contradicting side. Because these contradicting parts are difficult to fulfill at the same time, tension and change always exist to some degree (Baxter & Montgomery, 1996; Montgomery & Baxter, 1998).

   Praxis.   The idea of praxis is that "people are at once actors and objects of their own actions" (Baxter & Montgomery, 1996, p. 12). More fully, this concept states that people are usually proactive in choosing their social behavior; however, at the same time, individuals are also reactive to the situations they encounter. Bakhtin's notion of dialectical praxis posited that parties communicatively react to dialectical requirements as a result of their past experiences. By doing so, they also recreate the dialectical circumstances that they will face in the future (Baxter & Montgomery, 1996; Canary & Zelley, 2000; Montgomery & Baxter, 1998a, 1998b).

   Totality.   Baxter and Montgomery (1996) suggested that one can fully understand concepts, events, and situations only when they are related or linked to other concepts, events, and situations. They envisioned that "totality" encourages parties in relationships to "think about the world as a process of relations or interdependencies" (Montgomery & Baxter, 1998b, p. 164). Consequently, at the same time, relationships are both an ongoing product and producer of social dialogue. Relationships are created by individuals' interactions with other elements in society, but they also create individuals and societies. Relationships, individuals, and societies additionally create cultures.

THE COMBINATION OF SOCIAL EXCHANGE PERSPECTIVE AND THE DIALECTICAL PERSPECTIVE IN EXPLORING ORGANIZATION–PUBLIC RELATIONSHIPS

In order to unfold a full picture of how organization–public relationships develop, I consider it necessary to combine both the social exchange perspective and dialectical perspective. Following are my reasons: First, both approaches recognize the *interdependence* in relationships. Social exchange theorists acknowledge that every relationship is embedded in a network of other relationships (Kelley & Thibaut, 1978; Thibaut & Kelley, 1959). The parties are aware that their satisfaction from the relationship comes from the reward and cost of their interactions with others. Dialectical theorists' concept of *centripetal* thinking reveals their understanding about people's need for interacting with each other.

Second, whereas social theorists emphasize the calculation of rewards and costs, causing the birth of relationship cultivation, the dialectical approach provides the understanding of why and when parties choose their cultivation behaviors. For example, the desire to retain autonomy in the relationship will enable parties to select less symmetrical behavior, in order to maintain some semblance of independence. The same rule applies that when the individual wants to sense a feeling of connectedness, he or she will want to reveal himself or herself more fully.

By combining the two approaches, I believe I can provide a more complete rationale of how relationships start, why organizations and their publics choose their cultivation strategies, and how the relationship outcomes differ among all the publics around the organization.

RELATIONSHIP MANAGEMENT IN PUBLIC RELATIONS

The Excellence Study has shown that public relations help an organization interact with its institutional environment. From the economic perspective, the so-called "externality" happens because when an organization pursues its profits, it also inevitably creates new problems to other social units in the society that the organization should resolve regardless the cost (L. Grunig et al., 2002; Hung, 2000b). The relationship with publics starts when there are consequential behaviors executed by an organization that affects its publics. The value of public relations can be identified by "measuring the quality of the relationships it establishes with the strategic components of its institutional environment" (L. Grunig et. al., 2002, p. 539). To reach that end, public relations programs need to be strategically managed, administered, and evaluated in order to help an organization cultivate quality relationships (L. Grunig et al., 2002).

Inspired by J. Grunig and Huang (2000), who illustrated the stages and forms of relationships (which include the relationship antecedents, maintenance/cultivation strategies, and relationship outcomes),[2] Hung (2002) developed a model for relationship management (see Fig. 21.1) by incorporating both exchange theory and the dialectical perspectives. Agreeing with Baxter and Montgomery's theory that a relationship is an ongoing process, each stage of relationship development is affected by the state of the previous stage.

Hung's model demonstrates the factors that drive the diverse usages of relationship cultivation strategies that lead to different relationship outcomes. In bringing supplement to J. Grunig and Huang's stage of antecedents in relationships with publics, Hung considered that an organization's relationships with publics start when an organization realizes its interdependence with other units in the institutional environment. As a result, an organization's intention and motivation to survive in this institutional environment affect the type(s) of relationships it aims to have with the publics. There are also other factors that determine how an organization interacts with publics, such as the relationship qualities in the previous stage, the degree of achievement of the organization's goals, and the publics' view of the organization's reputation. From the dialectical perspective, the different expectations of stakeholders inside and outside the organization may contradict with the organization's management's objectives, and the socioeconomic-political environment will affect the organization's decisions in the choices of the relationship cultivation strategies with publics. Hence, the types of relationships an organization intends to develop with its publics determine the use of the cultivation strategies symmetrically or asymmetrically. After the use of the cultivation strategies, the types of relationships that ensue may be different from the organization's original expectations. In the same vein, the cultivation strategies an organization employs to interact with publics will also affect the quality of the resulting relationships. In the following section, I discuss the major concepts in relationship management: types of organization-public relationships, relationship cultivation strategies, and relationship outcomes.

---

[2]In the relationship antecedent stage, the authors suggested the use of continuous environmental scanning to identify strategic publics that were created from an organization's decision and behaviors. After identifying publics, the organization should develop various strategies in developing and cultivating quality relationships. Through co-orientational measures and observations by third parties, the organization will be able to evaluate how well the relationships are developed.

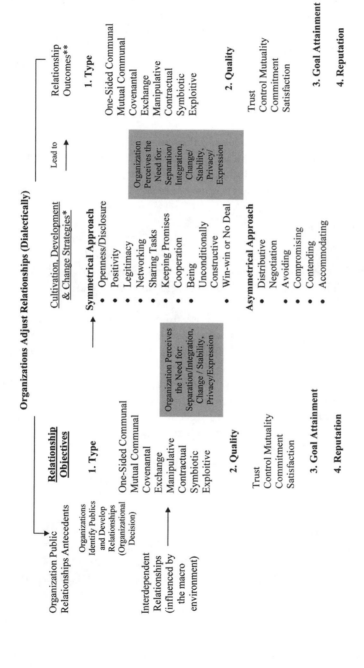

Organizations Adjust Relationships (Dialectically)

Organization Public
Relationships Antecedents

Organizations
Identify Publics
and Develop
Relationships
(Organizational
Decision)

Interdependent
Relationships
(influenced by
the macro
environment)

**Relationship
Objectives**

1. Type

One-Sided Communal
Mutual Communal
Covenantal
Exchange
Manipulative
Contractual
Symbiotic
Exploitive

Organization Perceives
the Need for:
Separation/Integration,
Change / Stability,
Privacy/Expression

2. Quality

Trust
Control Mutuality
Commitment
Satisfaction

3. Goal Attainment

4. Reputation

Cultivation, Development
& Change Strategies*

Symmetrical Approach
• Openness/Disclosure
• Positivity
• Legitimacy
• Networking
• Sharing Tasks
• Keeping Promises
• Cooperation
• Being
  Unconditionally
  Constructive
• Win-win or No Deal

Asymmetrical Approach
• Distributive
  Negotiation
• Avoiding
• Compromising
• Contending
• Accommodating

Organization
Perceives the
Need for:
Separation/
Integration,
Change/
Stability,
Privacy/
Expression

Lead to
→

Relationship
Outcomes**

1. Type

One-Sided Communal
Mutual Communal
Covenantal
Exchange
Manipulative
Contractual
Symbiotic
Exploitive

2. Quality

Trust
Control Mutuality
Commitment
Satisfaction

3. Goal Attainment

4. Reputation

* Organizations sometimes do not have relationships with some publics. Therefore, these are strategies for organizations
  to develop, maintain, and change relationships with different publics.
** Relationships can be most effectively evaluated by both organizations and their publics.

FIG. 21.1.   The relationship management model.

Types of Organization–Public Relationships

Mills and Clark (1982, 1986, 1994) developed two major types of relationships that are used in the study of organization–public relationships (Hon & J. Grunig, 1999): communal and exchange relationships. In communal relationships, benefits are given in order to please the other. Even though this may sound like an exchange relationship, members who give benefits do not expect the other's return or obligation to pay back (Mills & Clark, 1994). An exchange relationship suggests that members benefit one another in response to specific benefits received in the past or expected in the future.

Hung (2002, 2005a) adopted Mills, Clark, and their colleagues' theories on communal and exchange relationships (Clark, 1984; Clark & Mills, 1979, 1993; Clark, Mills, & Corcoran, 1989; Clark, Ouellette, Powell, & Milberg, 1987; Clark, Powell, & Mills, 1986; Clark & Taraban, 1991; Clark & Waddell, 1985; Mills & Clark, 1982, 1986, 1994) and developed the six types of relationships:[3]

- *Exploitive relationships* arise when one takes advantage of the other, when the other follows communal norms, or when one does not fulfill his or her obligation in an exchange relationship (Clark & Mills, 1993).
- *Manipulative relationships* occur when an organization, with the knowledge of what publics want, applies asymmetrical or pseudo-symmetrical approaches to communicate with publics to serve its own interests (Hung, 2005a).
- *Symbiotic relationships* happen when organizations, realizing their interdependence in the environment, work together with certain publics toward the common interest of surviving in the environment. However, both parties acknowledge this interdependence and understand the influence of their behavior on one another.
- *Contractual relationships* start when parties agree on what each should do in the relationships. This is akin to writing a contract at the beginning of a relationship. Contractual relationships cannot promise equal relationships (Hung, 2005a).
- *Covenantal relationships* mean that both sides commit to a common good by their open exchanges and the norm of reciprocity. Individuals in the relationship always provide the others with an opportunity to "ask for insight, to provide criticism, and to place a claim upon some of the individual's time" (Bennett, p. 9).
- *Mutual communal relationships:* Hon and J. Grunig (1999) defined communal relationships as "both parties provide benefits to the

---

[3]For detailed discussions on types or organization–public relationships, see Hung (2005a).

other because they are concerned for the welfare of the other—
even when they get nothing in return" (p. 21). Yet, what they identified is a more sophisticated level of relationships; what Mills and
Clark (1994) defined as "mutual communal relationships (i.e., relationships in which each person has a concern for the welfare of
the other)" (p. 30). Mutual communal relationships are different
from covenantal relationships, in that the latter emphasizes open
exchanges between the two parties, whereas the former emphasizes the psychological intention to protect the welfare of each
other (Hung, 2005a).

As cited from Hung (2005a), J. Grunig (personal communication,
April 18, 2001) developed a continuum describing the different types of
relationships from exploitive relationships to communal relationships
(see Fig. 21.2). In Fig. 21.2, the two ends of the continuum represent the
concern for oneself (exploitive relationships) and the concern for others
(communal relationships). Between the two extremes, there exist other
types of relationships, such as contractual relationships, exchange relationships, and covenantal relationships, depending on how both sides
agree to the way they interact. Hung (2002, 2005a) expanded this continuum by adding symbiotic relationships and manipulative relationships, and dividing communal relationships into mutual communal
and one-sided communal (see Fig. 21.3). Hung's (2002, 2003b, 2005a)
research findings showed that an organization enjoys win–win relationships with its publics when it develops mutual communal, covenantal relationships, or exchange relationships.

Dimensions of Public Relations and Relationship Cultivation Strategies

Public Relations Dimensions.   J. Grunig (1976) adapted Thayer's
(1968) ideas of communication types and developed identified two patterns of public relations practice: synchronic and diachronic public relations. The purpose of synchronic public relations was to "synchronize

Concern for   Concern for
Self Interest   Others' Interest

| Exploitive | Contractual | Exchange | Covenantal | Communal |
| Relationships | Relationships | Relationships | Relationships | Relationships |

FIG. 21.2.   J. Grunig's continuum of types of relationships. (From "Exploring
Types of Organization–Public Relationships and Their Implications for Relationship
Management in Public Relations," by C. J. F. Hung, in press, *Journal of Public Rela-
tions Research.*)

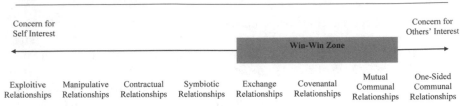

FIG. 21.3.   The modified continuum of types of relationships. (From "Exploring Types of Organization–Public Relationships and Their Implications for Relationship Management in Public Relations," by C. J. F. Hung, 2005a, *Journal of Public Relations Research*.)

the behavior of a public with that of the organization so that the organization can continue to behave in the way it wants without interference" (J. Grunig & L. Grunig, 1992, p. 287). The purpose of diachronic communication, however, represented communication that benefits both the organization and the public (J. Grunig & L. Grunig, 1992).

J. Grunig extended these two types into the four models of public relations: press agentry, public information, two-way asymmetrical communication, and two-way symmetrical communication (J. Grunig & Hunt, 1984). In these four models, J. Grunig (2001) contended that the two-way symmetrical model was best described by Murphy's mixed-motive model, in which "organizations try to satisfy their own interests while simultaneously trying to help a public satisfy its interests" (p. 12).

J. Grunig (2001) suggested the necessity of moving beyond the typology to develop more flexible variables. Therefore, he developed four underlying variables that defined the models, which he called the "maintenance strategies" (p. 29) for public relations practices: symmetrical and asymmetrical communication, one-way and two-way communication, mediated and interpersonal communication, and ethical communication. These variables describe the nature of communication between organizations and their publics in more detail than does the static typology of models. In addition, dimensions of interpersonal communication and mediated communication are practiced more often in Asian cultural settings. J. Grunig, L. Grunig, Sriramesh, Huang, and Lyra's (1995) research findings suggested that the use of personal influence appears common in Taiwan and India in media relations and lobbying.

Relationship Cultivation Strategies

In this section, I explain the choice of using the term *relationship cultivation* and then describe the strategies that have been adopted in public relations research. Literature in interpersonal communication (e.g., Canary & Stafford, 1994) and public relations (e.g., J. Grunig & Huang, 2000;

Hon & J. Grunig, 1999; Hung, 2000a; Ki, 2004) have used the term *maintenance* in developing strategies for quality relationships. J. Grunig (personal communication, February 26, 2002) considered using the term *cultivation* in place of *maintenance*. Hung (2004a) provided Dindia and Canary's (1993) definitions on relational maintenance and Montgomery's (1993) and Baxter and Montgomery's (1996) dialectical perspective on relationships to explain the rationale of using cultivation.

Dindia and Canary (1993) identified the four most commonly used definitions for the term *relationship maintenance:*

> (1) to keep a relationship in existence
>
> (2) to keep a relationship in a specified state or condition
>
> (3) to keep a relationship in satisfactory condition
>
> (4) to keep a relationship in repair. (p. 163)

Hung (2004a) adopted the third and the fourth definitions in her study on relationships between an organization and its publics, because the first definition could not provide any strategic aspect on the behaviors of maintaining relationship. The second definition, from the dialectical perspective, denies the constant changes and tensions in relationships. The third and the fourth definitions provide the context of the relationship that an organization has with its publics, inasmuch as the third definition illustrates the *efforts* an organization puts to make the relationship pleasant and happy with the publics. Finally, as acknowledged by Dindia and Canary (1993) and Baxter and Montgomery (1996), relationships are not always stable and a damaged relationship is possible. In Hung's (2002, 2003b) research on types of relationships, an exploitive relationship that an organization develops in maximizing its benefits not only damages the relationship between the two parties but also ruins the organization's reputation. As a result, organizations should not only maintain a relationship in its present state; rather, they also have to restore a failed or deteriorated relationship. Consequently, in responding to Dindia and Canary's (1994) points for keeping a relationship in a satisfactory condition and that one should strive for the effort in repairing a damaged relationship, I agree with J. Grunig (personal communication, February 26, 2002) that behaviors in relationships are an ongoing cultivation process. Therefore, the term *cultivation strategies* fits more in the context of relationship management.

Hence, based on the work of Canary and Stafford (1994), Plowman (1995), and Huang (1997), Hon and J. Grunig (1999) and J. Grunig and Huang (2000) conceptualized symmetrical and asymmetrical relationship strategies. Symmetrical strategies encompass the following:

Access: Members of publics or opinion leaders provide access to public relations practitioners. Public relations representatives or senior managers provide representatives of publics similar access to organizational decision-making processes.

Positivity: Organizations do whatever is necessary to make publics feel more content in the relationships.

Openness or disclosure: According to Canary and Stafford (1994), openness concerns the willingness to engage in direct discussions about the nature of relationships. Even though openness cannot guarantee a good quality relationship (Hung, 2000a), Bok (1989), in discussing secrets in power difference relationships, pointed out those with greater power have the obligation to prove that preservation of information is in the interest of those with less power.

Assurances of legitimacy: Earning legitimacy from publics means that organizations need to legitimize publics first (L. Grunig, 1992). Hon and J. Grunig (1999) maintained that assurances of legitimacy involve efforts by the parties in the relationship to express that they are committed to maintaining the relationship. Benefits stemming from legitimizing publics include more satisfaction and commitment from both sides (Hung, 2000a).

Networking: This strategy pertains to the effort that organizations exert in order to build networks or coalitions with the same groups as their publics, such as environmentalists, unions, or community groups. Hung (2000a) showed that networking serves as a catalyst in relationship building, especially in China, because personal relationships have been considered important in Chinese society (Hung, 2000a, 2000b, 2002).

Sharing of tasks: Organizations and publics do their fair share to solve problems that concern the other. Hon and J. Grunig (1999) provided examples of tasks—such as managing community issues, providing employment, making a profit, and staying in business—that are in the interests of either the organization, the public, or both.

Dual concern: Dual concern strategies are relevant for public relations practices, inasmuch as they take into consideration the role of balancing the interests of publics with the interests of the organization. These strategies also can be called mixed-motive or collaborative advocacy (Hon & J. Grunig, 1999).

Some dual concern strategies are asymmetrical because they emphasize the organization's interest over the public or vice versa, and will not be effective in developing and maintaining the most positive relationships over the long term. Such strategies include:

- *Contending:* The organization attempts to persuade the public to accept its position.

- *Avoiding:* The organization physically or psychologically ignores the conflict with publics.
- *Accommodating:* The organization, to some degree, gives in on its position and gives up its goals.
- *Compromising:* The organization partially meets the public's expectations, but both sides are not completely satisfied with the outcome.
- *Distributive:* Distributive strategies asymmetrically impose one's position onto that of the other party without concern for his or her welfare.

Plowman (1995) identified the following three symmetrical strategies:

Cooperating: Both the organization and the public work to bring together their interests and to reach a mutually beneficial relationship.

Being unconditionally constructive: The organization does whatever it considers is best for the relationship, even if it has to give up some of its position and even if the public does not respond to the organization's good intention.

Stipulating win-win or no deal: If the organization and public cannot find a solution that benefits both, they agree not to make a deal rather than to make a decision that is not beneficial for both parties.

In addition to these cultivation strategies, Hung's (2002) research on multinational and Taiwanese companies' relationship cultivation in China also identified another strategy:

Keeping promises: According to Hung, multinational companies in China utilized keeping promises to achieve dependability (one dimension of trust) between themselves and their Chinese publics; Taiwanese companies used this strategy to enhance dependability and competence (another dimension of trust).

Relationship Outcomes (Relationship Quality)

Hon and J. Grunig (1999) suggested six relationship outcomes to provide the first step for developing an ongoing audit of organization–public relationships. These six relationship outcomes include control mutuality, trust, satisfaction, commitment, communal relationship, and exchange relationship as the indicators of relationship. Yet, Hon and J. Grunig (1999) also mentioned that both communal and exchange relationships are types of relationships that affect the different degrees of the other four relationship indicators: control mutuality, trust, commitment, and satisfaction. Communal and exchange relationships were discussed in the previous section on types of relationships. As a result, here I mention only the rest of the relationship qualities defined by Hon and J. Grunig (1999):

> *Control mutuality* refers to how much each party of the relationship agrees on his or her rightful power to influence each other.
>
> *Trust* is about the confidence and willingness of both parties within the relationship to open themselves to each other. There are three dimensions in discussing trust: integrity, dependability, and competence. If one believes that the organization has integrity, it would mean that one believes the organization to be fair and just; whereas if one believes that the organization has dependability and competence, one also believes that the organization is willing and able to do what it says it will.
>
> *Satisfaction* is measure of how favorably each party of the relationship feels toward the other. The favorable feeling would be result from the reinforcement of one's positive expectations of the relationship.
>
> *Commitment* is how much each party of the relationship believes and feels that the relationship is worth putting forth an effort to maintain and promote. Two dimensions of commitment are continuance commitment (which refers to a certain line of action) and affective commitment (which is an emotional orientation).

These four relationship qualities have been adopted extensively in different contexts and studies over the years. For example, Brunner (2000) and Hon and Brunner (2002) used the indicators to examine a university's diversity issue. Jo et al. (2004) evaluated university–student relationships. Hung (2002) explored how multinational and Taiwanese companies practiced relationship management in China.

MOVING FROM CONCENTRATING ON MEASURING RELATIONSHIP OUTCOMES TO RELATIONSHIP CULTIVATION STRATEGIES

In the model presented in Fig. 21.1, I showed that the so-called relationship management cannot be accomplished by measuring the relationship outcomes. There are other various factors that define the quality of the relationship between an organization and its publics. Hence, when we conclude that Hon and J. Grunig (1999) successfully developed the measure for evaluating organization–public relationships, the next step for the future challenge on the study of organization–public relationships should be the concentration on *how* to sustain and cultivate quality relationships. Hon and J. Grunig (1999) and J. Grunig and Huang

(2000) developed a theoretical framework for relationship cultivation strategies. Yet, few studies have yet been conducted with a focus on relationship cultivation strategies, except for Hung's (2003a, 2004a, 2004b) study of cultural influence on relationship cultivation and both multinational and Taiwanese companies' relationship management in China. In the following section, I discuss how the types of relationships an organization intends to develop with its strategic publics affect the choice of relationship cultivation, and what strategies an organization uses in cultivating quality relationships (i.e., trust, control mutuality, commitment, and satisfaction). In exploring these two topics, 40 qualitative interviews were conducted with CEOs, vice presidents, and public relations managers from 18 multinational[4] and 18 Taiwanese companies[5] in seven cities in mainland China, Hong Kong, and Taipei on their relationship management with their strategic publics. I present findings on how the types of relationships have an effect on the choices of the cultivation strategies, and then discuss how the dimensions of public relations practices and the cultivation strategies enhance the quality of relationships.

Types of Relationships and Their Influence on the Cultivation Strategies

In discussing the types of relationships, I mentioned that organizations have win–win relationships with their publics when they develop mutual communal, covenantal relationships, or exchange relationships. In a win–win relationship, organizations tend to employ the cultivation strategies of *positivity, assurance of legitimacy,* and *being unconditionally constructive*. Moreover, in their goal of fostering win–win relationships, organizations reported that they tend to be willing to engage in dialogue with publics, listen to publics, treat publics as "partners," give positive feedback to publics, and be unconditionally constructive to publics. The research findings also proved that when an organization is more unconditionally constructive, publics tend to be more supportive and more responsive to the organization.

Sharing of tasks was the most frequently reported strategy practiced to establish communal relationships. The research showed that an organization is more willing to provide assistance when it hopes to have some contributions to the community. One may argue that organizations should not and would not unlimitedly devote and contribute to the publics without expecting anything in return, given that organizations have the bottom line to mind. Yet, participants in the research ac-

---

[4]These 18 multinational companies were on the 2001 Fortune Global 500 list.
[5]These 18 Taiwanese companies were on the 2001 Taiwan Commonwealth 1000 list.

knowledged that the development of communal relationships likely lead to the building of mutual communal relationships, inasmuch as publics, through long-term observations of an organization's benevolent behavior, will gradually reciprocate.

Exchange relationships work when each party legitimizes the other in the relationship, because when an organization is asking a favor from the publics, the first step should be to legitimize the publics or the other way around. In addition, when legitimacy is absent, one side may easily exploit the other. From a for-profit organization's perspective, to make profits from an exchange relationship with consumers it is essential to know what consumers need and desire to buy in a product. Therefore, providing access to open communication with publics and cooperating with publics are two evident strategies to nurture exchange relationships with publics.

In symbiotic relationships, both the symmetrical and asymmetrical strategies are used. Hung (2002) found that, in this type of relationships, organizations and their publics do not gain direct benefits from interacting with each other. However, this does not mean that there is no cooperation in the relationships. Although they do not directly profit from each other, through collaboration the benefit can be gained from a third party. Nevertheless, when one organization realizes it has more power in the relationship, the asymmetrical approach in relationship cultivation can change a symbiotic relationship to an exploitive or manipulative relationship.

Table 2.1 summarizes how the different types of relationships influence the choice of relationship cultivation strategies. This table illustrates that, when organizations take their publics' interests into consideration, they usually prefer to develop an amicable relationship with the publics. As a result, they will be more willing to listen to and provide positive feedback to their publics. On the other hand, in a negative relationship (e.g., an exploitive relationship), one party is self-serving and neglectful of others. This type of relationship makes use of asymmetrical communication.

Although the research shows that, in positive types of relationships, organizations tend to use symmetrical strategies in cultivating relationships, from the dialectical perspective, relationship development is an ongoing process. Asymmetrical strategies are sometimes necessary, if the expected outcome is for the benefit of both sides. Thus, we cannot conclude that organizations that want to cultivate positive relationships such as communal relationships, mutual communal relationships, and covenantal relationships will use only symmetrical cultivation strategies. However, numerous studies have shown that symmetrical communication helps organizations to be more effective (J. Grunig, 1992; L. Grunig et al., 2002; Huang, 1997; Hung, 2002, 2004c; Sha, 1999).

TABLE 21.1

Cultivation Strategies in Different Types of Relationships

Type of Relationships	Cultivation Strategies
Covenantal/win-win relationships	Dialogues and being attentive Positivity Assurances of legitimacy Being unconditionally constructive
Communal relationships	Sharing of tasks
Exchange relationships	Legitimacy Access Cooperation
Exploitive relationships	Asymmetrical strategies
Manipulative relationships	Asymmetrical strategies
Symbiotic relationships	Symmetrical strategies Asymmetrical strategies*

*In Hung's (2002) study, there are not many examples showing asymmetrical strategies in a symbiotic relationship. Future research is needed to explore how parties in a symbiotic relationship cultivate relationships.

In fact, the combination of symmetrical and asymmetrical strategies in achieving a positive relationship also indicates the dialectical context of relationships. The dialectical approach values multivocal strategies and does not consider that the traditional view on so-called progress can explain the dynamics in relationships. Instead of using the term *progress, dialogic complexity* is employed to describe the constant changes in a relationship that may make it more open, less intimate, or more uncertain (Baxter & Montgomery, 1996). The application of asymmetrical communication in cultivating positive relationships can be described by the process of dialogic complexity and the phenomenon of praxis because the multinational and Taiwanese companies reacted according to how their publics behaved under the existing conditions.

What a public relations scholar or practitioner should bear in mind, however, is that the dialectical approach only describes the dynamics of relationships and does not imply that all good relationships contain the phenomena of all the contradictions, changes, and so on. As a result, scholars and practitioners should consider that conflicts inherent in a relationship are natural and may bring positive outcomes, as long as organizations and their publics are determined to keep cultivating good relationships with each other.

Strategies and Dimensions in Cultivating Quality Relationships

Hung (2002) did a study on how multinational and Taiwanese companies build and maintain relationships with their publics in China. The following is a more detailed discussion on the communication dimension used for each relationship quality.

Integrity (As One Dimension of Trust). The research findings showed that two-way (ongoing dialogues), symmetrical (positivity, legitimacy, and sharing of tasks), and ethical communication (openness) were utilized in reach integrity. Multinational companies employed interpersonal communication (e.g. networking) in addition to mediated communication to achieve integrity.

Dependability (As One Dimension of Trust). Multinational companies employed more interpersonal, mediated, and ethical communication. Taiwanese companies, on the other hand, used one-way and asymmetrical communication (e.g., avoiding). The latter is an interesting finding, because Hung discerned in her research that the Taiwanese companies interviewed unilaterally avoided making some difficult promises in order to protect the companies' reputations.

Competence (One Dimension of Trust). Both multinational and Taiwanese companies used two-way symmetrical communication in this dimension (positivity, access, keeping promises, and sharing tasks). The difference was that multinational companies used mediated communication, whereas Taiwanese companies employed asymmetrical communication (contending) and interpersonal communication (face-to-face communication) in this dimension.

The finding that both symmetrical and asymmetrical approaches were applied in achieving competence can be viewed from two perspectives. First, scholars focusing on goal achievement in communication competence (McCroskey, 1984; Monge, Bachman, Dillard, & Eisenberg, 1981; Parks, 1994; Spitzberg & Cupach, 1984) contended that communication competence refers to whether one has the ability to bring about appropriate behaviors in a given situation or has the wisdom to exhibit the appropriate behaviors. This concept helps explain the necessity of using asymmetrical communication when the symmetrical approach cannot achieve the cooperation of the other party.

Second, from the dialectical aspect, relationships are not static. The downs in the relationship offer the opportunity for a relationship to reverse course and go up. Applying asymmetrical communication does not terminate a relationship. Rather, the positive side of a conflict helps to bring to both sides a chance to understand each other. The asymmetrical strategy forces the other side to listen and cooperate to achieve a win-win solution.

Control Mutuality.   The findings in this aspect showed much difference between multinational and Taiwanese companies. Multinational companies applied two-way (networking) and symmetrical communication (legitimacy and cooperation). For Taiwanese companies, besides two-way (access) and symmetrical communication (openness, legitimacy, and sharing tasks), participants' companies also used one-way (obligation to others), interpersonal (networking), mediated (access), and ethical communication (taking others' interests into consideration).

Commitment.   Two-way, symmetrical (sharing of tasks, cooperation, and being unconditionally constructive), and interpersonal communication (networking) were used by both multinational and Taiwanese companies in showing commitment to the publics. Besides these three dimensions, multinational companies applied asymmetrical (accommodation) and mediated communication (press releases to the publics). Taiwanese companies, however, used interpersonal communication in demonstrating their commitment.

It might be worthwhile to explore the phenomenon of applying asymmetrical communication in assuring commitment in a relationship. Hung (2002) found commitment to be the strongest indicator among all the relationship qualities in the relationship antecedents. With their commitment to maintaining and cultivating relationships, organizations might want to make some concessions to accommodate the publics and to be more unconditionally constructive in winning publics' cooperation.

Satisfaction.   Two-way (access) and symmetrical (positivity, legitimacy, sharing of tasks, cooperation, and being unconditionally constructive) communication were applied by both multinational and Taiwanese companies. Multinational companies also used interpersonal (networking) and mediated communication. Taiwanese companies used interpersonal and asymmetrical communication (contending).

DIALECTICS IN RELATIONSHIP MANAGEMENT

Relationships are not static. Organizations, serving their own interests, as well as their publics', usually face contradictions in relationships; therefore, the nature of a relationship changes. Baxter and Montgomery (1996) emphasized that one should evaluate a relationship based on its *process*. Hung's (2002) research showed that there were ups and downs in the relationships between an organization and its publics. However, as acknowledged by the research participants, these tensions and conflicts can bring some positive outcomes for organizations.

Baxter and Montgomery's relational dialectics encompasses four tenets: contradictions, change, praxis, and totality. These four tenets intertwine in explaining the dynamics in relationships. In the following, I will elaborate more of the phenomenon of relational dialectics in the following discussion.

Contradiction

The core concept of dialectics is contradiction, which states that there are interdependent and opposing tensions coexisting in relationships; therefore, these tensions pull people together and push them apart. In Hung's (2002, 2005b) research in China, the different principles in human relationships perceived by publics and the organizations have created fluctuations in relationships. The human relationship in Chinese society is still dominated by the principle of "affection, reason, and law," which is totally opposite from the principles in many countries from which multinational companies come. The emphasis on affection results in Chinese people commonly applying *guanxi* in facilitating business. However, many participants from multinational companies believe that everything should be done by rules, and that personal feelings should not be involved too much in business.

Change

Dialectical contradiction is the agent of change. The nature of relationships with publics changes because of the contradiction resulting from the respective differences in expectations. Baxter and Montgomery (1996) argued that the changes in relationships could be consequences of social influences and physical environmental influences.

In fact, when going beyond the description of the concept of dialectics, the element of change offers an explanation of how organizations reach quality relationships in the wake of conflicts in relationships. Stroh (1999) described how small changes bring chaos to the environment. She also acknowledged that, through strategic management in communication, these changes will eventually evolve into positive chaos. Organizations should recognize the continuing dynamics in the relationship-building process and tactfully deal with the conflicts in a positive manner. Hung (2002) asserted that because of the development of consumerism in China—in which consumers became more aware of their rights and sometimes behaved in ways that the companies considered irrational—organizations should employ a cooperative attitude in dealing with the conflicts with publics. Through offering more channels of communication and educating publics in a positive manner, the relationships between them could be improved, regardless of the constant changes in relationships.

From a more philosophical viewpoint, Baxter and Montgomery (1996) said that a relationship between two identities starts when there is a disparity between the two. A similar version was held by Hon and J. Grunig (1999), who viewed a relationship as starting when there is a consequence on its publics caused by an organization's behaviors, about which they hold different expectations. The dialectical approach views the relational consequence to be a product of centrifugal–centripetal forces in relationships, when both organizations and publics are interdependent but hold different views and interests.

Voloshinov and Bakhtin (1973) believed that "A word is a bridge thrown between myself and another" (p. 73). For Baxter and Montgomery (1996), the function of communication is to bridge the relational gap. Communication should be used in dealing with the consequences from the interactions between an organization and its publics. The outcome of communication is not the end of a relationship; rather, it should lead the relationship to another level.

CONCLUSION

In this chapter, the focus of the discussion on relationship management was relationship cultivation. J. Grunig (2001) commented that the models of public relations are the relationship cultivation strategies in public relations. The Excellence Study and other numerous studies in the past 2 decades have ascertained that two-way symmetrical communication helps contribute to organizational effectiveness. I also demonstrated via the research findings reviewed in this chapter that two-way and symmetrical communication dimensions nurture quality relationships. A basic model of relationship management in public relations was also presented in this chapter. Future research is needed for expanding or revising this model.

Moreover, public relations has always been considered as a boundary spanning function (J. Grunig, 1992; J. Grunig & Hunt, 1984; L. Grunig et al., 2002). Building solid, win–win relationships with strategic publics by listening to publics' concerns, garnering public supports, and helping to incorporate publics' opinions in the decision-making process in order to safeguard public interests is not just a one-time assignment. Likewise, research has demonstrated that relationship cultivation and building is a long-term process. I concur with Baxter and Montgomery's (1996) argument that relationship cultivation is not a linear development but a process of dialogic complexity. The dialectical approach for relationship management in public relations acknowledges that the ongoing interplay between contradictory expectations makes organization–public relationships a dynamic social entity. Thus, the combination of the social exchange and the dialectical perspectives in evaluating relationship management clearly pinpoints the importance for an organization to have constant dialogues with publics, especially those whose values and interests may conflict with the organization. The social exchange perspective reminds organizations not to overemphasize their bottom lines, whereas the dialectical approach embraces "multivocality," in which different social entities' voices are acknowledged. It is evident that strategic public relations can contribute to the organizational effectiveness and bottom line by reconciling the tension resulting from different expectations of publics inside and outside an organization through relationship building and cultivation. CEOs who can recognize this strategic value of public relations in the contemporary dynamic environment of organizations would agree that public relations fulfills a more strategic function than merely disseminating messages.

REFERENCES

Bakhtin, M. M. (1981). *The dialogic imagination: Four essays*. Austin: University of Texas Press.

Ball, R. A. (1979). The dialectical method: Its application to social theory. *Social Forces, 57*, 785–798.

Ballinger, J. (1991). *Relational dimensions of public–organization relationships*. Unpublished master's thesis. San Diego State University, CA.

Baxter, L. A. (1988). A dialectical perspective on communication strategies in relationship development. In S. Duck (Ed.), *Handbook of personal relationships: Theory, research and interventions* (pp. 257–273). New York: Wiley.

Baxter, L. A. (1990). Dialectical contractions in relationship development. *Journal of Social and Personal Relationships, 7*, 69–88.

Baxter, L. A. (1993). The social side of personal relationships: A dialectical perspective. In S. Duck (Ed.), *Understanding relationship process* (pp. 139–165). Newbury Park, CA: Sage.

Baxter, L. A. (1994). A dialogic approach to relationship maintenance. In D. J. Canary & L. Stafford (Eds.), *Communication and relational maintenance* (pp. 233–251). San Diego, CA: Academic Press.

Baxter, L. A., & Montgomery, B. M. (1996). *Relating: Dialogues & dialectics*. New York: Guilford.

Baxter, L. A., & Montgomery, B. M. (1998). A guide to dialectical approaches to studying personal relationships. In B. M. Mongtomery & L. A. Baxter (Eds.), *Dialectical approaches to studying personal relationships* (pp 1–15). Mahwah, NJ: Lawrence Erlbaum Associates.

Bennett, J. B. (2001). Teaching with hospitality. *Teaching and learning news, 10*(3), 88–89.

Bok, S. (1989). *Secrets: On the ethics of concealment and revelation*. New York: Vintage.

Broom, G. M., Casey, S., & Ritchey, J. (1997). Toward a concept and theory of organization–public relationships. *Journal of Public Relations Research, 9*, 83–93.

Broom, G. M., Casey, S., & Ritchey, J. (2000). Concept and theory of organiza-tion–public relationships. In J. A. Ledingham & S. D. Bruning (Eds.), *Public relations as relationship management: A relational approach to the study and practice of public relations* (pp. 3–22). Mahwah, NJ: Lawrence Erlbaum Associates.

Bruning, S. D., & Galloway, T. (2003). Expanding the organization–public rela-tionship scale: Exploring the role that structural and personal commitment play in organization–public relationships. *Public Relations Review, 29,* 309–319.

Bruning, S. D., & Ledingham, J. A. (1999). Relationships between organizations and publics: Development of a multi-dimensional organization–public rela-tionship scale. *Public Relations Review, 25,* 157–170.

Brunner, G. (2000). *Measuring students' perceptions of the University of Florida's commitment to public relationships and diversity.* Unpublished doctoral disser-tation, University of Florida, Gainesville.

Canary, J. D., & Stafford, L. (1992). Relational maintenance strategies and eq-uity in marriage. *Communication Monographs, 59,* 243–267.

Canary, J. D., & Stafford, L. (1993). Preservation of relational characteristics: Maintenance strategies, equity, and locus of control. In P. J. Kalbfleisch (Ed.), *Interpersonal communication: Evolving interpersonal relationships* (pp. 237–259). Hillsdale, NJ: Lawrence Erlbaum Associates.

Canary, J. D., & Stafford, L. (1994). Maintaining relationships through strategic and routine interaction. In D. J. Canary & L. Stafford (Eds.), *Communication and relational maintenance* (pp. 3–22). San Diego, CA: Academic Press.

Canary, J. D., & Stafford, L. (1997, July). *Equity and interdependence predictions of relational maintenance strategy use.* Paper presented at the meeting of the International Network on Personal Relationships, Miami University, Oxford, OH.

Canary, D. J, & Zelley, E. D. (2000). Current research programs on relational maintenance behaviors. In M. E. Roloff & G. D. Paulson (Eds.), *Communication yearbook 23* (pp. 305–340). Thousand Oaks, CA: Sage.

Clark, M. S. (1984). Record keeping in two types of relationships. *Journal of Per-sonality and Social Psychology, 47,* 549–557.

Clark, M., & Mills, J. (1979). Interpersonal attraction in exchange and commu-nal relationships. *Journal of Personality and Social Psychology, 37,* 12–24.

Clark, M. S., & Mills, J. (1993). The difference between communal and exchange relationships: What it is and is not. *Personality and Social Psychology Bulletin, 19,* 684–691.

Clark, M. S., Mills, J., & Corcoran, D. (1989). Keeping track of needs and inputs of friends and strangers. *Journal of Personality and Social Psychology Bulletin, 15,* 533–542.

Clark, M. S., Ouellette, R., Powell, M. C., & Milberg, S. (1987). Recipient's mood, relationship type, and helping. *Journal of Personality, and Social Psychology, 53,* 94–113.

Clark, M., Powell, M., & Mills, J. (1986). Keeping track of needs in two types of relationships. *Journal of Personality and Social Psychology, 51,* 333–338.

Clark, M. S., & Taraban, C. B. (1991). Reactions to and willingness to express emotions in communal and exchange relationships. *Journal of Experimental Social Psychology, 27,* 324–336.

Clark, M. S., & Waddell, B. (1985). Perception of exploitation in communal and exchange relationships. *Journal of Social and Personal Relationships, 2,* 403–413.

Coleman, J. S. (1998). Social capital in the creation of human capital. *American Journal of Sociology, 94,* 95–120.

Coombs, W. T. (2000). Crisis management: Advantages of a relational perspective. In J. A. Ledingham & S. D. Bruning (Eds.), *Public relations as relationship management: A relational approach to the study and practice of public relations* (pp. 73–94). Mahwah, NJ: Lawrence Erlbaum Associates.

Deutsch, M. (1985). *Distributive justice: A social-psychological perspective.* New Haven, CT: Yale University Press.

Dindia, K., & Canary, D. (1993). Definitions and theoretical perspectives on maintaining relationships. *Journal of Social and Personal Relationships, 10,* 163–173.

Ferguson, M. A. (1984, August). *Building theory in public relations: Interorganizational relationships as a public relations paradigm.* Paper presented to the Association for Education in Journalism and Mass Communication, Gainesville, FL.

Foa, U. G., Converse, J. R., Törnblom, K. Y., & Foa, E. B. (1993). *Resource theory: Explorations and applications.* San Diego, CA: Academic Press.

Grunig, J. E. (1976). Organizations and public relations: Testing a communication theory. *Journalism Monographs, 46.*

Grunig, J. E. (1992). *Excellence in public relations and communication management.* Hillsdale, NJ: Lawrence Erlbaum Associates.

Grunig, J. E. (2001). Two-way symmetrical public relations: Past, present, and future. In R. H. Heath & G. M. Vasquez (Eds.), *Handbook of public relations* (pp. 11–30). Newbury Park, CA: Sage.

Grunig, J. E., & Grunig, L. A. (1992). Models of public relations and communications. In J. E. Grunig (Ed.), *Excellence in public relations and communication management* (pp. 285–326). Hillsdale, NJ: Lawrence Erlbaum Associates.

Grunig, J. E., Grunig, L. A., Sriramesh, K., Huang, Y. H., & Lyra, A. (1995). Models of public relations in an international setting. *Journal of Public Relations Research, 7,* 163–186.

Grunig, J. E., & Huang, Y. H. (2000). From organizational effectiveness to relationship indicators: Antecedents of relationships, public relations strategies, and relationship outcomes. In J. A. Ledingham & S. D. Bruning (Eds.), *Public relations as relationship management: A relational approach to the study and practice of public relations* (pp. 23–54). Mahwah, NJ: Lawrence Erlbaum Associates.

Grunig, J., & Hung, C. J. F. (2002, March). *The effect of relationships on reputation and relationships on reputation: A cognitive, behavioral study.* Paper presented at the Conference of Public Relations Society of America, Educator's Academy, Miami, FL.

Grunig, J. E., & Hunt, T. (1984). *Managing public relations.* New York: Holt, Rinehart & Winston.

Grunig, L. A. (1992). Activism: How it limits the effectiveness of organizations and how excellent public relations departments respond. In J. E. Grunig (Ed.), *Excellence in public relations and communication management: Contributions to effective organizations* (pp. 483–501). Hillsdale, NJ: Lawrence Erlbaum Associates.

Grunig, L. A., Grunig, J. E., & Dozier, D. (2002). *Excellent public relations and effective organizations: A study of communication management in three countries.* Mahwah, NJ: Lawrence Erlbaum Associates.

Hatfield, E., Traupmann, J., Sprecher, S., Utne, M., & Hay, M. (1985). Equity in close relationships. In W. Ickes (Ed.), *Compatible and incompatible relationships* (pp. 91–117). New York: Springer-Verlag.

Hazelton, V., & Kennan, W. (2000, March). *Toward a social capital theory of public relationships*. Paper presented at the Conference of the Public Relations Society of America Educators' Academy, Miami, FL.

Hinde, R. A. (1997). *Relationships: A dialectical perspective*. East Sussex, London: Psychology Press.

Hon, L., & Brunner, B. (2002). Measuring public relationships among students and administrators at the University of Florida. *Journal of Communication Management, 6*(3), 227–238.

Hon, L. C., & Grunig, J. E. (1999). *Measuring relationships in public relations*. Gainesville, FL: Institute for Public Relations.

Huang, Y. H. (1997). *Public relations strategies, relational outcomes, and conflict management strategies*. Unpublished doctoral dissertation, University of Maryland, College Park.

Huang, Y. H. (2001a). OPRA: A cross-cultural, multiple-item scale for measuring organization–public relationships. *Journal of Public Relations Research, 13,* 61–90.

Huang, Y. H. (2001b). Values of public relations: Effects on organization–public relationships mediating conflict resolution. *Journal of Public Relations Research, 13,* 265–302.

Hung, C. J. F. (2000a, March). *Organization–public relationships, relationship maintenance strategies, and relationship outcomes*. Paper presented at the Conference of the Public Relations Society of America, Educator's Academy, Miami, FL.

Hung, C. J. F. (2000b, October). *Global public relations: A study of public relations in China from economic systems perspectives*. Paper presented at the Conference of the Public Relations Society of America, Educators' Academy, Miami, FL.

Hung, C. J. F. (2002). *The interplays of relationship types, relationship cultivation, and relationship outcomes: How multinational and Taiwanese companies practice public relations and organization–public relationship management in China*. Unpublished doctoral dissertation, University of Maryland, College Park.

Hung, C. J. F. (2003a, May). *Culture, relationship cultivation strategies and relationship qualities: A qualitative on multinational companies' relationship management in China*. Paper presented at the Public Relations Division of the 53rd Annual Conference of International Communication Association, San Diego, CA.

Hung, C. J. F. (2003b, October). *How to develop a quality relationship? Types of relationships and their effects on relationship cultivation strategies*. Paper presented at the Conference of the Public Relations Society of America, Educator's Academy, New Orleans, LA.

Hung, C. J. F. (2004a). Cultural influence on relationship cultivation strategies: Multinational companies in China. *Journal of Communication Management, 8*(3), 264–281.

Hung, C. J. F. (2004b). *Relationship cultivation strategies and relationship outcomes: A comparative study on multinational and Taiwanese companies' relationship building in China*. Paper presented at the 54th International Communication Association, New Orleans, LA.

Hung, C. J. F. (2004c). Relationship building, activism, and conflict resolution: A case study on the termination of licensed prostitution in the Taipei City. *Asian Journal of Communication, 13*(2), 21–49.

Hung, C. J. F. (2005a). Exploring types of organization–public relationships and their implication for relationship management in public relations. *Journal of Public Relations Research, 17*(4), 393–426.

Hung, C. J. F. (2005b, May). *Exploring the dynamics of organization–public relationships from the dialectical perspective.* Paper presented at the Public Relations Division of the 55th Annual Conference of International Communication Association, New York.

Jo, S., Hon, L. C., & Brunner, B. R. (2004). Organization–public relationships: Measurement validation in a university setting. *Journal of Communication Management, 9*(1), 14–27.

Jo, S., & Kim, Y. (2003). The effect of web characteristics on relationship building. *Journal of Public Relations Research, 15*(3), 199–224.

Kelley, H. H. (1979). *Personal relationships: Their structure and processes.* Hillsdale, NJ: Lawrence Erlbaum Associates.

Kelley, H. H., & Thibaut, J. W. (1978). *Interpersonal relations.* New York: Wiley.

Ki, E. J. (2004, May). *Relationship maintenance strategies on web sites: How do different industries utilize relationship maintenance strategies?* Paper presented at the 2004 Annual Conference of the International Communication Association, New Orleans.

Ki, E. J., & Shin, J. H. (2005, May). *The status of organization–public relationship research in public relations: Analysis of published articles between 1985 and 2004.* Paper presented at the 2005 Annual Conference of the International Communication Association, New York.

Kim, H. (2005, May). *Organizational structure and internal communication as antecedents of employee–organization relationships: A multilevel analysis.* Paper presented at the 2005 Annual Conference of the International Communication Association, New York.

Kim, Y. (2001). Searching for the organization–public relationship: A valid and reliable instrument. *Journalism and Mass Communication Quarterly, 78*(4), 799–810.

Ledingham, J. A., & Bruning, S. D. (1998). Relationship management and public relations: Dimensions of an organization-public relationship. *Public Relations Review, 24*, 55–65.

Ledingham, J. A., & Bruning, S. D. (2000). *Public relations as relationship management: A relational approach to the study and practice of public relations.* Mahwah, NJ: Lawrence Erlbaum Associates.

Ledingham, J. A., Bruning, S. D., & Wilson, L. J. (1999). Time as an indicator of the perceptions and behavior of members of a key public: Monitoring and prediction organization–public relationships. *Journal of Public Relations Research, 11*, 167–183.

Len-Rios, M. (2001). *Playing by the rules: Relationships with online users.* [Research paper submitted to the Institute for Public Relations for the 2000 Ketchum Walter K. Lindenmann Scholarship]. Gainesville, FL: Institute for Public Relations.

McCroskey, J. C. (1984). Communication competence: The elusive construct. In R. N. Bostrom (Ed.), *Competence in communication* (pp. 259–268). Beverly Hills, CA: Sage.

Millar, F. E., & Rogers, L. E. (1987). Relational dimensions of interpersonal dynamics. In M. E. Roloff & G. R. Miller (Eds.), *Interpersonal processes: New directions in communication research* (pp. 117–139). Newbury Park, CA: Sage.

Mills, J., & Clark, M. S. (1982). Communal and exchange relationships. *Review of Personality and Social Psychology, 3*, 121–144.

Mills, J., & Clark, M. S. (1986). Communications that should lead to perceived exploitation in communal and exchange relationships. *Journal of Social and Clinical Psychology, 4*, 225–234.

Mills, J., & Clark, M. (1994). Communal and exchange relationships: Controversies and research. In R. Erber & R. Gilmour (Eds.), *Theoretical frameworks for personal relationships* (pp. 29–42). Hillsdale, NJ: Lawrence Erlbaum Associates.

Monge, P. R., Bachman, S. G., Dillard, J. P., & Eisenberg, E. M. (1981). Communicator competence in the workplace: Model testing and scale development. In M. Burgoon (Ed.), *Communication yearbook 5* (pp. 505–527). Beverly Hills, CA: Sage.

Montgomery, B. M. (1993). Relationship maintenance versus relationship change: A dialectical dilemma. *Journal of Social and Personal Relationships, 10,* 205–223.

Montgomery, B. M., & Baxter, L. A. (1998a). *Dialectical approaches to studying personal relationships.* Mahwah, NJ: Lawrence Erlbaum Associates.

Montgomery, B. M., & Baxter, L. A. (1998b). Dialogism and relational dialectics. In B. M. Montgomery & L. A. Baxter (Eds.), *Dialectical approaches to studying personal relationships* (pp. 155–183), Mahwah, NJ: Lawrence Erlbaum Associates.

Parks, M. R. (1994). Communicative competence and interpersonal control. In M. L. Knapp & G. R. Miller (Eds.), *Handbook of interpersonal communication* (2nd ed., pp. 589–620). Thousand Oaks, CA: Sage.

Plowman, K. D. (1995) *Congruence between public relations and conflict resolution: Negotiating in the organization.* Unpublished doctoral dissertation, University of Maryland, College Park.

Portes, A. (1998). Social capital: Its origins and applications in modern sociology. *Annual Review of Sociology, 24*(1), 1–24.

Rawlins, W. K. (1989). A dialectical analysis of the tensions, function, and strategic challenges of communication in young adult friendships. In J. A. Anderson (Ed.), *Communication yearbook 12* (pp. 157–189). Newbury Park, CA: Sage.

Rusbult, C. E., Drigotas, S. M., & Verette, J. (1994). The investment model: An interdependence analysis of commitment processes and relationship maintenance phenomena. In D. J. Canary & L. Stafford (Eds.), *Communication and relational maintenance* (pp. 115–139). San Diego, CA: Academic Press.

Sha, B. L. (1999). *Cultural public relations: Identity, activism, globalization, and gender in the Democratic Progressive Party on Taiwan.* Unpublished doctoral dissertation, University of Maryland, College Park.

Spitzberg, B. H., & Cupach, W. R. (1984). *Interpersonal communication competence.* Beverly Hills, CA: Sage.

Stafford, L., & Canary, D. J. (1991). Maintenance strategies and romantic relationship type, gender, and relational characteristics. *Journal of Social and Personal Relationships, 8,* 217–242.

Stroh, U. (1999, May). *Communication management in a millennium of chaos and change.* Paper presented at the meeting of the International Communication Association, San Francisco.

Thayer, L. (1968). *Communication and communication systems.* Homewood, IL: Irwin.

Thibaut, J. W., & Kelley, H. H. (1959). *The social psychology of groups.* New York: Wiley.

Thomlison, T. D. (2000). An interpersonal primer with implications for public relations. In J. A. Ledingham & S. D. Bruning (Eds.), *Public relations as relationship management: A relational approach to the study and practice of public relations* (pp. 177–204). Mahwah, NJ: Lawrence Erlbaum Associates.

Toth, E. L. (2000). From personal influence to interpersonal influence: A model for relationship management. In J. A. Ledingham & S. D. Bruning (Eds.), *Public relations as relationship management: A relational approach to the study and practice of public relations* (pp. 205–220). Mahwah, NJ: Lawrence Erlbaum Associates.

Voloshinov, V. N., & Bakhtin, M. M. (1973). *Marxism and the philosophy of language.* Cambridge, MA: Harvard University Press.

Wood, J. T. (1996). *Everyday encounters: An introduction to interpersonal communication.* Belmont, CA: Wadsworth.

Chapter 22

Effective Government Affairs in China: Antecedents, Strategies, and Outcomes of Government Affairs

Yi-Ru Regina Chen
University of Macau, SAR

This chapter is written for public relations scholars, practitioners, and students who have interest in government affairs for business organizations, especially multinational corporations (MNCs) in China. Although there is a plethora of books on public relations or doing business in China on the market, none of them, to my best knowledge, has delineated insights of government affairs for MNCs in China from an integrated perspective of public relations and corporate political activity. It is my hope that this chapter, which provides a combination of succinct analysis and recommendations, casts some new insights on business–government interaction.

This chapter addresses how organizations can effectively interact with government in their task environments. The purposes of this chapter are to provide a brief literature review on government affairs from public relations and other relevant fields and then to suggest how to expand the Excellence Theory to this particular context. This chapter consists of three parts. It first examines the literature on corporate political activities, beginning with an overview of theories and models of corporate political involvement and extending to public relations studies on government affairs. Then, the chapter proposes a theoretical model of effective government affairs to expand the Excellence Theory to the particular context of governments. The conceptual model of government affairs in the chapter is developed based on theoretical propositions and empirical data from Chen's (2005) research that examined government affairs practices by 25 MNCs in China through long interviews. The MNCs in her study covered a variety of industries and three business entry models to China's market: wholly owned foreign subsidiaries, joint ventures, and a combination of the two. The chapter finally suggests future directions for expanding the Excellence Theory in relation to government relations.

PUBLIC AFFAIRS, CORPORATE POLITICAL INVOLVEMENT, GOVERNMENT RELATIONS, AND LOBBYING

Several disciplines examine the business–government interaction, including business management, political science, public affairs, and public relations. Business management has the most extensive body of research on corporate political activities and corporate responses to social and political issues from the perspective of corporations. Because business–government interaction is a subject studied by multiple disciplines, several terms are associated with the subject, including *corporate public affairs, corporate political involvement, lobbying,* and *corporate government affairs.*

Public affairs is a function of an organization that deals with its external environment. Hoewing (1998) maintained that, in its broadest sense, public affairs could be defined as "the management function that interprets the corporation's noncommercial conditions and directs the company's response to those conditions" (p. 61). Although public affairs has been widely recognized and utilized as an essential function of a corporation, what constitutes public affairs varies from company to company. A survey (1984) conducted by the Public Affairs Council showed that corporate public affairs in the United States typically has four major functions: government relations, political action, community involvement and corporate responsibility, and international political development (as cited in J. Grunig & Hunt, 1984).

Getz (2002) examined corporate public affairs research in the past two decades and identified three topics commonly explored in examinations of the nature of corporate public affairs: motivation of corporate political involvement, corporate political strategies, and the corporate capacity for rational political actions to attain desired outcomes. These three topics, which Mitnick (2001) called "threads,"[1] reflect various aspects of corporate public affairs and constitute the body of knowledge of corporate political affairs.

Corporate political involvement can be broadly defined as "[corporate] participation in the formulation and execution of public policy at

---

[1]As Getz (2002) cited, the idea of threads was coined by Mitnick during his communication with Getz.

various levels of government" (Sethi, 1982, p. 32). Corporations are involved in political processes by taking corporate political actions, initiating corporate political activities, and employing corporate political strategies. Lobbying is the most commonly practiced corporate political strategy. As Jaatinen (1999) defined, lobbying is "a process to influence political decision-making on a certain issue in the interest of a group by communicating with publics relevant to the political process, including decision-makers and officials, competitors, the mass media, citizens, and the constituents of the lobbyists" (p. 22).

Government affairs, or government relations, is an essential subset of public affairs (Wilcox, Cameron, Ault, & Agee, 2003). A 1992 survey conducted by the Foundation for Public Affairs concluded that government relations, including both federal and state governments, was the prototypical function in the 163 corporations that participated in the study. Dominguez (1982) defined government relations as "a function through which the company can actively participate in all phases of government with optimum resource utilization and maximum effectiveness" (p. 48). This function is maximized by communication techniques and establishment of corporation–government and corporation–employee relationships (J. Grunig & Hunt, 1984; Mack & Edwards, 1989; Wilcox et al., 2003).

In summary, public affairs, a specialty of public relations, is a function that oversees an organization's activities with its external environment. Corporate political involvement and government relations are two components of public affairs. Government affairs is a mediating function that fosters corporate political involvement in the government. Lobbying is a political strategy frequently practiced by corporations to influence a public policy.

LITERATURE REVIEW OF CORPORATE PUBLIC AFFAIRS BY THEORETICAL BASES

Getz (2002) classified works in corporate public affairs by their theoretical bases: atheoretical work, and works in political science, economics, sociology, and management. Political economy and public relations are two other theoretical bases of corporate public affairs studies and, thus, they are introduced in this section to build on Getz's list. Each individual theory base has applied different premises and taken different approaches when examining the three threads mentioned previously.

Atheoretical Work

Getz (2002) noted that atheoretical work dominated the research in the field at the early stage and has been providing carefully researched descriptions of the activities of the firms that are politically engaged as the political environment evolves (i.e., the focus of studies shifts from descriptions of U.S. corporations in U.S. democracy to the descriptions of political actions in the European Union and multinational corporations' political actions in a global context). Most of the descriptive work is published by management scholars. Getz (2002) claimed that Epstein's (1969) *The Corporation in American Politics* is the classical and most influential work of this sort that reports corporate political activities in U.S. society. Even though atheoretical work has contributed to the understanding of political actions, the results of this type of work has never been systematically explained or interpreted within theoretical frameworks.

Political Science

Political scientists have studied the process of governing and efforts to influence governmental activities from the interest group approach (Getz, 2002). The interest group theory posits that "the democratic public policy process is an attempt to reach compromise between the competing goals of a multitude of interest groups" (p. 308). This line of corporate public affairs research conceptualizes corporate interests as profit making or maintaining dominant ideology that fosters profits. Essentially, corporations participate in the political battle to secure their profit or to prevent unfavorable ideology (e.g., antibusiness, Keynesian, and prosocialist) from gaining momentum in the political arena (Clawson, Karson, & Kaufmann, 1986; Eismeier & Pollock, 1987; Plotke, 1992).

According to Getz's (2002) analysis, the interest group theory only explains one of the three threads of corporate political activities: the corporation's motivation for political involvement. The interest group theory suggests that business needs to participate in the political process to ensure that public policies or governmental actions do not damage business interests, and maintain the status quo business ideology in society because other interest groups are (or could be) representing their interests and ideology in the political process.

Economics

Economists have examined corporate political participation based on a cost–benefit calculation. Four economic theories are widely applied in approaching the issues of corporate political actions: collective action theory, public choice theory, game theory, and transaction costs theory (Getz, 2002). The first three theories provide different explanations of why corporations are politically active. The last three theories contribute to the understanding of how businesses choose political strategies.

Collective action theory explains the cost–benefit calculation of a corporation's political involvement by the size of the group to which the corporation belongs. The larger the group to which a corporation belongs is, the less likely the corporation is to engage in a political process if there are no incentives or sanctions involved (Olson, 1965). Public choice theory defines political process as a market-like exchange of self-interest between public officials and private actors, and predicts the behavior of individual political actors by their perceived incentives and constraints associated with a particular policy (Getz, 2002). Following the self-interest exchange assumption, firms enter the political process when they perceive a potential benefit or cost in a governmental policy. In addition, corporations must understand what constitutes incentives and constraints on a policy decision-making process as perceived by each individual actor to determine what the effective strategies would be to the actor.

Game theory suggests that (a) corporations engage in political activities when they anticipate their opponents are politically active, and (b) corporations choose political strategies and targeted political decision makers based on their expectations regarding their opponents' strategies and targets (Austen-Smith & Wright, 1992). Getz (2002) argued that game theory contributes to the dynamic and social nature of political activity. Transaction costs economists focus on finding the most effective organizational arrangement that reduces the most transaction costs, resulting from transferring goods or services across a technologically separable interface (Williamson, 1985). Transaction costs theory posits that firms practice political strategies (e.g., having an in-house public affairs function vs. contracting it out, and acting collectively with others in political advocacy vs. independently) that require little transaction cost.

Political Economy

Political economy theory emphasizes that economics cannot be separated from politics, and that these two reinforce each other (Gilpin, 2001; Strange, 1991). Political economy theory argues that industry-leading corporations tend to be politically active to make the economic structures in places where they conduct business more desirable to them. It also indicates that a corporation's economics determines its political influence on government (Lawton, 1997) and, thus, its political strategies should be developed accordingly.

Sociology

Sociologists study human behaviors in organizations and relations between organizations (Getz, 2002). Resource dependence theory and institutional theory are applied to explain business political actions. Resource dependence theory argues that the interdependence between corporations and governments in resources result in corporate political activities (Baysinger, 1984). Political activity is not used to reduce a corporation's dependence on government but rather to manage the uncertainty associated with dependence and, thereby, to minimize negative effects of dependence on the corporation (Getz, 2002). In addition, level of corporate dependence shapes corporate political strategies (Kotter, 1979).

Institutional theory posits that corporations use political activity to obtain informal and formal institutional resources critical to an organization's success, including legitimacy and laws and governmental policies favorable to organizational structures or processes (DiMaggio & Powell, 1983; Oliver, 1991). As for the selection of strategies, this theory argues that the ability and choice to act independently depends on institutional rules, as well as relative political capital (e.g., direct communication channels to and ongoing relationships with public officials) of the firm and its opponents. Political capital is produced by organizational resources (e.g., advanced technology and economic and social power) (Getz, 2002).

Management

According to Getz's (2002) analysis, management theorists focus on the behavior of organizations, as guided by their top management, to achieve maximum effectiveness and efficiency. Four management theories have been employed in business public affairs research: agency theory, behavioral theory of the firm, business strategy, and population ecology. Agency theory deals with problems derived from agent-principal relationships and strategies that the principal employs to reduce the problems (Eisenhardt, 1989; Keim & Baysinger, 1993; Mitnick, 1993). Agency theory in business public affairs focuses on the agency relationship—the firm as the principal and the political decision maker as the agent—and treats the relationship as the product of business political activity. Because it is structurally impossible for corporations to make policy decisions, the motivation of having political action is to create agents who act on the corporations' behalf and, further, to maintain a good agency relationship (Mitnick, 1993). This theory models political influence as a means of agent control and suggests that political strategies should be chosen based on the agency problems the firm is facing and attempts to resolve (Getz, 2002).

Behavioral theory of the firm and business strategy theory posit that an organization's decision of political engagement and activities is a result of the organization's characteristics and strategic thinking. In addition, organizational characteristics and strategic thinking also determine an organization's capability for rational political action. Population ecology theory argues that an organization's political activity is affected by other similar organizations in its external environment because they all extract resources from the same environment (Hannan & Carroll, 1992; Hannan & Freeman, 1989). This theory is used to examine the reasons that drive organizations to participate in political arena independently or collectively, as well as the organization's capability for rational action (Getz, 2002).

Public Relations

Public relations scholars consider corporate political activities as a corporation's response to political issues in order to manage its interdependence with publics who can enhance or constrain the corporation's goal achievement. From an open system perspective, public relations scholars maintain that organizations obtain resources from the outside environment, incorporate those resources into their operations, and discharge products or services to the outside environment (J. Grunig & Hunt, 1984; L. Grunig,, Grunig, & Dozier, 2002). Interdependence results because of the mutual needs between organizations and publics in their environment. Relationships that assist organizations in managing interdependence contribute to organizational effectiveness by allowing the organizations to balance their goals with the demands of their publics (L. Grunig et al., 2002).

Relationships also serve as the foundation of corporate political actions. Quality organization–public relationships gain support from the publics to an organization. The support builds up public momentum, which leads to successful lobbying and corporate political action. As Keim (1981) asserted, organizations must begin with developing an informed and motivated constituency and establishing contacts with political decision makers, regardless of which corporate political strategies they choose to apply. Communication assists relationship building. Therefore, public relations research in government affairs focuses on these two aspects: communication and organization–public relationships.

It is clear that pubic relations distinguishes from other theoretical bases when analyzing business–government relationships. Public relations emphasizes business–government relationships as an organizational tool to manage its interdependence with government. Other theoretical bases focus on the competitive nature of business–government relationships and treat corporate political activity as means to gain benefits or reduce costs by influencing public policies. Therefore, government affairs from the public relations perspective is a regular function of an organization to constantly manage its publics in the external environment. On the other hand, government affairs from other theoretical views is a corporate response to political issues.

PUBLIC RELATIONS RESEARCH ON GOVERNMENT AFFAIRS

Compared with disciplines of business management and political science, public relations literature has fewer studies on business–government interaction. This is because most public relations theories are general frameworks that can be applied across situations and publics, such as investors, consumers, employees, communities, media, and governments. The Public Relations Society of America's (1995) book, *Practical Public Affairs in an Era of Change*, is the first book entirely dedicated to public affairs studies from the public relations perspective. It introduces lobbying and political actions in the United States. It furthermore discusses the impacts of communication techniques, media relations, and public releases on public affairs; issues management and anticipatory management of public affairs; shadow constituencies, the CEOs, and activist groups in public affairs; lobbying; ethics, corporate social responsibility, corporate philanthropy, and public affairs; and international public affairs. Lerbinger's (2006) book *Corporate Public Affairs* is the second one of this type.

Other studies on public affairs in the body of public relations research can be categorized along three lines: the nature of government affairs in the United States and other countries, application of public relations theories to governments or other political publics, and corporate issues management of public issues. The first line of research investigates public affairs practices worldwide. Various public relations books and journal articles discuss the practice of public affairs in the United States and provide useful guidelines for practitioners. Johnson (1992) surveyed lobbyists in Washington, DC, to examine the relationship between lobbying and public relations by identifying which public relations models practiced by lobbyists. Kraus (1995) introduced the practice of government relations in the 1990s and beyond and pinpointed factors affecting contemporary government relations. This article provides an overview and useful recommendations of government relations practice in the United States. Mack (1995) explained different forms of U.S. lobbying and political actions and discussed the relationship between money and politics in the United States. Pinkham (2001) noted a decline of public trust toward corporations and provided guidance of practicing public affairs under this social sentiment.

Lange's (2000) research reported the profile of public affairs practitioners in the Netherlands. Similarly, Hang and Koppang (1997) examined how lobbying was practiced in a European context, Norway. They concluded that, in Norway, company CEOs and public relations managers ran corporate lobbying increasingly through companies' independent political actions. In Sriramesh and Vercic's (2003) edited book and Sriramesh's (2004) edited book, public relations scholars systematically introduced the political systems of 17 countries in Asia, Australia, Africa, Europe, and the Americas. However, only the chapters on Japan and Chile provide cases to illustrate government relations programs practiced in the nations (Ferrari, 2003; Inoue, 2003). Chen's (2005) research delineated government affairs practiced by MNCs in China.

As explained previously, public relations theories tend to be generic. Therefore, the second line of the public relations research on government relations examines the applications of these theories to corporate communication with government. The Excellence Study systematically examined the propositions of excellent factors in organizational communication with governments in the United States, Canada, and United Kingdom. Jaatinen (1999) examined lobbying in Finland and developed a model of effective lobbying strategies by applying the situation theory (J. Grunig & Hunt, 1984) and two-way symmetrical public relations (J. Grunig & L. Grunig, 1992). Chen (2005) analyzed government affairs practices by MNCs in China based on the public relations theories, including relationship management, the situational theory, and the strategic management of public relations.

The third line of public relations research on public affairs focuses on corporate management of public issues through communication. Scholars prescribe the management or rhetorical approach to examine this topic. The management approach of managing issues places emphasis on environmental scanning, two-way communication, strategic thinking, organization–public relationships, and organizational culture (Chase, 1984; J. Grunig & Repper, 1992; Heath, 1994, 1997, 1998). Studies of public affairs from a rhetorical approach concluded that advocacy is a necessary part of the political process that produces cocreation of meaning and public policy (Cheney, 1992; Heath, 1992; Toth & Heath, 1992). The best argument will be accepted and used to produce policy. Thus, public relations practitioners manage public issues by framing the best argument with appropriate frames and effective symbols in discussion. In addition, they communicate and negotiate the relationships with organizational publics through the process (Vasquez, 1996).

A CONCEPTUAL MODEL OF GOVERNMENT AFFAIRS

A theoretical or descriptive work on government affairs is informative but of little value to the theory building. The findings of several government affairs studies in different nations support the Excellence Theory in relation to the specific applications of generic principles considering a nation's conditions, including its economic system, political system, media, culture, level of development, and activism. To go beyond mere description of different government affairs practices in various countries, one should systematically explain the practical differences by linking them to contextual factors in a large social environment suggested by the theoretical bases of corporate public affairs. Based on the data from government affairs practices by MNCs in China, Chen (2005) developed a normative model of effective government affairs that contains the antecedents, strategies, and outcomes of government affairs. Figure 22.1 presents the model. The model first identifies six antecedents that affect the development of government affairs practice. It then illustrates the substance of strategic government affairs practice shaped by the antecedents. Finally, the model pinpoints the outcomes of effective government affairs. The following sections discuss each component of the model in detail, with evidence from Chen's (2005) research.

Antecedents of Government Affairs

Six variables are identified as antecedents of government affairs performed by MNCs in China: organizational economics, structural factors of a host country, corporation–government relationships, contextual features of an issue, characteristics of the government agencies involved, and organizational characteristics (Chen, 2005). These factors affect the development of an MNC's effective government affairs in China. It should be noted, however, that no one antecedent can determine an MNC's government affairs practice by itself. That is, when shaping strategic government affairs practice, MNCs always take the combination of the six antecedents (if applicable) into consideration.

Organizational Economics

Business–government relations is the best exemplar of political economy theory that demonstrates how economics and politics reinforce each other. Therefore, economics is the first identified antecedent of corporate government affairs. Evidence from Chen's (2005) research indicated that even though studied MNCs operated in a common political system of China, the economic circumstances of the MNCs shaped their individual needs and ways to interact with the Chinese government, as well as their relative levels of influence on the public policy. This conclusion echoed Kennedy's (2005) assertion on corporate lobbying in China. A firm's economic circumstances contain its organization-specific and industrial economic characteristics. Findings of the same study suggested that organization-specific economic characteristics include: wholly owned or joint-venture ownership, organizational importance, business scope, and phase of business development. Industrial economics consist of level of regulation and governmental priority of the industry.

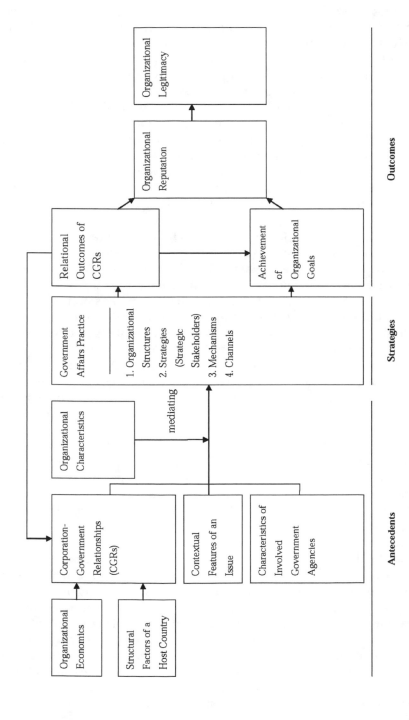

FIG. 22.1. Model of government affairs.

487

Organization-Specific Economics: Ownership Types.   The owner-ship of an organization affects its interaction with the government, which, in turn, often determines the mechanism of government affairs (e.g., internal government affairs function or contracting it out) in an MNC in China. State-owned organizations naturally have government support, whereas private companies must make efforts to form allies in the government. As a result, MNCs entering China with joint ventures (with Chinese state-owned companies) often have governmental sup-port, just like state-owned companies, or, at least, they can use their Chinese partners to seek government favors or access to government of-ficials. MNCs with only wholly owned foreign subsidiaries in China have to seek support with the government by themselves through mak-ing substantial effort in government affairs.

Organization-Specific Economics: Organizational Importance. Organizational importance is determined by a corporation's influence in the industry or its investment in a host market. According to resource dependence theory and political economy theory, the more important a firm is to a host government, the more influence it has on the govern-ment's decision making. For example, Chen (2005) found that indus-try-leading MNCs have significant access to top-level government officials in the central government. Furthermore, their positions as in-dustry leaders produce organizational credibility that enhances govern-ment officials' trust in them. Government officials seek information or resources from those MNCs. Consequently, dependence and frequent cooperation have formed. Dependence and cooperation, in turn, render advantages to the MNCs in government affairs.

Chen (2005) also noted that in contemporary China—where eco-nomic growth is highly valued by different levels of the Chinese govern-ment—attracting foreign direct investment in its district is one of the top priorities of the government. As a result, MNCs with massive invest-ment in China receive support and services from government officials.

Organization-Specific Economics: Business Scope.   Chen (2005) concluded that MNCs in pursuit of government procurement (e.g., aerospace MNCs) evidently pay closer attention to government affairs than do those that do not target governments as customers. Govern-ment's purchases of corporate output increase the government's impact on business, which, in turn, spurs corporate political activities with the Chinese government. This finding is consistent with the conclusion of studies conducted in the United States that industries whose inputs have to be purchased by governments put many resources on their po-litical action committees (PACs; e.g., Boies, 1989; Master & Baysinger, 1985; Zardkoohi, 1985). Again, resource dependence theory explains the motivation of MNCs in pursuit of government purchases or national projects to emphasize government affairs.

Organization-Specific Economics: Phase of Business Development. Lieberthal and Lieberthal (2003) argued that MNCs' China operations evolve through three distinct periods: the entry, country development, and global integration. Each phase has a different goal, and based on that fact the role of the MNC's China office and the profile of its ideal China manager vary. In the entry phase, the main goal of an MNC is to establish a presence in China through a right business model emphasizing its competitive values. The MNC's China office should provide support to its business units as they enter the market and make effort to establish the corporate brand with local and national government. In the country development phase, an MNC strives to expand operation in China to several initiatives and localities. As a result, its China office contributes to the organizational effectiveness by building brand awareness with strategic publics, especially customers; coordinating lobbying and negotiation with the Chinese government across business units; articulating "one face to China"; and managing awareness of its China operation at corporate headquarters. In the phase of global integration, an MNC aims to fully integrate its China operations into regional and global efforts. The role of the China office, then, is to implement further regional and global strategies for its operations and, thus, the senior China manager must be able to work with several business divisions across nations. Results of Chen's (2005) study show that MNCs in the entry phase of their China operations expect their government affairs to assist the firms effectively solving problems in the license-application process, whereas government affairs of those in their country development phase primarily focuses on issues management, relationship management, and business development to coordinate business units and government authorities. This finding suggests that corporations should design and alter their government affairs practices according to the goal of their business stages.

Industrial Economics: Level of Regulation.   Highly regulated industries require companies to practice government affairs in an attempt to influence industrial policy-formulation processes, because the government has a great impact on business operations in these industries. In addition, effective MNCs in highly regulated industries are keen to new policy changes and strategically adjust their business plans in line with revised policies to earn benefits (or reduce costs) from the changes and remain competitive in the industries. In the United States, empirical work has found that firms in highly regulated industries were more likely to form a PAC (Andres, 1985; Boies, 1989; Masters & Baysinger,

1985). In China, highly regulated industries (e.g., automobile, aerospace, banking, insurance, and express shipping) allow limited foreign investment mainly for political, economic, or national security reasons. With China's accession to the World Trade Organization, the country has had to gradually relax some restrictions on foreign ownership and establishment of business in currently highly regulated industries. Therefore, MNCs in these industries actively engage in relevant policy-formulation processes by various means (Chen, 2005). MNCs in loosely regulated industries, on the other hand, have low motivation to be politically active in China.

Industrial Economics: Governmental Priority of the Industry.   In business–government interdependence, governments depend on resources held by corporations, such as monetary capital and technology. Resource dependence theory posits that when an organization holds resources desired by a government, the organization has great bargaining power in relation to the government. The great bargaining power, as suggested by political economy theory, shapes the organization's relationship with the government and affects the policy formulation. As a result, governmental priority of industry affects a firm's government affairs. Luo (2000) observed that many MNCs benefit from the structural transformation of various industries in China. MNCs in the industries that were encouraged by the Chinese government have received various incentives for investment from the government, including basic infrastructure service and significant reductions in taxes and fees. Chen (2005) further noted that in addition to the incentives, government officials tend to be accommodative to the needs of MNCs to maintain their investment. Consequently, these MNCs have advantages in interacting with the government officials that are not available to MNCs in the industries with low governmental priority or local companies in China.

Structural Factors of a Host Country

In addition to a company's economic circumstances, the structural factors of a host country also affect business–government relations. There is a strong consensus that a corporation's external environment influences the calculation of benefits and costs of its political involvement. However, what constructs an organization's external environment might vary in different situations (Schuler & Rehbein, 1997). Taking China as an example, evidence from Chen's (2005) research indicates that two structural factors of China significantly shape government affairs practice by MNCs: China's authoritarian political system and its socialist market economy. The influence of the political system on government affairs is self-explanatory. A nation's political system shapes its political process and indicates influential actors in the process. China currently implements an authoritarian political system ruled by the Communist Party of China (CPC). Influential actors in Chinese politics are elite party members and middle- and top-level government officials (Chen, 2005). Unlike in democratic countries where policymakers, government officials, and interest groups are politically involved, China's lesser diversity of political actors has positive and negative effects on the practice of corporate government affairs. The positive effect is that corporations only need to lobby on two parties, which often have the same position on a policy, to influence the outcome of a policy. The negative effect rests on the difficulty of identifying party members and government officials who are politically influential in individual policymaking.

China is an emerging market under a socialist market economy. To implement a free market economy in a socialist setting, China has adopted a socialist market economy that allows business enterprises to be subject to market mechanisms (i.e., supply and demand) under governmental guidance of macrocentral planning (Suliman, 1998). Emerging markets, according to the World Bank, are those in which "GDP per capita income is below $8,000 per annum but potentially dynamic and rapidly growing economies, where MNEs [multinational enterprises] can seek lucrative opportunities for medium to long-term investments" (as cited in Luo, 2002, p. 4). This unique economic system has profound influence on business–government relations.

A socialist market economy increases government control of market developments and intervention in business operations, and thus increases the importance of government affairs to organizational effectiveness. Luo (2002) found that MNCs and host governments are highly cooperative in emerging markets because of recent shifts in policies of emerging-market governments, deregulation and liberalization of national economics, and intense competition pressure for attracting foreign direct investment. In addition, weak legal infrastructures, a common characteristic of emerging markets, leads to "unique commercial practice and business culture that are people-oriented and socially-embedded" (Luo, 2002, pp. 5–6). This feature well explains the emphasis that MNCs place on government relations to foster their operations in China, where the interpretation and enforcement of laws are heavily subject to responsible government officials (Chen, 2005). In summary, China's political and economic systems explain not only the importance of government affairs to corporations but also the special applications of Chinese government affairs.

Business–Government Relationships

Most corporate political literature focuses on the competitive-cooperation dimension of business–government relationships based on resource dependence, and how the dependence affects the dynamics between corporations and governments. Scholars who subscribe to a conflictual-based paradigm argue that MNCs and host governments form adversarial relationships in which each seeks the maximum gain of self-interest from the bargain based on their respective power (e.g., Fagre & Wells, 1982; Moran, 1985; Pfeffer & Salancik, 1978). Dunning (1997) and Stopford (1994) began to address cooperation between MNCs and host governments that creates synergy and better payoffs for both parties when they have complementary resources and compatible interest. To properly delineate the complexity of business–government relations, Luo (2002) proposed a typology that classifies relationships between MNCs and host governments into four categories based on their various degrees of competition and cooperation (coopetition): estranger, contender, partner, and coopetitor. Luo further maintained that each type of MNC has its own political tactics. For instance, MNCs having low competition with host governments (estranger and partner) tend to employ less confrontational tactics when responding to governmental regulations. Those with high competition (contender and coopetitor) are more likely to act aggressively (Luo, 2002).

Public relations highlights another perspective on business–government relationships—interdependence. That is, even though corporations and governments do not compete or collaborate with each other for resources, they must be independent to each other to survive in the environment (i.e., corporations seek legitimacy of operations from governments and governments need taxes paid by corporations to maintain administrative operations). Public relations scholars argue that managing the interdependence requires corporations to build quality, long-term relationships with governments by balancing firms' goals with the expectations of the governments. This corporate behavior, in turn, strengthens mutual understanding, trust, satisfaction, control, and commitment to each other. Therefore, public relations adds another dimension of business–government relationships: asymmetry versus symmetry. Asymmetrical business–government relationships often lead to emphasis on the competition and respective power and resources held by each party involved when practicing government affairs. Parties in a symmetrical business–government relationship tend to value mutual understanding, and thus are willing to depend on effective communication (discussions) in government affairs.

Contextual Features of the Issue

Effective government affairs must be contingent on a given issue (Jaatinen, 1999). Interview data with MNCs in China suggest several aspects of an issue that should be considered: types of the issue, levels of the issue, and stages of the issue. MNCs frequently face three types of issues concerning the Chinese government: administrative or operational, policy or regulatory, and business (Chen, 2005). Administrative or operational issues include issues that involve government administration or affect a corporation's normal operation. License applications, governmental inspections, and power shortages are issues of this type. Policy or regulatory issues are those resulting from existing policies or regulations. Business issues include those that affect a corporation's business development in China, such as government procurement.

Levels of the issue refer to the magnificence of an issue in terms of its impact. An issue's level can be a local, provincial, or national. It can also be company-specific or industrial. An issue's level determines not only the appropriate level of communication channel between a corporation and government officials, but also the mechanism of lobbying (i.e., lobbying independently or collectively). An issue usually evolves through three stages: emergence, formulation, and implementation (Buchholz, 1988; Getz, 1993). The emergence stage of the issue life cycle covers the period of time from when business firms, the government, or active interest groups begin to create certain social expectations, to when the expectations become political issues. The goal of organizational political action in this stage is to mold public opinion that is positive to the organization's position on the issue through communication strategies (Buchholz, 1988). The formulation stage involves the development of means for dealing with the political issues, such as laws, regulations, or public policies (Getz, 1993). The main task of this stage is to influence the formulation of policy by participation strategies (Buchholz, 1998). The implementation stage occurs when the political decision made is put into effect. In this stage, corporations will comply with the policies through organizational readjustments or lobby to amend the policies (Buchholz, 1988).

Characteristics of the Government Agencies

Effective government affairs should also be contingent on its target audience: the government agencies involved in a given issue. In public relations, effective programs require public relations practitioners to frame messages that are understandable and attractive to the target audience (Cutlip, Center, & Broom, 2000). In government affairs, the business–government interdependence in resource and knowledge sharing produces various degrees of cooperation and competition at the same time. As a result, exchange of interest and power always shape business–government interaction. Along with the communication capability of government officials, government affairs practitioners need to take officials' political interest, policy agendas, and levels at the hierarchy (i.e., the central, provincial, and local) into account to make government affairs effective.

Post, Preston, and Sachs (2002) observed the complexity of governance and management of foreign operation in China. This complex governance allows government officials at each level of government, with whom multinational corporations have to deal, to have their administrative and jurisdictional power. Since the first economic reform in 1979, the economic development of each region shapes the distribution of political power and resources of provincial and local authorities in China. As a result, from a political economy perspective, it is natural that the central government has an economic priority somewhat different from the ones of provincial or local governments. Different economic priorities indicate different stakes of governments from corporations, which affect the corporations' government affairs strategies. For instance, provincial authorities welcome foreign companies to bring job opportunities, taxes, and revenues to their jurisdictions, whereas the central government emphasizes high and sustainable aggregate economic growth of the nation with minimal dependence on foreign companies (Post et al., 2002). Chen (2005) found that provincial authorities often assist foreign firms in overcoming policy restrictions regulated by the central government to secure their own stakes in the operation of foreign enterprises. For example, a silicon-chemistry MNC planned to enter China by building a wholly owned subsidiary in an export processing zone of the Shanghai area. The Chinese central government rejected the MNC's application and proposed that the MNC build a joint venture. The zone administrative officials actively worked with the MNC's manager to lobby the central government on the application. Eventually, the MNC was able to establish a factory in the zone as its wholly owned subsidiary.

Corporations can become allies with provincial or local governments having compatible interests when lobbying with the central government. They can also use the central government's power granted by the hierarchy to solve their disagreement with provincial or local governments. Unlike the relationship between state and federal governments in the United States, Chinese central government has the highest administrative power and can override the decisions of provincial and local governments if it wishes. Similarly, provincial governments have power over local governments. In the case of a multi-industry MNC in Chen's (2005) study, its government affairs professionals sometimes escalated its conflicts with a government department (e.g. the customer) to the department's supervising authority (e.g., the Ministry of Commerce) in search of a solution.

Organizational Characteristics

As the behavior theory of the firm asserts, organizational characteristics determine an organization's ability and willingness to be engaged in political activities and practice certain strategies. Therefore, I included organizational characteristics to the conceptual model of government affairs and followed Schuler and Rehbein's (1997) rationale to treat these factors as "a filter of the environmental influences" (p. 120). That is, external factors (i.e., organizational economics, a host government's structural factors, business–government relationships, a given issue, and characteristics of government agencies) initially indicate quantity of political involvement and possible political actions of a firm. However, a firm's characteristics (e.g., structure, recourses, routines, policies, philosophy, and history) significantly affect how the firm interprets the external factors and actually interact with the government (Cyert & March, 1963; Schuler & Rehbein, 1997). Corporate political scholars suggest many organizational characteristics that affect corporate political activities: organizational structure, organizational resources (Meznar & Nigh, 1995), political experience (Schuler & Rehbein, 1997), organizational size and age (Cook & Fox, 2000; Meznar & Nigh, 1995), an organization's stakeholder dependence (Meznar & Johnson, 1996; Schuler & Rehbein, 1997), strategic thinking (Mahon, 1989), diversification and centralization of management (Shaffer & Hillman, 2000), and locus of control for business–government decisions (Mahini & Wells, 1986).

In studying 25 MNCs in China, Chen (2005) concluded that a corporation's management mechanism, expectation of government affairs, and culture determine the integration of government affairs into the strategic management of the corporation. Chen found two management mechanisms in MNCs: centralized and decentralized strategic management. Centralized strategic management allows top management to develop the strategic management for all products of the firm. Decentralized strategic management places the responsibility for business management on special business units throughout the firm to develop individual business plans for each product line or group of products that are strategically interrelated (Marx, 1990). MNCs with products in different industries are more likely to use the decentralized mechanism. The government affairs function was found to be less likely to participate in the overall strategic management of firms with decentralized management mechanism.

The Excellence Study (Dozier, J. Grunig, & L. Grunig, 1995; L. Grunig et al., 2002) also identified organizational expectation and culture as the factors affecting the participation of public relations to an organization's overall strategic-management process. Organizational expectation refers to the top management's expectation of government affairs to give input in the strategic management as its service to the organization. To form this expectation, government affairs must first demonstrate its managerial expertise and advanced government affairs experience in China to get it a seat at the decision-making table. Organizational culture profoundly affects an organization's behavior, including political involvement. The finding of Chen's (2005) study showed that the organizational culture, which emphasizes the interests of the organization's publics, promotes the participation of government affairs in a firm's strategic management.

Strategies of Government Affairs

Government affairs practices consist of four aspects: organizational structures and mechanisms of government affairs, communication channels to political publics, and political strategies of government affairs. Chen's (2005) examination of the government affairs practices by MNCs in China yielded the following results. For organizational structure of government affairs, China's complicated government structure resulted in the MNCs having two levels of government affairs within their corporations: the corporate and the local. The corporate level focuses on the company's overall management of the interaction with the central government. The local function concentrates on the relationship with local governments that influence the MNCs' local operations. At the corporate level, there was a department, a team, or a single staff member coordinating the government affairs practices for the companies. An interesting result was that government affairs was housed in the department of finance and accounting in the electronics MNC and in the office of the general manager in the auto MNC. At the local level, the government affairs practice was managed by the chief representatives or managers in the different departments (or both) in the local branches or special business units.

The data indicated that the MNCs could interact with the government through three lobbying mechanisms, five levels of communication channels, and seven strategies. The MNCs could lobby the government independently; collectively with other affected companies or industry associations; or with the help from their embassies, chambers of commerce, and other home-government bodies. The communication channels, from top to bottom, were nation to nation negotiation, government official to government official negotiation, worldwide CEO to government official negotiation, country CEO to government official negotiation, and special business unit president to government official negotiation.

The Western literature suggests several corporate political strategies: constituency building, advocacy advertising, lobbying, coalition building, reporting research results or public poll results, and personal services (Getz, 1993; Keim & Zeithaml, 1986). Chen (2005) identified the seven political strategies used by MNCs in China: lobbying, political accommodation, social accommodation, personal relationships, organizational credibility, personal services, and cooperation. *Political accommodation* refers to the extent to which an MNC has been responsive and contributive to governmental concerns of a host country, whereas *social accommodation* represents an MNC's contributions to fulfill social needs of a host country (Luo, 2002). MNCs in China often can show their political accommodation by providing services or solutions to the problems facing host governments. Political and social accommodation signifies the MNC's commitment to the long-term development of a host country. Social accommodation was demonstrated by corporate donations or philanthropy projects (Chen, 2005). In addition, she found that MNCs in China use personal relationships between their employees and respective governmental counterparts to facilitate positive outcomes of business–government conflicts.

The difference between commonly practiced political strategies in the Western countries and those in China exemplifiers how a nation's political system, economic system, level of development, and culture affect government affairs practices in the nation. With an authoritarian political system in China, advocacy advertising and grassroots lobbying are not applicable in the nation because the Chinese general population has little influence on policymaking. This fundamental difference in political systems also makes MNCs' strategic publics in government affairs in China (e.g., government officials, embassies, chambers of commerce, and universities) different from those in democratic countries (e.g., legislators, the media, and the interest groups). China's level of development and economic system make political and social accommodation effective in achieving organizational goals. As a developing country, China has been facing numerous political and social problems. Contributions to the resolution of these problems are perceived as a substantial "public favor" by Chinese officials (Chen, 2004, 2005; Peng & Luo, 2000). The public favor often cultivates business–government relationships and spurs government support. Government support, in turn, directly contributes to a foreign corporation's financial performance because of China's socialist market (Chen, 2004). Chinese culture, specifically *gaunxi*, makes personal relationships more significant in the Chinese context of business–government interaction than in the U.S. context. For example, in the *guanxi*-oriented society of China, individuals emphasize their relationships with others that serve as access to build mutuality, trust, and commitment through interactions among the parties involved. Therefore, quality personal relationships (between government affairs practitioners and their counterparts in the government) are directly translated into positive business–government relationships, but they are not the only cultivation for business–government relationships (Chen, 2005).

Outcomes of Government Affairs

Figure 22.1 shows that when an MNC practices effective government affairs to effectively manage issues with the Chinese government, the results are improved MNC–government relationships and achievement of the firm's goals. Quality relationships with the Chinese government have a crucial role in achieving organizational goals. This is because quality business–government relationships produce a favored status and support from Chinese authorities to its objective in a specific policy, access to the policy-making process, and stability and predictability in operations in spite of political and economic turbulence (N. Chen, 1996; Y. Chen, 2005; Hung, 2002; Luo, 2000; Post et al., 2002). In addition, Luo (2001) found that MNCs' cooperative relationships with Chinese regional and national government officials significantly improve the MNCs' financial and sale-based performance. Current relational outcomes become an antecedent that shapes government affairs programs for the next issue.

Quality relationships and achievement of goals build on an organization's reputation, which, in turn, establishes the legitimacy of the organization in terms of its business operations in a society (Luo, 2002; Pfeffer & Salancik, 1978; Suchman, 1995). This aspect is especially important for foreign companies to develop their businesses in a host nation, such as China, for the long term. The Chinese government has historically opposed foreign companies, and it has been cautious not to depend much on foreign corporations (Kronick, 2005). Quality relationships between foreign companies and the Chinese government cultivated by showing political and social accommodation not only can neutralize this opposition but also can form positive corporate reputations that legitimize the companies (Luo, 2002). Achieving organizational goals in a legal and socially responsible way produces economic gains to the Chinese society. This approach also establishes organizational legitimacy of a firm among government officials, who set economic growth as a priority, and the Chinese people, who benefit from the nation's economic development.

FURTHER DIRECTIONS FOR EXPANDING THE EXCELLENCE THEORY

One purpose of this chapter was to expand the Excellence Theory to a particular context—government affairs. This chapter fulfilled the purpose by providing empirical data from China to examine the theory and developing a conceptual model of government affairs. Most propositions of the Excellence Theory were supported across various publics of an organization (e.g., employees, media, investors, community, customers, and members). However, the Excellence study found government relations to be anomalous by posting correlations counter to theory: the significantly negative correlations (a) between excellent factors of public relations and conflict avoidance with government, (b) between managerial role expertise in the communication department and positive relationship outcomes with government, and (c) overall communication excellence to the outcomes of government relations programs (i.e., organizational sales; L. Grunig et al., 2002). L. Grunig et al. (2002) explained these unexpected results of government relations via two post hoc reasons. First, government relations of the studied organizations were mainly dominated by CEOs or lawyers rather than communication or public relations managers. Second, government affairs practitioners or lobbyists depended heavily on personal networking and experience when practicing government relations. These two reasons caused communication excellence to have little influence on the effectiveness of government relations programs.

Chen's (2005) study on Chinese government affairs provided additional evidence to confirm the applicability of the Excellence Theory to public relations programs with government. She identified a positive relationship between communication excellence and outcomes of government affairs by MNCs in China. Government relations programs of MNCs in China are usually dominated by government affairs practitioners with public relations background or experience with working in government authorities (Chen, 2005). This phenomenon is due to China being a *guanxi*-oriented society with a weak legal infrastructure, in which *people*—not laws—play a crucial role in government affairs. In addition, Chen (2005) observed some MNCs in China begin to emphasize their organizations' relationships with the government along with their government affairs practitioners' personal relationships with government officials. As a result, MNCs in China often see government affairs as a part of public relations or corporation communications. Furthermore, communication excellence (e.g., strategic origins of communication programs, managerial role expertise, communication tactics, environmental-scanning research, and symmetrical communication) contributes to the outcomes of government affairs (Chen, 2005). These findings show that the Excellence Theory stands true in government affairs when the function is dominated by public relations practitioners or communicators.

Chen's (2005) model of government affairs contributed to the body of knowledge of public relations by identifying the antecedents, strategies, and outcomes of government affairs programs of MNC foreign subsidiaries in China. It also answered L. Grunig et al.'s (2002) call for a normative theory of excellent global public relations. The model clearly demonstrates how a nation's conditions (e.g., political system, economic system, culture, and level of development) affect government relations practice in the nation by pinpointing the antecedents and their influence on shaping an MNC's government affairs practice.

Three future directions for expanding the Excellence Theory in relation to government affairs should be highlighted. First, I propose to conduct quantitative studies to test the generalizability of the model to all MNCs in China, to other types of companies in China, or to contexts other than China. The model, developed based on the interview data, serves as an initial attempt to provide a systematic guidance of how to develop an effective government affairs practice for an MNC in China. Quantitative studies should be conducted to refine the model and also yield information generalizable to profit all types of companies in China or companies in other countries.

Second, it is clear that culture is one salient factor affecting government affairs in China. However, it was not the focus of Chen's (2005) study. Scholars should examine the relationship between culture and government relations to further build a normative theory of global public relations. For example, culture is a multilevel concept. In the case of government affairs of MNCs in China, culture can refer to the Chinese culture (macrolevel), an MNC's organizational culture (mesolevel), and the culture of Chinese government official (*guan chang wen hua*, 官場文化; mesolevel). It requires ongoing research to fully understand the interplay of culture at different levels and its influence on special applications of generic principles of public relations in Chinese government affairs.

Third, additional research on activism is needed to refine the model of government affairs in China. With an authoritarian political system, the level of activism in China is relatively low and China's civil society is weak (Kennedy, 2005). As a result, strategic publics of MNCs in China's political environment now are government officials and elite party members. However, the increasing development of activism in China, resulting from the nation's rapid development and integration of globalization, may create additional strategic publics in the political process for MNCs to deal with, such as consumer activists or interest groups (Hung & Chen, 2004). When activist groups have become strong enough to express their concerns, they will affect the dynamics of business–government interaction and corporate political activities. For example, in recent years, nonprofit organizations have begun to be established in China. After reaching a certain level of development, these nonprofit organizations will start to advocate the interest for specific groups in the public policy arena. Some MNCs in China have been assisting the development of nonprofit organizations in attempt to have them represent the MNCs' interest in the future (Chen, 2005). Research, therefore, is needed to understand how the level and nature of activism in China affects Chinese government relations and furthermore to propose refinement of the model.

REFERENCES

Andres, G. J. (1985). Business involvement in campaign finance: Factors influencing the decision to form a corporate PAC. *Political Science, 18*, 213–220.

Austen-Smith, D., & Wright, J. R. (1992). Counteractive lobbying. *American Journal of Political Science, 38*, 25–44.

Baysinger, B. D. (1984). Domain maintenance as an objective of business political activity: An expanded typology. *Academy of Management Review, 9*, 248–258.

Boies, J. L. (1989). Money, business, and the state: Material interest, Fortune 500 corporations, and the size of political action committees. *American Sociological Review, 54*, 821–833.

Buchholz, R. A. (1988). *Public policy issues for management.* Englewood Cliffs, NJ: Prentice-Hall.

Chase, W. H. (1984). *Issue management: Origins of the future.* Stamford, CT: Issue Action.

Chen, N. (1996). Public relations in China: The introduction and development of an occupational field. In H. Culberton & N. Chen (Eds.), *International public relations: A comparative analysis* (pp. 121–154). Mahwah, NJ: Lawrence Erlbaum Associates.

Chen, Y. R. (2004). Effective public affairs in China: MNC-government bargaining power, corporate strategies for influencing foreign business policy formulation. *Journal of Communication Management, 8*, 395–413.

Chen, Y. R. (2005). *Excellent public affairs in an era of marketization: Issues management, business lobbying, and the management of government relations in China.* Unpublished doctoral dissertation, University of Maryland, College Park.

Cheney, G. (1992). The corporate person (re)presents itself. In E. L. Toth & R. L. Heath (Eds.), *Rhetorical and critical approaches to public relations* (pp. 165–183). Hillsdale, NJ: Lawrence Erlbaum Associates.

Clawson, D., Karson, M. J., & Kaufmann, A. (1986). The corporate pact for a conservative America: A data analysis of 1980 corporate PAC donations in sixty-six conservative congressional elections. In L. E. Preston (Ed.), *Research in corporation social performance and policy, 8* (223–245. Greenwich, CT: JAI.

Cook, R. G., & Fox, D. R. (2000). Resources, frequency and methods: An analysis of small and medium-sized firms' public policy activities. *Business and Society, 39*, 94–113.

Cutlip, S. M., Center, A. H., & Broom, G. M. (2000). *Effective public relations* (8th ed.). Upper Sadder River, NJ: Prentice-Hall.

Cyert, R. M., & March, J. G. (1963). *A behavioral theory of the firm.* Englewood Cliffs, NJ: Prentice-Hall.

DiMaggio, P., & Powell, W. W. (1983). The iron cage revisited: Institutional isomorphism and collective rationality in organizational fields. *American Sociological Review, 48*, 147–160.

Dominguez, G. S. (1982). *Government relations.* New York: Wiley.

Dozier, D. M., Grunig, L. A., & Grunig, J. E. (1995). *Manager's guide to excellence in public relations and communication management.* Hillsdale, NJ: Lawrence Erlbaum Associates.

Dunning, J. H. (1997). *Governments, globalization and international business.* Oxford, England: Oxford University Press.

Eisenhardt, K. M. (1989). Agency theory: An assessment and review. *Academy of Management Review, 14,* 57–74.

Eismeier, T. J., & Pollock, P. H., III. (1987). Strategy and choice in Congressional elections: The role of PACs. *American Journal of Political Science, 30,* 197–213.

Epstein, E. M. (1969). *The corporation in American politics.* Englewood Cliffs, NJ: Prentice-Hall.

Fagre, N., & Wells, L. T. (1982). Bargaining power of multinationals and host governments. *International Organization, 39*(1), 32–47.

Ferrari, M. A. (2003). Public relations in Chile: Searching for identity amid imported models. In K. Sriramesh, & D. Vercic, D. (Eds.), *The global public relations handbook* (pp. 378–398). Mahwah, NJ: Lawrence Erlbaum Associates.

Getz, K. A. (1993). Selecting corporate political tactics. In B. M. Mitnick (Ed.), *Corporate political agency: The construction of competition in public affairs* (pp. 242–273). Newbury Park, CA: Sage.

Getz, K. A. (2002). Political affairs and political strategy: Theoretical foundations. *Journal of Public Affairs, 1,* 305–329.

Gilpin, R. (2001). *Global political economy: Understanding the international economic order.* Princeton, NJ: Princeton University Press.

Grunig, J. E., & Grunig, L. A. (1992). Models of public relations and communication. In J. E. Grunig (Ed.), *Excellence in public relations and communication management* (pp. 285–326). Hillsdale, NJ: Lawrence Erlbaum Associates.

Grunig, J. E., & Hunt, T. (1984). *Managing public relations.* New York: Holt, Rinehart & Winston.

Grunig, J. E., & Repper, F. C. (1992). Strategic management, publics, and issues. In J. E. Grunig (Ed.), *Excellence in public relations and communication management* (pp. 117–158). Hillsdale, NJ: Lawrence Erlbaum Associates.

Grunig, L. A., Grunig, J. E., & Dozier, D. M. (2002). *Excellent public relations and effective organizations: A study of communication management in three countries.* Mahwah, NJ: Lawrence Erlbaum Associates.

Hang, M., & Koppang, H. (1997). Lobbying and public relations in a European context. *Public Relations Review, 23,* 233–247.

Hannan, M. T., & Carroll, G. R. (1992). *Dynamics of organizational populations.* New York: Oxford University Press.

Hannan, M. T., & Freeman, J. (1989). *Organizational ecology.* Cambridge, MA: Harvard University Press.

Heath, R. L. (1992). The wrangle in the market place: A rhetorical perspective of public relations. In E. L. Toth & R. L. Heath (Eds.), *Rhetorical and critical approaches to public relations* (pp. 37–61). Hillsdale, NJ: Lawrence Erlbaum Associates.

Heath, R. L. (1994). *Management of corporate communication: From interpersonal contacts to external affairs.* Hillsdale, NJ: Lawrence Erlbaum Associates.

Heath, R. L. (1997). *Strategic management: Organizations and public policy challenges.* Thousand Oaks, CA: Sage.

Heath, R. L. (1998). New communication technologies: An issues management point of view. *Public Relations Review, 24,* 273–288.

Hoewing, R. L. (1998). Dynamics and role of public affairs. In P. Lesly (Ed.), *Lesly's handbook of public relations and communications* (5th ed., pp. 61–70). Chicago: NTC Business.

Hung, C. J. F. (2002). *The interplays of relationship types, relationship cultivation, and relationship outcomes: How multinational and Taiwanese companies* practice public relations and organization–public relationship management in China. Unpublished doctoral dissertation, University of Maryland, College Park.

Hung, C. J. F., & Chen, Y. R. (2004). Glocalization: Public relations in China in the era of change. In K. Sriramesh (Ed.), *Public relations in Asia: An anthology* (pp. 29–62). Singapore: Thomson Learning.

Inoue, T. (2003). An overview of public relations in Japan and the self-correction concept. In K. Sriramesh & D. Vercic (Eds.), *The Global public relations handbook* (pp. 68–85). Mahwah, NJ: Lawrence Erlbaum Associates.

Jaatinen, M. (1999). *Lobbying political issues: A contingency model of effective lobbying strategies.* Unpublished doctoral dissertation, Inforviestinta Oy, Helsinki.

Johnson, J. H. (1992). *The association of lobbying and public relations in Washington, D.C.* Unpublished master's thesis, University of Maryland, College Park.

Keim, G. D. (1981). Foundations of a political strategy for business. *California Management Review, 23*(3), 41–48.

Keim, G. D., & Baysinger, B. D. (1993). Efficacy of business political activity: Competitive considerations in a principle-agent context. In B. M. Mitnick (Ed.), *Corporate political agency: The construction of competition in public affairs* (pp. 125–147). Newbury Park, CA: Sage.

Keim, G. D., & Zeithaml, C. P. (1986). Corporate political strategy and legislative decision making: A review and contingency approach. *Academy of Management Review, 11,* 828–853.

Kennedy, S. (2005). *The business of lobbying in China.* Cambridge, MA: Harvard University Press.

Kotter, J. P. (1979). Managing external dependence. *Academy of Management Review, 4,* 87–92.

Kraus, M. (1995). Government relations in the 90s and beyond. In L. B. Dennis (Ed.), *Practical public affairs in an era of change* (pp. 89–100). New York: University Press of America/PRSA.

Kronick, S. (2005). Corporate social responsibility with Chinese characteristics. *PR Magazine, 1,* 94–96.

Lange, R. (2000). Public affairs practitioners in the Netherlands: A profile study. *Public Relations Review, 26,* 15–29.

Lawton, T. C. (1997). *Technology and the new diplomacy: The creation and control of EC industrial policy for semiconductors.* Aldershot, England: Avebury.

Lerbinger, O. (2006). *Corporate public affairs: Interacting with interest groups, media, and governments.* Mahwah, NJ: Lawrence Erlbaum Associates.

Lieberthal, K., & Lieberthal, G. (2003). The great transition. *Harvard Business Review, 81,* 70–81.

Luo, Y. (2000). *Multinational corporations in China: Benefiting from structural transformation.* Copenhagen, Denmark: Copenhagen Business School Press.

Luo, Y. (2001). Toward a cooperative view of MNC-host government relations: Building blocks and performance implications. *Journal of International Business Studies, 32,* 401–419.

Luo, Y. (2002). *Multinational enterprises in emerging markets.* Copenhagen, Denmark: Copenhagen Business School Press.

Mack, C. S. (1995). Lobbying and political action. In L. B. Dennis (Ed.), *Practical public affairs in an era of change* (pp. 101–114). Lanham, MD: University Press of America.

Mack, C. S., & Edwards, R. A. (1989). *Lobbying and government relations.* New York: Quorum.

Mahini, A., & Wells, L. T., Jr. (1986). Government relations in the global firms. In M. E. Porter (Ed.), *Competition in global industries* (pp. 291–312). Boston: Harvard Business School Press.

Mahon, J. F. (1989). Corporate political strategy. *Business in the Contemporary World, 2,* 50–63.

Marx, T. G. (1990). Strategic planning for public affairs. *Long Range Planning, 23,* 9–16.

Master, M. F., & Baysinger, B. D. (1985). The determinants of funds raised by political action committees: An empirical examination. *Academy of Management Journal, 28,* 654–664.

Meznar, M. B., & Johnson, J. H., Jr. (1996). Multinational operations and stakeholder management: Internationalization, public affairs strategies, and economic performance. *Journal of International Management, 2,* 233–261.

Meznar, M. B., & Nigh, D. (1995). Buffer or bridge? Environmental and organizational determinants of public affairs activities in American firms. *Academy of Management Journal, 38,* 975–996.

Mitnick, B. M. (1993). Strategic behavior and the creation of agent. In B. M. Mitnick (Ed.), *Corporate political agency: The construction of competition in public affairs* (pp. 90–124). Newbury Park, CA: Sage.

Moran, T. (1985). *Multinational corporations: The political economy of foreign direct investment.* Lexington, MA: Lexington.

Oliver, C. (1991). Strategic responses to institutional processes. *Academy of Management Review, 16,* 145–179.

Olson, M. (1965). *The logic of collective action: Public good and the theory of groups.* Cambridge, MA: Harvard University Press.

Peng, M. W., & Luo, Y. (2000). Managerial ties and firm performance in a transition economy: The nature of a micro-macro link. *Academy of Management Journal, 43,* 486–501.

Pfeffer, J., & Salancik, G. (1978). *The external control of organizations: A resource dependence perspective.* New York: Free Press.

Pinkham, D. G. (2001). How'd we get to be the bad guys? Managing the public affairs under fire. *Public Relations Quarterly, 46*(2), 12–15.

Plotke, D. (1992). The political mobilization of business. In M. P. Petracca (Ed.), *The politics of interest groups transformed* (pp. 175–198). Boulder, CO: Westview.

Post, J. E., Preston, L. E., & Sachs, S. (2002). *Redefining the corporation: Stakeholder management and organizational wealth.* Stanford, CA: Stanford University Press.

Schuler, D. A., & Rehbein, K. (1997). The filtering role of the firm in corporate political involvement. *Business and Society, 36,* 116–139.

Sethi, S. P. (1982). Corporate political activism. *California Management Review, 24*(3), 32–42.

Shaffer, B., & Hillman, A. J. (2000). The development of business–government strategies by diversified firms. *Strategic Management Journal, 21,* 175–170.

Sriramesh, K. (Ed.). (2004). *Public relations in Asia: An anthology.* Singapore: Thomson Learning.

Sriramesh, K., & Vercic, D. (Eds.). (2003). *The global public relations handbook.* Mahwah, NJ: Lawrence Erlbaum Associates.

Stopford, J. M. (1994). The growing interdependence between transnational corporations and governments. *Transnational Corporations, 3*(1), 53–76.

Strange, S. (1991). An eclectic approach. In C. N. Murphy & R. Tooze (Eds.), *The new international political economy* (pp. 33–49). Boulder, CO: Lynne Rienner.

Suchman, M. C. (1995). Managing legitimacy: Strategic and institutional approaches. *Academy of Management Review, 20,* 571–610.

Suliman, O. (1998). *China's transition to a socialist market economy.* Westport, CT: Quorum.

Toth, E., & Heath, R. (Eds.) (1992). *Rhetorical and critical approaches to public relations.* Hillsdale, NJ: Lawrence Erlbaum Associates.

Vasquez, G. M. (1996). Public relations as negotiation: An issue development perspective. *Journal of Public Relations Research, 8,* 57–77.

Wilcox, D. L., Cameron, G. T., Ault, P. H., & Agee, W. K. (2003). *Public relations: Strategies and tactics* (7th ed.). Boston: Pearson Education.

Williamson, O. E. (1985). *The economic institutions of capitalism.* New York: Free Press.

Zardkoohi, A. (1985). On the political participation of the firm in the electoral process. *Southern Journal of Economics, 51,* 804–817.

Chapter 23

The Relationship Between Culture and Public Relations

Krishnamurthy Sriramesh
Nanyang Technological University, Singapore

In presenting the literature review on corporate culture and public relations, we (Sriramesh, Grunig, & Buffington, 1992) began our chapter by quoting Smircich's (1983) succinct statement: "[C]ulture is an idea whose time has come" (p. 339). Organizational management literature had begun to accept the relevance of this concept at the dawn of the 1980s. We had contended that the time had come for the public relations body of literature to also integrate culture into its pedagogy because of the significance of this variable to human communication and relationship building.

Sadly, culture has yet to be integrated into the public relations body of knowledge. It appears that culture's time has not yet come after all for our field. Much of the literature and scholarship in our area continues to be ethnocentric with a predominantly American, and to a lesser extent British and Western European, bias, even though studies have begun to explore the status of public relations in different regions of the world, especially in the past 5 years. In 1992, we had written: "[T]o communicate to [with] their publics in a global marketplace, public relations practitioners will have to sensitize themselves to the cultural heterogeneity of their audiences.... The result will be the growth of a culturally richer profession" (Sriramesh & White, 1992, p. 611). Unfortunately, well into the 21st century, our hope has not yet materialized. The reality is that in a rapidly globalizing world, our field will ignore culture at its own peril. This is true of the other "environmental variables" that emanated from the excellence project, such as the political system, media system, economic system, and level of activism. We know conceptually that these variables do contribute significantly to

507

making organizational environments around the world dynamic and challenging. It is important to recognize that there may be other variables, or local variations of the previously cited variables, that need to be identified and integrated to the body of literature.

The mandate given to this chapter is to assess the role of one of the environmental variables—culture—on public relations. It is important to recognize at the very outset that we discuss these highly interrelated sociopolitical variables in isolation only for the sake of conceptual clarity and convenience of explanation. Each of these environmental variables influences the other. As a result, studying their relationship with public relations has not been, and will not be, an easy challenge. In fulfilling the given mandate, the chapter first reviews the research studies that have assessed the nexus between culture (both societal and corporate) and public relations. Next, it offers suggestions to build on these initial attempts and give the culture concept the primacy it deserves in the public relations body of knowledge. In doing so, this chapter challenges public relations scholars to integrate this important variable into the public relations body of knowledge and pedagogy, thus extending the robust foundations offered by the excellence project.

THE EXCELLENCE PROJECT AND CULTURE

One can state with a great deal of confidence that the excellence project spawned research linking culture with public relations. When the project began in 1987, culture had not yet been discussed as a determinant of public relations strategies or practice in the then-fledgling body of knowledge of the field. There was no mention of this variable in the 1988 *Body of Knowledge* report commissioned by the Public Relations Society of America (PRSA). When public relations practitioners needed to enter a new market and interact with publics of a different culture, they often depended on anecdotal evidence to design strategies that were sensitive to the local culture. To a great extent, this continues to be the case, even today, because of the anemic growth of knowledge in this aspect of public relations.

We (Sriramesh & White, 1992) began our literature review for the excellence project by discussing whether public relations practice is *culture free* or *culture specific*—terms we had borrowed from Tayeb (1988). Scholars advocating the former had argued that organizational characteristics (e.g., organizational structure) and their contextual factors are stable across societies. Hickson, Hinings, McMillan, and Schwitter (1974) articulated the culture-free thesis best: "[W]hether the culture is Asian or European or North American, a large organization with many employees improves efficiency by specialising their activities but also by increasing, controlling and coordinating specialities" (pp. 63-64). Scholars advocating the *culture-specific* approach (Hofstede, 1991; Ouchi, 1981; Pascale & Athos, 1981; Tayeb, 1988) had countered this argument by stating that organizations are made up of individuals who are acculturated differently at home, school, and the workplace, which makes each individual a unique personality offering different sets of opportunities and challenges to managers. Organizations, which are themselves cultures, face the challenge of harnessing these individual personalities to their mutual benefit, which is not an easy task.

There can be little doubt that organizations are culture bound. The linkage between culture and public relations is logical and very obvious. Culture affects communication, and is affected by it. Because public relations is fundamentally a communication activity, it is logical to conclude that culture affects public relations also—hence, the need to conceptually link culture with public relations. In order to do so effectively, we believed it was important to distinguish between *societal* culture (Sriramesh & White, 1992) and *corporate* culture (Sriramesh et al., 1992). Drawing the distinction between these two types of culture is important because public relations professionals deal with *external* and *internal* publics who are acculturated differently by society and by organizations, respectively. As members of a society, external publics are imbued with cultural idiosyncrasies specific to a region. Internal publics, although acculturated to the culture of the larger society, also become acculturated to certain unique characteristics that are specific to the organization within which they operate. These two types of culture influence not only the way people communicate but also how they respond to communication within the organization.

Having made this basic distinction, we began an extensive review of literature from fields such as anthropology, organizational psychology, and sociology that helped identify conceptual linkages between public relations and these two types of culture. The next two sections offer a review of studies that have empirically analyzed the relationship between these two types of cultures and public relations thus far.

Societal Culture

The review of literature on societal culture conducted for the Excellence Study included the four cultural dimensions that Hofstede (1984) had identified at that time: power distance, uncertainty avoidance, masculinity/femininity, and individualism/collectivism. Hofstede (1991) later added a fifth dimension that he first termed *Confucian dynamism* but later labeled *long-term orientation*. A few other studies that used the conceptual framework proposed by the Excellence Study later included the fifth dimension as well.

We ended our literature review with two conceptual propositions that linked societal culture with public relations. The first stated, "[S]ocietal cultures that display lower levels of power distance, authoritarianism, and individualism, but have higher levels of interpersonal trust among workers, are most likely to develop the excellent public relations practices identified in this book" (Sriramesh & White, 1992, p. 611). Because we had no empirical data at that time, we chose to keep this conceptual proposition very broad. Now that we have over a decade of data, albeit from only a few countries, it is possible to rephrase this proposition or divide it into several propositions. For example, it is possible that societies with higher levels of collectivism also can develop excellent public relations practices as long as the levels of other dimensions (e.g., power distance) are lower. Subcultures and countercultures also play a key role in public relations. As discussed later, these are some of the avenues and challenges for future researchers.

The second proposition stated:

> [A]lthough such occurrences are rare, organizations that exist in societal cultures that do not display these characteristics that are conducive to the spawning of excellent public relations programs also may have excellent public relations programs if the few power holders of the organization have individual personalities that foster [a more] participative organizational culture even if this culture is atypical to [the] mainstream societal culture. (Sriramesh & White, 1992, p. 612)

With this proposition, we wanted to highlight the fact that an organization can develop an internal culture that is different from the mainstream culture of the society in which it exists, and that this happens more often than one might expect.

It is important to note that the Excellence Study did not attempt to gather data on the dimensions of societal culture and, therefore, did not try to empirically link these dimensions with public relations. Despite the dire need to do so, we refrained from garnering empirical data on societal culture for several reasons. The scope of data gathering for the project had already expanded—especially with the inclusion of the employee questionnaire to elicit information for determining the organizational culture of the sample that was important. Including societal culture as another variable to be studied would have increased the project's scope exponentially and affected the efficacy of data gathering. Furthermore, like scores of anthropologists and Hofstede, we recognized that culture is a malleable concept that is hard to define and harder to measure. Therefore, we thought it would be best to design individual studies that break down societal culture to manageable parts and study its impact on public relations with some depth. A few studies have done this, as reviewed in this chapter.

Although the Excellence Study did not gather empirical evidence on the relationship between societal culture and public relations, the literature review and conceptualization based on the project have spawned several studies that have contributed to the body of knowledge. Although these studies have not been large in number, they have contributed significantly toward extending the body of knowledge beyond Anglo–Saxon cultures. In doing this, they have helped reduce, at least to some extent, the extreme ethnocentricity of the field. These studies have principally used one or more of Hofstede's dimensions of culture and attempted to link them with public relations practice.

An ethnographic analysis of southern Indian organizations was among the first studies to assess the impact of societal culture on public relations (Sriramesh, 1992). That study focused in particular on the impact of *power distance* on public relations practice. Inequality exists in all societies and there are differences in power among people of different strata in every society. Like Mulder (1977), from whom he had borrowed the concept of power distance, Hofstede (1984) viewed power distance mostly as a form of oppression by the more powerful. Whereas this may be true in many societies, there is also an implicit practice of *deference to authority* by the less powerful that is often seen in some societies. In the study in India, for example, even though the CEO of a private bank wanted to bring a more participative culture in his bank, there was more discomfort from the lower ranks because of their deference to authority (Sriramesh, 1996). However, the study also found that more than half the public relations managers agreed that employees lose respect for a manager who consults them before making decisions, signifying that managers also exhibited high levels of power distance. Interestingly, high levels of power distance also resulted in lower status accorded public relations by organizations. Societal culture was found to affect corporate culture.

In her study of public relations in South Korea, Rhee (1999) used all five dimensions of culture that Hofstede (1984, 1991) had identified. Her data suggested that except for the masculinity/femininity dimension, the other four dimensions identified by Hofstede correlated strongly with the public relations variables identified by the Excellence Study. She noted that "[A]lthough conceptually affiliated with high power distance,… Confucianism may not be detrimental to achieving excellence in public relations" (p. 185). She reasoned that certain key characteristics of Confucianism, such as the focus on harmonious living and placing high value on family morals, logically linked Confucianism with excellence in public relations.

Kim (2003) used documentary analysis and personal interviews to assess the extent to which Confucian dynamism affected the global as well as domestic public relations practices of a South Korean multinational corporation. Her data revealed that the organization changed its public relations strategies by region. It predominantly used the personal influence model, and to a lesser extent the mixed-motive model, in relating to domestic publics, whereas it used the two-way models for its international publics. Interestingly, the corporation also reported that it employed different cultural strategies for domestic and global audiences. Its domestic public relations strategies were largely driven by Confucian culture, whereas its global public relations strategies were designed to be "as rational as possible" (p. 90). In other words, societal culture had a greater bearing on its domestic public relations strategies, whereas its global strategies were driven by what the author called "pragmatism" that one could construe as cultural relativism.

As Hofstede himself admitted, his dimensions of culture do not measure the variable in its entirety, and so it is important that researchers go beyond these dimensions when attempting to link culture with public relations. This has been lacking in most of the small number of studies that currently exist on culture and public relations. Conducting country-specific studies focusing only on culture will greatly help identify these nuances. In our analysis of public relations in Japan (Sriramesh & Takasaki, 2000), we found that the concept of *wa* (harmony) had a significant impact on public relations practice. Superior–subordinate relationships in Japanese organizations were influenced by the concept of *amae* (the desire to depend on another's goodness), in which the manager attempts to satisfy the *amae* of subordinates, who in turn reciprocate the gesture by remaining loyal. *Amae*, we argued, contributes to a strong corporate culture, which directly influences an organization's internal and external communication. We also found that *tataeme* (the public persona and behavior of an individual) and *honne* (the private self) play a crucial role in the way the Japanese communicate. The Japanese are reluctant to express disagreement publicly (practicing *tataeme*) because of the fear that it may destroy *wa* (social harmony). Instead, they prefer to engage in communication in informal and social settings (e.g., in a bar or restaurant) to build stable relationships, thus practicing *honne*.

The concept of *guanxi*, a uniquely Chinese cultural characteristic, is among the more widely discussed cultural dimensions (Aw, Tan, & Tan, 2002; Chen, 1996; Huang, 2001; Hung, 2003; Kipnis, 1997; Tan, 2000). *Guanxi* appears to be the Chinese manifestation of the personal influence model of public relations. Like the personal influence model, *guanxi* involves building interpersonal relationships with strategic individuals such as journalists and government officials, often by doing favors for them. Such relationship building helps open the "gates" so that, when needed, these individuals can be relied on to return the favor, whether it be by publishing a news story or approving a government license.

In an analysis of public relations in three Asian cultures, we exhorted scholars to build a global theory of public relations by taking into account the *native's point of view* on how public relations is practiced within different political, economic, and cultural contexts. We had hoped that our three-nation comparison would be "the harbinger of many more such attempts because finding the uniqueness in public relations practices of a country is as important as finding commonalities among different countries" (Sriramesh, Kim, & Takasaki, 1999, p. 289). However, as is dealt with at some length later in this chapter, there have been very few studies that specifically evaluate the relationship between societal culture and public relations. Furthermore, there appear to be no studies on this topic from Latin America, Central America, Africa, the Caribbean, or Eastern Europe—at least in English.

In one of the few non-Asian studies that have linked societal culture with public relations, Vercic, Grunig, and Grunig (1996) used the first four of Hofstede's dimensions and interpersonal trust (Tayeb, 1988) to assess the impact of Slovenian culture on public relations. They gathered data through "lengthy personal interviews" with three executives of Pristop Communications, the leading public relations agency in Slovenia. The authors discovered that the interviewees often disagreed among themselves about basic Slovenian cultural idiosyncracies. The authors attributed these disagreements to factors such as the difficulty of describing one's own culture, the rapid changes that the Slovenian society had been undergoing after becoming an independent nation in 1990, and the varying changes that each of the interviewees had experienced personally because of these rapid postindependence sociopolitical changes.

This is further evidence that it is very challenging to measure culture. Vercic et. al.(1996) summarized one of the key findings of their study: "whereas Sriramesh and White's (1992) propositions suggest that societal culture shapes public relations ... [the Slovenian data] suggested that a professional public relations culture may loosen the grip of societal culture on practitioners, freeing them to help transform that larger culture" (pp. 55–56). This is a significant finding and one that is of great importance to the field because the impact of public relations in shaping societal culture has yet to be explored, although it should be a significant area of research in the era of globalization where public relations professionals may be accused of cultural imperialism when they communicate with foreign markets on behalf of multinational corporations.

Vasquez and Taylor (2000) studied the relationship among Hofstede's four dimensions and the models of public relations by surveying 134 members of a Midwestern city's PRSA chapter in the United States. They found that the power distance perceived by respondents was low and concluded that "American practitioners in this study were not working under heavily controlled or authoritative management" (p. 443). However, the authors seemed perplexed that their respondents preferred the one-way models, which led them to ask: "Do public relations professionals practice one-way models because their organizations force them to?" (p. 443). Relying on their data, the authors affirmed that "the answer would have to be no" (p. 443). What the authors seem to have overlooked in this seeming contradiction is the fact that authoritarian corporate cultures can, and do, exist in egalitarian societal cultures (Sriramesh et al., 1992; Sriramesh, Grunig, & Dozier, 1996). Therefore, in a relatively egalitarian societal culture such as the United States, it is easy to find many organizations with varying degrees of authoritarian corporate cultures. Numerous studies have repeatedly stressed that it is often the case that public relations managers do not set communication policies, which is often the primary reason why they have no control over the public relations strategies they employ.

It is clear from this review that even though it is a small body of literature, much of the literature linking culture with public relations emanates from studies conducted in Asia. A significant gap exists because few studies in English have linked societal culture and public relations in Latin America, the Caribbean, or Africa. These are serious deficiencies that need to be addressed by the global community of scholars if the public relations body of knowledge is to become holistic and comprehensive.

CORPORATE CULTURE AND PUBLIC RELATIONS

In 1986, Downey remarked that "[A] great deal has been written of late about corporate culture" (p 7). The author contended that the term *corporate culture* had become a buzzword and that this increased attention had created "armies of corporate culture vultures" (p. 7). He posited that corporate culture "is the consequence of corporate identity" (p. 7). One would have to take serious issue with the author that corporate culture had become an "overused" term in 1986. In the 1980s, management scholars had just begun to discuss it as an important variable affecting organizational processes. Almost 20 years later, the public relations body of knowledge has yet to fully identify the relationship between public relations and corporate culture.

Notwithstanding Downey's comment, the term *corporate culture* was very new to the public relations field in 1987 when the Excellence Study began. Based on our literature review for the Excellence Study, we had made three propositions that conceptually linked public relations with corporate culture (Sriramesh et al., 1992). We largely relied on the work of scholars such as Ouchi (1981) and Pascale and Athos (1981) to identify two principal dimensions of organizational culture that we termed *authoritarian* and *participative* (Sriramesh et al., 1996). We then gathered data to link organizational culture with public relations that led to the following conclusion reported by Grunig, Grunig, and Dozier (2002):

> [P]articipative culture is neither a necessary nor a sufficient condition for excellent public relations. An authoritarian culture does not make excellent public relations impossible because it does not correlate negatively with the Excellence factor. At the same time, a participative culture provides a more supportive, nurturing environment for excellent public relations than does an authoritarian culture. Nevertheless, a participative culture does not produce an excellent public relations department unless that department possesses the knowledge and skills to practice public relations symmetrically. (p. 496)

One of the conclusions of the Excellence Study was that public relations practitioners would find it easier to conduct strategic public relations in participatory rather than authoritarian cultures.

Cameron and McCollum (1993) also assessed the linkage between public relations and organizational culture. They used personal interviews and a survey to assess the link between the efficacy of internal communication and shared beliefs among managers and employees. They posited that "consensus between employees and management at the level of constructs, ideals, and beliefs is both a product and facilitator of communication between management and employees" (p. 244). Their data suggested that employees are more receptive to communication initiated by management when they perceive that they and organizational managers share similar beliefs about the organization's mission. The authors extrapolated from these findings that public relations practitioners should facilitate greater two-way communication between management and employees that would ultimately result in a stronger corporate culture.

Grunig's (1995) critique of the corporate culture of the U.S. Department of State, based on her analysis of a sex discrimination class-action suit by women in the foreign service, is a good example of a different genre of research on corporate culture. Instead of measuring indicators of corporate culture as is typical of corporate culture studies, she used "primary and secondary sources to … look at the subcultures that may exist within the larger organizational context" (p. 139). She found that organizational leaders, formal written codes, and the court order had all wanted, or required, the State Department to cease all sex discrimination. However, these seemingly powerful forces appeared to have consistently been overruled by "a grimly determined counterculture" that sought to "undermine significantly the emancipatory efforts of organizational management and the court" (p. 157).

Save for the previously discussed studies, one cannot find published information of empirical research that has specifically linked corporate culture with public relations. Everett's (1990) essay, although reaffirming some of the conceptualization of the Excellence Study (both essays seem to have been prepared around the same time, even though they were published on different dates), also offered a deeper understanding of the relationship between ethnoecology and public relations. Everett saw organizations as sociocultural systems, just as we (Sriramesh & White, 1992) had done. The significance of Everett's contribution is in the way he logically linked organizations with ethnoecology. Stating that "the view of organizations as sociocultural systems places such concepts squarely in the domain of organizational ethnography," the author contended that "it is this relationship that is best explored using the theoretical features and methodological tools of ethnoecology" (p. 248). He concluded that "an adequate understanding of organizational adaptation [with its environment] necessarily requires an account of interactions of the organizational culture and the organizational environment" (p. 248). It is pertinent to note here that organizational ethnography, a critical tool, has not been the preferred methodology for even a handful of studies in our field.

A few other studies have made references to the direct or indirect linkage between corporate culture and public relations or communication in organizations. Reber and Cameron (2003) mentioned corporate culture as a determinant of public relations and noted that "organizational characteristics ... [such as] harmony among staff" (p. 444) contribute to the willingness among organizations to enter into dialogue with their stakeholders. However, these authors did not gather empirical evidence on specific indicators of corporate culture, because it was not the primary focus of their study. Although Negandhi and Robey (1977) were not studying the impact of corporate culture on public relations, their remark—that studies focusing on the importance of multinational corporations to economic development have limited efficacy in increasing our understanding of organizational behavior in multicultural settings—is pertinent to our field. The authors posited that researchers should focus also on specific management practices in individual firms (that often reflect corporate culture), which have a greater impact in increasing our insight into effective management practices globally.

The preceding review of literature on societal and corporate culture educates us primarily about how much we still do not know about the link between public relations and these two concepts. In keeping with the theme of this book, the next section explores avenues for future research in this area and challenges the scholarly community to give culture the attention it deserves.

BEYOND THE EXCELLENCE PROJECT: THE FUTURE

Robust theories generate intellectual debates and provide avenues for further research, thereby advancing the body of knowledge. As arguably the largest and most influential research project in the field of public relations, one can state with a great deal of confidence that the Excellence Study has certainly achieved both of these lofty goals vis-à-vis culture and public relations. Among other things, it has provided the conceptual linkage between public relations and sociopolitical variables (environmental variables), of which culture is a significant one. In addition, the study has provided empirical data on the linkage between public relations and two dimensions of corporate culture—authoritarian and participative. Finally, it also has provided the conceptual foundation for many studies that have contributed to the advancing of the field by gathering empirical data from different parts of the world on the relationship between culture and public relations.

However, as the preceding review clearly shows, we are far from making definitive, and predictive, linkages between the each of the environmental variables and public relations based on empirical evidence. Even though culture is the most researched of these environmental variables, in reality we have barely touched the surface of the impact of culture on public relations based on data from a variety of nations and cultures from all parts of the globe. In other words, few scholars seem to have built on the foundations of the Excellence Study. The next section provides some avenues for future research pertaining to culture and public relations.

Expanding the Dimensions of Societal Culture

Hofstede (1984) himself admitted that his seminal study had serious limitations because culture, being malleable, was hard to define and even harder to measure. Defining culture as "the collective programming of the mind which distinguishes the members of one group from another" (p. 21), the author admitted that the five dimensions of culture that he had identified were not comprehensive, but were the only ones that he was able to measure. Scholars who have tried to link societal culture with public relations have almost exclusively relied on Hofstede's dimensions. This is partly because of the lucidity with which he described and operationalized these constructs. In large part, scholars have also relied on Hofstede's dimensions because of the ease of replicating his reliable and valid survey instrument.

As useful as all these studies have been in advancing our body of knowledge, it would not be an exaggeration to state that there is a dire need to explore other cultural dimensions that often may be unique to a society, and then explore their relationship with public relations, as we did in the study in Japan (Sriramesh & Takasaki, 2000). Whereas Hofstede sought to study cultural dimensions that were common across cultures, we should not overlook the importance of cultural character-istics that are often unique to a single culture and determine its linkage with public relations. It is pertinent to note here that although Hofstede (1984) recognized that the corporation he studied had "a distinct corpo-rate identity—a company subculture" (p. 41), for the most part he pre-sented his data as representing the societal culture of the mangers from the 39 countries he studied. His study has often been the target of valid criticism that it did not recognize the impact of the corporate culture of the organization he termed HERMES on his findings. It is important to note in this context that quantitative methods have their own limita-tions in studying culture, which is why many ethnographers have re-lied almost exclusively on qualitative methods (Mishler, 1986). This is also why Everett's (1990) advocacy of organizational ethnoecology is pertinent and useful for our field.

The concept of *guanzi* and *mianzi* from Chinese culture are good ex-amples of successful efforts to expand the number of societal cultural dimensions that affect public relations. As mentioned earlier, the con-cept of *guanzi* has been mentioned by several scholars as affecting public relations in Chinese cultures. However, the depth of this concept as well as the manifestation of the concept vis-à-vis public relations have not yet been fully explored. For example, Huang (2000) offered *Gao guanxi*, which represents the exploitation of personal relations or human net-works for personal gain, as a cultural extension of *guanxi* in Chinese so-cieties. However, its presence and any variations in manifestation have not yet been widely studied by other scholars. This is the case with *mianzi* (face) also, which has yet to be deeply studied and integrated into public relations pedagogy, even though it is very relevant in many Asian cultures. Even some studies conducted in Chinese societies often merely refer to these concepts as influencing communication without empiri-cally testing their presence and manifestation. Many, however, take the easy route and indicate these cultural constructs as areas that should be studied in "future research." For example, Lee (2004) studied corporate image in a *Chinese-based context* (emphasis added) and yet did not assess the link between culture and corporate image. Instead, the author sug-gested *mianzi* and *guanxi* as avenues for future research!

The concepts of *wa, amae, tatamae,* and *honne* have added to our ex-panding knowledge of Japanese culture and its impact on public rela-tions (Sriramesh & Takasaki, 2000). However, we have yet to explore the relationship between public relations and concepts such as *onjoshugi* (managerial paternalism) discussed by Raz (2002). The author men-tioned *katachi de hairu* or "entering self-fulfilment through the rules" as one of the ways Japanese employees (*kobun*) define their relationship with the organization. Yoshikawa (1993) discussed the intermediated communication pattern that Japanese people often have used to bring credibility to interpersonal communication. Sometimes, even an introductory letter from a third person who knows the principals often serves the purpose of breaking the ice between two people and gets the communication underway. The business card (*meishi*) also serves a similar important role. We have yet to study individual societal cultures deeply enough to bring out the impact of such unique dimensions on public relations.

Interpersonal Trust

Although in the literature review for the excellence project we (Sriramesh & White, 1992) identified interpersonal trust as a key dimension of societal culture and one that has a great influence on public relations practice, only one study (Vercic et al., 1996) has so far studied the impact of this dimension on public relations. In fact, the significance of interpersonal communication on public relations activities is one of the most important, yet least studied, linkages in the public relations body of knowledge.

In the early 1990s, the "personal influence model" was introduced as a potential fifth model of public relations, extending the original four models proposed by Grunig and Hunt (1984). Although studies in three diverse cultures (Huang, 1990; Lyra, 1991; Sriramesh, 1988; Sriramesh, 2000; Sriramesh & Grunig, 1988) initially confirmed the presence of this model and studies from other countries have done so since then, there is clearly a dearth of research that assesses the different ways in which culture affects the interpersonal relationships that the personal influence model describes—in both public relations strategy and practice. Trust is a key ingredient that gives credibility to a source in any communication. Interpersonal trust, then, should take primacy in the way public relations practitioners practice the personal influence model in building relationships with key stakeholders. There can be little doubt that the strategies of developing and maintaining interpersonal trust are culture specific. However, the body of knowledge of public relations has yet to study the linkage among culture, interpersonal trust, and public relations.

Relationship Patterns

The notion of relationship building is related to interpersonal trust, although this linkage has not yet been recognized in the literature. Scholars (Hon & Grunig, 1999; Huang, 2001; Hung, 2003; Ledingham &

Bruning, 2000) have proposed relationship management as one of the key activities of public relations practitioners. Hon and Grunig offered six relationship outcomes and suggested ways of measuring them: trust, control mutuality, relationship commitment, relationship satisfaction, communal relationships, and exchange relationships. However, culture—although fundamental to any relationship building effort (including all the six outcomes listed by Hon & Grunig)—has yet to be integrated into the discussion of relationship building.

Hung's (2003) is among only two empirical studies that have attempted to integrate culture and relationship building. She found that Chinese cultural characteristics such as family orientation and relational orientation (role formalization, relational interdependence, face, favor, relational harmony, relational fatalism, and relational determination) influenced the relationship cultivation strategies of a sample of multinational companies operating in China. Based on her empirical data from an earlier study (Huang, 1997), Huang (2001) added *face and favor* as a fifth relationship dimension, which is laudable. However, the impact of culture on the other four dimensions remains as yet to be established empirically, even though conceptually it appears very logical that such a relationship should exist.

Furthermore, it is also important to assess the cross-cultural nature of relationship building, as we live in an increasingly globalizing world. F. Kluckhohn (1953) identified three relationship patterns. She stated that the *individual* pattern is typical of Western cultures in which the existence of nuclear families ensures that an individual's relationship within the family is limited in scope and intensity. The *collateral* pattern represents cultures in which the family sphere is wider than that of a nuclear family (to include grandparents, uncles, cousins, etc.) and the intensity of relationship is also greater than the individual pattern. The *linear* pattern is indicative of even a wider circle of family members to include distant relatives that may often include the tribe or clan. Future studies should assess the impact that acculturation into one of these patterns has on the way that organizational decision makers and public relations practitioners of different cultures manage their relationships with key publics on behalf of the organization.

HIGH- AND LOW-CONTEXT CULTURES

Hall was among the first to identify the differences between high- and low-context cultures. Despite its importance to success in communication, the relationship between high and low context in culture remains one of the underresearched concepts in public relations. There is a need to assess how context affects interpersonal communication and relationship building, which is crucial to the success of public relations outreach with external publics. Furthermore, context must affect organizational communication internally (perhaps as an indicator of the corporate culture of an organization) and therefore also needs to be studied. Myths, stories, rights, and rituals are all discussed as ingredients of corporate culture. These also provide the context for internal communication in organizations and therefore need to be studied and integrated into public relations pedagogy.

Finally, we also need to keep in mind that culture affects, and is affected by, other environmental factors identified by the Excellence Study, such as political system, economic system and level of development, media system, and activism. This relationship is yet to be empirically established and incorporated into the public relations body of knowledge. For example, the spiral of silence theory, which is influenced by the political system of a society, invariably affects the level of openness and communication patterns of individuals of a culture. These are as yet unexplored and certainly are not integrated into the body of knowledge, despite their relevance and importance.

CONCLUSION

The Freedom Forum called the 20th century "democracy's century," because at the dawn of the century there was not a single democratic country (with universal adult suffrage), whereas by the end of the century there were 119 countries (covering about 58% of the world population) with some form of democratic political system (Freedom House, 2000). It is no coincidence that modern public relations flourished concomitantly with political pluralism in the 20th century. Yet, we have yet to empirically link political systems with public relations practice based on data from different parts of the world. For example, in a study of organizations in Shanghai, we found the impact of political ideology on public relations in the form of the *lun zi pai bei* system (Sriramesh & Enxi, 2004). Because those Chinese who are now in their 50s grew up during the cultural revolution, when many did not have access to higher education, the Chinese government has an affirmative program that actively promotes employees based on seniority (measured in the number of years one has worked in an organization) rather than on professional qualifications or suitability for the position. As a result, we found instances in which the public relations managers of some government agencies had previously been steel mill workers, school teachers, and even chefs!

If the 20th century was democracy's century, the 21st century has exploded as the century of globalization. In such an environment, where peoples of various cultures are becoming ever more interdependent, it is sad and alarming that the concept of culture is being treated almost as an afterthought in many disciplines, including public relations. For example, the *Journal of Public Relations Research*—arguably the premier journal oriented to empirical research in our field—welcomed the new millennium by publishing a special issue titled *Public Relations* Values [emphasis added] *in the New Millennium*. The thoughtful essays in that volume, from the leading scholars of our field, discussed the values of the profession because "professions are based on values and a body of knowledge to teach and enhance values" (Toth & Pavlik, 2000, p. 1). Even though values of every profession are steeped in culture, only one of these essays made a mention of culture, albeit briefly, to argue that "[individualistic] Anglo cultures need symmetrical public relations even more than organizations in collective cultures" (Grunig, 2000, p. 39).

The other essays in this special issue very articulately discussed the importance of activist values (Dozier & Lauzen, 2000), feminist values (L. Grunig, Toth, & Hon, 2000), rhetorical values (Heath, 2000), and postmodernist values (Holtzhausen, 2000). It is an indication of how culture's time has not yet come in our field that all these discussions seem to have been presented almost completely devoid of any attention to the impact of culture, even though concepts such as values and ethics are so deeply rooted in culture, as are all human beings. All the rhetorical theories currently discussed in public relations literature are based in Western philosophy, even though Indian and Chinese culture, for example, have a more ancient history that includes rhetorical principles. Public relations scholars—especially from other parts of the world such as Asia, Africa, Latin America, and the Caribbean, most of which have longer histories of human habitation—should take it up as a challenge to integrate the cultural values of their societies into the public relations body of knowledge and help expand it. This appears to be the only way of reducing the extreme ethnocentricity that exists in the current body of knowledge of public relations.

Ethnocentricity in scholarship spills over to public relations education as well. The Commission on Public Relations Education (CPRE), set up by the Public Relations Society of America (PRSA), delivered a report, aptly entitled *Public Relations Education for the 21st Century: A Port of Entry*, at the annual conference of PRSA in October 1999. The commission stated that one of its goals was to "determine the knowledge and skills needed by practitioners in a technological, *multicultural and global society* [emphasis added], and then to recommend learning outcomes" (CPRE, 1999, n.p.). Although the goal was laudable, the recommendations fell far short of the kind of global outlook that the rapidly globalizing 21st century demands (See Sriramesh, 2002, 2003 for a critique of the report and avenues for expanding public relations curricula to include multiculturalism). One hopes that the forthcoming revision of the report will be more sensitive to the dire need to integrate cultural diversity into the public relations curriculum. Issues such as cultural diversity and multiculturalism should not be the sole domain of books on international or global public relations, but rather must be integrated into all books, such as those addressing public relations campaigns, writing, and cases. This is the only way to educate students in the United States (often accused of being ethnocentric) to become effective citizens and communicators in an increasingly globalizing world.

Finally, the format of this volume itself is indicative of how the field has treated, and continues to treat, cultural diversity highlighted by globalization—almost as an afterthought. It appears from the table of contents of this book that most of the 25 chapters in the first four sections deal with public relations almost in isolation of culture or the other environmental variables. We know conceptually that all these variables do play a significant role in the way public relations practitioners operate as professionals. Yet, the mindset of this field has always been to first identify the strategic principles of public relations (based on Western experiences) and then attempt to juxtapose them with the environments of other countries.

The challenge before us is to conduct public relations research studies indigenous to other parts and cultures of the world such as Asia, Africa, Latin America, and the Caribbean. This is the only way of reducing the ethnocentricity of the body of knowledge, thus making it more culturally diverse and holistic. Students who receive training in such a holistic system would truly be "global citizens," which is what it will take for them to succeed in, and be effective contributors to, a global and culturally integrated world.

REFERENCES

Aw, A., Tan, S. K., and Tan, R. (2002, July). *Guanxi and public relations: An exploratory qualitative study of the public relations-Guanxi phenomenon in Singapore firms*. Paper presented to the Public Relations Division of the International Communication Association, Seoul, South Korea.

Cameron, G. T., & McCollum, T. (1993). Competing corporate cultures: A multi-method, cultural analysis of the role of internal communication. *Journal of Public Relations Research*, 5(4), pp. 217–250.

Chen, N. (1996). Public relations in China: The Introduction and development of an occupational field. In H. Culberton & N. Chen (Eds.). *International public relations: A comparative analysis* (pp. 121–154). Mahwah, NJ: Lawrence Erlbaum Associates.

Collectivism, collaboration, and societal corporatism as core professional values in public relations. *Journal of Public Relations Research*, 12(1), 2–48.

CPRE. (1999). Public relations education for the 21st century: A port of entry. Retrieved May 23, 2005, from http://www.prsa.org/_Resources/resources/pre21.asp?ident=rsrc6

Downey, S. M. (1986). The relationship between corporate culture and corporate identity. *Public Relations Quarterly, 31*(4), 7–12.

Dozier, D. M., & Lauzen, M. M. (2000). Liberating the intellectual domain from the practice: Public relations, activism, and the role of the scholar. *Journal of Public Relations Research, 12*(1), 2–22.

Everett, J. L. (1990). Organizational culture and ethnoecology in public relations theory and practice. *Public Relations Research Annual*, pp. 235–252.

Freedom House. (2000). *Democracy's century: A survey of global political change in the 20th century*. Retrieved June 4, 2005, from http://www.freedomhouse.org/reports/century.html

Grunig, J. E. (2000). Collectivism, collaboration, and societal corporatism as core professional values in public relations. *Journal of Public Relationships Research, 12*(1), 23–48.

Grunig, J. E., & Hunt, T. (1984). *Managing public relations*. New York: Holt, Rinehart, & Winston.

Grunig, L. A. (1995). The consequences of culture for public relations: The case of women in the foreign service. *Journal of Public Relations Research, 7*(2), 139–161.

Grunig, L. A., Grunig, J. E., & Dozier, D. M. (2002). *Excellent public relations and effective organizations: A study of communication management in three countries*. Mahwah, NJ: Lawrence Erlbaum Associates.

Grunig, L. A., Toth, E. L., & Hon, L. C. (2000). Feminist values in public relations. *Journal of Public Relations Research, 12*(1), 49–68.

Heath, R. L. (2000). A rhetorical perspective on the values of public relations: Crossroads and pathways toward concurrence. *Journal of Public Relations Research, 12*(1), 69–92.

Hickson, D. J., Hinings, C. R., McMillan, C. J., & Schwitter, J. P. (1974). The culture-free context of organization structure: A tri-national comparison. *Sociology, 8*, 59–80.

Hofstede, G. (1984). *Culture's consequences*. Beverly Hills, CA: Sage.

Hofstede, G. (1991). *Culture and organization: Software of the mind*. London: McGraw-Hill.

Holtzhausen, D. R. (2000). Postmodern values in public relations. *Journal of Public Relations Research, 12*(1), 93–114.

Hon, L. C., & Grunig, J. E. (1999). *Guidelines for measuring relationships in public relations*. Gainesville, FL: Institute for Public Relations.

Huang, Y. H. (1990). *Risk communication, models of public relations and anti-nuclear activities: A case study of a nuclear power plant in Taiwan*. Unpublished master's thesis, University of Maryland, College Park.

Huang, Y. H. (1997, May). *Toward the contemporary Chinese philosophy of public relations: A perspective from the theory of global public relations*. Paper presented to the Public Relations Division at the 47th Annual Conference of the International Communication Association, Quebec, Canada.

Huang, Y. H. (2000). The personal influence model and *gao guanxi* in Taiwan Chinese public relations. *Public Relations Review, 26*, 216–239.

Huang, Y. H. (2001). OPRA: A cross-cultural, multiple-item scale for measuring organization–public relationships. *Journal of Public Relations Research, 13*(1), 61–90.

Hung, C. J. F. (2003, May). *Culture, relationship cultivation, and relationship outcomes: A qualitative evaluation on multinational companies' relationship management in China*. Paper presented at the Public Relations Division in the 53rd Annual Conference of International Communication Association, San Diego, CA.

Kim, H. S. (2003). Exploring global public relations in a Korean multinational organization in the context of Confucian culture. *Asian Journal of Communication, 13*(2), 65–95.

Kipnis, A. (1997). *Producing guanxi: Sentiment, self, and subculture in a North China village.* Durham, NC: Duke University Press.

Kluckhohn, F. (1953). Dominant and variant value orientations. In C. Kluckhohn & H. Murray (Eds.), *Personality in nature, society, and culture* (pp. 342–357). New York: Knopf.

Ledingham, J. A., & Bruning, S. D. (2000a). A longitudinal study of organization–public relationships: Defining the role of communication in the practice of relationship management. In J. A. Ledingham & S. D. Bruning (Eds.), *Public relations as relationship management: A relational approach in the study and practice of public relations* (pp. 55–69). Mahwah, NJ: Lawrence Erlbaum Associates.

Ledingham, J. A., & Bruning, S. D. (Eds.). (2000b). *Public relations as relationship management: A relational approach to the study and practice of public relations.* Hillsdale, NJ: Lawrence Erlbaum Associates.

Lee, B. K. (2004). Corporate image examined in a Chinese-based context: Study of a young educated public in Hong Kong. *Journal of Public Relations Research, 16*(1), 1–34.

Lyra, A. (1991). *Public relations in Greece: Models, roles and gender.* Unpublished master's thesis, University of Maryland, College Park.

Mishler, E. G. (1986). *Research interviewing: context and narrative.* Cambridge, MA: Harvard University Press.

Mulder, M. (1977). *The daily power game.* Leyden: Martinus Nijhoff.

Negandhi, A. R., & Robey, D. (1977). Understanding organizational behavior in multinational and multicultural settings. *Human Resource Management, 16*(1), 16–24.

Ouchi, W. G. (1981). *Theory Z: How American business can meet the Japanese challenge.* Reading, MA: Addison-Wesley.

Pascale, R. T., & Athos, A. G. (1981). *The art of Japanese management.* New York: Simon & Schuster.

Public Relations Body of Knowledge Task Force Report. (1988). *Public Relations Review, XIV*(1), 3–40.

Raz, A. E. (2002). *Emotions at work: Normative control, organizations, and culture in Japan and America.* London: Harvard University Press.

Reber, B. H., & Cameron, G. T. (2003). Measuring contingencies: Using scales to measure public relations practitioner limits to accommodation. *Journalism and Mass Communication Quarterly, 80*(2), 431–446.

Rhee, Y. (1999). *Confucian culture and excellent public relations: A study of generic principles and specific applications in South Korean public relations practice.* Unpublished master's thesis, University of Maryland, College Park.

Smircich, L. (1983). Concepts of culture and organizational analysis. *Administrative Science Quarterly, 28,* 339–358.

Sriramesh, K. (1989, November). *Culture and communication: Corporate culture as a determinant of symmetrical communication in organizations.* Paper presented to the panel of Symmetrical Communication for Professionals in Development organized by the Association for the Advancement of Policy, Research, and Development in the Third World, San Juan, Puerto Rico.

Sriramesh, K. (1992). The impact of societal culture on public relations: Ethnographic evidence from India. *Public Relations Review, 18*(2), 201–211.

Sriramesh, K. (1996). Power distance and public relations: An ethnographic study of southern Indian organizations. In H. Culbertson & Ni Chen (Eds.), *International public relations: A comparative analysis* (pp. 171–190). Hillsdale, NJ: Lawrence Erlbaum Associates.

Sriramesh, K. (2000). The models of public relations in India. *Journal of Communication Management, 4*(3), 225–239.

Sriramesh, K. (2002). The dire need for multiculturalism in public relations education: An Asian perspective. *Journal of Communication Management, 7*(1), 54–70.

Sriramesh, K., (2003). The missing link: Multiculturalism and public relations education. In K. Sriramesh & D. Vercic (Eds.), *The global public relations handbook: Theory, research, and practice* (pp. 505–521). Mahwah, NJ: Lawrence Erlbaum Associates.

Sriramesh, K., & Enxi, L. (2004). Public relations practices and socio-economic factors: A case study of different organizational types in Shanghai. *Journal of Communication Studies, 3*(4), 44–77.

Sriramesh, K., & Grunig, J. E. (1988, November). *Toward a cross-cultural theory of public relations: Preliminary evidence from India.* Paper presented to the panel on New Frontiers in the International Management Environment, Association for the Advancement of Policy, Research and Development in the Third World, Myrtle Beach, NC.

Sriramesh, K., Grunig, J. E., & Buffington, J. (1992). Corporate culture and public relations. In J. E. Grunig (Ed.), *Excellence in public relations and communications management: Contributions to effective organizations* (pp. 577–596). Hillsdale, NJ: Lawrence Erlbaum Associates.

Sriramesh, K., Grunig, J. E., & Dozier, D. (1996). Observation and measurement of organizational culture: Development of indices of participative and authoritarian cultures. *Journal of Public Relations Research, 8*(4), 229–262.\

Sriramesh, K., Kim, Y., & Takasaki, M. (1999). Public relations in three Asian cultures: An analysis. *Journal of Public Relations Research 11*(4), 271–292.

Sriramesh, K., & Takasaki, M. (2000). The impact of culture on Japanese public relations. *Journal of Communication Management 3*(4), 337–352.

Sriramesh, K., & White, J. (1992). Societal culture and public relations. In J. E. Grunig (Ed.), *Excellence in public relations and communications management: Contributions to effective organizations* (pp. 597–616). Hillsdale, NJ: Lawrence Erlbaum Associates.

Tan, S. L. (2000). *Guanxi and public relations in Singapore: An exploratory study.* Unpublished master's thesis, Nanyang Technological University, Singapore.

Tayeb, M. H. (1988). *Organizations and national culture: A comparative analysis.* London: Sage.

Toth, E. L., & Pavlik, J. V. (2000). Public relations values in the new millennium. *Journal of Public Relations Research, 12*(1), 1–2.

Vasquez, G. M., & Taylor, M. (2000). What cultural values influence American public relations practitioners? *Public Relations Review, 25*(4), 433–449.

Vercic, D., Grunig, L. A., & Grunig, J. (1996). Global and specific principles of public relations: Evidence from Slovenia. In H. Culbertson & N. Chen (Eds.), *International public relations: A comparative analysis* (pp. 31–66). Mahwah, NJ: Lawrence Erlbaum Associates.

Yoshikawa, M. J. (1993). Japanese and American modes of communication and implications for managerial and organizational behavior. In W. Dissanayake (Ed.), *Communication theory: The Asian perspective* (pp. 150–182). Singapore: The Asian Media Information and Communication Centre.

Chapter 24

The Application
of Situational Theory in Croatia

Ana Tkalac
University of Zagreb

The world is globalizing and public relations is globalizing with it. It is the major challenge of public relations theory and research to account for these processes. What both academics and practitioners need to understand is how public relations knowledge developed in one part of the world operates in the rest of the world.

Vercic, Grunig, and Grunig (1996) proposed that public relations body of knowledge consists of globally applicable general principles and locally adaptable specific applications of these principles. In that context, it is both intellectually interesting and pragmatically valuable to identify which theoretical concepts in public relations belong to the core of generalized elements. Specifically in this context, this chapter first addresses a question of general applicability of situational theory of publics and then proposes some of its extensions.

Situational theory of publics originally developed in the United States, which is considered to have the most developed public relations academic and practitioner communities. For this chapter, the theory's applicability in other parts of the world has been applied to Croatia, a country in which both public relations education and practice are perceived as being less developed than in situational theory's country of origin (Hajoš and Tkalac, 2004).

As this chapter demonstrates, the situational theory of publics has sustained its test of globalization (as it has done before, cf. Vercic, 1997). It can be considered a truly global theory that has a core of generally useful rules that enable us to understand organizational environments regardless of their economic, political, and social development. It is the theory's specific application to concrete situations that needs to be contextualized. As this chapter also shows, the theory's further use around the globe will bring to it new challenges to address, and in that way enable its further growth.

THE CROSS-SITUATIONAL PARADIGM VERSUS THE SITUATIONAL PARADIGM

From the very beginnings of systematic, scientific research of communication, one of the most important questions was—and still is—how to predict human behavior. Modern social psychology in its analysis starts from the supposition that behavior greatly depends on the attitudes people hold (i.e., behavior results from decisions based on attitudes). In exploring attitudes and their link to behavior, the dominant paradigm was (for a long time) the classical, cross-situational theory of attitudes. According to the previously mentioned theory, human behavior is mostly directed by attitudes that a person transfers from one situation to another, meaning that a person always acts consistently with his or her enduring, stable attitudes.

According to this traditional approach to attitudes and behavior, one of the main functions of communication is modifying cross-situational attitudes in order to reprogram certain behaviors. The number of studies concentrated on the process of communication (i.e., the causal relationship between attitudes and behavior) is very big, but only a limited number of these studies actually add proof to the hypothesis of the classical theory of attitudes (Eagly & Chaiken, 1993).

It has been more than 70 years since LaPierre (1934) published his famous article (quoted in most subsequent attitudes studies) in which he pointed toward the inconsistency of expressed attitudes and behavior. In order to assess how much expressed attitudes actually correlate with behavior, LaPierre took a Chinese couple to 251 restaurants along the American West Coast, registering that only once was the couple refused service. Six months later, LaPierre sent questionnaires to restaurant owners in order to investigate their readiness to serve Chinese guests. All of the questioned restaurant owners answered that they would not serve Chinese guests. Thirty years later, Festinger (1964) described the relationship between attitudes and behavior as one of the most important and enduring problems in the area of attitude research and theory. However, after a thorough literature analysis, he found only three articles that investigated this problem. Festinger, like many scientists before him, concluded that there was insufficient evidence to support the theoretical link between attitudes and behavior. Seibold (1975) analyzed 16 additional empirical studies published after Festinger's attempt and noted that only one study demonstrated a high level of correlations between verbally expressed attitudes and respondents' behavior.

Even in 1963, DeFleur and Westie recognized the effects that situational variables have on the relationship between attitudes and behavior. In their studies, they defined the so-called situational factors (group norms, roles, situation definitions, and other social limitations) that affect verbal behavior or an observable action in specific situations. As a result of this trend, attitude theories have become more complex in the last 20 years and at the same time oriented toward "situational" explanations.

Many attitude researchers based their studies on multivariate theories of behavior, including in them different variables, mostly situationally influenced. That way, behavior was explained additionally, with variables that included individual judgment of consequences of a certain behavior, normative pressures, or situational limitations (Seibold, 1975). Situational theories of behavior predict that behavior is affected by internal intentions (attitudes) as well as by external limitations (i.e., the effects that surroundings have in a certain situation). The situational theory of communication behavior described in this text is based on the assumption that the way a person perceives a situation also defines if and how this person communicates about a situation, and at the same time determines if this person has an attitude relevant for the situation (Grunig, 1983). According to this theory, attitudes affect perception but at the same time are the results of this perception.

THE SITUATIONAL THEORY OF PUBLICS

In public relations, the process of communications is one of the main areas of research, so it is clear why there is a need for a comprehensive theory of communication behavior and why it is important to understand the connection between communication and attitudes. The cross-situational theory of attitudes has not offered a satisfactory answer that clearly and consistently explains the connection among attitudes, communication, and behavior. This is one of the major reasons for the development of a theory that has probably been one of the most researched in public relations–James Grunig's situational theory of publics.

For almost 40 years, the situational theory of communication behavior has developed, changed, been empirically tested, and been reconceptualized in order to adequately and correctly represent the elements of the process of communication, and behavior that is a result of this process. The situational theory also offers an explanation of how communication behavior can be used to segment the general public into smaller groups of publics that show the highest likelihood of communication on a certain topic. The theory predicts behavioral and cognitive effects of communication, as well as attitudes that are usually connected to certain types of communication and types of publics for which these consequences are most likely. The theory additionally describes situations in which publics are developed, from an unconnected group of individuals to an activist group that, with its public opinion, affects the decisions of an organization (Grunig, 1997).

Situational theory of publics was originally developed in order to help predict differential responses important in the area of public relations (Grunig, 1997). Specifically, the main goal of the theory has been to forecast the public's reactions to certain issues and problems. The idea was to try and predict the quantity and type of their communication behavior; the effects of communications on cognitions, attitudes, and behavior; as well as the likelihood of publics' participation in pressuring an organization (Grunig, 1982, 1983, 1992, 1997; Grunig & Hunt, 1984).

According to Grunig (1979, 1982, 1992, 1997; Grunig & Hunt, 1984) the theory began with the premise made by John Dewey and Herbert Blumer that the development of a public is a result of a mutual problem that a group of people share, and that has equal or similar consequences on this group of people.

The theory comprises of two dependent variables (active and passive communication behavior) and three independent variables (problem recognition, constraint recognition, and level of involvement; Grunig, 1982, 1983, 1992, 1997; Grunig & Hunt, 1984). More recent studies have added cognitive effects as well as attitudinal and behavioral effects to the list of dependent variables (Cameron, 1992; Slater, Chipman, Auld, Keffe, & Kendall, 1992). Dependent variables can also be defined as information seeking and information processing (Grunig, 1992, 1997; Grunig & Hunt, 1984).

The main assumption of the theory is that people who communicate actively have a higher likelihood of developing organized cognitions, a higher probability of having an attitude toward an attitude object, and a higher frequency of engaging in certain behaviors connected to the situation (Grunig, 1982, 1983). Grunig expected, basing his predictions on theories of decision making in economy and psychology, that seeking information is more likely in situations in which people make original decisions than in situations in which their decisions are habitual. Situational theory, consequently, presupposes that as in theories of cognitive dissonance, people actively seek additional information in situations in which they recognize a problem (Grunig, 1983, 1997). The first variable of the theory was therefore named *problem recognition*.

The second variable, called *constraint recognition*, was developed through Grunig's research of the decision-making process and communication behavior during the late 1960s and 1970s (Grunig, 1997). At this stage, communication behavior was already conceptualized as intentional and active (i.e., as a problem-solving tool). In his study a few years later (1976), Grunig added Krugman's concept of level of involvement (1965, cited in Grunig, 1976) to the theory, in order to explain passive and active communication behavior, namely information processing and information seeking.

At the same time, Grunig added a fourth variable that he, using Carter's terminology (1965, cited in Grunig, 1976), named *reference criterion*. Reference criterion was, at the time, defined as a solution taken from previous situations and applied in new ones. The role of reference criterion was to reduce the need to seek additional information in new situations. Even though previous conceptualizations indicated that reference criterion has a certain value in predicting cognitions and attitudes, subsequent research showed that the influence that a reference criterion has on communication behavior is limited (Grunig & Disborow, 1977). It seemed that the reference criterion is more of an effect of communication behavior than its cause, which led to further analysis of this variable as a dependent instead of an independent one (Grunig, 1983). Grunig concluded at this stage that the referent criterion is positively correlated with communication, probably because it is a result of problem recognition, involvement, and constraint recognition, and not because it causes behavior. Because none of the results in situational theory research seemed to satisfactorily explain the existence of the reference criterion, this variable was replaced with two new cognitive variables—cognitive breadth and cognitive depth—which can also be combined into a unison variable–cognitive schema (Grunig & Childers, 1988).

Even though graduate students (many of them working with James Grunig) have been adding various variables to the situational theory, the "basic" model of the theory is still comprised of the three independent variables and two dependent variables (active and passive communication behavior). Research done within the framework of the situational theory has added cognitive and behavioral effects as well as attitudes to the list of dependent variables (Grunig & Childers, 1988). Two dependent variables—active and passive communication behavior—are also named *information seeking* and *information processing*. Information seeking describes what Clarke and Kline (according to Grunig, 1997, p. 9) named "premeditated information seeking," that is, "planned scanning of the environment for messages about a specified topic." Information processing describes what Clarke and Kline (according to Grunig, 1997, p.. 9) named "message discovery," that is, "the unplanned discovery of a message followed by continued processing of it."

All of the described variables help explain in which cases individuals or groups activate the two types of communication behavior (Grunig, 1982, 1983, 1992, 1997; Grunig & Hunt, 1984). As mentioned before, information seeking is defined as the process of intentional seeking of information with the purpose of reaching a decision on the direction of the behavior. Individuals who communicate actively seek information and are trying to understand it once they find it. Because of this, the likelihood of forming cognitions or ideas about a situation is higher. On the other hand, individuals or publics that communicate passively do not purposefully seek information. These individuals process information that they receive accidentally, and often do not try to understand this information, which leads to loosely structured cognitions on a certain issue.

According to the situational theory, people will seek and process information more often when the level of involvement is high, when problem recognition is high, and when constraint recognition is low (Grunig 1983). This combination of situational perceptions stimulates a person into actively seeking information about the situation. A certain combination of situational perception also encourages passive communication, because it becomes more likely that the person will pay attention to and remember information that she or he receives accidentally without any effort. However, level of involvement has a smaller influence on information processing than on information seeking. Most of the time, people are not in an active search of information that does not concern them. On the other hand, there is an equal possibility that people will accidentally process information in situations of lower involvement as they do in situations of higher involvement, especially if they recognize a problem in lower involvement situations (Grunig, 1983).

In previous formulations of the theory (Grunig, 1982, 1983), non-existence of a referent criterion also meant a higher likelihood of information seeking and processing. People who perceive their own involvement in a situation will be motivated to communicate because they need information in order to plan their behavior in certain situations. Because none of the research actually confirmed or proved the existence of a referent criterion, it was important to try and discover a variable that could serve in its place. A line of research conducted in Croatia and described in this text (Tkalac and Pavicic, 2002; Tkalac 2003, 2005) proposed the concept of cognitive schemas as a possible alternative to the referent criterion. Even though the situational theory of publics (as well as other situational theories) is based on the assumption that behavior is mostly explained situationally, it is clear that certain elements of decision making have to be constant. For this purpose, Grunig has, in some of his work (Grunig, 1997), used the term *cognitive schema*, a concept that has recently resurfaced in social psychology. As a potential, partial substitute to cross-situational attitudes, it could be the possible missing link in the incomplete association of attitudes and behaviors.

COGNITIVE SCHEMAS

Research shows that situational attitudes predict behavior better than do cross-situational attitudes (Fishbein & Ajzen, 1975). In the area of attitude research, the nomenclature is sometimes unclear (e.g., the distinction between situational and cross-situational attitudes), which allows the concept of cognitive schemas to become a possible alternative.

Individual members of a public, organize their cognitions and attitudes into complex units of knowledge (i.e., cognitive schemas). Schemas represent constructs of knowledge that are wider than individual cognitive units (e.g., attributes, propositions, or mental representations). Schemas are sets of cognitive units that are formed through coding information from short-term memory into long-term memory, where they are organized into more complex structures (Fiske & Taylor, 1991).

Cognitive schemas are structures that includes all cognitions on a certain object including all characteristics and relations between characteristics of the object in question (Fiske & Taylor, 1991). Every stimulus situation provides more information than can be processed, so the main purpose of using a schema is to direct attention toward relevant elements of the situation. When relevant information is missing in a certain situation, schemas "feel the gaps" and offer matrixes of cognitive schemas. Thoughts without matrixes lead to small and unsystematic changes, whereas the existence of such plans results in systematic cognitive changes.

Using cognitive schemas to predict behavior in certain situations offers new possibilities in the area of attitude and communicational behavior research. If schemas represent matrixes of change, then a higher level of elaboration and development of schemas suggests a bigger possibility of systematic cognitive change. The hypothesis that thoughts based on a highly elaborated schema polarize attitudes more than do thoughts with a weakly elaborated schema was tested in some studies (Britton & Tesser, 1982, cited in Petty & Krosnick ,1995), but the results were still unclear. Schemas as constructs are dynamic and likely to change in spite of the fact that these changes are rarely the result of an individual message. Schemas help people in assimilating new information (i.e., they help in making sense of the information through the already existing schemas). Schemas can also alter information through placing information or groups of information in already formed but incorrect schemas.

Research in the area of public relations has rarely proved revolutionary change caused by communication programs when the cognitive schemas of the publics are concerned, at least not in the way it was discussed in the past (Grunig & Childers, 1988). It is a lot more probable that specific communication programs simply add a new unit to cognitive associations of individuals. Once people accumulate cognitions and attitudes, they continue to place them in long-term memory and associate them with existing schemas. If we associate cognitive schemas with reputation, it is important to remember that cognitive schemas have a long life. This makes it crucial to acquire a good reputation early, because later it becomes very difficult to replace it (Grunig, 1993).

The assumption that cognitive schemas could serve as a predictor in the theory and, as such, help forecast the existence of attitudes and their link to communication behavior motivated three separate studies of the situational theory in Croatia (Tkalac, 2003, 2005; Tkalac & Pavicic, 2002). The conceptual assumption in this research was that the situational theory is a better tool for solving certain communication problems than is the classical cross-situational theory, and that it offers a superior framework for planning communication programs with various publics of the organization. One of the major suppositions of this line of research incorporated the reconceptualization of the situational theory so that it included cognitive schemas as independent variables (i.e., predictors of communication behavior).

VARIABLES AND PUBLICS OF THE SITUATIONAL THEORY

The situational theory of publics is based on the assumption that publics form around certain issues, situations, or topics that are a result of the behavior of the organization. The theory predicts (studies that confirm these predictions include Cameron, 1992; Grunig, 1982, 1983, 1989; Hamilton, 1992) that a higher level of problem recognition and a lower level of constraint recognition increase active information seeking and passive information processing. The level of involvement increases the possibility of information seeking but has a lower level of impact on information processing. In other words, people rarely seek information about situations that do not concern them; however, the possibility of accidental processing of such information is big, especially if the situation in question is perceived as problematic.

Because people get involved more actively in information seeking than information processing, information seeking and variables that precede it more frequently lead to communication effects than does information processing. The situational theory predicts (Cameron, 1992; Grunig, 1982, 1983; Hamilton, 1992) that people who communicate actively have a higher chance of having an attitude or engage into behavior connected to the situation, and—what is specially significant for the Croatian studies (Tkalac, 2003, 2005; Tkalac and Pavicic, 2002)—a higher chance of having organized cognitions (Grunig, 1982; Grunig & Ipes 1983).

In the selection of communication issues used to test the theory, typically a number of issues are selected, and these issues connect particular publics to a certain extent. In the original formulation of the theory, the basic premise was that each organization as well as each situation will formulate specific profiles of various publics (considering dependent and independent variables). However, most of the studies up to this point have showed that publics consistently form four groups that Grunig (1989) named: all-issue publics (publics active on every issue), apathetic publics (publics that communicate very little on any of the topics), single-issue publics (publics active in one or a small group of issues, mostly issues that are connected to only a small portion of the population), and hot-issue publics (publics active only on an issue that has an influence on almost everyone in the population and that has high media coverage).

Numerous studies have been conducted through the years that concentrated on validating the situational theory. In spite of many confirming results, certain parts of the theory are still open for debate. Situational theory, according to its author (Grunig, 1997) still does not include the valence of attitudes in any form (i.e., the direction and the intensity of attitudes are not included in any part of the theory). To this potential omission Grunig offered a twofold explanation. On one side, reasons for excluding attitude valence are philosophical and associated with the fact that deterministic theories assume that attitudes control behavior. Situational theory was developed under a symmetrical worldview (asymmetrical, in this context, means that messages are being constructed in order to present organizations positively no matter what the truth really is). On the other side, attitude valence was excluded because of pragmatic reasons. Research showed (Grunig, 1997) that communication behavior cannot be (exclusively) explained by attitudes. People do not seek or process information in order to confirm their existing attitudes; they seek information because this information is of relevance to them. According to the situational theory, cognitions, attitudes, and behavior are a result of communication.

Critics of the situational theory (Cameron, 1992; Vasquez, 1994) have concluded that, for the complete understanding of publics and communication with those publics, it is necessary to understand the way they think. Even though attitudes, cognitions, and behaviors are (according to the theory) a result of communication behavior, and not its source, even the author of the theory agrees that it is necessary to include these variables in the theory. The idea of testing a conceptualization of the theory that uses cognitive schemas as a potential substitute for attitudes was one of the major incentives for the research conducted in Croatia (Tkalac, 2003, 2005; Tkalac & Pavicic, 2002).

The author of the situational theory of publics, James Grunig, has through the years developed a methodology for measuring specific variables of the theory as well as the results of communication (Grunig, 1975, 1977, 1979, 1982, 1983, 1989). It is important to mention that even though Grunig is the creator of the situational theory of publics as an integrated concept, other scientists have used certain variables and ideas. Problem recognition, for example, exists in many models of decision making, whereas constraint recognition can be compared to Bandura's concept of personal efficacy (1977). Involvement as a concept has been a key component of various theories for more than 40 years, especially in the areas of persuasion and communication (Petty & Cacioppo, 1986).

STUDIES OF THE SITUATIONAL THEORY CONDUCTED IN CROATIA

The first study (Tkalac & Pavicic, 2002) attempted to test the situational theory in a context of a Croatian institution, with an aim to explore the feasibility of using cognitive schemas as a dependent variable in the theory. The applied purpose was to segment publics that arise from four issues connected to the organizational reputation of a Croatian institution—the Graduate School of Economics and Business—and to describe their cognitive schemas, attitudes, and behavioral intentions. The second study (Tkalac, 2003) was aimed at exploring the communication behavior of publics of the government of Croatia. Research was conducted in July 2002, on a sample of 1,200 respondents. The sample used in the study was a representative, stratified sample of the population that included all citizens of Croatia over the age of 15. A variety of controversial issues connected to the policy of the government led to formation of first strong activist groups in Croatia, as well as various other publics. The third study (Tkalac, 2005) was conducted in 2004, and represented a continuation of the first study from 2002, in order to analyze potential change that had happened during the ensuing 2 years.

In all three studies, selected issues followed the methodology of the situational theory (Grunig, 1982, 1983, 1989). For example, the study of the government publics included: (a) the problem of unemployment in Croatia; (b) the problem of international relations between Croatia and Slovenia; (c) governmental solutions toward Croatian inductees in Haag; (d) governmental involvement in the privatization of the biggest national oil company; and (e) the issue of legalizing homosexual marriages in Croatia. Three independent variables were measured with Likert-type scales applied in previous studies of the situational theory

(Grunig, 1979, 1982, 1983, 1989). Cognitive schemas were measured through a methodology most commonly applied in the area of cognitive and social psychology (Slater et al., 1992). Craik and Lockhart (1972) introduced the concept of depth of processing in order to explain the construct previously known in cognitive psychology as long-term memory. For these authors, "depth of processing" means that people apply a higher level of semantic or cognitive analysis on incoming information. Researchers in the area of cognitive psychology later concluded that the original concept of depth, introduced by Craik and Lockhart, could more precisely be defined as width of processing, where width is determined by the number of elaborations (Anderson & Reder, 1979). Anderson and Reder (1979) differentiated between the concepts of width and depth in a sense that width is the number of elaborations and depth–the quality of elaborations. The increase in the width of processing can be defined as the increase of the number of "cognitive units" in memory, whereas the depth of processing can be defined as the organization level of these cognitive units into schemas–bigger and more complex units of knowledge (Anderson, 1983).

In a variety of research studies (in the areas of both cognitive psychology and public relations), cognitive schemas have often been measured through open-ended questions. Answers to open-ended questions were then coded through different methods that emphasized width, depth, or another dimension of schemas. Because the concepts of width and depth of cognitive schemas did not receive complete support in previous test of the theory (Grunig & Childers, 1988), all three studies described here (Tkalac, 2003, 2005; Tkalac & Pavicic, 2002) used a different concept–the level of elaboration of cognitive schemas. The level of elaboration was defined on a five-point scale and depended on the number and type of responses given by the respondents.

The dependent variables of the situational theory (information seeking and information processing) were, in all three studies, measured by multiple Likert-type scales developed and used in previous investigations of the situational theory (Grunig, 1979, 1982, 1983, 1989). Attitudes toward specific situations as well as toward the institutions in general were also measured through Likert-type scales. It is important to mention here that the situational approach greatly differs from the classic cross-situational approach in the assessment of attitudes. The situational theory does not assign motivation exclusively to attitudes and values. The value of attitudes in decision making is not underestimated, but the theory proposes that decisions are also formed according to specific situational elements. An important assumption of the theory is that people are rarely interested in situations or issues that do not concern them (i.e., they do not feel the need to communicate about those issues). A significant implication of this assumption is that elaborate public relations programs are often misdirected as an attempt of the organization to communicate with publics that do not reciprocate this communication (Grunig, 1997).

The logic behind big media actions in public relations is based primarily on the idea that communication programs can change the level of problem recognition, involvement, and constraint recognition. Change in these variables in certain publics should lead to indirect behavioral change and bring it closer to what the organization needs. The basic assumption of the situational theory, however, rejects this connection, because people cannot be under the influence of messages they do not seek or process.

In all three Croatian studies, the correlation between the level of elaboration of cognitive schemas and independent situational variables—information processing and information seeking—pointed toward a possible connection between the situational theory and cognitive schema complexity. In the government study (Tkalac, 2003) correlations between each of the five situational issues and information processing were statistically significant ($p < 0.001$). The correlation between level of schema elaboration and information seeking was statistically significant in four out of five situations. The hypothesis according to which the situational perception variables are not significantly correlated with the existence of an attitude toward specific issues was also confirmed in all three studies (Tkalac, 2003, 2005; Tkalac & Pavicic, 2002). According to the situational theory and the conceptualization of described studies, active publics should have a higher likelihood of situational attitudes than should passive publics, and both active and passive communication behavior should be significantly correlated with the existence of attitudes. However, none of the Croatian studies confirmed these predictions. According to the situational theory, the intensity of attitudes and membership to a specific public is not connected. Active publics should have an equal chance of having intense attitudes as should passive publics (i.e., evaluation intensity does not depend on the readiness for active or passive communication). In this segment, the results of the studies were mixed. In all three studies, correlations between information processing and attitude intensity were occasionally significant and occasionally not. Information seeking did not correlate with attitude intensity in any of the situations.

Croatian studies of the situational theory (Tkalac, 2003, 2005; Tkalac & Pavicic, 2002) partially confirmed the assumption that cognitive schemas could serve as a predictor in the theory. Inconsistent connections between attitude direction and intensity on one side and situational variables on the other additionally emphasized the importance of cognitive schemas.

CONCLUSION

Reasons why the situational theory is important in any context (American, Croatian, or other) are dual. On one side, situational theory offers an explanation why people communicate and when the possibility of communication is the highest. On the other side, the theory also explains how predicted communication behavior can be used for segmenting a population into specific publics (that communicate on one or more situational issues). Situational theory offers a conceptual explanation of the situation in which the likelihood of cognitive effects is the highest, as well as the existence of attitudes and behavior. The theory also explains in which situations publics transform from an unconnected group of individuals into organized activist groups that influence organizational and business decisions through their public opinion (Grunig, 1997).

Situational theory predicts various types of communication behavior depending on the membership to a certain category of public. The theory segments publics according to the level of activity (or passivity) of their communication behavior and according to the effects their behavior has on an organization. The applied purpose of the described research was primarily focused on segmenting publics around issues connected to the Graduate School of Business and Economics (Tkalac, 2005; Tkalac & Pavicic, 2002) and the Croatian government (Tkalac, 2003), as well as the description of their cognitive schemas and attitudes. On the other hand, the theoretical framework of the studies was based on potentially including cognitive schemas into the theory and determining the relationship between attitudes and membership to a certain public.

Research based in social psychology has for a number of years been dominated by the deterministic view according to which it is attitudes that rule people's behavior. According to the paradigm described earlier (the assumption that communication can change attitudes), communication can indirectly change behavior. It is clear why practitioners (and not only practitioners) in various organizations hope this paradigm to be true, where public relations programs are concerned. However, years of research in the area of attitude formation and change do not support this assumption. Communication and attitude research has, through years, led to a conceptualization that is situational and teleological more than it is deterministic and cross-situational.

Croatian studies of the situational theory (Tkalac, 2003, 2005; Tkalac & Pavicic, 2002) as well as previous applications of the theory have shown that communication with active publics is more likely than with passive publics, and that active publics have a higher likelihood of having cognitions, attitudes, and demonstrating behavior than have passive publics. Passive publics can hold attitudes more often than cognitions, but these attitudes are often weak. It is more likely that communication will cause a change in cognitions of active publics. This does not mean that a specific communication program will necessarily be efficient in causing change that the organization wants. Active publics communicate with a large number of sources of information, so their attitudes, cognitions, and behavior are formed from a bigger pool of information. The results of the Croatian research also show (as do the previous studies of the theory) that active publics have a higher likelihood of creating attitudes and cognitions than have apathetic publics.

All of this highlights the importance of elaborated cognitions as effects of communication on one side and as mediating variables toward attitudes and behavior on the other. Cognitive variables have high value when public relations programs are concerned, because they can be modified in the short term, unlike attitudinal and behavioral change, that is based mostly on long-term processes. Cognitive effects can be measured immediately and then used in order to evaluate communication program results (with the possibility of potential program correction).

In the described context, the situational theory becomes even more useful, because the variables of the theory offer a possibility of predicting when active communication will occur. Active communication, as cognitions, represents a variable on its own, but at the same time represents an important mediating variable because it produces elaborated cognitions that intervene in the formation of attitudes and behavior.

Research conducted in Croatia adds to the attempt of testing the relationship between cognitive schemas and situational as well as cross-situational attitudes. Results of the studies confirm (strongly, if not completely) theoretical predictions according to which active publics have elaborated cognitive structures and situational attitudes more often than cross-situational attitudes.

The program of research offered under the framework of the situational theory approaches publics as a group of people defined through their motivation to communicate about problems that involve them, that they recognize, and about which they can do something. At the same time, people are less motivated by attitudes or values in their communication behavior. As was already mentioned, people are rarely interested in situations that do not include them. The situational theory therefore suggests that many practitioners are working hard for no use, because it is very difficult to communicate with a public that does not want to communicate. Grunig argued (1997) that the attempt to change levels of constraint recognition, problem recognition and involvement through communication—and, by this change, behavior—is impossible. People cannot be under the influence of messages they do not want or even process.

Certain critics of the theory (Slater et al., 1992) suggested that valence of support should be added to the theory based on their belief that how a public evaluates a problem influences the effect of the message. Results of Croatian studies (Tkalac 2003, 2005; Tkalac & Pavicic, 2002), however, helped in showing that attitudes (especially their valence) are not adequate variables for explaining communication behavior. As previous research indicated, these studies affirmed that cognitions and attitudes mostly form (or organize) only after the communication process. This helps explain why cognitions, attitudes, and behavior can (just as the theory suggests) be viewed as a result of communication behavior. On the other hand, attitudes should not be ignored, because they are also essential in completing the picture on how publics think, behave, and communicate, which is necessary for good communication.

Good communication is partially culturally determined and therefore subject to local applicability; yet, the underlying mechanisms of human behavior and its explanation are universal. In such a way, situational theory of publics belongs to core elements of the global public relations body of knowledge.

REFERENCES

Anderson, J. R. (1983). *The architecture of cognition*. Cambridge, MA: Harvard University Press.

Anderson, J. R., & Reder, L. M. (1979). An elaborative processing explanation of depth of processing. In L. S. Cermak & F. I. M. Craik (Eds.), *Levels of processing in human memory* (pp. 385–403). Hillsdale, NJ: Lawrence Erlbaum Associates.

Cameron, G. T. (1992). Memory for investor relations messages: An information-processing study of Grunig's situational theory. *Journal of Public Relations Research, 4*(1), 45–60.

Craik, F. I. M., & Lockhart, R. S. (1972). Levels of processing: A framework for memory research. *Journal of Verbal Learning and Verbal Behavior, 11,* 671–684.

DeFleur, M. L., & Westie, F. R. (1963). Attitude as a scientific concept. *Social Forces, 42,* 17–31.

Eagly, A., & Chaiken, S. (1993). *The psychology of attitudes*. Fort Worth, TX: Harcourt Brace Jovanovich.

Festinger, L. (1964). Behavioral support for opinion change. *Public Opinion Quarterly, 28,* 227–236.

Fishbein, M., & Ajzen, I. (1975). *Belief, attitude, intention and behavior: An introduction to theory and research*. Boston, MA: Addison-Wesley.

Fiske, S. T., & Taylor, S. E. (1991). *Social cognition* (2nd ed.). New York: McGraw-Hill.

Grunig, J. E. (1975). Some consistent types of employee publics. *Public Relations Review, 1*(4), 17–36.

Grunig, J. E. (1976). Communication behaviors occurring in decision and non-decision situations. *Journalism Quarterly, 53,* 252–263.

Grunig J. E. (1977). Review on research on environmental public relations. *Public Relations Review, 3*(3), 36–58.

Grunig J. E. (1979). A new measure of public opinion on corporate social responsibility. *Academy of Management Journal, 22,* 738–764.

Grunig J. E. (1982). The message-attitude-behavior relationship: Communication behaviors of organizations. *Communication Research, 9,* 163–200.

Grunig, J. E. (1983). Communication behaviors and attitudes of environmental publics: Two studies. *Journalism Monographs, 81.*

Grunig, J. E. (1989). Sierra Club study shows who become activists. *Public Relations Review, 15*(3), 3–24.

Grunig, J. E. (1992). Systems of internal communication. In J. Grunig (Ed.), *Excellence in public relations and communications management* (pp. 531–575). Hillsdale, NJ: Lawrence Erlbaum Associates.

Grunig, J. E. (1993). Image and substance: From symbolic to behavioral relationships. *Public Relations Review, 19*(2), 121–139.

Grunig, J. E. (1997). A situational theory of publics: Conceptual history, recent challenges and new research. In D. Moss, T. MacManus, & D. Vercic (Eds.), *Public relations research: An international perspective* (pp. 3–48, 282–288). London: International Thomson Business Press.

Grunig, J. E., & Childers, L. (1988, August). *Reconstruction of a situational theory of communication: Internal and external concepts as identifiers of publics for AIDS.* Paper presented at the Association for Education in Journalism and Mass Communication Conference, Portland, OR.

Grunig, J., & Disborow, J. B. (1977). Developing a probabilistic model for communication decision making. *Communication Research, 4,* 145–168.

Grunig, J. E., Hunt, T. (1984). *Managing public relations.* New York: Holt, Rinehart & Winston.

Grunig, J. E., & Ipes, D. A. (1983). The anatomy of a campaign against drunk driving. *Public Relations Review, 9*(2), 36–53.

Hajoš, B., & Tkalac, A. (2004). Croatia (Chapter 6). In B. van Ruler & D. Vercic (Eds.), *Public relations and communications management in Europe: A nation by nation introduction to public relations theory and practice* (pp. 83–94). New York: Mouton de Gruyter.

Hamilton, P. K. (1992). Grunig's situational theory: A replication, application and extension. *Journal of Public Relations Research, 4,* 123–150.

LaPierre, R. (1934). Attitudes vs. actions. *Social forces, 13,* 230–237.

Petty, R. E., & Cacioppo, J. T. (1986). The elaboration likelihood model of persuasion. In L. Berkowitz (Ed.), *Advances in experimental social psychology* (Vol. 19, pp. 123–205). San Diego, CA: Academic.

Petty, R. E., & Krosnick, J. A. (Eds.). (1995). *Attitude strength: Antecedents and consequences.* Hillsdale, NJ: Lawrence Erlbaum Associates.

Seibold, D. R. (1975). Communication research and the attitude-verbal report-overt behavior relationship: A critique and theoretic reformulation. *Human Communication Research, 2,* 3–32.

Slater, M. D., Chipman, H., Auld, G., Keffe, T., & Kendall, P. (1992). Information processing and situational theory: A cognitive response analysis. *Journal of Public Relations Research, 4*(4), 198–203.

Tkalac, A. (2003). *Public relations in attitude formation and change: The application of the situational theory of communication behavior.* Unpublished doctoral dissertation, University of Zagreb.

Tkalac, A. (2005). *Re-applying the situational theory: Second study.* Unpublished manuscript.

Tkalac, A., & Pavicic, J. (2002). How global is the situational theory of publics: The case of Croatia. In *9th International Public Relations Research Symposium in conjunction with 2002 Euprera Annual Congress: The status of public relations knowledge in Europe and around the World* (pp. 174–182). Bled, Slovenia: Pristop Communications, Ljubljana.

Vasquez, G. M. (1994). Testing a communication theory-method-message-behavior complex for the investigation of publics. *Journal of Public Relations Research*, 6(4), 267–291.

Vercic, D. (1997). Towards fourth wave public relations: A case study. In D. Moss, T. Macmanus, & D. Vercic (Eds.), *Public relations research: An international perspective* (pp. 264–279). London: International Thomson Business Press.

Vercic, D., Grunig, L., & Grunig, J. (1996). Global and specific principles of public relations: Evidence from Slovenia. In H. Culbertson & N. Chen (Eds.), *International public relations: A comparative analysis* (pp. 31–65). Mahwah, NJ: Lawrence Erlbaum Associates.

Chapter 25

A Retrospective on *World Class*:
The Excellence Theory
Goes International

Robert I. Wakefield
Brigham Young University

The study on excellence in public relations management surely ranks as the most comprehensive compilation of benchmark information that the public relations industry has ever enjoyed. Until the Excellence Study began in the late 1980s, most of the research had examined narrow aspects of the practice rather than exploring it holistically. Furthermore, no scholar or group had ever attempted such a thorough search of theories from related domains to determine how they might apply. Over several years, the excellence team gathered theories inside and outside of the field and tested them against all aspects of the practice. The result was a set of principles to guide and measure excellence in public relations and among its practitioners well into the 21st century.

As thorough as the Excellence Study was, however, its earlier stages seemed to overlook one of the rapidly expanding arenas of the practice: international public relations. In 1989, when I, the author of this chapter, entered the PhD program at the University of Maryland, the Excellence Study was in its data collection phase. On the team were Jon White, a consultant in the United Kingdom, and Krishnamurthy Sriramesh, a PhD candidate from India. They contributed significant international perspectives and collaborated on a chapter in the excellence book about the influences of culture on the practice (J. Grunig, 1992). Yet, culture is just one of the many variables that affect international public relations, and adding a more comprehensive study of this complex area was no doubt beyond the already broad scope of the excellence project.

545

Entering the PhD. program, I had a great desire to delve into international public relations research. With previous public relations experience in two organizations, I was excited about the roadmaps that the Excellence Study offered to the practice. Having also spent 3 years in Asia, my interests tended toward understanding how public relations is effectively structured and practiced in multinational entities. Therefore, I wanted to contribute this important facet of research to the excellence endeavor. In hearing of this desire, Doctors Jim and Lauri Grunig jumped in with their full support. Starting with little information, we embarked on a project to determine how the Excellence Study would hold up in multinationals across the cultural, economic, and political borders that comprise the international public relations environment.

This chapter outlines our international research track within the excellence framework, and then analyzes it according to the global environment of today—more than 10 years after the research began. This international project was not officially part of the Excellence Study, but it was based on those principles. And although I personally invested great struggles into this research, the work was a communal knowledge-building process that spanned many nations. Through my decade of wanderings from Maryland to Utah to Hawaii, the Grunigs continued to offer advice, encouragement, and contacts. Dejan Vercic, a practitioner and scholar from Slovenia; fellow Maryland PhD. traveler Frank Marra; Michael Morley of Edelman Worldwide; international practitioners John Reed, Barbara Burns, and Deanna Pelfrey; and many others contributed by giving advice or participating in the project that is discussed in this chapter. It is summarized here to provide insight into what the research has produced, along with some suggestions on what remains to be done to build greater understanding of effective international practice.

RESEARCH ON EXCELLENCE IN INTERNATIONAL PUBLIC RELATIONS

In the early 1990s, literature searches revealed little information specific to the international practice of public relations. In fact, one American executive said, "There simply is no such thing as international public relations" (Angell, 1998. p. 8). Another countered that "international public relations is one of the most rapidly growing areas of the profession, and one of the least understood" (Pavlik, 1987, p. 64). If the practice was indeed moving rapidly across borders with little understanding, it seemed critical to build the base of knowledge so that multinational organizations would be able to maximize their relationship building and avoid costly, or perhaps deadly, mistakes.

What little research there was at the time, Culbertson (1996) divided into two categories. The first he called *comparative public relations*, which explores the similarities and differences in the practice of public relations between countries or cultures. "Its primary purpose," he said, "is to identify more or less universal problems that challenge many or all nations, and to search for generic principles that apply widely" (p. 2). Following Geertz' (1973) concept of "thick description," comparative research is somewhat like building a puzzle piece by piece (or nation by nation) until the whole is understood. Such comparisons offer important accumulative glimpses into the practice of public relations around the world. They also give insight to multinational organizations that, to maintain long-term profitability, need to understand how the nuances of culture, politics, and economics affect their worldwide operations.

Culbertson's (1996) second category was *international public relations*, which "focuses on the practice of public relations in an international or cross-cultural context" (p. 2). In other words, where the unit of analysis for comparative researchers is the nation, for international researchers it is the organization and its processes. Within this context, he said, are intergovernmental diplomacy and alliance building; transnational economic transactions, like investment trading; interactions among citizens of the nations through tourism, sports events, the arts, and other means; and international organizations, such as the United Nations or the World Bank. Culbertson acknowledged that there was scant research in this second area (and even his and Chen's groundbreaking 1996 book, *International Public Relations*, concentrated mostly on the comparative realm).

It seems strange that as recently as the mid-1990s there was still scant theory building to guide the behaviors and public relations practices of multinational entities. These large organizations nowadays have an enormous impact on the international arena and can become easy targets for activists in various countries, regions, or even globally. It is crucial for these entities to better understand local cultures and global interactions so as to proactively communicate and build relationships wherever they operate. Yet, in the 1990s it seemed that without such guidance, multinationals were subjecting themselves to mistakes that, in such a complex and dynamic environment, could be catastrophic.

Larry Foster, who for 30 years worked for Johnson & Johnson and was its public relations supervisor during the Tylenol crisis many years ago, warned his fellow practitioners about the vulnerability of such a condition. After leaving Johnson & Johnson and while serving as consultant to multinational organizations, he said:

> There are ... some dark and disturbing clouds on the horizon. The darkest is the tendency of many large multinational companies to make inter-

national public relations management the victim of benign neglect. As a result of this neglect, the international public relations/public affairs function has not developed in large corporations as it should. While this may seem to bode well for the public relations agencies and consultancies that are filling the void ... over the long term it can spell trouble. (Foster, 1999, p. 3)

There is plenty of evidence that the neglect of relationship building and crisis anticipation has brought trouble to major multinational organizations. Coca-Cola's crippling crisis from improper handling of a dioxin scare in Europe in 1999 has been well documented (Wakefield, 2000a). The crisis was fostered in part by the company's overconfidence in estimating its relationships with multicultural publics. This resulted in financial losses that took several years to retrieve, the company being dropped from *Fortune*'s annual Most Admired Companies list, and the resignation of its chief executive, Douglas Ivester. However, Coca-Cola is hardly alone. Crises suffered by Union Carbide in Bhopal, Nestle in Africa, Royal Dutch Shell in Norway, McDonald's in Yugoslavia, Nike and other shoe manufacturers in Southeast Asia, and even Disney in France all stemmed from the challenges of operating across cultural boundaries.

BALANCING GLOBAL AND LOCAL OPERATIONS

One of the most difficult challenges for multinationals is the delicate navigation between global imperatives and local action in implementing and communicating their mission. In the early 1990s, theoretical precedent had already been established around this basic issue. Not only had this balance been addressed in such disciplines as comparative management (Adler, Doktor, & Redding, 1986) and marketing (Baalbaki & Malhotra, 1993), but it was sneaking into public relations treatises as well (see Dilenschneider, 1992; Ovaitt, 1988). Anderson (1989) observed a preference among organizations toward one of two poles: the philosophy that programs can and should be created at a central headquarters and be implemented in all markets with only minor adaptations, or the placement of resources and decision-making authority in the local markets, where local communicators best understand the needs of their audiences.

Authors usually defended one side or other of this equation. For example, Anderson argued for global mandates, demanding "that programs in distinctive markets be interrelated" (1989, p. 413). Dilenschneider (1992) insisted that public relations should be performed by locals who best understand the customs and laws of each nation. Most multinationals leaned toward one of the poles, and Americans particularly tended to see the choice as an either/or proposition—either centralizing everything or allowing unmonitored local autonomy.

In practice, polarization was shown to be damaging. Centralization often imposes programs that are inappropriate for local conditions. It also breeds disunity when people of diverse, and often conflicting, perspectives are forced to comply (Botan, 1992). Local autonomy, by contrast, indicates that the multinational perceives little need to strengthen the brand through global consistency. There is little chance for coordination, and handing operations entirely to locals fosters a "not invented here" mentality that undermines the organization (Hill, 1992). Kinzer and Bohn agreed that "lack of global ... coordination within the corporation risks a public relations disaster" (1985, p. 5).

Some experts proposed that successful multinationals respond to *both* global and local imperatives. Traverse-Healy (1991) said that an international public relations program should centralize policies and messages and then localize strategies to adapt to language, customs, and politics. Morley later asserted, "There is not likely to be a phrase you will hear in ... public relations as often as 'think global, act local' ... The idea is that a good product, service, or communications strategy can achieve global success as long as it is customized to meet local tastes" (1998, p. 29).

If both central and local programs are needed, then the key to successful international practice would be to discover which combination of global and local variables is the most effective. If practitioners could attain a theoretical understanding of which combination works best, they would be more valuable to the multinational organizations they serve. Therefore, the critical question going into our research was: What strategies or tasks would be important for the global scale, and what things were best handled in the various markets? Again, cues to this issue came from the more advanced research of related disciplines.

The Excellence Study had already identified contingency theory as important to public relations practice because it allows adaptation for rapidly changing environments. This theory seemed especially relevant to the uncertainties faced by multinational entities in an even more complex and dynamic global realm (Negandhi, 1983). For one thing, Lauri Grunig characterized publics in the global environment as "increasingly more unfamiliar and more hostile ... more organized and more powerful (L. Grunig, 1992, p. 130).

One salient contingency model was Brinkerhoff and Ingle's (1989) *theory of structured flexibility*, created for the developmental management domain after considerable research of such organizations as the United States Agency for International Development. Their theory identified a combination of functions that were generic to good performance—that could be universally applied—or that were "specific" to local contingencies. Their generic variable included creation of short- and long-term objectives, consensus on policies, establishment of responsibilities, overall strategic plans, and budget management. The specific variable accounted for the flexibility to modify and implement centralized themes in specific regions or countries as necessary.

FOUNDATION FOR INTERNATIONAL EXCELLENCE

Incorporating structured flexibility into international public relations, it was possible to attach the field to the contingency discussions of the Excellence Study. Because the effectiveness study was upholding scrutiny in the U.S. domestic arena, and because many of its variables had been drawn from more universal theories that had originated or been accepted outside the United States, these excellence variables would serve as valuable points of departure for an exploration into international practice. Thus, in the early 1990s, we began to develop the foundation for our research on excellence in international public relations.

The research project incorporated eight major variables from the Excellence Study into propositions on global effectiveness—called the *generic* variables in accordance to Brinkerhoff and Ingle's (1989) model of structured flexibility. Six additional propositions were developed relative to local, or *specific*, effectiveness.[1] For the generic realm of the multinational organization, we proposed that:

1. The multinational organization has an overarching global philosophy—but not overpowering edicts—based on communication that fosters trust and seeks mutual benefits or understanding between the multinational and its publics worldwide.
2. This same symmetrical philosophy is reflected within the organizational culture and internal communication worldwide. Management fosters participation and two-way communication among all of its employees.
3. Public relations is a strategic management function worldwide, working with the dominant coalition both at headquarters and in each of the local units to make decisions related to communication,

---

[1]The concept of applying generic and specific variables into international public relations was first broached by Jim Grunig and me as part of my comprehensive exams at the University of Maryland. Because it took me 7 whole years to complete my dissertation (Wakefield, 1997—the dreaded ABD/full-time work scenario), the generic-specific concept was first *publicly* presented by Vercic, Grunig, and Grunig (1993) and then published in Culbertson's book on international public relations (1996). Although we had complete consensus on the generic-specific concept, we did not collaborate on exactly which variables apply; Dejan Vercic and the Grunigs included one more generic variable and one less specific variable than I did.

and not subordinated to simply carrying out or communicating the wishes of senior managers.

4. The public relations function is integrated, meaning that practitioners worldwide report to the public relations unit at headquarters as well as to their own local management and work under a unified single umbrella.
5. Public relations is not subordinated to marketing, legal or other departments so that it can properly carry out its strategic mission.
6. Senior practitioners in the lead public relations position at headquarters and in every local unit will be trained in public relations and able to perform managerial roles of boundary spanning and advising senior management (obviously, some variations will be necessary in given cultures where public relations training may not be available).
7. Hiring and promotional practices will value and foster diversity by offering equal opportunities to women and to whatever minorities may be resident within given cultures where the multinational operates.
8. Because multinationals face turbulent, dynamic environments, public relations is structured to be globally adaptable to rapid changes anywhere in the world that would affect the organization's operations or reputation.

To be tested was our proposal that the successful multinational would value and implement these generic principles universally; however, the entities with excellent public relations also would create strategies and interact with publics in response to the specific factors. It would be unlikely, however, for local practitioners to establish strategies and actions if they did not understand which factors affected their local practice. To identify these factors, we again examined theories outside of public relations and settled on six specific variables. These are summarized in the following list, as we explained them at the beginning of our study:

1. The level of development within a given country.
2. The local political situation.
3. The cultural environment.
4. Language differences.
5. The potential for activism.
6. The role of the mass media.

Level of Development

While examining public relations practice in Slovenia, Vercic et al. (1993) determined that level of development is one factor affecting local practice. Botan explained that economic and technological factors in a given country affect the "development of the information infrastructure" (1992, p. 154). Level of development also determines the type of public relations activity. In developed nations, public relations often is a tool for marketing, subordinated to the marketing function; in developing nations, it typically assists the government in rallying citizens. Development also influences literacy rates and the media that are available for an entity's communications with its publics (Botan, 1992).

Political Situation

Development is often linked to political environment: the less development, the greater the tendency there is toward authoritarianism. Vercic et al. (1993) argued that public relations is not possible in such a regime because one-way propaganda dominates its information spectrum and violence or severe punishment is used to enforce behaviors. This environment restricts the honest dialogue prerequisite to effective public relations. Sharpe (1992) disagreed, saying public relations is practiced in countries like China and Turkey despite these constraints. In fact, Jia (1992) cited government estimates that more than 100,000 practitioners were working across the economic spectrum of China even before the great influx of Western public relations agencies. Political environment, then, seemed to be fertile ground for additional research.

Cultural Environment

The concept of culture is hard to define, but its influence on communication has been widely accepted for decades. Hall said, "Culture is communication and communication is culture" (1959, p. 191). Grunig and Hunt (1984) and Sriramesh and White (1992) then viewed communication and public relations as synonymous.

One path of cultural study stems from Hofstede's (1980) dimension theories, which have since been dissected by numerous scholars. Hofstede developed four categories to distinguish one culture from another: individualistic versus collective societies; the gap between the powerful and the masses (power distance); the extent to which a society avoids or welcomes uncertainty; and the prevalence of typically masculine activities (aggression, competition, etc.) versus feminine characteristics (cooperation and compromise) within a culture.

Hampden-Turner and Trompenaars (1993) interpreted Hofstede's dimensions differently than most other scholars. They claimed, for example, that the highly individualistic U.S. society is actually the most codified in the world, valuing lawsuits and short-term results more than relationships and complex long-term perspectives. American multinationals, therefore, are concerned only about stockholder satisfaction and worry less about building relationships with publics than do their European or Asian counterparts, who seem much more attuned to their place within the broader society.

Language Differences

Language has an obvious effect on public relations. Many nations have multiple official languages and differing dialects, taxing budgets and resources to make required translations (Newsom, VanSlyke Turk, & Kruckeberg, 1996). English has become a universal language; "nearly a quarter of the world's population is already fluent or competent in English, and this figure is steadily growing" (Crystal, 1997, pp. 4–5). Yet, its dominance is often resented. Crystal commented, "If English is your mother tongue, you may have mixed feelings about the way it is spreading around the world.... And if you live in a country where the survival of your own language is threatened by the success of English, you may feel envious, resentful, or angry" (p. 2).

Even with a global language, intercultural misunderstandings can arise and be tragic or even fatal. In 1990, when an Avianca Airlines plane crashed on Long Island and killed 72 people, misinterpretation of one word between American flight controllers and Colombian pilots was largely responsible (Pinsdorf, 1991). This reality of miscommunication across cultures argues for giving local practitioners the autonomy to communicate directly with their publics rather than being forced to parrot global verbiage. Although consistency in organizational messages is important, the messages must be broad enough to allow for local adaptation.

Potential for Activism

Publics are the heart of public relations, and activist publics provoke organizational response. Strategic guidelines should be created for interactions with activists around the world, both for organizational protection and to pursue mutual advantages. However, as Traverse-Healy noted, "The public is 'out there'... and therefore 'out there' is where the action has to be" (1991, p. 34). Therefore, activism is a key factor that affects local practice.

Activism varies greatly from country to country. Authoritarian regimes stifle public debate, and activism is scarce in countries like India, with its great power distance, or Japan, where saving face is important (Funakawa, 1997; Sriramesh, 1992). Nations and organizations that previously curbed or ignored activist movements are now forced to respond as the groups band together to impose change. Activist publics have become organized and powerful, and they insist that mainstream organizations satisfy their expectations (Friedman, 2000).

It is more difficult to respond to activists internationally than domestically. It is difficult to identify international publics and issues, trace their movements across borders, and communicate across cultural and language barriers (Nigh & Cochran, 1994). To reduce the potential for significant damage, organizations must identify and communicate with activists early and often in every locale where they operate (Rose, 1991).

Role of the Mass Media

Some may debate the role of media, but few would argue their influence on world affairs. Pavlik explained that media coverage "leads to action, not because of its effect on the ostensible audience, but because others believe it will influence its audience" (1987, p. 107). Most media initially had only local or national influence, but modern technologies have carried media and their ideologies across the world with increasing speed and lower costs. Of course, the Internet has revolutionized all media and the way people interact with them. Even in the early 1990s, Epley maintained that "instant communication has made the planet's populace more knowledgeable and opinionated than ever before" (1992, p. 110). Interest groups have learned how to manipulate media to achieve their ends, and although media do not intentionally favor these groups they like the conflicts behind activist events (Pires, 1989).

Still, international public relations often comes down to local action (but perhaps in many locations at the same time). Epley stated that international practitioners must transcend "infatuation with modern gadgetry and learn how to use these new sophisticated communication vehicles to narrow our scope and better define very specific messages to targeted audiences" (1992, p. 115). Haywood added that "communication is extremely local and very personal" (1991, p. 22).

THE RESEARCH PROCESS

After identifying and including these generic and specific variables into our excellence foundation, it was time to test the variable among multinational organizations whose success depends on understanding all the important nuances of operating across cultural, political, and economic boundaries. The intent was to create a normative theory of excellence in international public relations. Normative theory would explain how public relations *should* be practiced, as distinguished from positive theory that describes how it *is* practiced. However, the best normative theories also guide actual practice (Grunig & Grunig, 1991), so we believed that creation of a good normative theory on international public relations would be useful for practitioners as well as for scholars.

The research began in the mid-1990s, and evolved into three cumulative studies that combined the wisdom of 79 public relations experts in 30 countries. My dissertation research, a Delphi study involving 23 veterans in the field from 18 nations, served as the initial international test of the excellence variables. That was followed by a survey of 31 experts in 11 more countries, replicating an instrument from the second round of the Delphi. This second study strengthened the reliability of the initial results. Then, in 1998, I was asked to conduct a study for Edelman Worldwide Public Relations, which offered an investigation into the philosophies and activities of 25 multinational corporations using the excellence variables as the measuring stick. This project ultimately led to a model for effective international public relations. Following is a more detailed summary of each of the research projects.

The Delphi Study

The Delphi method collects knowledge from experts in a process in which there is an "incomplete state of knowledge concerning ... the nature of the problem" (Delbecq, Van de Ven, & Gustafson, 1975, p. 5). We felt that this was an exploration into what would be effective in international public relations, and thus a Delphi study was appropriate. The method involves experts without having to gather them in one place— perfect for a study that included respondents from 18 nations.

The study progressed in two rounds, the minimum necessary for gathering sufficient data to validate the Delphi. In the first round, 50 potential respondents were given the 14 propositions along with questions about the propositions: Do you agree with the statement; does the proposition apply in your country; if so, why, and if not, why not; can it hold up in an organization that crosses borders; and so on. The experts were asked to respond to these statements and questions based on their knowledge of the practice in their country. The purpose was to generate significant dialogue from the respondents, including specific examples as to why the propositions would or would not be appropriate or useful in the given countries.

Once the responses came back from the first round, we identified patterns of agreement in addition to the "outliers"—those comments that departed significantly from the norm. The comments, typical and atypical, then were converted into 78 declarative statements, presented in at least one of the respondents' own words, which were sent again to the respondent group for the second round. Attached to each statement was a Likert scale that measured to what extent the respondents agreed or disagreed with the comment. From this process it was possible to reach conclusions about how well the 14 propositions held up to international scrutiny.

Results of the Delphi

As we had hoped before the study commenced, the Delphi achieved solid agreement between the respondents. One indicator was that 34 of the 78 declarative statements received mean scores above 4 or below 2 on the 5-point Likert scale (5.0 or 1.0 representing complete consensus for or against the statement). Although our qualitative study was not seeking statistical significance, these clusters represented concurrence on several issues (to see what statements earned the strongest consensus, see Table 25.1).

TABLE 25.1

Responses to Declarative Statements

Statements that received the most consensus (4.5 or higher, 1.4 or lower):

- International PR is exponentially more complex than domestic PR.
- Two-way symmetrical communication is desirable.
- Organizations should be more concerned with sales turnover than with public credibility (generated strong disagreement).
- If headquarters involves local practitioners in planning, it can gain insights about local conditions and resources and profit from global thinking.
- PR should be separate from marketing, working independently but closely with marketing, etc.
- An ideal qualification for PR education and training would be clear understanding of local politics, media, culture, language, etc.
- Headquarters must understand and have empathy for local cultures to ensure that decisions do not insult local populations or harm the organization.
- A local component of a multinational organization should build relationships with local media.

Statements that received the least consensus (2.8 to 3.2 on 5-point scale):

- Most multinationals don't care about benefits of external publics.
- Multinational PR programs should be run inside the multinational organization, not be handed over to an outside PR firm.
- It's cheaper to hire a local PR firm than to hire an inside PR staff person.
- When talking about strategic planning, a PR background will hardly suffice.
- If development means GNP per capita, it doesn't affect PR practice.
- In political systems without freedom of speech and other freedoms, there is no room for PR.

Most of the panelists shared surprisingly similar thoughts about the practice, regardless of their country of origin, suggesting that certain fundamental principals of public relations are becoming universal. Although most of the panelists viewed the propositions as primarily normative, the study did unearth several examples of where the principles are applied in daily practice. Several respondents, particularly those in Europe, also commented that the public relations field is gradually moving closer to that ideal that would allow the propositions to be practicable.

Seven of the eight generic propositions generated concurrence. It was seen as desirable for multinationals to perpetuate two-way communication throughout the world, both internally and with their external publics. It was generally agreed, however, that multinationals rarely achieve this ideal. A common global strategy was seen as wise, as long as it was not imposed from the top down. The respondents also saw a great need to use the multinational diversity of the public relations staff in planning and implementing global programs. The respondents concurred that a globally integrated public relations unit would be ideal but was improbable in today's business environment. There was also consensus on the notion that public relations staff in the excellent multinational organization would be well trained according to "international standards of public relations education," and would never be subordinated to marketing or any other department. Finally, there was unanimous consent that the multinational more than domestic organizations must anticipate and adapt quickly to potential issues.

The one generic proposition that generated a wide range of opinions was about the hiring of diverse practitioners, including those who represent the minority groups in the various countries. The majority of respondents agreed with this ideal, but strongly concurred that multinationals should consider local cultural mores in the hiring and placement of employees. Their thoughts were best represented by the declarative statement "The only criterion for hiring should be, is this the best person for the position?" Interestingly, Nancy Adler (1993), a cross-cultural management scholar, has written that multinationals are breaking down long-standing employment norms in many nations.

The six specific variables proposed as potential influences on local public relations also elicited support from the diverse section of respondents. The novel element was that some of the specific variables—particularly activism and the role of media—are rapidly spreading influences far beyond individual countries and must therefore be considered in global public relations programming. Other variables—like culture, language, and developmental differences—require different local approaches not only between countries but within countries as well.

Follow-Up of Delphi's Second Round

Qualitative studies do not require large samples to ensure reliability, but after completing the initial Delphi I wanted to determine how well the initial results would hold up in even more cultures. So, using additional contacts I had made in the field since starting the study, I sent out the declarative statements from the second round of the Delphi. The attempt generated 31 responses from 11 different countries than in the initial pool. This pushed the total sampling to 54 responses from 29 countries. The results yielded similar comments toward each of the propositions from the first study.

The Edelman Project

The final study was completed in 1998. Edelman Worldwide, one of the larger public relations firms across the globe, had several clients who were expanding their operations and were asking how to structure and carry out their international public relations to be most effective. A few months earlier, Edelman executive Michael Morley and I had presented together at a conference of the Counselors Academy of Public Relations Society of America. Aware of my research, he asked me to conduct a study for his organization and its clients.

The research consisted of lengthy telephone interviews with public relations supervisors in 25 multinational corporations headquartered in 12 nations in North and South America, Europe, Asia, and Australia. Eighteen of the companies were on the 1997 Fortune Global 500 list, and the smallest earned close to $2 billion in annual earnings that year. The interviews included questions about each entity's public relations structuring and programs, communication between headquarters and local public relations units, budget centers and processes for public relations programs around the world, processes for anticipating and dealing with major issues or challenges, uses of public relations agencies, and strengths and weaknesses of agency assistance.

One of the significant impacts of the Edelman research was to verify the applicability of the Excellence Study in international public relations. Although the Excellence Study was a groundbreaking compilation of theories, it was seen by some practitioners as abstract and not relevant to the everyday realities of public relations (Dozier, Grunig, & Grunig, 1995). Although evidence was already accumulating against these claims, the Edelman study offered confirmation of the excellence variables from senior public relations people who were orchestrating the strategic activities around the world.

GLOBAL EXCELLENCE: MODEL OF WORLD-CLASS PUBLIC RELATIONS

With their cumulative data, the three studies helped answer the question of what comprises public relations excellence in multinational organizations. Certainly, there is no "one-size-fits-all" prescription; organizations will always differ in philosophies and structures depending on the industry in which they operate, country of origin, size and financial resources, and many other factors. However, the three studies disclosed certain universal fundamentals that can give multinational organizations of any type greater chances for success with their public relations. The Edelman study in particular clearly delineated variances of success in the public relations practices of various organizations based on these principles. Most of the fundamentals stem right back to the excellence variables identified more than 15 years ago.

With these characteristics of excellence in place, it was possible to develop a model for public relations practice in the multinational. The model could be used to evaluate a multinational's public relations program and predict its potential for achieving and maintaining a solid reputation around the world, as opposed to just in the organization's home country.

To distinguish the model from any domestic equivalents, I called it the *model of world-class public relations*. The term may seem like a cliché, but it was borrowed from the ranks of international business. Harvard professor Rosa Beth Moss Kanter (1995), in a book entitled *World Class*, said that successful multinational entities incorporate the best available thinking and resources from anywhere in the world, not just from hometown roots. She referred to such an entity as cosmopolitan. Clear evidence of the cosmopolitan organization, she said, is that its headquarters will look like the United Nations rather than the "good-old boy" network from Ohio. Using this same reasoning, I placed the term *world class* into the model of global public relations excellence.

Based on this model, the public relations program for every company that participated in the Edelman study—or any other corporation, for that matter—could be placed into one of four classifications. The categories range from virtually no resources or qualified personnel to full global staffing of highly qualified personnel who actively cooperate to accomplish mutual goals. Of course, local public relations officers should always work closely with their unit managers, but these same local officers are also integral to a global team that builds understanding and preserves reputation throughout the world. Consider, for example,

what a tremendous waste it is for an organization to hire qualified practitioners in all local units only to restrict their activities to adapting and
carrying out global vision set by someone else. Wouldn't it be better to
harness the ideas of these diverse personnel into the entire global strategic team? That is what the global strategic team is about—using the
public relations staff (and perhaps agency resources, as well) throughout the world in a horizontal planning and implementation capacity,
while simultaneously having each individual carry out his or her own
local assignments as well.

At first, the four classifications were based on stages of evolution. For
example, multinationals with virtually no international public relations were *early evolution;* as the program expanded it would fall into
the *moderate evolution* phase. Even greater resources and sophistication
converted to *advanced evolution,* and the full-scale programs were in the
complete evolution category. However, while the Edelman research was
under way, two companies were severely affected by the collapse of Korea's economy. As a result, both firms had been forced to drastically reduce their public relations staffs around the world, and their
international public relations program dropped from an advanced
evolution state to barely emerging status.

However, after musing over the Korean example and after discussions
with Lauri Grunig, I dropped the term *evolution* from the model. The
term connotes slow but constant growth, yet the classifications do not
represent such phases; rather, they depict the current status of public relations in the multinational, which could be different from what it was
last year or will be next year. As a result, the names of the categories
were changed to *dormant program, emerging program, sophisticated program,* and *world-class program.* These classifications are explained in
Table 25.2.

Core Findings from the Edelman Study

Once the model was developed, it became possible to make interesting
observations about the multinational corporations that participated in
the Edelman study. These are included here because it indicated that
many of even the largest multinationals had insufficient public relations programs at the end of the 20th century. For example, only 4 of the
25 firms had reached world-class status. Seven of the companies in the
study fell into the sophisticated category, eight were in emerging status,
and five more had not broken away from a dormant state. Certainly,
these conditions would support the assertion made earlier by Larry Foster, that "many large multinational companies ... make international
public relations management the victim of benign neglect," which, "over
the long term ... can spell trouble" (Foster, 1999, p. 3).

TABLE 25.2

Four Classifications of the Model of World-Class Public Relations

Dormant program	• No real support from dominant coalition for PR. • Functions mostly as one-way publicity/marketing support. • Few/no PR resources and activities outside headquarters. • No cooperation between headquarters and local units. • No strategy for handling PR issues across borders. • All international PR is reactive.
Emerging program	• Growing resources, but staffs still incomplete in local units. • PR at headquarters still conducts mostly one-way publicity tasks and has little or no authority to influence local PR. • Still little interaction between headquarters and local units. • Local PR people are not trained or are not well qualified. • International PR is still reactive.
Sophisticated program	• Good support from dominant coalition. • PR function becoming strategic; combines traditional publicity efforts with two-way communication and emphasis on reputation management. • Qualified staff or use of PR agencies in most local units. • Some cooperation between headquarters PR and local units. • Local PR beginning to be subject to global guidelines. • Proactive international PR valued but not often achieved.
World-Class program	• Dominant coalition sees PR as core international function and supports it completely. • PR protects reputation first, then supports marketing. • Full-time PR officers in all major markets, often supplemented by PR agencies. • PR training is prerequisite for hiring at headquarters and in local units; development and team building is ongoing. • PR officers function as global team, with frequent, purposeful interaction between headquarters and local units and among local units. • Headquarters PR person is team leader for achieving PR goals both globally and locally. • Information sharing is fostered, with ideas and solutions coming from any source on the global team. • Global team cooperatively sets global PR guidelines, and every unit creates and carries out strategies based on those guidelines; budgeting available at headquarters and locally. • Global PR team anticipates and is prepared to expedite, even across borders, any contingency that arises.

Three other findings contradicted what might be considered conventional wisdom about public relations in the multinational. First, corporate size had little correlation with public relations status. One Fortune Global 500 firm that has been in dozens of national markets for years was entrenched in the dormant state. The only U.S.-based firm that showed world-class status was also the only U.S. firm not listed among the Global 500. Second, the European corporations seemed far more advanced in their international public relations than did American firms. This is probably because the European firms are inherently more attuned to the international environment; their managers grew up surrounded by several different countries and languages, and from their earliest stages the corporations must look beyond their own borders to increase their marketplace. Therefore, European managers recognize the innate varieties in their publics and have organized their public relations with a more holistic, international approach from the outset. Third, and perhaps surprisingly, the corporations with more advanced international public relations—those that have the most in-house public relations resources—also make the most effective use of public relations agencies.

TOWARD THE FUTURE

The studies conducted from 1995 to 1998 disclosed considerable knowledge about the practice of international public relations and helped to show the validity of the excellence theories in the global arena. The variables held up well over three tests and proved to be a solid basis for effective practice in multinational organizations. In addition, we verified that level of development, political environments, culture and language, activism, and the media affect public relations practices in the local units but are also causing a need for advanced programming and coordination on a global level.

However, it must be understood that all of these studies were early explorations into the poorly framed world of international public relations. They were qualitative approaches with small sample sizes and mostly open-end questions. Therefore, although the studies certainly identified worldwide patterns of thought and consensus among public relations experts, they should still be viewed with what some scholars call "systematic doubt" (Agar, 1980).

So, what does it all mean—particularly as we look at the situation a decade later? Pauly (1991) referred to qualitative research as a "conversation." In our research to date, we fostered early conversation about how to effectively organize and practice public relations in the multinational. The dissertation has never been published beyond the University of Maryland, but parts of the three studies have been presented in the

United States, Europe, and Asia. In addition to presentations at the International Public Relations Research Symposium in beautiful Bled, Slovenia (Wakefield, 1999, 2000b), some of the information has been presented at an annual conference of the Public Relations Society of America (PRSA), a PRSA Counselors Academy conference, and in conferences in the Netherlands, Switzerland, and the Philippines. Before he passed away in 2001, Patrick Jackson (1999, 2000) twice summarized the studies in his popular *pr reporter* newsletter.

Building theoretical understanding in such a broad and expanding domain as international public relations is a mammoth undertaking, however, and there is tremendous room for future research. More people need to join the conversation, and many more topics can be addressed. Following are just a few of the possibilities.

Update of the Delphi and *World-Class* Model

The first potential study is to replicate the original research to determine whether it is still applicable. The world at large and the world of commerce have changed, with the advent of the Internet, increases in travel tempered somewhat by the post-9/11 environment, greater clout and sophistication of globally connected activist networks, and many other global adjustments just since the onset of the new century. Given these dynamics, it would be interesting to conduct the Delphi study again—or at least disseminate the second-round instrument—to see if opinions about the propositions have persisted over the years or changed with the new environment.

It also would be useful to re-examine the validity of the model of world-class public relations created after the Edelman study. One way to do this would be to conduct in-depth interviews of either the companies in the original study or a sampling of different corporations. To further validate the results, it would be beneficial to visit the participating companies for a few days to observe whether the actual practices mirror what was reported by the public relations officers.

Particular aspects of the Edelman study also deserve additional exploration in the future. As mentioned earlier, for example, the study identified two companies whose public relations structures and resources had been reduced as a result of an economic crisis in their home country. This brings up the question as to the dynamics of public relations in multinational organizations: Do most multinational entities face rapid or continual changes in their public relations structures, or did these companies represent anomalies? Because the Edelman study was a one-time snapshot into the practice, one or more additional studies are needed to help answer this question. Another fruitful area of research surrounds the questions raised but not clarified in the study, about how multinationals use public relations agencies and whether they find this usage valuable.

Influence of the Internet

At the outset of this research quest in the early 1990s, only the military and academics knew much about the Internet. Today it is difficult to imagine how the world got along without it. It has penetrated the developed world and reaches into even some of the most remote villages of Africa and the Pacific. It has facilitated great communication and marketing opportunities and unprecedented vulnerabilities for multinational organizations. The entire world comes to the individual at the click of a rodent, and with that comes power to communicate directly and civilly with organizations or to pressure corporations anywhere in the world. With the Internet, borders lose meaning. And, as revolutionary and incredible as the Internet is, this world information system is always at risk of viruses and security issues that could threaten multinationals as well (Cha, 2005).

Researchers are studying the influence of the Internet on the public relations practice, but it would be interesting to re-examine our international excellence studies in light of the fact that it has entered the arena. For example, questions about the role of the media would no doubt generate completely different discussion because the Internet now exists as both another media conduit and a competitor (Chester & Larson, 2005). Today, most media sources can be accessed from anywhere in the world or multinationals can bypass them entirely in favor of more direct communication with their publics.

What does this mean for public relations practice? How has the Internet changed the role of the mass media? What are the implications of the rapidly proliferating media conglomerates, which combine traditional media venues with the Internet and focus on profitability rather than on providing information? These questions and others could use additional exploration. In addition, Micklethwait and Wooldridge (2000) argued that the Internet has fused media, politics, economics, and other power centers to the point that it is impossible to change one of these areas without impacting the others. What influence does this new situation have on multinational organizations operating in countries that have lost the ability to control their people and information?

The Role of Activism

One outgrowth of the Internet is the connectivity and power it offers to activist groups. A decade ago, activists could pressure for change either by enduring the bureaucratic pace of legislation, approaching media to obtain coverage, or trying direct intervention like standing at head-quarters and protesting (Rose, 1991). Activism that started in one location usually stayed there, and multinationals could hide negative incidents in one country from the rest of the world. With the Internet, this is not possible. Information goes global in hours, if not minutes, as activists quickly rally other groups to help apply pressure. Even governments that previously could terrorize their citizens and hide human rights abuses are finding it more difficult as activists swarm in from around the world—literally and virtually—to expose the misdeeds.

Friedman (2000) referred to this phenomenon of activists who go into countries other than their own to pressure for change as *globalution*, or revolution from beyond. Although he did not have a name for the activists who are involved in this phenomenon, perhaps they could be called *globalutionaries*. These global activist movements were major catalysts behind the fall of the Suharto regime in Indonesia, and international activist pressure has frustrated such entities as Nike, Wal-Mart, and other companies.

This growing power and reach of activists provides another significant topic for future research. In comparison to the international excellence research, where activism was seen as a specific variable, have the international connections and combined pressuring of activist groups turned the activity into a generic variable? Does activism now demand attention from headquarters, with carefully developed global strategies that include continual communication and feedback from the local units? From where does communication with these activist groups need to originate—headquarters, host countries, or both?

Another possible research track relates to the excellence foundation of two-way symmetrical communication. Previously, scholars have argued that this theory is impractical because publics do not have power equal to the large organizations; therefore, communication between the big multinationals and their publics could never be symmetrical. With the increasing power of activism, however, has this balance shifted so that organizations can no longer afford to ignore them? All of these questions merit additional and updated research.

The Conversation Goes On

Certainly, additional topics could be suggested. International public relations is still in the early phases of theory building, with much to be discovered. As I have suggested, for example, is there truly a developing universal foundation for the practice of public relations worldwide? Are American corporations beginning to structure their public relations programs looking at the world first and then their home country, as opposed to the traditional way it has been done in most companies? Given

the increasingly insatiable appetite for short-term stockholder communication among today's multinational organizations, will the entities
continue (or in some cases, begin) the strategic, long-term relationship-building function that is clearly shown to be the most effective aspect of public relations?

These questions and many more will be critical to the future of public
relations, particularly as more and more of it is practiced across cultural, political, and economic borders that make up the world of international public relations. Again, as Pauly (1991) implied, let that
conversation continue.[2]

REFERENCES

Adler, N. (1993). Competitive frontiers: Women managers in the Triad. *International Studies of Management and Organizations, 23*(2), 3–23.

Adler, N., Doktor, R., & Redding, S. (1986). From the Atlantic to the Pacific century:
Cross-cultural management reviewed. *Journal of Management, 12,* 295–318.

Agar, M. (1980). *The professional stranger: An informal introduction to ethnography.* San Diego, CA: Academic Press.

Anderson, G. (1989). A global look at public relations. In B. Cantor (Ed.), *Experts
in action* (2nd ed., pp. 412–422). White Plains, NY: Longman.

Angell, R. (1990). "International PR": A misnomer. *Public Relations Journal,
46*(10), 8.

Baalbaki, I., & Malhotra, N. (1993). Marketing management bases for international market segmentation: An alternate look at the standardization/cus-
tomization debate. *International Marketing Review, 10*(1), 19–44.

Botan, C. (1992). International public relations critique and reformulation.
Public Relations Review, 18(2), 149–159.

Brinkerhoff, D., & Ingle, M. (1989). Between blueprint and process: A structured
flexibility approach to development management. *Public Administration and
Development, 9*(5), 487–503.

Cha, A. (2005, June 26). Viruses, security problems undermine Internet. *Washington Post.* Retrieved June 26, 2005, from www.washingtonpost.com/
wp-dyn/content/article/2005/06/25/AR2005062501284.html

Chester, J., & Larson, G. (2005). Sharing the wealth: An online commons for the
non-profit sector. In R. McChesney, R. Newman, & B. Scott (Eds.), *The future
of media: Resistance and reform in the 21st century* (pp. 185–205). New York:
Seven Stories Press.

Crystal, D. (1997). *English as a global language.* Cambridge, England: Cambridge University Press.

Culbertson, H. (1996). Introduction. In H. Culbertson & N. Chen (Eds.), *International public relations: A comparative analysis* (pp. 1–16). Mahwah, NJ: Lawrence Erlbaum Associates.

---

[2]Meanwhile, I express my great gratitude to my advisors and friends, Jim and Lauri
Grunig. They truly have changed the nature and scope of research in the public relations
field and have guided it into the realm of an actual domain, rather than just the few studies
that existed when they began their work. Not only are the Grunigs valuable scholars in
this broad field, but they are genuinely good human beings and valuable friends to the
many graduate students who have gone through their program over the years. May their
days together in retirement be full of continuous symmetrical communication!

Delbecq, A., Van de Ven, A., & Gustafson, D. (1975). *Group techniques for program planning: A guide to nominal group and Delphi processes*. Glenview, IL: Scott, Foresman.

Dilenschneider, R. (1992). *A briefing for leaders: Communication as the ultimate exercise of power*. New York: HarperCollins.

Dozier, D., Grunig, L., & Grunig, J. (1995). *Manager's guide to excellence in public relations and communication management*. Mahwah, NJ: Lawrence Erlbaum Associates.

Epley, J. (1992). Public relations in the global village: An American perspective. *Public Relations Review, 18*(2), 109–116.

Foster, L. (1999). 1998 Atlas award lecture on international public relations. In *International Section Monograph, II* (p. 1). New York: Public Relations Society of America.

Friedman, T. (2000). *The Lexus and the olive tree*. New York: Anchor.

Funakawa, A. (1997). *Transcultural management: A new approach for global organizations*. San Francisco: Jossey-Bass.

Geertz, C. (1973). *The interpretation of cultures*. New York: Basic Books.

Grunig, J. (1992). *Excellence in public relations and communication management*. Hillsdale, NJ: Lawrence Erlbaum Associates.

Grunig, J., & Grunig, L. (1991). Conceptual differences in public relations and marketing: The case of health-care organizations. *Public Relations Review, 17*(3), 257–278.

Grunig, J., & Hunt, T. (1984). *Managing public relations*. New York: Holt, Rinehart & Winston.

Grunig, L. (1992). Strategic public relations constituencies on a global scale. *Public Relations Review, 18*, 127–136.

Hall, E. (1959). *The silent language*. Garden City, NY: Doubleday.

Hampden-Turner, C., & Trompenaars, A. (1993). *The seven cultures of capitalism*. New York: Doubleday.

Haywood, R. (1991). Are the issues converging? In M. Nally (Ed.), *International public relations in practice* (pp. 21–25). London: Kogan Page.

Hill, R. (1992). *We Europeans*. Brussels: Europublications.

Hofstede, G. (1980). *Culture's consequences*. Beverly Hills, CA: Sage.

Jackson, P. (1999). How smart multinationals practice PR on a global level—and what all organizations can learn from their experience. *pr reporter tips & tactics, 37*(13), 1–2.

Jackson, P. (2000). Managing global relationships done best not by central mandate but single strategy carried out locally to emphasize cultural sensitivities; is all PR then similar? *pr reporter, 43*(43), pp. 1–4.

Jia, G. (1992, November). *China's public relations frontier*. Paper presented at the National Conference of the Public Relations Society of America, Kansas City, MO.

Kanter, R. (1995). *World class: Thriving locally in the global economy*. New York: Simon & Schuster.

Kinzer, H., & Bohn, E. (1985). *Public relations challenges of multinational corporations*. Paper presented to the International Communications Association Conference, Honolulu, HI.

Micklethwait, J., & Wooldridge, A. (2000). *A future perfect: The challenge and hidden promise of globalization*. New York: Crown Business.

Morley, M. (1998). *Managing your global reputation*. London: Macmillan.

Negandhi, A. (1983, Fall). Cross-cultural management research: Trend and future directions. *Journal of International Business Studies*, pp. 17–28.

Newsom, D., VanSlyke Turk, J., & Kruckeberg, D. (1996). *This is PR: The realities of public relations*. Belmont, CA: Wadsworth.

Nigh, D., & Cochran, P. (1994). Issues management and the multinational enterprise. *Management International Review, 27*(1), 4–12.

Ovaitt, F. (1988). PR without boundaries: Is globalization an option? *Public Relations Quarterly, 33*(1), 5–9.

Pauly, J. (1991). A beginner's guide to doing qualitative research in mass communication. *Journalism Monographs, 125*, 1–29.

Pavlik, J. (1987). *Public relations: What research tells us*. Newbury Park, CA: Sage.

Pinsdorf, M. (1991). Flying different skies: How cultures respond to airline disasters. *Public Relations Review, 17*(1), 37–56.

Pires, M. (1989). Working with activist groups. *Public Relations Journal, 45*(4), 30–32.

Rose, M. (1991). Activism in the 90s: Changing roles for public relations. *Public Relations Quarterly, 36*(3), 28–32.

Sharpe, M. (1992). The impact of social and cultural conditioning on global public relations. *Public Relations Review, 17*(1), 69–83.

Sriramesh, K. (1992). Societal culture and public relations: Ethnographic evidence from India. *Public Relations Review, 18*(2), 201–211.

Sriramesh, K., & White, J. (1992). Societal culture and public relations. In J. Grunig (Ed.), *Excellence in public relations and communication management* (pp. 597–614). Hillsdale, NJ: Lawrence Erlbaum Associates.

Traverse-Healy, T. (1991). The corporate aspect. In M. Nally (Ed.), *International public relations in practice* (pp. 29–40). London: Kogan Page.

Vercic, D., Grunig, L., & Grunig, J. (1993a). *Global and specific principles of public relations: Evidence from Slovenia*. Paper presented to the International Conference on the State of Education and Development, the Association for the Advancement of Policy, Research and Development in the Third World, Cairo, Egypt.

Vercic, D., Grunig, L., & Grunig, J. (1996). Global and specific principles of public relations: Evidence from Slovenia. In H. Culbertson & N. Chen (Eds.), *International public relations: A comparative analysis* (pp. 31–65). Mahwah, NJ: Lawrence Erlbaum Associates.

Wakefield, R. (1997, November). *International public relations: A theoretical approach to excellence based on a worldwide Delphi study*. Unpublished doctoral dissertation, University of Maryland, College Park.

Wakefield, R. (1999). World-class public relations: A model for effective public relations in the multinational. Paper presented at the 6th annual International Public Relations Research Symposium, Bled, Slovenia.

Wakefield, R. (2000a). World-class public relations: A model for effective public relations in the multinational. *Journal of Communication Management, 5*(1), 59–71.

Wakefield, R. (2000b). Preliminary Delphi research on international public relations programming. In D. Moss, D. Vercic, & G. Warnaby (Eds.), *Perspectives on public relations research* (pp. 179–208). London: Routledge.

VI

Challenges to Educators

Public Relations Knowledge and Professionalism: Challenges to Educators and Practitioners

Donald K. Wright
University of South Alabama

Judy VanSlyke Turk
Virginia Commonwealth University

The 1992 Excellence Study identified 14 characteristics of excellent public relations programs at the organizational, departmental, and individual practitioner levels (Grunig, 1992). At the individual level, the potential to practice excellent public relations is, according to the study, indicated by knowledge of the two-way symmetrical model of public relations, knowledge of the managerial role played by practitioners, and professionalism. According to Ehling (1992):

> [P]otential depends in large part on the body of knowledge and professionalism that practitioners bring to bear on public relations problems.... Practitioners with more education in and knowledge of public relations are more likely to be in the dominant coalition, to be in the manager role, and to practice the two-way symmetrical model of communication—all attributes of excellent public relations. (p. 439)

This chapter looks at how professionalism in public relations has evolved and been influenced by what the Excellence Study told us about what excellent, effective public relations look like and how practitioners can carry out excellent public relations. The chapter also identifies some of the challenges facing educators and practitioners as public relations seeks greater levels of professionalism.

PROFESSIONALISM AND PUBLIC RELATIONS

Interpretation of the word *profession* is confusing, because the term doesn't explicitly identify a body or group that is immediately identifiable by all. Although there rarely is any doubt about the traditional professions of medicine, law, and the clergy, multiple questions present themselves throughout many other fields. Some view *profession* as a synonym for *occupation*, and consider people professionals if they're paid for what they do. Others differentiate occupations from professions by saying a profession requires specialized knowledge and academic preparation, whereas an occupation does not. However, because certain occupational groups continually strive for recognition as professions, one can assume that, in society's eyes at least, the words *profession* and *occupation* are not similar.

The essence of the professional idea and the professional claim, according to Hughes (1965), is that professionals claim to know the nature of certain matters better than other people. In his early work on medical education and professional organization, Flexner (1915) applied these six criteria to distinguish professions from occupations:

- A profession is intellectual and has great personal responsibility for the proper exercise of choice and judgment.
- Professions are learned and based on a substantial body of knowledge.
- A profession is practical, because its knowledge can be applied to real-life situations.
- Professions have techniques, or skills, that can be taught and applied to problem solving.
- Professions are organized into associations or groups of practitioners for various professional purposes, including those of guiding the education of students and regulating entrance to the profession.
- A profession is guided by altruism—concerns for the patients or clients who come to it for help. Its purpose is to benefit society.

Carr-Saunders and Wilson (1933) supported and amplified Flexner's criteria and stipulated these characteristics for professions:

- The activity consists of intellectual operations with large individual responsibility.
- Raw materials of the work are drawn from science and learning.
- The learning is practically applied.
- The technique is communicable by education.
- A tendency toward self-organization exists.
- Practitioners are increasingly altruistic.

Defining a profession often invites controversy, according to Cogan (1955), who claimed that reactions to definitions of professions are either "polarized toward an enthusiastic and uncritical acceptance or toward a rancorous and defensive rejection" (p. 105). Literature throughout the social sciences is full of similar opinions discerning between professions and occupations or vocations (Cogan, 1953; Engberg, 1968; Greenwood, 1966; Liberman, 1956; Marshall, 1939; McGlothlin, 1964; Tawney, 1920). Viewing matters in terms of journalism and mass communication, Gerald (1963) listed the following characteristics as necessary: a technique acquired by prolonged and specialized intellectual training, rendering of specialized service to the community, fixed remuneration by fee or salary, a sense of responsibility developed among practitioners for the technique that they possess, and manifest concern for competence and honor in the profession as a whole.

Much like journalism, public relations falls within a group of occupations that may never meet all of the criteria of traditional professions but endeavor to acquire some characteristics of professionalization. Hughes (1965) pointed out that a number of vocational groups do this in the hopes that they will merit professional standing in the eyes of their clients and the public. He cited librarians who strive to become experts on the effects of reading, bibliography, and reference, rather than serving only as custodians and distributors of books; social workers attempting to show that their work could not be done by amateurs; and even older occupations such as nursing, whose practitioners always seek to upgrade their place in the medical system.

Some occupations exaggerate their own importance, perhaps presuming that society will overlook such arrogance and think more highly of their services. Thus, garbage collectors are known as sanitation engineers, janitors have become building service managers, and so on. Sutherland (1966) claimed that even some common thieves can be considered professionals because they meet many requirements of traditional professions. By extension, personal service functionaries like barbers, bellhops, shoeshine stand operators, and taxi drivers also could be classified as professionals. Engberg (1968) went to exorbitant extremes, suggesting people could be classified as professionals if they were to profess, by means of newspaper classified advertising, to walk your dog. These dog walkers' entitlement to professional status would increase if they belonged to a group of dog walkers. Greater professionalization would exist if this dog-walking group was part of a national organization that published a newsletter.

Wilensky (1964) approached the problem of differentiating professions from occupations by critically examining the argument that many occupations are becoming professionalized. Etizoni (1969) introduced the concept of "semi-professions" as an alternative way of classifying occupations that exhibit evidence of professionalization but fail to meet all the criteria of the traditional professions.

Where does public relations stand in this debate over professional recognition? Is there a place for it as a traditional profession? Is it a semi-profession? Is it a trade? Although one could argue that public relations is intellectual, practical, and skilled, others might point to its lack of professional criteria. No specialized intellectual training is necessary to practice public relations. Even in the United States, where university programs in public relations have flourished in recent decades, there still is nothing to prevent someone not trained through these programs from becoming successful in public relations. Most CEOs of the world's largest public relations firms and most of the world's senior-level corporate communications officers do not hold university degrees in public relations. Although technical skills are required for public relations practice, it isn't essential that these skills be acquired through prescribed professional education. Because many who practice public relations lack knowledge and skills taught through public relations education, professional education and continuing education in public relations have blossomed. Both of these topics are covered later in this chapter.

Marston (1968) appears to have been the first public relations author to list characteristics that he said distinguished professions from occupations. These were: a defined area of competence, an organized body of knowledge, self-consciousness, competence of entrants determined by controlled access, continuing education, support for research, aid in education of competent replacements, and independence. Cutlip and Center (1978) suggested that public relations possessed some of Marston's recommended attributes, but also pointed out that "Even though practitioners continue to be beset with all sorts of complexes and doubts as to their own worthiness, movement in these professional directions is apparent" (p. 581). In 1985, Cutlip, Center, and Broom discussed professionalism and public relations and said there was a "general consensus" that a profession needed at least four of the following five criteria: acquisition of specialized educational preparation based on theory and research, with an emphasis on knowledge over skill; production of a unique and essential service; an emphasis on public service and social responsibility; practitioners with autonomy as well as personal responsibility, expecting individual accountability; and enforceable codes of ethics and standards of performance. Grunig and Hunt (1984) argued that professionalism for public relations would be attained when practitioners have a set of professional values, membership in a strong professional organization, adherence to professional norms, an intellectual tradition associated with an established body of knowledge, and technical skills acquired through prescribed professional education.

Although it is possible for someone who practices public relations to meet the aforementioned requirements of professionalism, it is still possible to practice the function without ascribing to any of them. Although some occupations require education in a prescribed field, a complete understanding of a body of knowledge, membership in a national professional society, licensing or accreditation, adherence to a prescribed code of ethics, and so forth, the reality of the situation in public relations is that all of these are much more voluntary than they are required. However, a good number of public relations practitioners have elected to follow the path of professionalization, suggesting, perhaps, that the question of whether public relations is a profession or not should be answered in terms of individuals and not the entire practice.

FORMAL PROFESSIONAL EDUCATION AND PUBLIC RELATIONS

A variety of research conducted over the past three decades has found that public relations practitioners function in three principal roles: as technicians, as managers, and as executives (Broom & Dozier, 1990; Broom & Smith, 1979; Wright, 1995). Prescribed professional education accommodates all three of these roles. Although some technicians might function only in that occupational role, most public relations people serve in a variety of different roles. It might be possible for a senior-level executive to counsel the CEO on a strategic issue in the morning, manage some organizational function in the afternoon, and perform some kind of technical task in the evening. Even though most novices in the field begin working as public relations technicians, most professional educational programs provide training in all three role areas.

Unfortunately, some who practice public relations do not understand the need for education that goes beyond the technician level. Educators have argued for decades that although public relations education should include a close association with technical practice, it also should be grounded in social inquiry (based on a well-defined body of knowledge), thoroughly explore theory and research, and address aspects of strategic management practice (Cutlip & Center, 1978; Grunig & Hunt, 1984). This disconnect between what public relations practitioners believe they want from universities and what academics actually deliver remains uncomfortably large. Few occupational groups support professional education in their fields less than is the case in public relations. There are many reasons for this disconnect, including the reality that most public relations education programs are small subsets of larger programs in journalism, mass communication, communication, or business. Also, it's rare for educators and practitioners to engage in meaningful dialogue about curriculum matters, and when any such exchange takes place it usually involves a small number of practitioners—frequently the same people time and time again—who differ from most of their peers in that they are truly supportive of public relations education.

However, specialized educational preparation—education that provides the technical and managerial knowledge and skills needed in a particular profession—clearly is a hallmark of professionalism. Drawing on the Excellence Study, Dozier, Grunig, and Grunig (1995) identified seven strategies that public relations and communications practitioners can employ to increase their knowledge and skills. Several—such as learning an employer's business and industry, regular reading of journals and books, and accreditation—are self-directed activities independent of any institution or organization. Higher education, offered through colleges and universities, is identified as providing the most in-depth knowledge.

Although higher education in public relations dates back to 1928, when the late Edward R. Bernays taught a course at New York University, it was not until post–World War II when courses and sequences began to develop at some universities. In 1973, public relations practitioners and educators began to formalize the content of academic programs offering undergraduate and graduate majors or degrees in public relations. In that year, a Commission on Public Relations Education was established by the Public Relations Division of the Association for Education in Journalism (now the Association for Education in Journalism and Mass Communication, or AEJMC). The seven-member commission was cochaired by the late J. Carroll Bateman of the Insurance Information Institute and the late Dr. Scott Cutlip, then on the faculty at the University of Wisconsin. Its members were evenly divided between practitioners and educators. The commission concluded its work in 1975 with a report, *A Design for Public Relations Education*, that recommended curricula for public relations at the undergraduate and graduate levels. The report received strong endorsement from the Public Relations Division.

The 1973–1975 commission spelled out the courses it saw as necessary for the educational preparation of students desiring to enter the practice of public relations. At the undergraduate level, it recommended liberal arts courses, communication studies courses (theory and process of communication, writing for the mass media, copy editing, and graphics of communication), and courses in public relations (introduction to public relations, publicity media and campaigns, public relations case problems, and internship or practicum; Commission on Public Relations Education, 1975).

At the graduate level, the commission noted that few doctoral-level programs existed, so it focused its attention on graduate study at the master's level. It called for a curriculum that focused the student's attention on research methods and existing research data while also requiring the student to engage in original research. Students were to select from media studies courses (mass media and society, advanced communication theory, etc.) and public relations studies such as public relations law and ethics, contemporary public relations problems, organization and management of public relations organizations and departments, and public opinion research and analysis of social trends. A thesis would be required (Commission on Public Relations Education, 1975).

In 1982, in response to rapid growth in the number of graduate programs in public relations, a 12-member Commission on Graduate Study in Public Relations—half practitioners and half educators—was created to design a model curriculum at the graduate level and to make recommendations as to the "manner in which graduate-level education in public relations can meet the needs of the profession as well as bring about the improvement of practice itself" (Commission on Graduate Study in Public Relations, 1985, p. 5). This commission was cochaired by Paul H. Alvarez, APR, Fellow PRSA, then the CEO of Ketchum, and Michael B. Hesse, PhD., APR, who was then the Chair of the Department of Advertising and Public Relations at the University of Alabama. Alvarez's status as a CEO of one of the world's 10 largest agencies gave this commission particular status within the professional community.

The commission's 1985 report and recommendations were more explicit, detailed, and structured than were those of the 1975 commission. It recommended that students earning master's degrees in public relations complete courses in five areas, one of which involved a thesis or comprehensive examination. The other four areas were research and theory, communication processes applied to public relations, public relations management, and a minor that would allow students to specialize in corporate public relations, government public relations, and the like (Commission on Graduate Study in Public Relations, 1985). The graduate curriculum would total a minimum of 30 semester credit hours.

Doctoral education received more attention in 1985 than it had in the 1975 commission report. The commission noted that the body of public relations knowledge is heavily dependent on research that focuses on public relations done by those who are the product of doctoral programs. Therefore, it recommended that the core curriculum of a public relations–oriented doctoral program emphasize research methodology and analysis of research data. Doctoral programs also should include, it said, specialized seminars in public relations on topics such as public relations management, organizational structure, public relations roles, interorganizational relations, and public relations law (Commission on Graduate Study in Public Relations, 1985).

As the Commission on Graduate Study in Public Relations was deliberating, the Public Relations Division of AEJMC examined the state of public relations education and concluded that the sweeping changes that had been employed in the public relations industry and the concurrent growth of undergraduate public relations programs necessitated a fresh look at how public relations education prepared students for public relations work. A 27-member Commission on Undergraduate Public Relations Education was created in 1983; this time, the commission was jointly sponsored by AEJMC's Public Relations Division, the Public Relations Society of America (PRSA), and PRSA's Educators Section (now Educator Academy).

The commission, cochaired by Betsy Ann Plank, then with Illinois Bell Telephone, and William P. Ehling, PhD., then on the public relations faculty at Syracuse University, conducted extensive research to determine what educators and practitioners believed should be the content of undergraduate public relations education. That research laid the framework and guidelines for the commission's discussions over the next 3 years (Commission on Undergraduate Public Relations Education, 1987).

This commission's recommendations were the most specific and detailed of any commission to date. It recommended that of the credit hours required for a bachelor's degree, a minimum of 54% should be in the liberal arts, with no more than 25% of the total number obtained through professionally oriented courses in public relations or related communication disciplines. Of this 25% in professional courses, at least half should be in courses clearly identifiable as public relations courses. The recommended undergraduate public relations curriculum thus included both professional education (technical/production, historical/institutional, and communications processes/structure) and public relations studies (public relations principles and theory, communication principles as applied to public relations, strategic planning and evaluative research, ethics, management principles involving goal setting and program implementation, and a supervised internship program; Commission on Undergraduate Public Relations, 1987).

The commission operationalized this curriculum model by identifying five public relations courses that together embodied the content it recommended. These five courses, it said, were the minimum for a quality public relations program at the undergraduate level. Soon after the commission's report was published, the PRSA Assembly approved a resolution that required colleges and universities that wished to establish or maintain chapters of the Public Relations Student Society of America (PRSSA) to offer at least these five courses in public relations.

All of these commissions had concluded their work before the findings of the 1992 Excellence Study were published. However, another commission—a Commission on Public Relations Education—was formed in 1997. It was comprised of 47 members, evenly divided between educators and practitioners, representing eight communications organizations: PRSA and its Educator Academy, the Institute for Public Relations, the National Communication Association, AEJMC, the Association for Women in Communication, the International Association of Business Communicators, the International Communication Association, and the International Public Relations Association.

The Excellence Study's findings—at least some of them—were reflected in this commission's 1999 report, *Public Relations Education for the 21st Century: A Port of Entry* (Commission on Public Relations Education, 1999). The commission noted that its recommendations had their roots in the work of earlier commissions. However, it also acknowledged that it was looking to the future by suggesting what public relations education must look like if it is to serve the needs of a public relations profession whose goal is excellence. The commission's vision statement touched on several of the characteristics of excellent public relations identified in the 1992 Excellence Study:

> In the future, public relations professionals will not only be skilled communicators but leaders who will help their organizations build and maintain relationships with strategic publics. They will fulfill dual roles of managing communication and counseling top management. (Commission on Public Relations Education, 1999, p. 12)

Some of the assumptions the commission said guided its work clearly reflect the excellence characteristics, notably that public relations communication is a two-way process, practitioners must be able to operate in a multicultural environment, and public relations has a fundamental responsibility and adds value to society (Commission on Public Relations Education, 1999).

This commission, cochaired by Dean Kruckeberg, PhD, APR, Fellow PRSA, and John L. Paluszek, APR, Fellow PRSA, conducted a major research study to learn what skills, knowledge, and concepts that practitioners and educators thought were currently being taught in public relations curricula; compare those with what practitioners and educators thought should be taught; and finally document the level of agreement between practitioners and educators. The findings of this research became the basis for a 4-day conference on public relations education that, in turn, became the basis for the commission's recommendations.

The commission identified a number of knowledge areas that graduates of public relations programs should know and understand:

- Communication and persuasion concepts and strategies.
- Communication and public relations theories.
- Relationships and relationship building.

- Societal trends.
- Ethical issues.
- Legal requirements and issues.
- Marketing and finance.
- Public relations history.
- Use of research and forecasting.
- Multicultural and global issues.
- Organizational change and development.
- Management concepts and theories.

The commission also identified skills necessary to enter the profession:

- Research methods and analysis.
- Management of information.
- Mastery of language in written and oral communication.
- Problem solving and negotiation.
- Management of communication.
- Strategic planning.
- Issues management.
- Audience segmentation.
- Informative and persuasive writing.
- Community relations, consumer relations, employee relations, other practice areas.
- Technological and visual literacy.
- Managing people, programs and resources.
- Sensitive interpersonal communication.
- Fluency in a foreign language.
- Ethical decision making.
- Participation in the professional public relations community.
- Message production.
- Working with a current issue.
- Public speaking and presentation.
- Applying cross-cultural and cross-gender sensitivity.

The commission recommended that the undergraduate public relations curriculum be grounded in a strong liberal arts and social science education, with a minimum of five courses required in public relations. However, the commission said that the ideal undergraduate curriculum would include seven public relations courses.

Although the majority of the commission's attention was focused on undergraduate education, which is understandable because of the large numbers of students being served, it did offer recommendations for public relations education at the graduate level. Its primary recommendation echoed findings of the Excellence Study: "[S]tudents studying for master's degrees in public relations (must) learn and appreciate the role of public relations as part of the management team, and learn relevant management and communications competencies and skills needed to build effective relationships between organizations and their publics" (Commission on Public Relations Education, 1999, p. 4). It also provided sample master's degree curricula, one a 30-credit-hour program and the other carrying 36 credits. Compared to the curricular recommendations at the undergraduate level, the content areas recommended at the master's level were aligned much more closely with positioning public relations as an integral part of the overall organizational and managerial structure and as part of an organization's dominant coalition, both consistent with the Excellence Study's findings.

The commission was even more brief in addressing doctoral education in public relations. It identified a core curriculum and called for specialized seminars in public relations and in related social, behavioral, and business sciences. Noting that graduates of doctoral programs were likely to pursue academic careers that would involve teaching, the commission recommended that doctoral students be prepared not only to conduct research but be given the opportunity to develop their teaching skills and to have some experience in the classroom as a part of their doctoral programs.

Unlike earlier commissions on public relations education, the 1999 commission was not sunsetted out of existence when its report was released. It continued to meet to monitor the state of public relations education and the degree to which its report influenced public relations curricula. In 2004, the commission reorganized, adding representatives of professional societies not included in its earlier incarnation (such as the Arthur W. Page Society). It agreed that it should take another formal look at public relations education and set a target date of October 2006 for issuing a new report. The commission's outline for its report indicates that this report will be even broader than the work of previous commissions; in addition to addressing undergraduate and graduate education, it will offer recommendations on professional certification, professional development, professional resources and support for public relations education, distance learning, international public relations education, diversity, use of information technology in public relations, and the role that chapters of the Public Relations Student Society of America play in public relations education.

Like the 1999 commission, this 2006 commission conducted a survey to inform its work. This time, the research focus was the impact of the 1999 commission report on public relations education and practice. Only one third of the 396 educators and practitioners who were mailed copies of the 1999 report even remembered receiving it, with educators far more likely to recall receiving it than were practitioners. And all of the practitioners who remembered receiving the report were either part-time faculty teaching public relations or frequent guest speakers in public relations classes.

One of the challenges facing the commission in the next phase of its work will be making its recommendations, whatever they may be, resonate more strongly with practitioners. Educators seem to get the message as to what an effective, excellent public relations curriculum ought to look like and can accomplish. However, there is clearly a great deal of work to be done before practitioners attach enough importance to public relations education as *the* port of entry into the profession and to advancing the professionalism of the discipline.

Although the work of these commissions is impressive and should be praised, the fact remains that a large percentage of public relations practitioners never studied the field at a university. Consequently, there is a huge disconnect between the goals and ideals of public relations education and the education that most people are receiving before entering public relations practice. This disconnect gives continuing education an especially important role in professionalizing public relations. It also echoes the importance of the individual in the public relations professionalism process, because in many cases whether or not practitioners are educated, accredited, follow codes of ethics, and so forth, all are decisions made by individual practitioners and not the practice.

DISCONNECT BETWEEN EDUCATION AND PRACTICE

As mentioned earlier, there is a large disconnect between public relations education and occupational practice. Ironically, only a very small number of the nation's senior-level public relations executives and managers studied public relations at a university, and many of those hired for entry-level jobs with corporations, agencies, and other organizations today are not graduates of university-based public relations programs.

Many educators claim the reason for this disconnect is because practitioners neither appreciate nor understand the importance of the theoretical aspects of the science beneath the art of the field. Practitioners, on the other hand, point out that much of public relations education is esoteric and out of touch with the bottom-line realities of the modern business world. Unlike business schools, where faculty members are encouraged to interact with practitioners to the point that professional service might account for half or more of a university professor's time, most university sequences of public relations rarely allocate more than 20% for professional service.

Public relations faculty members at many universities also have been somewhat discouraged from networking with practitioners at conferences and other gatherings due to the extremely small travel budgets available to many professors. Similar restrictions usually do not exist in other professional fields, such as business and law. Although some public relations educators have been able to travel adequately and network with practitioners, most of them only do so because they earn additional income from consulting, which they are willing to spend on professional travel.

Public relations education also has too often been treated like a "second-class citizen" in many of the nation's larger journalism schools. It is not uncommon to find universities in which journalism faculty members outnumber public relations faculty members four to one, but student enrollment figures show three or four times as many public relations majors as journalism majors.

Another reason for this disconnect relates to the inability of educators and practitioners to agree on a common research agenda. Whereas practitioners have stressed the need for practical and applied studies, many educators have insisted on providing more abstract and theoretical research. Although there sometimes have been opportunities to combine the theoretical with the practical, these opportunities are not frequent enough. Perhaps, in some ways, the Excellence Study might have been more effective if it could have addressed strategic communication management needs in clearer and more precise language. Even today, when some practitioners talk about the Excellence Study, they refer to it as "that 700-page book." Although the seminal and theoretical benchmarking of the Excellence Study made massive contributions to our body of knowledge, it might have been more effective in the eyes of practitioners if information could have been delivered in more "user-friendly" ways.

CONTINUING EDUCATION

The role of continuing education in public relations is equally perplexing. Because such a huge majority of those who practice public relations never studied the field in college, one would imagine that practitioners would be flocking to universities and professional societies for knowledge essential to function effectively in the field. In reality, this has been the exception rather than the rule. Continuing education needs of working public relations practitioners have turned to two main sources: traditional university-based undergraduate and graduate programs and professional development opportunities provided by a number of professional associations.

Even though several of the aforementioned commissions and a number of others have encouraged practitioners who lack formal public relations education or training to pursue one of these options, few do. Geographical circumstances frequently prevent some interested practitioners from studying public relations at a university. Although there are highly regarded, university-based undergraduate and graduate public relations degree programs near some of the nation's largest cities, many of the top universities in public relations education are located in remote areas, making it virtually impossible for practitioners to attend. Recently, some universities have established distance learning programs and a number of Internet-based, online courses have been created by some colleges. Although some working practitioners do manage to take courses and even receive university degrees, generally this is the exception rather than the rule.

The continuing education that practitioners receive through traditional university programs covers the three major roles of public relations practice: technicians, managers, and executives. This also is the case with training and development offered by various professional associations. PRSA and IABC have long been noted for providing what many call lowest-common-denominator professional development training—mainly offerings designed for technicians. Both organizations do offer some training for managers and executives, but their professional development thrust clearly is elsewhere, perhaps because revenue is important to both associations in order to support their fairly large staffs, and enrollment generally is higher at professional development seminars on general topics.

PRSA's current professional development workshop offerings include courses and seminars in writing, media relations, employee communications, planning, and programming at the technician level, plus managerial-level offerings in strategic communication management, crisis communication strategy, leadership, and management. Ragan Communications offers a similar list of workshops. Ragan and PRSA also provide various teleseminars. PRSA and IABC both have accreditation programs and supply training courses related to these.

PRSA does offer a workshop called "Inside the Mind of the CEO," but most of the nation's executive-level public relations professional development training is run by the Institute for Public Relations, the Arthur W. Page Society, and a consortium of companies who have formed the San Francisco Academy. Many consider the San Francisco Academy and the Public Relations Executive Forum—cosponsored by Page and the Institute—to be the standard setters in training and development for public relations at the executive level.

Founded in 1991, the San Francisco Academy annually runs an intense course that involves about 20 upwardly mobile, high-potential, emerging public relations executives who are on career paths leading to senior-level corporate communications positions. The academy's students meet two days each month for a year, and its list of "graduates" includes a number of people who currently hold senior vice president positions in public relations and corporate communications. Currently associated with the Haas Executive Development Center at the business school of the University of California, Berkeley, the San Francisco Academy previously held academic affiliation with the School of Journalism and Communications at the University of Florida. Monthly San Francisco Academy sessions are currently held throughout the nation.

The Public Relations Executive Forum began in 1992 and consists of a weeklong course condensed into 2½ days. Some have described it as a mini-version of the academy. Now entering its 14th year, the Executive Forum has attracted more than 300 high-potential, mid-level communications executives who are on career tracks leading toward senior-level corporate communications or public relations positions. More than 100 Fortune 200 companies have sent representatives through the Executive Forum seminars that are restricted to 30 people apiece. One of the cosponsors—the Institute for Public Relations—is based at the School of Journalism and Communications at the University of Florida; the other—the Arthur W. Page Society—is a select membership organization for senior public relations and corporate communications executives from Fortune 500 companies. All Executive Forum seminars are held in Chicago.

In 2005, the Institute and Page joined with the Council of Public Relations Firms to create the Public Relations Leadership Forum. Based in Atlanta, this annual seminar program was designed for high-potential public relations managers who work at public relations agencies and corporate communications professionals who spend a considerable part of their time working with agencies.

There are several possible reasons why the San Francisco Academy, Executive Forum, and Leadership Forum programs have been more successful than have similar seminars planned within PRSA and, in some cases, by various universities. First and foremost, organizations such as the Arthur W. Page Society (which cosponsors the forum programs) are a much more senior-level groups than is PRSA. Once the province of the nation's senior-level practitioners, PRSA has evolved over the past 25 years into much more of a mid-level management organization. The president of the Page Society usually is the chief public relations officer of a Fortune 100 company or the CEO of a major agency. It's been decades since the PRSA president has held such a job.

Another reason for the success of these continuing education programs is the extensive research that goes into planning and developing curricula for the Academy and the forums. Committees annually review program topics and faculty in attempts to make certain that students receive cutting-edge and up-to-date information in these courses.

CONCLUSIONS

Although the Excellence Study clearly has had an impact on knowledge and professionalism in public relations, the debate as to whether or not public relations is a profession continues. Clearly, public relations has some characteristics of professionalism, but the voluntary nature of education, accreditation, certification, professional development training, and more cloud the issue.

The Excellence Study and research stimulated us because of it have made valuable contributions to the public relations body of knowledge, but practitioners are not required to study or read any of this material unless they elect to take courses, pursue accreditation, and so on. Unfortunately, many practitioners also are less than inspired by the lengthy and somewhat esoteric approaches provided by the Excellence Study.

Although formal, university-based public relations education has evolved for more than half a century, there appears to be a huge disconnect between what universities are providing and what those who practice public relations want. When people want to become physicians they go to medical schools; when they want to become attorneys they go to law school. This is also the case in engineering, nursing, accounting, and many other occupational groups. In public relations, however, having a university degree in the field is too often the exception and not the rule.

The great challenge for educators would appear to be for them to do several things differently to advance both public relations education and the profession. This different approach might include, but not necessarily be limited to, working more closely with a wide range of practitioners as well as with peer academicians. Certainly, at some point, educators will need to face the reality that only a small percentage of those who practice public relations studied it at a university. Although this has provided many opportunities for those who offer effective continuing education opportunities in public relations, it also could provide opportunities for many universities and individual professors. Perhaps the next "commission" studying public relations education should face this issue head on.

Professional education in the "traditional" professions of medicine, law, and the clergy is concentrated at the graduate level, but public relations education remains primarily focused as an undergraduate field of study. Perhaps the time has come for public relations students to focus more of their undergraduate educations on the arts, letters, business, and sciences, with a course or two in communication and public relations. After graduating with a well-rounded undergraduate degree, they then would study public relations at the master's level in much the way law, religion, and medicine are learned.

Educators also must face the reality that much of the research being conducted and published through public relations education is not considered valuable by practitioners. Practitioners and educators alike should be encouraged to come together for dialogue addressing this uncomfortable reality. An annual conference coordinated through the Institute for Public Relations that attracts educators and practitioners to the University of Miami each March is making major strides in trying to bring about such a dialogue.

Finally, one way or another, public relations educators need to play a greater role in their own destiny. For more than half a century, public relations education has functioned as a small fish in someone else's educational pond. For much of that time, public relations educators have chafed at being subsumed under a college, school, or department of speech, communication, journalism, or mass communications. The various commissions that have made recommendations regarding public relations curricula have maintained that public relations' academic home doesn't matter; that it is what is taught, not where, that is important. However, perhaps it is time to proclaim that it *does* matter, and that it is time for public relations to be, at the least, a stand-alone department within a school or college. The Commission on Public Relations Education, expected to issue new guidelines and recommendations in 2006, has the opportunity to take the lead in moving public relations education into its own educational pond.

REFERENCES

Broom, G. M., & Dozier, D. M. (1990). *Using research in public relations: Applications to program management.* Englewood Cliffs, NJ: Prentice-Hall.

Broom, G. M., & Smith, G. D. (1979). Testing the practitioner's impact on clients. *Public Relations Review, 5*(3), 47–59.

Carr-Saunders, A. M., & Wilson, P. A. (1933). *The professions.* Oxford, England: Clarendon.

Cogan, M. L. (1953). Towards a definition of profession. *Harvard Educational Review, 23,* 33–50.

Cogan, M. L. (1955, January). The problem of defining a profession. *Annals of the American Academy of Political Science,* pp. 103–116.

Commission on Graduate Study in Public Relations. (1985). *Advancing public relations education.* New York: Foundation for Public Relations Research and Education.

Commission on Public Relations Education. (1975). *A design for public relations education.* New York: Foundation for Public Relations Research and Education.

Commission on Public Relations Education. (1999). *Public relations education for the 21st century: A port of entry.* New York: Public Relations Society of America.

Commission on Undergraduate Public Relations Education. (1987). *Design for undergraduate public relations education.* Chicago: Illinois Bell Telephone.

Cutlip, S. M., & Center, A. H. (1978). *Effective public relations.* (4th ed.). Englewood Cliffs, NJ: Prentice-Hall.

Cutlip, S. M., Center, A. H. & Broom G. M. (1985). *Effective public relations*. (5th ed.). Englewood Cliffs, NJ: Prentice-Hall.

Dozier, D. M., Grunig, L. A., & Grunig, J. E. (1995). *Manager's guide to excellence in public relations and communication management*. Hillsdale, NJ: Lawrence Erlbaum Associates.

Ehling, W. P. (1992). Public relations education and professionalism. In J. E. Grunig (Ed.), *Excellence in public relations and communication management* (pp. 439–464). Hillsdale, NJ: Lawrence Erlbaum Associates.

Engberg, E. (1968, November). Can the professions save us? *The Center Magazine*, pp. 5–8.

Etizoni, A. (Ed.). (1969). *The semi-professions and their organization: Teachers, nurses, social workers*. New York: Free Press.

Flexner, A. (1915, June 26). Is social work a profession? *School and Society*, pp. 903–917.

Gerald, J. E. (1963). *The social responsibility of the press*. Minneapolis: University of Minnesota Press.

Greenwood, E. (1966). The elements of professionalization. In H. M. Vollmer & D. L. Mills (Eds.), *Professionalization*. Englewood Cliffs, NJ: Prentice-Hall.

Grunig, J. E. (Ed.). (1992). *Excellence in public relations and communication management*. Hillsdale, NJ: Lawrence Erlbaum Associates.

Grunig, J. E., & Hunt, T. (1984). *Managing public relations*. New York: Holt, Rinehart & Winston.

Hughes, E. C. (1965). The professions. In K. S. Lynn (Ed.), *The professions in America* (pp. 1–8). Boston: Houghton Mifflin.

Liberman, M. (1956). *Education as a profession*. Englewood Cliffs, N.J.: Prentice-Hall.

Marshall, T. H. (1939, August). Professionalism in relation to social structure. *Canadian Journal of Economics and Political Science*.

Marston, J. (1968). Hallmarks of a profession. *Public Relations Journal, 22*, 22–27.

McGlothlin, W. J. (1964). *The professional schools*. New York: Center for Applied Research in Education.

Sutherland, E. (1966). Professional theft. In H. M. Vollmer & D. L. Mills (Eds.), *Professionalization*. Englewood Cliffs, NJ: Prentice-Hall.

Tawney, R. H. (1920). *The acquisitive society*. New York: Harcourt, Brace & World.

Wilensky, H. (1964). The professionalization of everyone. *American Journal of Sociology, 70, 2*, 132–143.

Wright, D. K. (1995). The role of corporate public relations executives in the future of employee communications. *Public Relations Review, 21*(3), 181–198.

Chapter 27

An Education Model to Prepare for Excellence in Public Relations: A Case Study of the Syracuse University Limited Residency/ Distance Learning Master's Program in Communications Management

Maria P. Russell
S.I. Newhouse School of Public Communications,
Syracuse University

What an organization needs is not just good people; it needs people who are improving with education.

—W. Edwards Deming, *Out of the Crisis*

BACKGROUND

In *The Work of Nations: Preparing Ourselves for 21st Century Capitalism,* former U.S. Secretary of Labor Robert Reich outlined the basic skills required of the future workforce, including these: Workers must be competent, life-long learners who can cope with change; individuals must have the ability to take initiatives, engage in abstract thinking and deal with nonroutine tasks, detecting problems and developing remedies for them; social skills are essential, because work is people-oriented; workers must be able to work in a team and communicate with coworkers in a facilitative fashion; and workers must learn that a multiskills approach must replace dependence on a single skill (Reich, 1992).

589

In the ongoing evolution of public relations as a profession, its leaders and practitioners are questioning how and where it will find its future workforce, how the workforce will be prepared, and how that workforce with "improve with education." This inquiry is taking place in public relations professional organizations both within national boundaries (e.g., the Public Relations Society of America, or PRSA) and in a global context (the Global Alliance). It can easily be argued that, in the 21st century and beyond, education—on its many levels and in its various forms, both formal and informal—will determine the future of this evolving discipline.

Since the 1992 publication of the landmark study by Dr. James Grunig (Grunig et al., 1992) of the University of Maryland with his team of scholars and senior practitioners, the concept of "excellence," drawn in parallel with the "excellence movement" of American business and industry, has scientifically identified the knowledge base needed by public relations practitioners of the future, and they echo the predictions of Robert Reich. In addition to being a capable *technician*, the Excellence Study reported, the evolving public relations professional must be a *manager* of communications, one who understands that the focus of endeavors must be on building relationships with key publics, not on communication activity as an end to itself. Three years later, Dr. David Dozier of San Diego State University, along with Grunig and Dr. Larissa Grunig, also of the University of Maryland, wrote *Manager's Guide to Excellence in Public Relations and Communications Management* (Dozier, Grunig, & Grunig, 1995) as an easily digestible way to help practitioners adapt to and adopt the international findings of the excellence project. Much of the literature today, both in professional publications and scholarly research journals, illustrate these studies, especially in the practitioner's need to get a seat at the management table, to speak the language of business, and to measure and evaluate the impact of communications on the ROI and long-term goals of the organizations of employers and clients.

However, how are practitioners to do this? Scholars have argued that:

> excellence begins at home. Without expertise for excellence in the communication department the expectations of the dominant coalition matter little. If your communication department is devoid of needed expertise, even the most demanding chief executive officer (CEO) will not be able to squeeze excellence from it. (Dozier et al., 1995, p. 63)

Their recommendations, based on interviews with leaders of excellent departments, urged professionals to fully know and understand the business of the organization; to develop a discipline of self-study (not only of public relations literature, but also of the literature relating to one's organization and industry); to participate in the workshops and seminars of professional associations; to mentor junior practitioners; to sponsor in-house workshops for staff; to seek and encourage others to earn professional accreditation; and to pursue and encourage the pursuit of formal higher education in public relations (Dozier et al., 1995). This chapter provides one model to prepare for excellence in public relations practice: the Syracuse University Independent Study Degree Program (ISDP) in communication management.

SUPPORT FROM INDUSTRY LEADERS

The push to move beyond the craft of public relations to the management of the function has been in the minds of many visionaries in the field for at least 25 years. A review of their thinking can be found by reading the collection of Vernon C. Schranz Lectures collected in a publication to celebrate the silver anniversary of the Ball State University series (Sharpe, 2004).

As early as 1979, Edward M. Block, then vice president of public relations for AT&T, told the Ball State audience, "The public relations function is simply one among the many extensions of the office of the chief executive" (Sharpe, 2005, p. 3). James L. Tolley, the retired vice president of public affairs of both Chrylser Corporation and American Motors Corporation, worried in 1988 that "we're supposed to be the great persuaders, but we haven't convinced the captains of industry that we belong at the helm with them" (Sharpe, 2004, p. 57). In 1993, Ann H. Barkelew, then senior partner at Fleishman-Hillard, warned her audience, "[W]hat we do has to be measured if we're ever going to find a 'place at the table'" (Sharpe , 2004, p. 89). By 2000, Daniel J. Edelman, founder of Edelman Public Relations Worldwide, felt confident enough to claim, "We've come a long way. There's greater awareness that public relations is essential for the success of the company ..." (Sharpe, 2004, p. 134). However, the corporate scandals that ensued led Willard (Bill) D. Nielsen, vice president of public relations for Johnson & Johnson, to remind his 2003 audience of the need to follow the words of Arthur W. Page and "conduct public relations as if the whole company depends upon it" (Sharpe, 2004, p. 155).

THE ROLE OF EDUCATORS AND ACADEMIC PROGRAMS

Public relations educators have been thinking about the "ideal" public relations curriculum since at least the mid-1970s. In 1975, a commission of educators and practitioners, led by the late J. Carroll Bateman, a counselor and past president of the Public Relations Society of America, and the late Dr. Scott M. Cutlip, then the retired dean of the University of

Georgia School of Journalism, issued its *Design for Public Relations Education*—a first in the field and a milestone in the evolution of the profession. Both undergraduate and graduate programs were examined (PRSA, 1975).

In the early 1980s, a new commission was established to update the initial study, providing more specific recommendations for graduate education. This update was published in 1985 (Foundation, 1985).

The next iteration of recommendations was published in 1987 under the leadership of an educator, Dr. William P. Ehling, then chair of the public relations department at Syracuse University's Newhouse School, and Betsy Ann Plank, of Illinois Bell, the first woman president of the PRSA. This study focused entirely on undergraduate education, and did not recommend specific courses; instead, it focused on course content. Also, this report reached out beyond the PRSA to include representation from other major professional and academic organizations, all of whom had a stake in quality education for public relations. The report strongly recommended that the basis of any public relations program be grounded in the liberal arts, with no more than 25% of the total credit hours for the baccalaureate degree coming from professional courses. The commission recommended that public relations students "especially those planning to enter the corporate world give strong consideration to *business* as a secondary area of concentrated study" (PRSA, 1987, p. 4).

The most recent commission (1999), cochaired by Dr. Dean Kruckeberg of the University of Northern Iowa and John Paluszek, of Ketchum Public Affairs, put heavy emphasis on the future of public relations education, extended its recommendations on graduate education, and introduced the topic of continuing education.

On the undergraduate level, the commission again strongly recommended a foundation in the traditional liberal arts and social sciences, and then urged that a minimum of five public relations courses make up the major and that the minor or double major be in the liberal arts, social sciences, or business. On the graduate level, it advised that the public relations curriculum should be complemented by courses in accounting, finance, marketing, and strategic planning.

The commission members pointed out that although

> the future is indeed bright for the field of public relations ... there is one major qualification—having enough trained people to meet the expanding demand for public relations services and counsel.... Law and medicine have methods, admittedly long-term, to deal with the supply and demand for their professionals. Public relations doesn't. (commission, 1999, p. 1)

The report continued by pointing to a model for meeting this demand as proposed by Dr. Clark Kerr, former chancellor of the University of

California at Berkeley: "Some new professions are being born; others are becoming more professional, for example, business and social work. The university becomes the chief port of entry for these professions. In fact a profession gains its identity by making the university the port of entry" (PRSA, 1999, p. 2).

The next iteration of the commission's research and recommendations is now under way, with a projected publication date in late 2006. Its areas of review will include undergraduate, graduate, and continuing education, as well as a new addition: distance learning.

TOWARD THE "IDEAL" PROFESSIONAL MASTER'S DEGREE PROGRAM

In preparation for developing the recommendations of the 1999 commission, the National Communication Association (NCA) devoted its summer 1998 annual conference to various topics in public relations education. One group of volunteer educators and practitioners was charged with developing a model for the "ideal" curriculum for a professional master's degree program; the author of this chapter chaired the effort (Russell, 1999).

An initial activity was to review the basic assumptions of the 1985/1987 commission reports and to revise them as the group saw fit. Here are the 1998 assumptions that later went to the commission:

- The professional master's program prepares individuals for public relations management, career development, and ongoing contributions to the profession and to society in a global context. It guides the individual in knowing and appreciating the role of public relations on the management team, in gaining relevant management and communications competencies, and in building effective relationships between organizations and their publics.
- Students should be placed within a problem-solving environment in which they use communication, social and behavioral science theory, and research techniques to analyze and solve public relations problems.
- To enter the master's degree program, individuals must hold an undergraduate degree in public relations or a related discipline or have significant experience. Flexible options can and should be provided to prepare students for advanced study and/or to enhance or build on their current competencies (Russell, 1999, p. 103).

The team developed a lengthy list of desired outcomes from the "ideal" master's program, including possession of a global perspective, knowledge of the role of public relations in a management team, an understanding of communications and public relations theory, a demonstration of research abilities, the possession of advanced interpersonal communication competencies, and an ability to be socially responsible. Others included the ability to manage projects and campaigns, the ability to use communication technologies, a willingness to contribute to the profession, the management of the strategic communication of the organization, responsiveness to diversity, and the intention to pursue continuing education (Russell, 1999).

In order to achieve these competencies, the team recommended that the following be the essential curriculum content areas:

- Public relations, organizational communication, and management theories.
- The integrated relationships between and among advertising, marketing, public relations, and organizational communication.
- Strategic planning and problem solving both at the macro and micro levels of budgeting, scheduling, and financial management.
- Crisis management.
- Management of communication and information technologies.
- Advanced media production and delivery skills.
- Applied research.
- Multicultural, international, and global issues.
- Leadership and team building.
- Constraints on the practice of public relations: legal, social, cultural, economic, and environmental.
- Applied and professional ethics.
- Specializations such as investor relations and employee communications.
- Training and consulting.
- Professional experience (Russell, 1999, p. 107).

THE SYRACUSE RESPONSE

Throughout this entire period, the author was examining these and other educational issues as chair of the public relations department at Syracuse University's Newhouse School (1990–1992, 1994–2002). In her travels both nationally and internationally, she was frequently asked by alumni about the latest developments in public relations education and given suggestions as to how to prepare students for the world of public relations work. Often there were wistful comments shared about the desire to earn a master's degree—followed quickly by a litany of problems encountered by the alum in trying to do so. These ranged from the lack of a good communications/public relations program in the alum's area; to the frustration of never being able to finish a semester because of the erratic nature of the public relations job, client demands, frequent out-of-town travel; to the problems of balancing work–family life issues. Clearly, these alumni knew that continuing education was important to their career advancement; they understood that the field was changing rapidly, the management side of the equation was gaining more emphasis, and learning must indeed be lifelong. Often they were frequent attendees in professional seminars, onetime classes, and in-house training programs. Many were accredited through the Universal Accreditation Board and were designated "Accredited in Public Relations," or APR, or other programs, including the International Association of Business Communicators designation of "Accredited in Business Communications," or ABC. The frustration arose not over understanding the need for an advanced education, but in rather how to accomplish the career milestone of a master's degree.

After considerable study of existing master's programs and primary research, Syracuse introduced an innovative approach that would address the current and future educational needs of public relations professionals, but do so in a flexible manner that allowed busy professionals to work full time, anywhere in the world, and still earn a master's degree from a highly regarded institution.

THE PURPOSE

What were we trying to accomplish?

- The enhancement of public relations skills.
- The development of critical management abilities.
- The offering of an interdisciplinary curriculum built on communication, social and behavioral sciences, research, theory, and management.
- A flexible format for experienced practitioners who could not follow the traditional routes to advanced degrees.

THE PRECEDENT

Syracuse University is considered a national pioneer in developing external degree programs, and has been widely emulated across the country. Beginning in 1966 with a single bachelor's degree designed especially for adults, the Independent Study Degree Program (ISDP) now offers nine fully accredited bachelor's and master's programs. Over 3,000 graduates, many of them distinguished in their fields, have earned degrees through these programs. On the school level, the public relations department is known as a national leader and has been recognized by *U.S. News and World Report* as one of the top three graduate schools for the study of public relations. It has one of the few programs in the United States offering public relations education on the baccalaureate, master's and doctoral levels, and serves as a national model in undergraduate curriculum design. Since 1970, three of its faculty members have been honored as outstanding educators by the Public Relations Society of America—more than any other institution's faculty.

THE PROGRAM

The curriculum was developed on the basis of a literature review, interviews with senior public relations managers, and a national survey of public relations practitioners. It aims to promote:

- Expanded knowledge in public relations theory, research, and management.
- Better understanding of strategic planning, counseling, and decision-making processes.
- A firmer grasp of business, finance, and marketing.
- Leadership, interpersonal, and small-group communications skills.

The format was a combination of limited residency and distance learning:

- Public relations core (4 courses, 12 credits).
- Management core (4 courses, 12 credits).
- Electives (2–3 courses, 6–9 credits).
- Cumulative experience (3-credit professional project or 6-credit thesis).

DELIVERY OF INSTRUCTION

The master's program draws on the interdisciplinary strengths and international reputations of the S.I. Newhouse School of Public Communications, the Maxwell School of Citizenship, and the Whitman School of Management. The program takes a minimum of 2 years to complete, with a week-long required residency on the Syracuse University campus at the start of the fall term (mid-August), a week-long required residency at Syracuse University's Lubin House in New York City in the spring term (early January), and a week-long required spring residency in Syracuse (mid-May). Students enroll in as many terms as meet their professional and personal schedules, but each enrollment requires the residency. During the residencies, faculty present an overview of the entire course and the guidelines for independent study. After returning to their communities, the participants study and complete assignments at their own pace, meeting predetermined deadlines over the 15-week semester. Access to faculty is ongoing through the use of traditional mail, e-mail, telephone, or facsimile transmission; midsemester meetings with faculty (optional) can be arranged. After completing 30–33 credit hours (10 or 11 3-credit courses), the student chooses to complete the program with either a 6-credit master's thesis or a 3-credit professional project.

THE FACULTY

ISDP faculty members are Syracuse University professors who have been invited to work with this special program on a continuous, year-round basis. They have been chosen based on distinction in their respective disciplines and proven ability to teach adult students. Complementing the academic faculty are distinguished communications practitioners who serve as visiting faculty, guest lecturers, and members of a policy-making advisory committee.

THE STUDENTS

Most students are attracted to the ISDP format because traditional college programs are not easily accessible to them. Either prospective students do not live near a campus program of interest, or their jobs or family situations make attendance in traditional daytime or evening classes impossible. Many have jobs that require extensive travel, or they may expect to be transferred at least once in the time it would take them to finish a degree. ISDP is not an easier path to a traditional degree. Add the difficulty of studying independently to the highly structured curricula and exacting academic standards, and it is clear that the ISDP format is not for everyone. Success in the program requires high scholastic aptitude, a superior command of written English, a lively interest in reading and research, and a capacity for self-directed study. The profile of our targeted student is a college graduate holding a baccalaureate degree from an accredited college or university in the liberal arts, mass communications, or public relations. He or she is an experienced professional in public relations or a related field, whose current position and/or career advancement plans require expanded knowledge and experience in counseling and decision-making processes, a firmer grasp of management and finance, a global perspective, strategic planning, and leadership. Participants must maintain a cumulative grade point average (GPA) of 3.0 (B) in order to remain in good standing in this program.

STUDENT TESTIMONIALS

The success of the program is reflected in the success of our graduates. I enjoyed the camaraderie with classmates and professors. The program is structured so that no one feels like an island, and there are numerous opportunities to discuss ideas, debate key concepts, and engage in teamwork activities. No matter what our duties are as public relations practitioners—agency consultants, corporate managers, or independent contractors—we're all part of a business. Syracuse integrates the thoughts and ideas of the profession with the latest concepts in strategic management and business acumen. This structure provides students with the knowledge to examine their own roles within an organization and apply these to the needs of the business. This is what makes public relations a valuable resource for executive management. (An associate director, communications, from Chicago, Illinois)

The program has enabled me to learn to think more strategically about communications management. It has also helped me to learn to think outside the box and understand the value of research in conjunction with day-to-day responsibilities. Moreover, as a result of the well-rounded curriculum, I am better prepared to comprehend, speak, and apply the terminology and concepts of finance and accounting within my professional environment.

If it hadn't been for the flexibility of this program, I wouldn't have been able to obtain my graduate degree without leaving my job. The flexibility of the program has enabled me to obtain and refine skills in the areas of strategic management, research, and general business practices. The ISDP program has not only been beneficial on a practical and professional level, but has also been a very enriching personal experience. (A public relations manager, from Rochester, New York)

The program was invaluable to me in supporting my personal goals in the workplace. It also expanded my view of public relations as an essential business component of the organization, and as far more than a publicity-generating machine. The classes in law, finance, crisis communications, and research were especially helpful. All in all, the program was one of the best professional decisions I have made. It reaffirmed my selection of public relations as a vibrant, thriving career that can use all my varied skills to the best advantage of my organization. SU [Syracuse University] has given me the tools to take my career to the next level. (A director of communications, from New York)

These testimonials encourage us to think that the Syracuse program is one model that addresses both the expressed needs of the practitioners and the findings of the Excellence Study.

REFERENCES

Deming, W. E. (1982). *Out of the crisis*. Cambridge, MA: MIT Press.

Dozier, D. M., Grunig, L. A., & Grunig, J. E. (1995). *Manager's guide to excellence in public relations and communication management*. Mahwah, NJ: Lawrence Erlbaum Associates.

Foundation for Public Relations Education Research and Education. (1985). *Advancing public relations: Recommended curriculum for graduate public relations education*. New York: Public Relations Society of America.

Grunig, J. E. (Ed.). (1992). *Excellence in public relations and communications management*. Mahwah, NJ: Lawrence Erlbaum Associates.

Public Relations Society of America and Association for Education in Journalism and Mass Communication. (1975). *Design for public relations education*. New York.

Public Relations Society of America. (1987). *Design for undergraduate public relations education: 1987 report of the Commission on Undergraduate Public Relations Education*. New York.

Public Relations Society of America. (1999). *Public relations education for the 21st century: A port of entry*. New York.

Reich, R. B. (2001). *The work of nations: Preparing ourselves for 21st century capitalism*. New York: Vintage Books.

Russell, M. P. (1999). Toward the ideal professional master's degree program. *Public Relations Review, 25*(1), 101–111.

Sharpe, M. L. (Ed.). (2004). *Building a reputation of excellence in public relations*. Papers presented at the Vernon C. Schranz Distinguished Lectureship in Public Relations, Muncie, IN.

Author Index

Note: *f* indicates figure; *n* indicates footnote; *t* indicates table.

Subject Index

Note: *f* indicates figure, *n* indicates footnote.

617